Lecture Notes in Computer Science   11920

Commenced Publication in 1973
Founding and Former Series Editors:
Gerhard Goos, Juris Hartmanis, and Jan van Leeuwen

Editorial Board Members

David Hutchison, UK
Josef Kittler, UK
Friedemann Mattern, Switzerland
Moni Naor, Israel
Bernhard Steffen, Germany
Doug Tygar, USA

Takeo Kanade, USA
Jon M. Kleinberg, USA
John C. Mitchell, USA
C. Pandu Rangan, India
Demetri Terzopoulos, USA

Advanced Research in Computing and Software Science
Subline of Lecture Notes in Computer Science

Subline Series Editors

Giorgio Ausiello, *University of Rome 'La Sapienza', Italy*
Vladimiro Sassone, *University of Southampton, UK*

Subline Advisory Board

Susanne Albers, *TU Munich, Germany*
Benjamin C. Pierce, *University of Pennsylvania, USA*
Bernhard Steffen, *University of Dortmund, Germany*
Deng Xiaotie, *Peking University, Beijing, China*
Jeannette M. Wing, *Microsoft Research, Redmond, WA, USA*

More information about this series at http://www.springer.com/series/7409

Ioannis Caragiannis · Vahab Mirrokni ·
Evdokia Nikolova (Eds.)

Web and Internet Economics

15th International Conference, WINE 2019
New York, NY, USA, December 10–12, 2019
Proceedings

 Springer

Editors
Ioannis Caragiannis (iD)
University of Patras
Rio, Greece

Vahab Mirrokni
Google Research New York
New York, NY, USA

Evdokia Nikolova
The University of Texas System
Austin, TX, USA

ISSN 0302-9743   ISSN 1611-3349 (electronic)
Lecture Notes in Computer Science
ISBN 978-3-030-35388-9   ISBN 978-3-030-35389-6 (eBook)
https://doi.org/10.1007/978-3-030-35389-6

LNCS Sublibrary: SL3 – Information Systems and Applications, incl. Internet/Web, and HCI

This Springer imprint is published by the registered company Springer Nature Switzerland AG
The registered company address is: Gewerbestrasse 11, 6330 Cham, Switzerland

Preface

This volume contains the regular papers and abstracts presented at the 15th Conference on Web and Internet Economics (WINE 2019) held during December 10–12, 2019, in New York (USA) at Columbia University.

Over almost 20 years, researchers in theoretical computer science, artificial intelligence, and economics have joined forces to tackle problems involving incentives and computation. These problems are of particular importance in application areas like the Web and the Internet that involve large and diverse populations.

WINE is an interdisciplinary forum for the exchange of ideas and scientific progress on incentives and computation arising from these various fields. WINE 2019 built on the success of the WINE series (named Workshop on Internet and Network Economics until 2013), which was held annually from 2005 to 2018.

The Program Committee, comprised of 42 top researchers from the field, reviewed 111 submissions and decided to accept 36 papers. Each paper had three reviews, with additional reviews solicited as needed. We are very grateful to the Program Committee for their insightful reviews and discussions. The review process was conducted entirely electronically via EasyChair – we gratefully acknowledge this support. We also thank Springer for providing the proceedings and offering support for the Best Paper Award.

The program included three invited talks by leading researchers in the field: Suchi Chawla (University of Wisconsin-Madison, USA), Michael I. Jordan (University of California, Berkeley, USA), and Tuomas Sandholm (Carnegie Mellon University, USA).

Our special thanks to the general chair Paul Goldberg, the local organizers Xi Chen and Omri Weinstein, and the poster chairs Santiago Balseiro and Jon Schneider.

October 2019

Ioannis Caragiannis
Vahab Mirrokni
Evdokia Nikolova

Organization

Program Committee

Elliot Anshelevich	Rensselaer Polytechnic Institute, USA
Haris Aziz	University of New South Wales, Australia
Santiago Balseiro	Columbia University, USA
Siddharth Barman	Indian Institute of Science, India
Ioannis Caragiannis	University of Patras, Greece
George Christodoulou	University of Liverpool, UK
Bart de Keijzer	University of Essex, UK
Argyrios Deligkas	University of Liverpool, UK
Edith Elkind	University of Oxford, UK
Aris Filos-Ratsikas	University of Liverpool, UK
Michele Flammini	Gran Sasso Science Institute and University of L'Aquila, Italy
Dimitris Fotakis	National Technical University of Athens, Greece
Yiannis Giannakopoulos	Technical University of Munich, Germany
Vasilis Gkatzelis	Drexel University, USA
Nikolai Gravin	Shanghai University of Finance and Economics, China
Nima Haghpanah	Pennsylvania State University, USA
Martin Hoefer	Goethe University Frankfurt, Germany
Ian Kash	University of Illinois at Chicago, USA
Thanasis Lianeas	National Technical University of Athens, Greece
Azarakhsh Malekian	University of Toronto, Canada
Evangelos Markakis	Athens University of Economics and Business, Greece
Vahab Mirrokni	Google, USA
Rad Niazadeh	Stanford University, USA
Evdokia Nikolova	University of Texas at Austin, USA
Sigal Oren	Ben-Gurion University, Israel
Renato Paes Leme	Google, USA
Ioannis Panageas	Singapore University of Technology and Design, Singapore
Giuseppe Persiano	University of Salerno, Italy
Georgios Piliouras	Singapore University of Technology and Design, Singapore
Maria Polukarov	King's College London, UK
Emmanouil Pountourakis	Drexel University, USA
Davide Proserpio	University of Southern California, USA
Alexandros Psomas	Simons Institute for the Theory of Computing, USA
Aviad Rubinstein	Stanford University, USA
Marco Scarsini	LUISS, Italy

Guido Schaefer	CWI Amsterdam, The Netherlands
Jon Schneider	Google, USA
Grant Schoenebeck	University of Michigan, USA
Marc Schroder	RWTH Aachen University, Germany
Nisarg Shah	University of Toronto, Canada
Samuel Taggart	Oberlin College, USA
Christos Tzamos	University of Wisconsin-Madison, USA
Adrian Vetta	McGill University, Canada
Matt Weinberg	Princeton University, USA
Song Zuo	Google, USA

Additional Reviewers

Aloisio, Alessandro
Azizan, Navid
Babichenko, Yakov
Beyhaghi, Hedyeh
Bilò, Vittorio
Birmpas, Georgios
Biswas, Arpita
Branzei, Simina
Brokkelkamp, Ruben
Burrell, Noah
Cai, Linda
Castro, Francisco
Chakraborty, Mithun
Chen, Louis
Cheung, Yun Kuen
Cseh, Ágnes
Dall'Aglio, Marco
Dasaratha, Krishna
Deng, Yuan
Dobzinski, Shahar
Du, Longyuan
Essaidi, Meryem
Fallah, Alireza
Fanelli, Angelo
Farajollahzadeh, Setareh
Fearnley, John
Feng, Yiding
Feng, Zhe
Ferraioli, Diodato
Fournier, Gaëtan
Freeman, Rupert
Garg, Jugal

Gergatsouli, Evangelia
Gurkan, Huseyin
Guruganesh, Guru
Hahn, Niklas
Hollender, Alexandros
Idem, Berk
Jabbari, Shahin
Khodabakhsh, Ali
Kleer, Pieter
Kodric, Bojana
Kontonis, Vasilis
Kotsialou, Grammateia
Krishna, Anand
Kroer, Christian
Lahaie, Sebastien
Lazos, Philip
Lee, Barton
Lenzner, Pascal
Leonardos, Stefanos
Li, Bo
Liu, Siqi
Lucier, Brendan
Ma, Hongyao
Mao, Jieming
Marmolejo Cossio, Francisco Javier
Mauras, Simon
Melissourgos, Themistoklis
Mohan, Divyarthi
Monachou, Faidra
Monnot, Barnabé
Moroz, Daniel
Mouzakis, Nikos

Munoz Medina, Andres
Nagarajan, Sai Ganesh
Papadigenopoulos, Orestis
Paparas, Dimitris
Patel, Neel
Patsilinakos, Panagiotis
Podimata, Chara
Protopapas, Nicos
Quattropani, Matteo
Raghavan, Manish
Rahimian, Amin
Rathi, Nidhi
Ray Chaudhury, Bhaskar
Schmand, Daniel
Schoepflin, Daniel
Schuldenzucker, Steffen
Schvartzman, Ariel
Serafino, Paolo
Sivan, Balasubramanian
Skoulakis, Stratis
Sotiraki, Katerina
Strangway, Tyrone
Suksompong, Warut

Syrgkanis, Vasilis
Tang, Zhihao Gavin
Tao, Biaoshuai
Tavafoghi, Hamidreza
Thomas, Clayton
Tsikiridis, Artem
Tziotis, Isidoros
Vaccari, Stefano
Vaidya, Tushar
Ventre, Carmine
Vinci, Cosimo
Voudouris, Alexandros
Wang, Xiao
Wilhelmi, Lisa
Williams, Cole
X. Ferreira, Matheus V.
Xiao, Shenke
Xu, Haifeng
Yu, Fang-Yi
Zhao, Mingfei
Zhou, Yun
Ziani, Juba

Contents

Regular Papers

Awareness of Voter Passion Greatly Improves the Distortion of Metric
Social Choice. 3
    Ben Abramowitz, Elliot Anshelevich, and Wennan Zhu

Autobidding with Constraints 17
    Gagan Aggarwal, Ashwinkumar Badanidiyuru, and Aranyak Mehta

Response Prediction for Low-Regret Agents. 31
    *Saeed Alaei, Ashwinkumar Badanidiyuru, Mohammad Mahdian,
    and Sadra Yazdanbod*

Computing Equilibria of Prediction Markets via Persuasion 45
    Jerry Anunrojwong, Yiling Chen, Bo Waggoner, and Haifeng Xu

Fair and Efficient Cake Division with Connected Pieces 57
    *Eshwar Ram Arunachaleswaran, Siddharth Barman, Rachitesh Kumar,
    and Nidhi Rathi*

A New Approach to Fair Distribution of Welfare 71
    Moshe Babaioff and Uriel Feige

From Darwin to Poincaré and von Neumann: Recurrence and Cycles
in Evolutionary and Algorithmic Game Theory. 85
    Victor Boone and Georgios Piliouras

On the Convergence of Swap Dynamics to Pareto-Optimal Matchings. 100
    Felix Brandt and Anaëlle Wilczynski

Hotelling Games with Random Tolerance Intervals 114
    Avi Cohen and David Peleg

Mix and Match: Markov Chains and Mixing Times for Matching
in Rideshare. 129
    *Michael Curry, John P. Dickerson, Karthik Abinav Sankararaman,
    Aravind Srinivasan, Yuhao Wan, and Pan Xu*

Persuasion and Incentives Through the Lens of Duality 142
    *Shaddin Dughmi, Rad Niazadeh, Alexandros Psomas,
    and S. Matthew Weinberg*

Convergence and Hardness of Strategic Schelling Segregation   156
  Hagen Echzell, Tobias Friedrich, Pascal Lenzner, Louise Molitor,
  Marcus Pappik, Friedrich Schöne, Fabian Sommer, and David Stangl

Automated Optimal OSP Mechanisms for Set Systems:
The Case of Small Domains.   171
  Diodato Ferraioli, Adrian Meier, Paolo Penna, and Carmine Ventre

The Pareto Frontier of Inefficiency in Mechanism Design   186
  Aris Filos-Ratsikas, Yiannis Giannakopoulos, and Philip Lazos

On the Price of Anarchy of Cost-Sharing in Real-Time
Scheduling Systems.   200
  Eirini Georgoulaki and Kostas Kollias

The Classes PPA-k: Existence from Arguments Modulo k   214
  Alexandros Hollender

On the Approximability of Simple Mechanisms for MHR Distributions   228
  Yaonan Jin, Weian Li, and Qi Qi

Topological Price of Anarchy Bounds for Clustering Games on Networks . . .   241
  Pieter Kleer and Guido Schäfer

Outsourcing Computation: The Minimal Refereed Mechanism   256
  Yuqing Kong, Chris Peikert, Grant Schoenebeck, and Biaoshuai Tao

On Core-Selecting and Core-Competitive Mechanisms for Binary
Single-Parameter Auctions   271
  Evangelos Markakis and Artem Tsikiridis

Scheduling Games with Machine-Dependent Priority Lists   286
  Marc Schröder, Tami Tamir, and Vipin Ravindran Vijayalakshmi

Optimal Search Segmentation Mechanisms for Online Platform Markets   301
  Zhenzhe Zheng and R. Srikant

On the Price of Anarchy for High-Price Links   316
  Carme Àlvarez and Arnau Messegué

Abstracts

Competition in Ride-Hailing Markets.   333
  AmirMahdi Ahmadinejad, Hamid Nazerzadeh, Amin Saberi,
  Nolan Skochdopole, and Kane Sweeney

Persuading Risk-Conscious Agents: A Geometric Approach   334
  Jerry Anunrojwong, Krishnamurthy Iyer, and David Lingenbrink

Scrip Systems with Minimal Availability   335
  Itai Ashlagi and Süleyman Kerimov

The Capacity Constrained Facility Location Problem   336
  Haris Aziz, Hau Chan, Barton E. Lee, and David C. Parkes

The Price of Anarchy in Routing Games as a Function of the Demand   337
  Roberto Cominetti, Valerio Dose, and Marco Scarsini

The Value of Personalized Pricing.   338
  Adam N. Elmachtoub, Vishal Gupta, and Michael L. Hamilton

Sophisticated Attacks on Decoy Ballots: A Devil's Menu.   339
  Hans Gersbach, Akaki Mamageishvili, and Oriol Tejada

Markets Beyond Nash Welfare for Leontief Utilities   340
  Ashish Goel, Reyna Hulett, and Benjamin Plaut

Capacity and Price Competition in Markets with Congestion Effects   341
  Tobias Harks and Anja Schedel

Equality of Power and Fair Public Decision-Making   342
  Nicole Immorlica, Benjamin Plaut, and E. Glen Weyl

How to Hire Secretaries with Stochastic Departures.   343
  Thomas Kesselheim, Alexandros Psomas, and Shai Vardi

Almost Quasi-linear Utilities in Disguise: Positive-Representation
an Extension of Roberts' Theorem   344
  Ilan Nehama

Information Design in Spatial Resource Competition   346
  Pu Yang, Krishnamurthy Iyer, and Peter I. Frazier

Author Index   347

Regular Papers

Awareness of Voter Passion Greatly Improves the Distortion of Metric Social Choice

Ben Abramowitz(✉), Elliot Anshelevich(✉), and Wennan Zhu(✉)

Rensselaer Polytechnic Institute, Troy, NY, USA
{abramb,anshee,zhuw5}@rpi.edu

Abstract. We develop new voting mechanisms for the case where voters and candidates are located in an arbitrary unknown metric space, and the goal is to choose a candidate minimizing social cost: the total distance of the voters to this candidate. Previous work has often assumed that only the ordinal preferences of the voters are known (instead of their true costs), and focused on minimizing distortion: the quality of the chosen candidate as compared to the best possible candidate. In this paper, we instead assume that a (very small) amount of information is known about the voter preference *strengths*, not just about their ordinal preferences. We provide mechanisms with much better distortion when this extra information is known as compared to mechanisms which use only ordinal information. We quantify tradeoffs between the amount of information known about preference strengths and the achievable distortion. We further provide advice about which type of information about preference strengths seems to be the most useful. Finally, we conclude by quantifying the *ideal candidate distortion*, which compares the quality of the chosen outcome with the best possible candidate that could ever exist, instead of only the best candidate that is actually in the running.

1 Introduction

One often hears about 'where candidates stand' on issues, calling to mind a spatial model of preferences in social choice [5,25,27,28,32,35]. In proximity-based spatial models, voters' preferences over candidates are derived from their distances to each of the candidates in some issue space. In particular, we consider voters and candidates which lie in an arbitrary unknown metric space. Our work follows a recent line of research in social choice which considers this setting [2–4, 10,15–17,19,22,24,26,33,36]. The distance between each voter and the winning candidate is interpreted as the cost to that voter. Naturally, one of the main goals is to select the candidate which minimizes the total Social Cost, i.e., the sum of costs of the voters.

The crucial observation in the work cited above is that the actual costs of the voters for the selection of each candidate (i.e., the distances in the metric space)

This work was partially supported by NSF award CCF-1527497.

I. Caragiannis et al. (Eds.): WINE 2019, LNCS 11920, pp. 3–16, 2019.
https://doi.org/10.1007/978-3-030-35389-6_1

are often unknown or difficult to obtain [11]. Instead, it is more reasonable to assume that voters only report *ordinal preferences*: orderings over the candidates which are induced by, and consistent with, latent individual costs. Because of this, past research has often focused on optimizing *distortion*: the worst-case ratio between the winning candidate selected by a voting rule aware of only ordinal preferences, and the best available candidate which minimizes the overall social cost. Many insights were obtained for this setting, including that there are deterministic voting rules which obtain a distortion of at most a small constant (5 in [2], and more recently 4.236 in [31]), and that no deterministic rule can obtain a distortion of better than 3 given access to only ordinal information.[1]

The fundamental assumption and motivation in the above work is that the *strength* or intensity of voter preferences is not possible to obtain, and thus we must do the best we can with only ordinal preferences. And indeed, knowing the exact strength of voter preferences is usually impossible. In many settings, however, *some* cardinal information about the ardor of voter preferences is readily available or obtainable, and is often used to affect outcomes and make better collective decisions. For example, a decision in a meeting may be decided in favor of a minority position if those in the minority are significantly more adamant or passionate about the issue than the apathetic majority, as revealed during discussion or debate. In political campaigns, the amounts of monetary donations, activists attending rallies, and other measures of "grass-root support" can cause a candidate to become a de-facto front-runner even before an official election or primary is ever held. Because of this, in this paper we ask the question: "How much can the quality of selected candidates be improved if we know some *small* amount of information about the *strength* of voter preferences?"

There are many different approaches for modeling, measuring, eliciting, and aggregating the strength or intensity of voter preferences [12, 18]. Such measures can be done through survey techniques, measuring the total amount of monetary contributions, amounts of excitement and time people spend volunteering or advocating for particular issues, etc (see Sect. 2). All such measures are by their very nature imprecise. And yet while it is unreasonable to assume that exact strength of preference is known for every voter, it is certainly possible to obtain insights such as "there are many more voters who are passionate about candidate A as compared to candidate B", or quantify the approximate amount of extreme preference strengths as opposed to the voters who are mostly indifferent. As we show in this paper, even such a small amount of information about aggregate preference strengths or the amount of passionate voters can greatly improve distortion, and allow mechanisms which provably result in outcomes that are close to optimal. In fact, knowing only a single additional bit of information for each voter (i.e., do they prefer A to B strongly, or not strongly?) is enough to greatly improve distortion.

---

[1] We focus on deterministic mechanisms in this paper; see Sect. 2 for a discussion of why.

Model and Notation. As in previous work on metric distortion, we have a set of voters $V = \{1, 2, \ldots, n\}$ and a set of candidates (or alternatives) C. These voters and candidates correspond to points in an arbitrary (unknown) metric space d. The voter preferences over the candidates are induced by the underlying metric, i.e., voters prefer candidates who are closer to them. Voter i prefers candidate P over candidate Q (i.e., $P \succ_i Q$) only if $d(i, P) \leq d(i, Q)$. Moreover, we assume that the strengths of voter preferences are induced by these latent distances. If i prefers P over Q, then the strength of this preference is $\alpha_i^{PQ} = \frac{d(i,Q)}{d(i,P)}$. The cost to voter i if candidate P is elected is $d(i, P)$, and the goal is to select the candidate minimizing the Social Cost: $SC(P) = \sum_{i \in V} d(i, P)$.

Given a set of preference strength thresholds $\{1 \leq \tau_1 < \tau_2 < \ldots < \tau_m\}$, voters report the largest threshold which their preference strength exceeds for each pair of candidates. We let $A_\ell^{PQ} = \{i \in V : d(i, P) \leq d(i, Q) \text{ and } \tau_\ell \leq \alpha_i^{PQ} < \tau_{\ell+1}\}$ and $B_\ell^{PQ} = \{j \in V : d(j, Q) \leq d(j, P) \text{ and } \tau_\ell \leq \alpha_j^{QP} < \tau_{\ell+1}\}$. When $\tau_1 = 1$ we know the preferred candidate of every voter, i.e., for voter i and each pair of candidates P and Q, we know whether i prefer P or Q. When $\tau_1 > 1$ we let C denote the set of voters with preference strength strictly less than τ_1 whose preferred candidate is unknown. When $m \to \infty$, we know the exact preference strength of every voter for every pair of candidates. For convenience in expressing some of our bounds, we also sometimes say $\tau_{m+1} = \infty$ and $\tau_0 = 1/\tau_1$.

In previous work on metric distortion only the ordinal preferences were known, i.e., whether $(P \succ_i Q)$ or $(Q \succ_i P)$. In this paper, however, we assume that we are also given some information about the preference strengths $\alpha_i^{PQ} = \frac{d(i,Q)}{d(i,P)}$ as well. Note that knowing these values still does not tell us how $d(i, P)$ compares with $d(j, P)$ for $i \neq j$, only how strongly each voter feels when comparing different candidates.

For a given voting rule $\mathcal{R}$ and instance $I = \{V, C, d\}$, let P_I be the winning candidate selected by $\mathcal{R}$ and let Z_I be the best available candidate (the one minimizing the Social Cost). Then, the *distortion of winning candidate* P_I is defined as

$$\delta_I = \frac{SC(P_I)}{SC(Z_I)}$$

The *distortion of a voting rule* $\mathcal{R}$ is defined by its behavior on a worst-case instance:

$$\delta = \max_I \delta_I = \max_I \frac{SC(P_I)}{SC(Z_I)}$$

Lower Bounds on Distortion with Preference Strengths. Before presenting our main results, we first provide lower bounds on the minimum distortion any deterministic mechanism can achieve given only preference strength information. First, note that even if all *exact* preference strengths were known to us, we still would not be able to choose the optimal candidate: knowing the relative strength of preference for every voter is not the same thing as knowing their exact distances to every candidate (i.e., we would only know $\alpha_i = \frac{d(i,P)}{d(i,Q)}$ and not

$d(i, P)$ and $d(i, Q)$ themselves). Proofs for all our results can be found in the full version of this paper at https://arxiv.org/abs/1906.10562.

Theorem 1. *No deterministic mechanism with only preference strength information can achieve a worst-case distortion less than $\sqrt{2}$.*

Theorem 2. *When given knowledge of m fixed thresholds, no deterministic mechanism can always achieve a distortion less than $\max\limits_{0 \leq \ell \leq m} \{\frac{\tau_\ell \tau_{\ell+1} + 2\tau_{\ell+1} - 1}{\tau_\ell \tau_{\ell+1} + 1}\}$.*

Our Contributions. In this work, we study the possible distortion with different levels of voter preference strength information. A summary of our results is shown in Table 1. We begin with the setting in which we are given the voters' ordinal preferences, as well as a threshold $\tau \geq 1$ of voter preference strength. In other words, for any two candidates P and Q, we know the number of voters who prefer P to Q, as well as how many of them prefer P to Q by at least a factor of τ (i.e., $d(i, P) < \frac{1}{\tau}d(i, Q)$). For the case that there are only two candidates, we provide a mechanism which achieves provably the best possible distortion of $\max\{\frac{\tau+2}{\tau}, \frac{3\tau-1}{\tau+1}\}$, as shown in Fig. 1. For the setting with more than two candidates, we get a distortion of $\min\{\max\{\frac{3\tau-1}{\tau+1}, \frac{\tau+2}{\tau}\} + 2, \max\{(\frac{3\tau-1}{\tau+1})^2, (\frac{\tau+2}{\tau})^2\}\}$ as shown in Fig. 2. Note that when $\tau = 1$, we get a distortion of 5. A recent paper [31] shows a deterministic algorithm that gives a distortion of 4.236.

Table 1. Distortion in different settings.

Distortion	Two candidates	More than two candidates
Preferences and a threshold τ	$\max\{\frac{\tau+2}{\tau}, \frac{3\tau-1}{\tau+1}\}$	$\min\{\max\{\frac{3\tau-1}{\tau+1}, \frac{\tau+2}{\tau}\} + 2,$ $\max\{(\frac{3\tau-1}{\tau+1})^2, (\frac{\tau+2}{\tau})^2\}\}$
m thresholds $\tau_1, \ldots, \tau_m$	$\max\limits_{1 \leq l \leq m} \{\frac{\tau_\ell \tau_{\ell+1} + 2\tau_{\ell+1} - 1}{\tau_\ell \tau_{\ell+1} + 1}\}$	$\max\limits_{1 \leq l \leq m} \{(\frac{\tau_\ell \tau_{\ell+1} + 2\tau_{\ell+1} - 1}{\tau_\ell \tau_{\ell+1} + 1})^2\}$
Exact preference strengths	$\sqrt{2}$	2

From Figs. 1 and 2, we can see that the distortion is minimized when $\tau = 1 + \sqrt{2}$ in both settings. With only voter preferences being known, the best known deterministic distortion bounds are 3 for two candidates [2], and 4.236 for multiple candidates [31]. Interestingly, if we are also allowed to choose a threshold τ, our results indicate that the optimal thing to do is to differentiate between candidates with a lot of supporters who prefer them at least $1 + \sqrt{2}$ times to other candidates, and candidates which have few such supporters. By obtaining this information, we can improve the quality of the chosen candidate from a 3-approximation to only a 1.83 approximation (for 2 candidates), and from a 4.236-approximation to a 3.35-approximation (for ≥ 3 candidates). This is a huge improvement obtained with relatively little extra cost in information gathering.

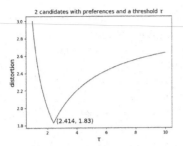

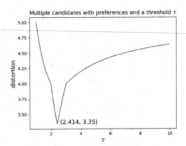

Fig. 1. Distortion for two candidates with preferences and a threshold τ.

Fig. 2. Distortion for more than two candidates with preferences and a threshold τ.

2   Related Work and Discussion

The concept of distortion was introduced by [34] as a measure of efficiency for ordinal social choice functions (see also [2,11] for discussion). Since then, two main approaches have emerged for analyzing the distortion of various voting mechanisms. One is assuming that the underlying unknown utilities or costs are normalized in some way, e.g., [6–9,11,13,14,20,29]. Especially, Amanatidis et al. [1] study distortion with queries of voters' preference strength, which is similar to our model, but with unit-sum or unrestricted utility functions. The second approach, which we take here, assumes all voters and candidates are points in a metric space [2–4,10,15–17,19,22–24,26,33,36]. In particular, when the latent numerical costs that induce voter preferences over a set of candidates obey the triangle inequality, it is known that simple deterministic voting rules yield distortion which is always at most a small constant (5 for the well-known Copeland mechanism [2], and recently 4.236 for a more sophisticated, yet elegant, mechanism [31]). While [2] showed that no deterministic mechanism can always produce distortion better than 3, closing this gap remains an open question.

Randomized vs Deterministic Mechanisms. In this paper we restrict our attention to deterministic social choice rules, instead of randomized ones as in e.g., [3,13,19,26], for several reasons. First, consider looking at our mechanisms from a social choice perspective, i.e., as voting rules that need to be adopted by organizations and used in practice. People are far more resistant to adopting randomized voting protocols. This is because an election with a non-trivial probability of producing a terrible outcome is usually considered undesirable, even if the *expected* outcomes are good. There are many exceptions to this, of course, but nevertheless deterministic mechanisms are easier to convince people to adopt. Second, consider looking at our mechanisms from the point of view of approximation algorithms, i.e., as algorithms which attempt to produce an approximately-optimal solution given a limited amount of information. For traditional randomized approximation algorithms with guarantees on the quality of the expected outcome it is possible to run the algorithm several times, take the best of the results, and be relatively sure that you have achieved an outcome close to the expectation. In this setting of limited information, however, we cannot know the "true" cost of a candidate even after a randomized mechanism chooses it, and thus cannot take the best outcome after several runs. Therefore, unless stronger approximation guarantees are given than simply bounds on the expectation, it is quite likely that the outcome of a randomized algorithm in our setting would be far from the expected value. While randomized algorithms are certainly worthy of study even in our setting, and many interesting questions about them exist, we choose to focus only on deterministic algorithms in this paper.

Attempts to exploit preference strength information have led to various approaches for modeling, eliciting, measuring, and aggregating people's preference intensities in a variety of fields, including Likert scales, semantic differential scales, sliders, constant sum paired comparisons, graded pair comparisons, response times, willingness to pay, vote buying, and many others (see [12,18,21] for summaries). In our work we specifically consider only a small amount of coarse information about preference strengths, since obtaining detailed information is extremely difficult. Intuitively, any rule used to aggregate preference strengths must ask under what circumstances an 'apathetic majority' should win over a more passionate minority [37], and we provide a partial answer to this question when the objective is to minimize distortion.

Perhaps most related to our work is that of [3] which introduced the concept of *decisiveness*. Using our notation, [3] proves bounds on distortion under the assumption that *every* voter has a preference strength at least α between their top and second-favorite candidates. We, on the other hand, do not require that voters have any specific preference strength between any of their alternatives, and provide general mechanisms and distortion bounds based on knowing a bit more about voters (arbitrary) preference strengths. In other words, while [3] limits the possible space of voter preferences and locations in the metric space, we instead allow those to be completely arbitrary, but assume that we are given slightly more information about them.

In our model, when voter preference strength is less than the smallest threshold ($\tau_1 > 1$), they effectively abstain because their preferred candidate is unknown, and so any reasonable weighted majority rule must assign them a weight of 0. Therefore, our work also bears resemblance to literature on voter abstentions in spatial voting (see [22] and references therein). While there are major technical differences in our model and that of [22], at a high level the model of [22] is similar to a special case of ours with only two candidates and a single threshold on preference strengths (and no knowledge of voter preferences otherwise), which we analyze in Sect. 4.

Finally, in this paper we assume that the preference strengths given to our algorithms are truthful, i.e., that the voters do not lie. While it would certainly be interesting and important to consider the case where voters may not be truthful (as in e.g., [9,19]), for many settings with preference strengths it is actually more reasonable to expect voters to be truthful than for settings with only ordinal votes. This is because preference strengths are often signaled passively (e.g., average response times to surveys) or expressing this intensity comes at a cost (e.g., time commitments, activism, or monetary contributions and payments). Even in debates and committees where a member signals their strong preference for A over B, this member is putting their reputation on the line in doing so, and so may not want to do this unless their preference is actually that strong, in order to not look foolish or inconsistent in the future.

3   Adding the Knowledge of a Single Threshold τ to Ordinal Preferences

3.1   Distortion with Two Candidates

In this section we begin by analyzing the case with only two possible candidates. In the section that follows, we use these results to form mechanisms with small distortion for multiple candidates. Suppose there are two candidates P and Q. We are given the voters' ordinal preferences, and a strength threshold τ, i.e., for every voter we only know two bits of information: whether they prefer P or Q, and whether their preference is strong ($> \tau$) or weak ($\leq \tau$). Note that our results still hold if we only have this knowledge in aggregate, i.e., if for both P and Q we know approximately how many people prefer P to Q strongly versus weakly, and vice versa.

Notice that preference strengths tell us little about the true underlying distances for voters with weak preference strengths, because the preference strength of a voter almost directly between P and Q who is very close to both can have the same preference strength as a voter who is very distant from both candidates. However, if a voter's preference strength is large, we know they must be fairly close to one of the candidates - and it is these passionate voters who contribute most to distortion.

Weighted Majority Rule 1. *Given voters' preferences and a threshold τ for two candidates, if $\tau \geq \sqrt{2}+1$, assign weight $\frac{\tau+1}{\tau-1}$ to all the voters with preference strengths $> \tau$ and weight 1 to all the voters with preference strengths $\leq \tau$. If $\tau < \sqrt{2}+1$, assign weight τ to all the voters with preference strengths $> \tau$ and weight 1 to all the voters with preference strengths $\leq \tau$. Choose the candidate by a weighted majority vote.*

The following theorem shows that the above voting rule produces much better distortion than anything possible from knowing only the ordinal preferences. Moreover, due to the lower bounds in the previous section, this is the best distortion possible (apply Theorem 2 with $\tau_1 = 1$ and $\tau_2 = \tau$).

Theorem 3. *With 2 candidates in a metric space, if we know voters' preferences and a strength threshold τ, Weighted Majority Rule 1 has a distortion of at most $\delta = \max\{\frac{\tau+2}{\tau}, \frac{3\tau-1}{\tau+1}\}$.*

Proof Sketch. Let P be the winning candidate, and Q the losing candidate. For all voters, consider their individual ratio of $\frac{d(i,P)}{d(i,Q)}$, regardless of which candidate they prefer. For voters who prefer P this is their preference strength, and for voters who prefer Q this is the reciprocal of their preference strength. If for all voters this is less than δ, then clearly we have a distortion of at most δ by just summing them up. However, for some voters this ratio is higher and for others it is lower. If we think of charging $SC(P)$ to $SC(Q)$, we should charge the voters for whom this ratio is lower to the voters for whom this ratio is higher. Clearly, for any voters who prefer P this ratio is less than 1 and so it is less than δ. For voters who prefer Q, some voters with weak preferences will allow us to save charge while others with stronger preferences will use up the extra charge. However, charging the voters to other voters is quite difficult in this setting. The main new technique in our proof is to use $d(P,Q)$ as a sort of numeraire or store of value. We first perform the charging for all voters for whom this ratio is small, and we use $d(P,Q)$ to quantify how much extra charge is saved. We then show that this quantity of charge stored in terms of $d(P,Q)$ is sufficient to expend the charge from the remaining voters, yielding a distortion at most δ.   □

Note that Weighted Majority Rule 1 is not the only rule that gives the optimal distortion for two candidates. Consider the following simpler rule:

Weighted Majority Rule 2. *Given voters' preferences and a threshold τ for two candidates, assign weight $\frac{\tau+1}{\tau-1}$ to all the voters with preference strengths $> \tau$ and weight 1 to all the voters with preference strengths $\leq \tau$.*

This rule gives the same distortion as Weighted Majority Rule 1 for two candidates, as we prove in the full version. When extending these rules to more than 2 candidates, however, Weighted Majority Rule 1 allows us to form better mechanisms, thus sacrificing a small amount of simplicity for an improvement in distortion. We discuss this in the next section.

Theorem 4. *Weighted Majority Rule 2 has a distortion of* $\max\{\frac{3\tau-1}{\tau+1}, \frac{\tau+2}{\tau}\}$.

3.2 Multiple Candidates (Given Preferences and a Threshold τ)

In this section, we discuss mechanisms with small distortion for multiple (≥ 3) candidates. We assume that we are given the ordinal preference ordering of each voter for all candidates, as well as an indication whether, for every pair of candidates, the voter has a strong preference ($> \tau$), or a weak preference ($\leq \tau$). While this certainly requires more than a single bit of information for every voter, we believe that such data is reasonably possible to collect: it is usually easy for voter to express whether they prefer option A to option B *strongly* or *weakly*, as opposed to trying to quantify exactly how strong their preference is. In reality we would need to compare only the obviously front-runner candidates in this way, and would not actually need this thresholded knowledge for *every* pair of candidates. As discussed in Sect. 1, this information could also be reasonably estimated from other sources, such as the amount of monetary donations, attendance to political rallies, the amount of "buzz" on social media, etc.

The mechanisms we consider are as follows. First, we create a weighted majority graph by choosing pairwise winners using Majority Rule 1. Then we study the distortion of the winner(s) in the uncovered set [30] in this majority graph. Recall that if a candidate P is in the uncovered set, it means that for any candidate Z, either P beats Z directly, or there exists another candidate Q such that P beats Q, and Q beats Z. The uncovered set is always known to be non-empty, and for example the Copeland mechanism always chooses a candidate in the uncovered set.

We begin with the following useful lemma due to Goel et al. [24].

Lemma 1 (Goel et al. 2017). *If a majority of voters prefer P to Q, then $SC(P) \le 2 \cdot SC(Z) + SC(Q)$ for any other possible candidate Z.*

We first show that while this lemma certainly does not hold for all pairwise majority rules, this lemma can be generalized specifically for Majority Rule 1. We then use this to prove bounds on the distortion of the above "uncovered set" mechanisms. This lemma is precisely why we use Majority Rule 1 instead of, for example, simpler rules such as Majority Rule 2, since while their distortion for two candidates remains the same, the theorem below fails to hold.

Theorem 5. *If Weighted Majority Rule 1 selects P over Q, then $SC(P) \le 2 \cdot SC(Z) + SC(Q)$ where Z can be any point in the metric space.*

All the complexity lies in the proof of the above theorem. Once it is proven, it is very easy to establish distortion bounds based on our weighted majority rule.

Theorem 6. *Suppose a weighted majority graph is formed by using Majority Rule 1 to choose pairwise winners. The distortion of the uncovered set of this graph is at most $\min\{\max\{\frac{3\tau-1}{\tau+1}, \frac{\tau+2}{\tau}\} + 2, \max\{(\frac{3\tau-1}{\tau+1})^2, (\frac{\tau+2}{\tau})^2\}\}$ in the multiple candidates setting when given voters' ordinal preferences and a threshold τ.*

4   Undecided Voters: Working Without Knowing Voter Preferences

Suppose there are two candidates P and Q and for all voters with preference strength greater than threshold τ, we know their preferred candidate. For all other voters we know *nothing* about their preferences. This is a strict generalization of the case where we just know voter preferences, since that is the case where $\tau = 1$. As with the case where we only know preferences, the only reasonable voting rule is to select the candidate preferred by more voters (in the case that there are only two candidates), out of those for whom we know preferences. This represents the case where voters abstain if their preference strength is not sufficiently high for them to be motivated enough to vote. In this section we consider mechanisms to deal with such undecided or unmotivated voters.

Weighted Majority Rule 3. *Given candidates P and Q and any single threshold $\tau \geq 1$, give all voters with preference strength at least τ a weight of 1 and all other voters a weight of 0. Select the candidate by weighted majority rule.*

Theorem 7. *With two candidates and only the preferences of voters with preference strength greater than τ, Weighted Majority Rule 3 achieves a worst-case distortion of $\max\{\frac{\tau+2}{\tau}, \tau\}$, and no deterministic mechanism can do better.*

If we can only select a single threshold for voter preference strengths, which should we choose? Intuitively, this is analogous to determining how difficult it should be to vote. If it takes a little bit of effort to vote, then you know that the voters who actually do participate have a significant interest in the outcome. However, if the barriers to voting are too high, then the outcome can be decided by a small fraction of the voters and fails to capture their collective preferences as a whole. In our setting the optimal choice of threshold is $\arg\min_{\tau}\{\max\{\frac{\tau+2}{\tau}, \tau\}\} = 2$, yielding a distortion of 2 (instead of 3 for the case when $\tau = 1$).

When there are more than two candidates, we again consider the distortion of the uncovered set.

Theorem 8. *With mutiple candidates and only the preferences of voters with preference strength greater than τ, if Weighted Majority Rule 3 is used to choose pairwise winners, then the distortion of the uncovered set of this graph is at most $\max\{(\frac{\tau+2}{\tau})^2, \tau^2\}$.*

5 Distortion with General Thresholds

In this section we generalize some of our results in the previous sections to deal with general preference strength thresholds. We are given thresholds $\{1 \leq \tau_1 < \tau_2 < \ldots < \tau_m\}$, and for every voter i and pair of candidates P and Q we know the pair of thresholds between which the preference strength of i falls into. In other words, the more thresholds we have, the less coarse our knowledge of voters preferences. We believe it is realistic to assume that we have one or two, perhaps three, such thresholds, and for most candidate pairs we can create a profile describing how devoted and fanatical their supporters are with respect to these thresholds. However, in this section we consider general sets of thresholds in order to provide bounds on distortion which are as general as possible. For convenience, we let $\tau_{m+1} = \infty$ and $\tau_0 = \frac{1}{\tau_1}$.

We begin as before, by analyzing the case with only 2 candidates P and Q, and then extending our results to multiple candidates.

Weighted Majority Rule 4

For all $\ell < k$, assign to all voters in A_ℓ and B_ℓ a weight of $\frac{(\delta+1)(\tau_\ell \tau_{\ell+1}-1)}{(\tau_\ell+1)(\tau_{\ell+1}+1)}$. For all $\ell \geq k$, assign voters in A_ℓ and B_ℓ a weight of $\left(\left(\frac{\tau_{\ell+1}-\delta}{\tau_{\ell+1}-1}\right) + \left(\frac{\delta\tau_\ell-1}{\tau_\ell+1}\right)\right)$. Lastly, assign all voters in C a weight of 0. Choose the candidate by a weighted majority vote.

Theorem 9. *Weighted Majority Rule 4 achieves the optimal distortion for two candidates with preference strength information.*

How much effort, time, and money, should someone charged with developing a voting protocol, or with choosing an alternative minimizing social cost, spend in order to understand the preference strengths of voters in more detail? With only ordinal preferences ($m = 1, \tau = 1$), the best distortion achievable is by simple majority vote, yielding a distortion of 3. However, if we are permitted any single threshold of our choice ($m = 1, 1 < \tau$), we can bring the distortion down significantly to 2. With any two thresholds of our choice ($m = 1, 1 \leq \tau_1 < \tau_2$), we can bring distortion down further to $5/3 \approx 1.67$, and as the number of thresholds permitted increases we see distortion converge to $\sqrt{2} \approx 1.4$. (See Fig. 3.) This is because in the limit when we know the exact preference strengths of all voters, distortion can be bounded by $\sqrt{2}$, as we show in the next section. Thus, there is not much incentive to spend a huge amount of money to understand exact preference strengths, as one or two carefully chosen thresholds already provide very good distortion.

For the general case with arbitrary thresholds and no extra assumptions, we can demonstrate a bound of δ^2 on the distortion for three or more candidates (Fig. 4). This is obtained simply by forming a pairwise majority graph based on the above weighted majority rule, and then taking any alternative in the uncovered set of the resulting graph. It remains an open question whether there exist weighted majority rules that can improve the bound on distortion in the general case using this method, as we can when we have a single threshold and preferences, or preferences alone. More generally, it is unknown how to get a tight bound on the distortion with multiple candidates using any rule, even in the simpler case with only ordinal preferences [31].

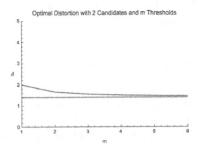
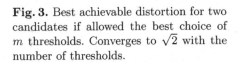
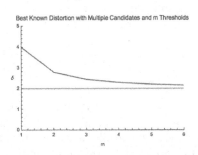

Fig. 3. Best achievable distortion for two candidates if allowed the best choice of m thresholds. Converges to $\sqrt{2}$ with the number of thresholds.

Fig. 4. Best known distortion for multiple candidates if allowed the best choice of m thresholds. Converges to 2 with the number of thresholds.

Exact Preference Strengths of All Voters. For completeness of analysis, we include the case when we know the exact preference strengths of all voters with respect to every pair of candidates. Suppose there are two candidates P and Q, and we are given the preference strengths of every voter. Denote A as the set of voters that prefer P to Q, and B as the set of voters that prefer Q to P. The preference strength of any $i \in A$ is denoted as α_i, and the preference strength of any $j \in B$ is denoted as β_j.

Weighted Majority Rule 5. *Assign weight $\frac{\sqrt{2}\alpha_i - 1}{\alpha_i + 1}$ to each voter $i \in A$ such that $\alpha_i > \sqrt{2}$, and weight $\alpha_i - 1$ to each voter $i \in A$ such that $\alpha_i \leq \sqrt{2}$. Assign weight $\frac{\sqrt{2}\beta_j - 1}{\beta_j + 1}$ to each voter $j \in B$ such that $\beta_j > \sqrt{2}$ and weight $\beta_j - 1$ to each voter $j \in B$ such that $\beta_j \leq \sqrt{2}$.*

Theorem 10. *Using Weighted Majority Rule 5, the distortion is always at most $\sqrt{2}$ for two candidates, and this is the best bound possible for any deterministic mechanism. Moreover, choosing a candidate from the uncovered set of a weighted majority graph obtained by using pairwise Rule 5 results in distortion of at most 2 for any number of candidates.*

6   Ideal Candidate Distortion

In addition to forming mechanisms with small distortion, we also have a secondary goal in this paper. Rather than only comparing the winning candidate to the best available candidate, we can also measure them against the ideal conceivable candidate Z_I^* who may not be an available option to vote upon. Z_I^* is the point in the metric space which minimizes social cost; it is the absolute best consensus of the voters, and it would be wonderful if that point corresponded to a candidate, but that may not be the case (i.e., Z_I^* may not be in $\mathcal{C}$). We introduce the notion of *ideal candidate distortion* as follows, where $I = \{\mathcal{V}, \mathcal{C}, d\}$ is any instance and P_I is the winner that our mechanism selects for an instance I:

$$\Delta = \frac{SC(P_I)}{SC(Z_I^*)}$$

As we show, while the ideal candidate distortion Δ is unbounded in general, for many simple voting rules it can be bounded as a function of the distortion of the winning candidate (δ_I). Intuitively, the distortion δ_I can only be high when the best available candidate (best in $\mathcal{C}$) is close to being the ideal possible candidate (best in the entire metric space).

A summary of our results on this topic is shown in Table 2. These results imply that if we are only given ordinal preferences, as in most previous work, and use certain mechanisms like the Copeland voting mechanism, then *either* the selected candidate is much closer to the best candidate in the running than the worst-case distortion bound indicates (say within a factor of $\delta_I = 3$ instead of the worst-case of 5 for the Copeland mechanism), *or* the selected candidate is not far from the *ideal* candidate, i.e., the best candidate that could ever exist (say within a factor of 6 if $\delta_I = 3$). So in the case when distortion is high, we at least can comfort ourselves with the fact that the selected candidate is not too far away from the best possible candidate that could ever exist, not just from the best candidate in the running.

Table 2. Ideal candidate distortion (Δ) bounds

Ideal candidates distortion	Two candidates	Multiple candidates
Only preferences	$\frac{2\delta_I}{\delta_I - 1}$	$\frac{4\delta_I}{\delta_I - 1}$
Preferences and a threshold τ	$\frac{2\delta_I}{\delta_I - 1}$	$\frac{4\delta_I}{\delta_I - 1}$
Exact preference strengths	$\frac{(\sqrt{2}+1)\delta_I}{\delta_I - 1}$	$\frac{2(\sqrt{2}+1)\delta_I}{\delta_I - 1}$

References

1. Amanatidis, G., Birmpas, G., Filos-Ratsikas, A., Voudouris, A.A.: Peeking behind the ordinal curtain: improving distortion via cardinal queries. arXiv preprint arXiv:1907.08165 (2019)
2. Anshelevich, E., Bhardwaj, O., Elkind, E., Postl, J., Skowron, P.: Approximating optimal social choice under metric preferences. Artif. Intell. **264**, 27–51 (2018)
3. Anshelevich, E., Postl, J.: Randomized social choice functions under metric preferences. In: IJCAI (2016)
4. Anshelevich, E., Zhu, W.: Ordinal approximation for social choice, matching, and facility location problems given candidate positions. In: WINE (2018)
5. Arrow, K.: Advances in the Spatial Theory of Voting. Cambridge University Press, Cambridge (1990)
6. Benade, G., Itzhak, N., Shah, N., Procaccia, A.D., Gal, Y.: Efficiency and usability of participatory budgeting methods (2018, unpublished manuscript)
7. Benade, G., Nath, S., Procaccia, A.D., Shah, N.: Preference elicitation for participatory budgeting. In: AAAI (2017)
8. Benade, G., Procaccia, A.D., Qiao, M.: Low-distortion social welfare functions. In: AAAI (2019)
9. Bhaskar, U., Dani, V., Ghosh, A.: Truthful and near-optimal mechanisms for welfare maximization in multi-winner elections. In: AAAI (2018)
10. Borodin, A., Lev, O., Shah, N., Strangway, T.: Primarily about primaries. In: AAAI (2019)
11. Boutilier, C.: Optimal social choice functions: a utilitarian view. Artif. Intell. **227**, 190–213 (2015)
12. Campbell, D.E.: Social choice and intensity of preference. J. Polit. Econ. **81**(1), 211–218 (1973)
13. Caragiannis, I., Nath, S., Procaccia, A.D., Shah, N.: Subset selection via implicit utilitarian voting. J. Artif. Intell. Res. **58**, 123–152 (2017)
14. Caragiannis, I., Procaccia, A.D.: Voting almost maximizes social welfare despite limited communication. Artif. Intell. **175**(9–10), 1655–1671 (2011)
15. Cheng, Y., Dughmi, S., Kempe, D.: Of the people: voting is more effective with representative candidates. In: EC (2017)
16. Cheng, Y., Dughmi, S., Kempe, D.: On the distortion of voting with multiple representative candidates. In: AAAI (2018)

17. Fain, B., Goel, A., Munagala, K., Prabhu, N.: Random dictators with a random referee: constant sample complexity mechanisms for social choice. In: AAAI (2019)
18. Farquhar, P.H., Keller, L.R.: Preference intensity measurement. Ann. Oper. Res. **19**(1), 205–217 (1989)
19. Feldman, M., Fiat, A., Golomb, I.: On voting and facility location. In: EC (2016)
20. Filos-Ratsikas, A., Micha, E., Voudouris, A.A.: The distortion of distributed voting. In: SAGT (2019)
21. Gerasimou, G.: Preference intensity representation and revelation. School of Economics and Finance Discussion Paper No. 1716 (2019)
22. Ghodsi, M., Latifian, M., Seddighin, M.: On the distortion value of the elections with abstention. In: AAAI (2019)
23. Goel, A., Hulett, R., Krishnaswamy, A.K.: Relating metric distortion and fairness of social choice rules. In: NetEcon (2018)
24. Goel, A., Krishnaswamy, A.K., Munagala, K.: Metric distortion of social choice rules: lower bounds and fairness properties. In: EC (2017)
25. Grofman, B., Merrill III, S.: A Unified Theory of Voting: Directional and Proximity Spatial Models. Cambridge University Press, Cambridge (1999)
26. Gross, S., Anshelevich, E., Xia, L.: Vote until two of you agree: mechanisms with small distortion and sample complexity. In: AAAI (2017)
27. Hinich, M.J., Enelow, J.M.: The Spatial Theory of Voting: An Introduction. Cambridge University Press, Cambridge (1984)
28. Lu, J., Zhang, D. K., Rabinovich, Z., Obraztsova, S., Vorobeychik, Y.: Manipulating elections by selecting issues. In: AAMAS (2019)
29. Mandal, D., Procaccia, A.D., Shah, N., Woodruff, D.P.: Efficient and thrifty voting by any means necessary. In: NeurIPS 2019
30. Moulin, H.: Choosing from a tournament. Soc. Choice Welfare **3**(4), 271–291 (1986)
31. Munagala, K., Wang, K.: Improved metric distortion for deterministic social choice rules. In: EC (2019)
32. Ordeshook, P.C., McKelvey, R.D.: A decade of experimental research on spatial models of elections and committees. In: Advances in the Spatial Theory of Voting, p. 99 (1990)
33. Pierczyński, G., Skowron, P.: Approval-Based Elections and Distortion of Voting Rules. arXiv preprint arXiv:1901.06709 (2019)
34. Procaccia, A.D., Rosenschein, J.S.: The distortion of cardinal preferences in voting. In: Klusch, M., Rovatsos, M., Payne, T.R. (eds.) CIA 2006. LNCS (LNAI), vol. 4149, pp. 317–331. Springer, Heidelberg (2006). https://doi.org/10.1007/11839354_23
35. Schofield, N.: The Spatial Model of Politics. Routledge, Abingdon (2007)
36. Skowron, P.K., Elkind, E.: Social choice under metric preferences: scoring rules and STV. In: AAAI (2017)
37. Willmoore, K., Carey, G.W.: The "intensity" problem and democratic theory. Am. Polit. Sci. Rev. **62**(1), 5–24 (1968)

Autobidding with Constraints

Gagan Aggarwal, Ashwinkumar Badanidiyuru[✉], and Aranyak Mehta

Google, Mountain View, USA
ashwinkumarbv@gmail.com

Abstract. Autobidding is becoming increasingly important in the domain of online advertising, and has become a critical tool used by many advertisers for optimizing their ad campaigns. We formulate fundamental questions around the problem of bidding for performance under very general affine cost constraints. We design optimal single-agent bidding strategies for the general bidding problem, in multi-slot truthful auctions. The novel contribution is to show a strong connection between bidding and auction design, in that the bidding formula is optimal if and only if the underlying auction is truthful.

Next, we move from the single-agent view to a full-system view: What happens when all advertisers adopt optimal autobidding? We prove that in general settings, there exists an equilibrium between the bidding agents for all the advertisers. As our main result, we prove a *Price of Anarchy* bound: For any number of general affine constraints, the total value (conversions) obtained by the advertisers in the bidding-agent equilibrium is no less than 1/2 of what we could generate via a centralized ad allocation scheme, one which does not consider any auction incentives or provide any per-advertiser guarantee.

Keywords: Automated bidder · Price of anarchy · Constrained optimization

1 Introduction

Autobidding is taking on an increasingly important role in online advertising [5] and has already become a critical tool used by many advertisers for optimizing their ad campaigns. Given its importance in the ad ecosystem, autobidding deserves fundamental investigation into algorithms and properties. In this paper, we formulate the questions of designing optimal bidding algorithms, study the interaction of bidding with the underlying auction, and study system equilibrium properties when all advertisers adopt autobidding.

The motivation behind autobidding is performance and product simplicity. The main idea is that instead of asking advertisers for fine-grained bids (e.g., a bid per keyword), the ad platform asks for higher level goals and higher level constraints. An *Autobidding agent* then converts these goals and constraints into per-query bids at serving time, based on predictions of performance of each

© Springer Nature Switzerland AG 2019
I. Caragiannis et al. (Eds.): WINE 2019, LNCS 11920, pp. 17–30, 2019.
https://doi.org/10.1007/978-3-030-35389-6_2

potential ad impression. Besides increased performance, these products also provide for a much simpler interaction with the ad system. For example, in some settings like Google's Universal App Campaigns (UAC) product [6], advertisers do not target at all, but only provide targets for cost-per-install and other goals. In other cases advertisers continue targeting via keywords to identify what queries are of interest, but let the system adjust bids based on predicted performance. In either case, the bidding agent will automatically adjust bids so as to give maximum performance for the campaign, even in a dynamically changing environment, as query volume and features change over time.

There are several autobidding products in the market. The simplest and oldest is that of budget optimization, in which the advertiser provides targeting and a (daily) budget, and the system bids on its behalf. This is a well-studied topic with significant related work. We now have increasingly sophisticated products which allow for performance-based optimization of campaigns, based on goals that advertisers may care more about, by leveraging predicted conversions (sales). For example, Target Cost-per-acquisition (tCPA), Enhanced-CPC (ECPC), and products aiming for deeper optimizations, such as Return on Ad Spend (ROAS), and post-install-value optimization (see, e.g., [5] for more detailed description of these products).

In this paper we formulate and answer several fundamental questions in autobidding. Specifically, (1) find an optimal bidding formula for very general constraints and connect it to the truthfulness of the underlying auction, and (2) quantify the price of anarchy in equilibrium when all advertisers adopt the optimal autobidding.

Remark: These are critical questions from an ad platform's point of view, but they are also interesting and novel from a purely theoretical view as several of the important autobidding products go beyond the classic profit-maximization setting and instead, follow the framework of maximizing value (e.g., number of conversions) under constraints on the average cost (of clicks or conversions) and a budget on total spend. One can consider such objectives and constraints as generalizations of the well-studied budget constraint – the difference now is that the cap on spend is not a fixed number (i.e., budget), but is a function of the specific items allocated (see Sect. 2 for details).

1.1 Overview, Results, and Techniques

In Sect. 2 we formulate the single agent bidding problem, for the general setting of value maximization under general affine constraints (in a multi-slot truthful auction). Specifically, given an advertiser's goals and constraints, and given predictions at query time, how should the bidding agent bid on behalf of the advertiser? This formulation generalizes all the autobidding products we mentioned above. Our two main results are:

- In Sect. 3 we show how to derive an optimal bidding formula assuming we have access to the cost-value landscape. In particular, we show that there is

a simple bidding formula which takes in the value for an item (including the predictions for probability of click or conversions), and converts it into a bid into the auction. While the technique of using LP duality to find an optimal allocation is not entirely new, our novel contribution here is to connect it to bidding, and more specifically, back to the truthfulness of the auction and show that the bidding formula is optimal if and only if the auction is truthful.
- In Sect. 5, we prove a "price-of-anarchy" result which is the most technically challenging and novel portion of the paper: For an autobidding setting with any number of general affine constraints, if all advertisers adopt autobidding, then the total value generated for all advertisers in equilibrium is at least a factor $1/2$ of the total value we could generate via a centralized ad allocation scheme – one which does not need to consider any pricing or auction incentives constraint, or have any per-advertiser optimization guarantee.

For this result, we extend the definition of liquid welfare [3,11] from the budgeted setting to the general affine constraints setting. Then, we use a charging argument, in which we use the structure of equilibrium bids, the truthfulness property of the underlying auction, as well as the nature of the affine constraints to bound the liquid welfare of global allocation in terms of the liquid welfare at equilibrium.

For the sake of completeness, we also provide two additional results, which may be considered as using somewhat standard techniques from the literature: Firstly, in Sect. 4, we show how a Multiplicative Weights Update based method of control feedback can help find the optimal parameters of the bidding formula assuming full access to the cost-value distribution. While the algorithm is a simple instantiation of MWU for solving LPs, which is standard, we do this by interpreting the hyperplanes generated by MWU with dual weights as the realization of a truthful auction, thus connecting truthfulness to the bidding formula.

Secondly, we show in Sect. 6 that, for multi-slot, general constraints setting, there exists a pure strategy bidding equilibrium, under certain technical smoothness assumptions. This result follows by defining a map from the space of dual variables to itself, using the optimal bidding formula, so that the fixed point of the map are the optimal parameters of the formula.

1.2   Related Work

Bidding algorithms have been studied previously in various forms and we describe some related work below. We have specifically two new contributions: the connection of bidding in auction with the truthfulness of the underlying auction, and analyzing the setting of multiple advertisers bidding optimally in a truthful auction and bounding the price of anarchy.

As mentioned above, perhaps the simplest autobidding product is budget optimization. This has been a well-studied topic, in particular [13] provided a formulation for this problem, and gave simple practical uniform bid strategies which achieve a constant factor of the optimal bidding under any auction –

however, they do not consider multiple bidders or equilibrium properties. Also somewhat related is work on back-end system optimization for budget management (not as a bidding agent); this includes work on ad allocation, budget throttling, and bid lowering, e.g., [4, 8, 12, 15–17].

Besides budget optimization bidding, previous literature includes several results on the so-called real-time bidding (RTB) in the context of display ads. A related paper is [9], which considers the problem of bidding algorithms for performance advertising. Similar to the work here, they use a Primal Dual formulation to find a bidding formula. However, there are some salient differences compared to our work: Firstly, their objective is *global value* maximization (sum over all bidders values) under volume constraints. Secondly, the pricing is simply first price, and it is not immediately clear how to extend this to second price auction (or a truthful auction for multiple slots). Bidding into an auction is a more difficult question, as bidders set prices for each other and thus have to be in equilibrium. Indeed, we show that no bidding formula can work in a non-truthful multi-slot auction, and even in a second price auction, the global value generated in an equilibrium solution can be bounded away from the global optimum by a factor of as much as 2.

There are several other interesting papers on RTB, e.g., [14, 19, 20]. The latter paper focuses on learning the underlying traffic distributions and using them to find a bid. The bidding question considered there is simple if the distribution is known (due to the simple nature of the constraints), but the innovation lies in learning the distributions from possibly partial feedback, which is not the focus of our work.

In another related work [7], the authors consider a different but related equilibrium question, in the setting of backend budget throttling (*aka* pacing, in which a budget constrained advertiser is throttled out of some subset of unprofitable auctions). The authors consider the question of whether there is a regret-free stable solution if we use optimal budget throttling for all budget constrained bidders in a single slot auction. However, they do not further analyze the price of anarchy in such a stable solution.

Finally, a very relevant line of work is that of solving online stochastic linear programs [10] and online stochastic convex programs [1]. The specific problems we study are actually instantiations of the more general problem they study, and they also use duality theory to find optimal allocations (in more general settings with stochastic input). We note two novel contributions in our work: Firstly, the connection to truthfulness, i.e., the dual based allocation gives rise to a bidding formula which is optimal if and only if the auction is truthful. And secondly, we study the equilibrium properties if every bidder uses this algorithm in a truthful auction, and prove a bound on the price of anarchy.

2   Preliminaries

There is a set of advertisers A bidding into an ad auction. There is a large set of queries I, each with potentially multiple slots (*aka* positions) S. For each query i, there is an auction which takes in bids and determines which advertisers show in which slots, and determines a cost-per-click (cpc_{is}^a) for each advertiser $a \in A$ and slot $s \in S$.

We define indices into different sets as follows. Let $i \in I$ be an query, $s \in S$ be a slot and $c \in C$ be a constraint. Let the click through rate (CTR), the probability that a user clicks on an ad of advertiser a on slot s of query i be ctr_{is}^a. Let the cost per click for winning slot s of query i be cpc_{is}^a. Let the value to a of a click on impression i be v_i^a – this is the estimate of the total downstream value accrued by a after the click, which we assume is independent of the slot s that the ad was in. Let x_{is}^a be indicator variable if slot s of impression i was allocated to a. Note that we will also abuse notation and refer to query i as an impression (which makes sense for the case when $|S| = 1$).

We study the problem of finding an optimal bidding strategy for each advertiser $a \in A$, assuming that the bids of all other advertisers are fixed. For this problem, even though all the parameters in the problem definitions are indexed by a, for simplicity we drop the index a when we study the optimal bidding strategy for a (here, and in Sects. 3 and 4). In Sects. 5 and 6 we will reintroduce the index a as we study what happens when all advertisers bid according to the proposed bidding formula.

The goal of an advertiser is to maximize its total value i.e. $\sum_{i,s} x_{is} ctr_{is} v_i$. Additionally we have several affine constraints on the spend of the advertiser. This can be formalized by integer program in Fig. 1, in which the index c stands for the constraints, and the v_{ic} are non-negative constants (one per query and constraint).

$$\max \sum_{i,s} x_{is} ctr_{is} v_i$$

$$\forall c, \ \sum_{i,s} x_{is} ctr_{is} cpc_{is} \leq B_c + \sum_{i,s} x_{is} ctr_{is} v_{ic}$$

$$\forall i, \sum_s x_{is} \leq 1$$

$$\forall i, s, x_{is} \in \{0, 1\}$$

Fig. 1. The Integer Program for value maximization for an advertiser under general affine constraints.

Next we show how many products in the industry can be modeled with the above set of constraints.

Budget Optimization: In this case there is a single constraint c with $v_{ic} = 0 \ \forall i$, and B_c is the budget B. So the constraint is simply $\sum_{i,s} x_{is} ctr_{is} cpc_{is} \leq B$. Here, v_i is sometimes taken to be 1 for all i, which means the goal would be to maximize clicks.

Target CPA: In the TCPA product the goal is to maximize the number of conversions subject to the constraint that average cost per conversion does not exceed an advertiser given target value T. Here once again we have a single constraint c. Here v_i represents the predicted number of conversions (*aka* acquisitions, or sale events) that the advertiser gets after a click on impression i (usually called $pcvr_i$, and also assumed to be independent of the slot s). We take $B_c = 0$ and $v_{ic} = T \cdot v_i$, $\forall i$. Note that we can rewrite the constraint which becomes $\frac{\sum_{i,s} x_{is} ctr_{is} cpc_{is}}{\sum_{i,s} x_{is} ctr_{is} v_i} \leq T$. This means that the ratio of the total expected spend to the total expected number of conversions should be at most T, as required.

Target on CPA and CPC: In some bidding products the goal is to maximize number of conversions, but we have two constraints. One is to ensure that average cost per conversion does not exceed T (the same as in TCPA) and the other is to ensure that average cost per click is at most M (both T and M are given by the advertiser). For the second constraint we set $B_c = 0$ and $v_{ic} = M$.

Note that the last two settings above can also be accompanied by a separate budget constraint.

We will also make an assumption throughout that the parameters of this problem are in general position.

3   Bidding Formula

In this section we show that there is an optimal bidding formula of the form $b(i) = \frac{v_i + \sum_c \alpha_c v_{ic}}{\sum_c \alpha_c}$, and this holds if and only if the auction is truthful. If an advertiser bids according to this bidding formula then they violate their constraints by at most $|C|$ impressions (where $|C|$ is the number of constraints) and get a value which is at least the value of an optimal bidding strategy minus the value of at most $|C|$ impressions.

To prove the result we consider Integer Program 1 and relax it to a Linear Program and also consider the corresponding dual LP.

Primal Linear Program

$$\max \sum_{i,s} x_{is} ctr_{is} v_i$$

$$\forall c, \ \sum_{i,s} x_{is} ctr_{is} cpc_{is} \leq B_c + \sum_{i,s} x_{is} ctr_{is} v_{ic}$$

$$\forall i, \ \sum_s x_{is} \leq 1$$

$$\forall i, s, x_{is} \geq 0$$

Dual Linear Program

$$\min \sum_i \delta_i + \sum_c \alpha_c B_c$$

$$\forall i, s \ \left| \begin{matrix} \delta_i + \\ \sum_c \alpha_c ctr_{is}(cpc_{is} - v_{ic}) \end{matrix} \right\} \geq ctr_{is} v_i$$

$$\forall i, \ \delta_i \geq 0$$

$$\forall c, \ \alpha_c \geq 0$$

Let $\{\alpha_c\}$ be the optimal dual solution. Define

$$\Delta_{is} = ctr_{is} v_i - \sum_c \alpha_c ctr_{is}(cpc_{is} - v_{ic})$$

Then the dual constraints can be written as $\delta_i \geq \Delta_{is} \ \forall i, s$.

Now define the bidding formula as

$$b(i) := \frac{v_i + \sum_c \alpha_c v_{ic}}{\sum_c \alpha_c}$$

This is the bid that the bidder puts into the auction for query i. The auction determines the slot and price for the bidder. We will assume that ties are broken arbitrarily. Note that the dual constraints can also be written as

$$\frac{\delta_i}{\sum_c \alpha_c} \geq ctr_{is}(b_i - cpc_{is}), \ \forall \ i, s \qquad (2)$$

We first note some properties of the optimal solution to the primal and dual programs.

Lemma 1. *Let $\{x_{is}\}$ and $\{\alpha_c\}$ be optimal solutions to primal and dual linear program. Then they satisfy the following properties.*

1. *$\delta_i = max(0, max_s(\Delta_{is}))$*
2. *If $\delta_i > 0$ and there is a unique s such that $\delta_i = \Delta_{is}$ then $x_{is} = 1$*
3. *If $\delta_i = 0$ with $b(i) < cpc_{is}, \forall s$ then $x_{is} = 0$.*
4. *There can be at most $|C|$ impressions i such that $\exists s \neq s'$ with $\delta_i = \Delta_{is} = \Delta_{is'}$.*
5. *There can be at most $|C|$ impressions i such that $\delta_i = 0$ and $\exists s, b(i) = cpc_{is}$.*

Proof. The proof follows from linear programming complementary slackness and will be included in the full version of the paper.

Theorem 1. *Bidding strategy $b(i)$ gives a solution which has value at least OPT minus value of $2|C|$ impressions and violates each constraint by at most $2|C|$ impressions if and only the auction is truthful.*

Proof. Fix a query i, for which the bidder's bid is b_i. A truthful auction will allocate the bidder to the slot which maximizes its profit given the bid, i.e., the slot s which maximizes $ctr_{is}(b_i - cpc_{is})$ (of course the cpcs are derived during the auction itself from other bidders). A non-truthful auction will, for some value of the bid b_i (and some values of other bidder bids) allocate the bidder to some other slot $s' \neq s$.

Now consider the LP. By Lemma 1 point 2 $x_{is} = 1$, precisely for the tight dual constraint. But, by Eq. (2), this is precisely the one which maximizes the profit. Therefore the LP allocation solution matches the solution that a truthful auction would choose with the same bids, and would not match the allocation of a non-truthful auction, for at least some values of bids.

Next we prove the bound on the value achieved by the bidding strategy to compare it to the optimal achievable value.

Value of bidding strategy

$$\geq \sum_{\delta > 0, \text{unique } s \text{ with } \delta_i = \Delta_{is}} ctr_{is} v_i$$

$$= \sum_{\delta > 0, \text{unique } s \text{ with } \delta_i = \Delta_{is}} x_{is} ctr_{is} v_i$$

$$= \sum_{i,s} x_{is} ctr_{is} v_i - \sum_{i,s,\delta=0 \text{ or } \Delta_{is} = \Delta_{is'}} x_{is} ctr_{is} v_i$$

$$\geq \sum_{i,s} x_{is} ctr_{is} v_i - |C| \cdot max_{is} ctr_{is} v_i$$

$$= OPT - 2|C| \cdot max_{is} ctr_{is} v_i$$

Here Eq. 1 is because bidder wins at least these impressions, Eq. 2 is from Lemma 1 point 2 and Eq. 4 is from Lemma 1 points 3, 4, 5. Next we show that the constraints are violated by at most $2|C|$ impressions. This is simple because by Lemma 1, Points 3, 4, 5 there are at most $2|C|$ impressions for which $x_{is} = 1$ and bidder doesn't win it or $x_{is} < 1$ and bidder wins it.

We will include an intuitive example illustrating the bidding formula in full version of the paper.

4   Bidding Algorithm

In this section we will give a bidding algorithm which computes the bidding formula and bids accordingly. The algorithm is an application of multiplicative weight update (MWU) method. While it is well known how to use MWU to solve a linear program we note that we specifically need a bidding formula which does not depend on other bidders bids. We show how feasibility oracle used in MWU to solve linear program translates to bidding formula and hence the bidding formula can be used to answer the separation oracle.

We use the MWU algorithm to solve $Ax \geq b$ subject $x \in P$ when a feasibility oracle for any $c, d, \exists? x \in P : c^T x \geq d$ is given. We borrow this from Sect. 3.2 of [2] (Included in full version of the paper). MWU in each step maintains a weight vector w of same number of rows as A and in each step multiplicatively updates w based on how much each constraint is violated from solution in previous step. Then in each step it asks oracle question of the form $w^T A x \geq w^T b$.

Let $\mathcal{V}$ be upper bound on what the OPT and let $\mathcal{V}_c$ be an upper bound on $|B_c + \sum_{i,s} x_{is} ctr_{is}(v_{ic} - cpc_{iks})|$.

Theorem 2. *In $T \geq O(\frac{1}{\delta^3})$ steps Algorithm 1 converges to a solution which satisfies the following.*

1. Value$\geq OPT - \delta \cdot \mathcal{V}$.

2. For each constraint we have $\sum_{i,s} x_{is} ctr_{is}(cpc_{is} - v_{ic}) \leq B_c + \delta \mathcal{V}_c$

Algorithm 1. Bidder

1: **for** $i = 1, \ldots, O(\frac{1}{\delta})$ **do**
2:    $\mathcal{V}_{OPT} = i \cdot \delta \cdot \mathcal{V}$ (Guess for the value of OPT)
3:

$$A = \begin{pmatrix} \cdots\cdots\cdots & ctr_{is}v_i/\mathcal{V} & \cdots \\ \cdots\cdots\cdots & \cdots & \cdots \\ \cdots\cdots\cdots & ctr_{is}(v_{ic} - cpc_{is})/\mathcal{V}_c & \cdots \\ \cdots\cdots\cdots & \cdots & \cdots \end{pmatrix} \qquad b = \begin{pmatrix} \mathcal{V}_{OPT}/\mathcal{V} \\ \cdots \\ -B_c/\mathcal{V}_c \\ \cdots \end{pmatrix}$$

    Where each row (except first one) of A corresponds to constraint c and column for impression/slot i, s.
4:    P be a convex constraints on x_{is} denoting $0 \leq x_{is}$ and $\sum_s x_{is} \leq 1$.
5:    Run algorithm MWU to check feasibility of $Ax \geq b$ such that $x \in P$.
6:    **for** $t = 1, \ldots T$ (Each step of MWU) **do**
7:       Let $w^t = (w_1^t, w_2^t, \ldots)$ be the weight vector maintained by MWU.
8:       Let $\alpha_c = (w_{c+1}^t/\mathcal{V}_c)/(w_1^t/\mathcal{V})$
9:       Define oracle O for $F = \exists? x \in P : w^T Ax \geq w^T b$.
        - Run bidder with bidding strategy $\frac{v_i + \sum_c \alpha_c v_{ic}}{\sum_c \alpha_c}$
        - Let $x_{is} = 1$ if bidder won the impression at slot s, otherwise $x_{is} = 0$.
        - Check if this solution $\{x_{is}\}$ satisfies $w^T Ax \geq w^T b$
10:   **end for**
11:   If algorithm MWU returns infeasibility then break
12: **end for**

Proof. Consider the value of i such that $OPT \geq i \cdot \delta \cdot \mathcal{V} \geq OPT - \delta \cdot \mathcal{V}$. We will fix this iteration for the remaining part of the proof. We know that for such i we have feasible solution for $Ax \geq b, x \in P$. By proof of MWU we know that as long as oracle O is implemented such that feasibility of $F = \exists? x \in P : w^T Ax \geq w^T b$ correctly then MWU returns a feasible solution. We show this by showing that this is equivalent to the bidding strategy in step 9.

First note that bidder in step 9 which produces solution $x_i = 1$ if and only if $\frac{v_i + \sum_c \alpha_c v_{ic}}{\sum_c \alpha_c} \geq cpc_{is}$. We will show that checking $w^T Ax \geq w^T b$ for the output of bidder is equivalent to solving F.

$$w^T Ax - w^T b = \left(\sum_{i,s} \frac{w_1^t x_{is} ctr_{is} v_i}{\mathcal{V}} + \sum_{i,s,c} \frac{w_{c+1}^t x_{is} ctr_{is}(v_{ic} - cpc_{is})}{\mathcal{V}_c} \right) - \frac{w_1^t \mathcal{V}_{OPT}}{\mathcal{V}} + \sum_c \frac{w_{c+1}^t B_c}{\mathcal{V}_c}$$

$$= \frac{w_1^t}{\mathcal{V}} \sum_c \alpha_c \sum_{i,s} x_{is} ctr_{is} \left(\frac{v_i + \sum_c \alpha_c v_{ic}}{\sum_c \alpha_c} - cpc_{is} \right) - \frac{w_1^t \mathcal{V}_{OPT}}{\mathcal{V}} + \sum_c \frac{w_{c+1}^t B_c}{\mathcal{V}_c}$$

It is easy to see that the right hand side is maximized when $x_{is} = 1$ when $\frac{v_i + \sum_c \alpha_c v_{ic}}{\sum_c \alpha_c} \geq cpc_{is}$ which is the exact set of impressions/slots won by the bidder. Hence it is enough to check for this vector if $w^T Ax \geq w^T b$ which completes the proof.

5   Price of Anarchy

In this section we show a factor $1/2$ price of anarchy of any bidder which optimizes for each bidder separately as opposed to optimizing globally for everyone. We consider the special case when each impression has a single slot and hence we will drop the subscript s from remaining part of this section.

5.1   Price of Anarchy Objective

We consider Liquid Welfare as defined in [3] as our objective function. This is defined as sum over all advertisers of the maximum revenue that can be got from an advertiser. This turns out to be the following.

$$\sum_a \left(\min_c B_a^c + \sum_i x_i^a ctr_i^a v_{ic}^a \right)$$

Let OPT be the welfare objective achieved by OPT and let ALG be the welfare objective achieved at equilibrium. Also for any subset S of bidders, define $OPT(S)$ to be the contribution of bidders in S to OPT's welfare objective. Define $ALG(S)$ analogously.

5.2   Price of Anarchy Is Bounded by 2

Let $c'(a)$ be one of the indices that decides the contribution of bidder a of OPT's welfare objective function. Let $C(a)$ be the set of constraints that are tight for bidder a (let $C(a)$ be empty if no constraints are tight). Let A_1 be the set of bidders who are completely unconstrained at equilibrium and let A_2 be the remaining bidders.

Bidders in A_1 are bidding infinity at equilibrium and are winning everything they are interested in. So for $a \in A_1$, a's contribution to ALG is $\sum_i v_i^a$ which is the maximum possible contribution that bidder a can make to the welfare objective.

$$ALG(A_1) >= OPT(A_1)$$

Next we split $OPT(A_2)$ into two parts and bound each separately. For this, define $O(a)$ to be the set of impressions allocated to bidder a in OPT, and let $A(a)$ be the set of impressions allocated to bidder a at equilibrium.

The proof is by a charging argument to bound the liquid welfare of the global allocation in terms of global welfare at equilibrium. For this, we consider two types of impressions – impressions where the global optimal allocation overlaps with the allocation at equilibrium (i.e. $O(a) \cap A(a)$), and the impressions where the two allocations differ (i.e. $O(a) - A(a)$). At first glance, it would appear that the efficiency contribution of the overlapping impressions is trivially equal, and that we need to only worry about the non-overlapping impressions. But interestingly, because the efficiency contribution of each bidder is the minimum over several "types" of value, the efficiency contribution of the same subset of impressions with identical winning bidders may not be equal, and may in fact be incomparable, for the two allocations. To overcome this difficulty, we identify a subset $C(a)$ of constraints, which can be used to characterize both the contribution to liquid welfare as well as the query-level equilibrium bids for bidder a. In particular, this subset has the following three properties:

– For a given bidder a, its bid at equilibrium is no less than a particular convex linear combination of the RHS of bidder a's constraints indexed by $C(a)$.

$$b^a(i) = \frac{v_i^a + \sum_c \alpha_c^a v_{ic}^a}{\sum_c \alpha_c^a} = \frac{v_i^a + \sum_{c \in C(a)} \alpha_c^a v_{ic}^a}{\sum_{c \in C(a)} \alpha_c^a} \geq \frac{\sum_{c \in C(a)} \alpha_c^a v_{ic}^a}{\sum_{c \in C(a)} \alpha_c^a}$$

Using this bound on bids for each impression we can bound the "portion" of OPT from $O(a) - A(a)$.

$$ALG \geq Total\_ALG\_Spend$$

$$\geq \sum_{a \in A_2} \sum_{i \in O(a) \cap A(a)} ALG\_Spend(i)$$

$$\geq \sum_{a \in A_2} \sum_{i \in O(a) - A(a)} ctr_i^a b^a(i) \tag{3}$$

$$\geq \sum_{a \in A_2} \sum_{i \in O(a) - A(a)} ctr_i^a \frac{\sum_{c \in C(a)} \alpha_c^a v_{ic}^a}{\sum_{c \in C(a)} \alpha_c^a}$$

$$= \sum_{a \in A_2} \frac{\sum_{c \in C(a)} \alpha_c^a \sum_{i \in O(a) - A(a)} ctr_i^a v_{ic}^a}{\sum_{c \in C(a)} \alpha_c^a}$$

– A bidder a's contribution to the welfare at equilibrium is equal to the sum of its "c-type" values for the impressions it gets at equilibrium for any $c \in C(a)$. This in turn implies that its contribution is also equal to the sum (over its equilibrium allocation) of any convex linear combination of its c-type values for $c \in C(a)$.

$$ALG(A_2) = \sum_{a \in A_2} \frac{\sum_{c \in C(a)} \alpha_c^a (B_c^a + \sum_{i \in A(a)} ctr_i^a v_{ic}^a)}{\sum_{c \in C(a)} \alpha_c^a}$$

$$\geq \sum_{a \in A_2} \frac{\sum_{c \in C(a)} \alpha_c^a (B_c^a + \sum_{i \in O(a) \cap A(a)} ctr_i^a v_{ic}^a)}{\sum_{c \in C(a)} \alpha_c^a} \tag{4}$$

– For a given bidder a, its contribution to global optimal allocation's welfare is no more than the sum over its global optimal allocation of any convex linear combination of its c-type values (over any subset of C including $C(a)$).

$$OPT(A_2) = \sum_{a \in A_2} (B_{c'(a)}^a + \sum_i x_i^a ctr_i^a v_{ic}^a) = \sum_{a \in A_2} (B_{c'(a)}^a + \sum_{i \in O(a)} ctr_i^a v_{ic}^a)$$

$$\leq \sum_{a \in A_2} \frac{\sum_{c \in C(a)} \alpha_c^a (B_c^a + \sum_{i \in O(a)} ctr_i^a v_{ic}^a)}{\sum_{c \in C(a)} \alpha_c^a} \tag{5}$$

We now split the right hand side into two parts and then use all the other inequalities to get the final bound.

$$OPT(A_2) \leq \sum_{a \in A_2} \frac{\sum_{c \in C(a)} \alpha_c^a (B_c^a + \sum_{i \in O(a) \cap A(a)} ctr_i^a v_{ic}^a)}{\sum_{c \in C(a)} \alpha_c^a}$$

$$+ \sum_{a \in A_2} \frac{\sum_{c \in C(a)} \alpha_c^a \sum_{i \in O(a) - A(a)} ctr_i^a v_{ic}^a}{\sum_{c \in C(a)} \alpha_c^a}$$

$$\leq ALG(A_2) + ALG$$

Where the first inequality is due to 5 and second is due to 3 and 4. Summing $ALG(A_2) + ALG + ALG(A_1) >= OPT(A_1) + OPT(A_2)$ giving $2ALG >= OPT$.

5.3 Tight Example for Factor 2

Here we give an example showing that factor 2 is tight. We have two advertisers $A = \{a1, a2\}$ and two impressions $I = \{i1, i2\}$. ctr is 1 for all ad impression pairs. Value for advertiser $a1$ are $v_1^{a1} = \epsilon + \epsilon^2, v_2^{a1} = 1 - \epsilon$ and for second advertiser are $v_2^{a1} = 1, v_2^{a2} = 0$. We have one constraint (special case of TCPA constraint) with $B_c^{a1} = B_c^{a2} = 0$ and $v_{ic}^a = v_i^a$ for $i \in I, a \in A$.

One can show that $\alpha_c^1 = \epsilon, \alpha_c^2 = \frac{2}{\epsilon^2}$ is a locally optimal bidding strategy. This gives allocation of both $i1$ and $i2$ to $a1$ giving it liquid welfare of $\epsilon + \epsilon^2 + 1 - \epsilon = 1 + \epsilon^2$. But globally optimal solution allocates $c1$ to $a2$ and $c2$ to $a1$ giving it liquid welfare of $1 - \epsilon + 1 = 2 - \epsilon$.

6 Equilibrium

In this section we consider special case when the space of impressions/slots is a measure space. We further assume that there is no point mass distribution except a special impression,slot i, s for each advertiser a which has small ϵ positive value, 0 cost, $v_{ic}^a = \epsilon$ and always allocated to advertiser a. Then we show that there is an equilibrium bidding given by our bidding formula and no advertiser wants to deviate. We use the special impression to upper bound the dual variables. We use the no point mass distribution to make sure that slack in each constraint is a continuous function of the dual variables. Based on these two we can invoke Brower's fixed point theorem to show the existence of an equilibrium.

Lemma 2. *In any optimal solution to the dual linear program the dual variables α_c^a are bounded by $\int_{i,s} ctr_{is}^a v_i^a d(i,s)/\epsilon$. Further the slack in primal constraint i.e $slack_c^a = B_c^a + \int_{i,s} x_{is}^a ctr_{is}^a (v_{ic}^a - cpc_{is}^a) d(i,s)$ is a continuous function of the bidding formula $\frac{v_i^a + \sum_c \alpha_c^a v_{ic}^a}{\sum_c \alpha_c^a}$.*

Proof. We first note that slack in primal constraint being a continuous function of bidding formula is just a manifestation of assumption that we don't have any point mass distribution. Next to prove a upper bound on α_c^a we first prove an upper bound on each δ_i^a. Note that dual LP objective is lower bounded by δ_i^a and primal objective is upper bounded by $\int_{i,s} ctr_{is}^a v_{ik}^a d(i,s)$. Hence we get $\delta_i^a \leq \int_{i,s} ctr_{is}^a v_i^a d(i,s)$.

Now consider the dual constraint corresponding to the special impression, slot i, s for advertiser a. Then we know that $cpc_{is}^a = 0$ and $v_{ic}^a = \epsilon$. Then consider the corresponding dual constraint. $\delta_i^a + \sum_c \alpha_c^a (cpc_{is}^a - v_{ic}^a) \geq v_i^a$. Substituting the values and rewriting we get $\sum_c \alpha_c^a \epsilon \leq \delta_i^a$ which implies $\alpha_c^a \leq \delta_i^a / \epsilon$. Now using the upper bound on δ_i^a we get the upper bound on α_c^a.

We next define a map from α_c^a to itself. Define it as follows.

$$\phi(\alpha_c^a) = min \left(\frac{\int_{i,s} ctr_{is}^a v_{is}^a}{\epsilon}, \alpha_c^a (1 + \eta)^{-slack_c^a} \right)$$

Here $0 < \eta < 1$ is any positive number. Since this map is continuous and bounded, by Brower's fixed point theorem we have a fixed point. At fixed point $\alpha_c^a > 0$ if and only if the constraint is tight. Hence by primal dual complementary slackness we have that the solution is also locally optimal for each advertiser.

References

1. Agrawal, S., Devanur, N.R.: Fast algorithms for online stochastic convex programming. In: Proceedings of the Twenty-Sixth Annual ACM-SIAM Symposium on Discrete Algorithms, SODA 2015, San Diego, CA, USA, 4–6 January 2015, pp. 1405–1424 (2015). https://doi.org/10.1137/1.9781611973730.93
2. Arora, S., Hazan, E., Kale, S.: The multiplicative weights update method: a metaalgorithm and applications. Theory Comput. **8**(1), 121–164 (2012)
3. Azar, Y., Feldman, M., Gravin, N., Roytman, A.: Liquid price of anarchy. In: Bilò, V., Flammini, M. (eds.) SAGT 2017. LNCS, vol. 10504, pp. 3–15. Springer, Cham (2017). https://doi.org/10.1007/978-3-319-66700-3_1
4. Buchbinder, N., Jain, K., Naor, J.S.: Online primal-dual algorithms for maximizing ad-auctions revenue. In: Arge, L., Hoffmann, M., Welzl, E. (eds.) ESA 2007. LNCS, vol. 4698, pp. 253–264. Springer, Heidelberg (2007). https://doi.org/10.1007/978-3-540-75520-3_24
5. Google Ads Help Center: About automated bidding. https://support.google.com/google-ads/answer/2979071. Accessed 12 Feb 2019
6. Google Ads Help Center: About universal app campaigns. https://support.google.com/google-ads/answer/6247380. Accessed Feb 13 2019
7. Charles, D.X., Chakrabarty, D., Chickering, M., Devanur, N.R., Wang, L.: Budget smoothing for internet ad auctions: a game theoretic approach. In: Proceedings of the Fourteenth ACM Conference on Electronic Commerce, EC 2013, Philadelphia, PA, USA, 16–20 June 2013, pp. 163–180 (2013)
8. Chen, P., et al.: Ad serving using a compact allocation plan. In: Proceedings of the 13th ACM Conference on Electronic Commerce, EC 2012, Valencia, Spain, 4–8 June 2012, pp. 319–336 (2012)

9. Chen, Y., Berkhin, P., Anderson, B., Devanur, N.R.: Real-time bidding algorithms for performance-based display ad allocation. In: Proceedings of the 17th ACM SIGKDD International Conference on Knowledge Discovery and Data Mining, San Diego, CA, USA, 21–24 August 2011, pp. 1307–1315 (2011)
10. Devanur, N.R., Jain, K., Sivan, B., Wilkens, C.A.: Near optimal online algorithms and fast approximation algorithms for resource allocation problems. J. ACM 66(1), 7:1–7:41 (2019). https://doi.org/10.1145/3284177
11. Dobzinski, S., Leme, R.P.: Efficiency guarantees in auctions with budgets. In: Esparza, J., Fraigniaud, P., Husfeldt, T., Koutsoupias, E. (eds.) ICALP 2014, Part I. LNCS, vol. 8572, pp. 392–404. Springer, Heidelberg (2014). https://doi.org/10.1007/978-3-662-43948-7_33
12. Feldman, J., Korula, N., Mirrokni, V., Muthukrishnan, S., Pál, M.: Online ad assignment with free disposal. In: Leonardi, S. (ed.) WINE 2009. LNCS, vol. 5929, pp. 374–385. Springer, Heidelberg (2009). https://doi.org/10.1007/978-3-642-10841-9_34
13. Feldman, J., Muthukrishnan, S., Pál, M., Stein, C.: Budget optimization in search-based advertising auctions. In: Proceedings 8th ACM Conference on Electronic Commerce (EC-2007), San Diego, California, USA, 11–15 June 2007, pp. 40–49 (2007)
14. Ghosh, A., Rubinstein, B.I.P., Vassilvitskii, S., Zinkevich, M.: Adaptive bidding for display advertising. In: Proceedings of the 18th International Conference on World Wide Web, WWW 2009, Madrid, Spain, 20–24 April 2009, pp. 251–260 (2009)
15. Karande, C., Mehta, A., Srikant, R.: Optimizing budget constrained spend in search advertising. In: Sixth ACM International Conference on Web Search and Data Mining, WSDM 2013, Rome, Italy, 4–8 February 2013, pp. 697–706 (2013)
16. Mehta, A.: Online matching and ad allocation. Found. Trends® Theor. Comput. Sci. 8(4), 265–368 (2013)
17. Mehta, A., Saberi, A., Vazirani, U., Vazirani, V.: Adwords and generalized online matching. J. ACM 54(5), 22 (2007)
18. Plotkin, S.A., Shmoys, D.B., Tardos, É.: Fast approximation algorithms for fractional packing and covering problems. In: 32nd Annual Symposium on Foundations of Computer Science, San Juan, Puerto Rico, 1–4 October 1991, pp. 495–504 (1991)
19. Ren, K., Zhang, W., Chang, K., Rong, Y., Yu, Y., Wang, J.: Bidding machine: learning to bid for directly optimizing profits in display advertising. IEEE Trans. Knowl. Data Eng. 30(4), 645–659 (2018)
20. Zhang, W., Yuan, S., Wang, J.: Optimal real-time bidding for display advertising. In: The 20th ACM SIGKDD International Conference on Knowledge Discovery and Data Mining, KDD 2014, New York, NY, USA, 24–27 August 2014, pp. 1077–1086 (2014)

Response Prediction for Low-Regret Agents

Saeed Alaei, Ashwinkumar Badanidiyuru$^{(\boxtimes)}$, Mohammad Mahdian,
and Sadra Yazdanbod

Google, Mountain View, USA
`ashwinkumarbv@gmail.com`

Abstract. Companies like Google and Microsoft run billions of auctions every day to sell advertising opportunities. Any change to the rules of these auctions can have a tremendous effect on the revenue of the company and the welfare of the advertisers and the users. Therefore, any change requires careful evaluation of its potential impacts. Currently, such impacts are often evaluated by running simulations or small controlled experiments. This, however, misses the important factor that the advertisers respond to changes. Our goal is to build a theoretical framework for predicting the actions of an agent (the advertiser) that is optimizing her actions in an uncertain environment. We model this problem using a variant of the multi-armed bandit setting where playing an arm is costly. The cost of each arm changes over time and is publicly observable. The value of playing an arm is drawn stochastically from a static distribution and is observed by the agent and not by us. We, however, observe the actions of the agent. Our main result is that assuming the agent is playing a strategy with a regret of at most $f(T)$ within the first T rounds, we can learn to play the multi-armed bandits game (without observing the rewards) in such a way that the regret of our selected actions is at most $O(k^4(f(T)+1)\log(T))$, where k is the number of arms.

Keywords: Ad auctions · Advertiser response prediction ·
Multi-armed bandit · Low regret

1 Introduction

Over the last two decades, the online advertising market has emerged as one of the most important application areas of auctions. Companies like Google and Microsoft run billions of auctions every day to sell advertising opportunities worth hundreds of millions of dollars. Rules of these auctions have undergone frequent change, often prompted by the release of new features (such as ads with additional site links or ads taking advantage of re-targeting lists) or by optimizations in the auction system (such as a new reserve price algorithm or a new algorithm for estimating click probabilities). Any such change can have

© Springer Nature Switzerland AG 2019
I. Caragiannis et al. (Eds.): WINE 2019, LNCS 11920, pp. 31–44, 2019.
https://doi.org/10.1007/978-3-030-35389-6_3

tremendous impact on the revenue of the company and the welfare of the advertisers and the users. Therefore, any proposed change to the auction system goes through a rigorous vetting process to evaluate its potential impacts and decide, based on the results of the evaluation and current business priorities, whether the proposal merits a launch.

Currently, the main tools used for evaluating a proposed launch is running simulations [16] or small controlled experiments [19]. These approaches, however, miss the important factor that the advertisers respond to changes. This is evident in the case of simulations, where the bids advertisers have submitted for the existing auction are used to simulate the new proposed auction. In the case of controlled experiments, the trouble is that the treatment often has to be applied to all or none of advertisers in an auction. This, together with the fact that advertisers overlap imperfectly on the set of auctions they participate in, makes it practically impossible to select random treatment and control groups of advertisers, treat all of the auctions the treatment set of advertisers participate in while leaving all auctions that the control group participate in untreated (See [3] for a discussion of a very similar problem in the context of social networks)[1]. In practice, experiments are run with a random set of auctions (typically 1% or less of all auctions) as the treatment group. This means that for each advertiser only a very small percentage of their auctions is treated, leading to a treatment effect that is well smaller than the noise in the system, and is hence practically unobservable by the advertiser.[2]

In this paper, our goal is to build a theoretical framework for predicting advertiser response based on observations about their past actions. Our model is driven by a few important considerations. First, the advertisers face an uncertain environment, and optimize their objective in presence of uncertainty. As in [17], we capture this by modeling the advertiser as an agent solving a regret minimization problem in a multi-armed bandit setting. In our motivating application, each arm can correspond to an ad slot the agent can purchase or to a discretized value of the bid the agent submits. We make no assumption on the type of algorithm the agent is using except that it has bounded regret. Second, we are concerned with an environment that is changing, and therefore requires the agent to respond to this change. We model this by assuming each arm has a cost, and in each round, the agent is informed about the cost before he has to choose which arm to play. This is the main point of difference between our model and the model in [17], and is an important element of our model, since without

---

[1] See [15] for an attempt to solve this problem by restricting the experiment to small micro-markets. Note that this has the obvious disadvantage of biasing the experiment toward a non-representative set of advertisers and auctions.

[2] See [9] for an interesting theoretical treatment of this setting. It turns out that assuming that the advertisers are fully rational and react even to a small change in the auction, even treating a small percentage of each advertiser's auctions is enough to extrapolate their response to a full treatment. In practice, however, there is too much noise and fluctuation in the system for advertisers to be able to observe and respond to a change that, for example, increases their cost per click by 10% in 1% of their auctions.

this, to predict which arm an agent is going to play, it is enough to look at their past history and select the arm that is played most often. The assumption that the cost of each arm is observed before the agent picks which arm to play is not entirely accurate in our motivating application, since advertisers only learn about the cost of their ad after it is placed. However, given that in practice costs change continuously over time, the advertisers can use the cost of each arm in the recent past as a proxy for its current cost. Therefore, we feel this assumption is a justified approximation of the real scenario.

Finally, we model the objective of our prediction problem. In our model, once the agent decides which arm to play, they receive a reward from that arm that is drawn stochastically from a static distribution.[3] This reward is observed by the agent but not by us. All we observe is the cost of the arms and the arm that the agent plays. Over time, we would like to be able to "predict" which arm the agent plays. We need to be careful about the way we capture this in our model. For example, if two of the arms always have the same cost and the same reward, the agent's choice between them is arbitrary and can never be predicted. Also, if an arm has never been played (e.g., since its cost has been infinity so far), we cannot be expected to predict the first time it is played. For these reasons, we evaluate our prediction algorithm by the regret of its actions. Our main result is an algorithm that by observing the actions of the agent learns to play the multi-armed bandit problem with a regret that is close to that of the agent. Furthermore, we show if the optimal arm, i.e., the arm with highest reward and lowest cost, is unique at every step, the number of predictions of our algorithm that is not exactly the same as the agent actions is upper bounded. Our upper bound depends on the distance between the optimal arm and the second optimal arm at every step.

Since we evaluate our algorithm by the regret of its actions, it can be seen as a regret minimization algorithm which is a very well studied subject. The distinguishing point of between our work and previous work in regret minimization is that in our setting the algorithm does not observe the payoffs (not even the payoff of the arm it selects) which is the essential input for regret minimization algorithms in the literature [6].

2 Related Work

The closest previous work to this paper is [17], where the authors study a model for learning an agent's valuations based on the agent's responses. Similar to this paper, [17] does not assume that the agent always chooses a myopically optimal action, but assumes that the agent chooses its actions using a no-regret learning

---

[3] In our motivating application, the reward can be the profit the advertiser makes if the user clicks on their ad and makes a purchase, or zero otherwise. In this case, the assumption that the reward distribution is static means that the profit per conversion and the conversion probability are fixed over time. This is not entirely accurate, but is a reasonable approximation of the reality, since while these parameters change over time, they tend to change at a slow pace.

algorithm. There are two main differences between the model in [17] and in our paper. The first difference is that [17] studies a single parameter setting where each agent reports a single bid, whereas we study a multi-parameter setting where the agent can pick one of many actions and the utility of each action might not be related to the others. Hence as a model one can reduce [17] to our model by disretization. Another key difference between the two papers is the metric. The goal of [17] is to study sample complexity of computing a set whose Hausdoff distance from the "rationalizable set" of valuations is not large. In the current paper the metric is regret of the algorithm with respect to the agent's valuation. Another related work is [10], where the authors study the problem of mimicking an opponent in a 2 player gaming setting when we cannot observe the payoff and the only thing that is observable is the action of the opponent.

As we discussed in the introduction, our results can be used for bid prediction if the arms correspond to discretized values for the bids the agents submits. There are a number of papers [5,8,18,21] on this subject that model different objectives and behaviors of the agents. However, most of them rely on an estimation of the agent's private values so they can be used for bid prediction. Also, most of these papers ignore the fact that the agents often faces an uncertain environment that they learn over time, and the optimizations happen in presence of uncertainty.

Another line of related work is on designing mechanisms for agents that follow no-regret strategies. For example [4] studies an auction design problem in such a model.

Outside of computer science there is also a rich literature in Economics studying inference in auctions under equilibrium assumptions. A survey of this literature can be found in [2]. This approach has been used to study a wide variety of settings such as arbitrary normal form games [14], static first-price auctions [11], extension to risk-verse bidders [7,12], sequential auctions [13] and sponsored search auctions [1,20].

3   Model

In this section we describe our theoretical framework for predicting advertiser response based on observations about their past actions. In our model, an agent (representing an advertiser in our motivating application) plays a multi-armed bandit game with k arms. In each of the time steps $t = 1, 2, \ldots$, each arm i has a cost c_i^t. These costs can be different in each time step, but they are observed by the agent and by us at the beginning of each time step. The reward (also called the value) of playing arm i in any time step is drawn from a distribution $\mathcal{D}_i$ with expected value $0 \leq v_i \leq 1$. The agent does not know $\mathcal{D}_i$ or v_i, but after playing an arm, privately observes its reward. In our motivating application, each arm can correspond to a bid value the advertiser can submit. The reward of an arm is the value the advertiser receives (e.g., by selling a product through the click-through on their ad), and the cost corresponds to the amount they have to pay for their ad. In this context, the assumptions that the costs are observed by the advertiser as well as the auctioneer, that the distribution $\mathcal{D}_i$ is unknown, and that the reward is observed by the advertiser but not by the auctioneer all make sense.

As the costs are different at each time step, the optimal action $o_t = \text{argmax}_{i \in [k]} \{v_i - c_i^t\}$ for the agent can also be different. Since the agent does not know v_i's, she might play an arm that is not necessarily optimal. Let a_t be the arm that the agent picks at step t. As a result of this choice, the agent accrues a regret of $ar_t = (v_{o_t} - c_{o_t}^t) - (v_{a_t} - c_{a_t}^t)$ at time step t. We assume that the agent uses an arbitrary bounded-regret strategy, i.e., her total regret $\sum_{t=1}^{T} ar_t$ up to time T is bounded by a function $f(T)$ for each time step T.

The goal is to design an algorithm that in each time step t, given the history of the agent actions up to this time step (i.e., the costs $c^1, \ldots, c^{t-1}$ and the actions $a_1, \ldots, a_{t-1}$ of the agent, but not the rewards the agent has received) and the costs c^t of the arms in this time step, picks an arm p_t. Because of this choice, the algorithm accrues a regret of $pr_t = (v_{o_t} - c_{o_t}^t) - (v_{p_t} - c_{p_t}^t)$ at step t. Our metric for the algorithm's performance is measured by the total regret it achieves as compared to the regret of the agent.

Our main result is that there exists an algorithm with a regret bound of $O(k^4(f(T) + 1) \log(T))$.

4 Prediction Algorithm

In this section, we describe our prediction algorithm. A key step in designing the algorithm is our assumption that the agent's regret is bounded by $f(t)$ for each time step t. This allows us to define a set of values for the agent that are consistent with their actions so far and their regret bound. A value vector v is consistent with the actions up to time t if there exists a regret vector r such that:

$$
\begin{aligned}
v_{a_\ell} - c_{a_\ell}^\ell &\geq v_i - c_i^\ell - r_\ell \; \forall \ell \in [t-1], \forall i \in [k] \\
\textstyle\sum_{j \leq \ell} r_j &\leq f(\ell) \qquad \forall \ell \in [t-1]
\end{aligned}
\tag{1}
$$

We denote the set of consistent values at time t with $CV(t)$. Note that for every $v \in CV(t)$, the optimal arm is $\text{argmax}_i \{v_i - c_i^t\}$. The main idea of the algorithm is to pick an arm which is the optimal arm for the largest portion of $CV(t)$. Formally, for each arm i define w_i as the probability that i is the optimal arm for a vector $v \in CV(t)$ chosen uniformly at random. At every time step t, our algorithm picks the arm i with the highest w_i.

The time complexity of our algorithm at each time step is equivalent to the time complexity of computing the volume of polynomially many k dimensional polytopes.

4.1 Regret Analysis

In this section we analyze the regret bound of Algorithm 1. In the main theorem of this section, Theorem 1, we show Algorithm 1's predictions for the first T rounds has a regret bound of $O(k^4(f(T) + 1) \ln(T))$. Note that after each

---

ALGORITHM 1: Prediction Algorithm

$CV(0) = \{v \mid 0 \leq v_i \leq 1, \forall i\}$;
for *each time step t* **do**
    $c^t \leftarrow$ costs of playing arms at time step t;
    $CV(t) \leftarrow$ the set of consistent values at time step t ;
    $w_i := Pr_{v \sim Unif(CV(t))}[v_i - c_i^t \geq v_j - c_j^t, \forall j]$;
    $p_t \leftarrow \arg\max_i w_i$;
end

---

action by the agent, the set of consistent values should satisfy the following new constraints.

$$\forall j \neq a_t, v_{a_t} - v_j + r_t \geq c_{a_t} - c_j$$

Lemma 1 will be used later in the proof of Theorem 1 to show that each time the prediction of the algorithm is wrong (meaning $a_t \neq p_t$) the set $CV(t)$ shrinks. Before stating the lemma, we need to define the following notations:

$$U_{ij}(t) = max_{v \in CV(t)}\{v_i - v_j\}$$

$$L_{ij}(t) = min_{v \in CV(t)}\{v_i - v_j\}$$

Lemma 1. *If the predicted arm p_t is not the arm a_t that is played by the agent, then*

$$c_{a_t}^t - c_{p_t}^t \geq L_{a_t p_t}(t) + \frac{1}{8k}(U_{a_t p_t}(t) - L_{a_t p_t}(t)).$$

Proof. Let us simplify the notations by omitting some of the indices: $a = a_t$, $p = p_t$, $L = L_{a_t p_t}$, $U = U_{a_t p_t}$, and $c = c_{a_t} - c_{p_t}$. Suppose

$$c < L + \frac{1}{8k}(U - L) \tag{2}$$

for the sake of contradiction. Using Inequality (2), we show an arm i exists such that its weight w_i is higher than the weight of the arm p. Therefore, we have a contradiction because the algorithm chooses an arm p such that $w_p = max_{i \in [k]} w_i$. Lemma 1 follows from this contradiction.

Let us define $G(z) = Pr_{v \sim Unif(CV(t))}[v_a - v_p < z]$ and $g(z) = \frac{dG(z)}{dz}$. We first show $g(z)$ is concave and non-negative in $[L_{ap}, U_{ap}]$.

Claim 1. *$g(z)$ is concave and non-negative in $[L_{ap}, U_{ap}]$.*

Proof. For simplicity and without loss of generality we suppose $CV(t)$ is full dimensional. Following the definition, $G(z)$ is the probability that a randomly drawn point from $CV(t)$ is in the half space $v_a - v_p < z$. In other words, $G(z)$ is ratio of the volume of intersection of $CV(t)$ and the half space $v_a - v_p < z$ over the volume of $CV(t)$, i.e.,

$$G(z) = \frac{\text{Vol}(CV(t) \cap \{v : v_a - v_p < z\})}{\text{Vol}(CV(t))}.$$

Now it is easy to see that the derivative of $G(z)$, $g(z)$, is the surface area of the intersection of the hyperplane $v_a - v_p = z$ and $CV(t)$. Therefore, the claim follows due to convexity of $CV(t)$.

Considering Inequality (2), the following claim proves an upper bound on the weight w_p of arm p and the next claim (Claim 3) shows a lower bound on the sum of weights of all arms except arm p, i.e, $\sum_{i \neq p} w_i$. These claims will lead to the contradiction we need.

Claim 2. $w_p \leq 2g(c)(c - L)$.

Proof. Note that

$$w_p \leq G(c) \tag{3}$$

because we have $w_p = Pr_{v \sim Unif(CV(t))}[\forall j, v_p - c_p \geq v_j - c_j]$ and so

$$w_p \leq Pr_{v \sim Unif(CV(t))}[v_p - c_p \geq v_a - c_a] = G(c).$$

It suffices for the proof to show $g(x) \leq 2g(c)$, $\forall x \in [L, c]$ because $G(c) = \int_L^c g(x)dx$. By Claim 1 we know that g is a non-negative and concave function in $[L, U]$. Therefore, we have

$$\forall x \in [L, c], \quad g(x) \leq g(c) - \gamma(c - x)$$

where γ is the derivative of g at point c. By concavity of g, we have $\gamma \geq \frac{g(U) - g(c)}{U - c}$. Therefore, for every $x \in [L, c]$, we have

$$g(x) \leq g(c) - \frac{g(U) - g(c)}{U - c}(c - x)$$
$$\leq g(c) + g(c) \cdot \frac{c - x}{U - c}$$
$$\leq 2g(c)$$

where the second inequality follows from the non-negativity of $g(U)$, and the last inequality holds because by Inequality (2), $c - L \leq U - c$, and therefore for every $x \in [L, c]$, $\frac{c - x}{U - c} \leq 1$.

Claim 3. $\sum_{i:i \neq p} w_i \geq \frac{g(c)}{2}(U - c)$.

Proof. Note that $\sum_i w_i = 1$. Therefore, by Inequality (3), we have

$$\sum_{i:i \neq p} w_i = 1 - w_p \geq 1 - G(c) = G(U) - G(c). \tag{4}$$

Since g is a non-negative concave function on $[L, U]$, we have

$$\forall x \in [c, U], \ g(x) \geq g(c) + \frac{g(U) - g(c)}{U - c}(x - c)$$

Therefore,

$$\begin{aligned}
G(U) - G(c) &= \int_c^U g(x)dx \\
&\geq \int_c^U \left(g(c) + \frac{g(U) - g(c)}{U - c} \right)(x - c)dx \\
&= \frac{g(c) + g(U)}{2}(U - c) \\
&\geq \frac{g(c)}{2}(U - c).
\end{aligned}$$

This, together with Inequality (4) complete the proof of Claim 3.

Now we show a contradiction using Claims 2, 3 and Eq. (2). Note that $g(c) > 0$ and $U - c > \frac{U-L}{2}$ by Claim 2 and Inequality (2), respectively. Therefore,

$$w_p \leq 2g(c)(c - L) \leq \frac{g(c)}{4k}(U - L) < \frac{g(c)}{2k}(U - c),$$

where the first and the second inequalities follow from Claim 2 and Inequality (2), respectively. On the other hand, using Claim 3 we know there exists an arm i such that

$$w_i \geq \frac{g(c)}{2k}(U - c).$$

Therefore, we have $w_i \geq \frac{g(c)}{2k}(U - c) > w_p$ which contradicts the way p is selected by Algorithm 1.

Theorem 1. *Total regret of Algorithm 1 for the first T rounds is bounded by* $O(k^4(f(T) + 1)\ln(T))$.

Proof. To prove the theorem, we show that

$$\sum_{t \leq T} pr_t \leq f(T) + k^2 \lambda H(T)(f(T) + 1) \tag{5}$$

for $\lambda > 2 + \frac{1}{1 - \delta(1 - \ln(\delta))}$ and $\delta = 1 - \frac{1}{8k}$. Here $H(T)$ denotes the harmonic series. Let v^* denote the actual value vector of the arms. By the definition of regret we have

$$\begin{aligned}
pr_t &= (v_{o_t}^* - c_{o_t}^t) - (v_{p_t}^* - c_{p_t}^t) \\
&= ((v_{o_t}^* - c_{o_t}^t) - (v_{a_t}^* - c_{a_t}^t)) + ((v_{a_t}^* - c_{a_t}^t) - (v_{p_t}^* - c_{p_t}^t)) \\
&= ar_t + ((v_{a_t}^* - c_{a_t}^t) - (v_{p_t}^* - c_{p_t}^t))
\end{aligned}$$

Let us define $er_t = \max(0, (v^*_{a_t} - c^t_{a_t}) - (v^*_{p_t} - c^t_{p_t}))$. Therefore,

$$\sum_{t \leq T} pr_t \leq \sum_{t \leq T} ar_t + \sum_{t \leq T} er_t \leq f(T) + \sum_{t \leq T} er_t.$$

Therefore, to prove Inequality (5), it is enough to show $\sum_{t \leq T} er_t \leq k^2 \lambda H(T)(f(T) + 1)$. We define $B_{\alpha\beta}(T) = \{t : t \leq T \text{ and } (a_t, p_t) = (\alpha, \beta)\}$. Note that we have

$$\sum_{t \leq T} er_t = \sum_{\alpha, \beta} \sum_{t \in B_{\alpha\beta}(T)} er_t$$
$$\leq k^2 \cdot \max_{\alpha, \beta} \{ \sum_{t \in B_{\alpha\beta}(T)} er_t \}. \tag{6}$$

Therefore, to prove Inequality (5), it is enough to show that for every α, β,

$$\sum_{t \in B_{\alpha\beta}(T)} er_t \leq \lambda H(T)(f(T) + 1).$$

Let us fix α and β. Suppose $l = |B_{\alpha\beta}(T)|$ and $B_{\alpha\beta}(T) = \{t_1, \ldots, t_l\}$ where $t_1 < \cdots < t_l$. We only consider cases where $\alpha \neq \beta$ because $\forall \alpha, \sum_{t \in B_{\alpha\alpha}} er_t = 0$. Therefore, using Lemma 1 we know $L(t_i) \leq c^{t_i}_\alpha - c^{t_i}_\beta$. That gives

$$er_{t_i} = \max(0, (v^*_\alpha - v^*_\beta) - (c^{t_i}_\alpha - c^{t_i}_\beta))$$
$$\leq \max(0, (v^*_\alpha - v^*_\beta) - L(t_i))$$

In following claim we show $(v^*_\alpha - v^*_\beta) - L(t_i)$ is bounded by $\frac{\lambda(f(t_i)+1)}{i}$.

Claim 4. *For every $t_i \in B_{\alpha\beta}(T)$, we have*

$$(v^*_\alpha - v^*_\beta) - L(t_i) \leq \frac{\lambda(f(t_i) + 1)}{i}.$$

Proof. The proof is by contradiction. Suppose there is a t_i such that

$$(v^*_\alpha - v^*_\beta) - L(t_i) > \frac{\lambda(f(t_i) + 1)}{i}. \tag{7}$$

Let t_i be the smallest such t_i. Therefore,

$$\forall j < i, \ (v^*_\alpha - v^*_\beta) - L(t_j) \leq \frac{\lambda(f(t_j) + 1)}{j}. \tag{8}$$

Let $\hat{v} \in CV(t_i)$ be a point that minimizes $v_\alpha - v_\beta$, i.e., $\hat{v}_\alpha - \hat{v}_\beta = L(t_i)$. Note that we have $i > 1$ because the values are bounded by 1. Let us recall the definition of $CV(t_i)$ here. A vector v is in $CV(t_i)$ if $\exists r \in \mathbb{R}^T$ such that:

$$\forall t \in [t_i - 1]\forall j : v_{a_t} - c^t_{a_t} \geq v_j - c^t_j - r_t$$
$$\forall t \in [t_i - 1] \ : \ \sum_{h \leq t} r_h \leq f(t)$$

This can be written as:

$$\forall t \in [t_i - 1] \forall j : \ (v_j - c_j^t) - (v_{a_t} - c_{a_t}^t) \le r_t$$
$$\forall t \in [t_i - 1] \quad : \ \sum_{h \le t} r_h \le f(t)$$

Since $\hat{v} \in CV(t_i)$, we have

$$\sum_{t < t_i} \max(0, (\hat{v}_{p_t} - c_{p_t}^t) - (\hat{v}_{a_t} - c_{a_t}^t)) \le \sum_{t < t_i} r_t \le f(t_i - 1)$$

Note that $B_{\alpha\beta}(t_i - 1) \subset [t_i - 1]$. Therefore, we get

$$\sum_{t_j \in B_{\alpha\beta}(t_i-1)} \max(0, (\hat{v}_\beta - c_\beta^{t_j}) - (\hat{v}_\alpha - c_\alpha^{t_j})) \le f(t_i - 1).$$

Note that we can write $(\hat{v}_\beta - c_\beta^{t_j}) - (\hat{v}_\alpha - c_\alpha^{t_j})$ as

$$((v_\alpha^* - v_\beta^*) - L(t_i)) - ((v_\alpha^* - v_\beta^*) - (c_\alpha^{t_j} - c_\beta^{t_j}))$$

because $\hat{v}_\alpha - \hat{v}_\beta = L(t_i)$. If we combine the above equations we get

$$f(t_i - 1) \ge \sum_{j < i} \max(0, ((v_\alpha^* - v_\beta^*) - L(t_i)) - ((v_\alpha^* - v_\beta^*) - (c_\alpha^{t_j} - c_\beta^{t_j})))$$

$$\ge \sum_{j < i} \max(0, \frac{\lambda(f(t_i) + 1)}{i} - ((v_\alpha^* - v_\beta^*) - (c_\alpha^{t_j} - c_\beta^{t_j}))) \qquad (9)$$

where the second inequality follows from Inequality (7). On the other hand, we have

$$(v_\alpha^* - v_\beta^*) - (c_\alpha^{t_j} - c_\beta^{t_j}) \le (v_\alpha^* - v_\beta^*) - \left((1 - \frac{1}{8k})L(t_j) + \frac{1}{8k}U(t_j) \right)$$

$$\le (1 - \frac{1}{8k})((v_\alpha^* - v_\beta^*) - L(t)), \qquad (10)$$

where the first inequality follows from Lemma 1 and the second inequality follows from the fact that $U(t_j) \ge v_\alpha^* - v_\beta^*$. Inequalities (9) and (10) imply:

$$f(t_i - 1) \ge \sum_{j < i} \max(0, \frac{\lambda(f(t_i) + 1)}{i} - ((1 - \frac{1}{8k})((v_\alpha^* - v_\beta^*) - L(t_j))) \quad (11)$$

Recall $\delta = 1 - \frac{1}{8k}$. If we apply Eq. (8) into Eq. (11) we get:

$$f(t_i - 1) \geq \sum_{j<i} \max\left(0, \frac{\lambda(f(t_i) + 1)}{i} - \delta\lambda\frac{f(t_j) + 1}{j}\right)$$

$$\geq \sum_{\lfloor \delta i \rfloor \leq j < i} \max\left(0, \frac{\lambda(f(t_i) + 1)}{i} - \delta\lambda\frac{f(t_j) + 1}{j}\right)$$

$$\geq \sum_{\lfloor \delta i \rfloor \leq j < i} \frac{\lambda(f(t_i) + 1)}{i} - \delta\lambda\frac{(f(t_j) + 1)}{j}$$

$$\geq \sum_{\lfloor \delta i \rfloor \leq j < i} \lambda(f(t_i) + 1)(\frac{1}{i} - \delta\frac{1}{j}),$$

where the last inequality follows from the fact that f is monotone and increasing. With some straightforward calculations on the above we get:

$$1 \geq \lambda(1 - \delta(1 + \sum_{\lfloor \delta i \rfloor \leq j < i} \frac{1}{j}))$$

It is easy to see $\sum_{\lfloor \delta i \rfloor \leq j < i} \frac{1}{j} \leq \ln(\frac{1}{\delta})$ since $\frac{7}{8} \leq \delta < 1$. Therefore,

$$1 \geq \lambda((1 - \delta) - \delta\ln(\frac{1}{\delta}))$$

which is a contradiction because $\lambda > \frac{1}{(1-\delta)-\delta\ln(\frac{1}{\delta})}$ and $(1 - \delta) - \delta\ln(\frac{1}{\delta}) > 0$. The claim follows from this contradiction.

By Claim 4,

$$\sum_{t_i \in B_{\alpha\beta}(T)} er_{t_i} \leq \sum_{t_i \in B_{\alpha\beta}(T)} \frac{\lambda(f(t_i) + 1)}{i}$$

$$\leq \lambda(f(T) + 1) \sum_{i \leq |l|} \frac{1}{i}$$

$$\leq \lambda(f(T) + 1)H(l) \leq \lambda(f(T) + 1)H(T),$$

which completes the proof of Theorem 1.

4.2 Bounding the Number of Wrong Predictions

Note that predicting the exact arm an advertiser would choose is not always feasible. If there is more than one optimal arm, finding which one the advertiser would choose is not possible. Therefore, we need an assumption that the optimal arm is unique in every time step.

The following theorem is a corollary of Theorem 1. It bounds the number of wrong predictions of Algorithm 1. In this theorem, the utility of an arm is defined as the value of the arm minus the cost of playing it.

Theorem 2. *If the utility of the optimal arm is higher than the utility of other arms by δ for every time step, then the number of mistakes is bounded by* $\frac{k^4(f(T)+1)\log(T)+f(T)}{\delta}$.

Proof. Let $m_o(t)$ be the number of wrong predictions in which the algorithm chooses the optimal arm, i.e., $p_t = o_t$. Note that in such time steps the agent has a regret of at least δ. Therefore, the overall regret of the agent is lower bounded by $m_o(t)\delta$, and so $m_o(t) \le \frac{f(t)}{\delta}$.

Let $m_a(t)$ be the number of wrong predictions in which the algorithm does not choose the optimal arm. In such time steps the algorithm has a regret of at least δ. Therefore, the overall regret of the algorithm is at least $m_a(t)\delta$. Using Theorem 1, we get

$$m_a(t) \le \frac{k^4(f(T)+1)\log(T)}{\delta}.$$

The total number of wrong predictions up to time step t is $m_o(t) + m_a(t) \le \frac{f(t)}{\delta} + \frac{k^4(f(T)+1)\log(T)}{\delta}$.

5 Lower Bound

In this section, we show a lower bound on the prediction regret that holds even when the regret of the agent is zero, that is, $f(T) = 0$. We prove that there is no algorithm that can predict the agent's actions with a regret bound lower than $\frac{k}{4}$, even when $f(T) = 0$.

Theorem 3. *Given any algorithm $\mathcal{A}$, there exists a sequence of costs in which we have* $\sum_{t \le k/2} pr_t \ge \frac{k}{4}$.

Proof. For simplicity suppose k is even. Consider the following sequence of cost vectors.

$$c^1 = (0, 0, H, H, \ldots, H, H)$$
$$c^2 = (H, H, 0, 0, H, \ldots, H)$$
$$\vdots$$
$$c^{k/2} = (H, H, \ldots, H, H, 0, 0)$$

where H is any constant bigger than 1. Formally, $c^t = (c_1^t, \ldots, c_k^t)$ where

$$c_i^t = \begin{cases} 0 & i \in \{2t, 2t-1\} \\ H & \text{otherwise} \end{cases} \tag{12}$$

Note that at each time step t, the algorithm has no information about arms $2t$ and $2t-1$. Therefore, the algorithm cannot do better than choosing at random. If we set the rewards for arms as follows

$$v_i^* = \begin{cases} 1 & i \text{ is even} \\ 0 & i \text{ is odd} \end{cases} \tag{13}$$

then the algorithm has a regret of $\frac{1}{2}$ at every step. Therefore, the total regret will be at least $\frac{k}{4}$.

6 Conclusion

In this paper, we studied a multi-armed bandits setting where in each step, a cost for playing each arm is announced to the agent. We proved that if we observe an agent that achieves a regret of at most $f(T)$, then even without observing any rewards, we can learn to play with a regret of at most $O(k^4(f(T) + 1) \log(T))$, where k is the number of arms.

We used this model to capture applications like ad auctions, where the goal is to understand and predict the behavior of an advertiser with unknown utility and unobserved rewards.

There are several problems that are left open. The most natural open question is to find the best regret bound achievable in our setting. The only lower bound we know is $O(k)$ in the case that $f(T) = 0$. Also, the broader question of predicting an selfish agent's actions in a dynamic environment without observing her rewards is open in more complicated settings.

References

1. Athey, S., Nekipelov, D.: A structural model of sponsored search advertising auctions. In: Sixth Ad Auctions Workshop (2010)
2. Athey, S., Haile, P.A.: Nonparametric approaches to auctions. In: Handbook of Econometrics. Elsevier (2007)
3. Backstrom, L., Kleinberg, J.: Network bucket testing. In: Proceedings of the 20th International Conference on World Wide Web, pp. 615–624. ACM (2011)
4. Braverman, M., Mao, J., Schneider, J., Weinberg, M.: Selling to a no-regret buyer. In: Proceedings of the 2018 ACM Conference on Economics and Computation, pp. 523–538 (2018)
5. Broder, A., Gabrilovich, E., Josifovski, V., Mavromatis, G., Smola, A.: Bid generation for advanced match in sponsored search. In: Proceedings of the Fourth ACM International Conference on Web Search and Data Mining, New York, NY, USA, pp. 515–524 (2011)
6. Bubeck, S., Cesa-Bianchi, N.: Regret analysis of stochastic and nonstochastic multi-armed bandit problems. CoRR abs/1204.5721 (2012)
7. Campo, S., Guerre, E., Perrigne, I., Vuong, Q.: Semiparametric Estimation of First-price Auctions with Risk Averse Bidders. Working papers, Centre de Recherche en Economie et Statistique (2003)
8. Cary, M., et al.: Greedy bidding strategies for keyword auctions. In: Proceedings of the 8th ACM Conference on Electronic Commerce, EC 2007, pp. 262–271. ACM, New York (2007). https://doi.org/10.1145/1250910.1250949
9. Chawla, S., Hartline, J., Nekipelov, D.: Mechanism design for data science. In: Proceedings of the Fifteenth ACM Conference on Economics and Computation, pp. 711–712. ACM (2014)
10. Feldman, M., Kalai, A., Tennenholtz, M.: Playing games without observing payoffs. In: ICS, pp. 106–110 (2010)
11. Guerre, E., Perrigne, I., Vuong, Q.: Optimal nonparametric estimation of first-price auctions. Econometrica 68(3), 525–574 (2000)
12. Guerre, E., Perrigne, I., Vuong, Q.: Nonparametric identification of risk aversion in first-price auctions under exclusion restrictions. Econometrica 77(4), 1193–1227 (2009)

13. Jofre-Bonet, M., Pesendorfer, M.: Estimation of a dynamic auction game. Econometrica **71**(5), 1443–1489 (2003)

14. Kuleshov, V., Schrijvers, O.: Inverse game theory: learning utilities in succinct games. In: Markakis, E., Schäfer, G. (eds.) WINE 2015. LNCS, vol. 9470, pp. 413–427. Springer, Heidelberg (2015). https://doi.org/10.1007/978-3-662-48995-6_30

15. Lang, K.J., Andersen, R.: Finding dense and isolated submarkets in a sponsored search spending graph. In: Proceedings of the Sixteenth ACM Conference on Conference on Information and Knowledge Management, pp. 613–622. ACM (2007)

16. Mizuta, H., Steiglitz, K.: Agent-based simulation of dynamic online auctions. In: 2000 Winter Simulation Conference Proceedings, vol. 2, pp. 1772–1777. IEEE (2000)

17. Nekipelov, D., Syrgkanis, V., Tardos, E.: Econometrics for learning agents. In: Proceedings of the Sixteenth ACM Conference on Economics and Computation, pp. 1–18. ACM (2015)

18. Pin, F., Key, P.: Stochastic variability in sponsored search auctions: observations and models. In: Proceedings of the 12th ACM Conference on Electronic Commerce, pp. 61–70 (2011)

19. Tang, D., Agarwal, A., O'Brien, D., Meyer, M.: Overlapping experiment infrastructure: more, better, faster experimentation. In: Proceedings of the 16th ACM SIGKDD International Conference on Knowledge Discovery and Data Mining, pp. 17–26. ACM (2010)

20. Varian, H.R.: Position auctions. Int. J. Ind. Organ. **25**(6), 1163–1178 (2007)

21. Xu, H., Gao, B., Yang, D., Liu, T.Y.: Predicting advertiser bidding behaviors in sponsored search by rationality modeling. In: Proceedings of the 22nd International Conference on World Wide Web, May 2013

Computing Equilibria of Prediction Markets via Persuasion

Jerry Anunrojwong[1,2(✉)], Yiling Chen[3], Bo Waggoner[4], and Haifeng Xu[3,5]

[1] Massachusetts Institute of Technology, Cambridge, USA
jerryanunroj@gmail.com
[2] Chulalongkorn University, Bangkok, Thailand
[3] Harvard University, Cambridge, USA
[4] University of Colorado Boulder, Boulder, USA
[5] University of Virginia, Charlottesville, USA

Abstract. We study the computation of equilibria in prediction markets in perhaps the most fundamental special case with two players and three trading opportunities. To do so, we show equivalence of prediction market equilibria with those of a simpler signaling game with commitment introduced by Kong and Schoenebeck [18]. We then extend their results by giving computationally efficient algorithms for additional parameter regimes. Our approach leverages a new connection between prediction markets and Bayesian persuasion, which also reveals interesting conceptual insights.

1 Introduction

Prediction markets allow participants to buy and sell financial contracts whose payoff is contingent on the outcome of a future event. The market aggregates these decisions, which reveal beliefs about the event, into a collective prediction. Researchers study their game-theoretic properties to understand how these markets function in practice as well as how to better design them to encourage information elicitation and aggregation.

The widely-studied *scoring-rule based markets (SRM)* [13] utilize *proper scoring rules* $R(\mathbf{p}, e)$, which assign a score to each prediction $\mathbf{p}$ on any given outcome e of the event. Each participant $t = 1, \ldots, T$ arrives and updates the market prediction from $\mathbf{p}^{t-1}$ to $\mathbf{p}^t$, and receives a payoff of her improvement in score, $R(\mathbf{p}^t, e) - R(\mathbf{p}^{t-1}, e)$, after the event outcome e is revealed.

Despite the apparent simplicity of this game, its equilibria have been challenging to describe. We have two primary motivations for doing so. First, prediction markets are popular in practice, and understanding the properties of their equilibria may be helpful in determining how to design such markets. Second, the SRM is a very simple but apparently deep extensive-form signaling game. Understanding it may lead to general insights regarding value of information and connections to other signaling settings. Therefore, this paper seeks algorithms and characterizations that further our understanding of these games.

I. Caragiannis et al. (Eds.): WINE 2019, LNCS 11920, pp. 45–56, 2019.
https://doi.org/10.1007/978-3-030-35389-6_4

The Alice-Bob-Alice (ABA) Game and Prior Work. Historically, equilibria of markets have proven difficult to describe even in the special but perhaps the most fundamental "Alice-Bob-Alice" (ABA) case. Here there are only two players and three trading opportunities. Alice observes a private signal from a set $\mathcal{A}$ while Bob receives a private signal from a set $\mathcal{B}$. They can be correlated with each other and with the (random) event being predicted, which has outcomes drawn from a set $\mathcal{E}$. Alice, participating at $t = 1$, can choose to predict truthfully, withhold information, or even bluff and make a knowingly false prediction. This might mislead Bob into a poor prediction at $t = 2$, leaving Alice the opportunity to improve the market score significantly at $t = 3$.

A sequence of works [5,6,9,11] focused on the popular log scoring rule and found conditions under which Alice fully reveals all information in stage 1 as well as cases where she reveals no information. Chen and Waggoner [7] generalized these results to a characterization of pairs (players' signals, scoring rule) under which the first player is always truthful (termed *informational substitutes*) or withholds all information (*informational complements*). All of the results mentioned so far extend to general prediction markets with any number of players, yet solving the Alice-Bob-Alice case was often the key step.

However, one major open problem left in [7] is the computational tractability of determining whether players' signals satisfy the substitutes condition, complements condition, or neither. The aforementioned papers also leave open what happens in the "neither" case, i.e. when Alice uses some nontrivial strategy in the first stage. To our knowledge, Kong and Schoenebeck [18] are the first to address these questions. It introduced a signaling game, the *Alice-Bob-Alice game with commitment*, that simplifies some aspects of prediction markets from an analysis perspective. Payoffs are defined as in the Alice-Bob-Alice SRM above. But instead of directly making a prediction in round 1, Alice reports according to some signaling scheme conditioned on her private information. Bob observes Alice's signal and Alice is assigned $\mathbf{p}^1$ = the posterior event distribution conditioned on this signal. Crucially, Alice must commit to this signaling scheme and it is known to Bob in advance, so she cannot bluff or mislead him by deviating to another signal or prediction. For this game, [18] gave a fully polynomial-time approximation scheme (FPTAS) for computing an optimal signaling scheme of Alice when the number of possible realizations of Alice's private information, $|\mathcal{A}|$, is constant, and the scoring rule satisfies a rather strong separability and smoothness condition.

Our Results. Our first result establishes a formal connection between ABA game with and without commitment. We prove that Alice's optimal commitment in the ABA game is also (up to negligible ϵ) part of an equilibrium in the corresponding prediction market (without commitment). This shows, perhaps surprisingly, that any equilibrium that can be achieved when Alice is forced to commit to a signaling scheme can also be achieved in a market without commitment or explicit signaling. In other words, finding equilibria in prediction markets reduces to a pure signaling problem.

Given this result, we focus our attention on designing algorithms for the ABA game with commitment. Here, we extend the results of [18] to several other cases, although we do not solve the Alice-Bob-Alice game in full generality. Our results are built upon an interesting connection between Alice's signaling problem and *Bayesian persuasion* [16,17]—in some sense, Alice's signaling scheme in round 1 is "persuading" Bob to make certain reports. We formalize this connection by proving that Alice's signaling problem reduces to Bayesian persuasion of a *privately informed* receiver, but with a persuasion objective that is specific to prediction markets. As a direct application of this connection, we exhibit an efficient and exact algorithm for Alice's optimal signaling in the case $|\mathcal{B}| = O(1)$ but under the assumption that the expected scoring function is piece-wise linear with polynomially many pieces. Though this restriction appears restrictive, we hope this result may serve as a stepping stone to future work. Next, we leverage techniques from algorithmic persuasion to design an FPTAS for the case $|\mathcal{A}| = O(1)$ under a natural smoothness assumption on the scoring function. This results strictly generalizes—and interestingly, also much simplifies—the main result of Kong and and Schoenebeck [18]. Finally, to show the generality of our technique, we use a similar idea to design an FPTAS for the case that both $|\mathcal{B}|, |\mathcal{E}| = O(1)$.

2   Preliminaries

2.1   Signals and Probabilities

A *signal* is a random variable, denoted by a capital letter, taking values in an *outcome space* written in calligraphics. In particular, there are four signals of interest in this paper: E, A, B, and S. The signal E is a future event we would like to predict having a finite set of outcomes $\mathcal{E}$. The goal of a prediction market is to elicit forecasts about E in the form of probability distributions in $\Delta(\mathcal{E})$, the probability simplex over $\mathcal{E}$. For an outcome $e \in \mathcal{E}$, we write $\Pr[e]$ as shorthand for $\Pr[E = e]$, and so on for the other signals.

In this paper, there will always be two players, Alice and Bob. Alice observes a signal A with finite outcome space $\mathcal{A}$, while Bob observes B in the finite space $\mathcal{B}$. There is a prior distribution $\mu(e, a, b)$ on the joint realizations of $e \in \mathcal{E}$, $a \in \mathcal{A}$, and $b \in \mathcal{B}$. The prior distribution is common knowledge to Alice and Bob. Alice will be choosing to send a signal S in space $\mathcal{S}$. A *signaling scheme* is represented as a function $\pi : \mathcal{S} \times \mathcal{A} \to [0, 1]$ where $\pi(s, a) = \Pr[S = s, A = a]$ such that π satisfies $\sum_{s \in \mathcal{S}} \pi(s, a) = \sum_{e,b} \mu(e, a, b)$ for all $a \in \mathcal{A}$.

2.2   Prediction Market Model

Proper Scoring Rules. A scoring rule is a function $R : \Delta(\mathcal{E}) \times \mathcal{E} \to \mathbb{R} \cup \{-\infty\}$ that assigns a score $R(\mathbf{w}, e)$ to the prediction $\mathbf{w}$ when the event E of our interest is realized to e. We write $R(\mathbf{w}'; \mathbf{w}) = \mathbb{E}_{E \sim \mathbf{w}} R(\mathbf{w}', E)$ for the expected score of prediction $\mathbf{w}'$ when E is drawn from $\mathbf{w}$. It is *strictly proper* if for all $\mathbf{w} \neq \mathbf{w}'$, $R(\mathbf{w}'; \mathbf{w}) < R(\mathbf{w}; \mathbf{w})$. That is, for any belief $\mathbf{w}$, one uniquely maximizes expected score by reporting $\mathbf{w}$. We rely on the following characterization.

Proposition 1 ([12,21,23]). *For every strictly proper scoring rule R, there exists a strictly convex function $G : \Delta(\mathcal{E}) \to \mathbb{R}$ such that $R(\mathbf{w}; \mathbf{w}) = G(\mathbf{w})$. Conversely, from every strictly convex G, one can construct a strictly proper scoring rule R such that $G(\mathbf{w}) = R(\mathbf{w}; \mathbf{w})$.*

Example 1. The log scoring rule is defined as $R(\mathbf{w}, e) = \log w_e$, i.e. the logarithm of the probability assigned to e. Its "expected score function" is $G(\mathbf{w}) = \sum_e w_e \log w_e = -H(\mathbf{w})$, the negative of Shannon entropy. The quadratic scoring rule is $R(\mathbf{w}, e) = 2w_e - \|\mathbf{w}\|_2^2$. Its expected score function is $G(\mathbf{w}) = \|\mathbf{w}\|_2^2$. Both are strictly proper.

Automated Prediction Market. In this paper we focus on the popular *automated scoring-rule market (SRM)* framework of [13]. The market is parameterized by a finite set of event outcomes $\mathcal{E}$, a strictly proper scoring rule R, and an initial prediction $\mathbf{p}^0 \in \Delta(\mathcal{E})$. The participants arrive in a fixed, predefined order. Each round $t = 1, \ldots, T$, the arriving participant observes the previous prediction $\mathbf{p}^{t-1}$ and replaces it with a prediction $\mathbf{p}^t$. At the end, the event outcome $E = e$ is observed and the arriving participant at time t is paid

$$R(\mathbf{p}^t, e) - R(\mathbf{p}^{t-1}, e). \tag{1}$$

One of the key properties this payoff rule inherits from R is "one-step" truthfulness:

Fact 1. *If every player arrives only once, then it is a strictly dominant strategy to set $\mathbf{p}^t$ to the player's true posterior belief conditioned on all information they have observed.*

This follows immediately because R is a proper scoring rule and the second term in (1) is not under the player's control.

However, if players participate multiple times, it might be beneficial to withhold information (or possibly even bluff). This motivates study of the *Alice-Bob-Alice (ABA) market*, a prediction market with two players and three rounds where Alice participates in rounds 1 and 3 while Bob participates in round 2. Despite its apparent simplicity, this special case captures many of the challenges of general markets and has been studied in e.g. [5,11,18].

Equilibrium in Markets. In the prediction market game, a strategy for Alice consists of a pair of possibly-randomized functions σ_1, σ_3 defining her predictions at rounds 1 and 3. We have $\sigma_1 : \mathcal{A} \to \Delta(\mathcal{E})$, i.e. Alice plays $\mathbf{p}^1 = \sigma_1(A)$. Next, $\sigma_3 : \mathcal{A} \times \Delta(\mathcal{E}) \times \Delta(\mathcal{E}) \to \Delta(\mathcal{E})$, where Alice at round 3 plays $\mathbf{p}^3 = \sigma_3(A, \mathbf{p}^1, \mathbf{p}^2)$. Similarly, a strategy for Bob is a possibly-randomized function $\sigma_2 : \mathcal{B} \times \Delta(\mathcal{E}) \to \Delta(\mathcal{E})$ where he plays $\mathbf{p}^2 = \sigma_2(B, \mathbf{p}^1)$.

For $t \in \{1, 2, 3\}$, define the expected net score for the prediction at round t to be

$$u_t((\sigma_1, \sigma_3), \sigma_2) = \mathop{\mathbb{E}}_{A, B, E, \sigma_1, \sigma_2, \sigma_3} \left[R(\mathbf{p}^t, E) - R(\mathbf{p}^{t-1}, E) \right].$$

Alice's total expected utility is $u_A((\sigma_1, \sigma_3), \sigma_2) := u_1 + u_3$. Similarly, Bob's expected utility is $u_B((\sigma_1, \sigma_3), \sigma_2) := u_2$.

A set of strategies $((\sigma_1, \sigma_3), \sigma_2)$ are a *Bayes-Nash equilibrium (BNE)* if each is a best response to the other, i.e. for all (σ_1', σ_3'), $u_A((\sigma_1', \sigma_3'), \sigma_2) \leq u_A((\sigma_1, \sigma_3), \sigma_2)$, and similarly for all σ_2', $u_B((\sigma_1, \sigma_3), \sigma_2') \leq u_B((\sigma_1, \sigma_3), \sigma_2)$.

In extensive-form games such as prediction markets, BNE can include "non-credible" threats. For example perhaps in BNE, Bob may threaten to reveal no information in the second round if Alice deviates from the equilibrium strategy. This is not credible because, if Alice were to actually deviate, Bob's best response would still be to predict truthfully according to his beliefs. Therefore, in this paper we focus on *perfect Bayesian equilibrium (PBE)*. Informally, a BNE $((\sigma_1, \sigma_3), \sigma_2)$ is a PBE if, off the equilibrium path, these strategies still best-respond according to some beliefs that are consistent with Bayesian updating on the player's own signal and some information about their opponent's signal. See the full version for a formal definition.

2.3 ABA Game with Commitment

Although prediction market equilibria generally capture relative value of information, there are several technical complications. First, in principle it could be that a prediction of Alice's does not reveal her signal for the coincidental reason that two signals give the same posterior belief. For example, in the case where both players receive a uniformly random bit and $E = A \oplus B$ (the XOR), Alice's posterior on E is uniformly random regardless of which signal she receives. Second is the question of *commitment*. It might be that equilibria of prediction markets do not completely reflect the relative value of information and idealized signaling schemes because Alice is unable to commit to such a scheme.

This motivates us to study the more mathematically clean *ABA game with commitment*. Introduced in [18], this "game" can be phrased as a single-player decision problem, fully specified by $\{G, \mu\}$ where: convex function $G : \Delta(\mathcal{E}) \to \mathbb{R} \cup \{-\infty\}$ is chosen by the designer; μ is the prior on (A, B, E). Alice makes the only decision in the game by selecting a signaling scheme $\pi : \mathcal{S} \times \mathcal{A} \to [0, 1]$. This signaling scheme is announced to Bob. Nature draws $(A, B, E) \sim \mu$ and draws $S \sim \pi(\cdot \mid A)$. Bob observes the signal S, updates to a posterior $\mathbf{p}_{S,B}$, and receives utility $R(\mathbf{p}_{S,B}, E) - R(\mathbf{p}_S, E)$. Then Alice receives utility $R(\mathbf{p}_S, E) - R(\mathbf{p}, E) + R(\mathbf{p}_{A,B}, E) - R(\mathbf{p}_{S,B}, E)$ in total. Crucially, this payoff structure makes the game constant-sum since for each $A = a, B = b, E = e$, the sum of Alice's and Bob's utilities equals $R(\mathbf{p}_{a,b}, e) - R(\mathbf{p}, e)$, which is fixed.[1]

The interpretation of these payoffs is that Alice comes to the prediction market, announces signal S, and predicts the posterior conditioned on S. Then, Bob arrives, sees S, announces B, and predicts the posterior conditioned on both S and B (via Bayesian update). Finally, Alice arrives, announces A, and

---

[1] This is a slight departure from the formalization of the game in [18]. There, Alice did not automatically observe Bob's signal, causing complications in the case where Bob's report $\mathbf{p}_{S,B}$ could be the same for two different outcomes $b, b' \in \mathcal{B}$.

predicts the posterior given both A and B. In other words, as phrased by [7,14], Alice receives the *marginal value* of signal S over the prior; then Bob receives the marginal value of B over S; and finally, Alice receives the marginal value of A over S, B.

2.4 Bayesian Persuasion

The ABA game turns out to be relevant to the Bayesian persuasion model. A persuasion game is played between a *sender* and a *receiver*. The receiver is faced with selecting an action i from $[k] = \{1, \cdots, k\}$. Both the sender and receiver utility depend on the receiver's action as well as a state of nature e supported on $\mathcal{E}$. Formally, the sender and receiver payoff function are $v(i, e)$ and $u(i, e)$ where $i \in [k]$ and $e \in \mathcal{E}$.

Particularly relevant to this work is the model of *Bayesian persuasion with a privately informed receiver*, first studied by Kolotilin *et al.* [17]. Here, the sender and receiver each observe a private signal regarding the state of nature E, which may be correlated with each other. Let $A \in \mathcal{A}$ and $B \in \mathcal{B}$ denote the (random) signal observed by the sender and receiver, respectively. The joint distribution of A, B, E is public knowledge and denoted as $\mu(e, a, b)$. The Bayesian persuasion model studies how the sender can maximize her expected utility by *committing* to a signaling scheme $\pi : \mathcal{S} \times \mathcal{A} \to [0, 1]$ to strategically influence the receiver's belief about e and consequently his optimal action.[2] Here, again, $\mathcal{S}$ is the set of signal outcomes. In Sect. 4, we will formalize the connection to prediction markets, which involves Alice "persuading" Bob to make certain reports but with a particular form of sender objectives specific to prediction markets.

3   Equivalence with and Without Commitment

In this section, we show that Alice's optimal signaling scheme in the ABA game with commitment yields an approximate PBE in the Alice-Bob-Alice prediction market (without commitment). Thus, we can next focus on solving the ABA game with commitment. In this section, to simplify technicalities, we assume that the proper scoring rule R has a *differentiable* convex expected score function G.

First, we formalize the sense in which Alice uses a signaling scheme even in a prediction market. This perspective has appeared in prior works on equilibria of markets, though a precise result may not have been stated. Informally, it says that in *any* equilibrium, Alice's equilibrium strategy can be written as reporting the posterior conditioned on a signal she draws from a private scheme. Recall from Fact 1 that, because Bob only participates once and the market uses a strictly proper scoring rule, his unique best response is always to report truthfully according to his information and beliefs.

---

[2] Such a signaling scheme is also called an *experiment* by Kolotilin *et al.* [17]. We remark that their model is a special case of the general model we described here, with independent A, B and binary receiver actions.

Lemma 1. *In perfect Bayesian equilibrium of the Alice-Bob-Alice prediction market, without loss of generality, Alice's strategy is to predict $\mathbf{p}_S$ for some signaling scheme π and associated random signal S.*

Therefore, from here on we will describe Alice's strategy in prediction markets as a signaling scheme π, keeping in mind that she does not publicly announce her signal and does not have to commit to the scheme.

Before we proceed, we will give some necessary definitions.

Definitions. First, let us define $V = \mathbb{E}_{A,B,E} \, R(\mathbf{p}_{A,B}, E) - R(\mathbf{p}, E)$ where $\mathbf{p}$ is the prior. This is the difference in expected score between the prior and the posterior conditioned on both players' signals (it can also be written $\mathbb{E}_{A,B} \, G(\mathbf{p}_{A,B}) - G(\mathbf{p})$). Next, let us define the notation $u_B(\pi'; \pi)$ as follows. In the prediction market game, suppose Alice draws from π while Bob believes she is drawing from π'. If $\mathbf{p}^1$ is in the support of π' given Bob's signal B, then he does a Bayesian update to an incorrect (in general) posterior belief $\mathbf{p}^2$ and reports it. If $\mathbf{p}^1$ is not in the support of Alice's π' strategy ("off the equilibrium path"), then Bob forms some belief over Alice's signal and uses this to again form an incorrect posterior belief $\mathbf{p}^2$. We define $u_B(\pi'; \pi)$ to be Bob's expected utility in this case, for some off-path beliefs of Bob.

The core idea occurs in the following lemma, which shows that, under some conditions, Alice prefers to deviate to the optimal signaling scheme.

Lemma 2. *Suppose that, in the ABA game with commitment, π^* brings Alice higher utility than π. Then in the Alice-Bob-Alice prediction market, if Alice plays π and always learns Bob's signal after his report, then Alice improves utility by deviating to π^*.*

To prove our main result, we also need the following continuity claim.

Lemma 3. *In the prediction market with differentiable G, fixing Bob's strategy, Alice's expected utility is continuous in π; and similarly, fixing Alice's strategy, Bob's expected utility is continuous with respect to each of his reports at the second stage (i.e. outcomes of $\mathbf{p}^2$) as well as each of the probabilities he places on each report.*

These results allow us to prove the main result of this section.

Theorem 1. *Let π^* be the optimal signaling scheme for the ABA game with commitment, i.e. the minimizer of $u_B(\pi; \pi)$. Then for any ϵ, there is an ϵ-PBE of the Alice-Bob-Alice prediction market in which Alice plays within ϵ of π^*.*

4   ABA Game with Commitment Is Bayesian Persuasion

In this section, we formally establish the connection between the ABA game with commitment (denoted as `ABA-Commit`) and the Bayesian Persuasion (BP) game with a privately informed receiver (denoted as `BP-Private`). Besides revealing interesting conceptual insights, this connection also enables us to directly employ ideas from Bayesian persuasion to design an efficient algorithm for the ABA game when the size of Bob's signal space is a constant and the expected score function G is k-piecewise linear.

4.1   Reducing ABA-Commit to BP-Private

We start by simplifying the equilibrium analysis of the ABA game with commitment. Since Bob has only one chance to participate in the ABA game, his optimal strategy is simply to reveal his original signal at $t = 2$ (assuming tie breaking in favor of more information) and Alice will also reveal all her information at $t = 3$. Therefore, the only non-trivial stage is Alice's optimal commitment at the first stage. Since the game is constant-sum, so maximizing Alice's utility is equivalent to minimizing Bob's utility. As a result, solving the ABA game with commitment boils down to compute *Alice's optimal commitment* (to a signaling scheme) at the first stage to minimize Bob's utility.

For convenience and clarity, we state the result for piecewise linear convex function G, however this connection holds for arbitrary convex G function (see remarks at the end of the theorem proof).

Theorem 2. *For any ABA-commit instance $\{G, \mu\}$ where G is k-piecewise linear and μ is the prior over (A, B, E), there is a BP-private instance such that Alice's optimal commitment is the same as the sender's optimal commitment in the BP-private instance, which is described as follows: (1) the instance has the same joint prior μ over the sender signal A, receiver signal B and event E; (2) The receiver utility function $U_G(i, e)$ is uniquely determined by G with action set $[k] = \{1, 2, \cdots, k\}$; (3) The sender utility as a function of any signaling scheme $\pi : \mathcal{S} \times \mathcal{A} \to [0, 1]$ is given by*

$$Sender\ Obj = \mathbb{E} \max_{s} \sum_{\substack{i \in [k] \\ e \in E}} [U_G(i, e) \cdot \Pr(e|s)] - \mathbb{E} \max_{s,b} \sum_{\substack{i \in [k] \\ e \in E}} [U_G(i, e) \cdot \Pr(e|s, b)]. \quad (2)$$

4.2   A Direct Application of the Reduction

As a direction application of the reduction in Sect. 4.1, we now show how to use this connection to compute Alice's optimal commitment when $|\mathcal{B}|$ is constant and the expected score function G is k-piecewise linear. Our algorithm is polynomial in k but exponential in the constant $|\mathcal{B}|$, as described in the following theorem.

Theorem 3. *When G is k-piecewise linear, there exists a $\mathrm{poly}(k^{|\mathcal{B}|}, |\mathcal{A}|, |\mathcal{E}|)$-time algorithm that computes Alice's optimal signaling scheme to commit to.*

In the introduction, we discussed the connection between ABA-commit with informational substitutes and complements. Two signals are strong substitutes if the optimal signaling scheme is to always reveal all information, and two signals are strong complements if the optimal signaling scheme is to always reveal no information. We can use the algorithm in this section to compute the signaling scheme exactly. Therefore, the following corollary is immediate.

Corollary 1. *If G is k-piecewise linear, then there exists a $\mathrm{poly}(k^{|\mathcal{B}|}, |\mathcal{A}|, |\mathcal{E}|)$-time algorithm that tests whether two signals A and B are strong substitutes, complements, or neither.*

5 FPTAS for Different Parameter Regimes

In this section, we develop Fully Polynomial Time Approximation Schemes (FPTAS) for the ABA game with commitment for different parameter regimes. These results cover a wider range of settings, and in particular, strictly generalize the main result of Kong and Schoenebeck [18]. Moreover, our algorithm is much simpler than that in [18] and is inspired by ideas that have also been used in the previous literature of algorithmic Bayesian persuasion.

While we do not use the explicit correspondence with the Bayesian persuasion instance developed in Sect. 4 here, we use key analytical techniques from the persuasion literature. Namely, the signaling scheme can be equivalently viewed as a distribution of posteriors and the only constraint on that distribution is the *Bayes-plausibility* constraint: the expectation of the posteriors equal the prior. We then show that under a Lipschitz-like constraint on G, a small perturbation of the posterior leads to a small perturbation of Alice's payoff. We can therefore discretize the space of posteriors within ϵ precision and show that there exists an approximately optimal signaling mechanism whose induced posteriors lie only on those grid points. When the total number of grid points are polynomially bounded, we obtain efficient algorithms. This idea has been employed in algorithmic persuasion (e.g., [4,8]).

We start by defining the continuity condition we need on the expected score function G.

Definition 1 (Local Hölder Continuity). *A function $G : \mathbb{R}^n \to \mathbb{R}$ is (α, β)-locally Hölder continuous if there exists $\alpha > 0, \beta \in (0,1]$ and some $c \in (0,1)$ such that $|G(\mathbf{x}) - G(\mathbf{y})| \leq \alpha |\mathbf{x} - \mathbf{y}|^\beta$ for any $\mathbf{x}, \mathbf{y}$ such that $|\mathbf{x} - \mathbf{y}| \leq c$.*

Note that local Hölder continuity is a natural and weak continuity assumption, which holds for almost any reasonable scoring rule. In particular, it is weaker than the standard Hölder continuity, which requires the above condition to hold for any $\mathbf{x}, \mathbf{y}$, not only those with $|\mathbf{x} - \mathbf{y}| \leq c$. Hölder continuity is then weaker than the Lipschitz continuity which corresponds to the case of $\beta = 1$. Moreover, we will see later that α does not have to be an absolute constant; only that α is polynomial-sized is enough for an FPTAS.

To obtain an FPTAS for the case with constant $|\mathcal{A}|$, Kong and Schoenebeck [18] defined another notion of continuity of G, which they call *niceness* condition formally described as follows. It turns out that *niceness* condition is a stronger requirement than the local Hölder continuity. So any function satisfying their condition also satisfies ours, including quadratic and log scoring rules.

Definition 2 (Niceness Condition [18]). *A function $G : \Delta_n \to \mathbb{R}$ is λ-nice if there exists a function $g : [0,1] \to \mathbb{R}$ such that $G(\mathbf{x}) = \sum_i g(x_i)$ for every $\mathbf{x} \in \Delta_n$, $g(0) = g(1) = 0$, g is convex, and there exists a constant $\lambda \in (0,1)$ such that for sufficiently small ϵ, $\max(|g(\epsilon), g(1 - \epsilon)|) \leq \epsilon^\lambda$.*

Proposition 2. *Any function that is λ-nice for some $\lambda \leq 1$ is $(n^{1-\lambda}, \lambda)$-locally Hölder continuous.*[3]

The niceness condition is a relatively strong requirement, especially as requires the expected score function G to be separable in all arguments $G(x) = \sum_i g(x_i)$. It happens to hold for log and quadratic scoring rules, but it is certainly not a property we generally expect to hold; the spherical scoring rule has $G(x) = (\sum_i x_i^2)^{1/2}$ which is not separable.

5.1 Constant Number of Alice's Signal Outcomes

We now consider the setting of [18] with constant size of Alice's signal space, i.e., $d \equiv |\mathcal{A}|$ is a constant. Kong and Schoenebeck [18] prove that when G satisfies the niceness condition, there is an FPTAS for this case. Here we exhibit another FPTAS for this setting based on the aforementioned idea from persuasion but under the (weaker) assumption of local Hölder continuity. This thus strictly generalizes the result in [18].

Let $\Delta_d \equiv \Delta(\mathcal{A})$ denote the set of all possible distributions over signal realizations of A. Let $\mathbf{p} \in \Delta_d$ denote a generic posterior distribution over Alice's signal space. Throughout we always use $|\mathbf{z}| = \sum_i |z_i|$ to denote the l_1 norm of a vector $\mathbf{z}$. For a function f, denote by $\{f(e)\}_{e \in \mathcal{E}}$ a vector of dimension $|\mathcal{E}|$ whose entries are $f(e)$ for $e \in \mathcal{E}$. We prove the following theorem.

Theorem 4. *Assume that $|\mathcal{A}|$ is a constant, and the G function is (α, β)-locally Hölder continuous for some $\alpha, \beta > 0$ and bounded within $[-L, L]$ for some L. Then there exists a $\text{poly}(|\mathcal{B}|, |\mathcal{E}|, 1/\delta, L)$-time algorithm that computes Alice's δ-optimal signaling scheme.*

5.2 Constant Number of Event Outcomes and Bob's Signal Outcomes

Next we exhibit an FPTAS for another parameter regime: both $n_E \equiv |\mathcal{E}|$ and $n_B \equiv |\mathcal{B}|$ are constant. The proof uses the same technique as in the previous section. The key idea is that Alice's signaling scheme can be viewed equivalently as a distribution over posterior distributions $\mathbf{v} \in \Delta(\mathcal{E} \times \mathcal{B})$ jointly over the event and the Bob's private signal, and that this distribution captures *all* of the information needed. Compared to Theorem 3, this result does not require k-piecewise linearity of G but requires that $|\mathcal{E}|$ is a constant. Moreover, this result is an FPTAS whereas Theorem 3 gives an exact algorithm.

Theorem 5. *Assume that $|\mathcal{E}|$ and $|\mathcal{B}|$ are constants, and the G function is (α, β)-locally Hölder continuous for some $\alpha, \beta > 0$ and bounded within $[-L, L]$ for some L. Then there exists a $\text{poly}(|\mathcal{A}|, 1/\delta, L)$-time algorithm that computes Alice's δ-optimal signaling scheme.*

---

[3] Note that if $\lambda > 1$ in the λ-nice condition, or if $\beta > 1$ in the (α, β)-local Hölder continuity condition, then G is identically zero so we are not interested in those trivial cases.

6   Conclusion and Directions

In this work, we took steps toward better understanding of equilibria of prediction markets, identifying informational substitutes and complements, and connections between these problems and other signaling games including Bayesian persuasion.

While these results extend the work of [18] in several ways – connecting Alice's optimal commitment to the original prediction market game, generalizing results for the case of fixed $|\mathcal{A}|$, and new algorithms for other cases – much open work still remains. A first direction is to give efficient algorithms with fewer assumptions, e.g. if $|\mathcal{B}|$ is bounded but we have fewer restrictions on G. A second direction is to prove intractability results, which do not yet exist for this game, although the problem appears quite challenging. It would also be interesting to understand whether the problem of testing whether signals are informational substitutes is tractable or not, and whether computing Alice's optimal signaling scheme is algorithmically easier than testing substitutes. Finally, one can ask how these results extend to larger prediction market games.

References

1. Abernethy, J., Chen, Y., Vaughan, J.W.: Efficient market making via convex optimization, and a connection to online learning. ACM Trans. Econ. Comput. **1**(2), 12 (2013)
2. Berg, J., Forsythe, R., Nelson, F., Rietz, T.: Results from a dozen years of election futures markets research. In: Handbook of Experimental Economics Results (2008)
3. Bergemann, D., Morris, S.: The comparison of information structures in games: Bayes correlated equilibrium and individual sufficiency. Technical report 2, May 2016
4. Bhaskar, U., Cheng, Y., Ko, Y.K., Swamy, C.: Hardness results for signaling in Bayesian zero-sum and network routing games. In: Proceedings of the 2016 ACM Conference on Economics and Computation, pp. 479–496. ACM (2016)
5. Chen, Y., et al.: Gaming prediction markets: equilibrium strategies with a market maker. Algorithmica **58**(4), 930–969 (2010)
6. Chen, Y., Reeves, D.M., Pennock, D.M., Hanson, R.D., Fortnow, L., Gonen, R.: Bluffing and strategic reticence in prediction markets. In: Deng, X., Graham, F.C. (eds.) WINE 2007. LNCS, vol. 4858, pp. 70–81. Springer, Heidelberg (2007). https://doi.org/10.1007/978-3-540-77105-0_10
7. Chen, Y., Waggoner, B.: Informational substitutes. In: 56th Annual IEEE Symposium on Foundations of Computer Science, FOCS 2016 (2016)
8. Cheng, Y., Cheung, H.Y., Dughmi, S., Emamjomeh-Zadeh, E., Han, L., Teng, S.H.: Mixture selection, mechanism design, and signaling. In: 2015 IEEE 56th Annual Symposium on Foundations of Computer Science, pp. 1426–1445. IEEE (2015)
9. Dimitrov, S., Sami, R.: Non-myopic strategies in prediction markets. In: Proceedings of the 9th ACM Conference on Electronic Commerce, EC 2008, pp. 200–209. ACM (2008)
10. Freeman, R., Pennock, D.M., Vaughan, J.W.: The double clinching auction for wagering. In: Proceedings of the 18th Conference on Economics and Computation (EC) (2017)

11. Gao, X.A., Zhang, J., Chen, Y.: What you jointly know determines how you act: strategic interactions in prediction markets. In: Proceedings of the 14th ACM Conference on Electronic Commerce, EC 2013, pp. 489–506. ACM (2013). https://doi.org/10.1145/2482540.2482592
12. Gneiting, T., Raftery, A.E.: Strictly proper scoring rules, prediction, and estimation. J. Am. Stat. Assoc. **102**(477), 359–378 (2007)
13. Hanson, R.: Combinatorial information market design. Inf. Syst. Front. **5**(1), 107–119 (2003)
14. Howard, R.A.: Information value theory. IEEE Trans. Syst. Sci. Cybern. **2**(1), 22–26 (1966)
15. Iyer, K., Johari, R., Moallemi, C.C.: Information aggregation and allocative efficiency in smooth markets. Manag. Sci. **60**(10), 2509–2524 (2014)
16. Kamenica, E., Gentzkow, M.: Bayesian persuasion. Am. Econ. Rev. **101**(6), 2590–2615 (2011)
17. Kolotilin, A., Mylovanov, T., Zapechelnyuk, A., Li, M.: Persuasion of a privately informed receiver. Econometrica **85**(6), 1949–1964 (2017)
18. Kong, Y., Schoenebeck, G.: Optimizing Bayesian information revelation strategy in prediction markets: the Alice Bob Alice case. In: 9th Innovations in Theoretical Computer Science Conference, ITCS 2018 (2018)
19. Lambert, N.S., et al.: An axiomatic characterization of wagering mechanisms. J. Econ. Theory **156**, 389–416 (2014)
20. Lambert, N.S., et al.: Self-financed wagering mechanisms for forecasting. In: Proceedings of the 9th ACM Conference on Electronic Commerce, EC 2008, pp. 170–179. ACM (2008)
21. McCarthy, J.: Measures of the value of information. Proc. Nat. Acad. Sci. **42**(9), 654–655 (1956)
22. Ostrovsky, M.: Information aggregation in dynamic markets with strategic traders. Econometrica **80**(6), 2595–2647 (2012)
23. Savage, L.J.: Elicitation of personal probabilities and expectations. J. Am. Stat. Assoc. **66**(336), 783–801 (1971)
24. Tetlock, P.E., Gardner, D.: Superforecasting: The Art and Science of Prediction. Broadway Books, New York (2016)
25. Witkowski, J., Freeman, R., Vaughan, J.W., Pennock, D.M., Krause, A.: Incentive-compatible forecasting competitions. In: AAAI (2018)

Fair and Efficient Cake Division
with Connected Pieces

Eshwar Ram Arunachaleswaran, Siddharth Barman, Rachitesh Kumar,
and Nidhi Rathi[(✉)]

Indian Institute of Science, Bengaluru, India
eshwarram.arunachaleswaran@gmail.com, {barman,nidhirathi}@iisc.ac.in,
rachiteshkumar@gmail.com

Abstract. The classic cake-cutting problem provides a model for
addressing fair and efficient allocation of a divisible, heterogeneous
resource (metaphorically, the cake) among agents with distinct preferences. Focusing on a standard formulation of cake cutting, in which
each agent must receive a contiguous piece of the cake, this work establishes algorithmic and hardness results for multiple fairness/efficiency
measures.

First, we consider the well-studied notion of envy-freeness and develop
an efficient algorithm that finds a cake division (with connected pieces)
wherein the envy is multiplicatively within a factor of $3 + o(1)$. The
same algorithm in fact achieves an approximation ratio of $3 + o(1)$ for
the problem of finding cake divisions with as large a Nash social welfare (NSW) as possible. NSW is another standard measure of fairness
and this work also establishes a connection between envy-freeness and
NSW: approximately envy-free cake divisions (with connected pieces)
always have near-optimal Nash social welfare. Furthermore, we develop
an approximation algorithm for maximizing the ρ-mean welfare–this unifying objective, with different values of ρ, interpolates between notions
of fairness (NSW) and efficiency (average social welfare). Finally, we
complement these algorithmic results by proving that maximizing NSW
(and, in general, the ρ-mean welfare) is APX-hard in the cake-division
context.

Keywords: Fair division · Envy-freeness · Nash social welfare

1 Introduction

Cake cutting is a fundamental problem in the fair-division literature. It models the task of allocating a divisible, heterogeneous resource among agents with
distinct preferences, but equal entitlements. Indeed, the classic work of Steinhaus, Banach, and Knaster [27]—which lays the mathematical foundations of

Siddharth Barman gratefully acknowledges the support of a Ramanujan Fellowship
(SERB - SB/S2/RJN- 128/2015) and a Pratiksha Trust Young Investigator Award.

fair division—addresses cake cutting. Over the years, this problem has not only inspired the development of many interesting mathematical connections and algorithms (see, e.g., [25]), but has also been found relevant in real-world settings, such as border negotiations and divorce settlements [11]. Implementations of cake-division methods on platforms (such as Adjusted Winner [1]) further substantiate the practical relevance of this framework.

Here, the cake is represented by the segment $[0, 1]$ and the cardinal preferences of the agents are specified via valuation functions over (the intervals of) the cake. We will throughout focus on the setting wherein the cake needs to be partitioned into exactly n connected pieces (intervals) and each of the n agents receives one of these intervals. This is a well-studied formulation of cake cutting and is motivated by applications wherein connectivity (across each allocated part of the resource) is a crucial requirement [11]; consider, e.g., land division, spectrum allocation, and non-preemptive interval scheduling.[1]

Achieving fairness and efficiency are two pivotal goals in this resource-allocation context [11,25]. The current work contributes to these objectives, with a focus on computational aspects of cake cutting. The fairness and efficiency objectives addressed in this work are detailed next.

A quintessential notion of fairness is envy-freeness: a division is said to be envy-free iff, under it, every agent prefers its own piece over that of any other agent [18]. The well-known result of Su [30] (see also [28] and [26]) shows that, under mild assumptions on agents' valuations, envy-free cake divisions with connected pieces always exist. However, this existential result stands without an algorithmic counterpart; Stromquist [29] has shown that such an envy-free solution cannot be computed in bounded time, if the valuations are specified by an adaptive adversary.[2] This negative result leads one to study relaxations/approximation guarantees, such as the ones considered in this work.

It is relevant to note that, while envy-freeness provides fairness guarantees on an individual level, in and of itself, this notion is not concerned with overall efficiency. By contrast, the concept of social welfare quantifies efficiency achieved by the agents as a whole. Social (utilitarian) welfare is defined as the sum of the values that the agents have for their own pieces. For this welfare objective, we establish (multiplicative) approximation guarantees in the cake-cutting setup.[3]

A balance between the utilitarian (Benthamite) objective and the egalitarian (Rawlsian/max-min) welfare is achieved through Nash social welfare (NSW), which is defined as the geometric mean of the agents' values [20,23]. This welfare function has traditionally been studied for homogeneous (divisible) goods, where it is known to possess strong fairness (envy-freeness) and (Pareto) effi-

---

[1] The other variant of the problem, wherein agents can receive disconnected pieces, has also been studied in prior work; see, e.g., [24] and references therein. Related results on this variant are discussed at the end of this section.

[2] Notably, for the complementary problem of finding envy-free solutions with *noncontiguous pieces*, the work of Aziz and Mckinzie [7] provides a hyper-exponential time algorithm.

[3] Here, without loss of generality and to connect social welfare with the other objectives studied in this work, we equate social welfare with the average (arithmetic mean) of the values obtained by the agents.

ciency properties [31]. The appeal of Nash social welfare continues to hold in the case of indivisible goods: Caragiannis et al. [13] have shown that (under additive valuations) Nash-optimal allocations of discrete goods satisfy a natural relaxation of envy-freeness and are Pareto efficient. The relevance of Nash social welfare, as a measure of fairness, motivates its study in the cake-cutting setup as well. Towards this end, this work develops algorithmic and hardness results for the problem of finding cake divisions that maximize Nash social welfare.

Generalized (Hölder) means provide a unified framework to address fairness and efficiency objectives. Specifically, with exponent parameter ρ, the ρ-mean welfare, $M_\rho(\cdot)$, is defined as $\left(\frac{1}{n}\sum_i v_i^\rho\right)^{1/\rho}$; here v_is denote the valuations obtained by the agents in an allocation. We address ρ-mean welfare for $\rho \in (0,1]$. In particular, this parameter range captures both Nash social welfare and social welfare: $\rho = 1$ gives us the arithmetic mean (average social welfare) and, as ρ tends to zero, the limit of M_ρ is equal to the geometric mean (the Nash social welfare).[4]

This paper addresses all of the above-mentioned notions of fairness and efficiency. In particular, we develop approximation algorithms for finding cake divisions, with connected pieces, under the following objectives: (i) multiplicatively bounding envy, (ii) maximizing Nash social welfare, and (iii) maximizing ρ-mean welfare, for $\rho \in (0,1]$. We complement these approximation guarantees by establishing hardness results for Nash social welfare and ρ-mean welfare maximization. Our contributions are summarized in the following list.

- **Envy-Freeness:** We develop an efficient algorithm that finds a cake division (i.e., a partition of the cake into n connected pieces along with a one-to-one assignment of these pieces among the n agents) such that for every agent a the value of its piece is at least $1/(3 + o(1))$ times a's value for any other agent's piece (Theorem 1). Our algorithm for finding an approximately envy-free allocation is rather direct (see Sect. 3 for a description). The explainability/simplicity of this algorithm is a notable feature, since it makes the developed method amenable for realistic implementations, such as the ones found on websites like Spliddit [19].
- **Nash Social Welfare:** Our algorithm for finding approximately envy-free divisions also provides a polynomial-time $(3 + o(1))$-approximation algorithm for the Nash social welfare maximization problem (Theorem 2).

  We further show that approximately envy-free cake divisions (with connected pieces) always have near-optimal Nash social welfare: if in a cake division the envy is (multiplicatively) bounded within a factor of α, then the Nash social welfare of the division is at least $\frac{1}{2\alpha}$ times the optimal.[5]

---

[4] Note that, for each ρ, the ρ-mean welfare is ordinally equivalent to CES (constant elasticity of substitution) welfare functions that have the form $\left(\sum_i v_i^\rho\right)^{1/\rho}$.

[5] In comparison to this generic connection between envy-freeness and Nash social welfare, the cake divisions computed specifically by our algorithm admit a stronger guarantee–they essentially achieve an approximation bound of three for both envy and Nash social welfare.

Connections between envy-freeness and Nash social welfare have been established in other fair-division settings: addressing fair allocation of homogeneous,[6] divisible goods under additive valuations, the work of Varian [31] shows that there always exists an allocation which is both envy-free and Nash optimal.[7] Also, Caragiannis et al. [13] have established that, when dividing indivisible goods, allocations that maximize Nash social welfare satisfy relaxations of envy-freeness. Our results show that analogous connections hold in the cake-division framework as well.

We complement the algorithmic result for Nash social welfare by showing that it is APX-hard to find a Nash optimal cake division with connected pieces (Theorem 4). This hardness result implies, in particular, that the problem of maximizing Nash social welfare does not admit a polynomial-time approximation scheme (PTAS), unless $P = NP$.

- **Generalized-Mean Welfare:** As mentioned previously, generalized means—$M_\rho(\cdot)$ with exponent parameter $\rho \in (0, 1]$—is a family of functions which captures both Nash social welfare and (average) social welfare. For this unified objective, we develop a $(2 + o(1))^{1/\rho}$-approximation algorithm that runs in time $n^{\mathcal{O}(1/\rho)}$; here n is the number of agents (Theorem 3). Hence, for average social welfare (i.e., the $\rho = 1$ case) we obtain a polynomial-time $(2 + o(1))$-approximation algorithm. We note that this instantiation improves upon the 8-approximation guarantee obtained specifically for social welfare in the work of Aumann et al. [6].

Our algorithm, for maximizing ρ-mean welfare, relies on "discretizing" the given cake-division instance to obtain an interval-scheduling problem, called the Job Interval Selection Problem (JISP). Then, we invoke the 2-approximation algorithm of Bar-Noy et al. [9] for JISP to obtain the stated approximation guarantee (Theorem 3).

We also establish that, for any fixed $\rho \in (0, 1]$, finding cake divisions that maximize ρ-mean welfare is APX-hard. This general result, though, holds for cake-division instances wherein the valuations are not necessarily normalized.[8] For the social welfare case (i.e., the $\rho = 1$ setting), our techniques can be adopted to establish APX-hardness even under normalized valuations. Hence, we can rule out a PTAS for the social welfare maximization problem. This strengthens the inapproximability result of Aumann et al. [6], which showed that efficient (in the social-welfare sense) cake cutting does not admit a fully polynomial-time approximation scheme (FPTAS).

Prior work has also studied the impact of envy-freeness on social welfare in the cake-cutting context. Specifically, Caragiannis et al. [12] along with Aumann and Dombb [5] establish bounds for price of envy-freeness, which is

---

[6] Hence, such goods do not correspond to a heterogenous cake.

[7] In fact, in the homogenous-goods case, such an allocation can be efficiently computed by solving the convex program of Eisenberg and Gale [16]. By contrast, finding a Nash optimal allocation is the cake-division setting is computationally hard.

[8] Agents' valuations are said to be normalized iff, for every agent, the value of the entire cake is equal to one.

defined as the ratio between the social welfare of an optimal allocation and the social welfare of the best envy-free allocation. We extend this framework to ρ-mean welfare and show that any (approximately) envy-free allocation provides an $\mathcal{O}(2^{\frac{1}{\rho}} n^{\frac{\rho}{\rho+1}})$-approximate solution to maximizing ρ-mean welfare, for $\rho \in (0,1]$. We note that our upper bound on the price of envy-freeness for the $\rho = 1$ instantiation (i.e., for social welfare) is essentially tight. This follows from considering the result of Aumann and Dombb [5], which establishes a $\Theta(\sqrt{n})$ bound on the price of envy-freeness, in the social-welfare context. Due to space constraints, technical details and proofs of some of the above-mentioned results are deferred to the full version of this work [4].

Additional Related Work. Another standard notion of fairness is proportionality. This criterion requires that every agent a receives a piece of value at least $1/n$ times a's value for the entire cake; here n is the total number of agents participating in the cake-cutting exercise. In contrast to envy-freeness, proportionality is an algorithmically tractable solution concept; see [24] and references therein. Though, given that an (approximately) envy-free allocation is also (approximately) proportional,[9] approximation guarantees for envy-freeness (such as the ones developed in this work) give us matching bounds for proportionality as well.

With respect to maximizing social welfare, the result closest to ours is that of Aumann et al. [6]. We reiterate that the current work improves upon the algorithmic and hardness bounds obtained in [6]. Bei et al. [10] develop approximation results for maximizing social welfare with proportionality as a constraint. By contrast, we focus on social welfare by itself.

Deng et al. [15] present an algorithm that finds an additive approximation to an envy-free cake division with connected pieces. This algorithm, however, runs in exponential (in the number of agents) time.

If disconnected pieces can be assigned to each agent, then an additive approximation to envy-free divisions can be computed efficiently, see, e.g., [22] and the reentrant version of the last diminisher protocol in [11]. Also, for the disconnected-pieces variant and under specific valuations types, Aziz and Ye [8] present an efficient algorithm for maximizing Nash social welfare. The results of Kurokawa et al. [21] and Cohler et al. [14] address the noncontiguous-pieces setup as well. In particular, for a class of valuations, Cohler et al. [14] develop an algorithm for maximizing social welfare subject to the envy-freeness constraint. Our results are incomparable with all of these prior works, since we solely focus on allocation of connected pieces.

2 Notation and Preliminaries

We consider the problem of dividing a cake (which metaphorically represents a divisible, heterogenous good) among n agents. In this setup, the cake is modeled

---

[9] We conform to the standard assumption that the valuations of the agents over the cake are sigma additive.

as the segment $[0, 1]$ and the (possibly) distinct cardinal preferences of the agents are expressed as valuation functions, $\{v_a\}_{a \in [n]}$, over the intervals contained in $[0, 1]$ (i.e., over the pieces of the cake). Specifically, for each agent $a \in [n]$ and interval $I = [x, y] \subset [0, 1]$, with $0 \le x \le y \le 1$, the function v_a maps I to agent a's value for it, $v_a(I) \in \mathbb{R}_+$.

Conforming to standard assumptions, this work addresses valuations $\{v_a\}_{a \in [n]}$ that are (i) nonnegative, (ii) normalized: the value of the entire cake is equal to one, $v_a([0, 1]) = 1$, (iii) divisible: for every interval $I = [x, y]$ and parameter $\lambda \in [0, 1]$, there exists a $z \in [x, y]$ with the property that $v_a([x, z]) = \lambda v_a([x, y])$, and (iv) sigma additive: $v_a(I \cup J) = v_a(I) + v_a(J)$, for all disjoint intervals $I, J \subset [0, 1]$.

This divisibility property ensures that the valuations are non-atomic, i.e., $v_a([x, x]) = 0$ for all $a \in [n]$ and $x \in [0, 1]$. Furthermore, this property allows us, as a convention, to regard two intervals to be disjoint even if they intersect exactly at an endpoint.

Our results hold as long as the valuations satisfy the above-mentioned properties and only require oracle access to the valuations. That is, our algorithms can be efficiently executed in the Robertson-Webb model [25], which supports oracle access to the valuations in the form of evaluation queries (which, given an agent a and an interval I, return $v_a(I)$) and cut queries (which, given an agent a, an initial point $x \in [0, 1]$, and value τ, return the leftmost point $y \in [x, 1]$ such that $v_a([x, y]) = \tau$).

However, for ease of presentation, instead of the Robertson-Webb model, we will restrict attention to a well-studied setting in which the valuations of the agents can be explicitly given as input. In particular, we will consider valuations that are induced by density functions: given a piecewise-constant density function $\nu_a : [0, 1] \mapsto \mathbb{R}_+$ for an agent $a \in [n]$, the valuation of any interval I is set to be $v_a(I) := \int_I \nu_a(x)\, \mathrm{d}x$. Valuations obtained by integrating piecewise-constant densities are said to be *piecewise-constant*. Indeed, such valuations can be given as input, say, in terms of the underlying density functions.

Problem Instances: A *cake-division instance*, with piecewise-constant valuations, is a tuple $\langle [n], \{v_a\}_{a \in [n]} \rangle$ where $[n] = \{1, 2, \ldots, n\}$ denotes the set of n agents and v_as specify the piecewise-constant valuations of the agents over the cake $[0, 1]$.

Allocations: As mentioned above, the goal here is to partition the cake into disjoint intervals and allocate them among the n agents. We will focus solely on assigning to each agent a single interval, i.e., we will require that the piece assigned to each agent is connected.

For a cake-division instance with n agents, an *allocation* is defined to be a collection of n pairwise-disjoint intervals, $\mathcal{I} = \{I_1, I_2, \ldots, I_n\}$, where interval I_a is assigned to agent $a \in [n]$ and $\cup_{a \in [n]} I_a = [0, 1]$.[10] We will use

---

[10] Note that the intervals are not indexed based on how their endpoints are ordered, rather the subscript of each interval in an allocation identifies the unique agent that owns this interval.

the term *partial allocation* to refer to collection of pairwise-disjoint intervals, $\mathcal{J} = \{J_1, J_2, \ldots, J_n\}$, that do not necessarily cover the entire cake, $\cup_a J_a \subsetneq [0,1]$.

The overarching objective of the current work is to find fair and efficient allocations. Relevant notions of fairness and efficiency are defined next.

Envy-Freeness: For a cake-division instance $\langle [n], \{v_a\}_{a \in [n]} \rangle$, an (partial) allocation $\mathcal{I} = \{I_1, \ldots, I_n\}$ is said to be *envy free* (EF) iff each agent prefers its own interval over that of any other agent, $v_a(I_a) \geq v_a(I_b)$ for all agents $a, b \in [n]$.

We will address a natural relaxation of envy-freeness; specifically, we study allocations in which the envy between the agents is multiplicatively bounded. Given $\alpha \geq 1$, an allocation $\mathcal{I} = \{I_1, \ldots, I_n\}$ is said to be *α-approximately envy free* (α-EF) iff $v_a(I_a) \geq \frac{1}{\alpha} v_a(I_b)$, for every pair of agents $a, b \in [n]$.

A 1-EF allocation is envy free and, the smaller the value of α, the stronger is the envy-freeness guarantee.[11]

Nash Social Welfare: For an allocation $\mathcal{I} = \{I_1, \ldots, I_n\}$, the *Nash social welfare* is defined to be the geometric mean of the agents' valuations, $\mathrm{NSW}(\mathcal{I}) := \left(\prod_{a=1}^{n} v_a(I_a) \right)^{1/n}$. In a cake-division instance, an allocation $\mathcal{I}^*$ is said to be a *Nash optimal allocation* iff $\mathcal{I}^* \in \arg\max_{\mathcal{I} \in \mathbb{I}} \mathrm{NSW}(\mathcal{I})$; here $\mathbb{I}$ denotes the set of all allocations.

Social Welfare and Generalized Mean: Social welfare is a standard measure of efficiency in the context of resource allocation. For an allocation $\mathcal{I} = \{I_1, \ldots, I_n\}$, we define *social welfare* to be the arithmetic mean[12] of the valuations, $\mathrm{SW}(\mathcal{I}) := \frac{1}{n} \sum_{a=1}^{n} v_a(I_a)$.

Generalized (Hölder) means, M_ρ, provide a family of functions which interpolate between fairness and efficiency objectives. The *ρ-mean welfare* of an allocation $\mathcal{I} = \{I_1, \ldots, I_n\}$ is defined as

$$\mathrm{M}_\rho(\mathcal{I}) := \left(\frac{1}{n} \sum_{a=1}^{n} [v_a(I_a)]^\rho \right)^{1/\rho}$$

We will develop algorithmic and hardness results for maximizing the ρ-mean welfare, with exponent $\rho \in (0,1]$. This parameter range, in particular, captures both NSW and SW: $\rho = 1$ gives us the arithmetic mean (social welfare) and, as ρ tends to zero, the limit of M_ρ is equal to the geometric mean (the Nash social welfare).

Overall, this paper is concerned with finding allocations (i.e., finding cake divisions with connected pieces) under the following objectives (i) bounding envy, (ii) maximizing Nash social welfare, and (iii) maximizing ρ-mean welfare, for $\rho \in (0,1]$.

---

[11] Also, note that α cannot be strictly less than one–the definition of an α-EF allocation requires $v_a(I_a) \geq \frac{1}{\alpha} v_a(I_b)$, even for $b = a$.

[12] Since the work develops multiplicative approximation guarantees, we can consider the average valuation, instead of the sum of valuations, as a utilitarian objective.

3   Finding Envy-Free and Nash Optimal Allocations

In this section, first we will develop an efficient algorithm for finding $(3 + o(1))$-EF allocations and, in tandem, obtain a polynomial-time $(3 + o(1))$-approximation algorithm for the Nash social welfare maximization problem. Subsequently, we will establish a generic connection between envy-freeness and Nash social welfare in the cake-cutting context: any α-approximately envy-free allocation provides a 2α-approximation to Nash social welfare.

Our algorithm, ALG, for finding approximately envy-free allocations starts by assigning an empty interval to each agent–it starts with the partial allocation consisting of empty sets. Then, the algorithm proceeds to assign successively higher valued pieces to the agents, i.e., it iteratively moves from one partial allocation to the next. Note that the initial partial allocation (consisting of empty intervals) is envy free. In fact, all the partial allocations, $\mathcal{P} = \{P_1, \ldots, P_n\}$, computed during ALG's execution, satisfy the following additive relaxation of envy-freeness, for a fixed constant $\varepsilon \in (0, 1/3]$:

$$v_a(P_a) \geq v_a(P_b) - \frac{\varepsilon}{n^2} \quad \text{for all } a, b \in [n] \tag{1}$$

ALG updates a partial allocation $\mathcal{P} = \{P_1, \ldots, P_n\}$ by considering the unassigned pieces of the cake. Specifically, given a partial allocation $\mathcal{P}$, write $\mathcal{U}_\mathcal{P} = \{U_1, U_2, \ldots, U_m\}$ to denote the minimum-cardinality collection of disjoint intervals that satisfy $\cup_i U_i = [0, 1] \setminus \cup_a P_a$. In other words, $\mathcal{U}_\mathcal{P}$ consists of the intervals that remain after the assigned intervals in $\mathcal{P}$ (i.e., P_as) are removed from $[0, 1]$. Since there are n intervals in $\mathcal{P}$, there can be at most $n + 1$ intervals in $\mathcal{U}_\mathcal{P}$.

ALG keeps iterating as long as there exists an unassigned interval $\widehat{U} \in \mathcal{U}_\mathcal{P}$ of high enough value for any agent. Then, part of $\widehat{U}$ is assigned to a judiciously-chosen agent $\widehat{a}$ who relinquishes the previous interval assigned to it, but now accrues a higher valuation. The criterion for selecting $\widehat{a}$ ensures that the above-mentioned invariant is maintained; this selection can be viewed as a *moving-knife procedure* applied within $\widehat{U}$ (see Fig. 1).

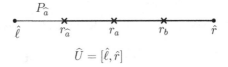

Fig. 1. An illustration of Step 4 in ALG

At the end, when the values of the unassigned intervals are not much larger than the value of the assigned ones, ALG merges each unassigned interval in $\mathcal{U}_\mathcal{P}$ with an adjacent interval in the (final) partial allocation $\mathcal{P}$ to obtain an

Algorithm 1. ALG

Input: A cake-division instance $\langle [n], \{v_a\}_a \rangle$ with piecewise-constant valuations and a fixed constant $\varepsilon \in (0, 1/3]$.
Output: A $\left(3 + \frac{9\varepsilon}{n}\right)$-approximately envy-free allocation.
1: Initialize partial allocation $\mathcal{P} = \{P_1, \ldots, P_n\}$ with empty intervals, i.e., $P_a = \emptyset$ for all $a \in [n]$. {Recall that $\mathcal{U}_\mathcal{P}$ denotes the set of unassigned intervals induced by any partial allocation $\mathcal{P}$.}
2: **while** there exists an agent $a \in [n]$ and an unassigned interval $\widehat{U} = [\hat{\ell}, \hat{r}] \in \mathcal{U}_\mathcal{P}$ such that $v_a(P_a) < v_a(\widehat{U}) - \frac{\varepsilon}{n^2}$ **do**
3:    Let $C := \left\{ b \in [n] \ : \ v_b(P_b) < v_b(\widehat{U}) - \frac{\varepsilon}{n^2} \right\}$ and, for every agent $b \in C$, set $r_b \in [\hat{\ell}, \hat{r}]$ to be the leftmost point such that $v_b([\hat{\ell}, r_b]) = v_b(P_b) + \frac{\varepsilon}{n^2}$.
4:    Select agent $\hat{a} \in \arg\min_{b \in C} r_b$.
5:    Update the partial allocation $\mathcal{P}$ by assigning $P_{\hat{a}} \leftarrow [\hat{\ell}, r_{\hat{a}}]$ and keeping the interval assignment of all other agents unchanged.
6:    Update $\mathcal{U}_\mathcal{P}$ to be the set of unassigned intervals induced by the current partial allocation $\mathcal{P}$.
7: **end while**
8: Associate each unassigned interval $U \in \mathcal{U}_\mathcal{P}$ with an assigned interval $P_a \in \mathcal{P}$ which is adjacent (either on the left or on the right) to U.
   {Note that any $P_a \in \mathcal{P}$ gets associated with at most two unassigned intervals, say U and U', and $U \cup P_a \cup U'$ is itself an interval}
9: For all $a \in [n]$, let interval I_a be the union of P_a and the unassigned intervals (if any) associated with it.
10: **return** allocation $\mathcal{I} = \{I_1, \ldots, I_n\}$

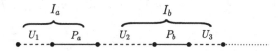

Fig. 2. An illustration of Steps 8 and 9 in ALG

approximately envy-free allocation (see Fig. 2). The algorithm is detailed below and we prove in Theorem 1 that it efficiently finds a $(3 + o(1))$-EF allocation.

The following lemma shows that the final partial allocation considered by ALG (in Step 8) satisfies the additive relaxation of envy-freeness considered in the Eq. (1), not only between the assigned intervals, but also against the unassigned ones. The proof of this lemma is deferred to the full version of the current paper [4].

Lemma 1. *For a given a cake-division instance $\langle [n], \{v_a\}_{a \in [n]} \rangle$, with piecewise-constant valuations, and given parameter $\varepsilon \in (0, 1]$, let $\mathcal{P} = \{P_1, \ldots, P_n\}$ be the final partial allocation considered by ALG (i.e., $\mathcal{P}$ is the partial allocation with which the while-loop terminates) and let $\mathcal{U}_\mathcal{P}$ be the set of unassigned intervals* *induced by* $\mathcal{P}$. *Then, for each agent* $a \in [n]$ *we have*

$$v_a(P_a) \geq v_a(Q) - \frac{\varepsilon}{n^2} \qquad \text{for all } Q \in \mathcal{P} \cup \mathcal{U}_{\mathcal{P}} \tag{2}$$

Using this lemma, we will now show that the allocation computed by ALG is $(3 + o(1))$-EF.

Theorem 1. *Given a cake-division instance* $\langle [n], \{v_a\}_{a \in [n]} \rangle$ *with piecewise-constant valuations, and constant* $\varepsilon \in (0, 1/3]$, *ALG computes a* $\left(3 + \frac{9\varepsilon}{n}\right)$-*approximately envy-free allocation in polynomial time.*

Proof. To bound the algorithm's time complexity note that in every iteration the selected agent's valuation (for the interval assigned to it) additively goes up by $\frac{\varepsilon}{n^2}$: in Steps 3 and 4, for the selected agent $\hat{a}$, we have $v_{\hat{a}}([\hat{\ell}, r_{\hat{a}}]) = v_{\hat{a}}(P_{\hat{a}}) + \frac{\varepsilon}{n^2}$. Since the total value of the cake for every agent is equal to one, ALG will iterate at most $\varepsilon^{-1} n^3$ times. Note that every step of the algorithm can be implemented efficiently and ε is set to be a constant. Hence, ALG runs in polynomial time.

Note that the collection of intervals, $\mathcal{P} = \{P_1, \ldots, P_n\}$, considered by ALG in Step 8 is indeed a partial allocation, i.e., the intervals P_as with which the while-loop terminates are pairwise disjoint. Let $\mathcal{U}_{\mathcal{P}}$ be the set of unassigned intervals induced by the final partial allocation $\mathcal{P}$. Also, write $\mathcal{I} = \{I_1, \ldots, I_n\}$ to denote the allocation returned by ALG; note that $P_a \subseteq I_a$ for all agents $a \in [n]$. Also, since $\mathcal{P}$ contains n intervals, $|\mathcal{U}_{\mathcal{P}}| \leq n + 1$.

Summing inequality (2) (see Lemma 1) across all intervals $Q \in \mathcal{P} \cup \mathcal{U}_{\mathcal{P}}$ gives us

$$(2n+1)\, v_a(P_a) \geq \sum_{Q \in \mathcal{P} \cup \, \mathcal{U}_{\mathcal{P}}} v_a(Q) - 2n\frac{\varepsilon}{n^2} = 1 - \frac{2\varepsilon}{n} \tag{3}$$

The last equality holds since $\bigcup_{Q \in \mathcal{P} \cup \, \mathcal{U}_{\mathcal{P}}} Q = [0, 1]$.

This inequality provides the following lower bound on the value attained by any agent $a \in [n]$ in the returned allocation $\mathcal{I} = \{I_1, \ldots, I_n\}$: $v_a(I_a) \geq v_a(P_a) \geq \frac{1}{2n+1} - \frac{2\varepsilon}{n(2n+1)}$. Therefore, with $n \geq 3$ and $\varepsilon \leq 1/3$,[13] we have the following bound:

$$\frac{3\varepsilon}{n} v_a(I_a) \geq \frac{\varepsilon}{n^2} \tag{4}$$

By construction, for each agent $b \in [n]$, the returned interval I_b is composed of P_b and at most two other unassigned intervals from $\mathcal{U}_{\mathcal{P}}$. Therefore, instantiating inequality (2) with $P_b \in \mathcal{P} \cup \mathcal{U}_{\mathcal{P}}$ and the (at most two) unassigned intervals associated with it, we get $3v_a(P_a) \geq v_a(I_b) - \frac{3\varepsilon}{n^2}$. That is, $3v_a(I_a) \geq v_a(I_b) - \frac{3\varepsilon}{n^2}$. Using this inequality and the bound (4), we obtain the desired approximate envy-freeness guarantee $\left(3 + \frac{9\varepsilon}{n}\right) v_a(I_a) \geq v_a(I_b)$ for all $a, b \in [n]$.

---

[13] For the $n = 2$ case one can efficiently find an envy-free allocation (i.e., a 1-EF allocation) by the cut-and-choose protocol [24].

Next, we will show that the allocations computed by ALG are not only $(3 + o(1))$-EF, but they also provide a $(3 + o(1))$-approximation to Nash social welfare.

The following theorem shows that an approximation ratio close to 3 can be obtained for the Nash social welfare maximization problem when the number of agents, n, is appropriately large. Such an approximation guarantee can also be achieved for constant values of n. This follows from the observation that, for the Nash social welfare maximization problem, one can compute an α-approximate solution (with $\alpha > 1$) in time $\left(\frac{n}{\log \alpha}\right)^{\mathcal{O}(n)}$; see the full version of this work for details [4]. Therefore, for any number of agents, maximizing Nash social welfare admits a polynomial-time $(3 + o(1))$-approximation algorithm. The proof of the this theorem appears in the full version of our work [4].

Theorem 2. *In cake-division instances with piecewise-constant valuations, the problem of maximizing Nash social welfare (with connected pieces) admits a polynomial-time $\left(3 + \frac{5}{n}\right)$-approximation algorithm; here n is the number of agents participating in the cake-cutting exercise.*

We conclude this section by formally stating that the approximately envy-free allocations always have near-optimal Nash social welfare. Note that, directly invoking this result for the $(3 + o(1))$-EF allocations computed by ALG, one would essentially obtain an approximation ratio of six for the Nash social welfare maximization problem. The proof of the following result is deferred to the full version [4].

In a cake-division instance, let $\widetilde{\mathcal{I}}$ be an α-approximately envy-free allocation and $\mathcal{I}^*$ be a Nash optimal allocation. Then,

(i) $\widetilde{\mathcal{I}}$ provides a 2α-approximation to Nash social welfare, i.e., $\mathrm{NSW}(\widetilde{\mathcal{I}}) \geq \frac{1}{2\alpha}\mathrm{NSW}(\mathcal{I}^*)$.

(ii) $\mathcal{I}^*$ is 4-approximately envy-free.

4 Approximation Algorithm for ρ-Mean Welfare Maximization

This section addresses cake-division with the objective of maximizing the ρ-mean welfare. We obtain an approximation algorithm for this problem via a simple reduction to the weighted job interval selection problem (JISP) [9,17].

The main result of this section is stated in the following theorem, the proof of which appears in the full version [4].

Theorem 3. *For $\rho \in (0, 1]$, $\varepsilon \in (0, 1)$ and cake-division instances $\mathcal{C} = \langle [n], \{v_a\}_{a \in [n]} \rangle$ with piecewise-constant valuations, there exists an algorithm that—in time $\left(\frac{n}{\varepsilon}\right)^{\mathcal{O}(\rho)}$—finds a $\left(2 + \frac{4\varepsilon e}{n}\right)^{\frac{1}{\rho}}$-approximation to the ρ-mean welfare maximization problem.*

Note that for any constant $\rho \in (0,1]$, Theorem 3 provides a constant-factor approximation algorithm that runs in polynomial time. In particular, for the $\rho = 1$ case (i.e., for average social welfare), we obtain a polynomial-time $(2 + o(1))$-approximation algorithm. As mentioned previously, this instantiation improves upon the 8-approximation guarantee obtained specifically for social welfare in the work of Aumann et al. [6].

5   Hardness of Maximizing Nash Social Welfare

This section asserts the APX-hardness of finding cake divisions (with connected pieces) that maximize Nash social welfare. That is, we have that, for a fixed constant $c \in (0,1)$, it is NP-hard to find an allocation (i.e., a cake division with connected pieces) whose Nash social welfare is within c times the optimal. This hardness result is obtained by developing a gap-preserving reduction from the Gap 3-SAT-5 problem [2,3]. The details of the reduction and the accompanying proof are deferred to the full version of this work [4]. The full version [4] also contains an analogous hardness result for the ρ-mean welfare objective.

Theorem 4. *Given a cake-division instance with piecewise-constant valuations, the problem of computing an allocation that maximizes Nash social welfare is* APX-*hard.*

6   Conclusions and Future Work

The current work studies cake-cutting from an algorithmic perspective and obtains approximation guarantees for multiple, well-studied notions of fairness and efficiency. In particular, we develop an efficient algorithm that computes $(3 + o(1))$-approximately envy-free allocations and, simultaneously, provides a $(3 + o(1))$-approximation to Nash social welfare. We complement this algorithmic result for Nash social welfare by proving that, in the cake-cutting context, maximizing this objective is APX-hard. Developing hardness results for (approximate) envy-freeness remains an interesting open problem.[14] Notably, the result of Deng et al. [15] shows that envy-free cake division (with connected pieces) is PPAD-hard, but this negative result holds under ordinal valuations–in this setup the preferences of each agent is specified via an explicit circuit which, given an allocation, identifies the agent's most preferred piece. Therefore, in and of itself, the result of Deng et al. [15] does not imply that envy-free cake division under cardinal valuations is PPAD-hard; complementarily, this result does not rule out an FPTAS for the contiguous-pieces version of envy-free cake-cutting under, say, piecewise-constant valuations.

Our approximation guarantee for ρ-mean welfare degrades as ρ tends to zero. Indeed, it does not match the approximation ratio achieved specifically for Nash

---

[14] Since an envy-free cake division always exists, the hardness results here will be in terms of complexity classes contained in TFNP.

social welfare. Tightening this gap is another interesting direction for future work. Computational results for maximizing ρ-mean welfare, with $\rho < 0$, will also be interesting. The $\rho \to -\infty$ case is particularly relevant, since it corresponds to egalitarian welfare, i.e., to the max-min (Santa Claus) objective. The work of Aumann et al. [6] proves that, in the cake-division framework, it is NP-hard to approximate egalitarian welfare within a factor of two. However, it remains open whether this problem admits a nontrivial approximation algorithm.

References

1. Adjusted winner. http://www.nyu.edu/projects/adjustedwinner/. Accessed 07 July 2019
2. Arora, S., Karger, D., Karpinski, M.: Polynomial time approximation schemes for dense instances of NP-hard problems. J. Comput. Syst. Sci. **58**(1), 193–210 (1999)
3. Arora, S., Lund, C., Motwani, R., Sudan, M., Szegedy, M.: Proof verification and the hardness of approximation problems. J. ACM (JACM) **45**(3), 501–555 (1998)
4. Arunachaleswaran, E.R., Barman, S., Kumar, R., Rathi, N.: Fair and efficient cake division with connected pieces. CoRR abs/1907.11019 (2019). http://arxiv.org/abs/1907.11019
5. Aumann, Y., Dombb, Y.: The efficiency of fair division with connected pieces. In: Saberi, A. (ed.) WINE 2010. LNCS, vol. 6484, pp. 26–37. Springer, Heidelberg (2010). https://doi.org/10.1007/978-3-642-17572-5_3
6. Aumann, Y., Dombb, Y., Hassidim, A.: Computing socially-efficient cake divisions. In: Proceedings of the 2013 International Conference on Autonomous Agents and Multi-Agent Systems, pp. 343–350. International Foundation for Autonomous Agents and Multiagent Systems (2013)
7. Aziz, H., Mackenzie, S.: A discrete and bounded envy-free cake cutting protocol for any number of agents. In: 2016 IEEE 57th Annual Symposium on Foundations of Computer Science (FOCS), pp. 416–427. IEEE (2016)
8. Aziz, H., Ye, C.: Cake cutting algorithms for piecewise constant and piecewise uniform valuations. In: Liu, T.-Y., Qi, Q., Ye, Y. (eds.) WINE 2014. LNCS, vol. 8877, pp. 1–14. Springer, Cham (2014). https://doi.org/10.1007/978-3-319-13129-0_1
9. Bar-Noy, A., Guha, S., Naor, J., Schieber, B.: Approximating the throughput of multiple machines in real-time scheduling. SIAM J. Comput. **31**(2), 331–352 (2001)
10. Bei, X., Chen, N., Hua, X., Tao, B., Yang, E.: Optimal proportional cake cutting with connected pieces. In: Twenty-Sixth AAAI Conference on Artificial Intelligence (2012)
11. Brams, S.J., Taylor, A.D.: Fair Division: From Cake-Cutting to Dispute Resolution. Cambridge University Press, Cambridge (1996)
12. Caragiannis, I., Kaklamanis, C., Kanellopoulos, P., Kyropoulou, M.: The efficiency of fair division. In: Leonardi, S. (ed.) WINE 2009. LNCS, vol. 5929, pp. 475–482. Springer, Heidelberg (2009). https://doi.org/10.1007/978-3-642-10841-9_45
13. Caragiannis, I., Kurokawa, D., Moulin, H., Procaccia, A.D., Shah, N., Wang, J.: The unreasonable fairness of maximum Nash welfare. In: Proceedings of the 2016 ACM Conference on Economics and Computation, pp. 305–322. ACM (2016)
14. Cohler, Y.J., Lai, J.K., Parkes, D.C., Procaccia, A.D.: Optimal envy-free cake cutting. In: Twenty-Fifth AAAI Conference on Artificial Intelligence (2011)
15. Deng, X., Qi, Q., Saberi, A.: Algorithmic solutions for envy-free cake cutting. Oper. Res. **60**(6), 1461–1476 (2012)

16. Eisenberg, E., Gale, D.: Consensus of subjective probabilities: the pari-mutuel method. Ann. Math. Stat. **30**(1), 165–168 (1959)
17. Erlebach, T., Spieksma, F.C.: Interval selection: applications, algorithms, and lower bounds. J. Algorithms **46**(1), 27–53 (2003)
18. Foley, D.K.: Resource allocation and the public sector (1967)
19. Goldman, J.R., Procaccia, A.D.: Spliddit: unleashing fair division algorithms. SIGecom Exch. **13**(2), 41–46 (2014)
20. Kaneko, M., Nakamura, K.: The Nash social welfare function. Econ. J. Econ. Soc. **47**(2), 423–435 (1979)
21. Kurokawa, D., Lai, J.K., Procaccia, A.D.: How to cut a cake before the party ends. In: Twenty-Seventh AAAI Conference on Artificial Intelligence (2013)
22. Lipton, R.J., Markakis, E., Mossel, E., Saberi, A.: On approximately fair allocations of indivisible goods. In: Proceedings of the 5th ACM Conference on Electronic Commerce, pp. 125–131. ACM (2004)
23. Nash Jr., J.F.: The bargaining problem. Econ. J. Econ. Soc. **18**(2), 155–162 (1950)
24. Procaccia, A.D.: Cake cutting algorithms. In: Handbook of Computational Social Choice, Chapter 13. Citeseer (2015)
25. Robertson, J., Webb, W.: Cake-Cutting Algorithms: Be Fair If You Can. AK Peters/CRC Press, Boca Raton (1998)
26. Simmons, F.: Private communication to Michael Starbird (1980)
27. Steinhaus, H.: The problem of fair division. Econometrica **16**, 101–104 (1948)
28. Stromquist, W.: How to cut a cake fairly. Am. Math. Mon. **87**(8), 640–644 (1980)
29. Stromquist, W.: Envy-free cake divisions cannot be found by finite protocols. Electron. J. Comb. **15**(1), 11 (2008)
30. Su, F.E.: Rental harmony: Sperner's lemma in fair division. Am. Math. Mon. **106**(10), 930–942 (1999)
31. Varian, H.R.: Equity, envy, and efficiency (1973)

A New Approach to Fair Distribution of Welfare

Moshe Babaioff[1] and Uriel Feige[2(✉)]

[1] Microsoft Research, Herzliya, Israel
moshe@microsoft.com
[2] Weizmann Institute, Rehovot, Israel
uriel.feige@weizmann.ac.il

Abstract. We consider transferable-utility profit-sharing games that arise from settings in which agents need to jointly choose one of several alternatives, and may use transfers to redistribute the welfare generated by the chosen alternative. One such setting is the Shared–Rental problem, in which students jointly rent an apartment and need to decide which bedroom to allocate to each student, depending on the student's preferences. Many solution concepts have been proposed for such settings, ranging from mechanisms without transfers, such as Random Priority and the Eating mechanism, to mechanisms with transfers, such as envy free solutions, the Shapley value, and the Kalai-Smorodinsky bargaining solution. We seek a solution concept that satisfies three natural properties, concerning efficiency, fairness and decomposition. We observe that every solution concept known (to us) fails to satisfy at least one of the three properties. We present a new solution concept, designed so as to satisfy the three properties. A certain submodularity condition (which holds in interesting special cases such as the Shared-Rental setting) implies both existence and uniqueness of our solution concept.

Keywords: Fairness · Envy-free · Shared-Rental · Anticore

1 Introduction

1.1 Background

We introduce a new solution concept for situations in which agents with cardinal preferences need to jointly choose one alternative from a set of alternatives, possibly compensating each other using transfers. This is a well studied setting in cooperative game theory, and we follow a normative approach that specifies properties that we wish our solution concept to have, and then design a solution concept that meets these specifications. To motivate our new solution concept and contrast it with well established previous solution concepts, we start with an example.

The reader is referred to the full version of the paper [1] for proofs, discussions and references that are omitted due to space limitations from the current version.

© Springer Nature Switzerland AG 2019
I. Caragiannis et al. (Eds.): WINE 2019, LNCS 11920, pp. 71–84, 2019.
https://doi.org/10.1007/978-3-030-35389-6_6

Suppose that three students jointly rent a three bedroom apartment for a total rent of r units of money. The students need to do two things. One is to jointly pay the rent, and the other is to solve the allocation problem, namely, decide which student gets which room, possibly compensating each other with money. We assume that the students are equals, in the sense that each student bears equal responsibility in paying the rent, and equal eligibility in receiving a room. Being equals, each student first pays $r/3$ towards the rent. It remains to solve the allocation problem, where this solution may possibly involve transfer of money among the students.

Remark 1. In cases in which no student receives a transfer larger than $r/3$, transfers may be implemented indirectly by having students pay unequal parts of the rent. However, in this paper we do not constrain transfers to be smaller than $r/3$, and the question of whether transfers are implemented as direct transfers among the students or as modification to rent payments is not a concern of the current paper.

A common approach for allocating rooms (and other goods) is using the *Random Priority* mechanism (a.k.a. *random serial dictatorship*), that we abbreviate as RP. A total order among the students is chosen uniformly at random, and each student in her turn chooses a room among those that are still available. RP has obvious advantages, being easy to implement in practice, agents (students in our case) have dominant strategies (given an agent's turn to choose, she should simply choose the available alternative that she most prefers), and being perceived as "fair" (all agents are treated equally from the mechanism's point of view). A significant drawback of RP is that it does not maximize welfare – the resulting allocation may produce less welfare (sum of utilities) than alternative allocations. Hence some economic efficiency is lost.

Let us consider a concrete example. Suppose that the students can express their valuation for rooms in units of money, and that they are risk neutral (they wish to maximize the expected received value). Suppose further that for some small $0 < \delta < \frac{1}{4}$, the value that each student derives by being given each of the rooms is as in the following table:

Example 1	Room 1	Room 2	Room 3
Student 1	$1 - \delta$	δ	0
Student 2	$1 - 2\delta$	2δ	0
Student 3	0	$\frac{1}{2} - \delta$	$\frac{1}{2} + \delta$

The maximum welfare allocation assigns room i to student i for every i, giving welfare of $\frac{3}{2} + 2\delta$. However, RP will result with probability half with an assignment in which student 2 gets room 1, giving welfare $\frac{3}{2}$, and hence the expected welfare of RP is δ lower than optimal.

The RP mechanism does not involve transfer of money among agents. In our language, we refer to it as an ANT, which is an abbreviation for Allocation mechanism with No Transfers. To overcome its weaknesses (shared by other ANTs as well), one often considers allocation mechanisms with transfers (abbreviated as AWT – Allocations With Transfers). AWTs allow for the following paradigm: first choose a maximum welfare allocation (thus creating the largest pie to divide: the maximum possible welfare to distribute among the agents), and then employ monetary transfers among the agents so as to distribute the high welfare to all agents, so as to satisfy some fairness criteria. In the example above, this would mean assigning room i to student i for every i, and then figuring out what the transfers should be so that the combination of allocation with transfers would be "fair".

To reason about transfers, we make the assumption that students have quasi-linear utilities: the utility of a student is simply the sum of her value for the room that she receives plus the transfer that she receives (the transfer may be negative if the student gives money rather than receives money). Moreover, we assume that the mechanism that computes the allocation and the transfers has access to the true valuations of the students. (This full information assumption is standard in cooperative game theory, and there are impossibility results showing that it cannot be avoided in our setting. See more details in [1].) Within such a setting, there is a well studied class of AWTs that is referred to as *envy free* solutions [4, 5, 10]). The basic principle is that one associates a transfer with each room (where the sum of transfers equals 0 – this is a *budget balance* condition) such that given the transfers, each student (weakly) prefers a different room. Then each student gets the room and associated transfers that she prefers, and no one prefers to switch with another agent. In the example above we can associate the following transfers with the rooms:

Room 1	Room 2	Room 3
$-\frac{2}{3} + 2\delta$	$\frac{1}{3} - \delta$	$\frac{1}{3} - \delta$

These transfers are indeed budget balanced and envy free, that is, each student i prefers her assigned room i (along with the associated payment) over any other room, leading to an allocation that maximizes welfare and in which supposedly every student is happy (as she got her most preferred one out of the three available options).

Let us consider a natural question. Suppose that the students initially intend to use the RP mechanism. Will the students be better off by using the envy free mechanism (that we abbreviate EF) instead of using RP? In some respects, the answer is no: RP is simpler to implement than EF, as it does not require students to disclose their valuation functions and to implement transfers. In other respects the answer is yes: EF generates higher welfare. But let us consider this last aspect more carefully. The social justification to maximize welfare is (in our opinion) the belief that the extra welfare will eventually get distributed to all members of the society that contributed to the increase in welfare. Is it the case that the increase in welfare (generated by moving from RP to EF) is distributed over the three students in a reasonable way? The answer is negative in our opinion.

- In RP, the sum of expected values derived by students 1 and 2 is 1. In EF, the sum of values increases to $1 + \delta$, but the sum of what they lose due to transfers is $\frac{1}{3} - \delta$. If $\delta < \frac{1}{6}$, each of the two students gets higher expected utility from RP than from EF. It is not true that the increase in welfare is distributed over all students in a way that *every* student (at least weakly) benefits.
- Student 3 contributes nothing to the increase in welfare when changing from RP to EF (in both cases her allocation is exactly the same – room 3). Nevertheless, under EF, student 3 not only gets her most preferred room, but also gets paid. Moreover, this payment is even larger than the total increase in welfare that EF offers compared to (the expected welfare of) RP.

Another aspect that we find troublesome with the EF solution is the following. In every Pareto efficient allocation, student 3 gets room 3 and the only question is which of the rooms 1 and 2 is allocated to which of the students 1 and 2. Hence the instance naturally decomposes into two subinstances, I_3 involving room 3 and student 3, and $I_{1,2}$ involving the other two students and two rooms. If one does this decomposition and then employs an EF mechanism on each component separately, student 3 does not receive any payments from the other students, and hence the resulting payments are different from those without the decomposition. Likewise, suppose that we had started with two separate instances, $I_{1,2}$ and I_3 as above, where every student prefers the rooms in her own instance over those in the other instance (it may even be that each instance concerns a different apartment). If we use EF mechanisms, then combining the two instances into one results in different payments compared to solving each of the instances separately. This sensitivity of the payments in EF mechanisms to composition and decomposition of instances (importantly, we are considering here cases in which composition and decomposition have no effect on the allocation itself) may lead to disagreements among the agents regarding what constitutes a single instance.

An allocation instance may have several different envy free solutions, but the above shortcomings are shared by *all* envy free solutions in the above example, provided that δ is sufficiently small.

Summarizing, ANT mechanisms such as RP need not maximize welfare. AWT mechanisms can address this weakness. A common AWT approach, that of envy free (EF) mechanisms has elegant conceptual properties when considered in isolation. However, when comparing its outcomes to those of RP, we identified several troubling aspects with its transfers. These include the fact that despite increase in welfare (compared to RP), some individual agents suffer loss in (expected) utility, the fact that agents who contribute nothing to the increase in welfare might receive payments (even beyond the total increase in welfare), and the fact that natural composition and decomposition properties are not respected by EF mechanisms.

Many other AWT approaches that have been proposed in the literature can be applied in the room allocation setting. They include (among others) the *Shapley value*, the *Nucleolus*, the *Nash bargaining* solution and the *Kalai-Smorodinsky (KS) bargaining* solution. Every AWT approach that we could find in the literature suffers from at least one of the troubling aspects listed above, see [1] for more details. Hence despite the many solution concepts that already exist, we find it appropriate to introduce a new AWT mechanism that does not suffer from any of the troubling aspects listed above.

1.2   The Model

We consider *transferable-utility profit-sharing games*, a setting that has been studied in previous work (e.g., by Moulin [7]). The room allocation problem of the previous section is a special case of this more general setting.

There is a set $\mathcal{N}$ of n *agents* (also referred to as *players*) and a set $\mathcal{A}$ of *alternatives*. Every agent $i \in \mathcal{N}$ has a valuation function $v_i : \mathcal{A} \to \mathbb{R}$. All valuation functions are expressed in the same units (of money). We let $v = (v_1, \ldots, v_n)$ denote the tuple of all the valuation functions. An NT (*no transfers*) *social choice function* f receives as input the pair $(\mathcal{A}, v)$ that includes the set of alternatives and the valuation functions, and outputs one of the alternatives from $\mathcal{A}$. A randomized NT social choice function may use randomization when choosing its output. Consequently, its output is a probability distribution over alternatives.

Given the tuple v of valuation functions, a set $S \subseteq \mathcal{N}$ of agents and an alternative $A \in \mathcal{A}$, the *welfare* $w_{S,v}(A)$ that alternative A offers to S is defined as $w_{S,v}(A) = \sum_{i \in S} v_i(A)$. An NT social choice function f *maximizes welfare* (with respect to $\mathcal{N}$) if the alternative $A^* \in \mathcal{A}$ that f selects satisfies $w_{\mathcal{N},v}(A^*) \geq w_{\mathcal{N},v}(A)$ for all $A \in \mathcal{A}$.

We allow transfer of money among agents. Such transfers are represented as a vector $p = (p_1, \ldots, p_n)$, where p_i is the payment to agent i, measured in units of money. We refer to the case of $p_i > 0$ as an *in-payment* (the amount of money of agent i increases), and to the case of $p_i < 0$ as an *out-payment* (the amount of money of agent i decreases). A transfer vector p is *budget balanced* if $\sum_{i=1}^{n} p_i = 0$. A *transfer function* g receives as input the triple $(\mathcal{A}, v, A^*)$ that includes the set of alternatives, the valuation functions, and an alternative chosen by an NT social choice function, and outputs a budget balanced transfer vector.

We assume that the utility functions of the agents are *quasi-linear*. Namely, for agent $i \in \mathcal{N}$ with valuation function v_i, her utility u_i from the pair of alternative A and transfer vector p is $u_i(A, p) = v_i(A) + p_i$. We further assume a setting of "full information upon request": the social planner may request information about valuation functions of agents (this information might be limited to the ordinal preferences of an agent over a set of alternatives, or might be as general as the full valuation function of an agent), and the agents reply truthfully to such requests.

Let us illustrate how the above model captures the example presented in Sect. 1.1, of three students renting a three bedroom apartment. $\mathcal{N}$ corresponds to the set of three students, and $\mathcal{A}$ corresponds to the set of six possible permutations over rooms, matching one room to one student. The valuation functions v_i are as in the example. An example of a randomized NT social choice function is the output of the *Random Priority* (RP) mechanism: once v is given (in fact, knowledge of ordinal preferences suffices here) RP induces a well defined probability distribution over alternatives. The envy-free allocation and transfers provided in the example are a solution (implicitly) involving an NT social choice function f and a transfer function g.

1.3   Our Contribution

For the setting described above, we wish to design a solution concept that has two components: an NT social choice function, and an associated transfer function. We have three goals. One is *economic efficiency*. This goal is easily attainable in our full information framework – we simply select a welfare maximizing alternative, which we denote by A^*. (If there are several welfare maximizing alternatives, A^* denotes one of them, selected arbitrarily.) Another goal is to achieve *fairness*, in the sense that the welfare will be shared "fairly" among all agents. Achieving this goal is made possible by the use of transfers. Those agents for which alternative A^* is undesirable can be compensated by in-payments, and the budget balance requirement can be met by extracting an equal amount of out-payments from those agents who do desire alternative A^*. The assumption that agents have quasilinear utility functions simplifies the accounting of the extent to which utility derived from payments can replace utility derived from the selected alternative. The third goal is that of *decomposability*, which basically means that if a large game involving multiple agents can be naturally decomposed into many smaller games over disjoint sets of agents, then the solution of the large game should also decompose into solutions of the smaller games. Equivalently, one should be able to solve each smaller game separately, and obtain a solution to the large game as the concatenation of the solutions to the smaller games.

Our contributions in this work are in setting the above three goals, proposing definitions for the fairness properties and decomposition properties that they refer to, proposing a solution concept that attains the above three goals, and providing sufficient conditions for its existence and uniqueness. Here is an informal statement of our main result when specialized to the Shared–Rental problem.

Theorem 1 (informal). *The* lex-max-WS *solution (introduced in our work) for the Shared–Rental problem maximizes welfare and satisfies the fairness and the decomposition properties alluded to above (and formally defined later in this paper). Moreover, in a well defined sense, it is the unique solution that satisfies these properties.*

Here are more details regarding our contributions, some of which are presented and/or discussed only in the full version of this paper [1]:

1. We propose a new notion of fair solutions, the *welfare-sharing core* (abbreviated WS-core). See Definition 1. It combines three principles that are briefly sketched below.

   (a) One principle is *domination* with respect to the utility agents can receive from a *disagreement point*, or *reference point*. This is mathematically similar to the familiar concept of *individual rationality* (IR), though conceptually there is a distinction between these two notions.

   (b) Another principle is that fairness entails not only lower bounds on the utilities that agents derive from the solution, but also natural upper bounds. We introduce a set-function W_{max}, where for a set S of agents, $W_{max}(S)$ is the welfare that S could derive from the alternative that is best for S. The same notion appears in [8], where is is referred to as *stand alone* utility. We require that the utility that a solution (with transfers) offers to a set S of agents does not exceed $W_{max}(S)$. This leads to the notion that we (and [8]) refer to as the *anticore*.

   (c) Another principle is that of *decomposability*, as discussed above (see Sect. 3 for more details). A key property of the anticore is that it decomposes: the anticore of a decomposable game is the concatenation of the anticores of each of the component games.

2. We show that in our setting, if W_{max} is submodular, then the WS-core is non-empty. See Theorem 1.

3. We propose to use egalitarian considerations (specifically, the lexicographically-maximal welfare-sharing rule, denoted *lex-max-WS*) for selecting a single solution from the WS-core, see Sect. 4. When W_{max} is submodular, we show (see Theorem 2, which relates to a previous result of Dutta and Ray [3]) that different egalitarian considerations (e.g., also the min-square rule, defined in Sect. 4) all lead to the same unique solution.

4. When W_{max} is submodular, we show that computing the *lex-max-WS* solution can be done in polynomial time. Moreover, it is a continuous function (with a small Lipschitz constant) of the valuation functions at points where the disagreement utility is a continuous function of the valuations.

5. We explain the similarities and differences between our new solution concept and several related notions. These include coalitional games and imputations; *cost-sharing* games; notions related to our notion of decomposability, such as *separability* and *consistency for reduced games*; previous notions referred to as the *anticore*; *egalitarian* solution concepts and *Lorenz ordering*; the *Shapley value*; the *Nucleolus*; *envy free* solutions; *Nash bargaining* and *Kalai-Smorodinsky (KS) bargaining*; *population monotonicity* and *resource monotonicity*.

6. We show that for the Shared–Rental problem W_{max} is submodular, and hence the *lex-max-WS* solution enjoys those properties shown above to be implied by submodularity.

2   The Welfare-Sharing Core

Our starting point is the (not necessarily new) premise that statements such as "this solution is fair" have no rigorous meaning on their own. Rather, the fairness of a solution needs to be judged in relation to a *reference context*. In our definition of fairness, the reference context will be the set $\mathcal{A}$ of alternatives together with a probability distribution π over $\mathcal{A}$ (which we will refer to as a *reference point*, or *disagreement point*). We now present the definition of the WS-core, and then follow it up with a discussion and comparison with related work.

A *solution* (A^*, p) is composed of a welfare maximizing alternative A^* and a budget balanced transfer vector $p = (p_1, \ldots, p_n)$. The *utility* that agent i derives from solution (A^*, p) is $u_i(A^*, p) = v_i(A^*) + p_i$. In our context, two solutions (A^*, p) and (A'^*, p') are *equivalent* if $u_i(A^*, p) = u_i(A'^*, p')$ for every agent i. Consequently, we sometimes refer to the utility vector $(u_1(A^*, p), \ldots, u_n(A^*, p))$ as the solution.

A solution will need to satisfy certain constraints, where these constraints are expressed as a function of the utilities that agents derive from the solution. We shall use $w_{S,v}(A) = \sum_{i \in S} v_i(A)$ to denote the welfare derived by a set S of agents from an alternative A, and $u_S(A^*, p) = \sum_{i \in S} u_i(A^*, p)$ to denote the utility derived by S from solution (A^*, p).

We associate two classes of constraints with solutions (A^*, p):

1. **Domination:** We assume that a probability distribution π over $\mathcal{A}$ is given, where $\pi(A)$ denotes the probability associated with alternative A. This distribution represents the alternative that would be chosen in the absence of agreement to use a mechanism with transfers. As such, the distribution π may depend on the valuations v, and we shall sometimes use the notation π_v to make this explicit. The value that agent i derives from π_v is $\sum_{A \in \mathcal{A}} \pi_v(A) v_i(A)$, and we refer to it as the agent's disagreement utility. The domination constraints require that $u_i(A^*, p) \geq \sum_{A \in \mathcal{A}} \pi_v(A) v_i(A)$ holds for every agent i.

2. **The anticore:** We introduce a welfare function over sets of agents, which we denote by W_{max}. For every $S \subseteq \mathcal{N}$ let $W_{max}(S) = \max_{A \in \mathcal{A}} [\sum_{i \in S} v_i(A)]$ indicate the maximum welfare achievable by S. The anticore constraints require that $u_S(A^*, p) \leq W_{max}(S)$ for every set $S \subseteq \mathcal{N}$.

Definition 1 (WS-core). *Suppose one is given a tuple v of valuation functions, a set $\mathcal{A}$ of alternatives, and a probability distribution π_v over $\mathcal{A}$. A solution (A^*, p) (composed of an alternative $A^* \in \mathcal{A}$ that maximizes welfare and a budget balanced vector p of transfers) is said to belong to the welfare-sharing core (WS-core) if the solution (A^*, p) satisfies the above two sets of constraints (domination and anticore) with respect to the given v and π_v.*

There are cases in which the WS-core is empty. However, in important special cases, the WS-core is nonempty. We first recall some standard terminology. A set function f is *monotone* if $f(S) \geq f(T)$ for all $T \subset S$. A set function f is *submodular* if for every two sets S and T it holds that $f(S) + f(T) \geq f(S \cap T) + f(S \cup T)$. Equivalently, f is submodular if it has the decreasing marginal returns property: for every item i and two sets $S \subset T$ it holds that $f(S \cup \{i\}) - f(S) \geq f(T \cup \{i\}) - f(T)$. A submodular function need not be monotone.

Our main existence result is the following:

Theorem 1. *Given a tuple v of valuation functions, a set $\mathcal{A}$ of alternatives, and a probability distribution π over $\mathcal{A}$, either one of the following conditions suffices in order for the WS-core to be nonempty.*

1. W_{max} *is submodular (though not necessarily monotone).*
2. $W_{max} - W_\pi$ *is monotone (though not necessarily submodular), where $W_\pi(S) = \sum_{i \in S} \sum_{A \in \mathcal{A}} \pi_v(A) v_i(A)$ is the expected value derived by set S from the disagreement distribution π. Note: if the disagreement utilities are 0, then a sufficient condition (though not necessary) for $W_{max} - W_\pi$ to be monotone is that the valuation functions are nonnegative.*

The proof of Theorem 1 appears in [1]. It is based on the following approach. Similar to proofs of the well known Bondareva-Shapley theorem [2,9], non-emptiness of the WS-core can be cast as a feasibility question for a certain linear program, which then translates to showing that the dual of the linear program is bounded. Each of the submodularity and monotonicity conditions listed above is shown to imply that the dual is bounded, thus proving the theorem.

3   Decomposability

In this section we introduce formal definitions for the notion of an instance being decomposable, and for two notions of decomposability for mechanisms: weak and strong.

Let $\mathcal{A}$ be a set of alternatives, $\mathcal{N}$ be a set of agents, and let $v = (v_1, \ldots, v_n)$ be a tuple specifying the valuation functions of the agents. We say that alternative $A \in \mathcal{A}$ is *Pareto optimal* with respect to a set $S \subset \mathcal{N}$ of agents if for every alternative $B \in \mathcal{A}$, either there is some agent $i \in S$ such that $v_i(A) > v_i(B)$, or for all agents $i \in S$ it holds that $v_i(A) = v_i(B)$.

Definition 2 (independent component, decomposable instance). *A set of players $S \subset \mathcal{N}$ is referred to as an* independent component *(or just component, for brevity) if for every alternative $A \in \mathcal{A}$ that is Pareto optimal with respect to S (given v) and for every alternative $B \in \mathcal{A}$ that is Pareto optimal with respect to $\bar{S} = \mathcal{N} \backslash S$, there is an alternative $C \in \mathcal{A}$ (possibly $C = A$ or $C = B$) such that for every agent $i \in S$ it holds that $v_i(C) = v_i(A)$, and for every agent $j \in \mathcal{N} \backslash S$ it holds that $v_j(C) = v_j(B)$. We say that an instance is* decomposable *if it has a component that is nontrivial (the component is neither empty, nor the whole instance).*

It is implicit in the above definition that if a decomposable instance has more than one Pareto optimal alternative, then there are agents that are indifferent among some choices of alternatives.

Observe that if $S \subset \mathcal{N}$ is a component then so is $\mathcal{N} \backslash S$. Definition 2 implies that if each of the two components S and $\mathcal{N} \backslash S$ selects a most preferred alternative on its own (such an alternative will be Pareto optimal with respect to the component), then there will be no conflicts between the two choices – we will be able to select a single alternative that is just as good, from the point of view of every player in every component.

As an example to the decomposition concept introduced above, consider the Shared–Rental problem example from Sect. 1.1, with valuation functions as in the table titled Example 1, and with $\delta < \frac{1}{4}$. In that example, there are two components, one containing Students 1 and 2, and the other containing Student 3. Every alternative A that is Pareto optimal for the first component assigns the first two rooms to the first two students, and every alternative B that is Pareto optimal for the second component assigns the third room to the third student. The two alternatives A and B can be replaced by one alternative C (in fact, in this simple example it will hold that $C = A$ as there is only one room in the second component), and every agent values C as being equally good as the alternative chosen by his own component.

A solution involves two aspects: a choice of alternative, and transfers. It is not hard to show that any alternative that maximizes welfare also maximizes welfare for each component separately. For a solution to qualify as "decomposable", it makes sense to in addition require that there are no transfers between components.

Definition 3 (weak decomposability). *Let $\mathcal{N}$ be the set of agents, let $\mathcal{A}$ be the set of alternatives, and let v be the tuple of valuation functions of the agents. A solution (A, p) is weakly decomposable if for every component $S \subset \mathcal{N}$ it holds that $\sum_{i \in S} p_i = 0$. Namely, the net transfer into the component is 0.*

As a trivial example, every solution that involves no transfers is weakly decomposable.

We also introduce a notion of *strong decomposability* that postulates that utilities of individual agents within a component are not influenced by decisions in other components. Unlike the notion of weak decomposability which is the property of a single solution, the notion of strong decomposability is a property of a mechanism and not just of a single solution. In the context of our work in which we assume "full information upon request", a *mechanism M* is a mapping from instances to solutions. The input to M is an instance I of arbitrary size, composed of a set $\mathcal{N}$ of agents, a set $\mathcal{A}$ of alternatives, and a tuple v of valuation functions of the agents. The output $M(I)$ is the proposed solution for the instance I, where the solution is composed of a winning alternative (in general, it is not required to be an alternative that maximizes welfare) and a vector of transfers. A mechanism can be randomized, in which case, given an input instance, the mechanism generates a distribution over solutions, and the proposed solution is a random sample from this distribution.

Definition 4 (strong decomposability). *We say that a mechanism M is strongly decomposable if for every decomposable instance I, the output of the* *mechanism is consistent with the outputs of the mechanism on each of the components separately, in the sense that for every agent $i \in S$, her utility in both cases is the same. (For randomized mechanisms, equality needs to hold for the expected utility.)*

It is not hard to show that for strong decomposable mechanism M that maximizes welfare and for every decomposable instance, the solution produced by M is also weakly decomposable.

The Anticore and Decomposition: A major benefit of the anticore is that it ensures decomposability properties. We remark that even though our notion of the anticore is the same as that of [8], the notion of decomposability was not defined in that or other previous work, and hence the connection between anticore and decomposability is a new contribution of the current paper. For weak decomposability (Definition 3) we have:

Proposition 1. *Every solution in the anticore is weakly decomposable.*

Proof. Let $\mathcal{N}$ be the set of agents, let $\mathcal{A}$ be the set of alternatives, let v be the tuple of valuation functions of the agents, and let $S \subset \mathcal{N}$ be a component. Consider an arbitrary solution (A^*, p) in the anticore, composed of a welfare maximizing alternative $A^* \in \mathcal{A}$ and a vector p of transfers. A^* also maximizes the welfare of each of the components S and $\bar{S}$ separately. By the anticore constraints, the net transfer into S is at most 0, and so is the net transfer into $\bar{S}$. Consequently, the net transfer into S is exactly 0. Hence the solution is weakly decomposable.

It is premature at this stage to address strong decomposability (Definition 4). This will be done later, in Proposition 3.

4   Selection from Within the Welfare-Sharing Core

The set of constraints corresponding to domination over a disagreement point are meant to achieve the property of having each agent (weakly) prefer (in terms of utility) every solution in the WS-core over the disagreement point. Our guideline for selecting a unique solution from within the WS-core (when the WS-core is nonempty) is that we wish this property to hold not only in a qualitative manner, but also in a quantitative manner, to the largest extent possible. Ideally, we would like it to be that for every agent, switching to our mechanism offers a worthwhile increase in utility compared to the disagreement point. This calls for an *egalitarian* distribution of the welfare gain among all agents, where the welfare gain is the difference in welfare between the maximum welfare alternative ($W_{max}(\mathcal{N})$) and the expected welfare generated by the disagreement point ($W_\pi(\mathcal{N})$). However, equal sharing of the welfare gain might not be in the WS-core, because it might violate the constraints of the anticore. Hence we aim to equalize the shares of the gain as much as possible, subject to satisfying the anticore constraints.

4.1   Selection Concepts

Before proceeding, let us establish some conventions and notation. We assume for convenience that the valuation function of each agent is such that at the disagreement point her expected value is 0. This can be enforced by applying an additive shift of $u_\pi(i)$ to each valuation function v_i. Given a solution (A^*, p), we let u_i denote the utility $u_i(A^*, p) = v_i(A^*) + p_i$ derived by agent i from the solution (where the valuation function v_i is such that the expected value offered by the disagreement point is 0). We shall sometimes refer to the vector $u = (u_1, \ldots, u_n)$ (rather than to (A^*, p)) as our solution, as this vector summarizes what the agents care about in a solution. An egalitarian solution will give every agent utility $u_i = \frac{W_{max}(\mathcal{N})}{n}$, but might not be in the WS-core. We present several approaches for how to relax the egalitarian requirement so as to select a solution within the WS-core (when it is nonempty).

- The *min-square* solution. Here we seek the unique solution within the WS-core minimizing $\sum_{i \in \mathcal{N}} (u_i)^2$. This solution minimizes the variance in the distribution of the welfare, subject to being in the WS-core.
- The *lexicographically-maximal* (*lex-max-WS*) solution. Given a vector $x \in R^n$, let $\hat{x}$ be the same vector with coordinates rearranged such that in the new order $\hat{x}_1 \leq \hat{x}_2 \leq \ldots \leq \hat{x}_n$. For two vectors $x \in R^n$ and $y \in R^n$ of equal sum of their entries, $x \geq_{Lex} y$ denotes that for the rearranged vectors $\hat{x}$ and $\hat{y}$ and for some $1 \leq k < n$ it holds that $\hat{x}_k > \hat{y}_k$, with $\hat{x}_i = \hat{y}_i$ for every $1 \leq i < k$. A solution u in the WS-core is *lexicographically maximal* if $u \geq_{Lex} u'$ for every other solution u' in the WS-core.
- A *Lorenz-maximal* solution. Given a vector $x \in R^n$, let $\hat{x}$ be the same vector with coordinates rearranged such that in the new order $\hat{x}_1 \leq \hat{x}_2 \leq \ldots \leq \hat{x}_n$. For two vectors $x \in R^n$ and $y \in R^n$ of equal sum, we say that x *Lorenz dominates* y (denoted by $x \geq_{Lor} y$) if for the rearranged vectors $\hat{x}$ and $\hat{y}$ it holds that $\sum_{i=1}^k \hat{x}_i \geq \sum_{i=1}^k \hat{y}_i$, for every $1 \leq k \leq n$. A Lorenz maximal solution is a solution in the WS-core that Lorenz-dominates every other solution in the WS-core. By definition, it also minimizes the so called *Gini index* of inequality [6].

The min-square solution exists whenever the WS-core is nonempty, and is unique (in terms of the utility that each agent receives). The same applies to the lexicographically-maximal solution, though the two solutions need not coincide. A Lorenz dominating solution need not exist. Out of the two solutions that do exist, we suggest picking the *lexicographically-maximal-Welfare-Sharing* solution, which we denote by *lex-max-WS*. (This choice is not of major significance to our work. Proposition 2 (with a different algorithm) and Proposition 3 also hold with respect to the min-square solution, and Corollary 1 shows that the two solutions coincide in many cases of interest.)

4.2   The Water Filling Algorithm

When W_{max} is submodular, the utilities in the *lex-max-WS* solution can be computed using an algorithm that we refer to as *water filling* (this is a generic name, used also elsewhere, for algorithms that increment variables at a uniform rate, subject to constraints). It proceeds in iterations. Initially (at iteration 0), all agents are *free* and every agent i starts with her disagreement utility $u_\pi(i)$. If any of the constraints of the anticore are tight (satisfied with equality) by this initial solution, then the set S_1 of agents involved in the tight constraints become *locked*. Thereafter, in every iteration $j \geq 1$ we do the following. If there are no free agents, the algorithm ends and outputs the utilities of the agents. If there are free agents, then the utility of every free agent is incremented by the same value x_j, where $x_j > 0$ is the smallest value that leads to some new anticore constraint becoming tight (equivalently, x_j is the largest increase that does not violate any of the anticore constraints). At this point, the set S_j of agents involved in a newly tight constraint become locked (some of these agents may have been locked already earlier), and iteration j ends. The proof of the following proposition appears in [1].

Proposition 2. *When W_{max} is submodular, the water filling algorithm computes the* lex-max-WS *solution. When W_{max} is not submodular, the water filling algorithm might fail to find the* lex-max-WS *solution, even when the WS-core is nonempty.*

4.3   Decomposability of *lex-max-WS*

The *lex-max-WS* solution lies in the anticore, and hence by Proposition 1 it is weakly decomposable. We now consider strong decomposability (see Definition 4). This property involves comparing the solutions generated for different instances. As the *lex-max-WS* solution for an instance depends on the disagreement point for the instance, we need to also relate between the disagreement points of different instances. For this purpose, we assume that there is a mechanism that given an instance outputs the disagreement point for that instance. For example, RP served as such a mechanism in Sect. 1.1.

Proposition 3. *When W_{max} is submodular, every mechanism M that satisfies both following properties is strongly decomposable.*

1. *For every instance M selects the respective* lex-max-WS *solution.*
2. *The disagreement utilities (that define the domination constraints for the WS-core) are the output of a disagreement mechanism that is strongly decomposable.*

The above proposition is proved by showing that the outcome of the water filling algorithm on the whole instance is identical to the concatenation of its outcomes on each component separately. See [1].

4.4   A Lorenz Dominating Solution

We next show that in the important case that W_{max} is submodular (e.g., in the Shared–Rental problem), a Lorenz dominating solution necessarily exists.

Theorem 2 below is an adaptation of a theorem of Dutta and Ray [3], which considers Lorenz minimal solutions and supermodular characteristic functions (we consider Lorenz maximal solutions and submodular characteristic functions). We provide a detailed proof of Theorem 2 rather than attempt to use the results of [3] as a blackbox, because in our setting we need to ensure that the solution dominates a given disagreement point, and this issue does not seem to have an analog in the setting of [3]. The proof of the following theorem appears in [1].

Theorem 2. *If W_{max} is submodular, then the* lex-max-WS *solution (which is in the WS-core) Lorenz-dominates all other solutions in the WS-core.*

Corollary 1. *If the function W_{max} is submodular then the WS-core is non-empty, a Lorenz dominating solution exists, it is unique, and it coincides with both the min-square solution and the lexicographically-maximal solution.*

Summarizing, when selecting a solution from the WS-core, we employ the egalitarian paradigm. In several natural settings (such as the Shared–Rental problem) W_{max} is submodular. In these cases, Theorem 2 offers a natural choice of a unique solution within the WS-core, because (essentially) all natural relaxations of the notion of being egalitarian (min-square, lexicographically-maximal, Lorenz-maximal) coincide. Moreover, in these cases the solution is computable in polynomial time, and also is continuous with a Lipshitz constant of 1 (see [1] for exact statements).

Acknowledgments. We thank Herve Moulin and Eyal Winter for helpful discussions. The work of Uriel Feige was supported in part by the Israel Science Foundation (grant No. 1388/16), and partly done at Microsoft Research, Herzeliya.

References

1. Babaioff, M., Feige, U.: A new approach to fair distribution of welfare. CoRR abs/1909.11346 (2019). http://arxiv.org/abs/1909.11346
2. Bondareva, O.N.: Some applications of linear programming methods to the theory of cooperative games (in Russian). Probl. Kybern. **10**(119–139), 2 (1963)
3. Dutta, B., Ray, D.: A concept of egalitarianism under participation constraints. Econometrica **57**(3), 615–635 (1989)
4. Foley, D.K.: Resource allocation and the public sector. Yale Econ. Essays **7**(1), 45–98 (1967)
5. Gal, Y.K., Mash, M., Procaccia, A.D., Zick, Y.: Which is the fairest (rent division) of them all? J. ACM **64**(6), 39:1–39:22 (2017)
6. Gini, C.: Concentration and dependency ratios. Riv. di Polit. Econ. **87**, 769–789 (1909). English translation, 1997
7. Moulin, H.: Egalitarianism and utilitarianism in quasi-linear bargaining. Econometrica **53**(1), 49–67 (1985)
8. Moulin, H.: An application of the Shapley value to fair division with money. Econometrica **60**(6), 1331–49 (1992)
9. Shapley, L.S.: On balanced sets and cores. Nav. Res. Logist. Q. **14**, 453–460 (1967)
10. Su, F.E.: Rental harmony: Sperner's lemma in fair division. Am. Math. Mon. **106**(10), 930–942 (1999)

From Darwin to Poincaré and von Neumann: Recurrence and Cycles in Evolutionary and Algorithmic Game Theory

Victor Boone[1] and Georgios Piliouras[2]($\boxtimes$)

[1] ENS de Lyon, Lyon, France
[2] SUTD, Singapore, Singapore
georgios.piliouras@gmail.com

Abstract. Replicator dynamics, the continuous-time analogue of Multiplicative Weights Updates, is the main dynamic in evolutionary game theory. In simple evolutionary zero-sum games, such as Rock-Paper-Scissors, replicator dynamic is periodic [39], however, its behavior in higher dimensions is not well understood. We provide a complete characterization of its behavior in zero-sum evolutionary games. We prove that, if and only if, the system has an interior Nash equilibrium, the dynamics exhibit Poincaré recurrence, i.e., almost all orbits come arbitrary close to their initial conditions infinitely often. If no interior equilibria exist, then all interior initial conditions converge to the boundary. Specifically, the strategies that are not in the support of any equilibrium vanish in the limit of all orbits. All recurrence results furthermore extend to a class of games that generalize both graphical polymatrix games as well as evolutionary games, establishing a unifying link between evolutionary

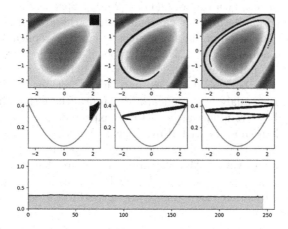

Fig. 1. One agent Rock-Paper-Scissor, see Sect. 3.4. Animation here (https://www.dropbox.com/s/c37cgiztlcryje6/foo.avi?dl=0)

© Springer Nature Switzerland AG 2019
I. Caragiannis et al. (Eds.): WINE 2019, LNCS 11920, pp. 85–99, 2019.
https://doi.org/10.1007/978-3-030-35389-6_7

and algorithmic game theory. We show that two degrees of freedom, as in Rock-Paper-Scissors, is sufficient to prove periodicity.

1   Introduction

Replicator dynamics is a basic model of evolution that is amongst the most well studied game theoretical models of adaptive behavior. It is the standard dynamic in evolutionary game theory [14,38] and enjoys formal connections to other classic evolutionary models such as the Price equation, the Lotka-Volterra equation of ecology and the quasispecies equation of molecular evolution [8,27]. Replicator also has strong, inherent connections to computer science and optimization theory. It is the continuous time-analogue of Multiplicative Weights Update [19], arguably the most widely studied online learning and optimization algorithm and a meta-algorithmic technique in itself with numerous applications [2]. Furthermore, it has diverse microcanonical foundations [35], i.e., it can emerge from numerous, simple (memoryless, best-response like) population dynamics, which enhance its plausibility as a model of emergent behavior. Finally, it has an interpretation as an inference dynamic [13,17]. Specifically, for systems governed by the replicator equations the maximum entropy principle (MaxEnt) can be derived rather than postulated as, e.g., in thermodynamics or statistical mechanics [16]. Given this impressive web of connections, it would not be unreasonable to think of replicator as a near-universal model of adaptive behavior, a proto-intelligence mechanism, emerging from simple physical processes and giving rise to self-organizing, ever-more complex and efficient systems. As such understanding its behavior in different contexts can simultaneously shed light to many of its related adaptive processes (Fig. 1).

Evolution as it turns out is a very efficient force of systemic optimization. Replicator dynamics is a regret minimizing dynamic in arbitrary games. Its regret converges to zero at a rate of $O(1/T)$ [20,22]. Specifically, its total regret remains bounded for all time. In cases of games where agents' interests are strongly aligned, such as potential, i.e., congestion games, replicator dynamics is known to perform admirably well. Not only does it converge to Nash equilibria [36] but typically to pure Nash [19]. Furthermore, it has been shown that pure Nash equilibria of higher social welfare have larger regions of attraction and hence an average case analysis of replicator dynamics where the initial condition is drawn uniformly at random can lead to an expected social welfare that can be much higher than those predicted by Price of Anarchy analysis [28]. Finally, even in games where the dynamics are non-equilibrating replicator dynamics may converge to limit cycles with optimal social welfare that dominate the performance of even the best Nash equilibrium by an arbitrary amount [12,18]. That is, replicator dynamic can significantly outperform even Price of Stability type of guarantees.

When we move to zero-sum games (and variants thereof) Price of Anarchy and more generally social welfare optimization type of results are no longer applicable. One would hope that in such games the Nash equilibria would be accurate predictors of the system behavior. If so equilibration would have not only a strong economic and algorithmic justification due to the celebrated maxmin theorem by von Neumann [24] and its connection to linear programming but also an evolutionary one. Unfortunately, this is not the case. [37] established experimentally that even small zero-sum games may have complex, non-equilibrating, chaotic type of behavior. More recently, [33] established that despite their chaotic behavior, these dynamics have also exploitable structure. Specifically, replicator dynamics in two-player zero-sum games with interior Nash equilibria are Poincaré recurrent. This means that almost all initial conditions return infinitely often arbitrarily close to their initial conditions. This result holds even for networks of zero-sum games, however, this class of games fails to capture the standard class of evolutionary zero-sum games. The immediate distinction between evolutionary games and standard multi-agent games is that evolutionary games only admit a single distribution over a simplex of strategies. These are games where a large population of animals compete against each other and where the frequencies of the different genotypes/strategies evolve according to the replicator dynamics. From the perspective of standard two-agent zero-sum games, the question reduces to analyzing symmetric zero-sum games (e.g. Rock-Paper-Scissors) under symmetric initial conditions. Due to the symmetric nature of the game, the symmetry of the initial condition is preserved by the dynamic. Thus, the dynamic evolves on a lower-dimensional manifold, which is a zero-measure set, hence the Poincaré recurrence result of [33] does not suffice to understand the behavior for such non-generic initial conditions. Our goal here is to completely understand the behavior of replicator dynamics in such settings and furthermore develop an expansive unifying framework for understanding dynamics both in evolutionary games as well as two-agent and multi-agent settings.

Our Results. We provide a complete characterization of the behavior of replicator dynamic in zero-sum evolutionary games. We prove that the dynamics exhibit Poincaré recurrence, if and only if, the system has an interior Nash equilibrium. If no interior equilibria exist, then all interior initial conditions converge to the boundary (Theorem 6). Specifically, the strategies that are not in the support of any equilibrium vanish in the limit of all orbits. All recurrence results furthermore extend to a class of games that generalize both graphical polymatrix games as well as evolutionary games (Theorem 5). Specifically, we allow for polymatrix edges with self-edges, where all polymatrix games are constant-sum, and all self-edges are antisymmetric games. To prove these results, we provide the most general to date set of game theoretic conditions under which replicator dynamics can be shown to be volume preserving (under a diffeomorphism, i.e. a differentiable transformation with invertible inverse) (Theorem 4). The other stepping stone in the direction of proving recurrence/convergence to the boundary is showing that the KL-divergence between the Nash equilibrium and the state of the system is invariant/strictly decreasing if the zero-sum games has/(does not have) an interior Nash. This argument mirrors arguments for the case of multiple agent replicator dynamics [22,33] Finally, we show that in this class of games, two degrees of freedom, as in Rock-Paper-Scissors, is sufficient to prove periodicity (Theorem 9). Furthermore, as we argue this does not follow from an immediate combination of Poincaré recurrence and the Poincaré-Bendixson theorem but requires more specialized arguments. The full version of this paper can be found here [9].

2   Related Work

Non-equilibration, Recurrence and Volume Preservation. In evolutionary game theory, numerous non-convergence results are known but they are usually restricted to small games [35]. [1] was the first paper to study both discrete and continuous-time evolutionary dynamics in zero-sum games and establish invariant for the dynamics, however, no formal recurrence or periodicity was shown. Constants of the motion exist for different classes of games (e.g. coordination/partnership games, null stable games) and dynamics [15,28,35] even for games with convergent dynamics. An orthogonal property of game dynamics is the preservation of volume of initial conditions (up to state space/speed transformation, see [15,22,35]). [33] and [31] showed that replicator dynamics in (network) zero-sum games (and affine variants thereof) exhibit a specific type of repetitive behavior, known as Poincaré recurrence by combining these two type of arguments. Recently, [22] proved that Poincaré recurrence also shows up in a more general class of continuous-time dynamics known as Follow-the-Regularized-Leader (FTRL). [21] established that the recurrence results for replicator dynamics extend to some biologically-inspired dynamically evolving zero-sum games. Perfectly periodic (i.e., cyclic) behavior for replicator may arise in team competition [32] as well as in network competition [23]. Our techniques build and extend upon these results by producing necessary, as well as sufficient conditions, for volume preservation, recurrence as well as periodicity.

Game Dynamics as Physics. Recently, [6] established a connection between game theory, online optimization in continuous-time (FTRL dynamics) and a ubiquitous class of systems in physics known as Hamiltonian dynamics, which exhibit conservation laws ("conservation of energy"). In the case of discrete-time dynamics such as MWU or gradient descent the system trajectories are first order approximations of the continuous-time dynamics. Energy conservation and recurrence no longer hold. Instead energy increases and the dynamics divergence to the boundary [4]. The dynamics exhibit volume expansion and Lyapunov chaos [10]. Despite this divergent, chaotic behavior, gradient descent with fixed step size, has vanishing regret in small zero-sum games [5]. More elaborate discretization techniques, based on leap-frogging (Verlet) symplectic integration technique for Hamiltonian dynamics, result in discrete-time algorithms of bounded regret in general games and Poincaré recurrence in zero-sum games respectively [3]. So far, it is not clear to what extent the connections with

Hamiltonian dynamics can be generalized; however, [26] have considered a class of piecewise affine Hamiltonian vector fields whose orbits are piecewise straight lines and developed the connections with best-reply dynamics.

Game Dynamics as Dynamical Systems. Finally, [29,30] initiated a program for linking game theory to topology, specifically to Conley's fundamental theorem of dynamical systems [11]. This approach shifts attention from Nash equilibria to a more general notion of recurrence, called chain recurrence, that generalizes both periodicity and Poincaré recurrence. [25] embeds this approach within an algorithmically tractable framework and uses it to develop new training algorithms for multi-agent AI settings.

3   Preliminaries and Definitions

3.1   Zero-Sum Games and Zero-Sum Polymatrix Games

A *graphical polymatrix game* is defined using a directed graph $G = (V, E)$ where V corresponds to the set of agents (or players) and where every edge corresponds to a *bimatrix game* between its two endpoints/agents. Each agent $i \in V$ has a set of *actions* $\mathcal{A}_i = \{1 \ldots n_i\}$ that he is allowed to select randomly under a distribution x_i called a *mixed stragegy*. The set of mixed strategies of player i is written $\mathcal{X}_i = \Delta \mathbb{R}^{n_i} = \{x_\alpha \in \mathbb{R}^{n_i}_{\geq 0} : \sum_\alpha x_\alpha = 1\}$; the state of the game is then defined by the concatenation of strategies of all players. We call *strategy space* the set of all possible strategies profiles, and write it $\mathcal{X} \equiv \prod_{i \in V} \mathcal{X}_i$.

The bimatrix game on edge (i, j) is described using a pair of matrices $A^{i,j} \in \mathbb{R}^{|\mathcal{A}_i| \times |\mathcal{A}_j|}$ and $A^{j,i} \in \mathbb{R}^{|\mathcal{A}_j| \times |\mathcal{A}_i|}$. The coefficient $(\alpha, \beta) \in \mathcal{A}_i \times \mathcal{A}_j$ of the matrix $A^{i,j}$ represents the reward player i gets when he plays α against player j playing β. As players can choose mixed strategies, their payoffs are random variables, yet we call *payoffs* again their expected payoffs. For instance, the payoff of player i against player j is $x_i \cdot A^{i,j} x_j$. We call *payoff of agent $i \in V$* under strategy profile x the sum of the payoffs agent i receives from every bimatrix game he participates in, and write it $u_i(x)$ or $u_i(x_i; x_{-i})$. More precisely,

$$u_i(x) = \sum_{j \,:\, (i,j) \in E} x_i \cdot A^{i,j} x_j \tag{1}$$

Sometimes, one can be interested in the payoff of agent i when deviating to action $\alpha \in \mathcal{A}_i$ under profile x. This quantity is usually denoted $u_{i,\alpha}(x)$ and corresponds to $\sum_{j=1}^{N} (A^{i,j} x_j)_\alpha$. Finally, we will compactify the definition of a N-player graphical polymatrix game by a tuple $\Gamma = (G, A)$ with G the underlying graph and A the block matrix built from $A^{i,j}$'s.

We say that a N-player graphical polymatrix game is *zero-sum* if the matrix A is antisymmetric. In the case $N = 2$ players $i, j = 1, 2$, it specifically means that $A^{1,2} = -(A^{2,1})^T$; in the case $N = 1$ player, that $A^{1,1} = A$ is antisymmetric. In our case, we allow the graph G to contain *self-loops*, and we call *diagonal games* the subgames induced by self-loops. Self-loop (1-agent) games make sense both in the content of evolutionary game theory as well as in classic (multi-agent) game theory. From the perspective of evolutionary game theory, 1-agent games are the norm where we study the frequencies of different competing genotypes within a single population. For example, Rock-Paper-Scissors could be different traits that exhibit a cyclic pattern of dominance. In the context of classic game theory a single agent self-loop added e.g. on top of a standard normal form game can capture effects like friction in dynamics (e.g. a matrix with zero diagonal and minus one in all other entries captures the effects of having cost for changing strategy). Specifically, if an agent changes her strategy from yesterday, then in the self-loop game, she experiences an additional cost of one. More generally, it allows to differentiate the performance of a strategy for an agent depending on his strategy in the previous time period in game dynamics such as replicator dynamics (Fig. 2).

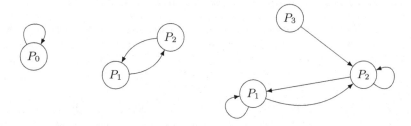

Fig. 2. From left to right, graphical representations of the evolutionary game setting, algorithmic game theory, and the merger of the two.

A very common notion in game theory is the one of *Nash equilibrium* (NE), defined in our case as a mixed strategy profile $x^* \in \mathcal{X}$ such that

$$u_i(x^*) \geq u_{i,\alpha_i}(x^*) \tag{2}$$

for every strategy $\alpha_i \in \mathcal{A}_i$ of every player $i \in \mathcal{N}$. We write $\mathrm{supp}(x_i^*) \equiv \{\alpha_i \in \mathcal{A}_i : x_{i,\alpha_i} > 0\}$ the support of $x_i^* \in \mathcal{X}_i$. A Nash equilibrium is said *interior* or *fully mixed* if $\mathrm{supp}(x_i^*)$ for every agent i is $\mathcal{A}_i$.

3.2   Replicator Dynamics

The *replicator equation* is one of the most well studied evolutionary processes. Its most usual formulation is:

$$\dot{x}_{i,\alpha} = \frac{dx_{i,\alpha}}{dt} = x_{i,\alpha}\left(u_{i,\alpha}(x) - u_i(x)\right) \tag{3}$$

for every player i and action $\alpha \in \mathcal{A}_i$. We will often translate (3) into *cumulative costs space* via the diffeomorphism from the interior of $\mathcal{X}$ to $\mathcal{C} \equiv \prod \mathbb{R}^{n_i - 1}$, used also in [33], that, for each player i, maps $x_i = (x_{i,1} \ldots x_{i,n_i})$ to $(\ln \frac{x_{i,2}}{x_{i,1}} \ldots \ln \frac{x_{i,n_i}}{x_{i,1}})$.

We will write this diffeomorphism $\boldsymbol{f}$ and its inverse $\boldsymbol{f}^{-1}$. $\mathcal{C}$ is called this way since one can show that it corresponds to the space of coordinates $\int_0^t u_{i,\alpha}(x(\tau))d\tau$ up to a re-centralization term (specifically, $\int_0^t u_{i,\alpha}(x(\tau))d\tau - \int_0^t u_{i,1}(x(\tau))d\tau$ for $\alpha > 1$).

3.3 Topology of Dynamical Systems

Flows. Since the strategy space is compact and the replicator dynamics Lipschitz-continuous, there exists a continuous function $\phi : \mathcal{X} \times \mathbb{R} \to \mathcal{X}$ called *flow of replicator dynamics (3)* such that for any point $x \in \mathcal{X}$, $\phi(x,-)$ defines a function of time corresponding to the trajectory of x. Conversely, fixing a time t provides a map $\phi^t \equiv \phi(-,t) : \mathcal{X} \to \mathcal{X}$, and the family $\{\phi^t : t \in \mathbb{R}\}$ is interestingly a subgroup of $(\mathcal{C}(\mathcal{X},\mathcal{X}), \circ)$. Moreover, if $\phi^t : A \to A$ and $\psi^t : B \to B$ are flows such that there exists a diffeomorphism g satisfying $g(\phi^t(x)) = \psi^t(g(x))$ for all $x \in A$, then ϕ^t and ψ^t are said to be *diffeomorphic* to each other.

Limit Sets. When $x \in \mathcal{X}$ is not a rest point of (3), we wish to grasp how the orbit of x will asymptotically behave. In general, its trajectory will not converge to a single point, but to a closed set called the ω-*limit (set) of* x, written $\omega(x)$. This set is formally defined as the set of points $y \in \mathcal{X}$ such that there exists a sequence (t_n) diverging to $+\infty$ such that $\phi(x,t_n) \to y$. One alternative definition is $\omega(x) = \bigcap_{t \geq 0} \bigcup_{\tau \geq t} \phi(x,\tau)$. The compactness of $\omega(x)$ is an immediate consequence of the compactness of $\mathcal{X}$, and $\lim_{t \to +\infty} \text{dist}(\phi(x,t), \omega(x)) = 0$.

Poincaré Recurrence. This paper is focused on a recurrent (periodic-like) behavior introduced by Poincaré in his studies of the three body problem. Thanks to Liouville's formula [38], divergent-free systems are volume preserving. Poincaré proved [34] that in volume-preserving dynamical systems with bounded orbits almost all trajectories return arbitrarily close to their initial position and do so infinitely often.

Theorem 1 (Poincaré recurrence). [7] *If a flow preserves volume and has only bounded orbits then for each open set, almost every point of the set returns back to it. In fact, almost every point returns infinitely often back to the set.*

3.4 Volume Conservation and Periodicity in Rock-Paper-Scissors

The front page figure shows the evolution of a set of initial conditions (black square) under replicator dynamics (3) in the (projected) cumulative payoff space; the game is the classic one agent Rock-Paper-Scissors with payoff matrix

$$\begin{pmatrix} 0 & 1 & -1 \\ -1 & 0 & 1 \\ 1 & -1 & 0 \end{pmatrix}$$

In the first row of the figure from left to right, we plot the evolution of a set at times $t = 0$, $t = 112$ and $t = 225$. The colormap represents the Kullback-Leibler divergence to the unique Nash equilibrium $x = (\frac{1}{3}, \frac{1}{3}, \frac{1}{3})$ (null vector in cumulative payoffs space). Observe that every point stays at the same color at which it started, i.e., its Kullback-Leibler divergence from the Nash equilibrium does not change. On the second row are the corresponding plots of the Kullback-Leibler divergence of points (y-axis) according to their first coordinate (y_1 in $\mathcal{C}$). The red curve is the minimum possible value for each y_1 values, that is, an analogue of *potential energy*. Intuitively, any initial condition will slide along an horizontal level set (of constant KL-divergence) and cannot escape outside the red curve. The third row shows an estimation of the volume of the cloud of points over time. This volume is estimated using a pruned Delaunay triangulation, more precisely, triangles with a diameter larger than some threshold value are deleted, and the volume is computed as the sum of the volume of each remaining triangle. Even though the shape of the initial condition is not preserved, the overall volume is constant over time. This spiralling snake shape results from periodic orbits of different periods.

4   Volume Conservation: Necessary and Sufficient Conditions

4.1   Games with Zero-Sum Self-loops Are Volume Conservative

Replicator dynamics in multi-games (with no loops) are volume conservative (even beyond replicator dynamics [22]). The reason becomes clear when we examine the differential equation satisfied by cumulative payoffs $y_{i,\alpha}$'s.

$$\frac{dy_{i,\alpha}}{dt}(t) = u_{i,\alpha+1}\left(f^{-1}(y)\right) - u_{i,1}\left(f^{-1}(y)\right) \tag{4}$$

Recall that f^{-1} acts like a set-wise product function, working locally at each player. Hence, as long as $u_{i,\beta}$ does not depend on x_i, $u_{i,\beta}$ is independent of $y_{i,\alpha}$ for any pair of actions α, β. The partial derivative $\frac{\partial \dot{y}_{i,\alpha}}{\partial y_{i,\alpha}}(y)$ is null. One can understand this as follows: *if the performance of an action only depends on the behavior of the rest of the agents then volume is preserved.* In single agent games, antisymmetry implies volume preservation [35]. We show that these results can be combined and that there is no need to have null diagonal games to get volume preservation in multi-agent games. The zero-sum property is enough to guarantee it.

Theorem 2. *Let ϕ be the flow of replicator dynamics (3) with N agents. Let $\psi(y,-) = f(\phi(f^{-1}(y),-))$ be the diffeomorphic flow onto cumulative payoffs space. If all diagonal games are zero-sum, then ψ is volume conservative.*

We know that if there are no games on the diagonal then volume is preserved. The intuition is that if each diagonal game preserves volume individually, there will be volume preservation; this is the main point. We rely on Liouville's formula to compute the divergence in the general case, and check that it is null if all diagonal games are zero-sum. This proves that in N-player polymatrix games with loops, as long as loops are antisymmetric games, the *quantity of information is preserved* in cumulative payoffs space. It also means that it will be hard to converge; for instance, no interior rest point cannot be locally attractive. Indeed, if that was the case, it would mean that locally, the volume would shrink around the rest point.

4.2 Volume Conservative Games Have Zero-Sum Self-loops

Interestingly, the inverse statement is also true. The preservation of information/volume in cumulative payoff space is specific to zero-sum diagonal games. We do not mean that a non-zero-sum game cannot preserve volume at some points, but rather that preserving volume at many points implies the zero-sum property. The precise number of points can be controlled by combinatorial Nullstellensatz arguments, and more precisely, the relation between a multivariate polynomial and the geometry of its vanishing set.

The argument is that the divergence of the vector field (in cumulative space) is a multivariate polynomial of variables $x_1 \ldots x_n$, and in particular, this polynomial vanishes exactly at points were the volume is preserved. So if the volume is conserved on an open ball, this polynomial is null and its coefficients are zeros. This imposes structure on the game, more precisely, that the game is equivalent (in a precise sense) to a zero-sum game.

Theorem 3. *Consider a 1-player game Γ. Let ϕ be the flow of replicator dynamics and ψ its diffeomorphic conjugate onto the cumulative payoffs space. If there exists an open set U of $\mathbb{R}^{|\mathcal{A}|-1}$ such that ψ is volume conservative at any point of U, then Γ is equivalent to a 1-player zero-sum game (summation of an antisymmetric matrix and a matrix of the form $\begin{pmatrix} 1 \cdots 1 \end{pmatrix}^T \begin{pmatrix} c_1 \cdots c_n \end{pmatrix}$).*

This result is easily generalizable to much more general games, for e.g. polymatrix games. The proof is very similar and we get the more stronger result.

Theorem 4. *A N-player (polymatrix)[1] game is volume conservative in cumulative payoffs space if, and only if its diagonal games are equivalent to zero-sum games (summation of an antisymmetric matrix and a matrix of the form $\begin{pmatrix} 1 \cdots 1 \end{pmatrix}^T \begin{pmatrix} c_1 \cdots c_n \end{pmatrix}$).*

This formally shows that volume preservation strongly correlates with zero-sum games. Furthermore, a polymatrix game that conserves volume on an open set *has* to conserve volume everywhere. Observe that we could have been less restrictive on the assumption relating the geometry of the vanishing set, so there is room to improve this result. The *take home idea* is that *if diagonal games are not zero-sum, the volume cannot be preserved at too many points*.

---

[1] The theorem straightforwardly extends to any game that can be rewritten as the sum of a N-player game in normal form and self-edges games (even without the polymatrix condition).

5 Limit Behavior: Poincaré Recurrence, Cycles and Convergence to Boundary

5.1 Zero-Sum Games with Interior Nash Are Poincaré Recurrent

We generalize a previous result from [33]. It is already known that zero-sum polymatrix games with no loops are volume conservative, and that they exhibit Poincaré recurrence behavior when there exists an interior Nash equilibrium. In fact, this is also true for polymatrix games allowing self-loops. The proof is the same in its structure, but the existence of self-loops necessitates the use of different arguments. The volume preservation is already given by Theorem 2 from the previous section. The idea is to prove that, under the assumption of the existence of an interior Nash, the Kullback-Leibler divergence is a constant of motion, and that this implies that every orbit is bounded in cumulative payoffs space. Then, the Poincaré recurrence theorem applies.

Theorem 5. *Consider a N-player zero-sum polymatrix game with self-loops. Assume there exists an interior Nash equilibrium, then replicator dynamics is Poincaré recurrent.*

The key idea is to show, generalizing [33], that for any interior equilibrium x^*, $\mathrm{KL}(x^*\|-)$ is a constant of motion. It follows that interior orbits remain bounded in cumulative payoffs space. Then the theorem follows directly from Poincaré recurrence theorem: the volume is preserved in cumulative payoffs space, while every orbit stays bounded. Hence, the system is Poincaré recurrent in cumulative payoffs space; and this property is transported to the strategy space via the diffeomorphism $\boldsymbol{f}^{-1}$.

The fact that $\mathrm{KL}(x^*\|-)$ is a constant of motion is not the important point; what is critical is that orbits *remain bounded*. The conservation of KL is no more than a tool to show boundedness.

5.2 Poincaré Recurrence and Evolutionary Game Theory

Given any (polymatrix) game, either there exists an interior Nash equilibrium, or no interior point is an equilibrium. The first case has been dealt with. As far as the second case is concerned, previous work [22] have shown that in the 2-players case, the absence of interior Nash equilibria enforces orbits to collapse to boundary. We show that this is also true for 1-player zero-sum games (i.e., for evolutionary game theory). Although not using the language of information theory, the results about the existence of strict Lyapunov functions and collapse to the boundary were first developed in [1]. In the full version [9], we provide alternative arguments to reduce this case to the more well studied two agent zero-sum games. In combination with our Poincaré recurrence results, this will result in a complete picture of all possible limit behaviors of the system.

Theorem 6 [1]. *Let be a 1-player zero-sum game with matrix A and with no interior Nash equilibrium, on which we write ϕ the flow of (3). Let x^* be a Nash* *equilibrium of maximal support. Then for any interior point $x \in \mathcal{X}$, the orbit $\gamma = \{\phi(x,t) : t \geq 0\}$ collapses to boundary. More precisely, for all $y \in \omega(x)$,* supp $y \subseteq$ supp x^*.

This theorem shows that in the absence of any interior equilibrium, every interior orbits collapses to the face spanned by supp(x^*) with a x^* of maximal support. It tells nothing about the behavior of orbits when coming close to this face. Do we have convergence, or do we get (Poincaré) recurrence/cycles on the boundary? In general, both are possible, depending on the initial condition.

Consider Rock-Paper-Scissor to which we add a dummy action, say Fork, which scores -10 against any other action (excepted Fork itself). That is, consider the 1-player zero-sum game with matrix (Fig. 3)

$$A = \begin{pmatrix} 0 & -1 & 1 & 10 \\ 1 & 0 & -1 & 10 \\ -1 & 1 & 0 & 10 \\ -10 & -10 & -10 & 0 \end{pmatrix}$$

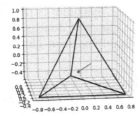 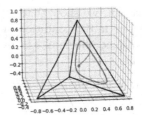

Fig. 3. Converging and non-converging orbits in the same game.

The Nash equilibrium is unique and $(\frac{1}{3}, \frac{1}{3}, \frac{1}{3}, 0)$. If one starts at $(\frac{1}{4}, \frac{1}{4}, \frac{1}{4}, \frac{1}{4})$, one converges to it. If one starts at $(\frac{3}{16}, \frac{5}{16}, \frac{1}{4}, \frac{1}{4})$, one collapses to a periodic orbit on the boundary.

Combining the results we have so far, we can prove a fairly complete theorem relating volume conservation, Poincaré recurrence and evolutionary game theory.

Theorem 7. *Let be a 1-player matrix game A under the flow of* replicator dynamics. *The volume is preserved in cumulative payoffs space if, and only if the game is equivalent to a zero-sum game; more precisely, if, and only if A can be written as $A = B + (1 \cdots 1)^T (A_{1,1} \cdots A_{n,n})$ with B an antisymmetric matrix.*

If that is the case, interior orbits exhibits Poincaré recurrent behavior if, and only if there exists an interior Nash equilibrium. If there is no interior equilibrium, every interior orbit collapses to the face spanned by the support of a Nash equilibrium of maximal support.

Proof. Let A be a single-agent matrix game under replicator dynamics. Assume the volume is conserved in cumulative payoff space. Then, by Theorem 3, A is equivalent to a zero-sum game $(A = B + (1 \cdots 1)^T (A_{1,1} \cdots A_{n,n})$ where B is an antisymmetric matrix.). Conversely, if A is equivalent in the above sense to a zero-sum game, one can assume without loss of generality that A is antisymmetric. Then, by Theorem 2, the volume is preserved at any point. This proves the first part of the theorem.

Now, assume A is antisymmetric. If there exists an interior Nash, by Theorem 5, the system is Poincaré recurrent. Conversely, if the system is Poincaré recurrent, there has to exist an interior Nash. Assume on the contrary that there is no such equilibrium. Let x^* be a Nash equilibrium. Consider the open ball $U = B(\frac{1}{n}(1 \ldots 1), \epsilon)$ with $\epsilon > 0$ small. We know that there exists an orbit γ intersecting U infinitely often. If ϵ is small enough, by taking x any point of γ, that means that

$$\limsup[\mathrm{dist}(\phi(x,t), \mathrm{bd}(\mathcal{X}))] > 0 \tag{5}$$

But by Theorem 6, γ should collapses to the boundary. This contradicts (5). □

6   Cycles in Dimension 3

In this section, we show that the flow ϕ of replicator dynamics is periodic for every interior initial condition of 1-player zero-sum games of dimension 3 with interior Nash equilibrium. The proof uses the Poincaré-Bendixson Theorem that we recall here.

Theorem 8 (Poincaré-Bendixson). *A limit set $\omega(x)$ of a $\mathcal{C}^1$ dynamical system over the plane, if non-empty and compact, that does not contain a rest point is a periodic orbit.*

In the following, we make the assumption that the game is a 1-player zero-sum game of dimension 3 that has an interior Nash equilibrium x^*.

Theorem 9. *Let be a 1-player zero-sum game of dimension 3 with matrix A. Assume there exists an interior Nash. Then, any interior point x belongs to a periodic orbit.*

Remark 1. Our proof relies on the Kullback-Leibler divergence. That is, in a Poincaré recurrent system, we used an argument specific to game theory to show that all interior orbits are periodic. Thinking of what Poincaré recurrent means, one may hope to get rid of the game theoretic proof and give a topological proof. The motivation is clear; for any open set, almost every orbit goes back arbitrarily close to its initial condition, and in addition, infinitely often. Therefore, we get what looks like a dense set of periodic orbits.

That is, if a point is not a rest point, because we are in dimension two, its orbit is infinitely-closely trapped between periodic orbits. As the counterexample below shows such arguments do not suffice to argue that all (interior) points are periodic. There, we claim that there is no hope to conclude that all orbits must be periodic based solely on topological arguments (Fig. 4).

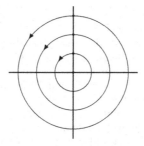

Fig. 4. On the complex plane, consider the ODE $\dot{z} = \mathbf{i}\, z$. The corresponding flow is $\phi(z,t) = z \cdot e^{\mathbf{i}t}$. Hence, every orbits are circles, excepted the single rest point at the origin. Add the *velocity regularizer* $\delta : z \mapsto \min\{1, \mathrm{dist}(z, \mathbf{i}\mathbb{N})\}$. The ODE becomes $\dot{z} = \mathbf{i}\,\delta(z)z$. Then, almost all orbits are still circles, so there is a dense set of periodic orbits and the system is Poincaré recurrent. Yet, if a point z has integer module, it is arbitrarily close to a periodic orbit, and its limit set is the rest point $\mathbf{i}|z|$.

Acknowledgments. Georgios Piliouras acknowledges MOE AcRF Tier 2 Grant 2016-T2-1-170, grant PIE-SGP-AI-2018-01 and NRF 2018 Fellowship NRF-NRFF2018-07. This work was partially done while Victor Boone was a visitor at SUTD under the supervision of Georgios Piliouras. Victor Boone thanks Bruno Gaujal and Panayotis Mertikopoulos for helping to arrange the visit and for their overall guidance and mentorship.

References

1. Akin, E., Losert, V.: Evolutionary dynamics of zero-sum games. J. Math. Biol. **20**, 231–258 (1984)
2. Arora, S., Hazan, E., Kale, S.: The multiplicative weights update method: a meta-algorithm and applications. Theory Comput. **8**(1), 121–164 (2012)
3. Bailey, J.P., Gidel, G., Piliouras, G.: Finite regret and cycles with fixed step-size via alternating gradient descent-ascent. arXiv e-prints arXiv:1907.04392, July 2019
4. Bailey, J.P., Piliouras, G.: Multiplicative weights update in zero-sum games. In: ACM Conference on Economics and Computation (2018)
5. Bailey, J.P., Piliouras, G.: Fast and Furious learning in zero-sum games: vanishing regret with non-vanishing step sizes. In: NeurIPS (2019)
6. Bailey, J.P., Piliouras, G.: Multi-agent learning in network zero-sum games is a Hamiltonian system. In: AAMAS (2019)
7. Barreira, L.: Poincare recurrence: old and new. In: XIVth International Congress on Mathematical Physics, pp. 415–422. World Scientific (2006)
8. Bomze, I.M.: Lotka-Volterra equation and replicator dynamics: new issues in classification. Biol. Cybern. **72**(5), 447–453 (1995)
9. Boone, V., Piliouras, G.: From Darwin to Poincaré and von Neumann: recurrence and cycles in evolutionary and algorithmic game theory. ArXiv (2019). http://arxiv.org/abs/1910.01334
10. Cheung, Y.K., Piliouras, G.: Vortices instead of equilibria in minmax optimization: chaos and butterfly effects of online learning in zero-sum games. In: COLT (2019)

11. Conley, C.C.: Isolated Invariant Sets and The Morse Index, Number 38. American Mathematical Soc., Providence (1978)
12. Gaunersdorfer, A., Hofbauer, J.: Fictitious play, shapley polygons, and the replicator equation. Games Econ. Behav. **11**(2), 279–303 (1995)
13. Harper, M.: Escort evolutionary game theory. Phys. D **240**(18), 1411–1415 (2011)
14. Hofbauer, J.: Evolutionary dynamics for bimatrix games: a Hamiltonian system? J. Math. Biol. **34**, 675–688 (1996)
15. Hofbauer, J., Sigmund, K.: Evolutionary Games and Population Dynamics. Cambridge University Press, Cambridge (1998)
16. Jaynes, E.T.: Information theory and statistical mechanics. Phys. Rev. **106**(4), 620 (1957)
17. Karev, G.P.: Replicator equations and the principle of minimal production of information. Bull. Math. Biol. **72**(5), 1124–1142 (2010)
18. Kleinberg, R., Ligett, K., Piliouras, G., Tardos, É.: Beyond the Nash equilibrium barrier. In: Symposium on Innovations in Computer Science (ICS) (2011)
19. Kleinberg, R., Piliouras, G., Tardos, É.: Multiplicative updates outperform generic no-regret learning in congestion games. In: ACM Symposium on Theory of Computing (STOC) (2009)
20. Kwon, J., Mertikopoulos, P.: A continuous-time approach to online optimization. J. Dyn. Games **4**, 125 (2017)
21. Mai, T., Panageas, I., Ratcliff, W., Vazirani, V.V., Yunker, P.: Cycles in zero sum differential games and biological diversity. In: ACM EC (2018)
22. Mertikopoulos, P., Papadimitriou, C., Piliouras, G.: Cycles in adversarial regularized learning. In: Proceedings of the Twenty-Ninth Annual ACM-SIAM Symposium on Discrete Algorithms, pp. 2703–2717. SIAM (2018)
23. Nagarajan, S.G., Mohamed, S., Piliouras, G.: Three body problems in evolutionary game dynamics: convergence, periodicity and limit cycles. In: Proceedings of the 17th International Conference on Autonomous Agents and MultiAgent Systems, pp. 685–693. International Foundation for Autonomous Agents and Multi-Agent Systems (2018)
24. von Neumann, J., Morgenstern, O.: Theory of Games and Economic Behavior. Princeton University Press, Princeton (1944)
25. Omidshafiei, S., et al.: α-rank: multi-agent evaluation by evolution. Sci. Rep. **9** (2019)
26. Ostrovski, G., van Strien, S.: Piecewise linear Hamiltonian flows associated to zero-sum games: transition combinatorics and questions on ergodicity. Regul. Chaotic Dyn. **16**(1–2), 128–153 (2011)
27. Page, K.M., Nowak, M.A.: Unifying evolutionary dynamics. J. Theor. Biol. **219**(1), 93–98 (2002)
28. Panageas, I., Piliouras, G.: Average case performance of replicator dynamics in potential games via computing regions of attraction. In: Proceedings of the 2016 ACM Conference on Economics and Computation, pp. 703–720. ACM (2016)
29. Papadimitriou, C., Piliouras, G.: From Nash equilibria to chain recurrent sets: an algorithmic solution concept for game theory. Entropy **20**(10), 782 (2018)
30. Papadimitriou, C., Piliouras, G.: Game dynamics as the meaning of a game. ACM SIGecom Exch. **16**(2), 53–63 (2019)
31. Piliouras, G., Nieto-Granda, C., Christensen, H.I., Shamma, J.S.: Persistent patterns: multi-agent learning beyond equilibrium and utility. In: AAMAS, pp. 181–188 (2014)
32. Piliouras, G., Schulman, L.J.: Learning dynamics and the co-evolution of competing sexual species. In: ITCS (2018)

33. Piliouras, G., Shamma, J.S.: Optimization despite chaos: convex relaxations to complex limit sets via Poincaré recurrence. In: Proceedings of the Twenty-Fifth Annual ACM-SIAM Symposium on Discrete Algorithms, pp. 861–873. SIAM (2014)
34. Poincaré, H.: Sur le problème des trois corps et les équations de la dynamique. Acta Math. **13**, 1–270 (1890)
35. Sandholm, W.H.: Population Games and Evolutionary Dynamics. MIT Press, Cambridge (2010)
36. Sandholm, W.H., Dokumacı, E., Lahkar, R.: The projection dynamic and the replicator dynamic. Games Econ. Behav. **64**(2), 666–683 (2008)
37. Sato, Y., Akiyama, E., Farmer, J.D.: Chaos in learning a simple two-person game. Proc. Nat. Acad. Sci. **99**(7), 4748–4751 (2002)
38. Weibull, J.W.: Evolutionary Game Theory. MIT Press, Cambridge (1995)
39. Zeeman, E.C.: Population dynamics from game theory. In: Nitecki, Z., Robinson, C. (eds.) Global Theory of Dynamical Systems. LNM, vol. 819, pp. 471–497. Springer, Heidelberg (1980). https://doi.org/10.1007/BFb0087009

On the Convergence of Swap Dynamics to Pareto-Optimal Matchings

Felix Brandt$^{(\boxtimes)}$ and Anaëlle Wilczynski

Technical University of Munich, 80538 Munich, Germany
{brandtf,wilczyns}@in.tum.de

Abstract. We study whether Pareto-optimal stable matchings can be reached via pairwise swaps in one-to-one matching markets with initial assignments. We consider housing markets, marriage markets, and roommate markets as well as three different notions of swap rationality. Our main results are as follows. While it can be efficiently determined whether a Pareto-optimal stable matching can be reached when defining swaps via blocking pairs, checking whether this is the case for *all* such sequences is computationally intractable. When defining swaps such that all involved agents need to be better off, even deciding whether a Pareto-optimal stable matching can be reached via *some* sequence is intractable. This confirms and extends a conjecture made by Damamme et al. (2015), who have furthermore shown that convergence to a Pareto-optimal matching is guaranteed in housing markets with single-peaked preferences. We show that in marriage and roommate markets, single-peakedness is not sufficient for this to hold, but the stronger restriction of one-dimensional Euclidean preferences is.

1 Introduction

One-to-one matchings, where individuals are matched with resources or other individuals, are omnipresent in everyday life. Examples include the job market, assigning offices to workers, pairing students in working groups, and online dating. The formal study of matching procedures is fascinating because it leads to challenging mathematical and algorithmic problems while being of immediate practical interest [see, e.g., 22,24].

One typically distinguishes between three different types of abstract one-to-one matching settings. In *housing markets* [28], each agent is matched with an object (usually referred to as a house). In *marriage markets* [16], agents are partitioned into two groups—say, males and females—and each member of one group is matched with an agent from the other group. Finally, in *roommate markets* [16], all agents belong to the same group and each agent is matched with another agent. In many applications, it is reasonable to assume that there is an initial assignment because agents already live in a house, are engaged in a relationship, and are employed by a company [see, e.g., 1,25]. Under these assumptions, an important question is whether sequences of individual agreements between small groups of agents can lead to socially optimal outcomes. In

© Springer Nature Switzerland AG 2019
I. Caragiannis et al. (Eds.): WINE 2019, LNCS 11920, pp. 100–113, 2019.
https://doi.org/10.1007/978-3-030-35389-6_8

this paper, we focus on atomic agreements which require the least coordination: *pairwise swaps*.

In general, we consider three different types of individual rationality for pairwise swaps. In housing markets, there is only one meaningful notion of swap rationality: two agents will only exchange objects if both of them are better off. By contrast, when matching agents with each other, one could require that all four agents involved in a swap or only two of them are better off. The latter requirement allows for two kinds of swap rationality: two agents who exchange their match are better off (e.g., a company and its subsidiary exchange employees without asking their consent) or two agents who decide to form a new pair are better off (e.g., two lovers leave their current partners to be together).

Social optimality in settings with ordinal preferences like that of matching markets is measured in terms of Pareto-optimality. We therefore study whether there exists a sequence of pairwise swaps that results in a Pareto-optimal matching that does not allow for further swaps (and hence is called stable). Whenever all sequences of pairwise swaps are of this kind, we say that the given type of swap dynamics converges.

It turns out that in all three types of matching markets and all three notions of swap rationality, it may not be possible to reach a Pareto-optimal stable matching from the initial assignment. We prove that deciding whether this is the case is NP-hard for two types of swap rationality while it can be solved in polynomial time for swaps based on blocking pairs. However, in the latter case, checking convergence is co-NP-hard. On the other hand, we show that when preferences are one-dimensional Euclidean—a natural but demanding restriction—swap dynamics for two types of swap rationality will always converge.

2   Related Work

Damamme et al. [14] investigated the dynamics of individually rational pairwise swaps in housing markets, where two agents are better off by exchanging their objects. Recently, variants of this problem that further restrict the agents' interactions using underlying graph structures have been examined [17,20,27].

In marriage and roommate markets, most of the literature focuses on deviations based on blocking pairs, where two agents decide to leave their old partners in order to be matched with each other. Blocking pairs are best known for their role in the definition of stability [16], but some papers also studied the dynamics of blocking pair swaps [2,26]. The notion of exchange stability, where two agents agree to exchange their partners has been investigated in both roommate markets [5,11] and marriage markets [12]. We consider both types of swaps, i.e., blocking pair swaps and exchange rational swaps, but focus on the study of dynamics that reach Pareto-optimal matchings.

In contrast to our definition of Pareto-optimality, some papers on swap dynamics have investigated matchings that are Pareto-optimal *among all reachable matchings* [7,17]. Other types of dynamics that have been considered in matching markets include pairwise swaps without local rationality constraints [7], Pareto improvements [8,25], local dynamics based on underlying graphs [18,19], and exchanges among more than two agents [7,9].

Perhaps closest to our work is a result by Damamme et al. [14] who proved that swap dynamics always converge to a Pareto-optimal matching in housing markets when the preferences of the agents are single-peaked. However, they left open the computational problem of deciding whether a Pareto-optimal stable matching can be reached for unrestricted preferences and conjectured this problem to be intractable. We solve this problem and extend it to marriage and roommate markets. Moreover, we prove that their convergence result for housing markets under single-peaked preferences does not extend to marriage and roommate markets, but can be restored when restricting preferences even further.

3   The Model

We are given a set N of agents $\{1, \ldots, n\}$ and a set O of objects $\{a, b, \ldots\}$ such that $|N| = |O| = n$. Each agent $i \in N$ has strict ordinal preferences, represented by a linear order $\succ_i$, over a set A_i of alternatives to be matched with. In the matching markets we consider, A_i is either a subset of the set of agents N or the set of all objects O. A tuple of preference relations $\succ = (\succ_1, \ldots, \succ_n)$ is called a *preference profile*.

We consider two restricted preference domains in this article: single-peaked preferences [10] and its subdomain of one-dimensional Euclidean preferences [13]. A preference profile $\succ$ is *single-peaked* if there exists a linear order $>$ over the alternatives in $A := \bigcup_{i \in N} A_i$ such that for each agent i in N and each triple of alternatives $x, y, z \in A_i$ with $x > y > z$ or $z > y > x$, $x \succ_i y$ implies $y \succ_i z$. A preference profile $\succ$ is *one-dimensional Euclidean (1-Euclidean)* if there exists an embedding $E : N \cup O \to \mathbb{R}$ on the real line such that for every agent $i \in N$ and any two alternatives $x, y \in A_i$, $x \succ_i y$ iff $|E(i) - E(x)| < |E(i) - E(y)|$.

One-dimensional Euclidean preferences form a subdomain of single-peaked preferences because every 1-Euclidean preference profile is singled-peaked for the linear order $>$ given by $x > y$ iff $E(x) > E(y)$. However, a single-peaked preference profile may not be 1-Euclidean, as illustrated in the example below.

Example 1. Consider an instance with four agents. Each agent $i \in N$ has preferences over the same set of alternatives $A_i = O = \{a, b, c, d\}$.

$$
\begin{aligned}
1: \quad & a \succ b \succ c \succ d \\
2: \quad & d \succ c \succ b \succ a \\
3: \quad & b \succ c \succ d \succ a \\
4: \quad & c \succ b \succ a \succ d
\end{aligned}
$$

Observe that this preference profile is single-peaked only w.r.t. the linear order $a < b < c < d$ (or its reverse order) because of the preferences of Agents

1 and 2. Suppose that this preference profile is 1-Euclidean w.r.t. an embedding E on the real line. Then, without loss of generality, we can assume that $E(a) < E(b) < E(c) < E(d)$. Since Agent 3 prefers b to c and Agent 4 prefers c to b, it must hold that $E(3) < E(4)$. However, $d \succ_3 a$, therefore $E(d) - E(3) < E(3) - E(a)$. It follows that $E(d) - E(4) < E(4) - E(a)$, implying that Agent 4 prefers d to a, a contradiction.

While assuming that all agents have 1-Euclidean preferences certainly represents a strong restriction, there are nevertheless some applications where this assumption is not unreasonable. For example, in job markets, preferences could be 1-Euclidean because employees prefer one workplace to another if it is closer to their home, or when pairing workers in offices with a joint thermostat, workers could prefer co-workers whose most preferred room temperature is closer to their own.

3.1 Matching Markets

In this article, we are considering three different settings where the goal is to match the agents either with objects—like in housing markets—or with other agents—like in marriage or roommate markets. In all cases, we assume that there is an initial matching. More formally,

- a *housing market* consists of a preference profile where $A_i = O$ for all $i \in N$, and an initial endowment given as a bijection $\mu : N \to O$,
- a *marriage market* consists of a preference profile where $N = W \cup M$ with $W \cap M = \emptyset$, $A_i = M$ for all $i \in W$ and $A_i = W$ for all $i \in M$, and an initial matching given as a bijection $\mu : W \to M$, and
- a *roommate market* consists of a preference profile with even n and $A_i = N \setminus \{i\}$ for all $i \in N$, and an initial matching given as an involution $\mu : N \to N$ such that $\mu(i) \neq i$ for all $i \in N$.

In marriage markets, we will sometimes denote the inverse function μ^{-1} of matching μ by μ for the sake of simplicity.

When allowing for indifferences as well as unacceptabilities in the preferences, the three settings form a hierarchy: housing markets are marriage markets where the "objects" are indifferent between all agents, and marriage markets are roommate markets where all agents of the same type are considered unacceptable. In this paper, however, we do not make either assumption and therefore these inclusion relationships do not hold.

The key question studied in this paper is whether Pareto-optimal matchings can be reached from the initial matching via local modifications. A matching is *Pareto-optimal* if there is no other matching μ' such that for every agent $i \in N$, $\mu'(i) \succeq_i \mu(i)$ and for at least one agent $j \in N$, $\mu'(j) \succ_j \mu(j)$.

3.2 Rational Swaps

We study sequences of matchings in which two pairs of the current matching are permuted. More formally, we assume that a swap w.r.t. two agents (i, j)

104   F. Brandt and A. Wilczynski

transforms a matching μ into a matching μ' where agents i and j have exchanged their matches, i.e., $\mu'(i) = \mu(j)$ and $\mu'(j) = \mu(i)$, while the rest of the matching remains unchanged, i.e., $\mu'(k) = \mu(k)$ for every $k \notin \{i, j, \mu(i), \mu(j)\}$ (see Fig. 1).

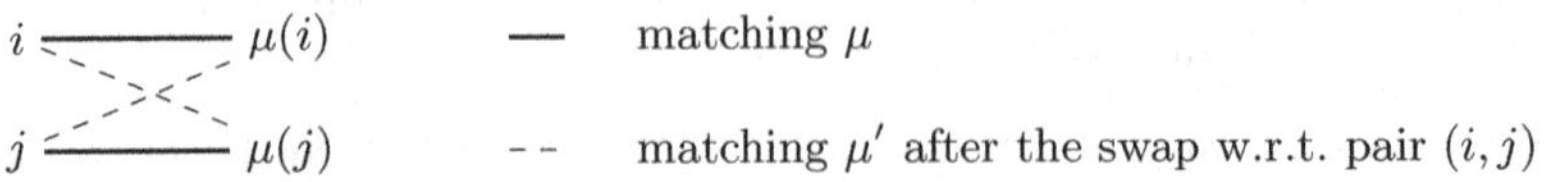

i ——————— $\mu(i)$ —   matching μ

j ——————— $\mu(j)$ --   matching μ' after the swap w.r.t. pair (i, j)

Fig. 1. Two matchings μ and μ' that differ in one swap.

We furthermore require these swaps to be *rational* in the sense that they result from an agreement among agents, and thus make the agents involved in the agreement better off.

The most natural notion of rationality in our definition of a swap is exchange-rationality, which requires that the two agents who exchange their matches are better off [5]. A swap w.r.t. agents (i, j) from matching μ is *exchange rational (ER)* if the agents who exchange their matches are better off, i.e.,

$$\mu(j) \succ_i \mu(i) \text{ and } \mu(i) \succ_j \mu(j). \hspace{2cm} \text{(ER-swap)}$$

Exchange-rationality is the only meaningful notion of swap rationality in housing markets because only one side of the market has preferences. However, several notions of rationality emerge in marriage and roommate markets, where agents are matched with each other. One could demand that only two of the agents who agree to form a new pair need to be better off. This notion of rational swaps is based on the classic idea of *blocking pairs*, which forms the basis of the standard notion of stability [16]. A swap w.r.t. agents (i, j) from matching μ between agents is *blocking pair (BP) rational* if one of the new pairs in μ' forms a blocking pair, where both agents are better off, i.e.,

$$[\mu(j) \succ_i \mu(i) \text{ and } i \succ_{\mu(j)} j] \quad \text{or} \quad [\mu(i) \succ_j \mu(j) \text{ and } j \succ_{\mu(i)} i]. \hspace{1cm} \text{(BP-swap)}$$

We usually refer to a *BP*-swap by mentioning the associated blocking pair $((i, \mu(j))$ or $(j, \mu(i)))$. The old partners of the blocking pair are also assumed to be matched together.[1]

Finally, in marriage and roommate markets, a stronger notion of rationality is that of a *fully rational swap*, which makes all four involved agents better off. A swap w.r.t. agents (i, j) from matching μ is *fully rational (FR)* if all four agents involved in the swap are better off, i.e.,

$$\mu(j) \succ_i \mu(i), \quad \mu(i) \succ_j \mu(j), \quad j \succ_{\mu(i)} i, \text{ and } \quad i \succ_{\mu(j)} j. \hspace{1cm} \text{(FR-swap)}$$

---

[1] Once the old partners are alone, they have an incentive to form a new pair. Roth and Vande Vate [26] therefore decompose *BP*-swaps into two steps. We do not explicitly consider these steps in order to always maintain a perfect matching [cf. 23].

Note that for marriage and roommate markets, an *FR*-swap w.r.t. pair of agents (i, j) from a matching μ is an *ER*-swap w.r.t. pair (i, j) or $(\mu(i), \mu(j))$ and also a *BP*-swap w.r.t blocking pair $(i, \mu(j))$ or $(j, \mu(i))$. We thus obtain the following implications:

$$BP\text{-swap} \quad \Leftarrow \quad FR\text{-swap} \quad \Rightarrow \quad ER\text{-swap}$$

The different types of swap rationality are illustrated in the following example.

Example 2. Consider a roommate market with six agents. The preferences of the agents are given below, where the initial assignment is marked with frames.

$$
\begin{array}{llllllllll}
1: & 4 \succ & \boxed{3} & \succ & 6 & \succ & 5 & \succ & 2 \\
2: & 3 \succ & 1 & \succ & \boxed{4} & \succ & 6 & \succ & 5 \\
3: & 6 \succ & 2 & \succ & \boxed{1} & \succ & 5 & \succ & 4 \\
4: & 5 \succ & 1 & \succ & 3 & \succ & \boxed{2} & \succ & 6 \\
5: & 2 \succ & \boxed{6} & \succ & 4 & \succ & 1 & \succ & 3 \\
6: & 4 \succ & 3 & \succ & 1 & \succ & 2 & \succ & \boxed{5}
\end{array}
$$

The swap w.r.t. pair $(1, 2)$, which matches Agent 1 with Agent 4 and Agent 2 with Agent 3, is an *FR*-swap because every involved agent is better off. Hence, this is also an *ER*-swap for pair $(1, 2)$ or $(3, 4)$ because they both prefer to exchange their partner. It is also a *BP*-swap for blocking pair $(2, 3)$ or $(1, 4)$ because they both prefer to be together than with their current partner.

The swap w.r.t. pair $(1, 6)$ is a *BP*-swap for blocking pair $(3, 6)$ because Agent 3, the old partner of Agent 1, prefers to be with Agent 6, as well as Agent 6 who prefers 3 to her old partner 5. This is not an *ER*-swap (and hence not an *FR*-swap) because neither the agents in pair $(1, 6)$ nor in pair $(3, 5)$ want to exchange their partners.

The swap w.r.t. pair $(4, 6)$ is an *ER*-swap for $(4, 6)$ because Agent 4 prefers the current partner of 6, i.e., Agent 5, to her current partner and 6 prefers the current partner of 4, i.e., Agent 2, to her current partner. This is not a *BP*-swap (and hence not an *FR*-swap) because it matches Agent 4 with Agent 5, who prefers to stay with her current partner, and Agent 6 with Agent 2, who prefers to stay with her current partner.

Stability can now be defined according to the different notions of rational swaps. A matching μ is σ-*stable*, for $\sigma \in \{FR, ER, BP\}$, if no σ-swap can be performed from matching μ. A sequence of σ-swaps, for $\sigma \in \{FR, ER, BP\}$, corresponds to a sequence of matchings $(\mu^0, \mu^1, \ldots, \mu^r)$ such that a σ-swap transforms each matching μ^t into matching μ^{t+1} for every $0 \le t < r$. Then, matching μ is σ-*reachable* from initial matching μ^0 if there exists a sequence of σ-swaps $(\mu^0, \mu^1, \ldots, \mu^r)$ such that $\mu^r = \mu$. When the context is clear, we omit σ and the initial matching μ^0.

A σ-*dynamics* is defined according to initial matching μ^0 and a type σ of rational swaps. The σ-dynamics is *finite* if all associated sequences of σ-swaps terminate in a σ-stable matching, and it is said to *converge* if it is finite for every initial matching μ^0.

In this article, we consider the following two decision problems related to the convergence of dynamics to a Pareto-optimal matching.

∃-σ-PARETOSEQUENCE / ∀-σ-PARETOSEQUENCE

Input: Matching market, type σ of rational swaps

Question: Does there exist a sequence of σ-swaps terminating in a Pareto-optimal σ-stable matching? /
Do all sequences of σ-swaps terminate in a Pareto-optimal σ-stable matching?

In order to tackle these questions, we also study the stability and convergence properties of the considered dynamics in the three types of matching markets.

4   Exchange Rational Swaps

In housing markets, every *ER*-swap represents a Pareto improvement. Hence, since the number of agents and objects is finite, *ER*-dynamics always converges and the existence of *ER*-stable matchings is guaranteed (simply because every Pareto-optimal matching happens to be *ER*-stable). However, it may be impossible to reach a Pareto-optimal matching from a given matching by only applying *ER*-swaps.

Proposition 1. *ER-dynamics may not converge to a Pareto-optimal matching in housing markets.*

Proof. Consider a housing market with three agents. The preferences of the agents are given below, where the initial assignment is marked with frames.

$$1 : \textcircled{a} \succ \boxed{b} \succ c$$
$$2 : \textcircled{b} \succ \boxed{c} \succ a$$
$$3 : \textcircled{c} \succ \boxed{a} \succ b$$

Observe that no *ER*-swap is possible in this instance, therefore the initial matching (framed objects) is the unique *ER*-reachable matching. However, there exists a unique Pareto-optimal matching (circled objects), and this matching is different from the initial one.   □

Nevertheless, Damamme et al. [14] have shown that *ER*-dynamics always converges to a Pareto-optimal matching in housing markets when the agents' preferences are single-peaked.

In marriage and roommate markets, an *ER*-stable matching may not exist, even for single-peaked preferences (Cechlárova [11] and Alcalde [5] provide counterexamples). However, it turns out that, when restricting preferences even further to 1-Euclidean preferences, an *ER*-stable matching always exists, and, moreover, the convergence to such a matching is guaranteed.

Proposition 2. *ER-dynamics always converges in marriage and roommate markets for 1-Euclidean preferences.*

Proof. Denote by $E : N \rightarrow \mathbb{R}$ the embedding of the agents on the real line such that their preferences are 1-Euclidean w.r.t. this embedding. Define as a potential function $f : \mu \rightarrow \mathbb{R}$ the function which assigns to each matching the sum of the distances on the real line between all the assigned pairs in the matching, i.e., $f(\mu) = \sum_{(i,j)s.t.\mu(i)=j} |E(i) - E(j)|$. Now consider a sequence of ER-swaps given by the sequence of matchings $(\mu^0, \mu^1, \ldots, \mu^r)$. Between each μ^t and μ^{t+1}, with $0 \leq t < r$, an ER-swap is performed, say w.r.t. pair (i,j) of agents. By definition of an ER-swap, agents i and j prefer to exchange their partners in μ^t, and thus, $\mu^t(j) \succ_i \mu^t(i)$ and $\mu^t(i) \succ_j \mu^t(j)$. This implies that $|E(i) - E(\mu^t(j))| < |E(i) - E(\mu^t(i))|$ and $|E(j) - E(\mu^t(i))| < |E(j) - E(\mu^t(j))|$. But i and $\mu^t(j)$ are matched in μ^{t+1}, as well as j and $\mu^t(i)$. Since the rest of the pairs remains unchanged between μ^t and μ^{t+1}, we get that $f(\mu^{t+1}) < f(\mu^t)$. Because the number of different matchings is finite, we can conclude that ER-dynamics always converges. □

In general, an ER-stable matching may not be Pareto-optimal, and thus the convergence to a Pareto-optimal matching is not guaranteed even when an ER-stable matching exists (note that determining whether there exists an ER-stable matching is NP-hard in both marriage and roommate markets [11,12]).

Proposition 3. *ER-dynamics may not converge to a Pareto-optimal matching, in marriage and roommate markets, even when an ER-stable matching exists.*

Proof. Consider a marriage market with three women and three men. The preferences are given below and the initial assignment is marked with frames.

$$w_1 : \boxed{\!\!\circled{m_1}\!\!} \succ \boxed{m_2} \succ m_3 \qquad m_1 : \circled{w_1} \succ \boxed{w_3} \succ w_2$$
$$w_2 : \circled{m_2} \succ \boxed{m_3} \succ m_1 \qquad m_2 : \circled{w_2} \succ \boxed{w_1} \succ w_3$$
$$w_3 : \circled{m_3} \succ \boxed{m_1} \succ m_2 \qquad m_3 : \circled{w_3} \succ \boxed{w_2} \succ w_1$$

No ER-swap is possible from the initial matching (framed agents), therefore the initial matching is the unique ER-reachable matching. However, there is another matching (circled agents) which is the unique Pareto-optimal matching.

Now, consider a roommate market with six agents. Preferences of the agents are given below, where the initial partner of each agent is marked with frames and "[...]" denotes an arbitrary order over the rest of the agents.

$$1 : \circled{3} \succ \boxed{2} \succ [\ldots] \qquad 4 : \circled{6} \succ \boxed{3} \succ [\ldots]$$
$$2 : \circled{5} \succ \boxed{1} \succ [\ldots] \qquad 5 : \circled{2} \succ \boxed{6} \succ [\ldots]$$
$$3 : \circled{1} \succ \boxed{4} \succ [\ldots] \qquad 6 : \circled{4} \succ \boxed{5} \succ [\ldots]$$

No ER-swap is possible from the initial matching (framed agents), thus the initial matching is the unique ER-reachable matching. However, there is another matching (circled agents) which is the unique Pareto-optimal matching. □

Note that the above preference profiles are not 1-Euclidean. In fact, they are not even single-peaked. Again, more positive results can be obtained by restricting the domain of admissible preferences.

Proposition 4. *Every ER-stable matching is Pareto-optimal when preferences are single-peaked in marriage and roommate markets.*

Proof. Let μ be an *ER*-stable matching. For any two agents i and j (in N for roommate markets, or both in either W or M for marriage markets) it holds that $\mu(i) \succ_i \mu(j)$ or $\mu(j) \succ_j \mu(i)$. Suppose there is another matching μ' such that $\mu'(i) \succeq_i \mu(i)$ for every $i \in N$ and there exists $j \in N$ such that $\mu'(j) \succ_j \mu(j)$. Then, there exists a Pareto improving cycle from μ to μ' along agents $(n_1, \ldots, n_k)$ such that each agent n_i, $1 \leq i \leq k$, is matched in μ' with agent $\mu(n_{(i \bmod k)+1})$. For marriage markets, the agents in $(n_1, \ldots, n_k)$ are restricted by definition to only one side of the market, but it impacts both sides since the agents exchange agents of the other side. But there is no problem of preferences of the matched agents because no agent is worse off in μ' compared to μ. The same holds for roommate markets. Since μ is *ER*-stable, it holds that $k > 2$. However, for single-peaked preferences, one can prove, by following the same proof by induction as Damamme et al. [14], that a Pareto improving cycle of any length cannot occur, contradicting the fact that μ is Pareto dominated. □

Propositions 2 and 4 allow us to conclude that sequences of *ER*-swaps will always terminate in Pareto-optimal matchings when preferences are 1-Euclidean.

Corollary 1. *ER-dynamics always converges to a Pareto-optimal matching in marriage and roommate markets for 1-Euclidean preferences.*

An interesting computational question is whether, given a preference profile and an initial assignment, a Pareto-optimal matching can be reached via *ER*-swaps. In the context of housing markets, the complexity of this question was mentioned as an open problem by Damamme et al. [14]. It turns out that this problem is computationally intractable for all kinds of matching markets considered in this paper.

Theorem 1. ∃-ER-PARETOSEQUENCE *is* NP-*hard in housing, marriage, and roommate markets.*

The proof is omitted due to space restrictions.

5   Blocking Pair Swaps

BP-swaps cannot occur in housing markets because objects can never be better off. We therefore focus on matching markets that match agents with each other in this section.

By definition of a blocking pair, any *BP*-stable matching is Pareto-optimal. Moreover, a *BP*-stable matching always exists in marriage markets by the Deferred Acceptance algorithm [16]. However, the convergence to such a state is not guaranteed, even for single-peaked preferences [23]. Nevertheless, there always exists a sequence of *BP*-swaps leading to a stable matching [26].[2] In roommate markets, even the existence of a *BP*-stable matching is not guaranteed [16], and actually this is the case even for single-peaked preferences.

---

[2] Assuming that the old partners also form a new pair does not alter this result.

Nevertheless, checking the existence of a stable matching in a roommate market can be done in polynomial time [21], and there always exists a sequence of BP-swaps leading to a stable matching when there exists one [15]. Therefore, by combining these facts with the observation that every BP-stable matching is Pareto-optimal, we get the following corollary.

Corollary 2. $\exists$-BP-PARETOSEQUENCE *is solvable in polynomial time in marriage and roommate markets.*

However, in general, determining whether all sequences of BP-swaps terminate in a Pareto-optimal matching, i.e., checking convergence of BP-dynamics to a Pareto-optimal matching, is hard. This is due to the hardness of checking the existence of a cycle in BP-dynamics.

Theorem 2. *Determining whether BP-dynamics can cycle in marriage and roommate markets is* NP-*hard.*

The proof is omitted due to space restrictions.

Corollary 3. $\forall$-BP-PARETOSEQUENCE *is* co-NP-*hard in marriage and roommate markets.*

Nevertheless, when preferences are 1-Euclidean, we can always reach a stable matching thanks to BP-dynamics in both settings.

Indeed, a marriage market under 1-Euclidean preferences is a particular case of a *correlated two-sided market* [4] where all the possible pairs are *globally ranked* [see, also 3]. In such a correlated market, the preferences of the agents are induced from the global order by taking into account the order over the pairs to which they belong. It has been proved that BP-dynamics always converges in correlated marriage markets [4]. Moreover, it is easy to see that from 1-Euclidean preferences, a global ranking over all possible pairs can be extracted by sorting all pairs according to the distance on the real line between the two partners.[3] Therefore, we obtain the following corollary.

Corollary 4. *BP-dynamics always converges in marriage markets for 1-Euclidean preferences.*

In roommate markets, there always exists a unique BP-stable matching under 1-Euclidean preferences [6]. We further prove that convergence to this matching is guaranteed using a potential function argument.

Proposition 5. *BP-dynamics always converges in roommate markets for 1-Euclidean preferences.*

---

[3] The presence of a global ranking over all possible pairs does not imply that preferences are 1-Euclidean. Consider for instance, in roommate markets, the following preference profile: $1 : 2 \succ 3 \succ 4$, $2 : 1 \succ 4 \succ 3$, $3 : 4 \succ 1 \succ 2$, $4 : 3 \succ 2 \succ 1$.

Proof. Denote by $E : N \to \mathbb{R}$ the embedding of the agents on the real line such that their preferences are 1-Euclidean w.r.t. this embedding. Let $d(\mu)$ be the $n/2$-vector of distances in E of all the different pairs in μ, i.e., $d(\mu) = (|E(i) - E(j)|)_{i,j \text{ s.t. } \mu(i)=j}$. Now consider a sequence of *BP*-swaps given by the following sequence of matchings $(\mu^0, \mu^1, \ldots, \mu^r)$. Then, between each pair of matchings μ^t and μ^{t+1} with $0 \leq t < r$, a *BP*-swap is performed, say w.r.t. blocking pair (i, j) of agents. By definition of a *BP*-swap, agents i and j prefer to be together than being with their partner in μ^t, so $j = \mu^{t+1}(i) \succ_i \mu^t(i)$ and $i = \mu^{t+1}(j) \succ_j \mu^t(j)$, which implies that $|E(i) - E(j)| < |E(i) - E(\mu^t(i))|$ and $|E(i) - E(j)| < |E(j) - E(\mu^t(j))|$. Therefore, $(|E(i) - E(j)|, |E(\mu^t(i)) - E(\mu^t(j))|)$ is lexicographically smaller than $(|E(i) - E(\mu^t(i))|, |E(j) - E(\mu^t(j))|)$. Since the rest of the pairs remains unchanged between μ^t and μ^{t+1}, $d(\mu^{t+1})$ is lexicographically strictly smaller than $d(\mu^t)$. Because the number of different matchings is finite, we conclude that *BP*-dynamics always converges. □

Since every *BP*-stable matching is Pareto-optimal, Corollary 4 and Proposition 5 imply the following corollary.

Corollary 5. *BP-dynamics always converges to a Pareto-optimal matching in marriage and roommate markets for 1-Euclidean preferences.*

6   Fully Rational Swaps

Just as in the case of *ER*-swaps and housing markets, *FR*-swaps always represent Pareto improvements because all involved agents are strictly better off after the swap. Hence, *FR*-stable matchings are guaranteed to exist because every Pareto-optimal matching is *FR*-stable and *FR*-dynamics always converges because the number of agents is finite.

In Sect. 4, we have shown that *ER*-dynamics always converges to a Pareto-optimal matching when the preferences of the agents are 1-Euclidean. It turns out that this does not hold for *FR*-dynamics.

Proposition 6. *A sequence of FR-swaps may not converge to a Pareto-optimal matching in marriage and roommate markets, even for 1-Euclidean preferences.*

Proof. Consider a marriage market with three women and three men. The preferences are given below, where the initial assignment is marked with frames.

$w_1 : (m_1) \succ \boxed{m_3} \succ m_2$ $\qquad\qquad$ $m_1 : (w_1) \succ \boxed{w_3} \succ w_2$

$w_2 : (m_3) \succ m_1 \succ \boxed{m_2}$ $\qquad\qquad$ $m_2 : (w_3) \succ w_1 \succ \boxed{w_2}$

$w_3 : (m_2) \succ \boxed{m_1} \succ m_3$ $\qquad\qquad$ $m_3 : (w_2) \succ \boxed{w_1} \succ w_3$

The initial matching is the only reachable matching, because no *FR*-swap is possible in this matching. However, there is another matching (circled agents) which is not reachable but which Pareto dominates this only reachable matching. The preferences are 1-Euclidean w.r.t. the following embedding on the real line.

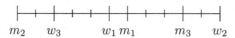

$$m_2 \quad w_3 \qquad w_1\, m_1 \qquad m_3 \quad w_2$$

Now, consider a roommate market with six agents. The preferences of the agents are given below, where the initial assignment is marked with frames.

$$
\begin{aligned}
&1 : ②\succ 3 \succ 4 \succ 5 \succ \boxed{6} && 4 : ③\succ 2 \succ \boxed{5} \succ 1 \succ 6\\
&2 : ①\succ \boxed{3} \succ 4 \succ 5 \succ 6 && 5 : ⑥\succ \boxed{4} \succ 3 \succ 2 \succ 1\\
&3 : ④\succ \boxed{2} \succ 1 \succ 5 \succ 6 && 6 : ⑤\succ 4 \succ 3 \succ 2 \succ \boxed{1}
\end{aligned}
$$

The initial matching is the only reachable matching, because there is no *FR*-swap from this matching. However, there is another matching (circled agents) which is not reachable but which Pareto dominates this only reachable matching. The preferences are 1-Euclidean w.r.t. the following embedding on the real line.

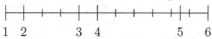

$$1 \quad 2 \qquad\quad 3 \quad 4 \qquad\qquad 5 \quad 6$$

□

The proof of Theorem 1 only dealt with instances in which *FR*-swaps are identical to *ER*-swaps. We thus immediately obtain hardness of ∃-FR-PARETOSEQUENCE.

Theorem 3. ∃-FR-PARETOSEQUENCE *is* NP-*hard in marriage and roommate markets.*

Table 1. Summary of the results on the existence of a stable matching (Stable), the guarantee of convergence (Conv) and the guarantee of convergence to a Pareto-optimal matching (Pareto) for the three different matching markets under study, according to different types of rational swaps and under different preference domains (General, single-peaked (SP), and 1-Euclidean (1-D)). The only meaningful type of rational swaps in housing markets are exchange-rational swaps; hence, the empty spaces.

Market	Prefs	Exchange rational swaps			Blocking pair swaps			Fully rational swaps		
		Stable	Conv	Pareto	Stable	Conv	Pareto	Stable	Conv	Pareto
Housing	General	✓	✓	– (Prop. 1)						
	SP	✓	✓	✓ [14]						
	1-D	✓	✓	✓						
Marriage	General	–	–	–	✓ [16]	–	–	✓	✓	–
	SP	– [11]	–	–	✓	–	–	✓	✓	–
	1-D	✓	✓	✓ (Prop. 2)	✓	✓	✓ (Cor. 4)	✓	✓	– (Prop. 6)
Roommate	General	–	–	–	– [16]	–	–	✓	✓	–
	SP	– [5]	–	–	–	–	–	✓	✓	–
	1-D	✓	✓	✓ (Prop. 2)	✓	✓	✓ (Prop. 5)	✓	✓	– (Prop. 6)

7   Conclusion

We have studied the properties of different dynamics of rational swaps in matching markets with initial assignments and, in particular, the question of convergence to a Pareto-optimal matching. For all considered settings, the dynamics may not terminate in a Pareto-optimal matching because *(i)* there is no stable matching, *(ii)* the dynamics does not converge, or *(iii)* the stable matching that is eventually reached is not Pareto-optimal. An overview of our results is given in Table 1.

Computationally, determining whether there exists a sequence of rational swaps terminating in a Pareto-optimal matching is NP-hard for fully rational swaps and exchange rational swaps in all matching markets (Theorems 1 and 3). For swaps based on blocking pairs, this problem can be solved efficiently (Corollary 2). However, the convergence to a Pareto-optimal matching is co-NP-hard to decide (Corollary 3). Since determining the existence of a sequence of fully rational or exchange rational swaps terminating in a Pareto-optimal matching is already hard, we did not investigate the complexity of convergence to a Pareto-optimal matching (which means that all sequences terminate) for these swaps. We leave it as an open problem that we conjecture to be hard.

The convergence to a Pareto-optimal matching in housing markets for exchange rational dynamics and single-peaked preferences [14] does not hold for more general settings where the "objects" are agents who have preferences. However, this convergence is guaranteed under 1-Euclidean preferences in marriage and roommate markets. Hence, the generalization of this convergence result to more general settings requires more structure in the preferences.

A natural extension of this work would be to study meaningful dynamics for hedonic games, where agents form groups consisting of more than two agents.

References

1. Abdulkadiroğlu, A., Sönmez, T.: House allocation with existing tenants. J. Econ. Theory **88**(2), 233–260 (1999)
2. Abeledo, H., Rothblum, U.G.: Paths to marriage stability. Discrete Appl. Math. **63**(1), 1–12 (1995)
3. Abraham, D.J., et al.: The stable roommates problem with globally-ranked pairs. In: Deng, X., Graham, F.C. (eds.) WINE 2007. LNCS, vol. 4858, pp. 431–444. Springer, Heidelberg (2007). https://doi.org/10.1007/978-3-540-77105-0_48
4. Ackermann, H., Goldberg, P.W., Mirrokni, V.S., Röglin, H., Vöcking, B.: Uncoordinated two-sided matching markets. SIAM J. Comput. **40**(1), 92–106 (2011)
5. Alcalde, J.: Exchange-proofness or divorce-proofness? Stability in one-sided matching markets. Rev. Econ. Design **1**(1), 275–287 (1994)
6. Arkin, E.M., Bae, S.W., Efrat, A., Okamoto, K., Mitchell, J.S.B., Polishchuk, V.: Geometric stable roommates. Inf. Process. Lett. **109**(4), 219–224 (2009)
7. Aziz, H.: Algorithms for Pareto optimal exchange with bounded exchange cycles. Oper. Res. Lett. **47**(5), 344–347 (2019)
8. Aziz, H., Brandt, F., Harrenstein, P.: Pareto optimality in coalition formation. Games Econ. Behav. **82**, 562–581 (2013)

9. Aziz, H., Goldwaser, A.: Coalitional exchange stable matchings in marriage and roommate markets (extended abstract). In: Proceedings of 16th AAMAS Conference, pp. 1475–1477. IFAAMAS (2017)
10. Black, D.: On the rationale of group decision-making. J. Polit. Econ. **56**(1), 23–34 (1948)
11. Cechlárová, K.: On the complexity of exchange-stable roommates. Discrete Appl. Math. **116**(3), 279–287 (2002)
12. Cechlárová, K., Manlove, D.F.: The exchange-stable marriage problem. Discrete Appl. Math. **152**(1–3), 109–122 (2005)
13. Coombs, C.H.: Psychological scaling without a unit of measurement. Psychol. Rev. **57**(3), 145–158 (1950)
14. Damamme, A., Beynier, A., Chevaleyre, Y., Maudet, N.: The power of swap deals in distributed resource allocation. In: Proceedings of 14th AAMAS Conference, pp. 625–633. IFAAMAS (2015)
15. Diamantoudi, E., Miyagawa, E., Xue, L.: Random paths to stability in the roommate problem. Games Econ. Behav. **48**(1), 18–28 (2004)
16. Gale, D., Shapley, L.S.: College admissions and the stability of marriage. Am. Math. Monthly **69**(1), 9–15 (1962)
17. Gourvès, L., Lesca, J., Wilczynski, A.: Object allocation via swaps along a social network. In: Proceedings of 26th IJCAI, pp. 213–219. IJCAI (2017)
18. Hoefer, M.: Local matching dynamics in social networks. In: Aceto, L., Henzinger, M., Sgall, J. (eds.) ICALP 2011. LNCS, vol. 6756, pp. 113–124. Springer, Heidelberg (2011). https://doi.org/10.1007/978-3-642-22012-8_8
19. Hoefer, M., Vaz, D., Wagner, L.: Dynamics in matching and coalition formation games with structural constraints. Artif. Intell. **262**, 222–247 (2018)
20. Huang, S., Xiao, M.: Object reachability via swaps along a line. In: Proceedings of 33rd AAAI Conference, pp. 2037–2044. AAAI Press (2019)
21. Irving, R.W.: An efficient algorithm for the "stable roommates" problem. J. Algorithms **6**(4), 577–595 (1985)
22. Klaus, B., Manlove, D.F., Rossi, F.: Matching under preferences. In: Brandt, F., Conitzer, V., Endriss, U., Lang, J., Procaccia, A.D. (eds.) Handbook of Computational Social Choice, Chap. 14. Cambridge University Press (2016)
23. Knuth, D.E.: Mariages stables. Les Presses de l'Université de Montréal (1976)
24. Manlove, D.F.: Algorithmics of Matching Under Preferences. World Scientific Publishing Company (2013)
25. Morrill, T.: The roommates problem revisited. J. Econ. Theory **145**(5), 1739–1756 (2010)
26. Roth, A.E., Vande Vate, J.H.: Random paths to stability in two-sided matching. Econometrica **58**(6), 1475–1480 (1990)
27. Saffidine, A., Wilczynski, A.: Constrained swap dynamics over a social network in distributed resource reallocation. In: Deng, X. (ed.) SAGT 2018. LNCS, vol. 11059, pp. 213–225. Springer, Cham (2018). https://doi.org/10.1007/978-3-319-99660-8_19
28. Shapley, L.S., Scarf, H.: On cores and indivisibility. J. Math. Econ. **1**(1), 23–37 (1974)

Hotelling Games with Random Tolerance Intervals

Avi Cohen$^{(\boxtimes)}$ and David Peleg

Weizmann Institute of Science, Rehovot, Israel
{avi.cohen,david.peleg}@weizmann.ac.il

Abstract. The classical Hotelling game is played on a line segment whose points represent uniformly distributed clients. The n players of the game are servers who need to place themselves on the line segment, and once this is done, each client gets served by the player closest to it. The goal of each player is to choose its location so as to maximize the number of clients it attracts.

In this paper we study a variant of the Hotelling game where each client v has a *tolerance interval*, randomly distributed according to some density function f, and v gets served by the nearest among the players *eligible* for it, namely, those that fall within its interval. (If no such player exists, then v abstains.) It turns out that this modification significantly changes the behavior of the game and its states of equilibria. In particular, it may serve to explain why players sometimes prefer to "spread out," rather than to cluster together as dictated by the classical Hotelling game.

We consider two variants of the game: *symmetric* games, where clients have the same tolerance range to their left and right, and *asymmetric* games, where the left and right ranges of each client are determined independently of each other. We characterize the Nash equilibria of the 2-player game. For $n \geq 3$ players, we characterize a specific class of strategy profiles, referred to as *canonical profiles*, and show that these profiles are the only ones that may yield Nash equilibria in our game. Moreover, the canonical profile, if exists, is uniquely defined for every n and f. In the symmetric setting, we give simple conditions for the canonical profile to be a Nash equilibrium, and demonstrate their application for several distributions. In the asymmetric setting, the conditions for equilibria are more complex; still, we derive a full characterization for the Nash equilibria of the exponential distribution. Finally, we show that for some distributions the simple conditions given for the symmetric setting are sufficient also for the asymmetric setting.

Keywords: Hotelling games · Pure nash equilibria · Uniqueness of equilibrium

1 Introduction

Background and Motivation. The Hotelling game, introduced in the seminal [14], is a widely studied model of spatial competition in a variety of con-

© Springer Nature Switzerland AG 2019
I. Caragiannis et al. (Eds.): WINE 2019, LNCS 11920, pp. 114–128, 2019.
https://doi.org/10.1007/978-3-030-35389-6_9

texts, ranging from the placement of commercial facilities, to the differentiation between similar products of competing brands, to the positioning of candidates in political elections. The well known toy example is as follows: two ice cream vendors choose a location on a beach strip. Beach goers are uniformly distributed on the beach, and each buys ice cream from the closest vendor. The goal of each vendor is to maximize the number of customers he receives. The well known result is that the only Nash equilibrium is for both vendors to locate at the median. This explains why sellers bunch together, but also why political candidates tend to have very similar platforms, converging on the opinion of the median voter.

However, there are many cases to which this observation does not apply. In the commercial setting, introducing price competition has been shown to cause competitors to differentiate in location [5,16]. Additional factors with a dispersing affect include transportation costs [16], congestion [1,12,17], and queues [15,18]. Nevertheless, those considerations do not apply to the political setting, and explaining how a polarized political space may emerge [13] remains a limitation of Hotelling's model. Our motivating question in this paper concerns identifying and understanding some of the factors of the Hotelling game that drive competitors to disperse rather then cluster together. Our results provide a possible explanation of why in some settings it would pay off for political candidates or firms to diverge from their competition.

The model we study is motivated by the following insightful observation, pointed out by several other authors [2,11,19]. One of the key assumptions at the basis of the Hotelling model is that clients will always go to the closest vendor, no matter how far he is. This assumption might be problematic in some settings. In the political context, for instance, the assumption means that voters may be willing to compromise their beliefs to an unlimited extent. In reality, this is not necessarily valid; it is possible that if no candidate presents sufficiently close opinions, the voter may simply abstain from voting. To address this issue, we adopt a modified variant of the Hotelling game, introduced and studied in [2, 11,19], in which clients (voters, in the political context) have a limited *tolerance interval*, and a client will choose only players (candidates, in the political context) that fall within her tolerance interval. In our model the interval boundaries are chosen randomly, as each client has a different tolerance threshold (reflecting different degrees of openness to other political views).

It is important to note that our model deviates from the previous models in two central ways. First, in our game, the player that the client chooses from among the eligible players (falling within her tolerance interval) is not arbitrary but rather the closest one (breaking ties uniformly at random). This expresses the intuition that while a voter may be open minded and willing to vote to a candidate with a vastly divergent standpoint, she would still rather vote to a candidate that closely agrees with her own opinions provided one exists. Similarly, the proverbial sunbather would prefer to visit a closer vendor, even if she is willing to travel a longer distance when necessary. In this sense, our model maintains

Hotelling's original intuition while capturing the realization that clients would not choose players that are too distant.

The second difference between our model and previous ones has to do with symmetry. Recently, a growing concern for the political discourse in western democracies is the phenomenon of *echo chambers* [13], namely, social media settings such as discussion groups and forums, in which one is exposed exclusively to opinions that agree with, and enhance, her own[1]. This phenomenon tends to "shorten" the tolerance intervals of individual voters. But more importantly, we note that the echo chamber effect is very likely to act in a *one-sided* manner, making a voter more receptive to views on one side of the political spectrum than the other. Hence in certain settings, it is unreasonable to assume that a client has the same tolerance bounds on both sides.

To take such settings into account, we consider two variants of the game: *symmetric games*, where clients have the same range of tolerance to their left and right, which expresses the willingness of a client to go a certain distance, with no preference of direction, and *asymmetric games*, where the left and right ranges of each client are determined independently of each other, which captures settings where the scope of views each client is exposed to may be biased due to media bias, one-sided echo chambers, or tendencies in her local environment.

It may be natural to expect our results to depend heavily on the distribution according to which client tolerances are chosen. Surprisingly, it turns out that most of our general findings apply to a wide class of distributions.

Contributions. In our model, the left and right tolerance ranges of each client are randomly distributed according to a given density f. Hence a game $G(n, f)$ is determined by the number of players n and the distribution function f. We consider two variants: symmetric games, where the left and right ranges of each client are equal, and asymmetric games, where the left and right ranges of each client are independent and identically distributed random variables.

We first characterize the Nash equilibria of the 2-player game (Theorem 2). For $n \geq 3$, we identify a specific class of strategy profiles, referred to as *canonical profiles*, where the distance between every pair of neighboring players is constant, and the distance from the leftmost player to 0 (a.k.a. the *left hinterland*) is the same as the distance from the rightmost player to 1 (the *right hinterland*).

We then show that canonical profiles are the only ones that may yield Nash equilibria in our game, namely, if there is an equilibrium then it must be canonical (Theorem 3). Moreover, the canonical profile, when it exists, is uniquely defined for every n and f. Hence, given a specific game $G(n, f)$, our problem is reduced to considering whether the canonical profile is a Nash equilibrium for given values of n and f.

---

[1] There are several reasons this phenomenon is increasingly prevalent online. First, exposure to content is curated by algorithms according to each user's personal preferences. Second, on social media, users are more likely to share with their network content that agrees with their own opinion. Third, it has become increasingly easier to join private discussion groups that consist of like-minded individuals.

In the symmetric setting we give simple conditions for the canonical profile to be a Nash equilibrium, and demonstrate their application for several distributions. In the asymmetric setting, the conditions for equilibria are more complex, but we show that for some distributions, existence of a Nash equilibrium in the symmetric setting implies its existence in the asymmetric setting (Theorem 4). Finally, we show that even though Theorem 4 does not apply for the exponential distribution, it is still possible to derive a full characterization of its Nash equilibria. Specifically, for the exponential distribution of parameter λ in the asymmetric setting, we show that a Nash equilibrium exists for the n-player game if and only if $\lambda \geq \lambda_{\min}(n)$, for some *threshold function* $\lambda_{\min}(n)$ (Theorem 5). Additionally, we show a way to efficiently approximate the values of $\lambda_{\min}(n)$ to any precision.

Related Work. Hotelling's model and its many variants have been studied extensively. Downs [7] extended the Hotelling model to ideological positioning in a bipartisan democracy. It is remarkable to note that even in Downs' original work it was stipulated that extremists would rather abstain than vote to center parties, but no mathematical framework was provided for this property of the model. Our work formalizes Downs' original intuition. Eaton and Lipsey [8] extended Hotelling's analysis to any number of players and different location spaces. Our model is a direct extension of their n-player game on the line segment. d'Aspremont et al. [5] criticized Hotelling's findings and showed that when players compete on price as well as location, they tend to create distance from one another, otherwise price competition would drop their profit to zero. Our results show a differentiation in location in the n-player Hotelling game without introducing price competition. A large portion of the Hotelling game literature is dedicated to models with price competition. We, however, exclusively consider pure location competition models since they apply more directly to certain settings, such as the political one. Eiselt, Laporte and Thisse [10] provide an extensive comparison of the different models classified by the following characteristics: the number of players, the location space (e.g., circle, plane, network), the pricing policy, the behavior of players, and the behavior of clients. (For more recent surveys see Eiselt et al. [9] and Brenner [3].)

Randomness in client behavior was introduced by De Palma et al. [6]. Their model assumes client behavior has an unpredictable component due to unquantifiable factors of personal taste, and thus clients have a small probability of "skipping" the closest player and buying from another. In their model, all players would locate at the center in equilibrium, reasserting Hotelling's conclusion. In our model, clients exhibit randomness in their choice of players as well, but in equilibrium players create a fixed distance from their neighbors.

Feldman et al. [11] introduced the Hotelling model with limited attraction, where, similarly to our model, clients are unwilling to travel beyond a certain distance. They considered a simplified variant of the model where each player has an attraction interval of width w for some fixed w. Their model admits an equilibrium for any number of players. Moreover, for most values of w, there exist infinitely many equilibria. (In contrast, our model admits at most a single

Nash equilibrium with a distinct structure.) Shen and Wang [19] extend the model of [11] to general distributions of clients. Ben-Porat and Tennenholz [2] consider random ranges of tolerance, and show that their game behaves like a cooperative game, since player payoffs are equal to their Shapley values in a coalition game. Their analysis relies on the fact that their game is a potential game, which does not hold for our model. As explained above, our model diverges from these studies in other ways. In particular, in our model, clients are not allowed to "skip" over players, and must choose the closest player within their tolerance interval, whereas the previous studies assume clients are indifferent between players within their range of tolerance. Also, our model introduces the notion of asymmetric ranges of tolerance, which has not been considered before.

2   Model

Consider a setting in which clients are uniformly distributed along the interval $[0, 1]$. A client is represented as a point $v \in [0, 1]$, denoting her preference along the interval $[0, 1]$. Clients are non-strategic. The strategic interaction in our model occurs between a finite set $N = \{1, \ldots, n\}$ of players. The set of strategies for a player is to choose a point in the interval $[0, 1]$. Let $s_i \in [0, 1]$ denote the strategy of player i, $1 \leq i \leq n$. A strategy profile is given by a vector of player locations $\mathbf{s} = (s_1, \ldots, s_n)$. Let $\mathbf{s}_{-i}$ denote the profile of actions of all the players different from i. Slightly abusing notation, we denote by $(s_i', \mathbf{s}_{-i})$ the profile obtained from a profile $\mathbf{s}$ by replacing its ith coordinate s_i with s_i'. We assume without loss of generality that $0 \leq s_1 \leq \cdots \leq s_n \leq 1$. For the sake of notational convenience, we denote $s_0 = 0$ and $s_{n+1} = 1$.

Each client v has left and right ranges of tolerance denoted B_v^R and B_v^L respectively. The *tolerance interval* of client v is defined as $I_v = [v - B_v^L, v + B_v^R]$. The client v supports the closest player within its tolerance interval. If there exists more than one closest player, then v chooses one of the closest players uniformly at random. Formally, $X(\mathbf{s}) = \{s_i \mid 1 \leq i \leq n\}$ is the set of locations occupied by a player under $\mathbf{s}$. For every client v the set of occupied locations inside v's tolerance interval is denoted $T_v(\mathbf{s}) = X(\mathbf{s}) \cap I_v$. Let $A_v(\mathbf{s}) = \arg\min_{x \in T_v(\mathbf{s})} |x - v|$ be the location v is attracted to. This set contains at most two locations, one to each side of v, but it is convenient to break ties by selecting the location on the left[2], i.e., if $A_v(\mathbf{s}) = \{s_i, s_j\}$ such that $s_i < s_j$, we modify $A_v(\mathbf{s})$ to be $\{s_i\}$. For every player i and location x, the attraction of v to location $x \in X(\mathbf{s})$ is given by

$$\omega_{v,x}(\mathbf{s}) = \Pr\left[v \text{ is attracted to a player in location } x\right] = \Pr\left[\{x\} = A_v(\mathbf{s})\right] .$$

We consider B_v^R, B_v^L to be non-negative random variables drawn from the same distribution $\mathcal{D}$ independently for all clients v. We consider two variants of

---

[2] There are at most $n - 2$ points which are at equal distances from the nearest player on the right and on the left, and given that there is a continuum of clients in total, modifying $A_v(\mathbf{s})$ in those points does not affect player utilities.

the game: *symmetric* and *asymmetric*. In the symmetric variant, $B_v^R = B_v^L$, for every client v. In the asymmetric variant, B_v^R and B_v^L are independent identically distributed random variables, for every client v. Throughout the paper, we denote by $f : [0,1] \rightarrow [0,1]$ the probability density function of $\mathcal{D}$, and the cumulative distribution function is denoted as $F : [0,1] \rightarrow [0,1]$. That is, $F(t) = \Pr[B_v^R \leq t] = \Pr[B_t^R \leq t]$. Additionally, for the analysis it is convenient to define $\bar{F}(t) = 1 - F(t) = \Pr[B_t^R \geq t]$.

Given a strategy profile $\mathbf{s} = (s_1, \ldots, s_n)$, two players $i, j \in N$ are said to be *colocated* if $s_i = s_j$. For $i \in N$, the set of i's colocated players is defined as $\Gamma_i = \{j \in N \mid s_j = s_i\}$, and the size of this set is $\gamma_i = |\Gamma_i|$. A player that is not colocated with other players is called *isolated*. Two players are called *neighbors* if no player is located strictly between them. A *left (resp., right) peripheral player* is a player that has no players to its left (resp., right). The players divide the line into *regions* of two types: *internal regions*, which are regions between two neighbors, and two *hinterlands*, which include the region between 0 and the left peripheral player, and the region between the right peripheral player and 1. (See Fig. 1, where the two hinterlands are marked by a.)

For $i \in N$, player i's *left* and *right neighbors* are $L(s_i) = \max_{x \in X(\mathbf{s})}\{x < s_i\}$ and $R(s_j) = \min_{x \in X(\mathbf{s})}\{x > s_i\}$, respectively. Namely, these are the closest occupied player locations on either side of player i. We define $L(s_i) = 0$ when i does not have a left neighbor and $R(s_i) = 1$ when i does not have a right neighbor. Define the *total utility at the location* of player i as

$$U_i(\mathbf{s}) = U_i^L(\mathbf{s}) + U_i^R(\mathbf{s}) = \int_{L(s_i)}^{R(s_i)} \omega_{v,s_i}(\mathbf{s})dv \ ,$$

where $U_i^L(\mathbf{s})$ and $U_i^R(\mathbf{s})$ are the *left* and *right* total utilities at player i's location,

$$U_i^L(\mathbf{s}) = \int_{L(s_i)}^{s_i} \omega_{v,s_i}(\mathbf{s})dv \qquad \text{and} \qquad U_i^R(\mathbf{s}) = \int_{s_i}^{R(s_i)} \omega_{v,s_i}(\mathbf{s})dv \ .$$

The total utility of player i represents the total amount of clients attracted to location s_i (either to player i itself or to some colocated player $j \in \Gamma_i$). The *utility*, *left utility* and *right utility* of player i are defined to be

$$u_i(\mathbf{s}) = u_i^L(\mathbf{s}) + u_i^R(\mathbf{s}) = \frac{U_i(\mathbf{s})}{\gamma_i} \ , \qquad u_i^L(\mathbf{s}) = \frac{U_i^L(\mathbf{s})}{\gamma_i} \qquad \text{and} \qquad u_i^R(\mathbf{s}) = \frac{U_i^R(\mathbf{s})}{\gamma_i} \ .$$

To summarize, our game is fully defined by the number of players n, the probability density function of client tolerances f, and whether the setting symmetric or asymmetric. Let $G^S = G^S(n, f)$ be the game under the symmetric setting, and let $G^A = G^A(n, f)$ be the game under the asymmetric setting. When making a claim that applies to both the symmetric and asymmetric setting we will use the notation $G = G(n, f)$.

Given a profile $\mathbf{s}$, $s_i' \in [0,1]$ is an *improving move* for player i if $u_i(s_i', \mathbf{s}_{-i}) > u_i(\mathbf{s})$. $s_i^* \in [0,1]$ is a *best response* for player i if $u_i(s_i^*, \mathbf{s}_{-i}) \geq u_i(s_i', \mathbf{s}_{-i})$ for every $s_i' \in [0,1]$. A profile $\mathbf{s}^*$ is a *Nash equilibrium* if no player has an improving move, i.e., for every $i \in N$ and every $s_i \in [0,1]$, $u_i(\mathbf{s}^*) \geq u_i(s_i, \mathbf{s}_{-i}^*)$.

3   Canonical Profiles as the only Possible Equilibria

In this section we characterize a specific class of strategy profiles, referred to as *canonical profiles*, and show that these profiles are the only ones that may yield Nash equilibria in our game (namely, if there is an equilibrium then it must be canonical). We then show that each game $G(n, f)$ admits a unique canonical profile, $s^{n,f}$, if one exists. This significantly simplifies later analysis and explains why the game presents similar behavior for every number of players $n \geq 3$. We conclude this section with a set of necessary and sufficient conditions for a given canonical profile to be a Nash equilibrium. Consequently, for every subclass of the game considered in the following sections, it suffices to consider these conditions to either find the entire set of Nash equilibria of a game $G(n, f)$ provided one exists, or prove that the game admits no Nash equilibrium.

Calculating Utilities. Note that the utilities in our game are locally defined, i.e., the utility of player i is independent of the location of players outside the interval $[L(s_i), R(s_i)]$. This is due to fact that a player i may only attract clients from within i's adjacent regions. Moreover, the attraction ω_{v,s_i} of a client $v \in [L(s_i), R(s_i)]$ to the location of player i depends only on the distance $|v - s_i|$, the length of the region v is inside, and whether it is a hinterland or an internal region. It follows that the game $G(n, f)$ is uniquely determined by the following two functions:

$$\mathcal{H}(x) = \int_0^x \Pr\left[B_t^R \geq t\right] dt \tag{1}$$

$$\mathcal{M}(x) = \int_0^{\frac{x}{2}} \Pr\left[B_t^L \geq t\right] dt + \int_{\frac{x}{2}}^x \Pr\left[B_t^L \geq t \wedge B_t^R < x - t\right] dt \tag{2}$$

Intuitively, $\mathcal{H}(x)$ (respectively, $\mathcal{M}(x)$) denotes the expected amount of support an isolated player gains from a hinterland (resp., an internal region) of length x. Note that in the symmetric setting, we have that $B_v^L = B_v^R$ for every client $v \in [0, 1]$ and therefore, for every $t \in [x/2, x]$, $\Pr[B_t^L \geq t \wedge B_t^R < x - t] = 0$. However, in the asymmetric setting, B_v^L and B_v^R are independent random variables and thus $\Pr[B_t^L \geq t \wedge B_t^R < x - t] = \Pr[B_t^L \geq t] \cdot \Pr[B_t^R < x - t]$. Recalling that $F(t) = \Pr[B_t^R \leq t]$ the next observation follows.

Observation 1. *For a symmetric game $G^S(n, f)$, the functions $\mathcal{H}$ and $\mathcal{M}$ are*

$$\mathcal{H}(x) = \int_0^x (1 - F(t)) dt \,, \qquad \mathcal{M}(x) = \int_0^{\frac{x}{2}} (1 - F(t)) dt \,.$$

For an asymmetric game $G^S(n, f)$, the functions $\mathcal{H}$ and $\mathcal{M}$ are

$$\mathcal{H}(x) = \int_0^x (1 - F(t)) dt \,, \qquad \mathcal{M}(x) = \int_0^{\frac{x}{2}} (1 - F(t)) dt + \int_{\frac{x}{2}}^x (1 - F(t)) F(x - t) dt$$

As B_v^L and B_v^R are drawn from the same distribution for all $v \in [0,1]$, we get

Lemma 1. *For any game* $G = G(n, f)$, *profile* **s** *and* $i \in N$,

$$U_i^L(\mathbf{s}) = \begin{cases} \mathcal{H}(s_i), & i \text{ is left peripheral;} \\ \mathcal{M}(s_i - L(s_i)), & \text{otherwise.} \end{cases}$$

$$U_i^R(\mathbf{s}) = \begin{cases} \mathcal{H}(1 - s_i), & i \text{ is right peripheral;} \\ \mathcal{M}(R(s_i) - s_i), & \text{otherwise.} \end{cases}$$

As an illustrative example, consider the profile $\mathbf{s} = (0.2, 0.5, 0.6)$ in a three player game $G(3, f)$. Then $u_1(\mathbf{s}) = \mathcal{H}(0.2) + \mathcal{M}(0.3)$, $u_2(\mathbf{s}) = \mathcal{M}(0.3) + \mathcal{M}(0.1)$ and $u_3(\mathbf{s}) = \mathcal{M}(0.1) + \mathcal{H}(0.4)$.

It is possible to define any game $G(n, f)$ by simply determining $\mathcal{H}(x)$ and $\mathcal{M}(x)$. In fact, these functions may be used to define many other variants of the Hotelling model not considered within the scope of this paper. Throughout this section, we will not use the explicit formulas for $\mathcal{H}(x)$ and $\mathcal{M}(x)$ and our results do not depend on these formulas. Instead, we derive our results based solely on the assumption that for the game under consideration, $\mathcal{H}(x)$ and $\mathcal{M}(x)$ satisfy the following properties:

(HM1) $\mathcal{H}$ and $\mathcal{M}$ are twice differentiable, concave and monotonically increasing, i.e., for $x \in [0,1)$, $\mathcal{H}'(x) > 0$, $\mathcal{M}'(x) > 0$, $\mathcal{H}''(x) < 0$ and $\mathcal{M}''(x) < 0$.
(HM2) For $x \in [0,1]$, $\mathcal{H}(x) \geq \mathcal{M}(x)$.
(HM3) $\mathcal{H}(0) = \mathcal{M}(0) = 0$.

Therefore, our results in this section are general and apply to any game $G(n, f)$ where (HM1), (HM2) and (HM3) are satisfied.

Optimizing Utilities Locally. We next extablish the optimal (maximum-utility) location of each player i when fixing the locations of the other players and assuming i can only move between its neighbors, but not "jump" over a neighbor. Consider a peripheral player, and suppose its neighbor is at distance $0 \leq x \leq 1$ from the endpoint. For $0 \leq t \leq x$, denote by $\theta_x(t)$ the utility of a peripheral player when its hinterland is of length t, and by $\mu_x(t)$ the utility of an internal player i with $s_i - L(s_i) = t$ and $R(s_i) - L(s_i) = x$. By Lemma 1,

$$\theta_x(t) = \mathcal{H}(t) + \mathcal{M}(x - t) \quad \text{and} \quad \mu_x(t) = \mathcal{M}(t) + \mathcal{M}(x - t).$$

Remark. To keep θ and μ continuous in the interval $[0, t]$, we disregard the fact that for $x = t$ and $x = 0$ the player is colocated with one of its neighbors, and assume all its payoff comes from the same interval of length t. By Lemma 5, this assumption does not affect the analysis of the Nash equilibria of the game.

Hereafter, proofs are deferred to the full paper.

Lemma 2. *Let* G *be game satisfying (HM1), (HM2), (HM3). For* $x \in [0,1]$,

(a) θ_x *and* μ_x *are strictly concave functions of* t.
(b) $t = x/2$ *is the unique maximum of* μ_x *in* $[0, x]$.

(c) If $\mathcal{H}'(x) > \mathcal{M}'(0)$, then θ_x is strictly increasing in $[0, x]$.
(d) If $\mathcal{H}'(x) \leq \mathcal{M}'(0)$, then t^* is the unique maximum of θ_x in $[0, x]$, where t^* is the unique solution of the equation $\mathcal{H}'(t^*) = \mathcal{M}'(x - t^*)$.

Let $\rho(x)$ denote the unique maximum of θ_x in the interval $[0, x]$. By Lemma 2, the function $\rho : [0, 1] \to [0, 1]$ is well defined, and is given by

$$\rho(x) = \begin{cases} x, & \text{if } \mathcal{H}'(x) > \mathcal{M}'(0); \\ t^*, & \text{if } \mathcal{H}'(x) \leq \mathcal{M}'(0), \end{cases}$$

where t^* is the unique solution of $\mathcal{H}'(t^*) = \mathcal{M}'(x - t^*)$. We next show several properties of $\rho(x)$ that will be used in the proofs of our main results.

Lemma 3. Let $x < y$, for $x, y \in [0, 1]$. Then

(a) If $\mathcal{H}'(x) \leq \mathcal{M}'(0)$, then $\mathcal{H}'(\rho(x)) \leq \mathcal{M}'(0)$.
(b) $\rho(x) \leq \rho(y)$.
(c) $\theta_x(\rho(x)) \leq \theta_y(\rho(y))$.

Nash Equilibria. Let us now characterize the stable profiles that lead to a Nash equilibrium for a given game $G(n, f)$. The pair $\langle a, b \rangle$, $a, b \in [0, 1]$, is called a *canonical pair* if a and b satisfy the following equations:

$$\mathcal{H}'(a) = \mathcal{M}'(b) \tag{3}$$
$$2a + (n - 1)b = 1 \tag{4}$$

A canonical pair induces a profile $\mathbf{s}^{n,f}$ for the game $G(n, f)$, such that

$$s_i^{n,f} = a + (i - 1)b$$

for every $i \in N$ (see Fig. 1). We refer to this profile as a *canonical profile*.

Fig. 1. A canonical profile.

Lemma 4. A game G satisfying (HM1), (HM2), (HM3) has a canonical pair if and only if $\mathcal{H}'(1/2) \leq \mathcal{M}'(0)$. Moreover, if such a pair exists then it is unique.

Theorem 2. Let G be a game satisfying (HM1), (HM2) and (HM3), and let $n = 2$. The game G has a unique Nash equilibrium, which is given by

$$\mathbf{s}^* = \begin{cases} \mathbf{s}^{n,f}, & \text{if } \mathcal{H}'(1/2) \leq \mathcal{M}'(0); \\ \left(\frac{1}{2}, \frac{1}{2}\right), & \text{otherwise.} \end{cases}$$

For $n \geq 3$ players, we show that the only possible Nash equilibrium is the canonical profile. We make use of the following claim.

Lemma 5. *Let G be a game satisfying (HM1), (HM2) and (HM3), and let $n \geq 3$. If $\mathbf{s}$ is a Nash equilibrium then no two players are colocated in $\mathbf{s}$.*

Theorem 3. *Let G be a game satisfying (HM1), (HM2) and (HM3), and let $n \geq 3$. If the game G admits a Nash equilibrium, then it is unique and equal to the canonical profile $\mathbf{s}^{n,f}$.*

Lemma 6. *Let G be a game satisfying (HM1), (HM2) and (HM3), and let $n \geq 3$. Let $\mathbf{s}^{n,f}$ be the canonical profile of G, with a corresponding canonical pair $\langle a, b \rangle$. Then $\mathbf{s}^{n,f}$ is a Nash equilibrium if and only if*

$$\mathcal{H}(a) + \mathcal{M}(b) \geq 2\mathcal{M}\left(\frac{b}{2}\right),$$

$$\mathcal{H}(\rho(a)) + \mathcal{M}(a - \rho(a)) \leq 2\mathcal{M}(b) .$$

4   Symmetric Range Distributions

In this section we consider the symmetric game $G^S(n, f)$, where the range of each client v satisfies $B_v^L = B_v^R$. We first show that the game satisfies assumptions (HM1), (HM2) and (HM3), which allows us to use all the results of Sect. 3.

Lemma 7. *Let $G^S(n, f)$ be a game such that f is continuously differentiable and has full support (i.e., $f(x) > 0$ for all $x \in [0,1]$), then $G^S(n, f)$ satisfies assumptions (HM1), (HM2) and (HM3).*

Due to Lemma 7, we may apply Theorems 2 and 3 to the game $G^S(n, f)$ and we thus obtain the following two corollaries.

Corollary 1. *Let $n = 2$, and let f be continuously differentiable and have full support (i.e., $f(x) > 0$ for all $x \in [0,1]$). Then the game $G^S(2, f)$ has a unique Nash equilibrium, which is given by*

$$\mathbf{s}^* = \begin{cases} \mathbf{s}^{n,f}, & \text{if } \bar{F}(1/2) \leq 1/2; \\ \left(\frac{1}{2}, \frac{1}{2}\right), & \text{otherwise,} \end{cases}$$

where $\mathbf{s}^{n,f}$ is the canonical profile, with a corresponding canonical pair $\langle a, b \rangle$, where a and b are given implicitly by the equation $\bar{F}(a) = \bar{F}(b/2)/2$.

Corollary 2. *Let $n \geq 3$. For every game $G^S(n, f)$ where f is continuously differentiable and has full support (i.e., $f(x) > 0$ for all $x \in [0,1]$), if G^S admits a Nash equilibrium then it is unique (up to renaming the players) and equal to the canonical profile $\mathbf{s}^{n,f}$, with a corresponding canonical pair $\langle a, b \rangle$, where a and b are given implicitly by the equation $\bar{F}(a) = \bar{F}(b/2)/2$.*

Lemma 8. *Under the symmetric game $G^S(n, f)$, the function $\rho : [0, 1] \to [0, 1]$ satisfies that $\rho(x) > x/3$, for all $x \in [0, 1]$.*

Lemma 9. *The game $G^S(n, f)$ as in Lemma 7, for $n \geq 3$, admits a Nash equilibrium if and only if $\mathcal{H}(\rho(a)) + \mathcal{M}(a - \rho(a)) \leq 2\mathcal{M}(b)$, where $\rho(a)$ is defined implicitly by the equation $\bar{F}(\rho(a)) = \bar{F}((a - \rho(a))/2)/2$.*

We conclude the discussion of symmetric games with a number of example distributions and their equilibria states.

Uniform Distribution. This distribution, in which the range boundary parameter B_v^L ($= B_v^R$) is drawn uniformly at random from $[0, 1]$, was considered by Ben-Porat and Tennenholtz [2] in a setting where clients are allowed to skip over players. Here we show that, if "skipping" is not allowed, as in our model, there is no Nash equilibrium for $n \geq 3$. For $n = 2$, the only Nash equilibrium is $(1/2, 1/2)$, where both players are colocated at the center. The probability density function and corresponding cumulative density function are defined as

$$f(x) = \begin{cases} 1, & x \in [0, 1]; \\ 0, & \text{otherwise,} \end{cases} \qquad F(x) = \begin{cases} x, & x \in [0, 1]; \\ 1, & x \geq 1; \\ 0, & \text{otherwise.} \end{cases}$$

Proposition 1. *For the game $G^S(n, f)$, where f is the uniform distribution, there exists a Nash equilibrium if and only if $n = 2$, and it is equal to the strategy profile $(1/2, 1/2)$.*

Linear Distribution. Here we consider any distribution whose density is linear and whose mass is entirely contained in $[0, 1]$. Specifically, assume $\int_0^1 (rx + q)dx = 1$, or rather $q = 1 - r/2$. For $f(x)$ to be non-negative in $[0, 1]$ we also need $-2 \leq r \leq 2$. Then take

$$f(x) = \begin{cases} rx + q, & x \in [0, 1]; \\ 0, & \text{otherwise,} \end{cases} \qquad F(x) = \begin{cases} \frac{r}{2}x^2 + qx, & x \in [0, 1]; \\ 1, & x \geq 1; \\ 0, & \text{otherwise.} \end{cases}$$

To make the analysis cleaner let us pick the two extreme examples of the parameters (r, q), namely, $(-2, 2)$ and $(2, 0)$.

Proposition 2. *The game $G^S(n, f)$, where f is the linear distribution with coefficients either $(r_1, q_1) = (-2, 2)$ or $(r_2, q_2) = (2, 0)$, has a Nash equilibrium if and only if $n = 2$. For r_1, q_1, the only Nash equilibrium is $(1/2, 1/2)$. For r_2, q_2, the only (canonical) Nash equilibrium is given by the canonical pair*

$$a = \frac{2\sqrt{2} + 1}{2\sqrt{2} + 2} \qquad and \qquad b = \frac{\sqrt{2} - 1}{1 + 1/\sqrt{2}}.$$

Remark. Intuitively, in the uniform distribution the players are forced to converge towards the center. In comparison, in the linear distribution corresponding to (r_2, q_2) it is likelier for clients to have a large range, which means more clients inside the hinterland will be covered by the peripheral player, so it will be beneficial for it to move closer to its neighbor and have fewer clients contested by another player, despite having a greater average distance to potential clients.

Pareto Distribution. The distribution Pareto(α, ξ) for parameters $\alpha > 0$ and $\xi > 0$ has density function and cumulative distribution function

$$f(x) = \begin{cases} 0, & x < \xi \; ; \\ \frac{\alpha \xi^\alpha}{x^{\alpha+1}}, & x \geq \xi \; , \end{cases} \qquad F(x) = \begin{cases} 0, & x < \xi \; ; \\ 1 - (\xi/x)^\alpha, & x \geq \xi \; . \end{cases}$$

Proposition 3. *For the game $G^S(n, f)$, where f is the density of Pareto(α, ξ), the canonical pair is given by*

$$a = \frac{2^{1/\alpha - 1}}{n - 1 + 2^{1/\alpha}} \qquad and \qquad b = \frac{1}{n - 1 + 2^{1/\alpha}} \; , \tag{5}$$

and it is a Nash equilibrium if and only if $\alpha \geq z$, where z is the unique solution of the equation $2^{1/z}(2 + 2^{1/z})^z = 8$ such that $0 < z < 1$.

Exponential Distribution. The exponential distribution with parameter $\lambda > 0$ has density function and cumulative density function

$$f(x) = \begin{cases} 0, & x < 0 \; ; \\ \lambda e^{-\lambda x}, & x \geq 0 \; , \end{cases} \qquad F(x) = \begin{cases} 0, & x < 0 \; ; \\ 1 - e^{-\lambda x}, & x \geq 0 \; . \end{cases}$$

Proposition 4. *For the game $G^S(n, f)$, where f is the density of the exponential distribution with parameter $\lambda > 0$, the canonical pair is given by*

$$a = \frac{1}{n}\left(\frac{1}{2} + \frac{(n-1)\ln 2}{\lambda}\right) \qquad and \qquad b = \frac{1}{n}\left(1 - \frac{2\ln 2}{\lambda}\right)$$

and it is a Nash equilibrium if and only if $\lambda \geq \ln 4 - n \ln(4\tau_1^6)$, where $\tau_1 = \frac{\sqrt[6]{2} + \sqrt{64 + \sqrt[3]{2}}}{8 \cdot 2^{5/6}} \approx 0.65$.

5   Asymmetric Range Distributions

In this section we consider the asymmetric game $G^A(n, f)$, where the range boundaries of each client v, B_v^L and B_v^R, are drawn independently at random. As in the previous section, we begin by showing that the game satisfies assumptions (HM1), (HM2) and (HM3), allowing us to use the results of Sect. 3.

Lemma 10.   *Let $G^A(n, f)$ be a game such that f is continuously differentiable and has full support (i.e., $f(x) > 0$ for all $x \in [0, 1]$), then $G^A(n, f)$ satisfies assumptions (HM1), (HM2) and (HM3).*

Due to Lemma 10, we may apply Theorems 2 and 3 to the game $G^A(n, f)$ and we thus obtain the following two corollaries.

Corollary 3. *Let $n = 2$, and let f be continuously differentiable and have full support (i.e., $f(x) > 0$ for all $x \in [0,1]$). Then the game $G^A(2, f)$ has a unique Nash equilibrium, which is given by*

$$\mathbf{s}^* = \begin{cases} \mathbf{s}^{n,f}, & \text{if } \bar{F}(1/2) \geq 1/2; \\ (\frac{1}{2}, \frac{1}{2}), & \text{otherwise,} \end{cases}$$

where $\mathbf{s}^{n,f}$ is the canonical profile, with a corresponding canonical pair $\langle a, b \rangle$, where a and b are given implicitly by the equation

$$\bar{F}(a) = \frac{1}{2}\left(\bar{F}\left(\frac{b}{2}\right)\right)^2 + \int_{\frac{b}{2}}^{b} \bar{F}(t)f(b-t)dt$$

Corollary 4. *Let $n \geq 3$. For every game $G^A(n, f)$ where f has full support (i.e., $f(x) > 0$ for all $x \in [0,1]$), if G^A admits a Nash equilibrium it is unique (up to renaming the players) and equal to the canonical profile $\langle a, b \rangle$ where a and b are given implicitly by the equation*

$$\bar{F}(a) = \frac{1}{2}\left(\bar{F}\left(\frac{b}{2}\right)\right)^2 + \int_{\frac{b}{2}}^{b} \bar{F}(t)f(b-t)dt$$

Lemma 11. *Under the asymmetric game $G^A(n, f)$, the function $\rho : [0,1] \to [0,1]$ satisfies that $\rho(x) > x/3$, for all $x \in [0,1]$.*

Lemma 12. *The game $G^A(n, f)$ admits a Nash equilibrium if and only if $\mathcal{H}(\rho(a)) + \mathcal{M}(a - \rho(a)) \leq 2\mathcal{M}(b)$, where $\rho(x)$ is defined implicitly by the equation $\bar{F}(\rho(x)) = \frac{1}{2}\left(\bar{F}\left((a - \rho(x))/2\right)\right)^2 + \int_{\frac{a-\rho(x)}{2}}^{a-\rho(x)} \bar{F}(t)f(a - \rho(x) - t)dt$.*

Theorem 4. *If $G^S(n, f)$ admits a Nash equilibrium and*

$$\frac{\partial}{\partial x}\left(\int_{\frac{x}{2}}^{x} \bar{F}(t)F(b-t)dt\right) \geq 0,$$

then $G^A(n, f)$ admits a Nash equilibrium.

Again we conclude with a couple of example distributions and their equilibria.

Uniform Distribution. This is the same as the uniform distribution for symmetric games, except that *both* range boundary parameters B_v^L and B_v^L need to be drawn uniformly at random. We have the following.

Proposition 5. *For the game $G^A(n, f)$, where f is the uniform distribution, there exists a Nash equilibrium if and only if $n = 2$, and it is equal to the strategy profile $(1/2, 1/2)$.*

Exponential Distribution. Finally, we consider the game $G^A(n, f)$ where f is the density function of the exponential distribution with parameter $\lambda > 0$. That is, the range of each client v is asymmetric and exponentially distributed, i.e., $B_v^L, B_v^R \in \text{Exp}(\lambda)$. Slightly abusing notation, we refer to this game as $G^A(n, \lambda)$. We dedicate special attention to this distribution for three main reasons. First, the exponential distribution is commonly considered in geometric models, and has been shown to apply to many real life situations. Second, the game $G^A(n, \lambda)$ is mathematically equivalent to a *fault-prone Hotelling game*, studied in our related paper [4]. In this game, faults occur at random along the line, and clients cannot visit players separated from them by a random fault. Hence, our results on the exponential distribution can be applied directly to fully characterize the equilibria of another interesting variant of the Hotelling model. Finally, this example demonstrates that even though the condition of Theorem 4 does not always apply, and the condition given for the existence of Nash equilibria in Lemma 12 is somewhat hard to work with, it is nevertheless possible to fully analyze certain useful classes of client range distributions.

By Corollary 3, if $n = 2$ then the game always admits a Nash equilibrium, which is the canonical profile if it exists, and $(1/2, 1/2)$ otherwise. For $n \geq 3$, the following theorem characterizes a *threshold function* $\lambda_{\min}(n)$ such that the game $G^A(n, \lambda)$ admits a Nash equilibrium if and only if $\lambda \geq \lambda_{\min}(n)$. The analysis is deferred to the full paper.

Theorem 5. $G^A(n, \lambda)$ for $n \geq 3$ admits a Nash equilibrium if and only if $\lambda \geq \lambda_{\min}(n) = (n+1)\alpha_0 - 2\ln((1+\alpha_0)/2)$, where $\alpha_0 \in (0, 1)$ is the unique constant given implicitly as the solution to the equations $e^{-\alpha}(1+\alpha) = e^{-2\beta}(1+\beta)$ and $e^{-\alpha}(1+\alpha/2) = e^{-\beta}(3/4 + \beta/2)$. Moreover, $\alpha_0 \approx 0.58813$, implying that a Nash equilibrium exists if and only if $\lambda \geq \lambda_{\min}(n) \approx 0.58813n + 1.04931$.

Acknowledgments. The authors would like to thank Shahar Dobzinski and Yinon Nahum for many fertile discussions and helpful insights, and the anonymous reviewers for their useful comments. This research was supported in part by a US-Israel BSF Grant No. 2016732.

References

1. Ahlin, C., Ahlin, P.D.: Product differentiation under congestion: hotelling was right. Econ. Inq. **51**(3), 1750–1763 (2013)
2. Ben-Porat, O., Tennenholtz, M.: Shapley facility location games. In: Devanur, N.R., Lu, P. (eds.) WINE 2017. LNCS, vol. 10660, pp. 58–73. Springer, Cham (2017). https://doi.org/10.1007/978-3-319-71924-5_5
3. Brenner, S.: Location (Hotelling) Games and Applications. Wiley Encyclopedia of Operations Research and Management Science. Wiley, New York (2010)
4. Cohen, A., Peleg, D.: Hotelling games with multiple line faults. CoRR, abs/1907.06602 (2019). http://arxiv.org/abs/1907.06602
5. d'Aspremont, C., Gabszewicz, J.J., Thisse, J.-F.: On hotelling's "stability in competition". Econometrica: J. Econometric Soc. **47**, 1145–1150 (1979)
6. De Palma, A., Ginsburgh, V., Thisse, J.-F.: On existence of location equilibria in the 3-firm Hotelling problem. J. Ind. Econ. **36**, 245–252 (1987)

7. Downs, A.: An economic theory of political action in a democracy. J. Polit. Econ. **65**(2), 135–150 (1957)
8. Eaton, B.C., Lipsey, R.G.: The principle of minimum differentiation reconsidered: some new developments in the theory of spatial competition. Rev. Econ. Stud. **42**(1), 27–49 (1975)
9. Eiselt, H.A.: Equilibria in competitive location models. In: Eiselt, H., Marianov, V. (eds.) Foundations of Location Analysis. International Series in Operations Research Management Science, vol. 155, pp. 139–162. Springer, Heidelberg (2011). https://doi.org/10.1007/978-1-4419-7572-0_7
10. Eiselt, H.A., Laporte, G., Thisse, J.-F.: Competitive location models: a framework and bibliography. Transp. Sci. **27**(1), 44–54 (1993)
11. Feldman, M., Fiat, A., Obraztsova, S.: Variations on the hotelling-downs model. In: 13th AAAI Conference on AI (2016)
12. Feldotto, M., Lenzner, P., Molitor, L., Skopalik, A.: From hotelling to load balancing: approximation and the principle of minimum differentiation. In: Proceedings of 18th AAMAS, pp. 1949–1951 (2019)
13. Garimella, K., De Francisci Morales, G., Gionis, A., Mathioudakis, M.: Political discourse on social media: echo chambers, gatekeepers, and the price of bipartisanship. In: Proceedings of 2018 WWW, pp. 913–922 (2018)
14. Hotelling, H.: Stability in competition. Econ. J. **39**(153), 41–57 (1929)
15. Kohlberg, E.: Equilibrium store locations when consumers minimize travel time plus waiting time. Econ. Lett. **11**(3), 211–216 (1983)
16. Osborne, M.J., Pitchik, C.: Equilibrium in hotelling's model of spatial competition. Econometrica: J. Econometric Soc. **55**, 911–922 (1987)
17. Peters, H., Schröder, M., Vermeulen, D.: Hotelling's location model with negative network externalities. Int. J. Game Theory **47**(3), 811–837 (2018)
18. Peters, H.J.M., Schröder, M.J.W., Vermeulen, A.J.: Waiting in the queue on Hotelling's main street (2015)
19. Shen, W., Wang, Z.: Hotelling-Downs model with limited attraction. In: Proceedings of 16th AAMAS, pp. 660–668 (2017)

Mix and Match: Markov Chains and Mixing Times for Matching in Rideshare

Michael Curry[1], John P. Dickerson[1], Karthik Abinav Sankararaman[1,2],
Aravind Srinivasan[1], Yuhao Wan[1,3], and Pan Xu[1,4(✉)]

[1] University of Maryland, College Park, MD, USA
{curry,john,srin}@cs.umd.edu
[2] Facebook, Inc., Menlo Park, CA, USA
karthikabinavs@gmail.com
[3] University of Washington, Seattle, WA, USA
yuhao.diane.wan@gmail.com
[4] New Jersey Institute of Technology, Newark, NJ, USA
pxu@njit.edu

Abstract. Rideshare platforms such as Uber and Lyft dynamically dispatch drivers to match riders' requests. We model the dispatching process in rideshare as a Markov chain that takes into account the geographic mobility of both drivers and riders over time. Prior work explores dispatch policies in the limit of such Markov chains; we characterize when this limit assumption is valid, under a variety of natural dispatch policies. We give explicit bounds on convergence in general, and exact (including constants) convergence rates for special cases. Then, on simulated and real transit data, we show that our bounds characterize convergence rates—even when the necessary theoretical assumptions are relaxed. Additionally these policies compare well against a standard reinforcement learning algorithm which optimizes for profit without any convergence properties.

1 Introduction

Rideshare firms such as Uber, Lyft, and Didi Chuxing dynamically match riders to drivers via an online, digital platform. Riders request a driver through an online portal or mobile app; a driver is matched by the platform to a rider based on geographic proximity, driver preferences, pricing, and other factors. The rideshare driver then picks up the rider at her request location, transfers her to her destination, and reenters the platform to be matched again—albeit at a new geographic location. Part of the larger *sharing economy*, rideshare firms are increasingly competitive against traditional taxi services due to their ease of use, lower pricing, and immediacy of service [12].

Matching riders to rideshare drivers is nontrivial. While the core process is a form of the well-studied online matching problem [21], current models developed in the EconCS, AI, and Operations Research communities [5,10,25] do not

© Springer Nature Switzerland AG 2019
I. Caragiannis et al. (Eds.): WINE 2019, LNCS 11920, pp. 129–141, 2019.
https://doi.org/10.1007/978-3-030-35389-6_10

completely capture the mobile aspects of both the drivers and riders. Drivers *and* riders are agents who move about a constrained space (e.g., city streets), becoming (in)active periodically due to the matching process. When a platform receives a request, it must make a near-real-time dispatch decision amongst nearby drivers who are available at the current time. The platform's goal is to maximize an objective (e.g., revenue or throughput) by servicing requests in an online fashion, subject to various real-world constraints and challenges like setting prices, predicting supply and demand, fairness considerations, competing with other firms, and so on [3,7,15].

In this paper, we study the dynamics of the nascent rideshare market under different *dispatch strategies*. Recent work uses Markov chains to model complex ride-sharing dynamics in a *closed-world* system—that is, a system with a fixed total supply of cars [3,5,25]. These assume the Markov chains reach their stationary distributions quickly, and thus all prior work optimizes for dispatch strategies in the limit. As a complement, the present paper characterizes—theoretically and empirically—when that limit assumption is valid under a variety of natural strategies.

Our Contributions. The main contribution in this paper is *to show both theoretically and empirically the convergence rate of many natural policies to the stationary distribution.* First, we model the dispatching problem in rideshare platforms as a Markov chain. The number of states in this Markov chain is exponential in the natural size of the problem; thus, unless the chain is *rapidly mixing*, the time taken to reach the stationary distribution is prohibitively large. Next, we consider two large natural classes of strategies and study the evolution of the driver distribution theoretically. We show that the Markov chains are rapidly mixing and give explicit bounds on the convergence rates. Then, we consider a special case of uniform arrival rates and compute the convergence rates *exactly*, including the constants. Finally, we conduct experiments on both simulated as well as a real-world large-scale dataset to corroborate our findings. In particular, even when the assumptions needed by the theory do not necessarily hold, simulations show that the convergence behavior does not change drastically, and experiments on real data show that the theory gives direct insight on the convergence properties in practice. Additionally, compared against a standard RL algorithm, these policies perform similarly. Hence, our policies are simpler and efficient to run with theoretical convergence guarantees while performing almost as good as more complicated algorithms without such properties.

2   Preliminaries

In this section, we define the formal model used throughout the paper. We begin with a brief primer on Markov chains, and then show how Markov chains can be used to model rideshare markets.

Definition 1 (Markov chain). *A Markov chain $\mathcal{M}$ is defined by a state space Ω and a transition matrix P. $P(\mathbf{x}, \mathbf{y})$ represents the probability of reaching state*

$\mathbf{y} \in \Omega$, *in one step, from state* $\mathbf{x} \in \Omega$. $P(\mathbf{x}, \mathbf{y})$ *does not depend on states which the process was in prior to* $\mathbf{x}$ *(i.e., it obeys the* Markov *property).*

A central concept in Markov chain analysis is the notion of a *limiting* distribution and a *stationary* distribution. For two distributions μ and ν on the state space Ω, the *total variation distance* between μ and ν is defined as $||\mu - \nu||_{TV} = \frac{1}{2}\sum_{\mathbf{x}\in\Omega}|\mu(\mathbf{x}) - \nu(\mathbf{x})|$. A distribution π^* is said to be a *stationary distribution* if $\pi^* = \pi^*P$. A distribution π^* is said to be a *limiting distribution* if for every initial state $\mathbf{x}$, we have that $\lim_{t\to\infty}||P^t(\mathbf{x}, \cdot) - \pi^*||_{TV} = 0$, where $P^t(\mathbf{x}, \cdot)$ denotes that distribution of states after t steps, starting at $\mathbf{x}$.

To use Markov chains as an algorithmic tool, we need to understand the *rate* of convergence to the stationary distribution, commonly called its *mixing time*.

Mixing Time $\tau(\epsilon)$. Consider an irreducible and aperiodic Markov Chain $\mathcal{M}$ with stationary distribution π^*. For a given t, let $d(t) = \max_{\mathbf{x}\in\Omega}||P^t(\mathbf{x}, \cdot) - \pi^*||_{TV}$. The mixing time of $\mathcal{M}$ is defined as $\tau(\epsilon) = \min\{t : d(t') \leq \epsilon, \forall t' \geq t\}$. We say $\mathcal{M}$ is *rapidly mixing* if $\tau(\epsilon) = O\left(poly\left(\log\frac{|\Omega|}{\epsilon}\right)\right)$.

In this paper, we consider a class of strategies (as motivated by, *e.g.,* [10]) for the rideshare problem and cast it as a natural Markov chain. We then consider an objective function which depends on the limiting distribution of this chain and study convergence properties of that objective function, using the mixing properties of the Markov chain. We use Markov chains and relevant tools as the central concepts in this paper. Levin and Peres [16] details classical results in this space. The first *algorithmic* usage of Markov chain Monte Carlo (MCMC) methods can be traced back to the classical works of Hastings [13], Metropolis et al. [22], Metropolis and Ulam [23], commonly known as the Metropolis-Hastings algorithm. MCMC methods are a powerful tool in machine learning and we refer the reader to the survey [2].

A Markov Chain Model of Rideshare. We now define our Markov-chain-based model of rideshare. Consider a two-dimensional grid $\mathcal{U}$ consisting of n points (e.g., geographic locations). A *request type* $r = (u, u')$, represented by an *ordered* pair of points, is a set of requests that start and end at locations $u \in \mathcal{U}$ and $u' \in \mathcal{U}$, respectively. Let $\mathcal{R} = \{r = (u, u')|u \in \mathcal{U}, u' \in \mathcal{U}\}$ be the set of all request types. Note that we allow request types $r = (u, u)$—that is, a request that both starts and ends at the same point $u \in \mathcal{U}$. This is just for notational convenience.

Given a time horizon T, at each time (or round) $t \in [T] \doteq \{1, 2, \ldots, T\}$, a request of type r is sampled from $\mathcal{R}$ with probability p_r.[1] Our goal is to design a *matching* (or dispatching) scheme—assigning a driver (or car) to a request—that maximizes an overall objective after T rounds. In this paper, we assume that the sampling distribution $\{p_r\}$ in every round is *identical and independently distributed* (IID) but *unknown* to the algorithms. For notational simplicity, we also use r to denote a specific online request of type r when the context is clear.

---

[1] We have $\sum_{r\in\mathcal{R}} p_r \leq 1$. Thus, with probability $1 - \sum_{r\in\mathcal{R}} p_r$, there is no request in any given time.

Dispatching Policy. Suppose the system has m identical drivers. We characterize the state of the system by a vector $\mathbf{x} \in \mathbb{Z}_+^n$, where x_u denotes the number of drivers in location u. Then, we can construct a Markov chain with state space $\Omega = \{\mathbf{x} : x_u \in \{0, 1, \ldots, c\}, \sum_u x_u = m\}$. In this paper, we assume that $m \ll c \cdot n$ for some constant capacity c. A *dispatching policy* (or strategy) σ is a mapping from $\Omega \times \mathcal{R}$ to $\mathcal{U} \cup \{\emptyset\}$ such that at time t and a state $\mathbf{X}^{(t)}$, when a request r comes, σ assigns that request r to a potential driver at location $u_\sigma = \sigma(\mathbf{X}^{(t)}, r)$.[2] Here $u_\sigma = \emptyset$ denotes that the policy σ rejects request r. We say σ successfully addresses the request $r = (u, v)$ at t if $X_{u_\sigma}^{(t)} \geq 1$ and $X_v^{(t)} < c$. If σ successfully addresses a request r, it receives a profit w_r.

Neighborhood of u. For each point $u \in \mathcal{U}$, let $\mathcal{N}(u)$ be the set of neighbors of u with Manhattan distance[3] exactly 1 to u, i.e., $\mathcal{N}(u) = \{u' \in \mathcal{U} : |u - u'|_M = 1\}$, where $|u - u'|_M$ denotes the Manhattan distance between u and u'. We can assign each request with origin u only to a driver in the set $\{u\} \cup \mathcal{N}(u)$.

Objective Functions. For a given policy σ, let $W(\sigma, t)$ be the expected profit obtained by the policy σ at time t. Denote $\mathbf{I_X} := \mathbf{I}(X_{u_\sigma}^{(t)} \geq 1, X_v^{(t)} < c)$ which is the indicator for the event $X_{u_\sigma}^{(t)} \geq 1$ and $X_v^{(t)} < c$. Thus the expected performance of σ at time t and the expected average performance of σ over T rounds is,

$$W(\sigma, t) = \mathbb{E}\left[\sum_{r=(u,v) \in \mathcal{R}} p_r \cdot w_r \cdot \mathbf{I_X} \right], \tag{1}$$

$$\widehat{W}(\sigma, T) = \tfrac{1}{T} \sum_{t=1}^{T} W(\sigma, t). \tag{2}$$

respectively. The randomness in the state $\mathbf{X}^{(t)}$ depends on two sources: the random arrival of requests from distribution $\{p_r\}$ and any internal randomness used in the execution of a randomized policy σ.

In this paper, our objective is to study a class of dispatching strategies that are both *effective* and *stable*. Specifically, suppose $\mathbf{x}_0$ is the initial state, $\mathbf{p} = \{p_r | r \in \mathcal{R}\}$ is the arrival distribution of the request types in each round, and $\mathbf{w} = \{w_r | r \in \mathcal{R}\}$ is the profit vector for the request types. We then wish to answer the following questions.

1. **Effectiveness.** For a given instance $\mathcal{I} = (\mathbf{x}_0, \mathbf{p}, \mathbf{w}, T)$, which non-adaptive strategy σ maximizes $W(\sigma, t)$ and $\widehat{W}(\sigma, T)$?
2. **Stability.** For a given non-adaptive strategy σ, do the limits $\lim_{t \to \infty} W(\sigma, t)$ and $\lim_{T \to \infty} \widehat{W}(\sigma, T)$ exist? If so, how fast do they converge to the respective limiting values?

3   Assumptions and Related Work

Rideshare is a recent and popular innovation; thus, the body of literature surrounding this paradigm is young and quickly growing. With that in mind, we

---

[2] The choice of u_σ can be random since σ can be a randomized policy.

[3] It is not critical for our purposes, but the experiments use New York city and road-distance is measured in Manhattan distance.

now explicitly motivate and list the assumptions we make in our paper, and then place our model in the greater body of related work.

Model Assumptions. First, we assume that the number of drivers in the system remains constant in the T rounds with no new driver either joining or leaving the system. This assumption is justified because (1) T rounds in the online phase is typically restricted to a few hours and (2) almost all trips are local (as described later in our experimental section on real data). Second, at time t when a request $r = (u, u')$ comes and is assigned to a driver at location v, we assume that (1) the system obtains a profit $w_r > 0$, which is proportional to the distance between u and u'; (2) at time $t + 1$, the number of drivers at v reduces by 1 and the number at u' increases by 1 (*i.e.*, the request is completed instantaneously). From the real dataset, we observe that most trips in the Manhattan area are local and are completed within 15 mins (*i.e.*, a short time period). Hence things do not change drastically by making this simplifying assumption. Third, we assume that all locations have the same capacity $c \in \mathbb{Z}_+$, an upper bound on the total number of drivers that can be present in each location at any time. Here c captures the maximum number of drivers allowed at any single location. Fourth, we make the following global *hot-spot assumption* about the requests. There exists a location $u^* \in \mathcal{U}$ such that $p_{(u^*,u)} > 0$ and $p_{(u,u^*)} > 0$ for all $u \in \mathcal{U}, u \neq u^*$. We call this location u^* the "hot-spot". This assumption naturally holds in many real scenarios, since most big cities have busy central locations. Finally, we assume IID arrivals of online requests. This is necessary for convergence—even for very simple dispatching policies. Consider the following example with two locations u and v in the system and a single driver. Define request types $r_a = (u, v)$ and $r_b = (v, u)$. Suppose the two online requests r_a and r_b arrive alternatively during odd and even rounds, and our dispatching policy is the simple greedy one: match a request r if there is one driver at the starting location of r, otherwise, reject it. Then the Markov chain will admit no stationary distribution, since it has a period of 2.

It is worth noting that the first, second and fifth assumptions are used in related work [3,5]. The third assumption is a generalization of prior works which all considered $c = m$.

Related Work. Research in rideshare platforms and similar allocation problems is an active area of research within multiple fields, including computer science, operations research and transportation engineering. State-independent policies were studied previously using theory from control and queuing systems [3,6,25]. Apart from using Markov-chain methods, many allocation and scheduling problems have been studied in the rideshare context using methods from combinatorial optimization and machine learning (*e.g.*, [8,10,14]). A large-scale mathematical and empirical study on the number of cars and the optimality of waiting times was recently analyzed by Alonso-Mora et al. [1]. In our work, we do not consider the waiting times; indeed, we assume that the match and the trips happen instantaneously. The role of pricing in the dynamics of drivers in rideshare platforms is also an active area of research in computational economics and AI/ML (*e.g.*, [4,20,27]). Although rideshare platforms face challenges that are unique and different from *bike-sharing* ecosystems, there are some similarities between the two. Both of these deal with a matching market where the agents are constantly moving around and hence it is important to characterize the *flow* patterns of these agents. A number of works study the prediction aspects as well as the dynamics of flow patterns in both bike-sharing (*e.g.,* [11,24]) as well as in ridesharing (*e.g.,* [15,26,30–32]) platforms.

Our problem is a form of *online matching in dynamic environments*, which is an active area of research within the AI/ML community. In particular, [9,19, 28,29] have studied algorithms for matching in various dynamic markets such as kidney exchange, spatial crowdsourcing, labor markets, and so on. Online matching in *static* environments has been extensively studied in the literature; see Mehta et al. [21] for a detailed survey. We use a reinforcement learning algorithm as a baseline in our experiments. Apart from a recent work by Lin et al. [18], which explores the fleet management problem in ride-share, this tool has not been explored much in this domain. However, reinforcement learning (RL) has found success in other applications and we refer the reader to a recent survey [17].

Comparison with Related Concurrent Work. In a recent work, Banerjee et al. [5] proposed an approximation framework for pricing in rideshare platforms. Our model shares many characteristics with theirs (*i.e.,* the first, second and fifth assumptions). The main difference is the focus of the paper. In particular, they are interested in finding the optimal (online) dispatching policy that has a *good* approximation ratio with respect to expected revenue at the stationary distribution. Thus they consider the *known IID* arrival assumption for online requests while we consider the stronger *unknown* IID arrival assumption. Moreover they assume that the number of cars tends to infinity, and seek approximation ratios in this limit. The main focus of this paper is instead to characterize the *rate* of convergence to the stationary distribution. We seek to understand when using the expected reward in the stationary distribution is a good measure, especially if the rate of convergence is slow and/or non-existent.

4   Dispatching Polices

In this section, we present our dispatching policies for matching riders to rideshare drivers. Specifically, we present two policies namely Samp(α) and Rand-Perm(ϕ). The main ideas of these are as follows.

When a request $r = (u, u')$ arrives, Samp(α) checks the availability of drivers in locations u and each of its neighbors in $\mathcal{N}(u)$ with respective probabilities α and $\frac{1-\alpha}{4}$, where $0 < \alpha < 1$ is a parameter. (Technically, nodes u on the boundary of the grid have less than 4 neighbors; we just assume that we do nothing if the realization is an invalid neighbor.)

When a request $r = (u, u')$ arrives, Rand-Perm(ϕ) will first check the availability of drivers at u and if there aren't any, then checks the neighbors in $\mathcal{N}(u)$ following a given order ϕ. Below, we present the theoretical results on their convergence rates.

Theorem 1 (Main Convergence Theorem). *For any policy* $\mathrm{Samp}(\alpha)$ *with* $\alpha > 0$ *and* $\mathrm{Rand\text{-}Perm}(\phi)$ *starting with any given initial state, the objective functions defined in* (1) *and* (2) *both converge to the same value with rates* $\Theta(\beta^t)$ *and* $\Theta(T^{-1})$, *respectively, for some* $\beta \in (0,1)$ *independent of* T *(possibly dependent on the other input parameters such as* m *and* n*).*

Theorem 1 refers to the absolute error bound of the objectives in (1) and (2) from its limit value. In particular, Theorem 1 states that as the number of rounds increases, the expected revenue in every timestep converges to a stable value *exponentially* quickly.

Markov Chains $\mathscr{M}(\mathrm{Samp}(\alpha))$ **and** $\mathscr{M}(\mathrm{Rand\text{-}Perm}(\phi))$. We make the simplifying assumption that for every $u \in \mathcal{U}$, the number of neighbors $|\mathcal{N}(u)| = 4$. Recall that $\Omega = \{\mathbf{x} : x_u \in \{0, 1, \dots, c\}, \sum_u x_u = m\}$. Define a Markov chain $\mathscr{M}(\mathrm{Samp}(\alpha))$ for $\mathrm{Samp}(\alpha)$ over Ω as follows. For any *ordered* pair $(\mathbf{x}, \mathbf{y})$ where $\mathbf{x}, \mathbf{y} \in \Omega$, we say $(\mathbf{x}, \mathbf{y})$ is a (u, u')-neighbor if $y_u = x_u - 1$, $y_{u'} = x_{u'} + 1$, and $x_v = y_v$ for every $v \notin \{u, u'\}$. The policy $\mathrm{Samp}(\alpha)$ induces the following transition probability between all possible (u, u')-neighbors.

$$q(u, u') \doteq \alpha p_{(u,u')} + \tfrac{1-\alpha}{4} \sum_{v \in \mathcal{N}(u)} p_{(v,u')}.$$

Thus the transition matrix for the Markov chain $\mathscr{M}(\mathrm{Samp}(\alpha))$ can be defined as follows.

$$P_\alpha(\mathbf{x}, \mathbf{y}) = q(u, u') \quad \text{iff } (\mathbf{x}, \mathbf{y}) \text{ is a } (u, u') \text{ neighbor} \tag{3}$$

Similarly, we can define a Markov chain $\mathscr{M}(\mathrm{Rand\text{-}Perm}(\phi))$ over Ω for $\mathrm{Rand\text{-}Perm}(\phi)$ as follows. For a given random permutation ϕ and $v \in \mathcal{N}(u)$, let $\phi(v)$ be the random order assigned by ϕ. Assume that $\mathrm{Rand\text{-}Perm}(\phi)$ checks the neighbors $\mathcal{N}(u)$ in the order $(\phi^{-1}(1), \phi^{-1}(2), \phi^{-1}(3), \phi^{-1}(4))$. For a given state $\mathbf{x}$, location u and random order ϕ, the respective *supportive neighbor* of u is defined as $\mathcal{N}_{\mathbf{x},\phi}(u) = \{v \in \mathcal{N}(u) : x_v = 0, x_{v'} = 0, \forall v' \in \mathcal{N}(v), \phi(v') < \phi(u)\}$. In other words, $\mathcal{N}_{\mathbf{x},\phi}(u)$ includes those neighbors v of u such that when we are at state $\mathbf{x}$ while a request r with origin v arrives, $\mathrm{Rand\text{-}Perm}(\phi)$ will surely match r to a driver at u if present. The resultant transition matrix for the Markov chain $\mathscr{M}(\mathrm{Rand\text{-}Perm}(\phi))$ is non-zero iff $(\mathbf{x}, \mathbf{y})$ is a (u, u') neighbor. The non-zero value is as follows.

$$P_\phi(\mathbf{x}, \mathbf{y}) = p_{(u,u')} + \sum_{r=(v,u'):v \in \mathcal{N}_{\mathbf{x},\phi}(u)} p_r. \tag{4}$$

We use the following lemma about $\mathscr{M}(\mathrm{Samp}(\alpha))$ and $\mathscr{M}(\mathrm{Rand\text{-}Perm}(\phi))$. The proof is deferred to the full version.

Lemma 1. *Under the hot-spot assumption, Markov chains* $\mathscr{M}(\mathrm{Samp}(\alpha))$ *and* $\mathscr{M}(\mathrm{Rand\text{-}Perm}(\phi))$ *defined in* (3) *and* (4) *are both irreducible and aperiodic for any given* $\alpha > 0$ *and permutation function* ϕ. *Additionally, both* $\mathscr{M}(\mathrm{Samp}(\alpha))$ *and* $\mathscr{M}(\mathrm{Rand\text{-}Perm}(\phi))$ *admit a unique limiting distribution* π^*, *which coincides with the unique stationary distribution.*

4.1 Proof of Theorem 1

We prove this theorem by first showing the convergence rate for the objective (1) for both the policies. Finally we show how this can be adapted to give the convergence rates for the objective (2).

Convergence Rate of $\mathrm{Samp}(\alpha)$ **for Objective** (1). We first show the convergence rates for $\mathscr{M}(\mathrm{Samp}(\alpha))$. From Lemma 1, we have that $\mathscr{M}(\mathrm{Samp}(\alpha))$ is irreducible and aperiodic when $\alpha > 0$ and thus, it admits a unique limiting distribution (say π^*), regardless of the initial state. Suppose $\mathbf{X}^{(t)}$ is the random state after t steps (let the starting state be $\mathbf{x}_0$), which follows the distribution $P^t(\mathbf{x}^{(0)}, .)$. Let $\mathbf{X}^{(\infty)}$ be the random state when $T \to \infty$, which follows the distribution π^*. For each $u, v \in \mathcal{U}$, define $\gamma_{u,v}$ as the probability that there is at least one driver at location u and there are less than c drivers at v in π^*. Thus by definition we have $\gamma_{u,v} = \Pr[X_u^{(\infty)} \geq 1, X_v^{(\infty)} < c] = \sum_{\mathbf{x} \in \Omega : x_u \geq 1, x_v < c} \pi^*(\mathbf{x})$. For each u, v and t, define $\gamma_{u,v}^{(t)} := \Pr[X_u^{(t)} \geq 1, X_v^{(t)} < c]$. We prove the following Lemma 2 which is used in the proof of the main theorem.

Lemma 2. *There exists a scalar $C > 0$, independent of t and $\beta \in (0, 1)$ such that $|\gamma_{u,v}^{(t)} - \gamma_{u,v}| \leq 2C\beta^t$ for any $u, v \in \mathcal{U}$ and initial state $\mathbf{x}_0$.*

Proof. Let $P^t(\mathbf{x}_0, \mathbf{y}) = \Pr[\mathbf{X}^{(t)} = \mathbf{y}]$ be the probability of reaching state $\mathbf{y}$ after t steps with initial state $\mathbf{x}_0$. Thus we have,

$$|\gamma_{u,v}^{(t)} - \gamma_{u,v}| = \left| \sum_{\mathbf{y}:y_u \geq 1, y_v < c} \Pr[\mathbf{X}^{(t)} = \mathbf{y}] - \gamma_{u,v} \right| \tag{5}$$

$$= \left| \sum_{\mathbf{y}:y_u \geq 1, y_v < c} P^t(\mathbf{x}_0, \mathbf{y}) - \sum_{\mathbf{z} \in \Omega : z_u \geq 1, z_v < c} \pi^*(\mathbf{z}) \right| \tag{6}$$

$$\leq \sum_{\mathbf{y}:y_u \geq 1, y_v < c} \left| P^t(\mathbf{x}_0, \mathbf{y}) - \pi^*(\mathbf{y}) \right| \tag{7}$$

$$\leq 2|P^t(\mathbf{x}_0, \cdot) - \pi^*|_{TV} \leq 2C\beta^t. \tag{8}$$

In Eq. (8), the first inequality is from the definition of total variation between two distributions while the second inequality is from the convergence theorem 4.9 in [16].   □

Convergence Rate of $\mathscr{M}(\mathrm{Rand\text{-}Perm}(\phi))$ **for Objective** (1). Recall that we proved in Lemma 1 that $\mathscr{M}(\mathrm{Rand\text{-}Perm}(\phi))$ admits a unique limiting distribution. For notational convenience, we overload π^* and P to denote the limiting distribution and transition matrix of $\mathscr{M}(\mathrm{Rand\text{-}Perm}(\phi))$. Set $\overline{\mathcal{N}}(u) = \{u\} \cup \mathcal{N}(u)$. Let $\mathbf{Y}^{(t)}$ be the random state in $\mathscr{M}(\mathrm{Rand\text{-}Perm}(\phi))$ after t steps starting with $\mathbf{y}_0$. For a given u and v let $\eta_{u,v}$ and $\eta_{u,v}^{(t)}$ be the respective probabilities, in the limiting distribution π^* and $\mathbf{Y}^{(t)}$, that there is at least one driver in $\overline{\mathcal{N}}(u)$ and less than c drivers at v. Therefore by definition we have that,

$$\eta_{u,v} = \Pr\left[\bigvee_{v \in \overline{\mathcal{N}}(u)} \left(Y_v^{(\infty)} \geq 1\right), \ Y_v^{(\infty)} < c \right] = \sum_{\mathbf{x}: \sum_{v \in \overline{\mathcal{N}}(u)} x_v \geq 1, x_v < c} \pi^*(\mathbf{x}),$$

$$\eta_{u,v}^{(t)} = \Pr\left[\bigvee_{v \in \overline{\mathcal{N}}(u)} \left(Y_v^{(t)} \geq 1\right), \ Y_v^{(t)} < c \right] = \sum_{\mathbf{x}: \sum_{v \in \overline{\mathcal{N}}(u)} x_v \geq 1, x_v < c} P^t(\mathbf{y}_0, \mathbf{x}).$$

Similar to Lemma 2, we have the following lemma for $\mathscr{M}(\mathrm{Rand\text{-}Perm}(\phi))$.

Lemma 3. *There exists a scalar $C > 0$ independent of t and $\beta \in (0,1)$ such that $|\eta_{u,v}^{(t)} - \eta_{u,v}| \leq 2C\beta^t$ for any $u, v \in \mathcal{U}$ and initial state $\mathbf{y}_0$.*

The proof of Lemma 3 is essentially the same as that of Lemma 2 since it does not use the properties of $\mathrm{Samp}(\alpha)$. Now we have all ingredients to prove main Theorem 1.

Proof. We focus on applying Lemma 2 to prove the results for $\mathcal{M}(\mathrm{Samp}(\alpha))$ in Theorem 1. A similar analysis applies to the case $\mathcal{M}(\mathrm{Rand\text{-}Perm}(\phi))$ by using Lemma 3.

Consider the case $\sigma = \mathrm{Samp}(\alpha)$ and a given $r = (u, u')$. Policy $\mathrm{Samp}(\alpha)$ implies that $u_\sigma = \sigma(\mathbf{X}^{(t)}, r)$ will be equal to u with probability α and any neighbor in $\mathcal{N}(u)$ with probability $\frac{1-\alpha}{4}$. Thus, we claim that

$$\lim_{t \to \infty} \mathbb{E}\left[\mathbf{I}(X_{u_\sigma}^{(t)} \geq 1, X_v^{(t)} < c)\right]$$

$$= \alpha \Pr[X_u^{(\infty)} \geq 1, X_v^{(\infty)} < c] + \tfrac{1-\alpha}{4} \textstyle\sum_{k \in \mathcal{N}(u)} \Pr[X_k^{(\infty)} \geq 1, X_v^{(\infty)} < c]$$

$$= \alpha \gamma_{u,v} + \tfrac{1-\alpha}{4} \textstyle\sum_{k \in \mathcal{N}(u)} \gamma_{k,v}$$

Let $W(\alpha) = \lim_{t \to \infty} W(\mathrm{Samp}(\alpha), t)$. Thus we claim that $W(\alpha)$ is

$$\lim_{t \to \infty} \mathbb{E}\left[\textstyle\sum_{r=(u,v) \in \mathcal{R}} p_r \cdot w_r \cdot \mathbf{I}(X_{u_\sigma}^{(t)} \geq 1, X_v^{(t)} < c)\right] \tag{9}$$

$$= \textstyle\sum_{r=(u,v) \in \mathcal{R}} p_r \cdot w_r \cdot \left(\alpha \gamma_{u,v} + \tfrac{1-\alpha}{4} \textstyle\sum_{k \in \mathcal{N}(u)} \gamma_{k,v}\right). \tag{10}$$

Now we bound the convergence rate of $W(\mathrm{Samp}(\alpha), t)$.

Let $\Delta(t) \doteq |W(\mathrm{Samp}(\alpha), t) - W(\alpha)|$ (we omit the subscript of α in $\Delta(t)$ here) and $w \doteq \max_{r \in \mathcal{R}} w_r$. We have

$$\Delta(t) = \left|\textstyle\sum_{r=(u,v) \in \mathcal{R}} p_r \cdot w_r \cdot \left(\alpha \Pr[X_u^{(t)} \geq 1, X_v^{(t)} < c]\right.\right. \tag{11}$$

$$+ \tfrac{1-\alpha}{4} \textstyle\sum_{k \in \mathcal{N}(u)} \Pr[X_k^{(t)} \geq 1, X_v^{(t)} < c]\Big) \tag{12}$$

$$- \textstyle\sum_{r=(u,v) \in \mathcal{R}} p_r \cdot w_r \cdot \left(\alpha \gamma_{u,v} + \tfrac{1-\alpha}{4} \textstyle\sum_{k \in \mathcal{N}(u)} \gamma_{k,v}\right)\Big| \tag{13}$$

$$\leq \textstyle\sum_{r=(u,v) \in \mathcal{R}} p_r \cdot w_r \cdot \left(\alpha |\gamma_{u,v}^{(t)} - \gamma_{u,v}| + \tfrac{1-\alpha}{4} \textstyle\sum_{k \in \mathcal{N}(u)} |\gamma_{k,v}^{(t)} - \gamma_{k,v}|\right) \tag{14}$$

$$\leq \textstyle\sum_{r=(u,v) \in \mathcal{R}} p_r \cdot w_r \cdot (2C\beta^t) \tag{15}$$

$$\leq 2wC\beta^t. \tag{16}$$

Inequality (15) is a direct application of Lemma 2 and the fact that $|\mathcal{N}(u)| \leq 4$ for each u; Inequality (16) is due to the fact that $\sum_{r \in \mathcal{R}} p_r \leq 1$.

Recall that $\widehat{W}(\alpha) = \lim_{T \to \infty} \widehat{W}(\mathrm{Samp}(\alpha), T)$. We can verify that $\widehat{W}(\alpha) = W(\alpha)$. Now we bound the convergence rate of $\widehat{W}(\mathrm{Samp}(\alpha), T)$. Let $\widehat{\Delta}(T) \doteq |\widehat{W}(\mathrm{Samp}(\alpha), T) - \widehat{W}(\alpha)|$. Then we have the following.

$$\widehat{\Delta}(T) \leq \tfrac{1}{T} \textstyle\sum_{t=1}^{T} \Delta(t) = \tfrac{1}{T} \textstyle\sum_{t=1}^{T} 2wC\beta^t \leq \tfrac{2wC}{T} \tfrac{\beta}{1-\beta}. \tag{17}$$

$\square$

A Special Case: Uniform Arrivals of Online Requests. We now focus on the policy, Samp(α), and consider a special case when the requests arrive as a uniform sample in each round (*i.e.*, $p_r = p$ for all $r \in \mathcal{R}$). Then we can compute explicit values of C and β. Note that in this case, the transition matrix for $\mathcal{M}(\text{Samp}(\alpha))$ is $P_\alpha(\mathbf{x}, \mathbf{y}) = \alpha p_{(u,u')} + \frac{1-\alpha}{4} \sum_{v \in \mathcal{N}(u)} p_{(v,u')} = p$.

Consider a given instance of the rideshare setting $\mathcal{I} = (\mathbf{x}_0, \mathbf{p}, \mathbf{w}, T)$ and Samp(α).

Let $W(\alpha) \doteq \lim_{t \to \infty} W(\text{Samp}(\alpha), t)$, and $\widehat{W}(\alpha) \doteq \lim_{T \to \infty} \widehat{W}(\text{Samp}(\alpha), T)$, where $W(\text{Samp}(\alpha), t)$ and $\widehat{W}(\text{Samp}(\alpha), T)$ are defined in Eqs. (1) and (2) respectively. From Lemma 1, we have that the limits in Eqs. (1) and (2) both exist and are the same for any given $\alpha > 0$ with the limiting value as in Eq. (18). Define $\Delta_\alpha(t) \doteq |W(\alpha) - W(\text{Samp}(\alpha), t)|$ and $\widehat{\Delta}_\alpha(T) \doteq |\widehat{W}(\alpha) - \widehat{W}(\text{Samp}(\alpha), T)|$. From Eqs. (10), (16) and (17) in the proof of Theorem 1 we have

$$W(\alpha) = \widehat{W}(\alpha) = \sum_{r=(u,v) \in \mathcal{R}} p_r \cdot w_r \cdot \left(\alpha \gamma_{u,v} + \frac{1-\alpha}{4} \sum_{k \in \mathcal{N}(u)} \gamma_{k,v} \right). \quad (18)$$

$$\Delta_\alpha(t) \le 2wC\beta^t, \quad \widehat{\Delta}_\alpha(T) \le \frac{1}{T} \sum_{t=1}^{T} \Delta_\alpha(t) \le \frac{2wC}{T} \frac{1}{1-\beta}. \quad (19)$$

In Eq. (18), $\gamma_{u,v}$ is the probability that location u has at least one driver and location v has fewer than c drivers in the limiting distribution π^*. In Inequalities (19), $w \doteq \max_{r \in \mathcal{R}} w_r$ and $C > 0$ and $\beta \in (0, 1)$ are two scalars which are independent of t and T, but may be related to parameters m and n. This yields the result for Samp(α); we can get similar results for the policy Rand-Perm(ϕ).

Observe that if $(\mathbf{x}, \mathbf{y})$ is a (u, u')-neighbor, then $(\mathbf{y}, \mathbf{x})$ is a (u', u)-neighbor and therefore we have $P_\alpha(\mathbf{y}, \mathbf{x}) = p$, implying that P_α is symmetric. This implies that $\mathcal{M}(\text{Samp}(\alpha))$ admits a unique uniform limiting distribution π^* over Ω (see more details in the full version). This enables us to get a closed-form expression for $W(\alpha)$ (Theorem 2), and derive explicit values of C and β (Theorem 3).

Theorem 2 (Closed-form expression for $W(\alpha)$). *Consider the uniform arrival distribution of the requests such that $p_r = p$ for all $r \in \mathcal{R}$ and $c = m$. Objectives defined in Eqs. (1) and (2) for Samp(α) both converge to $\frac{mp}{n+m-1} \sum_{r \in \mathcal{R}} w_r$ for any given $\alpha > 0$.*

The condition $c = m$ in Theorem 2 implies that there is no constraint on the maximum number of drivers in any location. The main idea of proof for Theorem 2 is to show that for any (u, v), $\gamma_{u,v} = \frac{m}{n+m-1}$ for the special case. We defer the full proof of Theorem 2 to the full version.

Theorem 3 (Explicit values of C and β). *Consider the uniform arrival distribution of the requests such that $p_r = n^{-2}$ for all $r \in \mathcal{R}$ and $c \le 2$. For any given $\alpha > 0$, Objectives in (1) and (2) for Samp(α) both converge with a rate upper bounded by (i.e., as least as fast as) $\frac{4m \sum_{r \in \mathcal{R}} w_r}{n^2 \exp(t/n^2)}$ and $\frac{4m \sum_{r \in \mathcal{R}} w_r}{T}$, respectively.*

We first show the following useful lemma with proof deferred to the full version. We use this to show the proof of Theorem 3. Consider the Markov Chain

$\mathscr{M}(\text{Samp}(\alpha))$ as defined in (3) and let $\tau(\epsilon)$ be the mixing time of $\mathscr{M}(\text{Samp}(\alpha))$ as defined in Sect. 2.

Lemma 4. $\tau(\epsilon) \leq n^2 \ln(2m/\epsilon)$ *when the arrival distribution of online requests is uniform such that* $p_r = n^{-2}$ *for all* $r \in \mathcal{R}$ *and* $c \leq 2$.

Proof. Setting $\tau(\epsilon) = t$ implies that $\epsilon \geq 2m\exp(-t/n^2)$ in Lemma 4. Let $\epsilon = 2m\exp(-t/n^2)$. Recall that the definition of $\tau(\epsilon) = \min\{t : d(t') \leq \epsilon, \forall t' \geq t\}$ where $d(t) = \max_{\mathbf{x}\in\Omega}||P^t(\mathbf{x},\cdot) - \pi^*||_{TV}$. Thus, we have $\max_{\mathbf{x}\in\Omega}||P^t(\mathbf{x},\cdot) - \pi^*||_{TV} \leq 2m(\exp(-1/n^2))^t$.

From the proof of Lemma 2 (The first inequality in (8)), we have $|\gamma_{u,v}^{(t)} - \gamma_{u,v}| \leq 2\max_{\mathbf{x}\in\Omega}||P^t(\mathbf{x},\cdot) - \pi^*||_{TV} = 4m\exp(-t/n^2)$. Recall that $W(\alpha) = \lim_{t\to\infty} W(\text{Samp}(\alpha),t)$ and $\Delta_\alpha(t) = |W(\text{Samp}(\alpha),t) - W(\alpha)|$. Thus the RHS in Eq. (16) can be upper-bounded by $\frac{4m\exp(-t/n^2)}{n^2}\sum_{r\in\mathcal{R}} w_r$. Similarly, we have that $\widehat{\Delta}_\alpha(T) \leq \frac{1}{T}\sum_{t=1}^{T}\Delta_\alpha(t) \leq \frac{4m\sum_{r\in\mathcal{R}} w_r}{T\cdot n^2}\frac{1}{1-\exp(-1/n^2)} \sim \frac{4m\sum_{r\in\mathcal{R}} w_r}{T}$. □

A Lower Bound on Convergence Rates. We show that even in very special cases, the convergence rate shown in Theorem 3 is *almost* optimal. When $c = 1$, we have the following lower bound where the dependence on t and T nearly matches our upper bounds. We defer the proof to the full version of the paper.

Theorem 4 (Lower bound for $\Theta(\beta^t)$). *There is an instance with uniform arrival distribution where* $p_r = n^{-2}$ *for all* $r \in \mathcal{R}$ *and* $c = 1$ *such that Objective* (1) *for* Samp(1) *has an asymptotic convergence rate equal to* $\frac{2m\sum_{r\in\mathcal{R}} w_r}{n^3 \exp(t/n)}$.

5   Conclusions and Future Research

In this paper, we considered the rideshare dispatching problem and the corresponding Markov chain for the evolution of the matching process. In turn, we characterized the driver distribution over time. In particular, we showed that the mixing time of this Markov chain is small, and gave explicit bounds on the convergence rate of various algorithms. Under practical assumptions, our theory shows that the convergence rates are fast, and in practice one would reach the stationary distribution in a short amount of time. To complement the theory we ran extensive experiments on both simulated and real datasets. Our theory gives accurate insight into rideshare dynamics in practice, and also complements a growing body of related research (e.g., [3,5,25]) that relies on assumptions that were, until now, underexplored and poorly understood. Still, relaxing any of the five commonly-made assumptions discussed in the preliminaries (Sect. 2) would be practically useful.

Acknowledgements. John Dickerson and Michael Curry were supported in part by NSF CAREER Award IIS-1846237 and DARPA SI3-CMD Award S4761. Aravind Srinivasan, Karthik Abinav Sankararaman and Pan Xu were supported in part by NSF CNS-1010789, CCF-1422569 and CCF-1749864, and by research awards from Adobe,

Amazon and Google. Yuhao Wan was supported via an REU grant, NSF CCF-1852352, and was advised by John Dickerson. John Dickerson and Aravind Srinivasan were both supported by a gift from Google and a seed grant from the Maryland Transportation Institute (MTI). Work done when Karthik was at the University of Maryland, College Park.

References

1. Alonso-Mora, J., Samaranayake, S., Wallar, A., Frazzoli, E., Rus, D.: On-demand high-capacity ride-sharing via dynamic trip-vehicle assignment. Proc. Nat. Acad. Sci. **114**(3), 462–467 (2017)
2. Andrieu, C., De Freitas, N., Doucet, A., Jordan, M.I.: An introduction to MCMC for machine learning. Mach. Learn. **50**(1–2), 5–43 (2003)
3. Banerjee, S., Freund, D., Lykouris, T.: Pricing and optimization in shared vehicle systems: an approximation framework. In: Proceedings of the 2017 ACM Conference on Economics and Computation, EC 2017, pp. 517–517. ACM, New York (2017). https://doi.org/10.1145/3033274.3085099. http://doi.acm.org/10.1145/3033274.3085099. ISBN 978-1-4503-4527-9
4. Banerjee, S., Johari, R., Riquelme, C.: Dynamic pricing in ridesharing platforms. SIGecom Exch. **15**(1), 65–70 (2016). https://doi.org/10.1145/2994501.2994505. http://doi.acm.org/10.1145/2994501.2994505. ISSN 1551–9031
5. Banerjee, S., Kanoria, Y., Qian, P.: State dependent control of closed queueing networks with application to ride-hailing. In: Proceedings of the 2018 ACM International Conference on Measurement and Modeling of Computer Systems, SIGMETRICS 2018 (2018). Complete working paper available at arXiv:1803.04959
6. Braverman, A., Dai, J.G., Liu, X., Ying, L.: Empty-car routing in ridesharing systems. arXiv preprint arXiv:1609.07219 (2016)
7. Cachon, G.P., Daniels, K.M., Lobel, R.: The role of surge pricing on a service platform with self-scheduling capacity. Manufact. Serv. Oper. Manage. **19**(3), 368–384 (2017)
8. Das, A., Gollapudi, S., Kim, A., Panigrahi, D., Swamy, C.: Minimizing latency in online ride and delivery services. In: Proceedings of the 2018 World Wide Web Conference, pp. 379–388. International World Wide Web Conferences Steering Committee (2018)
9. Dickerson, J.P., Sandholm, T.: Futurematch: combining human value judgments and machine learning to match in dynamic environments. In: Twenty-Ninth AAAI Conference on Artificial Intelligence (2015)
10. Dickerson, J.P., Sankararaman, K.A., Srinivasan, A., Xu, P.: Allocation problems in ride-sharing platforms: online matching with offline reusable resources. In: Proceedings of the Thirty-Second AAAI Conference on Artificial Intelligence AAAI 2018, pp. 1007–1014 (2018)
11. Ghosh, S., Varakantham, P., Adulyasak, Y., Jaillet, P.: Dynamic repositioning to reduce lost demand in bike sharing systems. J. Artif. Intell. Res. **58**, 387–430 (2017)
12. Hahn, R., Metcalfe, R.: The ridesharing revolution: Economic survey and synthesis. Technical report (2017)
13. Hastings, W.K.: Monte carlo sampling methods using markov chains and their applications. Biometrika **57**, 97–109 (1970)
14. Jia, Y., Xu, W., Liu, X.: An optimization framework for online ride-sharing markets. In: 2017 IEEE 37th International Conference on Distributed Computing Systems (ICDCS), pp. 826–835. IEEE (2017)

15. Laptev, N., Yosinski, J., Li, L.E., Smyl, S.: Time-series extreme event fore-casting with neural networks at uber. In: International Conference on Machine Learning, vol. 34, pp. 1–5 (2017)
16. Levin, D.A., Peres, Y.: Markov Chains and Mixing Times. American Mathematical Society (2017)
17. Li, Y.: Deep reinforcement learning: An overview. arXiv preprint arXiv:1701.07274 (2017)
18. Lin, K., Zhao, R., Xu, Z., Zhou, J.: Efficient large-scale fleet management via multi-agent deep reinforcement learning. In: Proceedings of the 24th ACM SIGKDD International Conference on Knowledge Discovery & Data Mining, pp. 1774–1783. ACM (2018)
19. Lowalekar, M., Varakantham, P., Jaillet, P.: Online spatio-temporal matching in stochastic and dynamic domains. Artif. Intell. **261**, 71–112 (2018). https://doi.org/10.1016/j.artint.2018.04.005. http://www.sciencedirect.com/science/article/pii/S0004370218302030. ISSN 0004-3702
20. Ma, H., Fang, F., Parkes, D.C.: Spatio-temporal pricing for ridesharing platforms. In: Proceedings of the 2019 ACM Conference on Economics and Computation, EC 2019 (2019)
21. Mehta, A., et al.: Online matching and ad allocation. Found. Trends® Theoret. Comput. Sci. **8**(4), 265–368 (2013)
22. Metropolis, N., Rosenbluth, A.W., Rosenbluth, M.N., Teller, A.H., Teller, E.: Equation of state calculations by fast computing machines. J. Chem. Phys. **21**(6), 1087–1092 (1953)
23. Metropolis, N., Ulam, S.: The monte carlo method. J. Am. Stat. Assoc. **44**(247), 335–341 (1949)
24. O'Mahony, E., Shmoys, D.B.: Data analysis and optimization for (citi) bike sharing. In: Twenty-ninth AAAI Conference on Artificial Intelligence (2015)
25. Ozkan, E., Ward, A.: Dynamic matching for real-time ridesharing. SSRN 2844451 (2017)
26. Qu, M., Zhu, H., Liu, J., Liu, G., Xiong, H.: A cost-effective recommender system for taxi drivers. In: Proceedings of the 20th ACM SIGKDD International Conference on Knowledge Discovery and Data Mining, pp. 45–54. ACM (2014)
27. Rong, J., Qin, T., An, B.: Dynamic pricing for reusable resources in competitive market with stochastic demand. In: Thirty-Second AAAI Conference on Artificial Intelligence (2018)
28. Sun, Y., Wang, J., Tan, W.: Online algorithms of task allocation in spatial crowd-sourcing. In: Proceedings of the 12th Chinese Conference on Computer Supported Cooperative Work and Social Computing, pp. 205–208. ACM (2017)
29. Tong, Y., She, J., Ding, B., Chen, L., Wo, T., Xu, K.: Online minimum matching in real-time spatial data: experiments and analysis. Proc. VLDB Endowment **9**(12), 1053–1064 (2016)
30. Verma, T., Varakantham, P., Kraus, S., Lau, H.C.: Augmenting decisions of taxi drivers through reinforcement learning for improving revenues. In: Twenty-Seventh International Conference on Automated Planning and Scheduling (2017)
31. Wen, J., Zhao, J., Jaillet, P.: Rebalancing shared mobility-on-demand systems: a reinforcement learning approach. In: 2017 IEEE 20th International Conference on Intelligent Transportation Systems (ITSC), pp. 220–225. IEEE (2017)
32. Yao, H., et al.: Deep multi-view spatial-temporal network for taxi demand prediction. In: Proceedings of the Thirty-Second AAAI Conference on Artificial Intelligence, AAAI 2018, pp. 2588–2595 (2018)

Persuasion and Incentives Through the Lens of Duality

Shaddin Dughmi[1], Rad Niazadeh[2], Alexandros Psomas[3(✉)],
and S. Matthew Weinberg[4]

[1] Department of Computer Science, University of Southern California,
Los Angeles, USA
shaddin@usc.edu
[2] Department of Computer Science, Stanford University, Stanford, USA
rad@cs.stanford.edu
[3] Simons Institute for the Theory of Computing, Berkeley, USA
alexpsomi@cs.berkeley.edu
[4] Department of Computer Science, Princeton University, Princeton, USA
smweinberg@princeton.edu

Abstract. Lagrangian duality underlies both classical and modern
mechanism design. In particular, the dual perspective often permits simple and detail-free characterizations of optimal and approximately optimal mechanisms. This paper applies this same methodology to a close
cousin of traditional mechanism design, one which shares conceptual and
technical elements with its more mature relative: the burgeoning field of
persuasion. The dual perspective permits us to analyze optimal persuasion schemes both in settings which have been analyzed in prior work,
as well as for natural generalizations which we are the first to explore
in depth. Most notably, we permit combining persuasion policies with
payments, which serve to augment the persuasion power of the scheme.
In both single and multi-receiver settings, as well as under a variety of
constraints on payments, we employ duality to obtain structural insights,
as well as tractable and simple characterizations of optimal policies.

1 Introduction

There are two primary ways of influencing the actions of strategic agents: through
providing incentives and through influencing beliefs. The former is the domain
of traditional *mechanism design*, and involves the promise of payments or goods
contingent on behavior. The latter is the domain of *information design*, or *persuasion*, and involves the selective provision of information pertaining to the
payoffs and costs of various actions. There are striking similarities and parallels
between the two worlds, both in terms of the domains in which they are studied—
for example in auctions [9, 10, 15] and routing [3]—as well in the mathematical
models and techniques used to characterize and compute optimal policies (e.g.

The full paper can be found at https://arxiv.org/abs/1909.10584.

© Springer Nature Switzerland AG 2019
I. Caragiannis et al. (Eds.): WINE 2019, LNCS 11920, pp. 142–155, 2019.
https://doi.org/10.1007/978-3-030-35389-6_11

[11,12,20]). Combining the approaches and techniques of mechanism design and persuasion leads to a more powerful toolkit for the design of economic systems, and this paper takes a step in that direction.

We work with two fundamental models of persuasion: the Bayesian Persuasion model of [19], and the multi-receiver private Bayesian persuasion model of [1] (further developed in [2] and [12]) which we generalize to allow externalities. In the spirit of mechanism design and principal-agent problems, we generalize both models by permitting payments, which serve as additional incentive for the receiver(s) to behave in accordance with the wishes of the sender (principal).

We then explore these models through the lens of *Lagrangian duality*, much in the spirit of the literature applying duality to auction theory and Bayesian mechanism design. In particular, we vary constraints on the payments (arbitrary, nonnegative, budget balanced) and the information/reward structure (symmetric vs asymmetric actions), and derive canonical and/or tractable optimal policies through duality.

The Persuasion Models. In the Bayesian persuasion model, there is a *receiver* who must select one of a number of actions, and a *sender* looking to influence the receiver's choice in order to maximize her own expected payoff. We adopt the perspective of the sender. A *state of nature*, drawn from a common knowledge prior distribution, determines the payoff of each action to each of the sender and the receiver. The sender has an informational advantage over the receiver: access to the realization of the state of nature. The problem facing the sender is that of computing and committing to the optimal *signaling scheme*: a randomized map from states of nature to signals. Once the state is drawn by nature, the signaling scheme is invoked and the corresponding signal is sent to the receiver; she then updates her prior belief and chooses the action maximizing her expected payoff. The multi-receiver private Bayesian persuasion model generalizes the previous model to multiple receivers. There is still a common knowledge prior distribution over states of nature, and a single sender with an informational advantage. We restrict attention to the special case of two actions $\{0, 1\}$ for each receiver. The state of nature determines a set function for the sender and a set function for each receiver: each set function maps the set of receivers taking action 1 to a payoff. A signaling scheme now is a randomized map from states of nature to a signal for each receiver. In both models, a simple revelation principle style argument shows that it suffices to restrict attention to schemes which are *direct* and *persuasive* (see e.g. [1,19]). A direct scheme is one in which signals correspond to action recommendations. Such a scheme is persuasive if it is a Bayes-Nash equilibrium for each receiver to follow the recommendation.

Adding Payments. We augment each model by allowing a special form of payment contract. In addition to committing to a direct signaling scheme, the sender also commits to a payment $p(i)$ for each action i. If the signaling scheme recommends action i, and the receiver follows the recommendation, she is then paid $p(i)$ by the sender (or pays the sender $-p(i)$ if $p(i) < 0$). If the receiver deviates from the scheme's recommendation, no payment is exchanged. Since payments are exchanged only when the receiver follows the recommendation, nonnegative payments can be viewed as augmenting the "persuasiveness" of the signaling scheme. Negative payments are less natural, although their consideration will be technically instructive.

We distinguish three classes of payment contracts: unrestricted (allowing arbitrary positive and negative payments), nonnegative, and budget balanced. For the latter, the sender's expected payment should be zero over states of nature and randomness in the signaling scheme, assuming the receiver(s) follow the recommendations of the scheme. Independent to our work, [21] also considers adding payments to Bayesian persuasion. They analyze a special case of Bayesian persuasion with two states of nature, and examine how adding a payment contract influences the optimal policy in that scenario. Our approach diverges from this work by considering more general settings of Bayesian persuasion and various classes of payment contracts.

Duality as a Unifying Lens. Persuasion and auction design share striking parallels. Indeed, both are economic design problems in which the outputs—recommendation(s) in the case of persuasion and allocations of goods in the case of an auction—are subjected to incentive constraints which at the surface appear quite similar in the two settings. This is made explicit by [11], who draw an analogy between persuasion and single-item auctions: actions are analogous to bidders, and recommending an action is analogous to allocating the item. Through this analogy, they were able to leverage techniques from auction theory—in particular Border's theorem [4]—to characterize and compute optimal signaling schemes for Bayesian persuasion when action payoffs are i.i.d. This analogy is imperfect, however, as illustrated by the impossibility result of [11] for independent non-identical action payoffs, contrasting the tractability of single-item auctions with independent bidders.

Despite being imperfect, however, this similarity is suggestive: if a Border's theorem based approach of optimization of interim rules can be applied to persuasion, why not the "virtual value" approach of [23] as well? Myerson's approach can be viewed through the more general lens of Lagrangian duality, in particular as a consequence of Lagrangifying the incentive constraints. The duality-based approach has been applied to much more general mechanism design settings, producing (often approximate) generalizations of Myerson's virtual-value characterization which have led to simple and approximately optimal mechanisms in a number of multi-parameter settings (e.g. [5,7,8,13,14,16,17,22], and classic results such as [24]). It is therefore natural that we embark on the same exploration for persuasion, as well as for models (such as ours) which combine the approaches of persuasion and mechanism design. As a best case scenario, we can hope for "simple" characterizations of optimal or near-optimal schemes, akin to those derived from duality in mechanism design. Particularly attractive are "canonical" characterizations which depend minimally on the details of the instance at hand.

Our Results. In Sect. 3, we apply Lagrangian duality to Bayesian persuasion, and derive some elementary properties of the primal/dual pair which enable our results to follow. Our first main result is in Sect. 4, and concerns (single-receiver) Bayesian persuasion with a prior distribution which is symmetric across n actions, and no payments are allowed. We show that a single dual variable naturally interpolates between two extreme schemes: at one extreme (λ equals zero) we get the (non-persuasive) scheme which always recommends the sender's ex-post preferred action, at the other extreme (λ very large) we get the (persuasive) scheme which recommends the receiver's ex-post preferred action. Intermediate values of λ yield schemes which point-wise optimize the sender payoff plus $n\lambda$ times the receiver's payoff. Moreover, there is a threshold λ^* below which the induced scheme is non-persuasive, and above which the scheme is persuasive. This λ^* induces the sender-optimal persuasive signaling scheme. This characterization is detail-free, in the sense that it reduces the prior distribution to a relative weighting of receiver to sender payoff. Furthermore, this optimal scheme is *Pareto efficient* in a strong (ex-post) sense: for every state θ, no outcome Pareto dominates the one picked by the scheme.

In Sect. 5, we use duality to characterize Bayesian persuasion schemes with payments. When arbitrary payments are allowed and the prior is symmetric, the optimal signaling scheme is canonical and does not depend on the prior: it always (i.e. in every state of nature) recommends the action that maximizes the sender utility plus $\frac{n}{n-1}$ times the receiver's utility. Payments accompanying this scheme are computed easily via a simple payment identity. Our main result in this section is a *dichotomy* for Bayesian persuasion with a symmetric prior, *but* non-negative payments: the optimal scheme is either the same as the aforementioned arbitrary-payment scheme (in the event that non-negative payments are needed), or else is the optimal no-payment signaling scheme. Finally, with only two actions and an arbitrary prior, we show that when arbitrary payments are allowed, the optimal scheme always recommends the action maximizing sender utility plus twice receiver utility. Again, all of our optimal schemes are ex-post Pareto efficient. We note that the strongest positive results of [11] (exact polynomial time solvability) hold in the setting of i.i.d. actions. Our results therefore extend and simplify theirs, while lending further insight.

Finally, we turn our attention to a multi-receiver private persuasion model with externalities. Again, we employ duality to analyze the optimal scheme in this setting. Our first main result shows that, when we allow budget balanced payments, there exists an optimal scheme which is "simple" in the following sense: It always recommends an action maximizing a weighted sum of sender utility and the receivers' marginal utility from following the recommendation of the scheme. The relative weighting is determined by a single dual variable. This characterization is interesting when contrasted with the optimal no-payment scheme, which is not as simple in general, and we show is sometimes strictly outperformed (in terms of sender expected utility) by the optimal budget-balanced scheme. Our second main result is a generalization of an algorithmic result of [12] to multi-receiver persuasion with *positive externalities*: when no payments are allowed, and sender and receiver utility functions lie in some cone of set functions $\mathcal{C}$, we use duality to exhibit a polynomial time reduction from optimal signaling to the optimization problem for set functions in $\mathcal{C}$. Due to the lack of space, these results are deferred to the full version of this paper.

2   Preliminaries

Bayesian Persuasion. Bayesian persuasion is a game between a sender, also termed as the *principal*, and a receiver, also termed as the *agent*. There is also a set of possible *states of nature* Θ. The true state of nature $\theta \in \Theta$ is drawn from a prior distribution μ_θ, known to both the sender and the receiver. The receiver has a set of possible *actions* $[n] = \{1, \ldots, n\}$ to pick. Based on the action i picked by the receiver and the true state of nature θ, the sender and the receiver gain *payoffs*[1], denoted by $s_\theta(i)$ and $r_\theta(i)$ respectively. In the Bayesian persuasion game, the sender commits to a *signaling scheme* ϕ, where in general ϕ is a mapping from Θ to distributions over possible *signals*, Σ. Then the sender observes $\theta \sim \mu_\theta$, and sends a signal $\sigma \in \Sigma$ to the receiver, where $\sigma \sim \phi_\theta$ for the observed θ. Given signal σ, the receiver updates her belief about the state of nature θ, and selects an action i_r that maximizes her expected payoff under this posterior distribution. In this paper, without loss of generality, and by applying the revelation principle [19], we focus on signaling schemes for which $\Sigma = [n]$. We use the notation $\phi_\theta(i)$ to denote the probability that the sender recommends action i conditioned on the state of nature being θ. A signaling scheme is said to *implement* ϕ_θ, if it samples signal $i \sim \phi_\theta$ given the state of nature θ.

Persuasive Signaling and Optimal Bayesian Persuasion. A signaling scheme is *persuasive* if the receiver is best off following the sender's recommendation, i.e. following the sender's recommendation maximizes the receiver's expected payoff under the receiver's posterior belief about the state of the nature (conditioned on the received signal). In the *optimal Bayesian persuasion problem*, we wish to find, over all persuasive schemes, the one that maximizes the sender's expected payoff.

Action Types. As typical in information structure design, we frequently think of each action as having a "type" depending on the state of nature.[2] That is, $\theta = [\theta_1, \ldots, \theta_n]$ is a vector in $[m]^n$, for some parameter m. Action i has type θ_i, which completely determines the sender and receiver payoffs should action i be selected, independent of θ_{-i}. More clearly, there exist m pairs of payoffs $(\xi_1^i, \rho_1^i), \ldots, (\xi_m^i, \rho_m^i)$ such that when the receiver selects action i with $\theta_i = j$, ξ_j^i is the payoff to the sender and ρ_j^i is the payoff to the receiver. Note that $s_\theta(i) = \xi_{\theta_i}^i$ and $r_\theta(i) = \rho_{\theta_i}^i$, and for universality we stick to this notation. Distributions in

---

[1] We use the words "payoff" and "reward" interchangeably in this paper.

[2] We refer the reader to [11] for a list examples of Bayesian persuasions and how types are defined in those.

this setting may be *independent*, if $\mu_\theta = \times_i \mu_{\theta_i}$ is a product distribution, where each μ_{θ_i} is a distribution over $[m]$. Distributions in this setting may also be *symmetric*, if μ_θ is invariant under all permutations. Distributions that are both independent and symmetric are *i.i.d.*

Bayesian Persuasion with Payments. We introduce a natural model of payments into the Bayesian persuasion problem. In addition to recommending an action i, the sender is allowed to "incentivize" the receiver to take the recommendation with an additional payment $p(i)$. Mathematically, it also makes sense to consider when payments are allowed to be negative (which corresponds to the sender "charging" the receiver $-p(i)$ in order to follow the recommendation). This certainly could be relevant for practice (e.g. if the sender/receiver can commit to contracts), but the non-negative payment model is clearly more natural. We study four different payment models: *zero payments* (i.e. classic Bayesian persuasion), *non-negative payments* (i.e. when the sender cannot charge the receiver), *budget-balanced payments* (i.e. the payment of the sender is zero in expectation) and *general payments* (i.e. payments are arbitrary real numbers). To unify the notation throughout the paper, we use $\mathcal{P}$ to denote the feasible set of payments, which plays the role of a different polytope for each relevant payment model (note that in all four models $\mathcal{P}$ is closed and convex). A signaling scheme *implements* (ϕ_θ, p) if given the observed state of nature θ, it samples $i \sim \phi_\theta$ and pays the receiver a (randomized) payment $p(i)$. Throughout this paper, it will be convenient to focus on specifying the *expected payments* for following the recommendation of action i, $P(i) \triangleq \sum_{\theta \in \Theta} \mu_\theta \phi_\theta(i) p(i)$ for any scheme. We similarly define the implementability of (ϕ_θ, P).[3]

Payment Identity and Optimal Payments. We conclude with an observation about persuasion with payments. Similar to auction design, there is a "payment identity" capturing which payments will make an implementable signaling scheme persuasive. In contrast to auctions, however, it is easy to see that *every* signaling scheme can be made persuasive with sufficiently high payments.

Observation 1. *Let μ_θ be any distribution over states of nature, and ϕ_θ be any signaling scheme (not necessarily persuasive). Then there exist thresholds $T_1, \ldots, T_n$ such that (ϕ_θ, p) is persuasive if and only if $P(i) \geq T_i$ for all i.*

Proof. Let $X_\phi(i, j)$ be the receiver's expected utility by taking action j when the scheme ϕ_θ recommends action i. Define $T_i = \max_{j \neq i}\{X_\phi(i, j) - X_\phi(i, i)\}$. Therefore, $X_\phi(i, i) + T_i \geq X_\phi(i, j)$ for all j, and any scheme that pays $P(i) \geq T_i$ is certainly persuasive when recommending i. Moreover, if $P(i) < T_i$, then there exists some j s.t. $X_\phi(i, i) + P(i) < X_\phi(i, j)$, and the scheme is not persuasive. □

---

[3] It is also easy to see how to implement payments $p(i)$ from $P(i)$ and an implementation of ϕ_θ: for a given state $\theta \in \Theta$, sample a payment $\frac{P(i)}{\phi_\theta(i)}$ whenever signal $i \sim \phi_\theta$ is recommended.

Definition 1. *We refer to the* $T_1, \ldots, T_n$ *in Observation 1 as the* optimal payments *for* ϕ, *and* $\max\{0, T_1\}, \ldots, \max\{0, T_n\}$ *as the* optimal non-negative payments *for* ϕ.

3   Lagrangian Duality and Bayesian Persuasion

In this section, we create a unified analysis toolbox for various Bayesian persuasion problems through the lens of LP duality. Specifically, we use Lagrangian duals to reveal the structures of the optimal signaling, á la successful instances of a similar technique in Bayesian mechanism design [7]. As a prerequisite, we heavily use linear programming techniques introduced in [19], and further improved in [11], and build a bedrock for the analyses in future sections.

3.1   LP for General Bayesian Persuasion with Payments

Linear programming formulations of Bayesian persuasion without payments have been introduced in numerous prior works (e.g. [11]). We now modify the program slightly to capture payments, by observing that whenever action i is recommended the receiver gets additional payoff $p(i)$ and the sender loses a payoff $p(i)$. The following program solves the sender's optimization problem.

$$\max \quad \sum_{\theta \in \Theta} \sum_{i \in [n]} \mu_\theta \phi_\theta(i) \left(s_\theta(i) - p(i)\right)$$

$$\sum_{\theta \in \Theta} \mu_\theta \phi_\theta(i) \left(r_\theta(i) + p(i)\right) \geq \sum_{\theta \in \Theta} \mu_\theta \phi_\theta(i) r_\theta(j), \qquad \forall i, j \neq i \in [n]$$

$$\phi_\theta \in \Delta_n, \ \forall \theta \in \Theta, \quad \text{and} \quad p \in \mathcal{P}$$

The first set of constraints, also called *persuasiveness constraints*, are similar to *Incentive Compatibility (IC)* constraints from auction design, and ensure that the receiver is best off (in expectation) by following the recommendation and paying the payment. The rest ensure that the scheme is in fact a valid distribution over recommendations, and the payments are feasible. While not yet a linear program, the above program can be made linear by a simple change of variables to expected payments $P(i)$:[4]

$$\max \quad \sum_{\theta \in \Theta} \sum_{i \in [n]} \mu_\theta \phi_\theta(i) s_\theta(i) - \sum_{i \in [n]} P(i) \quad \text{(LP-General-with-Payments)}$$

$$P(i) + \sum_{\theta \in \Theta} \mu_\theta \phi_\theta(i) r_\theta(i) \geq \sum_{\theta \in \Theta} \mu_\theta \phi_\theta(i) r_\theta(j), \qquad \forall i, j \neq i \in [n]$$

$$\phi_\theta \in \Delta_n, \ \forall \theta \in \Theta, \quad \text{and} \quad P \in \mathcal{P}$$

where we abuse the notation by using $\mathcal{P}$ to denote the feasible polytope of average.

---

[4] Recall that $P(i) = \sum_{\theta \in \Theta} \mu_\theta \phi_\theta(i) p(i)$.

3.2   The Partial Lagrangian Dual

One of the main tools we use in this paper is taking the *partial Lagrangians* of the linear programs of the Bayesian persuasion problem. Basically, similar to [7], we do not take a "complete dual" of the LP formulation, instead "Lagrangifying" only the persuasiveness constraints, and leave all feasibility constraints in the primal. To take the partial Lagrangians, we apply the method of Lagrangian multipliers by (*a*) introducing dual variables $\lambda(i,j)$ for every pair of actions $i, j \in [n]$ with $i \neq j$, (*b*) multiplying the persuasiveness constraints with duals $\lambda(i,j)$, and (*c*) moving the persuasiveness constraints to the objective. By rearranging the terms we have the following observation.

Observation 2. *Assigning dual variables $\lambda(i,j)$ to the persuasiveness constraint guaranteeing that the receiver prefers to take action i over action j when i is recommended gives the following partial Lagrangian.*

$$\mathcal{L}_\lambda(\phi, P) = \sum_{\theta \in \Theta, i \in [n]} \mu_\theta \phi_\theta(i) \left(s_\theta(i) + r_\theta(i) \sum_{j \neq i} \lambda(i,j) - \sum_{j \neq i} \lambda(i,j) r_\theta(j) \right)$$
$$+ \sum_{i \in [n]} P(i) \left(\sum_{j \neq i} \lambda(i,j) - 1 \right). \tag{1}$$

We remind the reader that the optimal signaling schemes and payments are solutions to the following min-max programs by applying strong duality ($\mathcal{D}$ denotes the appropriate dual feasible polytope):

$$\max_{\forall \theta : \phi_\theta \in \Delta_n, P \in \mathcal{P}} \left(\min_{\lambda \in \mathcal{D}} \mathcal{L}_\lambda(\phi, P) \right) = \min_{\lambda \in \mathcal{D}} \left(\max_{\forall \theta : \phi_\theta \in \Delta_n, P \in \mathcal{P}} \mathcal{L}_\lambda(\phi, P) \right). \tag{2}$$

Definition 2. *(Dual-adjusted receiver payoff). For any assignment of dual variables $\lambda \in \mathcal{D}$, define $r_\theta^\lambda(i) \triangleq r_\theta(i) \sum_{j \neq i} \lambda(i,j) - \sum_{j \neq i} \lambda(i,j) r_\theta(j)$.*

We conclude by Proposition 1, which we repeatedly use to extract various properties of the corresponding optimal policy.

Proposition 1. *[Strong Duality for Bayesian Persuasion] There exist dual variables $\lambda(.,.)$ such that the optimal signaling scheme, for every state of nature θ, recommends the action maximizing the dual-adjusted receiver payoff, i.e. $s_\theta(i) + r_\theta^\lambda(i)$. Moreover, if $\lambda(i,j) > 0$, then when action i is recommended, the receiver is indifferent between following the recommendation and taking action j instead (Complementary Slackness).*[5]

3.3   Exploiting Symmetries

When viewing actions by their types (recall this means that we view states of nature as a profile $[\theta_1, \ldots, \theta_n]$, with each $\theta_i \in [m]$), some of our results consider symmetric settings, where $\mu_{\theta_1, \ldots, \theta_n} = \mu_{\theta_{\pi(1)}, \ldots, \theta_{\pi(n)}}$ for any permutation

---

[5] We will not actually make use of complementary slackness in this paper, but include it here for completeness.

$\pi : [n] \rightarrow [n]$. It is well-known that symmetric LPs admit symmetric solutions (e.g. [18]), and this fact has indeed been exploited in prior work on signaling and auctions [6,11]. The proof of this is straight-forward (we provide a proof in the full version). First, we state clearly what we mean by symmetric solutions.

Definition 3. *We say that a signaling scheme* (ϕ, P) *is symmetric if* $P(i) = P(j)$ *for all* i, j *and we have* $\phi_{[\theta_1,...,\theta_n]}(i) = \phi_{[\theta_{\pi(1)},...,\theta_{\pi(n)}]}(\pi^{-1}(i))$ *for all permutations* π *and for all* i, θ. *We say that a dual solution* λ *is symmetric if* $\lambda(i,j) = \lambda(k,\ell)$ *for all* i, j, k, ℓ.

Proposition 2. *Let* μ_θ *be a symmetric instance of Bayesian Persuasion, with any of the four referenced constraints on payments (none, non-negative, budget-balanced, or arbitrary). Then there exists an optimal symmetric primal and an optimal symmetric dual for* μ_θ.

With Proposition 2 in hand, we can now draw further conclusions regarding the format of the Lagrangian function $\mathcal{L}$ in the special case that μ_θ is symmetric:

Corollary 1. *When* μ_θ *is symmetric, there exists a constant* λ *such that the optimal scheme, on every state of nature* θ, *selects an action* i *maximizing* $s_\theta(i) + n\lambda r_\theta(i)$. *Moreover, for the same* λ *and some constant* C, *the Lagrangian takes the following form:*

$$\mathcal{L}_\lambda(\phi, P) = \sum_{\theta \in \Theta, i \in [n]} \mu_\theta \phi_\theta(i) \left(s_\theta(i) + n\lambda r_\theta(i) \right) + \sum_{i \in [n]} P(i) \left((n-1)\lambda - 1 \right) - \lambda C.$$

Proof. Consider an optimal and symmetric dual solution, which is guaranteed to exist by Proposition 2, in which $\lambda(i,j) = \lambda$ for all $i \neq j$. Then we get the following simplified form for $\mathcal{L}$:

$$\mathcal{L}_\lambda(\phi, P) = \sum_{\theta \in \Theta, i \in [n]} \mu_\theta \phi_\theta(i) \left(s_\theta(i) + r_\theta(i) \sum_{j \neq i} \lambda - \sum_{j \neq i} \lambda r_\theta(j) \right)$$
$$+ \sum_{i \in [n]} P(i) \left(\sum_{j \neq i} \lambda - 1 \right)$$
$$= \sum_{\theta \in \Theta, i \in [n]} \mu_\theta \phi_\theta(i) \left(s_\theta(i) + r_\theta(i)(n-1)\lambda - \lambda \sum_{j \neq i} r_\theta(j) \right)$$
$$+ \sum_{i \in [n]} P(i) \left((n-1)\lambda - 1 \right)$$
$$= \sum_{\theta \in \Theta, i \in [n]} \mu_\theta \phi_\theta(i) \left(s_\theta(i) + n\lambda r_\theta(i) \right) + \sum_{i \in [n]} P(i) \left((n-1)\lambda - 1 \right) - \lambda C,$$

Where we have defined $C = \sum_{\theta \in \Theta} \mu_\theta \phi_\theta \sum_{j \in [n]} r_\theta(j)$. It is now easy to see that the signaling scheme maximizing $\mathcal{L}_\lambda$ necessarily on every state of nature θ recommends an action maximizing $s_\theta(i) + n\lambda r_\theta(i)$. $\square$

4   Symmetric Actions and No Payments

Here, we consider the standard symmetric setting without payments. We show how to derive structure on the optimal scheme by making use of duality. In any symmetric instance of Bayesian persuasion, there exists an optimal dual solution $\lambda^*(i,j)$ such that $\lambda^*(i,j) = \lambda^* \geq 0$ for all $i \neq j$ by applying Proposition 2. Now, by plugging directly into Corollary 1 and observing that $P(i) = 0$ for all i, we get that the Lagrangian for the optimal dual takes the following form:

$$\mathcal{L}_\lambda(\phi) = \sum_{\theta \in \Theta, i \in [n]} \mu_\theta \phi_\theta(i) \left(s_\theta(i) + n\lambda r_\theta(i) \right) - \lambda C. \tag{3}$$

We immediately conclude that the optimal scheme recommends, for every state θ, an action maximizing $s_\theta(i) + n\lambda^* r_\theta(i)$. With a little more work, we can conclude something stronger about the exact value of λ^*.

Definition 4 (λ-scaled welfare maximizer). *For a given multiplier λ, define ϕ^λ to be the scheme with $\phi_\theta^\lambda(i) = 0$ if $i \notin \arg\max_j\{s_\theta(j) + n\lambda r_\theta(j)\}$, and $\phi_\theta^\lambda(i) = 1/|\{\arg\max_j\{s_\theta(j) + n\lambda r_\theta(j)\}|$ if $i \in \arg\max_j\{s_\theta(j) + n\lambda r_\theta(j)\}$. In other words, ϕ^λ recommends a uniformly random action in $\arg\max_j\{s_\theta(j) + n\lambda r_\theta(j)\}$.*

Proposition 3. *Let λ^* be the smallest $\lambda \geq 0$ such that the scheme ϕ^λ is persuasive for μ_θ. Then ϕ^{λ^*} is the optimal scheme for μ_θ.*

The proof will follow from the following. We claim that the persuasiveness of ϕ^λ is monotone increasing in λ (larger λ is more persuasive), while the sender payoff is monotone *decreasing* in λ. Together this immediately concludes that the optimal persuasive scheme is ϕ^{λ^*}. We'll first need a technical lemma.

Lemma 1. *Let ϕ^1, ϕ^2 be symmetric schemes and let μ_θ be symmetric. Let the expected receiver payoff for accepting recommendation ϕ^1 for μ_θ be at least as large as the expected receiver payoff for accepting recommendation ϕ^2 for μ_θ. Then if ϕ^2 is persuasive, so is ϕ^1.[6]*

Lemma 2. *If ϕ^λ is persuasive, then $\phi^{\lambda+\delta}$ is persuasive, for all $\delta \geq 0$. Furthermore, the sender's expected payoff when the receiver follows ϕ^λ is monotone non-increasing in λ.*

Proof. For the first part of the lemma, first observe that ϕ^λ is symmetric for all λ. Further observe that the receiver's expected payoff for following the recommendation is monotone in λ: On every state of nature θ, the recommended action maximizes $s_\theta(i) + n\lambda r_\theta(i)$. The first part now immediately follows by Lemma 1. For the second part, simply observe that on every state of nature θ, the recommended action maximizes $s_\theta(i) + n\lambda r_\theta(i)$. As λ increases, the sender payoff for the recommended action decreases. □

---

[6] Note that this does *not* hold generally, and absolutely requires the symmetry assumptions.

5   Optimal Single Agent Signaling with Payments

In this section we study the single receiver Bayesian persuasion game with payments. While we consider our "main results" to be the case where payments are constrained to be non-negative, it's instructive to study general (positive or negative) payments. We characterize the optimal signaling scheme with payments in the general setting, drawing similar conclusions to [7] for optimal auctions. This is not a main result, but may be of independent interest. An easy corollary of this characterization, however, immediately allows us to claim something interesting in the case of two actions. The optimal scheme, for all states θ, recommends the action i maximizing $s_\theta(i) + 2r_\theta(i)$ (paying the optimal payments), and this holds for any distribution.

A deeper application of this result lets us characterize the optimal scheme for a single receiver with n symmetric actions. In this setting, we show that the optimal scheme recommends the action i maximizing $s_\theta(i) + \frac{n}{n-1}r_\theta(i)$ (paying the optimal payments).[7] When payments are non-negative, we prove that the optimal scheme is always either the optimal scheme without payments at all, or the optimal scheme with arbitrary payments.

5.1   The General Setting with Payments

The Langrangian function for an arbitrary polytope $\mathcal{P}$ is given by Eq. 1. Recall that for every choice λ of the Lagrange multipliers, $\max_{\phi,P} \mathcal{L}_\lambda(\phi, P)$ is an upper bound to the performance of the optimal persuasive scheme. Strong duality further implies that this bound is tight for some choice of the Lagrange multipliers.

Observe that if payments are allowed to be arbitrary, then $\max_{\phi,P} \mathcal{L}_\lambda(\phi, P)$ is unbounded whenever the coefficient for $P(i)$ is non-zero for any i (as we can simply set $P(i)$ to be $+\infty$ or $-\infty$. Therefore, we certainly have $\sum_{j \neq i} \lambda(i, j) = 1$ in the optimal dual, for all actions i. This means that for each action i, the dual variables $\lambda(i, .)$ form a distribution over actions other than i. The Lagrangian becomes $\mathcal{L}_\lambda(\phi, P) = \sum_{\theta \in \Theta} \sum_{i \in [n]} \mu_\theta \phi_\theta(i) \left(s_\theta(i) + r_\theta(i) - \mathbb{E}_{j \sim \lambda(i,.)}[r_\theta(j)] \right).$

For every choice of multipliers $\lambda(i, j)$, the scheme ϕ that maximizes $\mathcal{L}_\lambda(\phi, P)$ recommends, for every state of nature θ, the action that maximizes $s_\theta(i) + r_\theta(i) - \mathbb{E}_{j \sim \lambda(i,.)}[r_\theta(j)]$.

Observation 3. *The optimal persuasive scheme ϕ recommends, at each state of nature θ, the action that maximizes $s_\theta(i) + r_\theta(i) - \mathbb{E}_{j \sim \lambda^*(i,.)}[r_\theta(j)]$, where λ^* is the optimal Lagrange multiplier.*

Observation 3 provides a general framework to reason about optimal signaling schemes with arbitrary payments. We repeat now a connection to optimal auction design: In optimal auction design, there are some cases where the optimal

---

[7] Further recall that the sender/receiver payoffs for action i are completely determined by action i's type. So this can also be phrased as recommending a uniformly random action with type k, where k maximizes $\xi_k + \frac{n}{n-1}\rho_k$ over all present types k.

dual is "canonical," and doesn't depend on the input distribution (e.g. single-dimensional) [23]. In such settings, one can identify simple structure of the optimal mechanism. The case is similar in signaling: some cases admit a canonical optimal dual that doesn't depend on the input distribution. In these cases, we obtain simple characterizations of the optimal scheme.

5.2 Two Actions, Arbitrary Payments

In the $n = 2$ case of only two actions, Observation 3 immediately allows us to derive the simple structure of the optimal signaling scheme.

Proposition 4. *When $n = 2$, for every distribution μ_θ, the optimal persuasive scheme with possibly negative payments always recommends the action i that maximizes $s_\theta(i) + 2r_\theta(i)$ (and pays the optimal payments).*

Proof. Observe that there are only two Lagrange multipliers, $\lambda(0,1)$ and $\lambda(1,0)$, and are both equal to 1 in the optimal dual (by Observation 3). Therefore, the Lagrangian can be further simplified:

$$\mathcal{L}_\lambda(\phi, P) = \sum_{\theta \in \Theta} \sum_{i \in [2]} \mu_\theta \phi_\theta(i) \left(s_\theta(i) + r_\theta(i) - \sum_{j \neq i} r_\theta(j) \right)$$

$$= \sum_{\theta \in \Theta} \sum_{i \in [2]} \mu_\theta \phi_\theta(i) \left(s_\theta(i) + 2r_\theta(i) - \sum_{j \in [2]} r_\theta(j) \right).$$

Observe that the term $\sum_{j \in [2]} r_\theta(j)$ does not depend on the action selected at all. So in order to maximize $\mathcal{L}_\lambda(\phi, P)$, the scheme must recommend the action maximizing $s_\theta(i) + 2r_\theta(i)$ for every state of nature θ. $\square$

5.3 Symmetric Actions

Here, we draw conclusions for the symmetric setting with payments. Again getting initial traction from a canonical form for the optimal dual.

Arbitrary Payments

When arbitrary payments are allowed, i.e. $\mathcal{P} = \mathbb{R}$, then the multiplier $(n-1)\lambda - 1$ of the payment variable $P(i)$ must be equal to zero for all i. Otherwise the Lagrangian would be unbounded. This immediately implies that for the optimal dual, we have $\lambda = \frac{1}{n-1}$, and the Lagrangian becomes

$$\mathcal{L}_\lambda(\phi, P) = \sum_{\theta \in \Theta, i \in [n]} \mu_\theta \phi_\theta(i) \left(s_\theta(i) + \tfrac{n}{n-1} r_\theta(i) \right) - \tfrac{1}{n-1} C.$$

The proof of the following proposition then immediately follows.

Proposition 5. *In the single sender, single receiver setting with symmetric actions and arbitrary payments, the optimal scheme recommends, on every state of nature θ, the action i that maximizes $s_\theta(i) + \tfrac{n}{n-1} r_\theta(i)$ (and pays the optimal payments).*

Non-negative Payments: A Dichotomy

When payments are restricted to be non-negative, it is no longer the case that λ is pinned down completely (in particular, λ must certainly be $\leq \frac{1}{n-1}$, or else setting $P(i) = +\infty$ would result in an unbounded Lagrangian, but it is indeed possible to have $\lambda < \frac{1}{n-1}$). Our next result shows that the optimal scheme in this scenario is essentially either the optimal scheme without any payments, or the optimal scheme for arbitrary payments (because the payments are already non-negative).

Proposition 6. *In the single sender, single receiver setting with i.i.d. actions and non-negative payments, the optimal scheme is either (1) the optimal no-payment scheme, or (2) recommends the action i that maximizes $s_\theta(i) + \frac{n}{n-1} r_\theta(i)$ (and pays the optimal non-negative payments).*

Proof. Let $\lambda^* \in [0, \frac{1}{n-1}]$ be the λ guaranteed by Corollary 1. Then there is an optimal scheme (ϕ^*, P^*) that maximizes $\mathcal{L}_{\lambda^*}(\phi, P)$ over all feasible (ϕ, P).

If $\lambda^* < \frac{1}{n-1}$, then $(n-1)\lambda^* - 1$ is strictly negative, and hence the multiplier of each payment variable $P(i)$ is strictly negative. Therefore, every scheme that maximizes $\mathcal{L}_{\lambda^*}(\phi, P)$ must have $P(i) = 0$ for all actions i. Hence, the scheme ϕ is in fact feasible and persuasive for the no-payments case, and must be the optimal scheme without payments (as every scheme without payments is also feasible for non-negative payments, and ϕ is optimal among all schemes with non-negative payments).

If $\lambda^* = \frac{1}{n-1}$, then we immediately observe that this is exactly the same Lagrangian as for arbitrary payments, and therefore the second part of the proposition follows. $\square$

Acknowledgements. Shaddin Dughmi is supported by NSF CAREER Award CCF-1350900. S. Matthew Weinberg is supported by NSF CCF-1717899.

References

1. Arieli, I., Babichenko, Y.: Private Bayesian persuasion. J. Econ. Theory **182**, 185–217 (2019)
2. Babichenko, Y., Barman, S.: Computational aspects of private Bayesian persuasion. In: Proceedings of the 8th ACM Conference on Innovations in Theoretical Computer Science (ITCS) (2017)
3. Bhaskar, U., Cheng, Y., Ko, Y.K., Swamy, C.: Hardness results for signaling in Bayesian zero-sum and network routing games. In: Proceedings of the 2016 ACM Conference on Economics and Computation, pp. 479–496. ACM (2016)
4. Border, K.C.: Implementation of reduced form auctions: a geometric approach. Econometrica J. Econometric Soc. **59**, 1175–1187 (1991)
5. Brustle, J., Cai, Y., Wu, F., Zhao, M.: Approximating gains from trade in two-sided markets via simple mechanisms. In: Proceedings of the ACM Conference on Economics and Computation. ACM (2017)

6. Cai, Y., Daskalakis, C., Weinberg, S.M.: Optimal multi-dimensional mechanism design: reducing revenue to welfare maximization. In: 2012 IEEE 53rd Annual Symposium on Foundations of Computer Science (FOCS), pp. 130–139. IEEE (2012)
7. Cai, Y., Devanur, N.R., Weinberg, S.M.: A duality based unified approach to Bayesian mechanism design. In: Proceedings of the Forty-Eighth Annual ACM Symposium on Theory of Computing, pp. 926–939. ACM (2016)
8. Cai, Y., Zhao, M.: Simple mechanisms for subadditive buyers via duality. In: Proceedings of the ACM Symposium on the Theory of Computation (STOC) (2017)
9. Daskalakis, C., Papadimitriou, C., Tzamos, C.: Does information revelation improve revenue? In: Proceedings of the 2016 ACM Conference on Economics and Computation, pp. 233–250. ACM (2016)
10. Dughmi, S., Immorlica, N., Roth, A.: Constrained signaling in auction design. In: Proceedings of the Twenty-Fifth Annual ACM-SIAM Symposium on Discrete Algorithms, pp. 1341–1357. Society for Industrial and Applied Mathematics (2014)
11. Dughmi, S., Xu, H.: Algorithmic Bayesian persuasion. In: Proceedings of the Forty-Eighth Annual ACM Symposium on Theory of Computing, pp. 412–425. ACM (2016)
12. Dughmi, S., Xu, H.: Algorithmic persuasion with no externalities. In: Proceedings of the 2017 ACM Conference on Economics and Computation, pp. 351–368. ACM (2017)
13. Eden, A., Feldman, M., Friedler, O., Talgam-Cohen, I., Weinberg, S.M.: The competition complexity of auctions: A bulow-klemperer result for multi-dimensional bidders. In: Proceedings of the ACM Conference on Economics and Computation. ACM (2017)
14. Eden, A., Feldman, M., Friedler, O., Talgam-Cohen, I., Weinberg, S.M.: A simple and approximately optimal auction for a buyer with complements. In: Proceedings of the ACM Conference on Economics and Computation. ACM (2017)
15. Emek, Y., Feldman, M., Gamzu, I., PaesLeme, R., Tennenholtz, M.: Signaling schemes for revenue maximization. ACM Trans. Econ. Comput. **2**(2), 5 (2014)
16. Fu, H., Liaw, C., Lu, P., Tang, Z.G.: The value of information concealment. In: Proceedings of the Twenty-Ninth Annual ACM-SIAM Symposium on Discrete Algorithms, pp. 2533–2544. Society for Industrial and Applied Mathematics (2018)
17. Haghpanah, N., Hartline, J.: Reverse mechanism design. In: Proceedings of the Sixteenth ACM Conference on Economics and Computation, pp. 757–758. ACM (2015)
18. Herr, K., Bödi, R.: Symmetries in linear and integer programs. arXiv preprint arXiv:0908.3329 (2009)
19. Kamenica, E., Gentzkow, M.: Bayesian persuasion. Am. Econ. Rev. **101**(6), 2590–2615 (2011)
20. Kolotilin, A., Mylovanov, T., Zapechelnyuk, A., Li, M.: Persuasion of a privately informed receiver. Econometrica **85**(6), 1949–1964 (2017)
21. Li, C.: A model of bayesian persuasion with transfers. Econ. Lett. **161**, 93–95 (2017)
22. Liu, S., Psomas, C.A.: On the competition complexity of dynamic mechanism design. In: Proceedings of the Twenty-Ninth Annual ACM-SIAM Symposium on Discrete Algorithms, pp. 2008–2025. Society for Industrial and Applied Mathematics (2018)
23. Myerson, R.B.: Optimal auction design. Math. Oper. Res. **6**(1), 58–73 (1981)
24. Rochet, J.C., Choné, P.: Ironing, sweeping, and multidimensional screening. Econometrica **66**, 783–826 (1998)

Convergence and Hardness of Strategic Schelling Segregation

Hagen Echzell, Tobias Friedrich, Pascal Lenzner$^{(\boxtimes)}$, Louise Molitor,
Marcus Pappik, Friedrich Schöne, Fabian Sommer, and David Stangl

Hasso Plattner Institute, University of Potsdam, Potsdam, Germany
{Hagen.Echzell,Marcus.Pappik,friedrich.schoene,Fabian.Sommer,
David.Stangl}@student.hpi.de,
{Tobias.Friedrich,Pascal.Lenzner,Louise.Molitor}@hpi.de

Abstract. The phenomenon of residential segregation was captured by Schelling's famous segregation model where two types of agents are placed on a grid and an agent is content with her location if the fraction of her neighbors which have the same type as her is at least τ, for some $0 < \tau < 1$. Discontent agents simply swap their location with a randomly chosen other discontent agent or jump to a random empty cell.

We analyze a generalized game-theoretic model of Schelling segregation which allows more than two agent types and more general underlying graphs modeling the residential area. For this we show that both aspects heavily influence the dynamic properties and the tractability of finding an optimal placement. We map the boundary of when improving response dynamics (IRD) are guaranteed to converge and we prove several sharp threshold results where guaranteed IRD convergence suddenly turns into a strong non-convergence result: a violation of weak acyclicity. In particular, we show threshold results also for Schelling's original model, which is in contrast to the standard assumption in many empirical papers. In case of convergence we show that IRD find equilibria quickly.

Keywords: Schelling segregation · Convergence of improving response dynamics · Potential games · Computational hardness

1 Introduction

Residential segregation is a well-known phenomenon in many major metropolitan areas where local location choices by many individuals with preferences over their direct residential neighborhood yield cityscapes which are severely segregated along ethnical lines (see Fig. 1(a)). There, local strategic choices on the micro level lead to an emergent phenomenon on the macro level. This paradigm of "micromotives" versus "macrobehavior" [34] was first investigated and modeled by Schelling who proposed a simple stylized model for analyzing residential segregation [32,33]. With two types of individual agents and a grid serving as residential area, he demonstrated the emergence of segregated neighborhoods

© Springer Nature Switzerland AG 2019
I. Caragiannis et al. (Eds.): WINE 2019, LNCS 11920, pp. 156–170, 2019.
https://doi.org/10.1007/978-3-030-35389-6_12

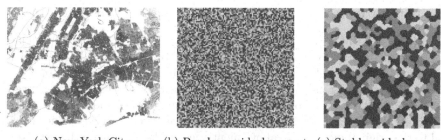

(a) New York City   (b) Random grid placement   (c) Stable grid placement

Fig. 1. (a) Residential segregation in New York City, color-coded by ethnicity. Every dot corresponds to a citizen. Snippet from the Racial Dot Map [10] based on 2010 US Census data. (b) Initial random placement on a grid in Schelling's model. (c) Equilibrium found for the instance in (b) with $\tau = \frac{1}{2}$ via IRD. (Color figure online)

under the following threshold behavior: agents are content with their current location if the fraction of agents of their own type in their neighborhood is at least τ, with $\tau \in (0,1)$ as a global parameter. Content agents do not move, discontent agents will swap their location with some other random discontent agent or perform a random jump to an unoccupied place. Schelling demonstrated by experiment that starting from a uniformly random distribution of the agents (see Fig. 1(b)) the induced random process yields a residential pattern which shows strong segregation (see Fig. 1(c)). While this is to be expected for intolerant agents, i.e., $\tau > \frac{1}{2}$, the astonishing finding of Schelling was that this also happens for tolerant agents, i.e., $\tau \leq \frac{1}{2}$. This explains why even in a very tolerant population segregation along racial, religious or socio-economical lines emerges.

Schelling's model became a landmark model in sociology and many variants of the model have been studied, e.g. Clark [12], Alba and Logan [1], Benard and Willer [5], Henry et al. [27] and Bruch [9]. A physical analogue was found by Vinković and Kirman [36] but Clark and Fosset [13] argued that such models do not enhance the understanding of the underlying social dynamics. In contrast, they promote agent-based models where the agents' utility function is inspired by real-world behavior. Such models can be easily simulated and many empirical studies have been conducted to investigate the influence of various parameters on the obtained segregation, e.g. the works by Fossett [18], which use the simulation framework SimSeg [19], Epstein and Axtell [17], Gaylord and d'Andria [22], Pancs and Vriend [31], Singh et al. [35] and Benenson et al. [6].

All these empirical studies consider a random process where discontent agents are activated at random and swap or jump to other randomly selected positions. In [19,31], agents change their location if this yields improved utility. This assumption of having rational agents matches the behavior of real-world agents more convincingly. In this papper we explore the properties of such strategic dynamic processes and the tractability of the induced optimization problems.

1.1 Related Work

Recently, a series of papers by Young [38], Zhang [39,40], Gerhold et al. [25], Brandt et al. [8,28], Barmpalias et al. [2,3] and Bhakta et al. [7] initiated a rigorous analysis of stochastic processes induced by Schelling's model. In these processes either two randomly chosen unhappy agents of different type swap positions [38–40] or a randomly chosen agent changes her type with a certain probability [2,3,7,8,28]. Both types of processes are closely related but not identical to the original model. The above mentioned works investigate the expected size of the obtained homogeneous regions and it is also shown that the stochastic processes starting from a uniform random agent placement converge with high probability to a stable placement. The convergence time was considered by Mobius & Rosenblat [29] who observe that the Markov chain analyzed in [38–40] has a very high mixing time. Bhakta et al. [7] show in the two-dimensional grid case a dichotomy in mixing times for high and very low τ values.

To the best of our knowledge, only a few papers have studied game-theoretic models of Schelling segregation. Pancs & Vriend [31] used different types of utility functions for their agents in extensive simulation experiments. On the theory side, Zhang [40,41] analyzed a model where the agents are endowed with a noisy single peaked utility function, which is a departure from the threshold behavior proposed by Schelling. Grauwin et al. [26] generalized the results. In contrast, the behavior of the original model is closely captured by a game-theoretic model which was proposed by Chauhan et al. [11]. The employed utility function depends on the type ratio in the neighborhood and increases linearly with the fraction of agents of the own type until a fraction of τ is reached. The authors of [11] investigate the convergence behavior of the induced sequential game where discontent agents are restricted either to performing only improving location swaps (Swap Schelling Game (SSG)) or are only allowed to jump to empty locations (Jump Schelling Game (JSG)). This corresponds to analyzing IRD, whose analysis is also our main contribution. We improve their main results in various ways by exactly characterizing when IRD convergence is ensured. In [11] an extension of Schelling's model is considered, where agents have preferences over different locations additionally strive for being close to their favorite one.

Very recently, Elkind et al. [16] studied a variant of the model in [11], where the agents are partitioned into stubborn agents who do not move and strategic agents who try to maximize the fraction of same-type agents in their neighborhood by jumping to a suitable empty location. This corresponds to a variant of the JSG with $\tau = 1$. They show that equilibria are not guaranteed to exist and that deciding whether equilibria or placements with certain social welfare exist is NP-hard. This relates to our hardness results for computing socially optimal states. They also prove that the price of anarchy and stability can be unbounded.

All mentioned works, with SimSeg [19] and Elkind et al. [16] as exceptions, assume that exactly two types of agents exist. In [19] and [16], agents only differentiate between agents of their own type and of other types. This is a very restricted point of view and this will correspond to our "one-versus-all" version.

1.2 Model and Notation

We consider a network $G = (V, E)$, with V the set of nodes and E the set of edges, which is connected, unweighted and undirected. The network G serves as the underlying graph modeling the residential area in which the agents will select a location. If every node in G has the same degree Δ, i.e., the same number of incident edges, then G is a Δ-*regular graph*. Let $deg_G(u)$ be the degree of a node $u \in V$ in G and let $\Gamma_G(u)$ denote the set of nodes $v \neq u$ so that an edge $\{u, v\}$ exists in E. We call $\Gamma_G(u)$ the *neighborhood* of u in network G. Let A be the set of agents and $P(A) = \{T_1, T_2, \ldots, T_k\}$ be any partition of A into k non-empty distinct sets, called *types*, which model racial/ethnic, religious or socio-economic groups. For $k = 2$ this corresponds to Schelling's original model [32,33] with two different types of agents. Let $t : A \mapsto P(A)$ be a surjective function such that $t(a) = T$ if $a \in T$. We say that agent a is of type $t(a)$. A state of our games is defined by an injective *placement* $p_G : A \mapsto V$ which assigns every agent to a node in the network G and we call $p_G(a)$ *agent a's location under placement p_G*. Two agents $a, b \in A$ are *neighbors under placement p_G* if $p_G(b) \in \Gamma_G(p_G(a))$. We denote the set of neighbors of a under placement p_G as $N_{p_G}(a)$. For any agent $a \in A$, we define $N_{p_G}^T(a) = \{b \in T \mid b \in N_{p_G}(a)\}$, as the set of agents of type T in the neighborhood of agent a under placement p_G.

For any agent $a \in A$ in a placement p_G, we define *agent a's positive neighborhood* $N_{p_G}^+(a)$ as $N_{p_G}^{t(a)}(a)$. For *agent a's negative neighborhood*, we define two different versions, called the *one-versus-all* and *one-versus-one* versions. In the one-versus-all version an agent wants a certain fraction of agents of her own type in her neighborhood, regardless of the specific types of neighboring agents with other types, so $N_{p_G}^-(a)$ is $N_{p_G}(a) \setminus N_{p_G}^+(a)$. In contrast to this, in the one-versus-one version an agent only compares the number of own-type agents to the number of agents in the largest group of agents with different type in her neighborhood. Thus, we define the negative neighborhood of an agent a under placement p_G as the set of neighboring agents of the type $T \neq t(a)$ that make up the largest proportion among all neighbors, i.e., $N_{p_G}^-(a) = N_{p_G}^T(a)$ such that $T \in P(A) \setminus \{t(a)\}$ and $|N_{p_G}^T(a)| \geq |N_{p_G}^{T'}(a)|$ for all $T' \in P(A) \setminus \{t(a)\}$. Notice that the one-versus-all and one-versus-one version coincide for $k = 2$, thus both versions generalize the two type case. If an agent a has no neighboring agents, i.e., $N_{p_G}(a) = \emptyset$, we say that a is *isolated*, otherwise a is *un-isolated*.

Let $\tau \in (0, 1)$ be the *intolerance parameter*. Similar to Schelling's model we say that an agent a is *content* with placement p_G if agent a is un-isolated and at least a τ-fraction of the agents in agent a's positive and negative neighborhood under p_G are in agent a's positive neighborhood. Hence, agent a is content if she is un-isolated and $\frac{|N_{p_G}^+(a)|}{|N_{p_G}^+(a)|+|N_{p_G}^-(a)|} \geq \tau$, otherwise a is *discontent* with placement p_G. We call the ratio $\mathrm{pnr}_{p_G}(a) = \frac{|N_{p_G}^+(a)|}{|N_{p_G}^+(a)|+|N_{p_G}^-(a)|}$ the *positive neighborhood ratio* of agent a. An agent's aim is to find a node in the given network where she is content or, if this is not possible, where she has the highest possible positive neighborhood ratio. Therefore, and analogous to [11], we define the *cost function* of an agent a in a placement p_G for network G as follows:

$$\text{cost}_{p_G}(a) = \begin{cases} \max\{0, \tau - \text{pnr}_{p_G}(a)\}, & \text{if } a \text{ is un-isolated}, \\ \tau, & \text{if } a \text{ is isolated}. \end{cases}$$

Thus, agent a is content with placement p_G, if and only if $\text{cost}_{p_G}(a) = 0$. The *placement cost*, denoted $\text{cost}_{p_G}(A)$, of a placement p_G in a network G is simply the number of all discontent agents: $\text{cost}_{p_G}(A) = |\{a \in A \mid \text{cost}_{p_G}(a) \neq 0\}|$.

The *strategy space* of an agent is the set of all nodes in the network G. An agent can change her strategy either via swapping with another agent who agrees or via jumping to another unoccupied node in network. This yields the *Swap Schelling Game (SSG)* and the *Jump Schelling Game (JSG)*.

For the SSG we will assume that all nodes of G are occupied. A *location swap*, or *swap*, of two agents $a, b \in A$ under placement p_G is to exchange the occupied nodes of both agents. This yields a new placement p'_G with $p'_G(a) = p_G(b)$, $p'_G(b) = p_G(a)$ and $p_G(x) = p'_G(x)$, for any other agent $x \in A \setminus \{a, b\}$. Two agents $a, b \in A$ would only agree to such a swap if it strictly decreases the cost of both agents, i.e., $\text{cost}_{p'_G}(a) < \text{cost}_{p_G}(a)$ and $\text{cost}_{p'_G}(b) < \text{cost}_{p_G}(b)$. Hence, swapping agents are always of different types. If for some placement p_G no improving swap exists, then we say that p_G is *swap-stable*.

In the JSG we assume that there exist empty nodes in the underlying graph and an agent can change her strategy to any currently empty node, which we denote as a *jump* to that node. An agent will only jump to another empty node, if this strictly decreases her cost. An equilibrium placement in the JSG where no agent can improve via jumping is called *jump-stable*.

If the game is clear from the context, we will simply say that a placement p_G is *stable*. If we have more than two different agent types we denote the one-versus-all version of the SSG and the JSG as $1 - k - SSG$ and $1 - k - JSG$, respectively and the one-versus-one version of both games as $1 - 1 - SSG$ and $1 - 1 - JSG$, respectively.

We analyze whether *improving response dynamics (IRD)*, i.e., the natural approach for finding equilibrium states where agents sequentially try to change towards better strategies until no agent can further improve, will converge. For showing this we employ *ordinal potential functions*. Such a function Φ maps placements to real numbers such that if an agent (or a pair of agents) under placement p_G can improve by a jump (or a swap) which results in placement p'_G then $\Phi(p_G) > \Phi(p'_G)$ holds. That is, any improving strategy change also decreases the potential function value. The existence of an ordinal potential function shows that a game is a *potential game* [30], which guarantees the existence of pure equilibria and that IRD must terminate in an equilibrium. In contrast, an *improving response cycle (IRC)* is a sequence of improving strategy changes which visits the same state of the game twice. The existence of an IRC directly implies that a potential function cannot exist and thus, that IRD may not terminate. However, even with existing IRCs it is still possible, that from any state of the game there exists a finite sequence of improving strategy-changes which leads to an equilibrium. In this case the game is *weakly acyclic* [37]. Thus, a strong non-convergence result is a proof that a game is not weakly acyclic.

1.3 Our Contribution

Our main contribution is a thorough investigation of the convergence behavior of IRD in variants of Schelling's model. Previous work, including Schelling's original papers and all the mentioned empirical simulation studies, assume that IRD always converge to an equilibrium. We challenge this by precisely mapping the boundary of when IRD are assured to find an equilibrium. We show that IRD behave radically different in the swap version compared to the jump version. Moreover, we show that this contrasting behavior can even be found within these two variants. We demonstrate the extreme cases of guaranteed IRD convergence and strong non-convergence results, i.e., that even weak acyclicity is violated. For this, we provide sharp threshold results where for some τ^* IRD are guaranteed to convergence for $\tau \leq \tau^*$ and we have non-weak-acyclicity for $\tau > \tau^*$, depending on the underlying graph. See Table 1.

Table 1. Results regarding IRD. "reg." stands for Δ-regular graphs, "arb" for arbitrary graphs, which model the residential area. "✓" denotes that IRD converge to an equilibrium, "o" denotes the existence of an IRC. "×" denotes that the version is not weakly acyclic. If τ is omitted, the result holds for any $0 < \tau < 1$.

	1-k-SSG	1-1-SSG	1-k-JSG	1-1-JSG
reg	✓(Theorem 2)	✓(Theorem 4) $\tau \leq \frac{1}{\Delta}$ o (Theorem 5) $\tau \geq \frac{6}{\Delta}$	✓(Theorem 7) $\tau \leq \frac{2}{\Delta}$ o (Theorem 8) $\tau > \frac{2}{\Delta}$	✓(Theorem 10) $\tau \leq \frac{1}{\Delta}$ o (Theorem 11) $\tau > \frac{2}{\Delta}$
arb	✓[11] $k = 2$, $\tau \leq \frac{1}{2}$ ×(Theorems 1 and 3) ow	×(Theorem 6)	×(Theorem 9)	×(Theorem 12)

In case of IRD convergence, we show that this happens after $\mathcal{O}(|E|)$ many jumps/swaps on a graph $G = (V, E)$ and in [15] we show via experiments that this bound is met by instances with randomly chosen initial placements.

Besides analyzing IRD, we start a discussion about segregation models with more than two agent types. Besides the simple generalization of differentiating only between own type and other types, i.e., the 1-k-SSG and 1-k-JSG, we propose a more natural alternative, called the 1-1-SSG and the 1-1-JSG, where agents compare the type ratios only with the largest subgroup in their neighborhood. The idea here is that a minority group mainly cares about if there is a dominant other group within the neighborhood.

Moreover, we investigate the influence of the underlying graph on the hardness of computing an optimal placement. We show that computing this is NP-hard for arbitrary underlying graphs if $\tau = \frac{1}{2}$ or if τ is sufficiently high. In contrast to this, we provide an efficient algorithm for computing the optimum placement on a 2-regular graph with two agent types. The number of agent types also has an influence: we establish NP-hardness even on 2-regular graphs if there are sufficiently many agent types.

All details omitted due to space constraints can be found in [15].

2 Schelling Dynamics for the Swap Schelling Game

In this section we analyze the convergence behavior of IRD for the SSG. The 1-k-SSG seems to be a straightforward generalization of the two type case. An agent simply compares the number of neighbors of her type with the total number of neighbors. Interestingly, our IRD convergence results for the 1-k-SSG with $k > 2$ for arbitrary networks for $\tau \leq \frac{1}{2}$ are in sharp contrast to the results for $k = 2$ proved in [11]: On arbitrary networks with tolerant agents, i.e., with $\tau \leq \frac{1}{2}$, and $k > 2$ types IRD convergence is no longer guaranteed.

For the 1-1-variant an agent compares the number of neighboring agents of her type with the size of the largest group of agents with a different type in her neighborhood. This captures the realistic setting where agents simply try to avoid being in a neighborhood where another group of agents dominates. We will show that even on a Δ-regular network an IRC exists for sufficiently high τ.

2.1 IRD Convergence for the One-versus-All Version

The existence of a potential function for the SSG on arbitrary networks with $\tau \leq \frac{1}{2}$ was shown before in [11]. We show that this bound is tight.

Theorem 1. *IRD are not guaranteed to converge in the SSG with $k = 2$ for $\tau \in \left(\frac{1}{2}, 1\right)$ on arbitrary networks. Moreover, weak acyclicity is violated.*

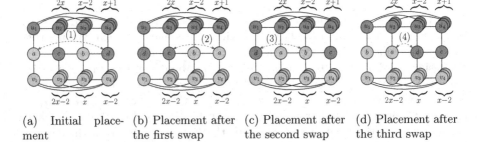

(a) Initial placement (b) Placement after the first swap (c) Placement after the second swap (d) Placement after the third swap

Fig. 2. An IRC for the SSG with $x = \max\left(\lceil \frac{1}{\tau - 0.5} \rceil, \lceil \frac{1}{2 - 2\tau} \rceil\right)$ for $\tau \in \left(\frac{1}{2}, 1\right)$. The agents types are marked orange and blue. Multiple nodes in series represent a clique of nodes of the stated size. Edges between cliques or between a clique and single nodes represent that all involved nodes are completely interconnected. (Color figure online)

Proof (sketch). We prove the statement by providing an IRC where in every step exactly one improving swap is possible. The construction is shown in Fig. 2. □

We now generalize the results from [11] to the 1-k-SSG for any $k \geq 2$.

Theorem 2. *IRD are guaranteed to converge in at most $|E|$ moves for the 1-k-SSG with $\tau \in (0, 1)$ on any Δ-regular network $G = (V, E)$.*

Proof (sketch). We show that $\Phi(p_G) = \frac{1}{2} \sum_{a \in A} |N_{p_G}^-(a)|$ is an ordinal potential function. A swap between two agents a and b changes the current placement p_G only in the locations of the involved agents and yields a new placement p_G'. It holds for agent a (and agent b likewise) $\frac{|N_{p_G}^+(a)|}{\Delta} < \frac{|N_{p_G'}^+(a)|}{\Delta}$. Thus, $|N_{p_G}^+(a)| < |N_{p_G'}^+(a)| \iff \Delta - |N_{p_G}^-(a)| < \Delta - |N_{p_G'}^-(a)| \iff |N_{p_G'}^-(a)| < |N_{p_G}^-(a)|$. Since $\Phi(p_G) \leq |E|$ and since $\Phi(p_G)$ decreases after every swap by at least 1 IRD find an equilibrium in at most $|E|$ many steps.   □

We contrast the above result by showing that guaranteed IRD convergence is impossible for any τ on arbitrary networks. This emphasizes the influence of the number of agent types on the convergence behavior of the IRD.

Theorem 3. *IRD are not guaranteed to converge in the 1-k-SSG with $k > 2$ for $\tau \in (0, 1)$ on arbitrary networks. Moreover, weak acyclicity is violated.*

Proof (sketch). We give an example of an IRC, where always exactly one improving swap exists. Together with Theorem 1 this yields the statement. See Fig. 3.
□

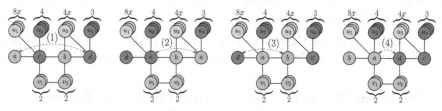

(a) Initial place-ment   (b) Placement after the first swap   (c) Placement after the second swap   (d) Placement after the third swap

Fig. 3. An IRC for the 1-k-SSG with $x > \frac{3}{4\tau} - 1$ for any $\tau \in (0, 0.5]$. Agent types are marked orange, blue and gray. Multiple nodes in series represent a clique of nodes of the stated size. Edges between cliques or between a clique and single nodes represent that all involved nodes are completely interconnected. (Color figure online)

2.2   IRD Convergence for the One-versus-One Version

Remember, that in the 1-1-SSG and 1-1-JSG, respectively, an agent only considers the largest group of different type neighboring agents. We start with a simple positive result for the 1-1-SSG.

Theorem 4. *IRD are guaranteed to converge in at most $\frac{|A|}{2}$ moves, where A is the set of agents, for the 1-1-SSG with $\tau \leq \frac{1}{\Delta}$ on any Δ-regular network $G = (V, E)$.*

Proof (sketch). Any agent a who is discontent has cost τ. Since a only considers a swap that decreases her cost, the cost of a can be at most $\max(0, \tau - \frac{1}{\Delta})$ after swapping, which means a is content. Each agent will participate in at most one swap. Therefore, the game converges after at most $\frac{|A|}{2}$ swaps.   □

If τ is high enough, then the 1-1-SSG is no longer a potential game.

Theorem 5. *IRD are not guaranteed to converge in the 1-1-SSG for $\tau \geq \frac{6}{\Delta}$ on Δ-regular networks.*

Proof (sketch). Consider Fig. 4 with $x > \frac{5(1-\tau)}{6\tau}$. We omit edges between the cliques u_1, u_2 and u_3 of gray agents. The highest degree in the graph is $6(x+1)$. To make the graph regular, we insert new nodes filled with agents such that each new agent is the only agent of its type, and connect these new nodes with existing nodes and each other as needed. From $x > \frac{5(1-\tau)}{6\tau}$ and $\Delta = 6(x+1)$ we obtain $\tau \geq \frac{6}{\Delta}$, where equality is reached if x is chosen as low as possible.   □

The situation is much worse on arbitrary graphs as the following theorem shows.

Theorem 6. *IRD are not guaranteed to converge in the 1-1-SSG for $\tau \in (0, 1)$ on arbitrary networks. Moreover, weak acyclicity is violated.*

Proof (sketch). We show the statement by giving an example for an IRC where in every step exactly one improving swap exists. Consider Fig. 4.   □

3   Schelling Dynamics for the Jump Schelling Game

We now analyze the convergence behavior of IRD for the JSG.

3.1   IRD Convergence for the One-versus-All Version

We first turn our focus to the 1-k-JSG, where an agent compares the number of neighbors of her type with the total number of neighbors, and prove a sharp threshold result for the convergence of IRD on Δ-regular graphs, for any $\Delta \geq 2$. Moreover, we show that the game is not weakly acyclic on arbitrary graphs.

Theorem 7. *IRD are guaranteed to converge in $\mathcal{O}(|E|)$ steps for the 1-k-JSG with $\tau \leq \frac{2}{\Delta}$ on any Δ-regular network $G = (V, E)$.*

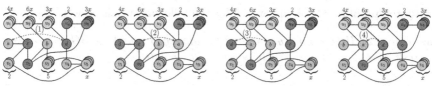

(a) Initial placement (b) Placement after the first swap (c) Placement after the second swap (d) Placement after the third swap

Fig. 4. An IRC with exactly one improving swap per step for the 1-1-SSG with $x >$ $\max\left(\frac{5(1-\tau)}{6\tau}, \frac{\tau}{1-\tau}\right)$ for any $\tau \in (0,1)$. Agents types are marked orange, blue and gray. Multiple nodes in series represent a clique of nodes of the stated size. Edges between cliques or between a clique and single nodes represent that all involved nodes are completely interconnected. (Color figure online)

Proof (sketch). For any Δ-regular network G we define the weight $w_{p_G}(e)$ of any edge $e = \{u, v\} \in E$ with $\frac{1}{2} - \frac{1}{2\Delta} < c < \frac{1}{2}$ as:

$$w_{p_G}(e) = \begin{cases} 1, & \text{if } u \text{ and } v \text{ are occupied by agents of different types for } p_G, \\ c, & \text{if either } u \text{ or } v \text{ , but not both, are empty for } p_G, \\ 0, & \text{otherwise.} \end{cases}$$

We prove that $\Phi(p_G) = \sum_{e \in E} w_{p_G}(e)$ is an ordinal potential function. An agent becomes content if she has two neighbors of her type. There is no incentive for agent y to decrease the number of same-type neighbors.   □

Actually Theorem 7 is tight and convergence is not guaranteed if $\tau > \frac{2}{\Delta}$.

Theorem 8. *The 1-k-JSG for $\tau > \frac{2}{\Delta}$ on Δ-regular graphs is no potential game.*

If the underlying network is an arbitrary network the situation is worse.

Theorem 9. *IRD are not guaranteed to converge in the 1-k-JSG for $\tau \in (0,1)$ on arbitrary networks. Moreover, weak acyclicity is violated.*

3.2 IRD Convergence for the One-versus-One Version

Now we turn to the 1-1-JSG. By using the same proof as in Theorem 4 with jumps instead of swaps we get the following positive result.

Theorem 10. *IRD are guaranteed to converge in at most $\frac{|A|}{2}$ moves for the 1-1-JSG with $\tau \leq \frac{1}{\Delta}$ on Δ-regular networks.*

The same IRC which proves Theorem 8 for the 1-k-JSG yields the next result.

Theorem 11. *IRD may not converge in the 1-1-JSG for $\tau > \frac{2}{\Delta}$ on Δ-regular graphs.*

Finally the proof of Theorem 9 works for the following result as well.

Theorem 12. *IRD are not guaranteed to converge in the* 1-1-*JSG for* $\tau \in (0,1)$ *on arbitrary networks and weakly acyclicity is violated.*

4 Hardness of Finding Optimal Placements

Here, we investigate the computational hardness of computing an optimal placement, i.e., a placement where as many agents as possible are content.

4.1 Hardness Properties for Two Types

We start with two types of agents and show that finding an optimal placement for the SSG in an arbitrary network G is NP-hard by giving a reduction from the BALANCED SATISFACTORY PROBLEM was introduced in [23,24] and proven to be NP-hard in [4]. This result directly implies that finding an optimal placement for the JSG with no empty nodes is NP-hard as well.

Theorem 13. *Finding an optimal placement of agents for the two types SSG in a network* G *is NP-hard for* $\tau = \frac{1}{2}$.

The proof of the above theorem relies on the fact that there are no empty nodes. The computational hardness of the JSG changes if many empty nodes exist. Obviously, it is easy to find an optimal placement if there are enough empty nodes to separate both types of agents completely and a suitable separator is known. Mapping the boundary for the transition from NP-hardness to efficient computation is a challenging question for future work.

Next we show that finding an optimal placement is hard for high τ via a reduction from MINIMUM CUT INTO EQUAL SIZE (MCIES) which was proven to be NP-hard in [21].

Theorem 14. *Finding an optimal placement in the SSG on an arbitrary network* $G = (V, E)$ *with maximum node degree* $\Delta_G = \max\{deg_G(v) \mid v \in V\}$ *is NP-hard for* $\tau > \frac{3\Delta_G}{3\Delta_G + 1}$.

Proof (sketch). Given a network $G = (V, E)$ and $W \in \mathbb{N}$. MCIES is the decision whether there is a partition V_1, V_2 with $V_1 \cup V_2 = V$, $V_1 \cap V_2 = \emptyset$ and $|V_1| = |V_2|$ such that $|\{\{v_1, v_2\} \in V \mid v_1 \in V_1, v_2 \in V_2\}| \leq W$. Let $\Delta_G = \max\{deg_G(v) \mid v \in V\}$ be the maximum node degree in G. We create a network $G' = (V', E')$ in which every node $v \in V$ is replaced by a clique C_v in G' of size $3\Delta_G + 1$. Each edge $\{u, v\} \in E$ will be replaced by an edge $\{u', v'\}$ between two nodes $u' \in C_u$ and $v' \in C_v$ such that each node in G' has at most one neighbor outside its clique. Therefore, the degree of nodes in G' is either $3\Delta_G$ or $3\Delta_G + 1$. We have two different agent types, each consisting of $\frac{|V'|}{2}$ agents. Let $\tau > \frac{\Delta_{G'} - 1}{\Delta_{G'}} = \frac{3\Delta_G}{3\Delta_G + 1}$. For a placement $p_{G'}$ to be optimal, all cliques C have to be uniform, i.e. assign agents of the same type to each node in C. $\qquad \square$

We used a placement cost function which counts the number of discontent agents. However, we remark that even if we change this definition into summing up the cost of all agents, i.e., $\text{cost}'_{p_G}(A) = \sum_{a \in A} \text{cost}_{p_G}(a)$, like *social cost*, the above hardness results still hold. This relates to the hardness results in [16] which hold for the JSG with $\tau = 1$ in the presence of stubborn agents.

We contrast the above results by providing an efficient algorithm for computing an optimal placement for the SSG on a 2-regular network with $k = 2$ by employing a well-known dynamic programming algorithm for SUBSET SUM [14,20].

Theorem 15. *Finding an optimal placement of agents of two types in the SSG on a 2-regular network with n nodes can be done in $\mathcal{O}(n^2)$ for $\tau > \frac{1}{2}$.*

Optimal placements for the JSG can be found with an analogous algorithm.

4.2 Hardness Properties for More Types

We now show that also the number of different agent types has an influence on the computational hardness of finding an optimal placement. We establish NP-hardness even on 2-regular networks if there are sufficiently many agent types by giving a reduction from 3-PARTITION which was proven to be NP-hard in [20].

Theorem 16. *Finding an optimal placement of agents with $k > 2$ types in the 1-1-SSG and 1-k-SSG on a 2-regular network with $\tau > \frac{1}{2}$ is NP-hard.*

We want to emphasize that solving the hardness question for optimal placements does not allow equivalent statements for computing stable placements.

Theorem 17. *For the SSG with two different types of agents there is a network G where no optimal placement is stable.*

Proof (sketch). We prove the statement by giving an example. See Fig. 5.   □

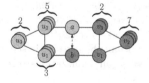 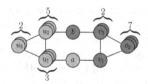

Fig. 5. The optimal placement (left) is not in equilibrium for $\tau > 0.9$ since agents a and b profit from swapping (right).

5   Conclusion and Open Questions

We provided tight threshold results for the IRD convergence for several game-theoretic versions of Schelling's segregation model. Furthermore, we found that the number of agent types and the underlying graph both have severe impact on the computational hardness of computing optimal placements.

It remains open whether IRD always converge for 1-1-SSG with $\tau \in \left(\frac{1}{\Delta}, \frac{6}{\Delta}\right)$, and for the 1-1-JSG with $\tau \in \left(\frac{1}{\Delta}, \frac{2}{\Delta}\right)$. Since most versions are not guaranteed to converge via IRD, the existence of stable placements for all graph types is an interesting open problem. For the 1-k-JSG and $\tau = 1$ it was shown in [16] that stable placements exist if the underlying network is a star or a graph with maximum degree 2 and that there are trees which do not admit stable placements. Unfortunately, our examples for IRCs or non-weak-acyclicity cannot be used as counter-examples since they all admit stable placements. We conjecture that equilibria always exist on regular and almost regular graphs but that for all versions for which we constructed IRCs on non-regular graphs there exist underlying graphs which do not admit stable placements.

Also the computational hardness of finding optimal placements deserves further study and could be extended to other interesting states, e.g., stable states with low segregation. Moreover, from a Mechanism Design point of view it could be interesting to study mechanisms which guide agents from a highly segregated state towards equilibria with low segregation.

Our IRD convergence results can be adapted to hold for the extended model in [11], where agents have single-peaked preferences over the locations. Moreover, we are positive that also our computational hardness results can be carried over.

Last but not least, we emphasize that there are many possible ways to model Schelling segregation with at least three agent types. For example, types could have preferences over other types which then yields a rich unexplored setting.

References

1. Alba, R.D., Logan, J.R.: Minority proximity to whites in suburbs: an individual-level analysis of segregation. Am. J. Sociol. **98**(6), 1388–1427 (1993)
2. Barmpalias, G., Elwes, R., Lewis-Pye, A.: Unperturbed schelling segregation in two or three dimensions. J. Stat. Phys. **164**(6), 1460–1487 (2016)
3. Barmpalias, G., Elwes, R., Lewis-Pye, A.: Digital morphogenesis via schelling segregation. In: 2014 IEEE 55th Annual Symposium on Foundations of Computer Science (FOCS), pp. 156–165. IEEE (2014)
4. Bazgan, C., Tuza, Z., Vanderpooten, D.: The satisfactory partition problem. Discret. Appl. Math. **154**(8), 1236–1245 (2006)
5. Benard, S., Willer, R.: A wealth and status-based model of residential segregation. Math. Sociol. **31**(2), 149–174 (2007)
6. Benenson, I., Hatna, E., Or, E.: From schelling to spatially explicit modeling of urban ethnic and economic residential dynamics. Sociol. Methods Res. **37**(4), 463–497 (2009)

7. Bhakta, P., Miracle, S., Randall, D.: Clustering and mixing times for segregation models on $\mathcal{Z}^2$. In: Symposium on Discrete Algorithms (SODA), pp. 327–340 (2014)
8. Brandt, C., Immorlica, N., Kamath, G., Kleinberg, R.: An analysis of one-dimensional schelling segregation. In: Proceedings of the Forty-Fourth Annual ACM Symposium on Theory of Computing (STOC), pp. 789–804. ACM (2012)
9. Bruch, E.E.: How population structure shapes neighborhood segregation. Am. J. Sociol. 119(5), 1221–1278 (2014)
10. Cable, D.: The racial dot map. Weldon Cooper Center for Public Service, University of Virginia (2013). https://demographics.coopercenter.org/Racial-Dot-Map/
11. Chauhan, A., Lenzner, P., Molitor, L.: Schelling segregation with strategic agents. In: Deng, X. (ed.) SAGT 2018. LNCS, vol. 11059, pp. 137–149. Springer, Cham (2018). https://doi.org/10.1007/978-3-319-99660-8_13
12. Clark, W.A.V.: Residential segregation in american cities: a review and interpretation. Popul. Res. Policy Rev. 5(2), 95–127 (1986)
13. Clark, W.A.V., Fossett, M.: Understanding the social context of the schelling segregation model. Proc. Natl. Acad. Sci. 105(11), 4109–4114 (2008)
14. Cormen, T.H., Leiserson, C.E., Rivest, R.L., Stein, C.: Introduction to Algorithms. MIT Press and McGraw-Hill, Cambridge (2001)
15. Echzell, H., et al.: Convergence and hardness of strategic schelling segregation. arXiv:1907.07513 (2019)
16. Elkind, E., Gan, J., Igarashi, A., Suksompong, W., Voudouris, A.A.: Schelling games on graphs. In: Proceedings of the Twenty-Eighth International Joint Conference on Artificial Intelligence, IJCAI 2019, pp. 266–272 (2019)
17. Epstein, J.M., Axtell, R.: Growing Artificial Societies: Social Science from the Bottom Up. The Brookings Institution, Washington, D.C. (1996)
18. Fossett, M.: Ethnic preferences, social distance dynamics, and residential segregation: theoretical explorations using simulation analysis. J. Math. Sociol. 30(3–4), 185–273 (2006)
19. Fossett, M.A.: SimSeg-a computer program to simulate the dynamics of residential segregation by social and ethnic status. Texas A&M University, Race and Ethnic Studies Institute Technical Report and Program (1998)
20. Garey, M.R., Johnson, D.S.: Computers and intractability. W. H. Freeman and Co., San Francisco (1979). A guide to the theory of NP-completeness, A Series of Books in the Mathematical Sciences
21. Garey, M., Johnson, D., Stockmeyer, L.: Some simplified NP-complete graph problems. Theor. Comput. Sci. 1(3), 237–267 (1976)
22. Gaylord, R.J., D'Andria, L.J.: Simulating Society: A "Mathematica" Toolkit for Modeling Socioeconomic Behaviour. Springer, Heidelberg (1998). https://doi.org/10.1007/978-1-4612-1726-8
23. Gerber, M.U., Kobler, D.: Partitioning a graph to satisfy all vertices. Technical report (1998)
24. Gerber, M.U., Kobler, D.: Algorithmic approach to the satisfactory graph partitioning problem. Eur. J. Oper. Res. 125, 283–291 (2000)
25. Gerhold, S., Glebsky, L., Schneider, C., Weiss, H., Zimmermann, B.: Computing the complexity for schelling segregation models. Commun. Nonlinear Sci. Numer. Simul. 13, 2236–2245 (2008)
26. Grauwin, S., Goffette-Nagot, F., Jensen, P.: Dyanmic models of residential segregation: an analytical solution. J. Public Econ. 96, 124–141 (2012)
27. Henry, A.D., Prałat, P., Zhang, C.Q.: Emergence of segregation in evolving social networks. Proc. Natl. Acad. Sci. 108(21), 8605–8610 (2011)

28. Immorlica, N., Kleinbergt, R., Lucier, B., Zadomighaddam, M.: Exponential segregation in a two-dimensional schelling model with tolerant individuals. In: Proceedings of the Twenty-Eighth Annual ACM-SIAM Symposium on Discrete Algorithms (SODA), pp. 984–993. SIAM (2017)
29. Mobius, M., Rosenblat, T.: Computing the complexity for schelling segregation models. Unpublished manuscript (2000)
30. Monderer, D., Shapley, L.S.: Potential games. Games Econ. Behav. **14**(1), 124–143 (1996)
31. Pancs, R., Vriend, N.J.: Schelling's spatial proximity model of segregation revisited. J. Public Econ. **91**(1), 1–24 (2007)
32. Schelling, T.C.: Models of segregation. Am. Econ. Rev. **59**(2), 488–493 (1969)
33. Schelling, T.C.: Dynamic models of segregation. J. Math. Sociol. **1**(2), 143–186 (1971)
34. Schelling, T.C.: Micromotives and Macrobehavior. WW Norton & Company, New York (2006)
35. Singh, A., Vainchtein, D., Weiss, H.: Schelling's segregation model: parameters, scaling, and aggregation. Demogr. Res. **21**(12), 341–366 (2009)
36. Vinković, D., Kirman, A.: A physical analogue of the schelling model. Proc. Natl. Acad. Sci. **103**(51), 19261–19265 (2006)
37. Young, H.P.: The evolution of conventions. Econ.: J. Econ. Soc. **61**, 57–84 (1993)
38. Young, H.P.: Individual Strategy and Social Structure: An Evolutionary Theory of Institutions. Princeton University Press, Princeton (1998)
39. Zhang, J.: A dynamic model of residential segregation. J. Math. Sociol. **28**(3), 147–170 (2004)
40. Zhang, J.: Residential segregation in an all-integrationist world. J. Econ. Behav. Organ. **54**(4), 533–550 (2004)
41. Zhang, J.: Tipping and residential segregation: a unified schelling model. J. Reg. Sci. **51**(1), 167–193 (2011)

Automated Optimal OSP Mechanisms for Set Systems
The Case of Small Domains

Diodato Ferraioli[1]([⊠]) [iD], Adrian Meier[2], Paolo Penna[2], and Carmine Ventre[3] [iD]

[1] Università degli Studi di Salerno, Fisciano, Italy
dferraioli@unisa.it
[2] ETH Zurich, Zürich, Switzerland
meiera@student.ethz.ch, paolo.penna@inf.ethz.ch
[3] King's College London, London, UK
carmine.ventre@kcl.ac.uk

Abstract. Obviously strategyproof (OSP) mechanisms have recently come to the fore as a tool to deal with imperfect rationality. They, in fact, incentivize people with no contingent reasoning skills to "follow the protocol" and be honest. However, their exact power is still to be determined. For example, even for settings relatively well understood, such as binary allocation problems, it is not clear when optimal solutions can be computed with OSP mechanisms.

We here consider this question for the large class of set system problems, where selfish agents with imperfect rationality own elements whose cost can take one among few values. In our main result, we give a characterization of the instances for which the optimum is possible. The mechanism we provide uses a combination of ascending and descending auctions, thus extending to a large class of settings a design paradigm for OSP mechanisms recently introduced in [9]. Finally, we dig deeper in the characterizing property and observe that the set of conditions can be quickly verified algorithmically. The combination of our mechanism and algorithmic characterization gives rise to the first example of automated mechanism design for OSP.

Keywords: Extensive form mechanisms · Bounded rationality

1 Introduction

The role of incentives in the design of algorithms has been a very active research area in the last two decades. Mechanism design has as its main objective the alignment of the objectives of the designer (e.g., optimality of the solution) with those of self-interested agents (e.g., maximize their utility). The crucial assumption made in the area is that these self-interested agents have perfect

D. Ferraioli—This author is partially supported by GNCS-INdAM and by the Italian MIUR PRIN 2017 Project ALGADIMAR "Algorithms, Games, and Digital Markets".

I. Caragiannis et al. (Eds.): WINE 2019, LNCS 11920, pp. 171–185, 2019.
https://doi.org/10.1007/978-3-030-35389-6_13

rationality: they will be able to ascertain that there is no point in strategizing, whenever the mechanism is proved to be truthful (a.k.a., strategyproof (SP)).

Unfortunately this might be too strong an assumption for practical applications of these theoretically sound mechanisms. Even for the well-known second-price auction, bidders lie when submitting sealed bids but are truthful when the mechanism is implemented via an ascending auction [14]. Intuitively, this means that it is easier to understand how to play the latter implementation of Vickrey auction, whilst the former can be confusing for agents with imperfect rationality. The recent definition of *obviously strategyproof (OSP)* mechanisms [16] formalizes how a different (extensive-form) *implementation* can make it *obvious* for an agent to decide what strategy to adopt. Roughly speaking, in OSP mechanisms, the utility for the *worst scenario* when truth-telling is at least as good as that of the *best scenario* when cheating. Li [16] proves that OSP mechanisms are obvious to understand for people without any contingent reasoning skill.

Research about the power of OSP mechanisms has barely scratched the surface. While it is clear that ascending/descending price auctions are OSP (as it is obvious for a bidder to decide whether to quit the auction or not), few general paradigms are known for the design of OSP mechanisms that return "good" (e.g., optimal) solutions. *Deferred-acceptance* (DA) mechanisms [18] are OSP (as they essentially are ascending price auctions), but unfortunately their performance (approximation guarantee) for several optimization problems is quite poor compared to what strategyproof mechanisms can do [6,9]. A combination of ascending and descending auctions has recently been given in [9] for the well-known scheduling related machines problem; the mechanism and its analysis rely on a generalization of the cycle monotonicity (CMON) technique, that allows to focus on the algorithmic component of OSP mechanisms.

A setting which is relatively better understood is the case of binary allocation problems, such as set systems. Here we are given a ground set of elements, each controlled by a selfish agent who privately knows the cost of the element, and a set of feasible solutions, i.e., subsets of elements in the ground set. The cost of each solution is the sum of the costs of its elements. The objective is to compute the feasible solution of minimum cost. Each agent can then be either selected or not. We normalize the utility of unselected agents to 0, whilst we use a quasi-linear utility for the selected agents, defined as the difference between the payment received from the mechanism and the cost of the element she contributes to the chosen solution. Li characterizes the class of OSP mechanisms for binary allocation problems, when the agents' domain is $[t_{\min}, t_{\max}]$, in terms of *personal clock auctions* (PCAs) – essentially, each agent faces either a descending or an ascending price auction. We are interested in the power of OSP mechanisms; in particular when can we design an OSP optimal mechanism for set systems?

To highlight the issues behind this question, let us consider a special set system, namely *path auctions*, as introduced in [19]. In this problem, each edge corresponds to a link that is owned by a selfish agent, the cost for using link i is some private nonnegative value t_i which is known only to agent i, and the goal is to pick the shortest path between two given nodes s and t.

Can we compute the shortest path whilst guaranteeing OSP? For a graph consisting of *parallel links*, we know from [16] that the answer is yes via a simple descending auction to select the cheaper edge. Already for *slightly* more general graphs, the answer is unclear. Consider, for example, the graph in Fig. 1(a). To make things even simpler let us restrict to a two-value domain $\{L, H\}$, i.e., edges cost either L or $H > 2L$. (Note that this means that we cannot rely on the PCA characterization, since our domains are not continuous.) In this setting, a simple OSP mechanism can be designed by querying the agents according to the *implementation tree* (i.e., a querying protocol where different actions are taken according to the answers received) in Figure 1(b). This algorithm is augmented with the following payments: H for edges in the selected path, 0 otherwise. It is not hard to see that, for every edge e, it is not possible that e is selected when she declares that her type is H and it is not selected when she says L. In particular, edge (s, t) is always selected when she says L, while the remaining edges are never selected when they declare H. Then, if e declares her true type, she receives a utility of $H - L$ if the true type is L and e is selected, and 0 otherwise; by inspection, she would receive at most the same utility when cheating. It turns out that this argument is enough to prove that the mechanism is indeed OSP. Does the same approach work, for example, on the *slightly* more general graph in Fig. 1(c)? Consider an edge e that is queried before the type of the remaining edges is known (that is, the first edge to be queried in a sequential mechanism, or an arbitrary edge in a direct revelation mechanism). Suppose that the type of this edge is L. If she declares her type truthfully, then the worst that may occur is that the corresponding path is not selected (that occurs when this path costs $H + L$ and the alternative path costs $2L$), and thus e receives utility 0. If this edge, instead, cheats and declares H, then it is possible that the corresponding path is selected (if it costs $H+L$ and the alternative path costs $2H$) and e receives utility $H - L$. Thus, it is not obvious for an edge e lacking contingent reasoning skills, to understand that being truthful is dominant. For which graphs can we then design an OSP optimal mechanism? The goal of this work is to answer this kind of questions for set system problems.

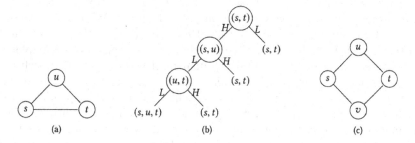

Fig. 1. Two instances of path auctions are shown in (a) and (c), while (b) is an OSP mechanism for instance (a).

Our Contribution. Our main result is a complete *characterization* of OSP optimal mechanisms for set system problems (which include path auctions as a special case). To prove our results, we adopt the CMON technique developed in [9]. CMON is a powerful technique in that it allows to abstract the OSP constraints (which depend on both the solution – e.g., the shortest path – and the implementation tree) and reduces the existence of OSP mechanisms to the absence of negative-weight cycles in a carefully defined graph. This is very similar to CMON for truthful mechanisms; the difference, however, is that whilst for SP it is enough to focus on cycles of length two for essentially all domains of interest [22], for OSP, 2-cycles are in general sufficient only for small domains (of up to three-values) [9]. Hence, while the necessary condition of our characterization holds irrespectively of the domain size, since non-negative 2-cycles are always necessary, our mechanism restricts the agents to have these small domains. The technical and conceptual challenge left open is then to what extent the necessary condition are sufficient for larger domains.

Before we discuss our characterization, we exemplify our approach on a restricted version of set systems, namely path auctions on graphs comprised of two parallel paths, whose edges have two-value domains. We show how the topology (i.e., number of edges of either path) and values in the domains can change the OSP-implementability of optimal algorithms. Specifically, we show that our observation for shortest path on the graph in Fig. 1(a) is not an accident as for all the graphs where a path is a direct edge, we can design an optimum OSP mechanism no matter what the alternative path looks like. Similarly, we prove that there are no OSP optimal mechanisms for the graph in Fig. 1(c) and all the graphs where the two paths are composed of the same number (larger than one) of edges. As for the graphs where neither path is direct and each has a different number of edges, the existence of an OSP mechanism returning the shortest path depends on the values in the domains.

We then generalize the setting to any set system problem, wherein agents have three-value (heterogeneous) domains and fully characterize the properties needed to design OSP mechanisms.

Main Theorem (informal). *There is an OSP optimal mechanism iff the set of feasible solutions are "aligned" with agent's subdomain.*

The intuition behind the characterization is simple. From OSP CMON, we know that if an OSP mechanism selects an agent e when she has a "high" cost then it must select e when she has a "low" cost (akin to monotonicity for strategyproofness). Therefore, to design an OSP optimal mechanism we need to define an implementation tree which satisfies this property. At each node of the tree, the domain of the agents is restricted to a particular subdomain, depending on the particular history; in turn, the set of possible type profiles also shrinks. Hence, there may solutions that become suboptimal for all type profiles in this set, and others that are still *alive* (i.e., optimal for at least one type profile in the set). When e is asked to separate a high cost from a low cost at node u of the tree, we then need the alive solutions to be "aligned" for the subdomain at u, which roughly means that it should never be the case that there are two bid profiles in this subdomain for which e belongs to an optimal solution when she has a high cost and is not part of an optimal solution when she has a low cost. The somehow surprising extra aspect is that even if the alive solutions were not aligned for one single subdomain then there would be no way to design an implementation tree to bypass this misalignment.

The technical definition of alignment has some nuisance to do with the particular ways in which the OSP monotonicity can be broken, but on the positive side, rather immediately suggests how to interleave ascending and descending phases to design an OSP optimal mechanism. This characterization precisely shows how OSP needs to look at the quality of solutions among set of instances (encoded by agent subdomains) rather than just the single instance and how this is needed to inform the shape of the implementation tree. Moreover, this characterization also enables us to give a *testing algorithm*, running in time polynomial in the size of the set system instance, which flags whether an OSP optimal mechanism for the instance at hand is possible or not. This coupled with our mechanism gives a sort of automated mechanism design result in that the designer has a blackbox, comprised of testing algorithm, and possibly our mechanism, to implement the optimal solution in an OSP way.

Related Work. The notion of OSP mechanism has been introduced recently by [16] and has received a lot of attention in the community. Several works have focused on understanding better the notion of OSP mechanism, and studying settings without money, namely matching and voting [2,4,17]. An early work on the approximation guarantee of OSP mechanisms is [10] where the authors consider OSP mechanisms for machine scheduling and facility location. A more recent study on the approximation guarantee of OSP mechanisms without money for machine scheduling is [15]. As mentioned above, a companion paper [9] introduces CMON and gives tight bounds for OSP mechanism for scheduling related machines. The use of verification [20] for OSP mechanisms is, instead, studied in [11]. The tradeoff between approximation guarantee (for machine scheduling) and relaxations of OSP is recently studied in [12].

Research in algorithmic mechanism design [5,13] has suggested to focus on "simple" mechanisms to deal with bounded rationality. For example, posted-price mechanisms received huge attention very recently and have been applied to many different settings [1,3,7,8] In these mechanisms one's own bid is immaterial for the price paid to get some goods of interest. However, posted price mechanisms do not fully capture the concept of simple mechanisms: e.g., ascending price auctions are not posted price mechanisms and still turn out to be "simple".

The automatic generation of mechanisms has been a classic desiderata in algorithmic mechanism design [23]: indeed, automated mechanisms are easier to use in practice, where inputs may quickly evolve. However, few results are known, even for SP mechanisms.

2   Preliminaries

A mechanism design setting is defined by a set of n *selfish agents* and a set of allowed *outcomes* S. Each agent i has a *type* $t_i \in D_i$, where D_i is called the *domain* of i. The type t_i is usually assumed to be *private knowledge* of agent i. We let $t_i(X) \in \mathbb{R}$ denote the *cost* of agent i with type t_i for the outcome $X \in \mathcal{S}$.

A *mechanism* is a process for selecting an outcome $X \in \mathcal{S}$. To this aim, the mechanism interacts with agents. Specifically, agent i is observed to take *actions* (e.g., saying yes/no) that may depend on her presumed type $b_i \in D_i$ (e.g., saying yes could "signal" that the presumed type has some properties that b_i alone might enjoy). We say that agent i takes *actions compatible with (or according to)* b_i to stress this. We highlight that the presumed type b_i can be different from the real type t_i.

For a mechanism $\mathcal{M}$, we let $\mathcal{M}(\mathbf{b})$ denote the outcome returned by the mechanism when agents take actions according to their presumed types $\mathbf{b} = (b_1, \ldots, b_n)$. In our context, this outcome is given by a pair $(f, \mathbf{p})$, where $f = f(\mathbf{b})$ (termed *social choice function* or, simply, *algorithm*) maps the actions taken by the agents according to $\mathbf{b}$ to a feasible solution in $\mathcal{S}$, and $\mathbf{p} = \mathbf{p}(\mathbf{b}) = (p_1(\mathbf{b}), \ldots, p_n(\mathbf{b})) \in \mathbb{R}^n$ maps the actions taken by the agents according to $\mathbf{b}$ to *payments* from the mechanism to the agents.

Each selfish agent i is equipped with a *utility function* $u_i \colon D_i \times \mathcal{S} \to \mathbb{R}$. For $t_i \in D_i$ and for an outcome $X \in \mathcal{S}$ returned by a mechanism $\mathcal{M}$, $u_i(t_i, X)$ is the utility that agent i has for outcome X when her type is t_i. We define utility as a quasi-linear combination of payments and costs, i.e., $u_i(t_i, \mathcal{M}(b_i, \mathbf{b}_{-i})) = p_i(b_i, \mathbf{b}_{-i}) - t_i(f(b_i, \mathbf{b}_{-i}))$.

A mechanism $\mathcal{M}$ is *strategy-proof* (SP) if it holds that $u_i(t_i, \mathcal{M}(t_i, \mathbf{b}_{-i})) \geq u_i(t_i, \mathcal{M}(b_i, \mathbf{b}_{-i}))$ for every i, every $\mathbf{b}_{-i} = (b_1, \ldots, b_{i-1}, b_{i+1}, \ldots, b_n)$ and every $b_i \in D_i$, with t_i being the true type of i. That is, in a strategy-proof mechanism the actions taken according to the true type are dominant for each agent.

We will be focusing on *single-parameter* settings, that is, the case in which the private information of each bidder i is a single real number t_i and $t_i(X)$ can be expressed as $t_i w_i(X)$ for some publicly known function w_i.

Obvious Strategyproofness. We now formally define the concept of obviously strategy-proof (deterministic) mechanism. This concept has been introduced in [16]. However, our definition is built on the more accessible ones given in [2] and [10]. As shown in [4,17], our definition is equivalent to Li's.[1]

Let us first formally model how a mechanism works. An *extensive-form mechanism* $\mathcal{M}$ is defined by a directed tree $\mathcal{T} = (V, E)$, called the *implementation tree*, such that:

- Every leaf ℓ of the tree is labeled with a possible outcome $X(\ell) \in \mathcal{S}$ of the mechanism;
- Every internal vertex $u \in V$ is labeled by an agent $S(u) \in [n]$;
- Every edge $e = (u, v) \in E$ is labeled by a subset $T(e) \subseteq D = \times_i D_i$ of type profiles such that:

---

[1] More in detail, our definition of implementation tree is equivalent to the concept of round-table mechanism in [17]. Consequently, our definition of OSP is equivalent to the concept of SP-implementation through a round table mechanism, that is proved to be equivalent to the original definition of OSP.

- The subsets of profiles that label the edges outgoing from the same vertex u are disjoint, i.e., for every triple of vertices u, v, v' such that $(u, v) \in E$ and $(u, v') \in E$, we have that $T(u, v) \cap T(u, v') = \emptyset$;
- The union of the subsets of profiles labelling the edges outgoing from a non-root vertex u is equal to the subset of profiles that label the edge going in u, i.e., $\bigcup_{v:\ (u,v) \in E} T(u, v) = T(\phi(u), u)$, where $\phi(u)$ is the parent of u in $\mathcal{T}$;
- The union of the subsets of profiles that label the edges outgoing from the root vertex r is equal to the set of all profiles, i.e., $\bigcup_{v:\ (r,v) \in E} T(r, v) = D$;
- For every u, v such that $(u, v) \in E$ and for every two profiles $\mathbf{b}, \mathbf{b}' \in T(\phi(u), u)$ such that $b_i = b'_i$, $i = S(u)$, if $\mathbf{b}$ belongs to $T(u, v)$, then $\mathbf{b}'$ must belong to $T(u, v)$ also.

Roughly speaking, the tree represents the steps of the execution of the mechanism. As long as the current visited vertex u is not a leaf, the mechanism interacts with the agent $S(u)$. Different edges outgoing from vertex u are used for modeling the different actions that agents can take during this interaction with the mechanism. As suggested above, the action that agent i takes may depend on her presumed type $b_i \in D_i$. That is, different presumed types may correspond to taking different actions, and thus to different edges. The label $T(e)$ on edge $e = (u, v)$ then lists the type profiles in which the type of $S(u)$ is one signalled by the actions assigned to e. In other words, when edge e is traversed, then the mechanism (and the other agents) can infer that the type profile must be contained in $T(e)$. The execution ends when we reach a leaf ℓ of the tree. The mechanism then returns the outcome that labels ℓ.

Observe that, according to the definition above, for every profile $\mathbf{b}$ there is only one leaf $\ell = \ell(\mathbf{b})$ such that $\mathbf{b}$ belongs to $T(\phi(\ell), \ell)$. For this reason we say that $\mathcal{M}(\mathbf{b}) = X(\ell)$. Moreover, for every type profile $\mathbf{b}$ and every node $u \in V$, we say that $\mathbf{b}$ is *compatible* with u if $\mathbf{b} \in T(\phi(u), u)$. Finally, two profiles $\mathbf{b}, \mathbf{b}'$ are said to *diverge* at vertex u if there are two vertices v, v' such that $(u, v) \in E$, $(u, v') \in E$ and $\mathbf{b} \in T(u, v)$, whereas $\mathbf{b}' \in T(u, v')$. For every node u in a mechanism $\mathcal{M}$ such that there are two profiles $\mathbf{b}, \mathbf{b}'$ that diverge at u, we say that u is a *divergent node*, and $i = S(u)$ the corresponding *divergent agent*. For each agent i, we define the *current domain* at node u, denoted $D_i(u)$, such that $D_i(r) = D_i$ for the root r and $D_i(u) = \cup_{\mathbf{b} \in T(\phi(u), u)} b_i$. In words, this is the set of types of i that are compatible with the actions that i took during the execution of the mechanism until node u is reached. Indeed, according to the definition above, at each node u in which i diverges, $\mathcal{M}$ partitions $D_i(u)$ in k subsets, where k is the number of children of u, and where for every child v of u, $D_i(v) \subset D_i(u)$ contains the types of bidder i compatible with the action that she takes when interacting with the mechanism at node u.

We are now ready to define obvious strategyproofness. An extensive-form mechanism $\mathcal{M}$ is *obviously strategy-proof (OSP)* if for every agent i with real type t_i, for every vertex u such that $i = S(u)$, for every $\mathbf{b}_{-i}, \mathbf{b}'_{-i}$ (with $\mathbf{b}'_{-i}$ not necessarily different from $\mathbf{b}_{-i}$), and for every $b_i \in D_i$, with $b_i \neq t_i$, such that $(t_i, \mathbf{b}_{-i})$ and $(b_i, \mathbf{b}'_{-i})$ are compatible with u, but diverge at u, it holds that

$u_i(t_i, \mathcal{M}(t_i, \mathbf{b}_{-i})) \geq u_i(t_i, \mathcal{M}(b_i, \mathbf{b}'_{-i}))$. Roughly speaking, an obviously strategy-proof mechanism requires that, at each time step agent i is asked to take a decision that depends on her type, the worst utility that she can get if at this time step she behaves according to her true type is at least the best utility achievable by behaving as she had a different type. Hence, if a mechanism is obviously strategy-proof, then it is also strategy-proof. Indeed, the latter requires that truthful behavior is a dominant strategy when agents know the entire type profile, whereas the former requires that it continues to be a dominant strategy even if agents have only a partial knowledge of profiles limited to what they observed in the mechanism up to the time they are called to take their choices.

We say that an extensive-form mechanism is *trivial* if for every vertex $u \in V$ and for every two type profiles $\mathbf{b}, \mathbf{b}'$, it holds that $\mathbf{b}$ and $\mathbf{b}'$ do *not* diverge at u. That is, a mechanism is trivial if it never requires agents to take actions that depend on their type. If a mechanism is not trivial, then there is at least one divergent node. On the other hand, every execution of a mechanism (i.e., every path from the root to a leaf in the mechanism implementation tree) may go through at most $\sum_i(|D_i| - 1)$ divergent nodes, the upper bound being the case in which at each divergent node u, the agent $i = S(u)$ separates $D_i(u)$ in $D_i(u) \setminus \{b\}$ and $\{b\}$ for some $b \in D_i(u)$.

Cycle-Monotonicity for OSP Mechanisms. In [9], a technique – that extends the well-known cycle monotonicity for strategyproofness [21] – is introduced to study whether a mechanism is OSP. We here recall their results, needed for our characterization.

Consider an extensive-form mechanism $\mathcal{M} = (f, \mathbf{p})$ with implementation tree $\mathcal{T}$.

Definition 1 (separating vertices). *A vertex u in the implementation tree $\mathcal{T}$ is $\alpha\beta$-separating for agent i if the following holds: Node u is labelled with i, i.e., $i = S(u)$; there are two profiles $(\alpha, \mathbf{a}_{-i})$ and $(\beta, \mathbf{b}_{-i})$ which are compatible with u but diverge at u, where $\mathbf{a}_{-i}, \mathbf{b}_{-i} \in D_{-i}(u) = \times_{j \neq i} D_j(u)$.*

Note that there might exist several $\alpha\beta$-separating vertices for agent i as the agent may be asked to separate a from b in different paths from the root to a leaf (but only once for every such path).

Definition 2 (OSP-graph). *Let f be a social choice function and $\mathcal{T}$ be an implementation tree. We define for every agent i, the OSP-graph $OSP_i^{(f,\mathcal{T})}$ as follows: There is a node for each type profile in D, and a directed edge $e = ((\alpha, \mathbf{a}_{-i}), (\beta, \mathbf{b}_{-i}))$ for every $\alpha, \beta \in D_i$, $\alpha \neq \beta$, and $\mathbf{a}_{-i}, \mathbf{b}_{-i} \in D_{-i}(u)$, where u is an $\alpha\beta$-separating vertex of $\mathcal{T}$. The weight of the edge is $w(e) = \alpha(f(\beta, \mathbf{b}_{-i})) - \alpha(f(\alpha, \mathbf{a}_{-i}))$.*

Definition 3 (OSP CMON). *We say that the OSP cycle monotonicity (OSP CMON) property holds if, for all i, the graph $OSP_i^{(f,\mathcal{T})}$ does not have negative weight cycles. Moreover, we say that the OSP two-cycle monotonicity (OSP 2CMON) holds if the same is true when considering cycles of length two only, i.e., cycles with two edges only.*

We now state the relationship between OSP CMON and OSP mechanisms.

Theorem 1 ([9]). *A mechanism with implementation tree T is an OSP mechanism for a social function f on finite domains if and only if OSP CMON holds.*

Theorem 2 ([9]). *Let $|D_i| \leq 3$ for each agent i. A mechanism with implementation tree T and social choice function f is OSP iff OSP 2CMON holds.*

Set Systems. In a *set system* $(E, \mathcal{F})$ we are given a set E of elements and a family $\mathcal{F} \subseteq 2^E$ of feasible subsets of E. Each element $i \in E$ is controlled by a selfish agent, that is, the cost for using i is known only to agent i and is equal to some non-negative value t_i. The social choice function f must choose a feasible subset in $\mathcal{F}$; we can use the same notation above for single-parameter agents with the restriction that $f_i(\mathbf{b}) \in \{0, 1\}$ to mean that the element controlled by agent i is either chosen by f, with $f_i(\mathbf{b}) = 1$, or not, with $f_i(\mathbf{b}) = 0$. Here our objective is social cost minimization, that is, $f^*(\mathbf{b}) \in \arg\min_{\mathbf{x}} \sum_{i=1}^{n} b_i(\mathbf{x})$. Several problems on graphs can be cast in this framework.

3 Warm-Up: Shortest Path with Two-Values Domains

Before stating our main results, we will illustrate our approach by providing a characterization for a simpler setting: specifically, we consider the path auction problem discussed in the introduction; this is a special case of a set system problem where the set of feasible solutions is the set of all the paths between the source node s and the destination node t in a given graph G. Moreover, we consider the case in which G has two parallel paths from the source to the destination; the first is comprised of a set T of t edges, that we will sometimes call top edges, whilst the second is comprised of a set B of b edges, that we will call bottom edges. Without loss of generality, we assume that $t \geq b$.

Proposition 1. *There is an OSP optimal mechanism for the shortest path problem on parallel paths and two-value domains $D = \{L, H\}^n$ if and only if either (1) $b = 1$ or (2) $t > b > 1$ and $\frac{H}{L} \leq \frac{t-1}{b-1}$.*

Proof (Sketch). Let us start by proving the sufficient condition. Consider the optimal mechanism that returns the bottom path in case of ties. By a case analysis, one can prove that under the hypotheses of the theorem: (i) For any top edge e, if the corresponding agent reports H, then the bottom path is chosen, i.e., $f_e(H, \mathbf{b}_{-e}) = 0$ for all $\mathbf{b}_{-e}$; (ii) For any bottom edge e, if the corresponding agent reports L, then the bottom path is chosen, i.e., $f_e(L, \mathbf{a}_{-e}) = 1$ for all $\mathbf{a}_{-e}$. Since $f_e(\cdot)$ is either 0 or 1 for this problem, the two items above imply that OSP 2CMON, and thus, by Theorem 2, OSP CMON holds for every agent e.

We next prove the necessity and show that when either (i) $t = b > 1$ or (ii) $t > b > 1$ and $\frac{H}{L} > \frac{t-1}{b-1}$, no optimal mechanism $\mathcal{M}$ can be OSP. Since $\mathcal{M}$ is optimal, it is not trivial and at some point it must separate L from H for at least one agent. We consider the first divergent agent e, and show via a simple case analysis, that OSP 2CMON is violated for this agent, thus implying that mechanism $\mathcal{M}$ is *not* OSP (Theorem 1). $\square$

4   Set Systems

In this section we characterize when OSP optimal mechanisms exist for set systems. We will formally define the concept of alignment introduced above, with a different and more technical terminology. The main message is that the feasibility of OSP optimal mechanisms depends on structural properties of the feasible solutions *and* the values in the agents' domains.

To this aim, let us first introduce the key concepts. Consider a set system problem $(E, \mathcal{F}, \mathbf{D})$. where $\mathbf{D} = (D_e)_{e \in E}$ denotes the domain. We next define some useful concepts and notation, to state our characterization and mechanism. Consider an arbitrary *subdomain* $\tilde{\mathbf{D}}$ of $\mathbf{D}$, that is, a type domain $\tilde{\mathbf{D}} = (\tilde{D}_e)_{e \in E}$ such that $\tilde{D}_e \subseteq D_e$ for all $e \in E$. We denote by $L(e, \tilde{\mathbf{D}}) = \min\{t \in \tilde{D}_e\}$ and $H(e, \tilde{\mathbf{D}}) = \max\{t \in \tilde{D}_e\}$ the lowest and the highest type for e according to the subdomain $\tilde{\mathbf{D}}$. Similarly, for any $P \subseteq E$, we let $L(P, \tilde{\mathbf{D}})$ and $H(P, \tilde{\mathbf{D}})$ be the lowest and the highest possible cost of P according to subdomain $\tilde{\mathbf{D}}$, i.e., $L(P, \tilde{\mathbf{D}}) = \sum_{e \in P} L(e, \tilde{\mathbf{D}})$ and $H(P, \tilde{\mathbf{D}}) = \sum_{e \in P} H(e, \tilde{\mathbf{D}})$. (When clear from the context, we omit the reference to $\tilde{\mathbf{D}}$ in these notations.) Finally, we let $\prec$ denote a total order among the feasible solutions in $\mathcal{F}$; this order will be used to select the optimal solution to return in case of ties.

Next concepts relate implementation trees and optimal solutions.

Definition 4 (selectable solution). *A feasible solution $P \in \mathcal{F}$ is said selectable for a subdomain $\tilde{\mathbf{D}}$ if for every other $P' \in \mathcal{F}$ it holds that $L(P \backslash P', \tilde{\mathbf{D}}) < H(P' \setminus P, \tilde{\mathbf{D}})$ or $L(P \setminus P', \tilde{\mathbf{D}}) = H(P' \setminus P, \tilde{\mathbf{D}})$ and $P \prec P'$.*

Any implementation tree gradually shrinks $\mathbf{D}$ to subdomains $\tilde{\mathbf{D}}$ by querying the agents. If the implementation tree has already shrunk to some $\tilde{\mathbf{D}}$, a selectable solution for $\tilde{\mathbf{D}}$ cannot be excluded a priori because, for some profile in $\tilde{\mathbf{D}}$, it is either the unique optimum or the optimum preferred according to the tie-breaking rule. Observe that at least one selectable solution exists for every $\tilde{\mathbf{D}}$.

While the above concept refers only to implementation tree and optimality, the next will turn out to be useful to study when there is a way to shrink $\mathbf{D}$ that returns an optimal solution but also that is compatible with OSP.

Definition 5 (strongly selectable solution). *A selectable solution P is said strongly selectable for a subdomain $\tilde{\mathbf{D}}$ if, for all $e \in P$, it continues to be selectable even for the subdomain $(\tilde{\mathbf{D}}_{-e}, H(e, \tilde{\mathbf{D}}))$, where $\tilde{\mathbf{D}}_{-f} = (\tilde{D}_e)_{e \neq f}$ and, with a slight abuse of notation, $H(e, \tilde{\mathbf{D}})$ denotes $\{H(e, \tilde{\mathbf{D}})\}$.*

In words, this means that solution P is still potentially optimum when any one of its elements has the largest possible cost $H(e, \tilde{\mathbf{D}})$ in $\tilde{\mathbf{D}}$.

The Analytical Characterization: Necessary Conditions. Our next two lemmas identify *necessary* conditions for the implementation tree of an OSP optimal mechanism for set systems. To this aim, we define the *obstacle domain set* $\mathcal{X}$ to contain $\mathbf{D}$ and, for each f with $|D_f| > 2$, $\tilde{\mathbf{D}}_f^{\top} = (\mathbf{D}_{-f}, \tilde{D}_f^{\top})$, where $\tilde{D}_f^{\top} = D_f \setminus L(f, \mathbf{D})$, and $\tilde{\mathbf{D}}_f^{\perp} = (\mathbf{D}_{-f}, \tilde{D}_f^{\perp})$, where $\tilde{D}_f^{\perp} = D_f \setminus H(f, \mathbf{D})$.

The first necessary condition roughly says that if there is a domain in the obstacle domain set $\mathcal{X}$ where elements of strongly selectable solutions can be excluded when they reveal their type to be as low as possible, then there is no implementation tree which yields an OSP optimal mechanism.

Lemma 1. *There is no OSP optimal mechanism for a set system problem if there is a domain $\tilde{\mathbf{D}} \in \mathcal{X}$ such that the following properties are both satisfied:*

(i) the set $\mathcal{S}$ of strongly selectable solutions for $\tilde{\mathbf{D}}$ contains at least one P with $f \in P$ such that $|\tilde{D}_f| > 1$;

(ii) for every $P \in \mathcal{S}$ and every $f \in P$ such that $|\tilde{D}_f| > 1$, there is $\bar{P}_f \in \mathcal{S}$ with $f \notin \bar{P}_f$ such that $\bar{P}_f$ remains selectable even for $(\tilde{\mathbf{D}}_{-f}, L(f, \tilde{\mathbf{D}}))$.

Proof (Sketch). Assume by contradiction that there is a domain $\tilde{\mathbf{D}} \in \mathcal{X}$ for which the conditions above are satisfied and yet there is an OSP optimal mechanism $\mathcal{M}$; let us denote with $\mathcal{T}$ its implementation tree.

Let $\mathcal{S}$ be the set of strongly selectable solutions defined in the statement, which is not empty by hypothesis. Consider the first node $u \in \mathcal{T}$ in which an agent $f \in \bigcup_{P \in \mathcal{S}} P$ diverges between $L(f, \tilde{\mathbf{D}})$ and $H(f, \tilde{\mathbf{D}})$ in the subtree compatible with the type of every agent $e \in \bigcup_{P \in \mathcal{S}} P$ being in $\tilde{D}_e$ and the type of every remaining agent e being $H(e, \tilde{\mathbf{D}})$. First, observe that, since the mechanism $\mathcal{M}$ is optimal, such a node u must exist.

Given the existence of u and f as above, we then apply the hypothesis (ii) to show a negative OSP 2-cycle.   □

The second necessary property regards domains $\tilde{\mathbf{D}} \in \mathcal{X}$ for which there are solutions that are selectable but *not* strongly selectable. For each such solution P there is an agent w, that we will call the *witness* of P, such that P is no longer selectable for $\tilde{\mathbf{D}}_{hw} = (\tilde{\mathbf{D}}_{-w}, H(w, \tilde{\mathbf{D}}))$.

The next lemma intuitively says that, if there exist domains where witnesses of solutions that are selectable but not strongly selectable can be excluded (included, respectively) when they reveal their type to be the lowest (highest, respectively) possible, then there is no implementation tree which yields an OSP optimal mechanism. Its proof uses ideas similar to that of Lemma 1.

Lemma 2. *There is no OSP optimal mechanism for a set system problem if there is a domain $\tilde{\mathbf{D}} \in \mathcal{X}$ such that the following properties are both satisfied:*

(i) the set $\mathcal{S}$ of selectable solutions for $\tilde{\mathbf{D}}$ has size $|\mathcal{S}| \geq 2$, and there is at least one $P \in \mathcal{S}$ such that P is not strongly selectable;

(ii) for every f for which there is at least one selectable solution to which it belongs and at least one selectable to which it does not belong (i.e., $f \in \bigcup_{(P,P') \in \mathcal{S} \times \mathcal{S}} P \setminus P'$) both the following are true:

- *there is $\bar{P}_f \in \mathcal{S}$ s.t. $f \notin \bar{P}_f$ and $\bar{P}_f$ is selectable for $\bar{\mathbf{D}} = (\tilde{\mathbf{D}}_{-f}, L(f, \tilde{\mathbf{D}}))$;*
- *there is $\check{P}_f \in \mathcal{S}$ s.t. $f \in \check{P}_f$ and $\check{P}_f$ is selectable for $\check{\mathbf{D}} = (\tilde{\mathbf{D}}_{-f}, H(f, \tilde{\mathbf{D}}))$.*

The Analytical Characterization: The Mechanism. The two necessary conditions suggest that it is possible to design an OSP optimal mechanism when both the following properties are satisfied for *some* subdomain $\tilde{\mathbf{D}}$ containing more than one instance. When all selectable solutions are also strongly selectable then there is an f such that every P' with $f \notin P'$ ceases to be selectable if the type of f is $L(f, \tilde{\mathbf{D}})$ (this is the negation of Lemma 1). Moreover, if there is at least one selectable solution that is not strongly selectable for $\tilde{\mathbf{D}}$, then there is f such that either every P' with $f \notin P'$ ceases to be selectable if the type of f is $L(f, \tilde{\mathbf{D}})$, or every P' with $f \in P'$ ceases to be selectable if the type of f is $H(f, \tilde{\mathbf{D}})$ (this is the negation of Lemma 2). We prove that these properties are indeed sufficient by proving that Algorithm 1 admit payments for an OSP optimal mechanism, that we call $\mathcal{M}_{\text{set}}^{\text{opt}}$, for set systems with *three-value domains*, i.e., with $D_e \subseteq \{L_e, M_e, H_e\}$ with $L_e < M_e < H_e$ for every e.

Theorem 3. *There is an OSP optimal mechanism for a set system problem with three-value domains if and only if there is no domain $\tilde{\mathbf{D}} \in \mathcal{X}$ for which conditions of Lemma 1 or of Lemma 2 hold.*

The "only if" direction follows from Lemmas 1 and 2. For the "if" direction, we will need the following lemma.

Lemma 3. *If the properties of Lemma 1 or of Lemma 2 are not satisfied for every domain $\tilde{\mathbf{D}} \in \mathcal{X}$, then they are not satisfied for every subdomain $\hat{\mathbf{D}}$ of $\mathbf{D}$.*

We are now ready to prove our main theorem.

Proof (Sketch of Theorem 3). According to Lemma 3, we can assume that for every subdomain of $\mathbf{D}$ the conditions of Lemmas 1 and 2 do not hold. The algorithm looks for an agent f we can safely ask for OSP-ness to diverge between their current $L(f)$ and $H(f)$; if f reveals type $L(f)$, then she will be securely selected, or if she reveals type $H(f)$, then she will be never selected. This shows that to each query that the mechanism does, there does not correspond a negative weight two-cycle in the OSP-graph of the queried agent. By Theorem 2 we can then conclude that $\mathcal{M}_{\text{set}}^{\text{opt}}$ is OSP.

Finally, the only solution in $\mathcal{P}$ at the end of the mechanism is by definition selectable for the final subdomain $\tilde{\mathbf{D}}$. To argue about optimality, we need to make sure that all the solutions excluded for bigger subdomains are not selectable for $\tilde{\mathbf{D}}$. The last key piece of the puzzle is a property of inheritance: the solutions removed for bigger subdomain, because they were not selectable, remain non-selectable for all the smaller domains. □

Note that the mechanisms $\mathcal{M}_{\text{set}}^{\text{opt}}$ runs in polynomial time, since it makes at most 2 queries to each agent. Interestingly, this mechanism is not a DA auction or a PCA. Indeed, it may require that single agents are involved first in an ascending phase and then in a descending phase or vice versa. In fact, it is not hard to see that this occurs even with a very simple example with only two feasible solutions, say P and Q, and three elements, x, y, and z, with $P = \{x, y\}$, and $Q = \{z\}$, with domains $D_x = D_y = D_z = \{L, M, H\}$, where $L = 1$, $M = 3$, and $H = 7$.

Input: $E, \mathcal{F}, \mathbf{D}$
Output: An optimal solution

1 Initialize $R = \{P \in \mathcal{F}: P \text{ not selectable for } \mathbf{D}\}$, $\mathcal{P} = \mathcal{F} \setminus R$ and $\tilde{\mathbf{D}} = \mathbf{D}$
2 **while** $|R| < |\mathcal{F}| - 1$ **do**
3   **while** *there is* $P \in \mathcal{P}$ *that is not strongly selectable for* $\tilde{\mathbf{D}}$ **do**
4   **if** $\exists f \in \bigcup_{P \in \mathcal{P}} P$ *s.t. every* $P \in \mathcal{P}$, *with* $f \notin P$, *is not selectable for*
                  $(\tilde{\mathbf{D}}_{-f}, L(f, \tilde{\mathbf{D}}))$ **then**
5   Ask f if her type is $L(f, \tilde{\mathbf{D}})$
6   **if** *yes* **then**
7                  $\tilde{\mathbf{D}} = (\tilde{\mathbf{D}}_{-f}, L(f, \tilde{\mathbf{D}}))$
8   Add to R and remove from $\mathcal{P}$ every P not selectable for $\tilde{\mathbf{D}}$
9   **else**
10                 $\tilde{\mathbf{D}} = (\tilde{\mathbf{D}}_{-f}, D_f \setminus L(f, \tilde{\mathbf{D}}))$
11   Add to R and remove from $\mathcal{P}$ every P not selectable for $\tilde{\mathbf{D}}$
12   **else**
13   Pick $f \in \bigcup_{P \in \mathcal{P}} P$ s.t. all $P \in \mathcal{P}$, with $f \in P$, are not selectable for
                  $(\tilde{\mathbf{D}}_{-f}, H(f, \tilde{\mathbf{D}}))$
14   Ask f if her type is $H(f, \tilde{\mathbf{D}})$
15   **if** *yes* **then**
16                 $\tilde{\mathbf{D}} = (\tilde{\mathbf{D}}_{-f}, H(f, \tilde{\mathbf{D}}))$
17   Add to R and remove from $\mathcal{P}$ every P not selectable for $\tilde{\mathbf{D}}$
18   **else**
19                 $\tilde{\mathbf{D}} = (\tilde{\mathbf{D}}_{-f}, D_f \setminus H(f, \tilde{\mathbf{D}}))$
20   Add to R and remove from $\mathcal{P}$ every P not selectable for $\tilde{\mathbf{D}}$
21   **if** $|R| < |\mathcal{F}| - 1$ **then**
22   Pick $f \in \bigcup_{P \in \mathcal{P}} P$ s.t. every $P \in \mathcal{P}$, with $f \notin P$, are not selectable for
                  $(\tilde{\mathbf{D}}_{-f}, L(f, \tilde{\mathbf{D}}))$
23   Ask f if her type is $L(f, \tilde{\mathbf{D}})$
24   **if** *yes* **then**
25             $\tilde{\mathbf{D}} = (\tilde{\mathbf{D}}_{-f}, L(f, \tilde{\mathbf{D}}))$
26   Add to R and remove from $\mathcal{P}$ every P that is not selectable for $\tilde{\mathbf{D}}$
27   **else**
28             $\tilde{\mathbf{D}} = (\tilde{\mathbf{D}}_{-f}, D_f \setminus L(f, \tilde{\mathbf{D}}))$
29   Add to R and remove from $\mathcal{P}$ every P that is not selectable for $\tilde{\mathbf{D}}$
30 Return the only solution in $\mathcal{P}$

Algorithm 1: The implementation tree of the optimal algorithm for mechanism $\mathcal{M}_{\text{set}}^{\text{opt}}$

The Algorithmic Characterization. Note that the obstacle domain set contains at most $2|E| + 1$ domains. So we can enumerate all elements in this set in time that is polynomial in the size of the set system instance. Observe also that it takes only polynomial time (in the number of feasible solutions) to verify whether a solution is (strongly) selectable or not. Hence, the *testing algorithm*, that for every domain in the obstacle domain set checks for whether the conditions of Lemmas 1 and 2 are satisfied, is a polynomial-time algorithm.

References

1. Adamczyk, M., Borodin, A., Ferraioli, D., de Keijzer, B., Leonardi, S.: Sequential posted price mechanisms with correlated valuations. In: Markakis, E., Schäfer, G. (eds.) WINE 2015. LNCS, vol. 9470, pp. 1–15. Springer, Heidelberg (2015). https://doi.org/10.1007/978-3-662-48995-6_1
2. Ashlagi, I., Gonczarowski, Y.A.: Stable matching mechanisms are not obviously strategy-proof. J. Econ. Theory **177**, 405–425 (2018)
3. Babaioff, M., Immorlica, N., Lucier, B., Weinberg, S.M.: A simple and approximately optimal mechanism for an additive buyer. In: FOCS 2014, pp. 21–30 (2014)
4. Bade, S., Gonczarowski, Y.A.: Gibbard-Satterthwaite success stories and obvious strategyproofness. In: EC 2017, p. 565 (2017)
5. Chawla, S., Hartline, J., Malec, D., Sivan, B.: Multi-parameter mechanism design and sequential posted pricing. In: STOC 2010, pp. 311–320 (2010)
6. Dütting, P., Gkatzelis, V., Roughgarden, T.: The performance of deferred-acceptance auctions. Math. Oper. Res. **42**(4), 897–914 (2017)
7. Eden, A., Feldman, M., Friedler, O., Talgam-Cohen, I., Weinberg, S.M.: A simple and approximately optimal mechanism for a buyer with complements. In: EC 2017, p. 323 (2017)
8. Feldman, M., Fiat, A., Roytman, A.: Makespan minimization via posted prices. In: EC 2017, pp. 405–422 (2017)
9. Ferraioli, D., Meier, A., Penna, P., Ventre, C.: Obviously strategyproof mechanisms for machine scheduling. In: ESA 2019 (2019)
10. Ferraioli, D., Ventre, C.: Obvious strategyproofness needs monitoring for good approximations. In: AAAI 2017, pp. 516–522 (2017)
11. Ferraioli, D., Ventre, C.: Probabilistic verification for obviously strategyproof mechanisms. In: IJCAI 2018 (2018)
12. Ferraioli, D., Ventre, C.: Obvious strategyproofness, bounded rationality and approximation: the case of machine scheduling. In: SAGT 2019 (2019)
13. Hartline, J., Roughgarden, T.: Simple versus optimal mechanisms. In: EC 2009, pp. 225–234 (2009)
14. Kagel, J., Harstad, R., Levin, D.: Information impact and allocation rules in auctions with affiliated private values: a laboratory study. Econometrica **55**, 1275–1304 (1987)
15. Kyropoulou, M., Ventre, C.: Obviously strategyproof mechanisms without money for scheduling. In: AAMAS 2019 (2019)
16. Li, S.: Obviously strategy-proof mechanisms. Am. Econ. Rev. **107**(11), 3257–3287 (2017)
17. Mackenzie, A.: A revelation principle for obviously strategy-proof implementation. Research Memorandum 014 (GSBE) (2017)
18. Milgrom, P., Segal, I.: Deferred-acceptance auctions and radio spectrum reallocation. In: EC 2014 (2014)
19. Nisan, N., Ronen, A.: Algorithmic mechanism design. Games Econ. Behav. **35**, 166–196 (2001)
20. Penna, P., Ventre, C.: Optimal collusion-resistant mechanisms with verification. Games Econ. Behav. **86**, 491–509 (2014)
21. Rochet, J.C.: The taxation principle and multitime Hamilton-Jacobi equations. J. Math. Econ. **14**(2), 113–128 (1985)

22. Saks, M., Yu, L.: Weak monotonicity suffices for truthfulness on convex domains. In: EC 2005, pp. 286–293 (2005)
23. Sandholm, T.: Automated mechanism design: a new application area for search algorithms. In: Rossi, F. (ed.) CP 2003. LNCS, vol. 2833, pp. 19–36. Springer, Heidelberg (2003). https://doi.org/10.1007/978-3-540-45193-8_2

The Pareto Frontier of Inefficiency in Mechanism Design

Aris Filos-Ratsikas[1,2]([✉]) [ID], Yiannis Giannakopoulos[3] [ID], and Philip Lazos[4] [ID]

[1] University of Liverpool, Liverpool, UK
Aris.Filos-Ratsikas@liverpool.ac.uk
[2] École Polytechnique Fédérale de Lausanne, Lausanne, Switzerland
[3] TU Munich, Munich, Germany
yiannis.giannakopoulos@tum.de
[4] Sapienza University of Rome, Rome, Italy
lazos@diag.uniroma1.it

Abstract. We study the trade-off between the Price of Anarchy (PoA) and the Price of Stability (PoS) in mechanism design, in the prototypical problem of unrelated machine scheduling. We give bounds on the space of feasible mechanisms with respect to the above metrics, and observe that two fundamental mechanisms, namely the First-Price (FP) and the Second-Price (SP), lie on the two opposite extrema of this boundary. Furthermore, for the natural class of anonymous task-independent mechanisms, we completely characterize the PoA/PoS Pareto frontier; we design a class of optimal mechanisms $\mathcal{SP}_\alpha$ that lie *exactly* on this frontier. In particular, these mechanisms range smoothly, with respect to parameter $\alpha \geq 1$ across the frontier, between the First-Price ($\mathcal{SP}_1$) and Second-Price ($\mathcal{SP}_\infty$) mechanisms.

En route to these results, we also provide a definitive answer to an important question related to the scheduling problem, namely whether non-truthful mechanisms can provide better makespan guarantees in the equilibrium, compared to truthful ones. We answer this question in the negative, by proving that the Price of Anarchy of *all* scheduling mechanisms is at least n, where n is the number of machines.

Keywords: Mechanism design · Price of anarchy · Price of stability · Pareto frontier

1 Introduction

The field of *algorithmic mechanism design* was established in the seminal paper of Nisan and Ronen [15] and has ever since been at the centre of research in

Supported by ERC Advanced Grant 321171 (ALGAME), the Swiss National Science Foundation under contract No. 200021_165522 and the Alexander von Humboldt Foundation with funds from the German Federal Ministry of Education and Research (BMBF). A full version of this paper is available at [8].

© Springer Nature Switzerland AG 2019
I. Caragiannis et al. (Eds.): WINE 2019, LNCS 11920, pp. 186–199, 2019.
https://doi.org/10.1007/978-3-030-35389-6_14

the intersection of economics and computer science. The research agenda put forward in [15] advocates the study of approximate solutions to interesting optimization problems, in settings where rational agents are in control of the input parameters. More concretely, the authors of [15] proposed a framework in which, not unlike classical approaches in approximation algorithms, algorithms that operate under certain limitations are evaluated in terms of their approximation ratio. In particular, in algorithmic mechanism design, this constraint comes from the requirement that agents should have the right incentives to always report their inputs *truthfully*. The corresponding algorithms, paired with appropriately chosen payment functions, are called *mechanisms*.

Another pioneering line of work, initiated by Koutsoupias [12] and popularized further by Roughgarden [18], studies the *inefficiency* of games through the notion of the *Price of Anarchy (PoA)*, which measures the deterioration of some objective at the worst-case Nash equilibrium. A more optimistic version of the same principle, where the inefficiency is measured at the *best* equilibrium, was introduced in [1], under the name of *Price of Stability (PoS)*.

Given the straightforward observation that mechanisms induce games between the agents that control their inputs, as well as the fact that truthfulness is typically a very demanding property, an alternative approach to the framework of Nisan and Ronen [15] is to design mechanisms that perform well *in the equilibrium*, i.e., they provide good PoA or PoS guarantees. This approach has been adopted, among others, by central papers in the field (e.g., see [17] and references therein) and is by now as much a part of algorithmic mechanism design as the original framework of [15]. An interesting question that has arisen in many settings is whether non-truthful mechanisms (evaluated at the worst-case equilibrium, in terms of their PoA) can actually outperform truthful ones (evaluated at the truth-telling, dominant strategy equilibrium), for a given objective.

While the literature that studies the concepts of PoA and PoS is long and extensive, there seems to be a lack of a *systematic approach* investigating the trade-off between the two notions *simultaneously*. More concretely, given a problem in algorithmic mechanism design, it seems quite natural to explore not only the best mechanisms in terms of the two notions independently, but also the mechanisms that achieve the best trade-off between the two. In a sense, this approach concerns a "tighter" optimality notion, as among a set of mechanisms with an "acceptable" Price of Anarchy guarantee, we would like to identify the ones that provide the best possible Price of Stability. Our main contribution in the current paper is the proposal of such a research agenda and its application on the canonical problem in the field, introduced in the seminal work of Nisan and Ronen [15], that of scheduling on unrelated machines.

1.1 Our Contributions

PoA/PoS trade-off: We propose the *research agenda of studying systematically the trade-off between the Price of Anarchy and the Price of Stability in algorithmic mechanism design*. Specifically, given a problem at hand and an objective function, we are interested in the trade-off between the PoA and the PoS of mechanisms for the given objective. We apply this approach on the prototypical problem of algorithmic mechanism design studied in [15], that of unrelated machine scheduling, where the machines are self-interested agents.

First, in Sect. 3, for the class of *all* possible mechanisms, we prove that PoA guarantees imply corresponding PoS lower bounds and vice-versa (Theorem 2), which allows us to quantify the possible trade-off between the two inefficiency notions in terms of a feasible region (see Fig. 1); we refer to the boundary of this region as the *inefficiency boundary*. Interestingly, two well-known mechanisms, namely the First-Price and the Second-Price mechanisms, turn out to lie on the extreme points of this boundary.

Next, in Sect. 4, for the well-studied class of task-independent and anonymous mechanisms, we are able to show a tighter feasibility region (Theorem 5). As a matter of fact, its inefficiency boundary turns out to *completely characterize* the achievable trade-off between the PoA and the PoS: we design a class of mechanisms (Sect. 4.2) called $\mathcal{SP}_\alpha$, parameterized by a quantity α, which are *optimal* in the sense that for any possible trade-off between the two inefficiency notions, there exists a mechanism in the class (i.e., an appropriate choice of α) that exactly achieves this trade-off (Theorem 6). In other words, we obtain an exact description of the *Pareto frontier of inefficiency* (see Fig. 2).

Our $\mathcal{SP}_\alpha$ mechanisms are simple and intuitive and are based on the idea of setting reserve prices *relatively* to the declarations of the fastest machines. While this is clearly not truthful, we prove that it induces the equilibria which are desirable for our results. More precisely, the choice of α enables us to "control" the set of possible equilibria in a way that allows us to achieve any trade-off on the boundary.

The Price of Anarchy of scheduling: Our results also offer insights in an other interesting direction. The inefficiency boundary result for general mechanisms is based on a novel monotonicity lemma (Lemma 1), which is quite different from the well-known *weak monotonicity* property [19]. Interestingly, we also use this lemma to prove a *general lower bound of n* on the PoA of *any* mechanism for the scheduling problem (Theorem 1), where n is the number of machines. This result contributes to the intriguing debate [4,10,11] of whether general mechanisms (that may be non-truthful, evaluated at the worst-case equilibrium) can outperform truthful ones (evaluated at the truth-telling equilibrium). Given that the best known truthful mechanism achieves an n-approximation, our results here provide a definitive, negative answer to the aforementioned question. As a matter of fact, in Theorem 4, we actually show that when evaluated at their worst-case equilibrium, truthful mechanisms are bound to perform even more poorly, as their PoA is unbounded.

Due to space constraints, all omitted proofs can be found in the full version of the paper [8].

1.2   Related Work

The (Selfish) Scheduling Problem: The scheduling problem on unrelated selfish machines is the prototypical problem studied by Nisan and Ronen [15] in 1999, when they introduced the field of algorithmic mechanism design. The authors consider the worst-case performance of truthful mechanisms on dominant strategy, truth-telling equilibria, and discover that the well-known Second-Price auction[1] has an approximation ratio of n for the problem, where n is the number of machines. Despite several attempts over the years, this is still the best-known truthful mechanism. On the other hand, the succession of the best proven lower bounds started with 2 in [15], improved to 2.41 in [5] and finally to 2.61 in [13]. Interestingly, Ashlagi et al. [2] showed a matching lower bound of n for *anonymous* mechanisms (i.e., mechanisms that do not take the identities of the machines into account) and whether there is a better mechanism that is not anonymous is still the most prominent open problem in the area.

The Truthful Setting vs the Strategic Setting: As we mentioned earlier, given that truthfulness is a very demanding requirement which imposes strict constraints on the allocation and payment functions, it is an interesting direction to consider whether *non-truthful* mechanisms could perform better, when evaluated in the worst-case equilibrium. In other words, for a given problem, one could ask the following question:

> *"Do there exist (non-truthful) mechanisms whose Price of Anarchy outperforms the approximation ratio guarantee of all truthful mechanisms?".*

To differentiate, we will refer to the traditional approach of Nisan and Ronen [15] as the *truthful setting* and to the setting where all mechanisms are explored (with respect to their Nash equilibria) as the *strategic setting.*

Koutsoupias [11] studied the truthful setting for the problem of unrelated machine scheduling *without money* but he explicitly advocated the strategic setting as a future direction. This was later pursued in Giannakopoulos, Koutsoupias and Kyropoulou [10] for the same problem, where the authors answered the aforementioned question in the affirmative. The same approach was taken in [4] following the results of [7] on the limitations of truthful mechanisms for indivisible item allocation. In the literature of auctions, the strategic setting was studied even in domains for which an optimal truthful mechanism (the VCG mechanism) exists, motivated by the fact that non-truthful mechanisms are being employed in practice, with the Generalized Second-Price auction used by Google for the Adwords allocation being a prominent example [3]. We refer the reader to the survey of Roughgarden [17] for more details.

Somewhat surprisingly, although the exploration of different solution concepts besides dominant strategy equilibria was already explicitly mentioned as a future direction in [15], the strategic setting for the scheduling problem was not

---

[1] In the related literature, this mechanism is often referred to as the Vickrey-Clarke-Groves (VCG) mechanism.

studied before our paper. As we mentioned earlier, the answer to the highlighted question above here is negative, but the setting proved out to be quite rich in terms of the achievable trade-off between the two different inefficiency notions.

To the best of our knowledge, ours is the first paper that proposes the systematic study of the trade-off between the Price of Anarchy and the Price of Stability. While preparing our manuscript, we became aware that a trade-off between the two notions was very recently considered also in [16], though in a fundamentally different setting: the authors of [16] study a special case of covering games, originally introduced by Gairing [9], which is not inherently a mechanism design setup. One the contrary, our interest is in explicitly studying this trade-off in the area of algorithmic mechanism design, thus choosing the prototypical scheduling problem as the starting point.

2   Model and Notation

Let $\mathbb{R}_{\geq 0} = [0, \infty)$ denote the nonnegative reals and $\mathbb{N} = \{1, 2, \ldots\}$ the positive integers. For any $n \in \mathbb{N}$, let $[n] = \{1, 2, \ldots, n\}$. In the *strategic scheduling* problem (on unrelated machines), there is a set $N = \{1, \ldots, n\}$ of *machines* (or *agents*) and a set $J = \{1, \ldots, m\}$ of *tasks*. Each machine i has a *processing time* (or *cost*) $t_{i,j} \geq 0$ for task j. The induced matrix $\mathbf{t} \in \mathbb{R}_{\geq 0}^{n \times m}$ is the *profile* of processing times. For convenience, we will denote by $\mathbf{t}_i = (t_{i,1}, \ldots, t_{i,m})$ the vector of processing times of machine i for the tasks and by $\mathbf{t}^j = (t_{1,j}, \ldots, t_{n,j})^{\mathrm{T}}$ the vector of processing times of the machines for task j, so that $\mathbf{t} = (\mathbf{t}_1, \ldots, \mathbf{t}_n) = (\mathbf{t}^1, \ldots, \mathbf{t}^m)^{\mathrm{T}}$. The machines are *strategic* and therefore, when asked, they do not necessarily report their true processing times $\mathbf{t}$ but they rather use *strategies* $\mathbf{s} \in \mathbb{R}_{\geq 0}^{n \times m}$. To emphasize the distinction, we will often refer to $\mathbf{t}$ as the profile of *true* processing times. Adopting standard game-theoretic notation, we use $\mathbf{t}_{-i}$ and $\mathbf{s}_{-i}$ to denote the profile of true or reported processing times respectively, without the coordinates of the i'th machine.

A (deterministic, direct revelation) *mechanism* $\mathcal{M} = (\mathbf{x}, \mathbf{p})$ gets as input a strategy profile $\mathbf{s} \in \mathbb{R}_{\geq 0}^{n \times m}$ reported by the machines and outputs *allocation* $\mathbf{x} = \mathbf{x}(\mathbf{s}) \in \{0, 1\}^{n \times m}$ and *payment* $\mathbf{p} = \mathbf{p}(\mathbf{s}) \in \mathbb{R}_{\geq 0}^n$: $x_{i,j}$ is an indicator variable denoting whether or not task j is allocated to machine j, and p_i is the payment with which $\mathcal{M}$ compensates machine i for taking part in the mechanism. Thus, the allocation rule needs to satisfy $\sum_{i \in N} x_{i,j}(\mathbf{s}) = 1$ for all tasks j.

The *utility* of machine i under a mechanism $\mathcal{M} = (\mathbf{x}, \mathbf{p})$, given true running times $\mathbf{t}_i$ and a reported profile $\mathbf{s}$ by the machines, is

$$u_i^{\mathcal{M}}(\mathbf{s}|\mathbf{t}_i) = p_i(\mathbf{s}) - \sum_{j=1}^{m} x_{i,j}(\mathbf{s}) t_{i,j},$$

that is, the payment she receives from $\mathcal{M}$ minus the total workload she has to execute. This is exactly the reason why machines may lie about their true processing times; they will change their report $\mathbf{s}_i$ and deviate to another $\mathbf{s}_i'$ if this improves the above quantity. A stable solution with respect to such best-response selfish behaviour is captured by the well-known notion of an equilibrium. Given a mechanism $\mathcal{M}$ and a strategy profile $\mathbf{s}$, we will say that $\mathbf{s}$ is a *(pure Nash) equilibrium*[2] of $\mathcal{M}$ (with respect to a true profile $\mathbf{t}$) if, for every machine i and every possible deviation $\mathbf{s}'_i \in \mathbb{R}^m_{\geq 0}$,

$$u_i^{\mathcal{M}}(\mathbf{s}|\mathbf{t}) \geq u_i^{\mathcal{M}}(\mathbf{s}'_i, \mathbf{s}_{-i}|\mathbf{t}).$$

Let $\mathcal{Q}_\mathbf{t}^{\mathcal{M}}$ denote the set of pure Nash equilibria of mechanism $\mathcal{M}$ with respect to true profile $\mathbf{t}$. As is standard in the literature, we focus on the case where $\mathcal{Q}_\mathbf{t}^{\mathcal{M}} \neq \emptyset$ for all $\mathbf{t} \in \mathbb{R}^{n \times m}_{\geq 0}$ (see, e.g.,[4,10,15]).

Our objective is to design mechanisms that minimize the *makespan*

$$C^{\mathcal{M}}(\mathbf{s}|\mathbf{t}) = \max_{i \in N} \sum_{j=1}^{m} x_{i,j}(\mathbf{s}) t_{i,j},$$

that is, the total completion time if our machines run in parallel. For a matrix $\mathbf{t}$ of running times, let $\mathrm{OPT}(\mathbf{t})$ denote the optimum makespan, i.e., $\mathrm{OPT}(\mathbf{t}) = \min_\mathbf{y} \max_{i \in N} \sum_{j=1}^{m} y_{i,j} t_{i,j}$ where $\mathbf{y}$ ranges over all feasible allocation of tasks to machines. It is a well-known phenomenon that equilibria can result in suboptimal solutions, and the following, extensively studied, notions where introduced to quantify exactly this discrepancy: the *Price of Anarchy* (PoA) and the *Price of Stability* (PoS) of a scheduling mechanism $\mathcal{M}$ on n machines are, respectively,

$$\mathrm{PoA}(\mathcal{M}) = \sup_{m \in \mathbb{N}, \mathbf{t} \in \mathbb{R}^{n \times m}_{\geq 0}} \frac{\sup_{\mathbf{s} \in \mathcal{Q}_\mathbf{t}^{\mathcal{M}}} C^{\mathcal{M}}(\mathbf{s}|\mathbf{t})}{\mathrm{OPT}(\mathbf{t})}$$

$$\mathrm{PoS}(\mathcal{M}) = \sup_{m \in \mathbb{N}, \mathbf{t} \in \mathbb{R}^{n \times m}_{\geq 0}} \frac{\inf_{\mathbf{s} \in \mathcal{Q}_\mathbf{t}^{\mathcal{M}}} C^{\mathcal{M}}(\mathbf{s}|\mathbf{t})}{\mathrm{OPT}(\mathbf{t})}.$$

For simplicity, we will sometimes drop the $\mathcal{M}$, $\mathbf{t}$ and $\mathbf{s}$ in the notation introduced in this section, whenever it is clear which mechanism and which true or reported profile we are referring to.

2.1 Task-Independent Mechanisms

For a significant part of this paper, we will focus on the class of anonymous, task-independent mechanisms. This is a rather natural class of mechanisms; as a matter of fact, two of the arguably most well-studied and used mechanisms in practice, namely the First-Price and Second-Price, lie within this class.

Definition 1 (Task-independence). *A mechanism $\mathcal{M} = (\mathbf{x}, \mathbf{p})$ is called task-independent if each one of its tasks is allocated independently of the others. Formally, there exists a collection of single-task mechanisms $\{\mathcal{A}_j\}_{j=1,\ldots,m}$, $\mathcal{A}_j = (\mathbf{y}^j, \mathbf{q}^j)$, such that, for any task j, any machine i, and for any strategy profile $\mathbf{s}$,*

$$\mathbf{x}^j(\mathbf{s}) = \mathbf{y}^j(\mathbf{s}^j) \qquad and \qquad p_i(\mathbf{s}) = \sum_{j=1}^{m} q_i^j(\mathbf{s}^j).$$

---

[2] We will be interested in pure Nash equilibria in this paper; we provide a discussion on different solution concepts in the full version.

We will refer to the single-task mechanisms $\mathcal{A}_j$ of the above definition as the *components* of $\mathcal{M}$. It is important to notice here that the definition does not require the mechanism to necessarily use the same component for all the tasks.

Another standard property in the literature of the problem is anonymity. The property can be defined generally (e.g., see [2,11]), but here we will define it for task-independent mechanisms. Since we are dealing with potentially non-truthful mechanisms, we need to handle the notion of anonymity in a more delicate way, in order to appropriately deal with ties.[3]

Definition 2 (Anonymity). *A single-task mechanism $\mathcal{A} = (\mathbf{x}, \mathbf{p})$ is anonymous if, for any permutation of the reports:*

- *The winning agent is permuted in the same way and receives the same payment. If there are multiple agents with the same bid, the winner is chosen to be the one with the largest index.[4]*
- *The payments of the agents that did not receive the task are permuted the same way. Additionally, losing agents with the same report receive the same payment.*

Formally, for any inputs $\mathbf{s}, \tilde{\mathbf{s}}$ such that $\tilde{\mathbf{s}} = \pi(\mathbf{s})$ for some permutation π, if s_{i^*} is the report of the winner in $\mathbf{s}$, then the winner in $\tilde{\mathbf{s}}$ has index $\max\{i \in N | \tilde{s}_i = s_{i^*}\}$. Additionally, let π' be any permutation such that $\tilde{\mathbf{s}} = \pi'(\mathbf{s}) = \pi(\mathbf{s})$. For any $i \neq i^*$ we have $p_{\pi(i)}(\tilde{\mathbf{s}}) = p_{\pi'(i)}(\tilde{\mathbf{s}}) = p_i(\mathbf{s})$. In particular, if all entries in $\mathbf{s}$ are distinct:

$$\mathbf{x}(\tilde{\mathbf{s}}) = \pi(\mathbf{x}(\mathbf{s})) \quad \text{and} \quad \mathbf{p}(\tilde{\mathbf{s}}) = \pi(\mathbf{p}(\mathbf{s})).$$

A task-independent mechanism $\mathcal{M}$ is anonymous, if all its components are anonymous (single-task) mechanisms.

Perhaps the simplest and most natural mechanism that one can think of is the following, which assigns the task to the fastest machine (according to the declared processing times) and pays her declaration.

Definition 3 (First-Price (FP) mechanism). *Assign each task j to the fastest machine $\iota(j)$ for it, i.e. $\iota(j) \in \arg\min_{i \in N} s_{i,j}$ (breaking ties arbitrarily), paying her her declared running time $s_{\iota(i),j}$; pay the remaining $N \setminus \{\iota(j)\}$ machines 0 for task j.*

Second-Price mechanisms have also been extensively studied and applied in auction theory, but also in strategic scheduling.

Definition 4 (Second-Price (SP) mechanism). *Assign each task j to the fastest machine $\iota(j)$ for it, i.e., $\iota(j) \in \arg\min_{i \in N} s_{i,j}$ (breaking ties arbitrarily), paying her the declared processing time of the second-fastest machine, i.e. $\min_{i \in N \setminus \{\iota(j)\}} s_{i,j}$; pay the remaining $N \setminus \{\iota(j)\}$ machines 0 for task j.*

---

[3] For a more detailed discussion of anonymity and tie-breaking, see Remark 1 of the full version.

[4] This is without loss of generality for our results; the tie-breaking could be any fixed total order on the machines that does not depend on the reports.

Notice that both FP and SP mechanisms are task-independent and anonymous. Furthermore, SP is truthful. For a more detailed discussion on the connection between the different solution concepts (truthfulness vs Nash equilibria) and inefficiency notions (Price of Anarchy vs Price of Stability vs approximation ratio), we refer the reader to Sect. 2.2 of the full version.

3   The Inefficiency of *All* Mechanisms

We start with a lower bound of n for the Price of Anarchy of the scheduling problem, which applies to *all* mechanisms. The lower bound will be based on the following monotonicity lemma. We note that this monotonicity property is different from the weak monotonicity (WMON) used in the literature of truthful machine scheduling, in the sense that (a) it is global, whereas WMON is local and (b) it applies to the relation between the true processing times and the equilibria of the mechanism, rather than the actual allocations.

Lemma 1 (Equilibrium Monotonicity). *Let $\mathcal{M}$ be any mechanism for the scheduling problem. Let $\mathbf{t}$ be a profile of true processing times and let $\mathbf{s} \in \mathcal{Q}_{\mathbf{t}}$ be an equilibrium under $\mathbf{t}$. Denote by S_i the set of tasks assigned to machine i by $\mathcal{M}$ on input $\mathbf{s}$. Consider any profile $\hat{\mathbf{t}}$ such that for every machine i, $\hat{t}_{i,j} \leq t_{i,j}$ if $j \in S_i$ and $\hat{t}_{i,j} \geq t_{i,j}$ if $j \notin S_i$. Then $\mathbf{s} \in \mathcal{Q}_{\hat{\mathbf{t}}}$, i.e., $\mathbf{s}$ is an equilibrium under $\hat{\mathbf{t}}$ as well.*

Proof. Assume by contradiction that $\mathbf{s} \notin \mathcal{Q}_{\hat{\mathbf{t}}}$, which means that for the profile of processing times $\hat{\mathbf{t}}$, there exists some machine i that has a beneficial deviation $\mathbf{s}'_i$, i.e., $u_i(\mathbf{s}'_i, \mathbf{s}_{-i}|\hat{\mathbf{t}}) > u_i(\mathbf{s}|\hat{\mathbf{t}})$. Let S'_i be the set of tasks assigned to machine i under report $\mathbf{s}' = (\mathbf{s}'_i, \mathbf{s}_{-i})$ (and underlying true reports $\hat{\mathbf{t}}$). The difference in utility for machine i between profiles $\mathbf{s}'$ and $\mathbf{s}$ is

$$\Delta u_i(\hat{\mathbf{t}}) \equiv u_i(\mathbf{s}'|\hat{\mathbf{t}}) - u_i(\mathbf{s}|\hat{\mathbf{t}}) = p_i(\mathbf{s}') - p_i(\mathbf{s}) + \sum_{j \in S_i \setminus S'_i} \hat{t}_{i,j} - \sum_{j \in S'_i \setminus S_i} \hat{t}_{i,j}.$$

By the fact that $\mathbf{s}'_i$ is a beneficial deviation, it holds that $\Delta u_i(\hat{\mathbf{t}}) > 0$. Now consider the profile of processing times $\mathbf{t}$ and the same deviation $\mathbf{s}'_i$ of machine i. The increase in utility now is

$$\Delta u_i(\mathbf{t}) = p_i(\mathbf{s}') - p_i(\mathbf{s}) + \sum_{j \in S_i \setminus S'_i} t_{i,j} - \sum_{j \in S'_i \setminus S_i} t_{i,j} \geq p_i(\mathbf{s}') - p_i(\mathbf{s})$$

$$+ \sum_{j \in S_i \setminus S'_i} \hat{t}_{i,j} - \sum_{j \in S'_i \setminus S_i} \hat{t}_{i,j} = \Delta u_i(\hat{\mathbf{t}}),$$

which holds because $t_{i,j} \geq \hat{t}_{i,j}$, if $j \in S_i$ and $t_{i,j} \leq \hat{t}_{i,j}$, if $j \notin S_i$. This implies that $\Delta u_i(\mathbf{t}) > 0$, which contradicts the fact that $\mathbf{s} \in \mathcal{Q}_{\mathbf{t}}$. $\square$

Using this lemma, we can prove our first lower bound:

Theorem 1. *For any scheduling mechanism $\mathcal{M}$ for n machines, it must be that* $\mathrm{PoA}(\mathcal{M}) \geq n$.

Proof. Let $\mathcal{M}$ be any mechanism and consider a profile of true processing times $\mathbf{t}$ with n machines and n^2 tasks, where $t_{i,j} = 1$ for all machines i and all tasks j. Let $\mathbf{s} = (s_1, s_2, \ldots, s_n)$ be a pure Nash equilibrium of $\mathcal{M}$ under $\mathbf{t}$. For each machine i, let S_i be the set of tasks assigned to that machine and note that there exists some machine k for which $|S_k| \geq n$. Let $T_k \subseteq S_k$ be any subset of S_k such that $|T_k| = n$.

Now consider the following profile $\hat{t}$ of processing times:

- For all $i \neq k$, $\hat{t}_{i,j} = 0$, for all $j \in S_i$ and $\hat{t}_{i,j} = t_{i,j}$, for all $j \notin S_i$.
- $\hat{t}_{kj} = 0$, for all $j \in S_k \backslash T_k$ and $\hat{t}_{kj} = t_{k,j}$, for all $j \notin S_k \backslash T_k$.

By Lemma 1, the profile $\mathbf{s} = (s_1, s_2, \ldots, s_n)$ is a pure Nash equilibrium under $\hat{t}$ and the allocation is the same as before, for a makespan of at least n, since machine k is assigned all the tasks in T_k. The optimal allocation will assign one task from T_k to each machine, the tasks from S_i to machine i for each $i \neq k$ and the tasks from $S_k \backslash T_k$ to machine k, for a total makespan of 1 and the Price of Anarchy bound follows.   □

3.1   PoA/PoS Trade-Off

In this section, we prove our main theorem regarding the trade-off between the Price of Anarchy and the Price of Stability. The theorem informally says that if the Price of Anarchy of a mechanism is small, then its Price of Stability has to be high.

Theorem 2. *For any scheduling mechanism $\mathcal{M}$ for $n \geq 2$ machines, and any positive real α,*

$$\mathrm{PoA}(\mathcal{M}) < \alpha \quad \Longrightarrow \quad \mathrm{PoS}(\mathcal{M}) \geq \frac{n-1}{\alpha} + 1.$$

By allowing α in Theorem 2 to grow arbitrarily large, we get the following:

Corollary 1. *Even for just two machines, if a scheduling mechanism has an optimal Price of Stability of 1, then its Price of Anarchy has to be unboundedly large.*

From the results of the section, as well as the trivial fact that $\mathrm{PoA}(\mathcal{M}) \geq \mathrm{PoS}(\mathcal{M})$ for any mechanism $\mathcal{M}$, we obtain a feasibility trade-off between the PoA and the PoS of scheduling mechanisms, which is illustrated in Fig. 1. We refer to the boundary of the shaded feasible region as the *inefficiency boundary*; the shape of the boundary follows from Theorem 2, as well as Theorem 1, since for $\mathrm{PoS}(\mathcal{M}) > 2 - \frac{1}{n}$ (or, in the language of Theorem 2, for $\alpha < n$), the best (i.e. largest) lower bound on the PoA is now given by Theorem 1.

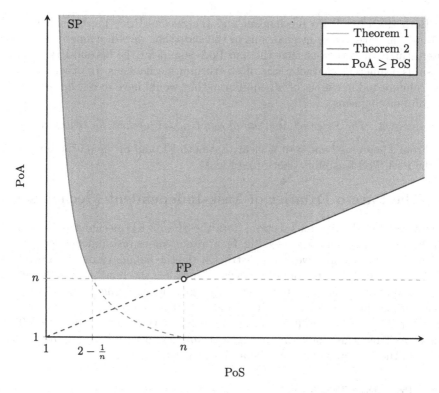

Fig. 1. The inefficiency boundary for general mechanisms, given by Theorem 2 (red line). Combined with the global PoA lower bound of Theorem 1 (green line) and the trivial fact that the PoS is at most the PoA (blue line), we finally get the grey feasible region. (Color figure online)

Mechanisms on the Extrema of the Inefficiency Boundary: When looking for mechanisms on the Pareto frontier, the first ones that come to mind are perhaps the First-Price (FP) and Second-Price (SP) mechanisms, defined in Sect. 2, which are straightforward adaptations of the well-known First-Price auction and Second-Price auction mechanisms from the auction literature.

It follows from known results in the literature for the First-Price auction (see, e.g., [6]) that in every pure Nash equilibrium of the FP, each task is allocated to the machine with the smallest *true* processing time for the task. For the Second-Price mechanism, again it follows from known observations in the literature that while the mechanism is truthful, it has several other pure Nash equilibria as well. More precisely, for a task $j \in J$ and any machine $i \in N$, there exists an equilibrium for which task j is allocated to machine i. Therefore, we have the following.

Theorem 3. *For the First-Price mechanism, the PoA and the PoS are both n. For the Second-Price mechanism, the PoA of the mechanism is unbounded and the PoS is 1.*

Both the First-Price mechanism and the Second-Price mechanism will be obtained as corner-case mechanisms in the class that we will define in Sect. 4.2. Interestingly, it turns out that the bad PoA bound for the Second-Price Mechanism is a inherent characteristic of all truthful mechanisms. In other words, if one is interested in the set of *all* equilibria, they would have to reach out beyond truthful mechanisms.

Theorem 4. *The Price of Anarchy of any truthful mechanism is unbounded.*

From Theorems 2 and 3, it is clear that both FP and SP lie on the boundary of the PoA/PoS feasibility space (see Fig. 1).

4   The Pareto Frontier of Task-Independent Mechanisms

As we noted in the previous section, both the SP and FP mechanisms, which lie on the inefficiency boundary (see Fig. 1), are anonymous task-independent mechanisms. In this section, we will construct a tighter boundary on the PoA/PoS trade-off for the class of anonymous task-independent mechanisms. Furthermore, we will show that this boundary is actually tight, by designing a class of optimal mechanisms that lie exactly on it, meaning that for each point on the boundary, there is a mechanism in our class that achieves the corresponding PoA/PoS trade-off. Thus, this results in a *complete characterization of the Pareto frontier* between the PoA and the PoS. For an illustration, see Fig. 2.

4.1   PoA/PoS Trade-Off

We start with the theorem that gives us the improved boundary on the space of feasible task-independent and anonymous mechanisms. This is the red line in Fig. 2.

Theorem 5. *For any task-independent anonymous scheduling mechanism $\mathcal{M}$ for n machines, and any real $\alpha > 1$,*

$$\mathrm{PoA}(\mathcal{M}) < (n-1)\alpha + 1 \quad \Longrightarrow \quad \mathrm{PoS}(\mathcal{M}) \geq \frac{(n-1)}{\alpha} + 1.$$

4.2   Optimal Mechanisms on the Pareto Frontier

Next, we will design a class of mechanisms, parameterized by a quantity α that will populate, in a smooth way, the boundary given by Theorem 5. Thus, these mechanisms achieve trade-offs that lie on the Pareto frontier of inefficiency for the class of task-independent and anonymous mechanisms.

Definition 5 (Second-Price mechanism with α-relative reserve price $(\mathcal{SP}_\alpha)$). *For $\alpha \geq 1$, $\mathcal{SP}_\alpha$ is the task-independent mechanism that, for each task j: finds a machine $k \in \arg\min_{i \in N} s_{i,j}$ and sets a reserve price at $r = \alpha \cdot s_{k,j}$; assigns the task to the fastest machine $\iota(j) \in \arg\min_{i \in N} s_{i,j}$ (breaking ties-arbitrarily); pays machine $\iota(j)$ the amount $\min\{\min_{i \in N \setminus \{\iota(j)\}} s_{i,j}, r\}$; pays nothing to the remaining machines $N \setminus \iota(j)$.*

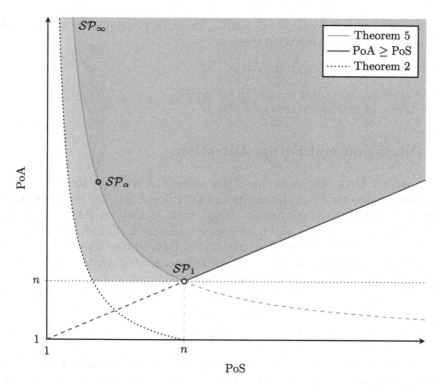

Fig. 2. The inefficiency boundary, for anonymous task-independent mechanisms, given by Theorem 5 (red line). Combined with the global PoA lower bound of Theorem 1 (green line) and the trivial fact that the PoS is at most the PoA (blue line), we finally get the grey feasible region. The family of mechanisms SP_α described in Sect. 4.2 lies exactly on this boundary (red line), thus completely characterizing the *Pareto frontier* in a smooth way with respect to parameter $\alpha \geq 1$: on its one end ($\alpha = 1$) is the First-Price mechanism FP = SP_1 and at the other ($\alpha \to \infty$) the Second-Price mechanism SP = SP_∞. (Color figure onlilne)

Informally, for each task j, the mechanism sets a reserve price which is α times larger than the smallest declared processing time, allocates the task to the fastest machine (according to the declarations) and pays the machine the minimum of the second-smallest declared processing time and the reserve price. What this mechanism achieves in terms of the equilibria that it induces is the following: assume that we create a *bucket* of tasks with *true* processing times at most α times larger than the smallest *true* processing time. Then, in every equilibrium of the mechanism, task j is allocated to some machine in the bucket and moreover, for any machine in the bucket, there exists some equilibrium under which SP_α allocates the task to that machine (see the full version for a formal handling of this intuition). Referencing our discussion in Sect. 3.1, we remark that in the case of FP = SP_1, the bucket contains only the fastest machine(s) for the task, and in the case of SP $= \mathcal{SP}_\infty$, the bucket contains the whole set of machines. We have the following theorem.

Theorem 6. *For $\mathcal{SP}_\alpha$ on n machines,*

- *the Price of Anarchy is at most $(n-1)\alpha + 1$,*
- *the Price of Stability is at most $\frac{n-1}{\alpha} + 1$.*

5   Discussion and Future Directions

On a general level, one could follow our agenda of studying the inefficiency trade-off between the Price of Anarchy and the Price of Stability for many other problems in algorithmic mechanism design, such as auctions [14,20], machine scheduling without money [10,11], or resource allocation [4], to name a few, for which the two inefficiency notions have already been studied separately.

In terms of the strategic scheduling setting, our work gives rise to a plethora of intriguing questions for future work, both on a technical and a conceptual level. The major open question is whether there exists a mechanism that achieves a better trade-off than that of Theorem 5, or in other words,

"Is the yellow region of Fig. 2 empty or not?"

If such a mechanism exists, it will most probably *not* be task-independent. Another question is whether we can remove anonymity from the statement for task-independent mechanisms. In that regard, we have come close, as captured by the following theorem.

Theorem 7. *For any task-independent scheduling mechanism $\mathcal{M}$ for n machines, and real $\alpha > 1$,*

$$\text{PoA}(\mathcal{M}) < (n-1)\frac{\alpha}{\sqrt{2}} + 1 \quad \Longrightarrow \quad \text{PoS}(\mathcal{M}) \geq \frac{(n-1)}{\alpha\sqrt{2}} + 1.$$

Another natural direction would be to consider different equilibrium notions, beyond pure Nash equilibria, or randomized scheduling mechanisms. We refer the reader to the discussion of the full version for a more insightful discussion of these avenues for future work.

References

1. Anshelevich, E., Dasgupta, A., Kleinberg, J., Tardos, É., Wexler, T., Roughgarden, T.: The price of stability for network design with fair cost allocation. SIAM J. Comput. **38**(4), 1602–1623 (2008). https://doi.org/10.1137/07068009
2. Ashlagi, I., Dobzinski, S., Lavi, R.: Optimal lower bounds for anonymous scheduling mechanisms. Math. Oper. Res. **37**(2), 244–258 (2012). https://doi.org/10.1287/moor.1110.0534

3. Caragiannis, I., et al.: Bounding the inefficiency of outcomes in generalized second price auctions. J. Econ. Theory **156**, 343–388 (2015). https://doi.org/10.1016/j.jet.2014.04.010
4. Christodoulou, G., Filos-Ratsikas, A., Frederiksen, S.K.S., Goldberg, P.W., Zhang, J., Zhang, J.: Social welfare in one-sided matching mechanisms (extended abstract). In: Proceedings of AAMAS, pp. 1297–1298 (2016). https://doi.org/10.1007/978-3-319-46882-2_3
5. Christodoulou, G., Koutsoupias, E., Vidali, A.: A lower bound for scheduling mechanisms. Algorithmica **55**(4), 729–740 (2009). https://doi.org/10.1007/s00453-008-9165-3
6. Feldman, M., Lucier, B., Nisan, N.: Correlated and coarse equilibria of single-item auctions. In: Proceedings of WINE, pp. 131–144 (2016). https://doi.org/10.1007/978-3-662-54110-4_10
7. Filos-Ratsikas, A., Frederiksen, S.K.S., Zhang, J.: Social welfare in one-sided matchings: random priority and beyond. In: Proceedings of SAGT, pp. 1–12 (2014). https://doi.org/10.1007/978-3-662-44803-8_1
8. Filos-Ratsikas, A., Giannakopoulos, Y., Lazos, P.: The Pareto Frontier of Inefficiency in Mechanism Design. CoRR abs/1809.03454, September 2018. https://arxiv.org/abs/1809.03454
9. Gairing, M.: Covering games: approximation through non-cooperation. In: Proceedings of WINE, pp. 184–195 (2009). https://doi.org/10.1007/978-3-642-10841-9_18
10. Giannakopoulos, Y., Koutsoupias, E., Kyropoulou, M.: The anarchy of scheduling without money. Theor. Comput. Sci. **778**, 19–32 (2019). https://doi.org/10.1016/j.tcs.2019.01.022
11. Lucier, B., Singer, Y., Syrgkanis, V., Tardos, E.: Equilibrium in combinatorial public projects. In: Proceedings of WINE, pp. 347–360 (2013).https://doi.org/10.1007/978-3-642-45046-4_28
12. Koutsoupias, E., Papadimitriou, C.: Worst-case equilibria. Comput. Sci. Rev. **3**(2), 65–69 (2009). https://doi.org/10.1016/j.cosrev.2009.04.003
13. Koutsoupias, E., Vidali, A.: A lower bound of $1+\varphi$ for truthful scheduling mechanisms. Algorithmica **66**(1), 211–223 (2013)
14. Lucier, B., Singer, Y., Syrgkanis, V., Tardos, E.: Equilibrium in combinatorial public projects. In: Proceedings of WINE, pp. 347–360 (2013). https://doi.org/10.1007/978-3-642-45046-4_28
15. Nisan, N., Ronen, A.: Algorithmic mechanism design. Games Econ. Behav. **35**(1/2), 166–196 (2001). https://doi.org/10.1006/game.1999.0790
16. Ramaswamy, V., Paccagnan, D., Marden, J.R.: Multiagent coverage problems: the trade-off between anarchy and stability. CoRR abs/1710.01409, July 2018. http://arxiv.org/abs/1710.01409
17. Roughgarden, T., Syrgkanis, V., Tardos, E.: The price of anarchy in auctions. J. Artif. Intell. Res. **59**, 59–101 (2017). https://doi.org/10.1613/jair.5272
18. Roughgarden, T., Tardos, É.: How bad is selfish routing? J. ACM **49**(2), 236–259 (2002). https://doi.org/10.1145/506147.506153
19. Saks, M., Yu, L.: Weak monotonicity suffices for truthfulness on convex domains. In: Proceedings of the 6th ACM Conference on Electronic Commerce, pp. 286–293 (2005). https://doi.org/10.1145/1064009.1064040
20. Syrgkanis, V., Tardos, E.: Composable and efficient mechanisms. In: Proceedings of the 45th Annual ACM Symposium on Theory of Computing, pp. 211–220 (2013). https://doi.org/10.1145/2488608.2488635

On the Price of Anarchy of Cost-Sharing in Real-Time Scheduling Systems

Eirini Georgoulaki[1] and Kostas Kollias[2]([✉])

[1] University of Athens, Athens, Greece
eirini.geo.98@gmail.com
[2] Google Research, Mountain View, USA
kostaskollias@google.com

Abstract. We study cost-sharing games in real-time scheduling systems where the operation cost of the server at any given time is a function of its load. We focus on monomial cost functions and consider both the case when the degree is less than one (inducing positive externalities for the jobs) and when it is greater than one (inducing negative externalities for the jobs). For the former case, we provide tight price of anarchy bounds which show that the price of anarchy grows to infinity as a polynomial of the number of jobs in the game. For the latter, we observe that existing results provide constant and tight (asymptotically in the degree of the monomial) bounds on the price of anarchy. We then switch our attention to improving the price of anarchy by means of a simple coordination mechanism that has no knowledge of the instance. We show that our mechanism reduces the price of anarchy of games with n jobs and unit server costs from $\Theta(\sqrt{n})$ to 2. We also show that for a restricted class of instances a similar improvement is achieved for monomial server costs. This is not the case, however, for unrestricted instances of monomial costs for which we prove that the price of anarchy remains super-constant for our mechanism.

1 Introduction

The model of cost-sharing in real-time scheduling systems was introduced by [29] in response to the emergence and popularity of cloud computing as well as to the efforts to reduce power consumption in large computing systems [2,6,9,19,20]. In the model studied in [29] there is a server and a collection of n jobs that are to be scheduled on the server. Each job j has a release time r_j and a deadline d_j. Time is slotted and each job gets to select which slot in $[r_j, d_j)$ it will be scheduled on. The server has a unit activation cost per time slot, which models the energy spent to keep the server open. This is an expressive model for many applications in cloud computing and data center optimization, which makes the understanding of the inefficiency of such a system and ultimately its improvement important tasks. In a more general model, the cost can depend on the load that the server has to process at any given time slot t, i.e., the energy spent will be

© Springer Nature Switzerland AG 2019
I. Caragiannis et al. (Eds.): WINE 2019, LNCS 11920, pp. 200–213, 2019.
https://doi.org/10.1007/978-3-030-35389-6_15

a function $c(l_t)$ that depends on the number of jobs l_t that are to be processed during t. This generalized model is the main focus of this work.

In the standard cost-sharing setting studied in [29], each of the jobs processed at time t assumes an equal share of the server cost $c(l_t)$ (or a proportional share for a more general setting where each job places a different load on the server). Given this rule, we would expect each job j to optimize for its individual cost share and declare the slot that minimizes the ratio of the server cost to the number of jobs (which is precisely the individual cost share) among all slots in its window $[r_j, d_j)$. When this is true for every job, we have an assignment that is a *Nash equilibrium* (NE). The inefficiency of a NE is captured by the *price of anarchy* (PoA) which is the worst case ratio of the total cost in a NE assignment over the total cost in the optimal assignment.

For the base case of unit server costs we have $c(0) = 0$ and $c(x) = 1$ for every $x > 0$. The PoA of such games was shown in [29] to be $\Theta(\sqrt{n})$ and the question of what happens when the server has a cost that depends on the load placed on it was posed as an open problem. A major part of our results focuses precisely on answering this question. We study cost functions of the form $c(x) = x^d$ for some parameter $d > 0$. Note that for $d < 1$ the cost share function $c(x)/x$ is monotonically decreasing and that for $d > 1$ it is monotonically increasing. The game we study here belongs to the class of *congestion games* [26], the PoA of which has received significant attention in the literature. Our games are equivalent to singleton congestion games with uniform resources arranged on a line and with strategy spaces that correspond to intervals on this line. We provide tight PoA bounds for the case of positive externalities (which is the best motivated case for our application of interest), i.e., $d < 1$, showing that the PoA is $\Theta(n^{(1-d)/2})$. For $d > 1$, the upper bound for general congestions games shows the PoA does not depend on the number of jobs and is at most $d^{\Theta(d)}$ (i.e., constant for fixed d). We observe that an early $d^{\Theta(d)}$ lower bound instance [4] designed for routing games applies to our setting, showing that the PoA is in fact $d^{\Theta(d)}$.

Subsequently, we focus on the design of *coordination mechanisms* for the problem in an effort to improve the PoA. A coordination mechanism [12] is a set of a-priori rules the system designer can set without knowledge of the instance. A coordination mechanism can, for example, modify the cost shares of jobs, expand or restrict their strategy spaces, etc. The modified rules of the game under the coordination mechanism will change the set of NE outcomes, hopefully to the improvement of the PoA. We design a simple coordination mechanism that merely expands the strategy space of each job by asking them to declare, not only a slot, but also a payment. It is clear that this mechanism requires no knowledge of the specifics of the instance and is very simple to implement. We show that this simple modification has a surprisingly strong impact on the PoA for the case of unit server costs, reducing it from infinity—specifically $\Theta(\sqrt{n})$—down to 2. For monomial cost functions of degree less than 1, we prove that our mechanism has super-constant PoA for general instances, however, we also prove that it does achieve an improvement from super-constant to constant for a special family of instances. Specifically, for instances such that the optimal solution uses a single slot (which includes, for example, instances with a common release time or a common deadline), our mechanism reduces the PoA from $\Theta(n^{(1-d)/2})$ to $\Theta(1)$. (Recall that for monomials of degree larger than 1, it is known that the PoA of congestion games is already constant [1,4] as a function of n without applying any coordination mechanism.)

1.1   Related Work

The work most closely related to our paper is the one in [29] where the model we study was introduced and various results were obtained for the case of constant (but possibly time-dependent) server costs with respect to the price of anarchy and the related concepts of the strong price of anarchy (inefficiency of equilibria with respect to coordinated deviations) and the price of stability (inefficiency of the best Nash equilibrium as opposed to the worst). Our work also has ties to literature on the price of anarchy of congestion games, cost-sharing in congestion games, and coordination mechanisms, all three of which we discuss below.

Congestion games were introduced by Rosenthal in [26] as a class of games that guarantee the existence of (pure) Nash equilibria. In a congestion game, there is a set of resources that the participants can use. Each one of the participants has a strategy space that allows them to select one of given subsets of resources, something that allows for various expressive models, including routing in networks. The cost of each resource, which is a function of the number of participants using it, is distributed equally among its users. The price of anarchy of a special case of congestion games was first studied in [23], where the price of anarchy was first introduced. A long sequence of follow-up work gave a strong understanding of the price of anarchy in congestion games [1,3,4,11,27]. Generalizations to weighted models have also been studied [1,7] albeit with the drawback that, in contrast to standard congestion games, existence of a (pure) Nash equilibrium is not guaranteed [16].

Cost-sharing aspects in the study of congestion games were brought into the picture to correct for the absence of equilibria in weighted games. The work in [22] shows how the Shapley value cost-sharing method can be applied to restore pure equilibria, whereas [17] shows that the more general class of generalized weighted Shapley values are the only ones that can guarantee this property. The price of anarchy of the induced games has been the subject of extensive study, with examples including [14,15,21,24,25,28]. Papers that use cost-sharing to improve the efficiency of equilibria include [10], which focuses on the price of stability, and [30], an approach which requires knowledge of the instance at hand.

A more general approach seeking to improve the price of anarchy is that of coordination mechanisms. A coordination mechanism gives the designer more freedom in designing the game. This freedom includes modifying the strategy spaces of the participants or changing how costs are defined on the resources. For example, coordination mechanisms were applied in a multiple machine makespan minimization scheduling setting in [12] by means of introducing different scheduling policies on different machines. Follow up work on coordination mechanisms includes [5,8,13,18].

1.2 Summary of Our Results and Roadmap

Section 2 presents our model and notation. In Sect. 3.1 we focus on the case of monomial cost functions of degree $d < 1$ and prove that the PoA is approximately $2n^{(1-d)/2}/(1 + d)$, where n is the number of jobs in the game. In Sect. 3.2 we discuss the case when $d > 1$ and observe that early results on congestion games [4] can be used to show that the PoA is $d^{\Theta(d)}$. Finally, in Sect. 4, we define our coordination mechanism and, in Sect. 4.1, we prove that it achieves a strong improvement on the PoA for the case of unit server costs (from $\Theta(\sqrt{n})$ to 2). Switching to monomials with $d < 1$, even though it is the case that the PoA grows to infinity for our mechanism as well, we are still able to show in Sect. 4.2 that we can reduce the PoA from $\Theta(n^{(1-d)/2})$ to $\Theta(1)$ for the class of *common slot instances*, in which the optimum uses a single slot (note that this class includes, among others, instances with a common release time or a common deadline). As stated earlier, the PoA for the case with $d > 1$ is already constant. Section 5 concludes the paper.

2 Preliminaries

The game is specified by the following parameters: (a) a cost function $c(x)$ that gives the cost at any given time step as a function of the number of jobs x that have to be processed at that time step, (b) a time horizon T that specifies the available time slots as $t = 1, 2, \dots, T$, and (c) a set of jobs J, with each $j \in J$ having an integer release time r_j and an integer deadline d_j such that $0 < r_j < d_j < T$.

Let s_j denote the slot declared by job j such that $r_j \leq s_j < d_j$ and let s denote the *assignment*, i.e., the vector of declared slots. The load on slot t, $l_t(s) = |\{j : s_j = t\}|$, is the number of jobs declaring slot t. The cost on slot t is then $c(l_t(s))$ and the *total cost* is:

$$C(s) = \sum_{t=1}^{T} c(l_t(s)).$$

An assignment s is a *Nash equilibrium* (NE) when for every job j we get:

$$\frac{c(l_{s_j}(s))}{l_{s_j}(s)} \leq \frac{c(l_t(s) + 1)}{l_t(s) + 1},$$

for every $t \neq s_j$ in $[r_j, d_j)$. This expression suggests that the cost share at the slot declared by j is at most the cost share j would get by deviating to any other slot in its interval. The inefficiency of equilibrium solutions is given by the *price of anarchy* (PoA), which is the worst case ratio of the total cost in a NE over the total cost in the optimal assignment:

$$PoA = \frac{\max_{s \text{ a NE}} C(s)}{\min_{s^*} C(s^*)}.$$

3   Monomial Cost Functions

3.1   Decreasing Cost Shares: $d < 1$

In this section we analyze the PoA for the case when the cost function equals x^d with $d < 1$, for which the cost share $c(x)/x$ is strictly decreasing. The main result of the section is the following theorem, which we prove in the two subsequent lemmas.

Theorem 1. *For games with n jobs and cost function $c(x) = x^d$ with $d < 1$, the worst case PoA is $\Theta(n^{(1-d)/2})$.*

Lemma 1. *Given a game with n jobs and cost function $c(x) = x^d$ with $d < 1$, for any NE s and any optimal assignment s^* we get:*

$$\frac{C(s)}{C(s^*)} = O\left(n^{\frac{1-d}{2}}\right).$$

Proof. Consider an optimal assignment s^* and focus on a slot t that holds $l_t(s^*) = l_t$ jobs in s^*. We will write $J(t)$ for the set including these l_t jobs. The jobs in $J(t)$ have a cost of $c(l_t)$ in s^* and we wish to bound the cost they can have in any given NE s.

We begin by proving the claim that, in the NE s and for any positive integer x, there exist at most 2 slots that have x jobs and include jobs from $J(t)$. We prove this claim by contradiction. Suppose there are at least 3 slots with x jobs that host jobs from $J(t)$. Pick any such 3 slots and let t' be the median. If $t' \geq t$, then we have at least two slots that are greater than or equal to t and hold x jobs including some from $J(t)$, otherwise we have at least two slots that are less than or equal to t with this property. We will treat the case when there are two slots that are greater than or equal to t. The other case is symmetric. Call these slots t' and t'' with $t'' > t'$. Consider some job $j \in J(t)$ that uses t'' in s. The allowed interval of j includes t, since it is scheduled on it in s^*, and t'', since it is scheduled on it in s. Since $t \leq t' < t''$, it follows that t' is also in the allowed interval for j. However, we can observe that j has an incentive to deviate from t'' to t' and improve its cost from $c(x)/x$ to $c(x+1)/(x+1)$. This contradicts the fact that s is a NE and proves our original claim that at most 2 slots can have jobs from $J(t)$ and exactly x jobs.

Given the above, we return to the task of upper bounding the total payments of jobs in $J(t)$ in s. By the claim in the previous paragraph, at most $2x$ jobs from $J(t)$ can pay $c(x)/x$ in s. This means at most 2 jobs can pay the maximum

$c(1)/1$, at most 4 jobs the second highest $c(2)/2$, etc. It follows that the total payments in s of the jobs in $J(t)$ are upper bounded by:

$$\sum_{j=1}^{h_t} 2c(j),$$

where h_t is the smallest integer such that $h_t^2 + h_t \geq l_t$. Then the ratio of the total cost paid by the jobs in $J(t)$ in s over the same cost in s^* is at most:

$$\frac{\sum_{j=1}^{h_t} 2c(j)}{c(l_t)}.$$

Suppose t is in fact the slot that maximizes this ratio, meaning the above expression is an upper bound on the PoA. We get:

$$\frac{C(s)}{C(s^*)} \leq \frac{\sum_{j=1}^{h_t} 2c(j)}{c(l_t)} = \frac{\sum_{j=1}^{h_t} 2j^d}{l_t^d}$$

$$\leq \frac{\int_0^{h_t+1} x^d dx}{l_t^d} \leq \frac{2(h_t+1)^{1+d}}{(1+d)l_t^d}$$

$$\leq \frac{2(h_t+1)^{1+d}}{(1+d)h_t^d(h_t-1)^d}$$

$$= O\left(h_t^{1-d}\right) = O\left(l_t^{\frac{1-d}{2}}\right) = O\left(n^{\frac{1-d}{2}}\right).$$

This completes the proof of the upper bound.   □

Lemma 2. *For every positive integer h and for every cost function $c(x) = x^d$ with $d < 1$, there exists a game with $n = h^2 + h$ jobs, and a NE s of that game, such that:*

$$\frac{C(s)}{C(s^*)} = \Omega\left(h^{1-d}\right) = \Omega\left(n^{(1-d)/2}\right),$$

where s^* is an optimal assignment of that game.

Proof. Our instance has $n = h^2 + h$ jobs and $2h+1$ slots. For ease of exposition we will shift time and call the slots $-h, -h+1, \ldots, -1, 0, 1, \ldots, h-1, h$. There exist j jobs that can use slots $[-j, 0]$ and j jobs that can use slots $[0, j]$ for $j = 1, 2, \ldots, h$. Observe that slot 0 is the only one that is common to all intervals. The optimal solution s^* would place all jobs on 0 for a total cost:

$$C(s^*) = (h^2 + h)^d = \Theta(n^d).$$

Consider the following assignment s, which as we will argue is a NE. Every one of the j jobs with interval $[-j, 0]$ selects slot $-j$ and every one of the j jobs with interval $[0, j]$ selects slot j. Note that the number of jobs on slot t is $|t|$. This fact implies the assignment is actually a NE, since the jobs on any slot t

share the slot with $|t| - 1$ other jobs, while every other slot t' between t and 0 has $|t'| \leq |t| - 1$ jobs. The cost of this assignment is:

$$C(s) = \sum_{j=1}^{h} 2j^d \geq 2 \int_1^h x^d dx = \frac{2}{d+1} \left(h^{d+1} - 1 \right) = \Theta \left(n^{(d+1)/2} \right).$$

Taking the ratio $C(s)/C(s^*)$ completes the proof.   □

Remark 1. From the proofs of Lemmas 1 and 2 it follows that the worst case PoA is in fact approximately:

$$\frac{2n^{\frac{1-d}{2}}}{1+d}.$$

3.2   Increasing Cost Shares: $d > 1$

We now discuss the PoA for the case when the cost function equals x^d with $d > 1$. In this case the cost share $c(x)/x$ is strictly increasing. We observe that the general upper bound on the PoA of congestion games and an early lower bound designed for routing games which applies to our model yield the following theorem.

Theorem 2 *([4] Theorem 4.3).* *For games with cost function $c(x) = x^d$ with $d > 1$, the worst case PoA is $d^{\Theta(d)}$.*

Note that the PoA is constant when d is fixed and is independent of the number of players n, in contrast to the unit and $d < 1$ cases. In this work, we are mostly interested in this behavior of the PoA as a function of n. However, observing the PoA as a function of d is also of interest and we note that the $d^{\Theta(d)}$ expression hides a gap. For example, for $d = 2$, the lower bound of [4] is 2, whereas the general upper bound for congestion games is $5/2$. The lower bound in [4] is a very natural instance, where, in the optimal solution, each slot has unit occupancy, whereas in the NE, slots become progressively more congested. This natural flavor of the instance could tempt us to conjecture that the lower bound is in fact tight for our setting, however, in the next result we show that this is not the case.

Lemma 3. *For games with cost function $c(x) = x^2$, the worst case PoA is strictly larger than 2.*

Proof. The game has the following slots in order: first a slot with label "6", then 2 slots with label "5", then 5 slots with label "4", then 20 slots with label "3", then 60 slots with label "2", then 120 slots with label "1", and, finally, another 120 slots with label "0". The labels of slots signify precisely how many jobs are on them in the NE s. The allowable slots of a job on a slot with label "x" are all slots with labels from "6" up to "$x - 1$". Clearly s is a NE. Simple calculations show that the total cost in s is 706.

Now consider the outcome s^* where all the jobs from slots with label "x", are spread as evenly as possible on the slots with label "$x - 1$". Again simple calculations show that the total cost of s^* is 352, which gives a PoA bound $C(s)/C(s^*) > 2$.   □

Identifying the precise PoA value as a function of d appears to be a challenging open problem that we leave as future work.

4   Coordination Mechanism

In this section we design a coordination mechanism that applies a simple modification to the game, without knowing anything about the instance, and significantly improves the PoA. For the case of constant (unit) costs, we show that the PoA is brought down to 2. For $c(x) = x^d$ with $d < 1$ we prove that the PoA is improved from super-constant to constant for the class of instances which have a single slot occupied in the optimal solution. This class includes instances with a common release time or a common deadline for all jobs, as well as instances with a batch of jobs centered around a common slot. We prove that, without this restriction, the PoA for $c(x) = x^d$ with $d < 1$ remains super-constant even under our mechanism. Note that for $d > 1$ the PoA is known to be constant even without applying any coordination mechanism.

Our mechanism changes the strategy space of each job j, from being simply a slot $s_j \in [r_j, d_j)$, to a pair (s_j, ξ_j) where $s_j \in [r_j, d_j)$ is again the declared slot and $\xi_j \geq 0$ is a payment. The mechanism will open slot t under strategies (s, ξ) if and only if:

$$\sum_{j:s_j=t} \xi_j \geq c(l_t(s)),$$

i.e., if the jobs selecting slot s cover the server cost with their declared payments. We assume every job j has an infinite cost for not being processed (i.e., when slot s_j is not opened), an assumption that is implicitly present in the base model as well, since jobs do not have the option of staying out of the game. In this framework, the NE condition asserts that each (s_j, ξ_j) are such that:

$$\sum_{j':s_{j'}=s_j} \xi_{j'} \geq c(l_{s_j}(s))$$

$$\text{and } \xi_j \leq \max\left\{0, c(l_t(s)+1) - \sum_{j':s_{j'}=t} \xi_{j'}\right\}, \forall t \in [r_j, d_j) \setminus \{s_j\}$$

$$\text{and } \xi_j \leq \max\left\{0, c(l_{s_j}(s)) - \sum_{j':s_{j'}=s_j, j' \neq j} \xi_{j'}\right\}. \tag{1}$$

The first inequality guarantees slot s_j is open, the second that there is no slot t that job j can move to, pay the minimum needed to open it (or keep it open), and get a lower payment, and the third that the job should pay as much as necessary to keep its current slot open.

Lemma 4. *Every NE* (s, ξ) *of our coordination mechanism is such that for every occupied slot t we have* $\sum_{j:s_j=t} \xi_j = c(l_t(s))$.

Proof. Suppose this is not the case. Then there exists some t such that:

$$\sum_{j:s_j=t} \xi_j > c(l_t(s)).$$

Consider any job j such that $s_j = t$ and $\xi_j > 0$. Clearly such a job must exist. We get:

$$\sum_{j':s_{j'}=s_j} \xi_{j'} > c(l_{s_j}(s)) \Rightarrow \xi_j > c(l_{s_j}(s)) - \sum_{j':s_{j'}=s_j, j'\neq j} \xi_{j'},$$

which violates (1) and gives a contradiction.   □

Using Lemma 4, we may simplify the NE condition (1) as:

$$\sum_{j':s_{j'}=s_j} \xi_{j'} = c(l_{s_j}(s)) \text{ and } \xi_j \leq c(l_t(s)+1) - \sum_{j':s_{j'}=t} \xi_{j'}, \forall t \in [r_j, d_j) \setminus \{s_j\}. \quad (2)$$

4.1 Unit Server Costs

Lemma 5. *Let* (s, ξ) *be a NE of our coordination mechanism in a game with unit server costs. Then for every job j, either* $\xi_j = 0$ *or every slot in* $[r_j, d_j) \setminus s_j$ *is unoccupied.*

Proof. Suppose $\xi_j > 0$. Then, by (2), we get that for any slot $t \in [r_j, d_j) \setminus \{s_j\}$:

$$1 - \sum_{j':s_{j'}=t} \xi_{j'} \geq \xi_j > 0. \quad (3)$$

However, by Lemma 4, we know that either t is unoccupied or $\sum_{j':s_{j'}=t} \xi_{j'} = 1$. From this, and given (3), we get that t is unoccupied.   □

Theorem 3. *The PoA of our coordination mechanism for unit server costs is* 2.

Proof. Focus on a slot t and the set of jobs $J(t)$ that use it in a given optimal assignment. The total cost paid by these jobs in the optimal assignment is 1. We will show that the same set of jobs pay at most 2 in any NE (s, ξ).

We examine two cases. First the case when slot t is open in (s, ξ). The jobs from $J(t)$ that use t in (s, ξ) pay at most 1, as given by Lemma 4 (they might be paying less than 1 as t might have additional jobs outside $J(t)$). The jobs in $J(t)$ that use other slots pay 0, as given by Lemma 5 and the fact that all of these jobs have an occupied slot in their windows other than the one they are using, namely, slot t. This proves that, in this case, the total payments of jobs in $J(t)$ are at most 1.

We now focus on the case when slot t is not open in (s, ξ). We first show that the jobs from $J(t)$ who are using slots larger than t are paying a total of at most 1. Focus on the smallest such slot t'. By the fact that (s, ξ) is a NE and using Lemma 4 we get that the total payments on t' are 1. Now focus on any slot $t'' > t'$ and any job $j \in J(t)$ that uses t''. Slot t' must be in the window of job j as both t'' and t satisfy this property and t' lies between them. Then, by Lemma 5 we get that $\xi_j = 0$. This proves that the total payment over all jobs j that use slots larger than t is 1. The proof is symmetric for slots smaller than t, which shows that for every slot t in an optimal solution and for the jobs $J(t)$ using it, the total payment of the jobs $J(t)$ in a NE is at most 2. This directly implies an upper bound of 2 for the PoA.

We now present a lower bound of 2 for the PoA. There exist two jobs j_1, j_2. Job j_1 can be scheduled at times 1 or 2, whereas job j_2 can be scheduled at times 2 or 3. Assigning job j_1 to slot 1, job j_2 to slot 3, and setting $\xi_1 = \xi_2 = 1$ gives rise to a NE with total cost 2. It is easy to verify that this is a NE as each job has only one alternative slot, slot 2, where again they would have to pay a unit cost. The optimal assignment places both jobs in slot 2 for total cost 1. □

We close with a note on existence of a NE for our mechanism. In fact we prove that for any optimal solution there exist payments that will yield a NE.

Theorem 4. *For unit server costs, our coordination mechanism induces games such that, for every optimal assignment s^*, there exists a vector of payments ξ such that (s^*, ξ) is a NE.*

Proof. We first claim that an optimal assignment s^* has the property that, on every occupied slot t, there exists at least one job such that no other slot in its allowed interval is occupied. If this is not true for some t, then moving all jobs j with $s_j = t$ to some other occupied slot in their intervals will decrease the total cost by 1, contradicting optimality of s^*. Given the above, we can find a job j on every slot t that has no other occupied slot in its interval and charge it the full cost of the slot by setting $\xi_j = 1$. Every other job pays 0. This solution will be a NE since the open slot costs are covered and all jobs who do not freeload, pay a unit cost and would pay the exact same cost if they were to deviate to any other slot in their intervals, since they are all unoccupied. □

4.2   Monomial Server Costs with $d < 1$

We first restrict ourselves to instances such that the optimal solution uses a single slot. Clearly this is the case if and only if there is some slot that is included in the interval of every job in the instance. This is the case, for example, when the jobs have common release times or deadlines. Note that by the instance in Lemma 2 (or simple modifications of it for the case of a common release time or a common deadline) we get that the PoA is infinite in the original game. In the next theorem we prove that our coordination mechanism reduces the PoA to a constant for every $d < 1$ for the instances under consideration which we call *common slot instances*.

Theorem 5. *For common slot instances and $c(x) = x^d$ with $d < 1$, the PoA of our coordination mechanism is $\Theta(1)$.*

Proof. For simplicity of exposition, suppose that, in a given game, we shift time so that the only slot used by the optimal solution s^* is slot 0. Let s be a NE of the game. For simplicity and without loss of generality (due to symmetry), suppose the non-negative slots have a larger or equal cost compared to the negative slots in s. If the number of non-negative slots used in s is 1, then a bound of 2 on the PoA of the instance follows trivially, so we assume there are at least 2 non-negative slots used in the game.

Let t and t' be used slots in s such that $0 < t < t'$. Let x be the number of jobs on t and y the number of jobs on t'. Observe that t must lie in the allowed interval of all jobs using t' since $0 < t < t'$ and these jobs use t' in s and 0 in s^*. This means each of these jobs has the option to move to t and pay the marginal contribution $c(x+1) - c(x)$. Also note that, by Lemma 4, at least one of the jobs on t' has to pay, in s, the average cost share $c(y)/y$. The above, combined with the equilibrium condition (2), imply:

$$c(x+1) - c(x) \geq \frac{c(y)}{y}. \tag{4}$$

Note that:

$$c(x+1) - c(x) = (x+1)^d - x^d$$
$$= x^{d-1} \frac{\left(1 + \frac{1}{x}\right)^d - 1}{\frac{1}{x}}$$
$$\leq x^{d-1} \lim_{x \to +\infty} \frac{\left(1 + \frac{1}{x}\right)^d - 1}{\frac{1}{x}}$$
$$= dx^{d-1}, \tag{5}$$

where the inequality follows by $d < 1$. Combining (4) with (5), we get:

$$dx^{d-1} \geq y^{d-1} \Rightarrow y \geq d^{\frac{1}{d-1}} x.$$

This suggests that every slot t must have at least $d^{1/(d-1)}$ (which is always larger than e) times the number of jobs as every other slot in $[0, t)$. This in turn implies that as we move from the largest slot closer and closer to 0, the number of jobs decreases by at least a factor $d^{1/(d-1)}$. We will write $\alpha = d^{1/(d-1)}$. Then, if h is the number of jobs on the last occupied slot, we get that the cost on non-negative slots is at most:

$$\sum_{j=0}^{+\infty} \left(\frac{h}{\alpha^j}\right)^d = h^d \sum_{j=0}^{+\infty} \left(\frac{1}{\alpha^d}\right)^j = \frac{h^d}{1 - \frac{1}{\alpha^d}} = \frac{h^d}{1 - d^{d/(1-d)}}.$$

Recall we have assumed that non-negative slots have at least as much cost as the negative ones, meaning the total cost of s is at most:

$$C(s) \leq \frac{2h^d}{1 - d^{d/(1-d)}}.$$

By the fact that we have h jobs on the largest slot, there at least h jobs in the game and we get:
$$C(s^*) \geq h^d.$$
Taking the ratio gives:
$$\frac{C(s)}{C(s^*)} \leq \frac{2}{1 - d^{d/(1-d)}},$$
which is a constant for every given d. □

Remark 2. For $c(x) = \sqrt{x}$ and for common slot instances with n jobs, our coordination mechanism reduces the PoA from $4n^{1/4}/3$ to at most 4.

We note that for common slot instances there always exists a NE. In fact, again we prove that any optimal solution can be a NE with the correct payment vector.

Theorem 6. *For $c(x) = x^d$ with $d < 1$ and common slot instances, our coordination mechanism induces games such that, for every optimal assignment s^*, there exists a vector of payments ξ such that (s^*, ξ) is a NE.*

Proof. An optimal assignment will clearly place all jobs on the same slot. Charging each job the fair share x^{d-1} results in a NE since $x^{d-1} < 1$ with 1 being the cost any job would have to pay to deviate to a different slot and open it. □

Earlier in the section we proved that our coordination mechanism reduces the PoA to a constant for common slot instances. On the contrary, we show that for general instances, the PoA remains super-constant even for our mechanism.

Theorem 7. *For a game with n jobs and $c(x) = x^d$ with $d < 1$, the worst case PoA of our mechanism is $\Omega(n^{d(1-d)})$.*

Proof. Consider a large number of jobs n such that n^d is integer. Our instance has n^d slots and n^d jobs $1, 2, \ldots, n^d$ such that job j can only be scheduled on slot j. All other $n - n^d$ jobs can be scheduled on any slot. Let s^* be the assignment where every one of the unrestricted jobs is scheduled in slot 1. We get:
$$C(s^*) = \left(n - n^d + 1\right)^d + \left(n^d - 1\right) = \Theta\left(n^d\right).$$
The first term of the sum comes from slot 1 and the second term comes from slots $2, 3, \ldots, n^d$ which hold one job each.

Now consider the following NE s. The unrestricted jobs are split equally among all slots, with each slot having $n^{1-d} - 1$ of them. The payments declared by the unrestricted jobs are 0 and the full cost of each slot is paid for by the corresponding restricted job. This outcome is a NE since the unrestricted jobs get to freeload while the restricted jobs can't move to a different slot and have to pay enough to keep their slot open and avoid the large cost of remaining unscheduled. We get:
$$C(s) = n^d \left(n^{1-d}\right)^d = \Theta\left(n^{2d-d^2}\right).$$

Taking the ratio $C(s)/C(s^*)$ completes the proof. □

5 Conclusion and Open Problems

In this work we tackled the problem of load-dependent server costs in real-time scheduling systems, a question that was posed as an open problem in [29]. We precisely characterized the price of anarchy for monomial cost functions. Furthermore, we came up with a novel coordination mechanism that achieved a spectacular improvement of the price of anarchy in the original model of unit server costs and in a restricted subclass of instances in our extended model.

There are several follow-up questions that emerge from our work. These include extending our results to wider classes of cost functions and settling the PoA gap between the constant bounds for $d > 1$ (e.g., between the 2.00568 lower bound we prove in this work and the standard 2.5 upper bound for $d = 2$). Most importantly, it is interesting to see whether coordination mechanisms of the type that we define here can yield similar improvements in other settings. Our mechanism relies on the simple idea of offloading the cost sharing aspect of the problem to the jobs themselves. This induces a setting where any deviation is charged the marginal contribution of the job on the new slot. Variants of the mechanism that impose, e.g., upper bounds on the cost share of a job/player might prove useful in these endeavors (for instance, such a modification would break the bad example in Lemma 7).

References

1. Aland, S., Dumrauf, D., Gairing, M., Monien, B., Schoppmann, F.: Exact price of anarchy for polynomial congestion games. SIAM J. Comput. **40**(5), 1211–1233 (2011)
2. Albers, S.: Energy-efficient algorithms. Commun. ACM **53**(5), 86–96 (2010)
3. Anshelevich, E., Dasgupta, A., Kleinberg, J.M., Tardos, É., Wexler, T., Roughgarden, T.: The price of stability for network design with fair cost allocation. SIAM J. Comput. **38**(4), 1602–1623 (2008)
4. Awerbuch, B., Azar, Y., Epstein, A. The price of routing unsplittable flow. In: Proceedings of the 37th Annual ACM Symposium on Theory of Computing, Baltimore, MD, USA, 22–24 May 2005, pp. 57–66 (2005)
5. Azar, Y., Fleischer, L., Jain, K., Mirrokni, V.S., Svitkina, Z.: Optimal coordination mechanisms for unrelated machine scheduling. Oper. Res. **63**(3), 489–500 (2015)
6. Bar-Noy, A., Guha, S., Naor, J., Schieber, B.: Approximating the throughput of multiple machines in real-time scheduling. SIAM J. Comput. **31**(2), 331–352 (2001)
7. Bhawalkar, K., Gairing, M., Roughgarden, T.: Weighted congestion games: the price of anarchy, universal worst-case examples, and tightness. ACM Trans. Econ. Comput. **2**(4), 14:1–14:23 (2014)
8. Caragiannis, I.: Efficient coordination mechanisms for unrelated machine scheduling. Algorithmica **66**(3), 512–540 (2013)
9. Chang, J., Gabow, H.N., Khuller, S.: A model for minimizing active processor time. Algorithmica **70**(3), 368–405 (2014)
10. Chen, H., Roughgarden, T., Valiant, G.: Designing network protocols for good equilibria. SIAM J. Comput. **39**(5), 1799–1832 (2010)

11. Christodoulou, G., Koutsoupias, E.: The price of anarchy of finite congestion games. In: Proceedings of the 37th Annual ACM Symposium on Theory of Computing, Baltimore, MD, USA, 22–24 May 2005, pp. 67–73 (2005)
12. Christodoulou, G., Koutsoupias, E., Nanavati, A.: Coordination mechanisms. In: Díaz, J., Karhumäki, J., Lepistö, A., Sannella, D. (eds.) ICALP 2004. LNCS, vol. 3142, pp. 345–357. Springer, Heidelberg (2004). https://doi.org/10.1007/978-3-540-27836-8_31
13. Cole, R., Correa, J.R., Gkatzelis, V., Mirrokni, V.S., Olver, N.: Decentralized utilitarian mechanisms for scheduling games. Games Econ. Behav. **92**, 306–326 (2015)
14. Gairing, M., Kollias, K., Kotsialou, G.: Tight bounds for cost-sharing in weighted congestion games. In: Halldórsson, M.M., Iwama, K., Kobayashi, N., Speckmann, B. (eds.) ICALP 2015. LNCS, vol. 9135, pp. 626–637. Springer, Heidelberg (2015). https://doi.org/10.1007/978-3-662-47666-6_50
15. Gkatzelis, V., Kollias, K., Roughgarden, T.: Optimal cost-sharing in general resource selection games. Oper. Res. **64**(6), 1230–1238 (2016)
16. Goemans, M.X., Mirrokni, V.S., Vetta, A.: Sink equilibria and convergence. In: 46th Annual IEEE Symposium on Foundations of Computer Science (FOCS 2005), 23–25 October 2005, Pittsburgh, PA, USA, Proceedings, pp. 142–154 (2005)
17. Gopalakrishnan, R., Marden, J.R., Wierman, A.: Potential games are necessary to ensure pure nash equilibria in cost sharing games. Math. Oper. Res. **39**(4), 1252–1296 (2014)
18. Immorlica, N., Li, L.E., Mirrokni, V.S., Schulz, A.S.: Coordination mechanisms for selfish scheduling. Theor. Comput. Sci. **410**(17), 1589–1598 (2009)
19. Irani, S., Pruhs, K.: Algorithmic problems in power management. SIGACT News **36**(2), 63–76 (2005)
20. Khandekar, R., Schieber, B., Shachnai, H., Tamir, T.: Real-time scheduling to minimize machine busy times. J. Sched. **18**(6), 561–573 (2015)
21. Klimm, M., Schmand, D.: Sharing non-anonymous costs of multiple resources optimally. In: Paschos, V.T., Widmayer, P. (eds.) CIAC 2015. LNCS, vol. 9079, pp. 274–287. Springer, Cham (2015). https://doi.org/10.1007/978-3-319-18173-8_20
22. Kollias, K., Roughgarden, T.: Restoring pure equilibria to weighted congestion games. ACM Trans. Econ. Comput. **3**(4), 21:1–21:24 (2015)
23. Koutsoupias, E., Papadimitriou, C.H.: Worst-case equilibria. Comput. Sci. Rev. **3**(2), 65–69 (2009)
24. Marden, J.R., Philips, M.: Optimizing the price of anarchy in concave cost sharing games. In: 2017 American Control Conference, ACC 2017, Seattle, WA, USA, 24–26 May 2017, pp. 5237–5242 (2017)
25. Marden, J.R., Wierman, A.: Distributed welfare games. Oper. Res. **61**(1), 155–168 (2013)
26. Rosenthal, R.W.: A class of games possessing pure-strategy nash equilibria. Int. J. Game Theory **2**(1), 65–67 (1973)
27. Roughgarden, T.: Intrinsic robustness of the price of anarchy. J. ACM **62**(5), 32:1–32:42 (2015)
28. Roughgarden, T., Schrijvers, O.: Network cost-sharing without anonymity. AACM Trans. Econ. Comput. **4**(2), 8:1–8:24 (2016)
29. Tamir, T.: Cost-sharing games in real-time scheduling systems. In: Christodoulou, G., Harks, T. (eds.) WINE 2018. LNCS, vol. 11316, pp. 423–437. Springer, Cham (2018). https://doi.org/10.1007/978-3-030-04612-5_28
30. von Falkenhausen, P., Harks, T.: Optimal cost sharing for resource selection games. Math. Oper. Res. **38**(1), 184–208 (2013)

The Classes PPA-k: Existence from Arguments Modulo k

Alexandros Hollender[(✉)]

Department of Computer Science, University of Oxford, Oxford, UK
alexandros.hollender@cs.ox.ac.uk

Abstract. The complexity classes PPA-k, $k \geq 2$, have recently emerged as the main candidates for capturing the complexity of important problems in fair division, in particular Alon's NECKLACE-SPLITTING problem with k thieves. Indeed, the problem with two thieves has been shown complete for PPA = PPA-2. In this work, we present structural results which provide a solid foundation for the further study of these classes. Namely, we investigate the classes PPA-k in terms of (i) equivalent definitions, (ii) inner structure, (iii) relationship to each other and to other TFNP classes, and (iv) closure under Turing reductions.

Keywords: Computational complexity · TFNP · Necklace splitting

1 Introduction

The complexity class TFNP is the class of all search problems such that every instance has a least one solution and any solution can be checked in polynomial time. It has attracted a lot of interest, because, in some sense, it lies between P and NP. Moreover, TFNP contains many natural problems for which no polynomial algorithm is known, such as FACTORING (given a integer, find a prime factor) or NASH (given a bimatrix game, find a Nash equilibrium). However, no problem in TFNP can be NP-hard, unless NP = co-NP [28]. Furthermore, it is believed that no TFNP-complete problem exists [31,33]. Thus, the challenge is to find some way to provide evidence that these TFNP problems are indeed hard.

Papadimitriou [31] proposed the following idea: define *subclasses* of TFNP and classify the natural problems of interest with respect to these classes. Proving that many natural problems are complete for such a class, shows that they are "equally" hard. Then, investigating how these classes relate to each other, yields a relative classification of all these problems. In other words, it provides a unified framework that gives a better understanding of how these problems relate to each other. TFNP subclasses are based on various non-constructive existence results. Some of these classes and their corresponding existence principle are:

- PPAD: given a directed graph and an unbalanced vertex (i.e. out-degree $\neq$ in-degree), there must exist another unbalanced vertex.

I. Caragiannis et al. (Eds.): WINE 2019, LNCS 11920, pp. 214–227, 2019.
https://doi.org/10.1007/978-3-030-35389-6_16

– PPA: given an undirected graph and vertex with odd degree, there must exist another vertex with odd degree (Handshaking Lemma).
– PPP: given a function mapping a finite set to a smaller set, there must exist a collision (Pigeonhole Principle).

Other TFNP subclasses are PPADS, PLS [24], CLS [11], PTFNP [19], EOPL and UEOPL [14]. It is known that PPAD $\subseteq$ PPADS $\subseteq$ PPP, PPAD $\subseteq$ PPA and UEOPL $\subseteq$ EOPL $\subseteq$ CLS $\subseteq$ PLS $\cap$ PPAD. Any separation of these classes would imply P $\neq$ NP, but various oracle separations exist [2,4,5,30] (see Sect. 2 for more details).

TFNP subclasses have been very successful in capturing the complexity of natural problems. The most famous result is that the problem NASH is PPAD-complete [7,10], but various other natural problems have also been shown PPAD-complete [6,8,9,25]. Many local optimisation problems have been proved PLS-complete [12,13,24,26,32]. Recently, the first natural complete problems were found for PPA [16,17] and PPP [34]. The famous FACTORING problem has been partially related to PPA and PPP [22].

Necklace-Splitting. The natural problem recently shown PPA-complete is a problem in fair division, called the 2-NECKLACE-SPLITTING problem [17]. For $k \geq 2$, the premise of the k-NECKLACE-SPLITTING problem is as follows. Imagine that k thieves have stolen a necklace that has beads of different colours. Since the thieves are unsure of the value of the different beads, they want to divide the necklace into k parts such that each part contains the same number of beads of each colour. However, the string of the necklace is made of precious metal, so the thieves don't want to use too many cuts. Alon's famous result [1] says that this can always be achieved with a limited number of cuts.

The corresponding computational problem can be described as follows. We are given an open necklace (i.e. a segment) with n beads of c different colours, i.e. there are a_i beads of colour i and $\sum_{i=1}^{c} a_i = n$. Furthermore, assume that for each i, a_i is divisible by k (the number of thieves). The goal is to cut the necklace in (at most) $c(k-1)$ places and allocate the pieces to the k thieves, such that every thief gets exactly a_i/k beads of colour i, for each colour i. By Alon's result [1], a solution always exists, and thus the problem lies in TFNP.

The complexity of this problem has been an open problem for almost 30 years [31]. While the 2-thieves version is now resolved, the complexity of the problem with k thieves ($k \geq 3$) remains open. The main motivation of the present paper is to investigate the classes PPA-k, which are believed to be the most likely candidates to capture the complexity of k-NECKLACE-SPLITTING. Indeed, in the conclusion of the paper where they prove that 2-NECKLACE-SPLITTING is PPA-complete, Filos-Ratsikas and Goldberg [15] mention:

> "What is the computational complexity of k-thief Necklace-splitting, for k not a power of 2? As discussed in [27,29], the proof that it is a total search problem, does *not* seem to boil down to the PPA principle. Right now, we do not even know if it belongs to PTFNP [19].

Interestingly, Papadimitriou in [31] (implicitly) also defined a number of computational complexity classes related to PPA, namely PPA-p, for a parameter $p \geq 2$. [...] Given the discussion above, it could possibly be the case that the principle associated with Necklace-Splitting for k-thieves is the PPA-k principle instead."

PPA-p. The TFNP subclasses PPA-p were defined by Papadimitriou almost 30 years ago in his seminal paper [31]. Recall that the existence of a solution to a PPA problem is guaranteed by a parity argument, i.e. an argument modulo 2. The classes PPA-p are a generalisation of this. For every prime p, the existence of a solution to a PPA-p problem is guaranteed by an argument modulo p. In particular, PPA-2 = PPA. Surprisingly, these classes have received very little attention. As far as we know, they have only been studied in the following:

- In [31] Papadimitriou defined the classes PPA-p and proved that a problem called CHEVALLEY-MOD-p lies in PPA-p and a problem called CUBIC-SUBGRAPH lies in PPA-3.
- In an online thread on Stack Exchange [21], Jeřábek provided two other equivalent ways to define PPA-3. The problems and proofs can be generalised to any prime p.
- In his thesis [23], Johnson defined the classes PMOD^k for any $k \geq 2$, which were intended to capture the complexity of counting arguments modulo k. He proved various oracle separation results involving his classes and other TFNP classes. While the PPA-p classes are not mentioned by Johnson, using Jeřábek's results [21] it is easy to show that PMOD^p = PPA-p for any prime p. In Sect. 6, we characterise PMOD^k in terms of the classes PPA-p when k is not prime. In particular, we show that PMOD^k only partially captures existence arguments modulo k.

Our Contribution. In this paper, we use the natural generalisation of Papadimitriou's definition of the classes PPA-p to define PPA-k for any $k \geq 2$. We then provide a characterisation of PPA-k in terms of the classes PPA-p. In particular, we show that PPA-k is completely determined by the set of prime factors of k. In order to gain a better understanding of the inner structure of the class PPA-k, we also define new subclasses that we denote PPA-$k[\#\ell]$ and investigate how they relate to the other classes. We show that PPA-$k[\#\ell]$ is completely determined by the set of prime factors of $k/\gcd(k, \ell)$.

Furthermore, we provide various equivalent complete problems that can be used to define PPA-k and PPA-$k[\#\ell]$ (Sect. 4). While these problems are not "natural", we believe that they provide additional tools that can be very useful when proving that natural problems are complete for these classes. In Sect. 7, we provide an additional tool for showing that problems lie in these classes: we prove that PPA-p^r (p prime, $r \geq 1$) and PPA-$k[\#\ell]$ ($k \geq 2$) are closed under Turing reductions. On the other hand, we provide evidence that PPA-k might not be closed under Turing reductions when k is not a prime power.

Finally, in Sect. 6 we investigate the classes PMOD^k defined by Johnson [23] and provide a full characterisation in terms of the classes PPA-k. In particular, we show that $\mathrm{PMOD}^k = \mathrm{PPA}$-$k$ if k is a prime power. However, when k is not a prime power, we provide evidence that PMOD^k does not capture the full strength of existence arguments modulo k, unlike PPA-k. This characterisation of PMOD^k in terms of PPA-k leads to some oracle separation results involving PPA-k and other TFNP classes (using Johnson's oracle separation results). We note that a significant fraction of our results were also obtained by Göös, Kamath, Sotiraki and Zampetakis in concurrent and independent work [20].

2 Preliminaries

TFNP. Let $\{0,1\}^*$ denote the set of all finite length bit-strings and for $x \in \{0,1\}^*$ let $|x|$ be its length. A computational search problem is given by a binary relation $R \subseteq \{0,1\}^* \times \{0,1\}^*$. The problem is: given an instance $x \in \{0,1\}^*$, find a $y \in \{0,1\}^*$ such that $(x,y) \in R$, or return that no such y exists. The search problem R is in FNP (*Functions in NP*), if R is polynomial-time computable (i.e. $(x,y) \in R$ can be decided in polynomial time in $|x| + |y|$) and there exists some polynomial p such that $(x,y) \in R \implies |y| \leq p(|x|)$. Thus, FNP is the search problem version of NP (and FNP-complete problems are equivalent to NP-complete problems under Turing reductions).

The class TFNP (*Total Functions in NP* [28]) contains all FNP search problems R that are *total*: for every $x \in \{0,1\}^*$ there exists $y \in \{0,1\}^*$ such that $(x,y) \in R$. With a slight abuse of notation, we can say that P lies in TFNP. Indeed, if a decision problem is solvable in polynomial time, then both the "yes" and "no" answers can be verified in polynomial time. In this sense, TFNP lies between P and NP.

Note that the totality of problems in TFNP does not rely on any "promise". Instead, there is a *syntactic* guarantee of totality: for any instance in $\{0,1\}^*$, there is always at least one solution. Nevertheless, TFNP can capture various settings where the instance space is restricted. For example, if a problem R in FNP is total only on a subset L of the instances and $L \in P$, then we can transform it into a TFNP problem by adding $(x,0)$ to R for all $x \notin L$.

Reductions. Let R and S be total search problems in TFNP. We say that R (many-one) reduces to S, denoted $R \leq S$, if there exist polynomial-time computable functions f, g such that

$$(f(x), y) \in S \implies (x, g(x,y)) \in R.$$

Note that if S is polynomial-time solvable, then so is R. We say that two problems R and S are (polynomial-time) equivalent, if $R \leq S$ and $S \leq R$. There is also a more general type of reduction. A Turing reduction from R to S is a polynomial-time oracle Turing machine that solves problem R with the help of queries to an oracle for S. Note that a Turing reduction that only makes a single oracle query immediately yields a many-one reduction.

PPA. The class PPA (Polynomial Parity Argument) [31] is defined as the set of all TFNP problems that many-one reduce to the problem LEAF [2,31]: given an undirected graph with maximum degree 2 and a leaf (i.e. a vertex of degree 1), find another leaf. The important thing to note is that the graph is not given explicitly (in which case the problem would be very easy), but it is provided implicitly through a succinct representation.

The vertex set is $\{0,1\}^n$ and the edges are given by a Boolean circuit $C : \{0,1\}^n \to \{0,1\}^n \times \{0,1\}^n$. For any $x \in \{0,1\}^n$, we abuse notation and interpret $C(x) = (y_1, y_2)$ as the set $\{y_1, y_2\} \setminus \{x\}$. Thus, $C(x)$ is the set of potential neighbours of x. We say that there is an edge between x and y if $x \in C(y)$ and $y \in C(x)$. Thus, every vertex has at most two neighbours. Note that the size of the graph can be exponential with respect to its description size.

The full formal definition of the problem LEAF is: given a Boolean circuit $C : \{0,1\}^n \to \{0,1\}^n \times \{0,1\}^n$ such that $|C(0^n)| = 1$ (i.e. 0^n is a leaf), find

- $x \neq 0^n$ such that $|C(x)| = 1$ (another leaf)
- or x, y such that $x \in C(y)$ but $y \notin C(x)$ (an inconsistent edge)

Type 2 Problems and Oracle Separations. We work in the standard Turing machine model, but TFNP subclasses have also been studied in the black-box model. In this model, one considers the type 2 versions of the problems, namely, the circuits in the input are replaced by black-boxes. In that case, it is possible to prove unconditional separations between type 2 TFNP subclasses (in the standard model this would imply $P \neq NP$). The interesting point here is that separations between type 2 classes yield separations of the corresponding classes in the standard model with respect to any generic oracle (see [2] for more details on this). This technique has been used to prove various oracle separations between TFNP subclasses [2,4,5,30]. In Sect. 6 we provide some oracle separations involving PPA-k and other TFNP subclasses.

On the other hand, any reduction that works in the type 2 setting, also works in the standard setting. Indeed, it suffices to replace the calls to the black boxes by the corresponding circuits that compute them. In this paper, our reductions are stated in the standard model, but they also work in the type 2 setting, because they don't examine the inner workings of the circuits.

3   Definition of the Classes

3.1   PPA-k: Polynomial Argument Modulo k

For any prime p, Papadimitriou [31] defined the class PPA-p as the set of all TFNP problems that many-one reduce to the following problem, that we call BIPARTITE-MOD-p: We are given an undirected bipartite graph (implicitly represented by circuits) and a vertex with degree $\neq 0 \mod p$ (which we call the *trivial solution*). The goal is to find another such vertex. This problem lies in TFNP: if all other vertices had degree $= 0 \mod p$, then the sum of the degrees of all vertices on each side would have a different value modulo p, which is impossible.

The problem remains well-defined and total if p is not a prime, and so we will instead define it for any $k \geq 2$. Let us now provide a formal definition of the problem. A vertex of the bipartite graph is represented as a bit-string in $\{0,1\} \times \{0,1\}^n$, where the first bit indicates whether the vertex lies on the "left" or "right" side of the bipartite graph. Given a vertex, a Boolean circuit C outputs the set of its neighbours (at most k, see Remark 1). Note that we can syntactically enforce that the graph is bipartite, i.e. a vertex $0x$ can only have neighbours of the type $1y$ and vice-versa.

Definition 1 (Bipartite-mod-k [31]). *Let $k \geq 2$. The problem* BIPARTITE-MOD-k *is defined as: given a Boolean circuit C that computes a bipartite graph on the vertex set $\{0,1\} \times \{0,1\}^n$ with $|C(00^n)| \in \{1,\ldots,k-1\}$, find*

- $u \neq 00^n$ *such that* $|C(u)| \notin \{0,k\}$
- *or* x,y *such that* $y \in C(0x)$ *but* $x \notin C(1y)$.

Here the trivial solution is the vertex 00^n. The first type of solution corresponds to a vertex with degree $\neq 0 \mod k$. The second type of solution corresponds to an edge that is not well-defined. We can always ensure that all edges are well-defined by doing some pre-processing. Indeed, in polynomial time we can construct a circuit C' such that all solutions are of the first type and yield a solution for C. On input $0x$ the circuit C' first computes $C(0x) = \{1y_1,\ldots,1y_m\}$ and then for each i removes $1y_i$ from this list, if $0x \notin C(1y_i)$.

Remark 1. Note that in this problem statement we take all degrees to lie in $\{0,1,\ldots,k\}$. This is easily seen to be equivalent to the more general formulation, since any vertex with degree higher than k can be split into multiple vertices that each have degree at most k, and a solution of the original problem is easily recovered from a solution in this new version. Note that since the set of neighbours is given as the output of a circuit, it will have length bounded by some polynomial in the input size and so this argument can indeed be applied.

Definition 2 (PPA-k [31]). *For any $k \geq 2$, the class* PPA-k *is defined as the set of all* TFNP *problems that many-one reduce to* BIPARTITE-MOD-k.

As a warm-up let us show the following:

Proposition 1 ([31]). PPA-2 = PPA

Proof. Recall that PPA can be defined using the canonical complete problem LEAF [2,31]: given an undirected graph where every vertex has degree at most 2, and a leaf (i.e. degree = 1), find another leaf. This immediately yields PPA-2 $\subseteq$ PPA, since BIPARTITE-MOD-2 is just a special case of LEAF where the graph is bipartite.

Given an instance of LEAF with graph $G = (\{0,1\}^n, E)$ we construct an instance of BIPARTITE-MOD-2 on the vertex set $\{0,1\} \times \{0,1\}^{2n}$ as follows.

For any $u \in \{0,1\}^n$ we have a vertex $x_u := 0u0^n$ on the left side of the bipartite graph. For any edge $\{u,v\} \in E$ (u,v ordered lexicographically) we have a vertex $y_{uv} := 1uv$ on the right side of the bipartite graph and we create the edges $\{x_u, y_{uv}\}$ and $\{x_v, y_{uv}\}$. All other vertices in $\{0,1\} \times \{0,1\}^{2n}$ are isolated. In polynomial time we can construct a circuit that computes the neighbours of any vertex. Furthermore, $w \in \{0,1\}^n$ is a leaf, if and only if x_w has degree 1. Finally, all vertices on the right-hand side have degree 0 or 2. □

3.2 PPA-$k[\#\ell]$: Fixing the Degree of the Trivial Solution

In the definition of the PPA-k-complete problem BIPARTITE-MOD-k (Definition 1) the degree of the trivial solution 00^n can be any number in $\{1, \ldots, k-1\}$. In this section we define more refined classes where the degree of the trivial solution is fixed. In Sect. 5, these classes will be very useful to describe how the PPA-k classes relate to each other. These definitions are inspired by the corresponding "counting principles" studied in Beame et al. [3] that were also defined in a refined form in order to describe how they relate to each other. We believe that these refined classes will also be useful to capture the complexity of natural problems. Note that for $k = 2$, the degree of the trivial solution will be always be 1 and thus the question does not even appear in the study of PPA.

Definition 3. *Let $k \geq 2$ and $1 \leq \ell \leq k-1$. The problem* BIPARTITE-MOD-$k[\#\ell]$ *is defined as* BIPARTITE-MOD-k *(Definition 1) but with the additional condition* $|C(00^n)| = \ell$.

Note that this condition can be enforced syntactically and so this problem also lies in TFNP.

Definition 4 (PPA-$k[\#\ell]$). *Let $k \geq 2$ and $1 \leq \ell \leq k-1$. The class* PPA-$k[\#\ell]$ *is defined as the set of all* TFNP *problems that many-one reduce to* BIPARTITE-MOD-$k[\#\ell]$.

If k is some prime p, then these classes are not interesting. Indeed, it holds that PPA-$p[\#\ell]$ = PPA-p for all $1 \leq \ell \leq p - 1$. This can be shown using the following technique: take multiple copies of the instance and "glue" the trivial solutions together. If p is prime, then any other degree of the glued trivial solution can be obtained (by taking the right number of copies). In fact this technique yields the stronger result:

Lemma 1. *If $\gcd(k, \ell_1)$ divides ℓ_2, then* PPA-$k[\#\ell_1]$ ⊆ PPA-$k[\#\ell_2]$.

Proof. Since $\gcd(k, \ell_1)$ divides ℓ_2, there exists $m < k$ such that $m \times \ell_1 = \ell_2$ mod k. Given an instance of BIPARTITE-MOD-$k[\#\ell_1]$, take the union of m copies of the instance, i.e. $m2^n$ vertices on each side (and any additional isolated vertices needed to reach a power of 2). Then, merge the m different copies of the trivial solution into one (by redirecting edges to a single one). This vertex will have degree $m\ell_1 = \ell_2$ mod k. Finally, apply the usual trick to ensure all degrees are in $\{0, 1, \ldots, k\}$ (Remark 1). □

In particular, we also get the nice result PPA-$k[\#\ell]$ = PPA-$k[\#\gcd(k,\ell)]$. Applying the result to the case $k = 6$, we get that PPA-6[#1] = PPA-6[#5], PPA-6[#2] = PPA-6[#4], as well as PPA-6[#1] $\subseteq$ PPA-6[#2] and PPA-6[#1] $\subseteq$ PPA-6[#2]. Thus, we have three "equivalence classes" $\{1,5\}$, $\{2,4\}$ and $\{3\}$ and the relationships $\{1,5\} \le \{2,4\}$ and $\{1,5\} \le \{3\}$. In Sect. 5, we will show that $\{2,4\}$ corresponds to PPA-3, $\{3\}$ to PPA-2 and $\{1,5\}$ to PPA-2 $\cap$ PPA-3.

Now let us introduce some notation that will allow us to precisely describe the relationship between PPA-k and the PPA-$k[\#\ell]$.

Definition 5. (& operation [5]). *Let R_0 and R_1 be two TFNP problems. Then the problem R_0 & R_1 is defined as: given an instance I_0 of R_0, an instance I_1 of R_1 and a bit $b \in \{0,1\}$, find a solution to I_b.*

This operation is commutative and associative (up to many-one equivalence). Indeed, R_0 & R_1 is many-one equivalent to R_1 & R_0, and $(R_0$ & $R_1)$ & R_2 is many-one equivalent to R_0 &$(R_1$ & $R_2)$. Since the & operation is associative, the problem $\&_{\ell=1}^{k} R_\ell$ is well-defined up to many-one equivalence. It is also equivalent to the following problem: given instances $I_1, \ldots, I_k$ of $R_1, \ldots, R_k$ and an integer $j \in \{1, \ldots, k\}$, find a solution to I_j.

We extend the & operation to TFNP subclasses in the natural way. Let C_0 and C_1 be TFNP subclasses with complete problems R_0 and R_1 respectively. Then C_0 & C_1 is the class of all TFNP problems that many-one reduce to R_0 & R_1. Note that the choice of complete problems does not matter. Intuitively, this class contains all problems that can be solved in polynomial time by a Turing machine with a single oracle query to either C_0 or C_1. The following result is easy to prove:

Lemma 2. *For all $k \ge 2$ we have* PPA-k = $\overset{k-1}{\underset{\ell=1}{\&}}$ PPA-$k[\#\ell]$.

Together with Lemma 1, this yields e.g. PPA-6 = PPA-6[#2] & PPA-6[#3].

4   Equivalent Definitions

In this section we show that PPA-k can be defined by using other problems instead of BIPARTITE-MOD-k. The totality of these problems is again based on arguments modulo k. By showing that these problems are indeed PPA-k-complete, we provide additional support for the claim that PPA-k captures the complexity of "polynomial arguments modulo k". While these problems are not "natural" and thus not interesting in their own right, they provide equivalent ways of defining of PPA-k, which can be very useful when working with these classes. In particular, we make extensive use of this equivalence in this work.

The TFNP problems we consider are the following:

- IMBALANCE-MOD-k: given a directed graph and a vertex that is *unbalanced-mod-k*, i.e. out-degree $-$ in-degree $\ne 0 \mod k$, find another such vertex.

- HYPERGRAPH-MOD-k: given a hypergraph and a vertex that has degree $\neq 0$ mod k, find another such vertex or a hyperedge that has size $\neq k$.
- PARTITION-MOD-k: given a set of size $\neq 0$ mod k and a partition into subsets, find a subset that has size $\neq k$.

As usual, the size of the graph (respectively hypergraph, set) can be exponential in the input size, and the edges (resp. hyperedges, subsets) can be computed efficiently locally. We also define the corresponding problems IMBALANCE-MOD-$k[\#\ell]$, HYPERGRAPH-MOD-$k[\#\ell]$ and PARTITION-MOD-$k[\#\ell]$ analogously. The formal definitions and the proof of the following result can be found in the full version.

Theorem 1. *Let* $k \geq 2$ *and* $1 \leq \ell \leq k - 1$.

- IMBALANCE-MOD-$k[\#\ell]$, HYPERGRAPH-MOD-$k[\#\ell]$, PARTITION-MOD-$k[\#\ell]$ *are* PPA-$k[\#\ell]$-*complete,*
- IMBALANCE-MOD-k, HYPERGRAPH-MOD-k, PARTITION-MOD-k *are* PPA-k-*complete.*

In his online post [21], Jeřábek proves that BIPARTITE-MOD-3, IMBALANCE-MOD-3 and PARTITION-MOD-3 are equivalent and (correctly) claims that the proof generalises to any other prime. Thus, our contribution is the definition of the problems for any $k \geq 2$ (and the ℓ-parameter versions) and the generalisation of the result to any $k \geq 2$ (not only primes) and to the ℓ-parameter versions of the problems, as well as to the new problem HYPERGRAPH-MOD-k.

The problem IMBALANCE-MOD-k is a generalisation of the PPAD-complete problem IMBALANCE [2,18]: given a directed graph and a vertex that is unbalanced (i.e. out-degree − in-degree $\neq 0$), find another unbalanced vertex. Since the latter trivially reduces to the former, Theorem 1 also yields[1]:

Corollary 1. *For all* $k \geq 2$, *we have* PPAD $\subseteq$ PPA-k.

Furthermore, if we set $k = 0$, then IMBALANCE-MOD-0 actually corresponds to IMBALANCE. Thus, in a certain sense we could define PPA-0 = PPAD. On the other hand, IMBALANCE-MOD-1 is a trivial problem.

5   Relationship Between the Classes

In this section, we present some results that provide deeper insights into how the classes relate to each other. For any $k \geq 2$, PF(k) denotes the set of all prime factors of k. The main conceptual result is that PPA-k is entirely determined by the set of prime factors of k:

Theorem 2. *For any* $k \geq 2$ *we have* PPA-$k = \underset{p \in \mathrm{PF}(k)}{\&} $ PPA-p.

---

[1] This observation was also made by Jeřábek for the classes PPA-p (p prime).

This equation can be understood as saying the following:

- Given a single query to an oracle for PPA-k, we can solve any problem in PPA-p for any $p \in \mathrm{PF}(k)$
- Given a single query to an oracle that solves any PPA-p problem for any $p \in \mathrm{PF}(k)$, we can solve any problem in PPA-k.

Corollary 2. *In particular, we have:*

- *For $k_1, k_2 \geq 2$, if $\mathrm{PF}(k_1) \subseteq \mathrm{PF}(k_2)$, then PPA-$k_1 \subseteq$ PPA-k_2.*
- *For all $k_1, k_2 \geq 2$, PPA-$k_1 k_2$ = PPA-k_1 & PPA-k_2.*
- *For all $k \geq 2$ and all $r \geq 1$ we have PPA-k^r = PPA-k.*

Using the PPA-$k[\#\ell]$ classes, we can formulate an even stronger and more detailed result. For any $k \geq 2$, $1 \leq \ell \leq k - 1$, we define $\mathrm{PF}(k, \ell) = \mathrm{PF}(k/\gcd(k, \ell))$. In this case the conceptual result says that PPA-$k[\#\ell]$ is entirely determined by the set of prime factors of $k/\gcd(k, \ell)$.

Theorem 3. *Let $k \geq 2$, $0 < \ell < k$. Then*

$$\text{PPA-}k[\#\ell] = \text{PPA-}\left(\prod_{p \in PF(k,\ell)} p\right)[\#1] = \bigcap_{p \in \mathrm{PF}(k,\ell)} \text{PPA-}p.$$

The proof of Theorem 3 can be found in the full version. It mainly relies on a technical result (Theorem 4) presented in the next section. Before we move on to that, let us briefly show that Theorem 2 follows from Theorem 3.

Proof (of Theorem 2). Using Lemma 2 and Theorem 3 we can write

$$\text{PPA-}k = \mathop{\&}_{\ell=1}^{k-1} \text{PPA-}k[\#\ell] = \mathop{\&}_{\ell=1}^{k-1} \left(\bigcap_{p \in PF(k,\ell)} \text{PPA-}p\right) = \mathop{\&}_{p \in \mathrm{PF}(k)} \text{PPA-}p$$

where the last equality follows by noting that $\mathrm{PF}(k, \ell) \subseteq \mathrm{PF}(k)$ for all ℓ, and $\mathrm{PF}(k, k/p) = \{p\}$ for all $p \in \mathrm{PF}(k)$. □

5.1 Proof Overview

In [3] Beame et al. investigated the relative proof complexity of so-called "counting principles". These counting principles are formulas that represent the fact that a set of size $\neq 0 \mod k$ cannot be partitioned into sets of size k. They investigated the relationship between these principles in terms of whether one can be proved from the other by using a constant-depth, polynomial-size Frege proof. Their main result is a full characterisation of when this is possible or not. As noted by Johnson [23], these counting formulas do not yield NP search problems, but they can be related to corresponding NP search problems (TFNP, in fact). Indeed, Johnson uses this connection to obtain some separation results between his PMOD^k classes (see Sect. 6) from Beame et al.'s negative results. Our contribution is using Beame et al.'s positive results in order to prove inclusion results about the PPA-$k[\#\ell]$ classes. More precisely, we modify their proofs to obtain polynomial-time reductions between our PARTITION-MOD-$k[\#\ell]$ problems. Thus, we obtain the following result which is proved in the full version.

Theorem 4. *Let* $k_1, k_2 \geq 2$ *and* $0 < \ell_i < k_i$ *for* $i = 1, 2$. *If* $\mathrm{PF}(k_2, \ell_2) \subseteq \mathrm{PF}(k_1, \ell_1)$, *then* PPA-$k_1[\#\ell_1] \subseteq$ PPA-$k_2[\#\ell_2]$.

6   Johnson's PMOD^k Classes and Oracle Separations

Inspired by the definition of the PPA-complete problem LONELY [2], Buss and Johnson [5] defined TFNP problems called MOD^p to represent arguments modulo some prime p. Their main motivation was to use these problems to show separations (in the type 2 setting) between Turing reductions with m oracle queries and Turing reductions with $m + 1$ oracle queries. In his thesis [23], Johnson generalised the definition of MOD^k to any $k \geq 2$ and defined corresponding classes PMOD^k. He also proved some separations between these classes and other TFNP classes in the type 2 setting (which yield oracle separations in the standard setting). It seems that Johnson was not aware of Papadimitriou's [31] PPA-p classes.

In this section, we study the classes PMOD^k and prove a characterisation in terms of the classes PPA-p. In particular, we show that PMOD^k does not capture the full strength of arguments modulo k, when k is not a prime power. This characterisation also allows us to use Johnson's separations to obtain some oracle separations involving PPA-k and other TFNP classes.

Informally, the problem MOD^k can be defined as follows. We are given a partition of $\{0, 1\}^n$ into subsets and the goal is to find one of these subsets that has size $\neq k$. If k is not a power of 2, then such a subset must exist. If k is a power of 2, then we instead consider $\{0, 1\}^n \setminus \{0^n\}$ and the problem remains total. The formal definition of MOD^k can be found in the full version.

Definition 6 (PMOD^k [23]). *For any* $k \geq 2$, *the class* PMOD^k *is defined as the set of all* TFNP *problems that many-one reduce to* MOD^k.

Note that the problem MOD^k is a special case of our problem PARTITION-MOD-k (which was indeed inspired by this definition). As a result, we immediately get that PMOD$^k \subseteq$ PPA-k. Unless k is a prime power, we don't expect this to hold with equality. The intuition is that restricting the size of the base set to always be a power 2 has the effect of only achieving a subset of the possible ℓ-parameter values of PPA-$k[\#\ell]$. Namely, only $\ell \in \{2^n \bmod k : n \in \mathbb{N}\}$ are achieved (for k not a power of 2).

The following result provides a full characterisation of PMOD^k in terms of the classes PPA-p. The proof can be found in the full version.

Theorem 5. *Let $k \geq 2$.*

- *if k is not a power of 2, then $\mathrm{PMOD}^k = \mathrm{PPA}\text{-}\widetilde{k}[\#1] = \cap_{p \in \mathrm{PF}(\widetilde{k})} \mathrm{PPA}\text{-}p$ where $\widetilde{k}$ is the largest odd divisor of k*
- *if k is a power of 2, then $\mathrm{PMOD}^k = \mathrm{PPA}\text{-}2$.*

Corollary 3. *In particular, we have:*

- *for all primes p and $r \geq 1$, $\mathrm{PMOD}^{p^r} = \mathrm{PPA}\text{-}p^r = \mathrm{PPA}\text{-}p$*
- *for all $k \geq 2$, $\mathrm{PMOD}^{2k} = \mathrm{PMOD}^k$*
- *for all odd $k \geq 3$, $\mathrm{PMOD}^k = \mathrm{PPA}\text{-}k[\#1] = \cap_{p \in \mathrm{PF}(k)} \mathrm{PPA}\text{-}p$*

If k is a prime power, then PMOD^k is the same as PPA-k. However, for other values of k, we argue that PMOD^k fails to capture the full strength of arguments modulo k. For example, $\mathrm{PMOD}^{15} = \mathrm{PPA}\text{-}15[\#1] = \mathrm{PPA}\text{-}3 \cap \mathrm{PPA}\text{-}5$, whereas PPA-15 = PPA-3 & PPA-5. This means that PPA-15 can solve any problem that lies in PPA-3 or PPA-5, while PMOD^{15} can only solve problems that lie *both* in PPA-3 and PPA-5. In particular, if $\mathrm{PMOD}^{15} = \mathrm{PPA}\text{-}15$, then it would follow that PPA-3 = PPA-5, which is not believed to hold (see oracle separations below). Even worse perhaps, is the fact that $\mathrm{PMOD}^{2k} = \mathrm{PMOD}^k$ for any $k \geq 2$. In particular, this means that $\mathrm{PMOD}^6 = \mathrm{PMOD}^3$, which indicates that PMOD^6 does not really capture arguments modulo 6.

Nevertheless, Johnson's oracle separation results (obtained from the corresponding type 2 separations as in [2]) also yield corresponding results for the PPA-k classes (using Theorem 5). We briefly mention a few of the results obtained this way. See Johnson [23, Chapter 8] for additional results. Relative to any generic oracle (see [2]):

- PPA-$p \not\subseteq$ PPA-q for any distinct primes p, q
- PPA-$k \not\subseteq$ PPP, PPA-$k \not\subseteq$ PLS, PPA-$k \not\subseteq$ PPADS for any $k \geq 2$
- PPP $\not\subseteq$ PPA-p, PLS $\not\subseteq$ PPA-p for any prime p

7 Many-One vs Turing Reductions

Theorem 6. *For any prime $p \geq 2$, PPA-p is closed under Turing reductions.*

In particular, PPA-p^r = PPA-p is also closed under Turing reductions. The proof can be found in the full version. Furthermore, we also obtain:

Corollary 4. *For all $k \geq 2$ and $0 < \ell < k$, PPA-$k[\#\ell]$ is closed under Turing reductions.*

Proof (of Corollary 4). Using Theorem 3, we have PPA-$k[\#\ell] = \bigcap_{p=1}^{d}$ PPA-p_i, where $\mathrm{PF}(k, \ell) = \{p_1, \ldots, p_d\}$. Consider a Turing reduction from some problem to PPA-$k[\#\ell]$. Since PPA-$k[\#\ell] \subseteq$ PPA-p_i, this yields a Turing reduction to PPA-p_i, in particular. By Theorem 6, it follows that there exists a many-one reduction to PPA-p_i, i.e. the problem lies in PPA-p_i. Since this holds for all p_i, the result follows. □

If k is not a prime power, then it is not known whether PPA-k is closed under Turing reductions. Using our results from Sect. 6, we can actually provide an oracle separation between PPA-k and the Turing-closure of PPA-k, i.e. an oracle under which PPA-k is not closed under Turing reductions. Let $R_1, \ldots, R_k$ be TFNP problems. Following Johnson [23] we define $\bigotimes_{j=1}^{k} R_j$ as the problem: given instances $(I_1, \ldots, I_k)$, where I_j is an instance of R_j, solve I_j for all j. As we did with the & operation, with a slight abuse of notation, we can also use the operation $\otimes$ with the PPA-k classes. In [23, Theorem 7.6.1], Johnson proved that for $m \geq 2$ and distinct primes $p_1, \ldots, p_m$, $\bigotimes_{i=1}^{m} \text{MOD}^{p_i}$ does not many-one reduce to $\&_{i=1}^{m} \text{MOD}^{p_i}$ in the type 2 setting. Together with our Theorems 2 and 5 this yields:

Theorem 7. *Let $k \geq 2$ not a power of a prime. Relative to any generic oracle, it holds that $\bigotimes_{p \in \text{PF}(k)} \text{PPA-}p \not\subseteq \text{PPA-}k$. In particular, relative to any generic oracle, PPA-k is not closed under Turing reductions.*

$S = \bigotimes_{p \in \text{PF}(k)} \text{PPA-}p$ corresponds to solving PPA-p for all prime factors p of k *simultaneously*. In particular, this can be done by using $|\text{PF}(k)|$ queries to PPA-k, i.e. a Turing reduction to PPA-k. Thus, S lies in the Turing closure of PPA-k, but not in PPA-k (relative to any generic oracle).

Acknowledgements. I would like to thank Aris Filos-Ratsikas and Paul Goldberg for helpful discussions and suggestions that helped improve the presentation of the paper. This work was supported by an EPSRC doctoral studentship (Reference 1892947).

References

1. Alon, N.: Splitting necklaces. Adv. Math. **63**(3), 247–253 (1987)
2. Beame, P., Cook, S., Edmonds, J., Impagliazzo, R., Pitassi, T.: The relative complexity of NP search problems. J. Comput. Syst. Sci. **57**(1), 3–19 (1998)
3. Beame, P., Impagliazzo, R., Krajíček, J., Pitassi, T., Pudlák, P.: Lower bounds on Hilbert's Nullstellensatz and propositional proofs. Proc. London Math. Soc. **3**(1), 1–26 (1996)
4. Buresh-Oppenheim, J., Morioka, T.: Relativized NP search problems and propositional proof systems. In: 19th CCC, pp. 54–67. IEEE (2004)
5. Buss, S.R., Johnson, A.S.: Propositional proofs and reductions between NP search problems. Ann. Pure Appl. Logic **163**(9), 1163–1182 (2012)
6. Chen, X., Dai, D., Du, Y., Teng, S.: Settling the complexity of Arrow-Debreu equilibria in markets with additively separable utilities. In: 50th FOCS, pp. 273–282 (2009)
7. Chen, X., Deng, X., Teng, S.H.: Settling the complexity of computing two-player Nash equilibria. J. ACM **56**(3), 1–57 (2009)
8. Chen, X., Paparas, D., Yannakakis, M.: The complexity of non-monotone markets. J. ACM **64**(3), 20:1–20:56 (2017)
9. Codenotti, B., Saberi, A., Varadarajan, K., Ye, Y.: The complexity of equilibria: hardness results for economies via a correspondence with games. Theor. Comput. Sci. **408**(2–3), 188–198 (2008)
10. Daskalakis, C., Goldberg, P.W., Papadimitriou, C.H.: The complexity of computing a Nash equilibrium. SIAM J. Comput. **39**(1), 195–259 (2009)

11. Daskalakis, C., Papadimitriou, C.H.: Continuous local search. In: 22nd SODA, pp. 790–804. SIAM (2011)

12. Dumrauf, D., Monien, B., Tiemann, K.: Multiprocessor scheduling is PLS-complete. In: 42nd Hawaii International Conference on System Sciences, pp. 1–10. IEEE (2009)

13. Fabrikant, A., Papadimitriou, C., Talwar, K.: The complexity of pure Nash equilibria. In: 36th STOC, pp. 604–612. ACM (2004)

14. Fearnley, J., Gordon, S., Mehta, R., Savani, R.: Unique end of potential line. In: 46th ICALP, pp. 56:1–56:15 (2019)

15. Filos-Ratsikas, A., Goldberg, P.W.: The complexity of splitting necklaces and bisecting ham sandwiches. arXiv preprint arXiv:1805.12559 (2018)

16. Filos-Ratsikas, A., Goldberg, P.W.: Consensus halving is PPA-complete. In: 50th STOC, pp. 51–64. ACM (2018)

17. Filos-Ratsikas, A., Goldberg, P.W.: The complexity of splitting necklaces and bisecting ham sandwiches. In: 51st STOC, pp. 638–649. ACM (2019)

18. Goldberg, P.W., Hollender, A.: The hairy ball problem is PPAD-complete. In: 46th ICALP, pp. 65:1–65:14 (2019)

19. Goldberg, P.W., Papadimitriou, C.H.: Towards a unified complexity theory of total functions. J. Comput. Syst. Sci. **94**, 167–192 (2018)

20. Göös, M., Kamath, P., Sotiraki, K., Zampetakis, M.: On the complexity of modulo-q arguments (2019), unpublished manuscript (private communication)

21. Jeřábek, E.: Theoretical Computer Science Stack Exchange. https://cstheory.stackexchange.com/q/37794. Accessed 20 Mar 2017

22. Jeřábek, E.: Integer factoring and modular square roots. J. Comput. Syst. Sci. **82**(2), 380–394 (2016)

23. Johnson, A.S.: Reductions and propositional proofs for total NP search problems. Ph.D. thesis, UC San Diego (2011)

24. Johnson, D.S., Papadimitriou, C.H., Yannakakis, M.: How easy is local search? J. Comput. Syst. Sci. **37**(1), 79–100 (1988)

25. Kintali, S., Poplawski, L.J., Rajaraman, R., Sundaram, R., Teng, S.: Reducibility among fractional stability problems. SIAM J. Comput. **42**(6), 2063–2113 (2013)

26. Krentel, M.W.: Structure in locally optimal solutions. In: 30th FOCS, pp. 216–221. IEEE (1989)

27. de Longueville, M., Živaljević, R.T.: The Borsuk-Ulam-property, Tucker-property and constructive proofs in combinatorics. J. Comb. Theor. Ser. A **113**(5), 839–850 (2006)

28. Megiddo, N., Papadimitriou, C.H.: On total functions, existence theorems and computational complexity. Theor. Comput. Sci. **81**(2), 317–324 (1991)

29. Meunier, F.: Simplotopal maps and necklace splitting. Discrete Math. **323**, 14–26 (2014)

30. Morioka, T.: Classification of search problems and their definability in bounded arithmetic. Master's thesis, University of Toronto (2001)

31. Papadimitriou, C.H.: On the complexity of the parity argument and other inefficient proofs of existence. J. Comput. Syst. Sci. **48**(3), 498–532 (1994)

32. Papadimitriou, C.H., Schaeffer, A.A., Yannakakis, M.: On the complexity of local search. In: 22nd STOC, pp. 438–445. ACM (1990)

33. Pudlák, P.: On the complexity of finding falsifying assignments for Herbrand disjunctions. Arch. Math. Logic **54**(7–8), 769–783 (2015)

34. Sotiraki, K., Zampetakis, M., Zirdelis, G.: PPP-completeness with connections to cryptography. In: 59th FOCS, pp. 148–158. IEEE (2018)

On the Approximability of Simple Mechanisms for MHR Distributions

Yaonan Jin[1], Weian Li[2], and Qi Qi[2($\boxtimes$)]

[1] Department of Computer Science, Columbia University, New York City, USA
jin.yaonan@columbia.edu
[2] Department of IEDA, Hong Kong University of Science and Technology,
Kowloon, Hong Kong
{wlibn,kaylaqi}@ust.hk

Abstract. We focus on a canonical Bayesian mechanism design setting: a seller wants to sell a single item to n bidders, whose values are drawn i.i.d. from a monotone-hazard-rate distribution. In the literature, three mechanisms receive particular attention: the revenue-optimal mechanism Myerson Auction (OPT), the welfare-optimal mechanism Second-Price Auction (SPA), and the most widely-used mechanism Anonymous Pricing (AP). In terms of revenue, we investigate how well the later two mechanisms can approximate Myerson Auction.

OPT vs. AP: over all $n \in \mathbb{N}_{\geq 1}$, the supremum ratio is 1.27, and the worst-case distribution is exponential-like. This answers an open question of Giannakopoulos and Zhu (WINE 18), who proved an asymptotically tight bound of $1 + \Theta\left(\frac{\log \log n}{\log n}\right)$ for large $n \in \mathbb{N}_{\geq 1}$. Thus, the approximability of AP is well understood.

OPT vs. SPA: for each $n \geq 2$, this ratio is upper-bounded by $\left(1 - (1 - 1/e)^{n-1}\right)^{-1} = 1 + 2^{-O(n)}$; an asymptotically matching lower bound can be reached by a truncated exponential distribution. This result settles an open problem asked of Allouah and Besbes (EC 18), who attained the supremum ratio of 1.40 over all $n \geq 2$. Both bounds together supplement the seminal result of Bulow and Klemperer (Am. Econ. Rev. 96).

Keywords: Approximation ratio · Myerson Auction · Anonymous Pricing · Second-Price Auction

1 Introduction

Extracting optimal revenue from selling a single item is a most basic problem in economics. The Bayesian version of this question was settled by Myerson [28]. Provided with symmetric bidders, Myerson Auction admits a concise and systematic format – Second-Price Auction with Anonymous Reserve. In that reserve-based

This work was supported by the Research Grant Council of Hong Kong (GRF Project no. 16215717 and 16243516).

I. Caragiannis et al. (Eds.): WINE 2019, LNCS 11920, pp. 228–240, 2019.
https://doi.org/10.1007/978-3-030-35389-6_17

auctions are quite prevalent in practice (e.g., eBay's auction), Myerson Auction is advocated by many as a triumph of auction theory. Nonetheless, both of Myerson Auction and Second-Price Auction with Anonymous Reserve still experience the following drawbacks.

- *Prior Dependency*: according to Wilson's doctrine [31], practical mechanisms should rely on least details of the input, hence being robust. On the contrary, Myerson Auction and Second-Price Auction with Anonymous Reserve both require an entire access to the bidders' distributions.
- *Privacy Concern*: in either mechanism, a bidder must propagate his value distribution to others. Also, even if a bidder were to lose the item, he still needs to submit his *true value* to the seller. Conceivably, these issues may stimulate the bidders to concern their privacy.
- *Synchronization*: for any auction scheme, all the bidders have to join in it simultaneously. Such synchronization may incur extra cost, or even make an auction non-implementable.

To remove the above complications, two even simpler mechanisms come to the rescue. Literally, Second-Price Auction with Anonymous Reserve composes of (a) Second-Price Auction and (b) Anonymous Pricing. Both mechanisms appear everywhere in the real life, and thus receive particular attention from the AGT, operations research and economics communities.

- Second-Price Auction is perhaps the most famous *prior-independent* mechanism. It is used in numerous scenarios, e.g., selling radio spectrum licenses [27] and the allocation of government or public goods [26]. Notably, this mechanism generates the optimal *social-welfare*, which further distinguishes it from any other mechanism.
- Anonymous Pricing addresses the second and third issues mentioned: (a) the bidders participate in this mechanism sequentially, and thus the synchronization issue automatically vanishes; (b) when a bidder arrives, he simply makes a take-it-or-leave-it decision, which would effectively conceal his private information. Besides, far less communication is involved in Anonymous Pricing. All these and other merits together make Anonymous Pricing the most widely-used mechanism in the real-world applications (e.g., eBay's buy-it-now pricing).

The significance and prevalence of Second-Price Auction and Anonymous Pricing have stimulated an abundance of research (e.g., see [2,3,5,6,14,16–18,20,23,24]) on the next question:

Under moderate assumptions on the value distributions, compared with Myerson Auction, *how much revenue can the two simple mechanisms guarantee?*

In this work, we concentrate on the natural setting where *symmetric* bidders draw their values independently and identically from a *monotone-hazard-rate* (MHR) distribution. By offering new insights into how to characterize the worst-case distributions, we settle the above question and respectively summarize the results as Theorems 1 and 2 in Sects. 3 and 4.

1.1   Further Related Work

This work fits in both of the "simple versus optimal" program (e.g., see also [4,7–10,29]) and the "robust mechanism design" program (e.g., see also [13, 15,22,30]). The approximability of Anonymous Pricing is also widely studied in various broader settings (e.g., see [17–19,21,25,28].

A technical objective of our work is to demonstrate the power of "reduction to worst-case distributions" in proving tight approximation ratios of simple mechanisms. Previously, such reductions were only developed for regular distributions (e.g., see [2,23,24]). Our reductions are the first ones applicable for MHR distributions. Given all these successes, this methodology may be further developed, resulting in an arsenal of tools for proving tight ratios in algorithmic mechanism design.

2   Notations and Preliminaries

Throughout this paper, we focus on the scenario where $n \in \mathbb{N}_{\geq 1}$ bidders compete for an indivisible item, and independently draw their values $\mathbf{v} = \{v_i\}_{i=1}^n$ for the item from a common distribution. This distribution would be denoted by its CDF F, and has a positive support $\mathsf{supp}(F) \subseteq \mathbb{R}_{\geq 0}$. In addition, the *monopoly price* p and the *monopoly quantile* q of this distribution are defined as follows[1]:

$$p \overset{\text{def}}{=} \underset{x \in [0,\infty]}{\arg\max} \left\{ x \cdot \left(1 - F(x)\right) \right\} \in \mathsf{supp}(F) \qquad q \overset{\text{def}}{=} \left(1 - F(p)\right) \in [0,1];$$

We always assume the distribution F satisfies the *monotone-hazard-rate* (MHR) property. To enable our proofs, however, we take into account the broader family of *regular* distributions as well. We introduce both concepts below, and then elaborate on the concerning mechanisms.

2.1   Distribution Families

Regular Distribution. By standard notions (e.g., see [23, Section 2.2]), the following properties hold for any regular distribution F:

- *Continuity*: the support $\mathsf{supp}(F)$ is a single interval, and only at its *right-endpoint* can the distribution F have probability mass.
- *Differentiability*: the CDF F is left- and right-differentiable everywhere in the interior of support $\mathsf{supp}(F)$; w.l.o.g., the corresponding PDF f exists, and is right-continuous everywhere.

We safely define the *virtual value* function $\varphi(x) \overset{\text{def}}{=} x - \frac{1-F(x)}{f(x)}$ on the support $x \in \mathsf{supp}(F)$. By definition, the distribution F is regular (i.e., $F \in \text{REG}$) iff

---

[1] When there are multiple alternative monopoly prices p's, we would break ties by choosing the largest one.

the function $\varphi(x)$ is non-decreasing. Under this assumption, $\varphi^{-1}(0)^2$ is exactly the monopoly price p. The monotonicity of $\varphi(x)$ indicates that the virtual value CDF $D(x)$ introduced below is well defined. (In Sect. 2.2, we will see that this concept helps us to formulate the revenues from the concerning mechanisms.)

$$D(x) \overset{\text{def}}{=} F\big(\varphi^{-1}(x)\big) \qquad \forall x \in \mathbb{R}.$$

MHR Distribution. Compared with the regularity, the *monotone-hazard-rate* (MHR) property is a stronger assumption on the distribution F, requiring[3] $G(x) = \ln\big(1 - F(x)\big)$ to be a *concave* and *decreasing* function on $\mathrm{supp}(F)$. The mentioned continuity and differentiability hold for all the MHR distributions. Further, the next fact will be useful in Sect. 4, and is rather a folklore in the literature (e.g., see [1]).

Fact 1. *Any* MHR *distribution F has a monopoly quantile $q \in [1/e, 1]$.*

Truncated Exponential Distribution. Given a monopoly price $p \in \mathbb{R}_{\geq 0}$ and a monopoly quantile $q \in [\frac{1}{e}, 1]$, the *truncated exponential* distribution $\mathrm{TR\bar{E}XP}(p, q)$ has a CDF of

$$\mathrm{TR\bar{E}XP}(p, q) \overset{\text{def}}{=} \begin{cases} 1 - e^{\frac{\ln q}{p} \cdot x} & \forall x \in (0, p) \\ 1 & \forall x \in [p, +\infty) \end{cases}.$$

This distribution will be useful in Sect. 4 to construct worst-case and lower-bound instances. Also, it is easy to check that this distribution belongs to the MHR family[4].

2.2 Mechanisms

We will focus on three basic mechanisms – Second-Price Auction, Anonymous Pricing and Myerson Auction – together with the (expected) revenues from them. The next lemma is known as the *revenue-equivalence theorem* (see [28]), which bridges any mechanism and its revenue formula via the virtual value function.

Lemma 1 (Revenue-Equivalence Theorem). *A mechanism can be fully determined by its allocation rule $\pi(\mathbf{v}) \in [0, 1]^n$, and the expected revenue is equal to* $\mathbb{E}\left[\sum_{i=1}^{n} \varphi(v_i) \cdot \pi_i(\mathbf{v})\right]$.

---

[2] Note that the virtual value function φ may not be strictly increasing, i.e., may be two different values $x < y$ both correspond to the same virtual value $\varphi(x) = \varphi(y)$. For ease of notation, throughout the paper we always break ties by choosing the largest value, namely $\varphi^{-1}(z) = \max\{x \geq 0 \,|\, \varphi(x) \leq z\}$.

[3] Here is another equivalent definition of the MHR property: $y = \frac{f(x)}{1 - F(x)}$ is a non-decreasing function on support $\mathrm{supp}(F)$. Intuitively, an MHR distribution has a tail decaying (at least) exponentially fast.

[4] Distribution $\mathrm{TR\bar{E}XP}(p, q)$ corresponds to a *linear* (and thus concave) function $G(x) = \ln\big(1 - F(x)\big) = \frac{\ln q}{p} \cdot x$.

*Anonymous Pricing (*AP*).* In such a mechanism, the item is labeled with a price $x \in (0, +\infty)$. W.l.o.g., in the lexicographic order[5], upon the arrival of each i-th bidder:

```
1. If the item remains unsold and v_i ≥ x, then bidder i
   wins the item
2. Otherwise, bidder i leaves forever
```

When the mechanism terminates, the item is sold out with probability $1 - \big(F(x)\big)^n$. For simplicity, we abuse the notation $\mathsf{AP}(x, F) = x \cdot \big[1 - \big(F(x)\big)^n\big]$ to denote the revenue. We figure out the optimum among this family of mechanisms, resulting in a revenue of

$$\mathsf{AP}(F) \overset{\text{def}}{=} \max\big\{\mathsf{AP}(x, F) : x \in \mathbb{R}_{\geq 0}\big\}.$$

*Second-Price Auction (*SPA*).* In this mechanism: the highest bidder $i^* \in \arg\max_{i\in[n]}\big\{v_i\big\}$ wins the item, and then pays the second-highest bid $\max_{i\in[n]\setminus\{i^*\}}\big\{v_i\big\}$. By Lemma 1, we can write down the revenue in terms of virtual value CDF D.

$$\mathsf{SPA}(F) = \mathbb{E}\big[\max_{i\in[n]}\{\varphi(v_i)\}\big] = \int_0^{+\infty}\big(1 - \big(D(y)\big)^n\big)\cdot dy - \int_{-\infty}^0\big(D(y)\big)^n\cdot dy.$$

*Myerson Auction (*OPT*).* As mentioned, in the concerning setting, Myerson Auction can be viewed as the composition of Anonymous Pricing and Second-Price Auction. Given the monopoly price p of the distribution F, and upon receiving values $\{v_i\}_{i=1}^n$, Myerson Auction runs as follows:

```
1. If v_i < p for all i ∈ [n], withhold the item
2. Otherwise,
   (a) W.l.o.g., v_σ1 ≥ v_σ2 ≥ ··· ≥ v_σn for some
       permutation {σ_i}_{i=1}^n
   (b) Bidder σ1 wins the item, with payment
       max{v_σ2, p}
```

Once again, the corresponding revenue can be formulated[6] in terms of virtual value CDF D.

$$\mathsf{OPT}(F) = \mathbb{E}\big[\max\{0, \varphi(v_{\sigma_2})\}\big] = \int_0^{+\infty}\big(1 - \big(D(y)\big)^n\big)\cdot dy.$$

From all of the above revenue formulas, one can infer the next Fact 2. Intuitively, we can "rank" distributions in a stochastic-domination sense. (For Anonymous Pricing and Second-Price Auction, one can verify Fact 2 via simple calculations about the first and second order statistics. As for Myerson Auction, a generalized result was proved by [12].)

---

[5] In different orders, the winner of the item may be different, but the corresponding revenue is always the same.

[6] For revenue formulas in more general settings, see [11, Section 4] and [23, Fact 1].

Fact 2 ([28]).   *Given two distributions F and $\overline{F}$ that $F(x) \geq \overline{F}(x)$ for all $x \in \mathbb{R}_{\geq 0}$, we have* $\mathsf{AP}(x, F) \leq \mathsf{AP}(x, \overline{F})$ *for all* $x \in \mathbb{R}_{\geq 0}$, $\mathsf{SPA}(F) \leq \mathsf{SPA}(\overline{F})$, *and* $\mathsf{OPT}(F) \leq \mathsf{OPT}(\overline{F})$.

3   Approximation Ratio of Anonymous Pricing

In this section, we concentrate on the Myerson Auction (OPT) vs. Anonymous Pricing (AP) problem, aiming to establish Theorem 1.

Theorem 1.   *To sell an item to $n \in \mathbb{N}_{\geq 1}$ bidders with values drawn i.i.d. from an MHR distribution, the supremum ratio of* Myerson Auction *to* Anonymous Pricing *is* 1.2683.

Recall the revenue of Anonymous Pricing: $\mathsf{AP}(x, F) = x \cdot \left[1 - \left(F(x)\right)^n\right]$. Since the Myerson Auction revenue and the Anonymous Pricing revenue both scale proportionally under scaling up the distributions, given a specific $n \in \mathbb{N}_{\geq 1}$, we formulate the concerning problem as the following program.

$$\sup_{F \in \mathsf{MHR}} \quad \mathsf{OPT}(F) \tag{P1}$$

$$\text{s.t.} \quad \mathsf{AP}(x, F) = x \cdot \left[1 - \left(F(x)\right)^n\right] \leq 1 \qquad \forall x \in \mathbb{R}_{\geq 0} \tag{C1.1}$$

After being rearranged, constraint (C1.1) becomes another equivalent constraint:

$$\ln\left(1 - F(x)\right) \leq H(x) \qquad \forall x \in \mathbb{R}_{\geq 0}, \tag{C1.2}$$

where $H(x) \overset{\text{def}}{=} \begin{cases} 0 & \forall x \in [0, 1] \\ \ln\left(1 - \sqrt[n]{1 - 1/x}\right) & \forall x \in (1, +\infty) \end{cases}$. Later, we will see that this transformation and the next technical lemma together enable the proof of Theorem 1.

Lemma 2. $H(x)$ *is a decreasing and strictly convex function on the interval* $(1, +\infty)$.

Worst-Case Distribution. As mentioned in Sect. 2.1, a distribution F satisfies the MHR property iff $y = \ln\left(1 - F(x)\right)$ is a concave function on the interval $\mathrm{supp}(F)$. Combining this fact, Lemma 2, and constraint (C1.2) together, we characterize the worst case of Program (P1).

First, in a worst case: *the concave function $y = \ln\left(1 - F(x)\right)$ is tangent to the strictly convex function $H(x)$ at $\left(a, H(a)\right)$, for some $a > 1$.* Due to constraint (C1.2) that curve $y = \ln\left(1 - F(x)\right)$ is point-wise upper bounded by curve $y = H(x)$, the concavity of $y = \ln\left(1 - F(x)\right)$ and the strict convexity of $y = H(x)$ together imply that the point of tangency $\left(a, H(a)\right)$ is *unique* (if exists).

If there is no such a point of tangency, constraint (C1.2) is strictly loose everywhere. After being scaled up, distribution F becomes another *feasible* MHR distribution $\overline{F}$, hence a larger revenue from Myerson Auction (see Fact 2). Apparently, we can always manipulate the scale-up factor, such that the resulting curve $y = \ln\left(1 - \overline{F}(x)\right)$ is tangent to curve $y = H(x)$.

Recall Fact 2, if $F(x) \leq \overline{F}(x)$ for all $x \in \mathbb{R}_{\geq 0}$, then $\mathsf{OPT}(F) \geq \mathsf{OPT}(\overline{F})$. Among all MHR distributions satisfying the mentioned "tangency" property, we need to find a distribution F_a^* that stochastically dominates all of the others (and thus, in view of the revenue monotonicity, gives a better Myerson Auction revenue than all of the others). Parameterize by $a > 1$, define tangent line

$$G_a(x) \overset{\text{def}}{=} H'(a) \cdot (x - a) + H(a).$$

Distribution F_a^* is given by $\ln\left(1 - F_a^*(x)\right) \equiv \min\left\{0, G_a(x)\right\}$, i.e.,

$$F_a^*(x) = \begin{cases} 0 & \forall x < a - \frac{H(a)}{H'(a)}, \\ 1 - e^{H'(a)\cdot(x-a)+H(a)} & \forall x \geq a - \frac{H(a)}{H'(a)}. \end{cases} \tag{1}$$

Moreover, we shall take into account the implicit condition that *support* $\mathsf{supp}(F_a^*)$ *is non-negative*, i.e., another constraint that $G_a(0) = H(a) - a \cdot H'(a) \geq 0$. In that $H(x)$ is a strictly convex function (recall Lemma 2), the following holds:

- $G_a(0)$ can be viewed as a *strictly* decreasing function of a.
- All feasible a's together form a *single* interval $(1, a_{\max}]$, where $a_{\max}$ is defined by letting $H(a_{\max}) - a_{\max} \cdot H'(a_{\max}) = 0$.

To sum up, for Program (P1): its optimal solution falls into the family of "exponential-like" distributions given by Eq. (1); its optimal objective value equals to that of the following *single-variable* optimization problem.

$$\sup_{a>1} \quad \mathsf{OPT}(F_a^*) \tag{P2}$$

$$\text{s.t.} \quad H(a) - a \cdot H'(a) \geq 0 \tag{C2}$$

Optimal Objective Values. Via case analysis, we next explicitly formulate the revenue of Myerson Auction $\mathsf{OPT}(F_a^*)$ as functions of a. By definition, on the interval $\left[a - \frac{H(a)}{H'(a)}, +\infty\right)$, distribution F_a has a virtual value function of

$$\varphi_a^*(x) = x - \frac{1-F_a^*(x)}{F_a^{*'}(x)} \overset{(1)}{=} x + \frac{1}{H'(a)} \equiv x - \frac{1}{|H'(a)|}.$$

(We shall notice that $H'(a) < 0$.) Hence, the virtual value CDF $D_a^*(x)$ is supported on $[s(a), +\infty)$, where $s(a) \overset{\text{def}}{=} a - \frac{H(a)}{H'(a)} + \frac{1}{H'(a)}$. In this range,

$$D_a^*(x) = F_a^*\left(x - 1/H'(a)\right) = 1 - e^{H'(a)\cdot(x-s(a))}.$$

Recall Sect. 2.2 that $\mathsf{OPT}(F_a^*) = \int_0^{+\infty} \left[1 - \left(D_a^*(y)\right)^n\right] \cdot dy$. In either case $s(a) > 0$ or $s(a) \leq 0$, the tight ratio is respectively the optimal objective value of Program (P3) and that of Program (P4).

$$\max_{a>1}\ s(a) + \int_{s(a)}^{+\infty} \left[1 - \left(D_a^*(y)\right)^n\right] \cdot dy$$

$$\text{s.t.}\ \ H(a) - a \cdot H'(a) \geq 0$$

$$s(a) = a + \frac{1}{H'(a)} - \frac{H(a)}{H'(a)} > 0$$

$$(P3)$$

$$\max_{a>1}\ \int_0^{+\infty} \left[1 - \left(D_a^*(y)\right)^n\right] \cdot dy$$

$$\text{s.t.}\ \ H(a) - a \cdot H'(a) \geq 0$$

$$s(a) = a + \frac{1}{H'(a)} - \frac{H(a)}{H'(a)} \leq 0$$

$$(P4)$$

Noticeably, the feasible space of either program is a non-empty bounded interval, since[7] **(a)** $s'(a) < 0$ for all $a \in (1, a_{\max}]$, **(b)** $s(a_{\max}) < 0$, and **(c)** $s(1^+) > 0$. (See footnote 7 for the proofs.) Also, the objective functions are obviously continuous functions in a. For these reasons, the optimum objective values of both programs are achievable, and we can find them numerically. Afterward, the *larger* objective value is exactly the revenue ratio of Myerson Auction to Anonymous Pricing, for any given $n \in \mathbb{N}_{\geq 1}$.

Supremum Ratio. In the rest of Sect. 3, we will catch the supremum ratio over all $n \in \mathbb{N}_{\geq 1}$: when $n \leq 44$, we offer the numerical results in Table 1; when $n \geq 44$, we exploit tools developed by [17], showing that the supremum ratio can never be reached. Hence, the supremum ratio of 1.2683 claimed in Theorem 1 is reached when $n = 17$.

Table 1. The ratios when $n \leq 44$; the worst case ($n = 17$) is marked in bold and italic.

n	2	3	4	5	6	7	8	9	10
ratio	1.1832	1.2206	1.2369	1.2460	1.2517	1.2558	1.2587	1.2610	1.2627

11	12	13	14	15	16	17*	18	19	20
1.2642	1.2654	1.2664	1.2672	1.2679	1.2682	*1.2683*	1.2682	1.2680	1.2676

21	22	23	24	25	26	27	28	29	30
1.2672	1.2667	1.2662	1.2656	1.2650	1.2643	1.2637	1.2630	1.2624	1.2617

31	32	33	34	35	36	37	38	39	40
1.2610	1.2603	1.2597	1.2590	1.2583	1.2577	1.2570	1.2564	1.2558	1.2551

41	42	43	44	...					
1.2545	1.2539	1.2533	1.2527	...					

Lemma 3 below can be easily summarized from [17], Theorem 2. We will adopt it to establish the next Lemma 4.

---

[7] More concretely, **(a)** given any $a \in (1, a_{\max}]$, we have $s'(a) = \frac{H(a)-1}{(H'(a))^2} \cdot H''(a) < 0$, where the inequality is due to $H(x) < 0$ and $H''(x) > 0$, for all $x \in (1, +\infty)$; **(b)** $s(a_{\max}) = a_{\max} - \frac{H(a_{\max})}{H'(a_{\max})} + \frac{1}{H'(a_{\max})} \overset{(\dagger)}{=} \frac{1}{H'(a_{\max})} < 0$, where $(\dagger)$ is due to the definition of $a_{\max}$; **(c)** $s(1^+) = 1 + \lim_{a \to 1^+} \frac{1 - H(a)}{H'(a)} = 1 + \frac{1-0}{+\infty} = 1 > 0$.

Lemma 3. *Define function* $\mathcal{G}_n(x) \overset{def}{=} x \cdot \left[1 - \left(1 - e^{-x}\right)^n\right]$ *on* $x \in \left[0, \mathcal{H}_n - 1\right]$, *where* $\mathcal{H}_n \overset{def}{=} \sum_{k=1}^{n} \frac{1}{k}$ *is the* n-*th harmonic number. For each* $n \geq 5$, *the revenue ratio of* Myerson Auction *to* Anonymous Pricing *is upper bounded by* $R_n \overset{def}{=} \frac{\mathcal{H}_n - 1}{\max\left\{\mathcal{G}_n(x) : x \in [0, \mathcal{H}_n - 1]\right\}} + \frac{(e-1)^{n-1}}{e^n - (e-1)^{n-1}}$.

Lemma 4. $R_n \leq R_{44} < 1.2683$ *for every* $n \geq 44$.

Remark. As mentioned in Sect. 1, Programs (P3) and (P4) basically do not admit a close-form optimal solution. Hence, the worst-case ratio (for each specific $n \geq 2$) can only be found numerically. Another observation is that the ratios are *unimodal* when $1 \leq n \leq 44$: it is increasing in n when $n \leq 17$ and is decreasing in n when $17 \leq n \leq 44$. Beyond that, we actually believe the ratios always decrease when $n \geq 17$.

4   Approximation Ratio of Second-Price Auction

In this section, we probe into the Myerson Auction (OPT) vs. Second-Price Auction (SPA) problem. The results are summarized in Theorem 2.

Theorem 2. *To sell an item to* $n \geq 2$ *bidders with values drawn i.i.d. from an* MHR *distribution, the following holds for the ratio of* Myerson Auction *to* Second-Price Auction:

1. The worst case is always achieved by a truncated exponential distribution.
2. The ratio is upper bounded by $\left(1 - (1 - 1/e)^{n-1}\right)^{-1} = 1 + 2^{-\Omega(n)}$, and there is a matching lower bound of $1 + 2^{-O(n)}$.

Actually, the upper-bound part of Theorem 2 is an implication of a result by Fu et al. [16]. Our main contributions are to characterize the worst-case distribution (see Sect. 4.1) and to establish a matching lower bound (see Sect. 4.2). Namely, via a novel reduction, we demonstrate that the *worst-case* distribution (in the MHR distribution family) is always a truncated exponential distribution. In that describing a truncated exponential distribution requires merely two parameters[8], we can exploit standard techniques to establish the whole theorem.

Upper Bound. Lemma 5 is basically a reformulation of [16], Corallary 1. Putting this together with Fact 1 completes the upper-bound part of Theorem 2.

Lemma 5 ([16]). *For any regular distribution* F *with monopoly quantile of* $q \in [0, 1]$, Second-Price Auction *generates at least* $\left[1 - \frac{1}{\sum_{i=0}^{n-1}(1-q)^{-i}}\right]$-*fraction as much revenue as* Myerson Auction.

---

[8] Actualy, one of the parameters has no effect on the ratio between Myerson Auction and Second-Price Auction.

Proof (Proof of Theorem 2 part 2). Recall Fact 1 that any MHR distribution F has a monopoly quantile of $q \in [1/e, 1]$. Thus, it follows from Lemma 5 that

$$\frac{\mathsf{SPA}(F)}{\mathsf{OPT}(F)} \geq 1 - \frac{1}{\sum_{i=0}^{n-1}(1-q)^{-i}} \geq 1 - \frac{1}{\sum_{i=0}^{n-1}(1-1/e)^{-i}} \geq 1 - (1-1/e)^{n-1}.$$

This completes the proof of Theorem 2 part 2. □

4.1 Worst Case

We reformulate Theorem 2 part 1 as the following Lemma 6.

Lemma 6. *Given any* MHR *distribution F with monopoly price $p \in \mathbb{R}_{\geq 0}$ and monopoly quantile $q \in [1/e, 1]$, the truncated exponential distribution* $\mathrm{TrExp}(p, q)$ *satisfies that*

$$\frac{\mathsf{SPA}(F)}{\mathsf{OPT}(F)} \geq \frac{\mathsf{SPA}\big(\mathrm{TrExp}(p,q)\big)}{\mathsf{OPT}\big(\mathrm{TrExp}(p,q)\big)}.$$

Proof. As mentioned in Sect. 2.2, we can formulate the Myerson Auction revenue and the Second-Price Auction revenue in terms of virtual value CDF D. That is,

$$\mathsf{OPT}(F) = \int_0^{+\infty} \left[1 - \big(D(y)\big)^n \right] \cdot dy,$$

$$\mathsf{SPA}(F) = \mathsf{OPT}(F) - \int_{-\infty}^0 \big(D(y)\big)^n \cdot dy. \tag{2}$$

To prove Lemma 6, we consider the distribution $\widehat{F} \stackrel{\text{def}}{=} \begin{cases} F(x) & \forall x \in (0, p) \\ 1 & \forall x \in [p, +\infty) \end{cases}$ and truncated exponential distribution $\overline{F} \stackrel{\text{def}}{=} \mathrm{TrExp}(p, q)$. Both new distributions have the same monopoly price p and monopoly quantile q as distribution F.

We first claim that $\frac{\mathsf{SPA}(\widehat{F})}{\mathsf{OPT}(\widehat{F})} \leq \frac{\mathsf{SPA}(F)}{\mathsf{OPT}(F)}$. Since $\widehat{F}(x) \geq F(x)$ for all $x \in \mathbb{R}_{\geq 0}$, it follows from Fact 2 that $\mathsf{OPT}(\widehat{F}) \leq \mathsf{OPT}(F)$. Due to the definition of monopoly price p, only values $x \in (0, p)$ are mapped to *negative* virtual values. Because $\widehat{F}(x) = F(x)$ for all $x \in (0, p)$, in terms of virtual value CDF, we observe that $\widehat{D}(x) = D(x)$ for all $x \in \mathbb{R}_-$, and thus $\int_{-\infty}^0 \big(\widehat{D}(y)\big)^n \cdot dy = \int_{-\infty}^0 \big(D(y)\big)^n \cdot dy$. Plugging everything into Eq. (2) settles our claim:

$$\frac{\mathsf{SPA}(\widehat{F})}{\mathsf{OPT}(\widehat{F})} = 1 - \frac{1}{\mathsf{OPT}(\widehat{F})} \cdot \int_{-\infty}^0 \big(\widehat{D}(y)\big)^n \cdot dy$$

$$\leq 1 - \frac{1}{\mathsf{OPT}(F)} \cdot \int_{-\infty}^0 \big(D(y)\big)^n \cdot dy = \frac{\mathsf{SPA}(F)}{\mathsf{OPT}(F)}.$$

Next, we turn to prove that $\frac{\text{SPA}(\overline{F})}{\text{OPT}(\overline{F})} \leq \frac{\text{SPA}(\widehat{F})}{\text{OPT}(\widehat{F})}$. For both distributions $\widehat{F}$ and $\overline{F}$, notice again that values $x \in (0, p)$ are mapped to *negative* virtual values. By contrast, the Myerson Auction revenue is determined by *positive* virtual values (corresponding to the probability mass at monopoly price p). Since $\lim\limits_{x \to p^-} \overline{F}(x) = \lim\limits_{x \to p^-} \widehat{F}(x) = 1 - q$ and $\overline{F}(p) = \widehat{F}(p) = 1$, we know $\text{OPT}(\overline{F}) = \text{OPT}(\widehat{F})$.

It remains to prove that $\text{SPA}(\overline{F}) \leq \text{SPA}(\widehat{F})$. Due to the MHR property, function $\widehat{G}(x) \overset{\text{def}}{=} \ln\left(1 - \widehat{F}(x)\right) = \ln\left(1 - F(x)\right)$ is a concave function on interval $x \in (0, p)$. By contrast, $\overline{G}(x) \overset{\text{def}}{=} \ln\left(1 - \overline{F}(x)\right) = \frac{\ln q}{p} \cdot x$ is a line segment on $x \in (0, p)$. Because both curves have the same endpoints $(0, 0)$ and $(p, \ln q)$, we know from the concavity of $\widehat{G}$ that $\overline{G}(x) \leq \widehat{G}(x)$, or equivalently,

$$\overline{F}(x) \geq \widehat{F}(x), \qquad \forall x \in (0, p).$$

Due to Fact 2, such domination relationship indicates that $\text{SPA}(\overline{F}) \leq \text{SPA}(\widehat{F})$. This completes the proof of Lemma 6 as $\frac{\text{SPA}(\overline{F})}{\text{OPT}(\overline{F})} \leq \frac{\text{SPA}(\widehat{F})}{\text{OPT}(\widehat{F})} \leq \frac{\text{SPA}(F)}{\text{OPT}(F)}$. □

4.2   Lower Bound

By Lemma 6, the worst case of the Myerson Auction vs. Second-Price Auction problem is reached by a truncated exponential distribution $\text{TREXP}(p, q)$. Recall Fact 1 that monopoly quantile $q \in [1/e, 1]$. For ease of notation, we let $t \overset{\text{def}}{=} -\ln q \in [0, 1]$, and scale monopoly price p to 1. Afterward, CDF F becomes

$$F(x) = \begin{cases} 1 - e^{-t \cdot x} & \forall x \in (0, 1), \\ 1 & \forall x \in [1, +\infty). \end{cases}$$

In the range of $x \in (0, 1)$: we reformulate virtual value function $\varphi(x) = x - \frac{1 - F(x)}{f(x)} = x - \frac{1}{t}$; note that $-\frac{1}{t} < \varphi(x) < 1 - \frac{1}{t}$. Virtual value CDF D is given by

$$D(x) = \begin{cases} 0 & x < -\frac{1}{t}, \\ 1 - e^{-(t \cdot x + 1)} & -\frac{1}{t} \leq x < 1 - \frac{1}{t}, \\ 1 - e^{-t} & 1 - \frac{1}{t} \leq x < 1, \\ 1 & x \geq 1. \end{cases} \tag{3}$$

Plugging this formula into Eq. (2) and then assigning $t \leftarrow \ln 2$ (i.e., $q \leftarrow 1/2$), then

$$\frac{\text{SPA}(\text{TREXP}(p, q))}{\text{OPT}(\text{TREXP}(p, q))} \overset{(2,3)}{=} 1 - \frac{\int_{-\frac{1}{t}}^{1-\frac{1}{t}} \left[1 - e^{-(t \cdot y + 1)}\right]^n \cdot dy + \left(1 - e^{-t}\right)^n \cdot \left(\frac{1}{t} - 1\right)}{1 - (1 - e^{-t})^n}$$

$$\leq 1 - \left(1 - e^{-t}\right)^n \cdot (1/t - 1)$$

$$= 1 - \left[(\ln 2)^{-1} - 1\right] \cdot 2^{-n} \qquad (\text{since } t = \ln 2)$$

$$\leq 1 - 2^{-(n+2)}. \qquad (\text{since } (\ln 2)^{-1} - 1 \approx 0.4427 > 0.25)$$

This indicates the lower-bound part claimed in Theorem 2.

References

1. Aggarwal, G., Goel, G., Mehta, A.: Efficiency of (revenue-)optimal mechanisms. In: Proceedings 10th ACM Conference on Electronic Commerce (EC-2009), Stanford, California, USA, 6–10 July 2009, pp. 235–242 (2009)
2. Alaei, S., Hartline, J.D., Niazadeh, R., Pountourakis, E., Yuan, Y.: Optimal auctions vs. anonymous pricing. In: IEEE 56th Annual Symposium on Foundations of Computer Science, FOCS 2015, Berkeley, CA, USA, 17–20 October 2015, pp. 1446–1463 (2015)
3. Allouah, A., Besbes, O.: Prior-independent optimal auctions. In: Proceedings of the 2018 ACM Conference on Economics and Computation, Ithaca, NY, USA, 18–22 June 2018, p. 503 (2018)
4. Beyhaghi, H., Golrezaei, N., Leme, R.P., Pal, M., Sivan, B.: Improved approximations for free-order prophets and second-price auctions. CoRR abs/1807.03435 (2018)
5. Blumrosen, L., Holenstein, T.: Posted prices vs. negotiations: an asymptotic analysis. In: Proceedings 9th ACM Conference on Electronic Commerce (EC-2008), Chicago, IL, USA, 8–12 June 2008, p. 49 (2008)
6. Bulow, J., Klemperer, P.: Auctions versus negotiations. Am. Econ. Rev. **86**, 180–194 (1996)
7. Cai, Y., Daskalakis, C.: Extreme value theorems for optimal multidimensional pricing. Games Econ. Behav. **92**, 266–305 (2015)
8. Cai, Y., Devanur, N.R., Weinberg, S.M.: A duality based unified approach to Bayesian mechanism design. In: Proceedings of the 48th Annual ACM SIGACT Symposium on Theory of Computing, STOC 2016, Cambridge, MA, USA, 18–21 June 2016, pp. 926–939 (2016)
9. Cai, Y., Zhao, M.: Simple mechanisms for subadditive buyers via duality. In: Proceedings of the 49th Annual ACM SIGACT Symposium on Theory of Computing, STOC 2017, Montreal, QC, Canada, 19–23 June 2017, pp. 170–183 (2019)
10. Chawla, S., Malec, D.L., Sivan, B.: The power of randomness in Bayesian optimal mechanism design. Games Econ. Behav. **91**, 297–317 (2015)
11. Correa, J.R., Foncea, P., Hoeksma, R., Oosterwijk, T., Vredeveld, T.: Posted price mechanisms for a random stream of customers. In: Proceedings of the 2017 ACM Conference on Economics and Computation, EC 2017, Cambridge, MA, USA, 26–30 June 2017, pp. 169–186 (2017)
12. Devanur, N.R., Huang, Z., Psomas, C.: The sample complexity of auctions with side information. In: Proceedings of the 48th Annual ACM SIGACT Symposium on Theory of Computing, STOC 2016, Cambridge, MA, USA, 18–21 June 2016, pp. 426–439 (2016)
13. Dhangwatnotai, P., Roughgarden, T., Yan, Q.: Revenue maximization with a single sample. Games Econ. Behav. **91**, 318–333 (2015)
14. Dütting, P., Fischer, F.A., Klimm, M.: Revenue gaps for static and dynamic posted pricing of homogeneous goods. CoRR abs/1607.07105 (2016)
15. Fu, H., Hartline, J.D., Hoy, D.: Prior-independent auctions for risk-averse agents. In: Proceedings of the Fourteenth ACM Conference on Electronic Commerce, EC 2013, Philadelphia, PA, USA, 16–20 June 2013, pp. 471–488 (2013)
16. Fu, H., Immorlica, N., Lucier, B., Strack, P.: Randomization beats second price as a prior-independent auction. In: Proceedings of the Sixteenth ACM Conference on Economics and Computation, EC 2015, Portland, OR, USA, 15–19 June 2015, p. 323 (2015)

17. Giannakopoulos, Y., Zhu, K.: Optimal pricing for MHR distributions. In: Christodoulou, G., Harks, T. (eds.) WINE 2018. LNCS, vol. 11316, pp. 154–167. Springer, Cham (2018). https://doi.org/10.1007/978-3-030-04612-5_11

18. Hajiaghayi, M.T., Kleinberg, R.D., Sandholm, T.: Automated online mechanism design and prophet inequalities. In: Proceedings of the Twenty-Second AAAI Conference on Artificial Intelligence, Vancouver, British Columbia, Canada, 22–26 July 2007, pp. 58–65 (2007)

19. Hartline, J.D.: Mechanism design and approximation. Book draft. October **122**, 4–5 (2013)

20. Hartline, J.D., Roughgarden, T.: Simple versus optimal mechanisms. In: Proceedings 10th ACM Conference on Electronic Commerce (EC-2009), Stanford, California, USA, 6–10 July 2009, pp. 225–234 (2009)

21. Hill, T.P., Kertz, R.P., et al.: Comparisons of stop rule and supremum expectations of IID random variables. Ann. Probab. **10**(2), 336–345 (1982)

22. Huang, Z., Mansour, Y., Roughgarden, T.: Making the most of your samples. SIAM J. Comput. **47**(3), 651–674 (2018)

23. Jin, Y., Lu, P., Qi, Q., Tang, Z.G., Xiao, T.: Tight approximation ratio of anonymous pricing. In: Proceedings of the 51st Annual ACM SIGACT Symposium on Theory of Computing, STOC 2019, Phoenix, AZ, USA, 23–26 June 2019, pp. 674–685 (2019)

24. Jin, Y., Lu, P., Tang, Z.G., Xiao, T.: Tight revenue gaps among simple mechanisms. In: Proceedings of the Thirtieth Annual ACM-SIAM Symposium on Discrete Algorithms, SODA 2019, San Diego, California, USA, 6–9 January 2019, pp. 209–228 (2019)

25. Krengel, U., Sucheston, L.: On semiamarts, amarts, and processes with finite value. Adv. Probab. **4**, 197–266 (1978)

26. Ledyard, J.O.: Public goods: a survey of experimental research (1994)

27. Milgrom, P.: Putting auction theory to work: the simultaneous ascending auction. J. Polit. Econ. **108**(2), 245–272 (2000)

28. Myerson, R.B.: Optimal auction design. Math. Oper. Res. **6**(1), 58–73 (1981)

29. Rubinstein, A., Weinberg, S.M.: Simple mechanisms for a subadditive buyer and applications to revenue monotonicity. In: Proceedings of the Sixteenth ACM Conference on Economics and Computation, EC 2015, Portland, OR, USA, 15–19 June 2015, pp. 377–394 (2015)

30. Vickrey, W.: Counterspeculation, auctions, and competitive sealed tenders. J. Finan. **16**(1), 8–37 (1961)

31. Wilson, R.: Game-theoretic analysis of trading processes. Technical report, Stanford University CA Institute for Mathematical Studies in the Social Sciences (1985)

Topological Price of Anarchy Bounds for Clustering Games on Networks

Pieter Kleer[1] and Guido Schäfer[1,2(✉)]

[1] Centrum Wiskunde & Informatica (CWI), Networks and Optimization Group,
Amsterdam, The Netherlands
{kleer,schaefer}@cwi.nl
[2] Department of Econometrics and Operations Research,
Vrije Universiteit Amsterdam, Amsterdam, The Netherlands

Abstract. We consider clustering games in which the players are
embedded in a network and want to coordinate (or anti-coordinate) their
choices with their neighbors. Recent studies show that even very basic
variants of these games exhibit a large Price of Anarchy. Our main goal is
to understand how structural properties of the network topology impact
the inefficiency of these games. We derive *topological bounds* on the Price
of Anarchy for different classes of clustering games. These topological
bounds provide a more informative assessment of the inefficiency of these
games than the corresponding (worst-case) Price of Anarchy bounds. As
one of our main results, we derive (tight) bounds on the Price of Anarchy
for clustering games on Erdős-Rényi random graphs, which, depending
on the graph density, stand in stark contrast to the known Price of Anarchy bounds.

Keywords: Clustering games · Coordination games · Price of
Anarchy · Random graphs · Nash equilibrium existence

1 Introduction

Motivation. Clustering games on networks constitute a class of strategic games
in which the players are embedded in a network and want to coordinate (or anti-
coordinate) their choices with their neighbors. These games capture several key
characteristics encountered in applications such as opinion formation, technology
adoption, information diffusion or virus spreading on various types of networks
(e.g., the Internet, social networks, biological networks, etc.).

Different variants of clustering games have recently been studied intensively
in the algorithmic game theory literature, both with respect to the existence and
the inefficiency of equilibria (see, e.g., [3,4,11,15,16,18,20,21]). Unfortunately,
several of these studies reveal that the strategic choices of the players may lead to
equilibrium outcomes that are highly inefficient. Arguably the most prominent
notion to assess the inefficiency of equilibria is the *Price of Anarchy (PoA)*
[19], which refers to the worst-case ratio of the optimal social welfare and the

© Springer Nature Switzerland AG 2019
I. Caragiannis et al. (Eds.): WINE 2019, LNCS 11920, pp. 241–255, 2019.
https://doi.org/10.1007/978-3-030-35389-6_18

social welfare of a (pure) Nash equilibrium. It is known that even the most basic clustering games exhibit a large (or even unbounded) Price of Anarchy (see below for details). These negative results naturally trigger the following questions: Is this high inefficiency inevitable in clustering games on networks? Or, can we trace more precisely what causes a large inefficiency? These questions constitute the starting point of our investigations: *Our main goal in this paper is to understand how structural properties of the network topology impact the Price of Anarchy in clustering games.*

In general, our idea is that a more fine-grained analysis may reveal topological parameters of the network which can be used to derive more accurate bounds on the Price of Anarchy; we term such bounds *topological Price of Anarchy bounds*. Given the many applications of clustering games on different types of networks, our hope is that such topological bounds will be more informative than the corresponding worst-case bounds. Clearly, this hope is elusive for a number of fundamental games on networks whose inefficiency is known to be *independent* of the network topology, the most prominent example being the selfish routing games studied in the seminal work by Rougharden and Tardos [22]. But, in contrast to these games, clustering games exhibit a strong *locality property* induced by the network structure, i.e., the utility of each player is affected only by the choices of her direct neighbors in the network. This observation also motivates our choice of quantifying the inefficiency by means of topological parameters (rather than other parameters of the game).

We derive topological bounds on the Price of Anarchy for different classes of clustering games. Our bounds reveal that the Price of Anarchy depends on different topological parameters in the case of symmetric and asymmetric strategy sets of the players and, depending on these parameters, stand in stark contrast to the known worst case bounds. As one of our primary benchmarks, we use Erdős-Rényi random graphs [13] to obtain a precise understanding of how these parameters affect the Price of Anarchy. More specifically, we show that the Price of Anarchy of clustering games on random graphs, depending on the graph density, improves significantly over the worst case bounds. To the best of our knowledge, this is also the first work that addresses the inefficiency of equilibria on random graphs.[1]

We note that the applicability of our topological Price of Anarchy bounds is not limited to the class of Erdős-Rényi random graphs. The main reason for using these graphs is that their structural properties are well-understood. In particular, our topological bounds can be applied to any graph class of interest (as long as certain structural properties are well-understood).

Our Clustering Games. We study a generalization of the unifying model of *clustering games* introduced by Feldman and Friedler [11]: We are given an undirected graph $G = (V, E)$ on $n = |V|$ nodes whose edge set $E = E_c \cup E_a$ is partitioned into a set of *coordination* edges E_c and a set of *anti-coordination*

---

[1] We note that Valiant and Roughgarden [23] study Braess' paradox in large random graphs (see Related Work).

edges E_a.[2] Further, we are given a set $[c] = \{1, \ldots, c\}$ of $c > 1$ colors and edge-weights $w : E \to \mathbb{R}_{\geq 0}$.[3] Each node i corresponds to a player who chooses a color s_i from her color set $S_i \subseteq [c]$. We say that the game is *symmetric* if $S_i = [c]$ for all $i \in V$ and *asymmetric* otherwise. An edge $e = \{i, j\} \in E$ is *satisfied* if it is a coordination edge and both i and j choose the same color, or if it is an anti-coordination edge and i and j choose different colors. The goal of player i is to choose a color $s_i \in S_i$ such that the weight of all satisfied edges incident to i is maximized.

We consider a generalization of these games by incorporating additionally: (i) individual player preferences (as in [21]), and (ii) different distribution rules (as in [3]): We assume that each player i has a *preference function* $q_i : S_i \to \mathbb{R}_{\geq 0}$ which encodes her preferences over the colors in S_i. Further, player i has a *split parameter* $\alpha_{ij} \geq 0$ for every incident edge $e = \{i, j\}$ which determines the share she obtains from e: if e is satisfied then i obtains a proportion of $\alpha_{ij}/(\alpha_{ij} + \alpha_{ji})$ of the weight w_e of e. The utility $u_i(s)$ of player i for choosing color $s_i \in S_i$ is then the sum of the individual preference $q_i(s_i)$ and the total share of all satisfied edges incident to i. We consider the standard utilitarian *social welfare* objective $u(s) = \sum_i u_i(s)$.

We use $\bar{\alpha}_e$ to denote the *disparity* of an edge $e = \{i, j\}$, defined as $\bar{\alpha}_e = \max\{\alpha_{ij}/\alpha_{ji}, \alpha_{ji}/\alpha_{ij}\}$, and let $\bar{\alpha} = \max_{e \in E} \bar{\alpha}_e$ refer to the maximum disparity of all edges. We say that the game has the *equal-split distribution rule* if $\bar{\alpha} = 1$ (equivalently, $\alpha_{ij} = \alpha_{ji}$ for all $\{i, j\} \in E$).

Our clustering games generalize several other strategic games, which were studied extensively in the literature before, such as *max cut games* and *not-all-equal satisfiability games* [15], *max k-cut games* [16], *coordination games* [4], *clustering games* [11] and *anti-coordination games* [20].

Main Contributions. We derive results for symmetric and asymmetric clustering games. Due to space restrictions, we elaborate on our main findings for symmetric clustering games only below; our results for the asymmetric case are discussed in Sect. 5. An overview of the bounds derived in this paper is given in Table 1.

1. Topological Price of Anarchy Bound. We show that the Price of Anarchy for symmetric clustering games is bounded as a function of the *maximum subgraph density* of G which is defined as $\rho(G) = \max_{S \subseteq V}\{|E[S]|/|S|\}$, where $|E[S]|$ is the number of edges in the subgraph induced by S. More specifically, we prove that $\text{PoA} \leq 1 + (1 + \bar{\alpha})\rho(G)$ and that this bound is tight (even for coordination games). Using this topological bound, we are able to show that the Price of Anarchy is at most $4 + 3\bar{\alpha}$ for clustering games on planar graphs and $1 + 2\rho(G)$ for coordination games with equal-split distribution rule. We also derive a (qualitatively) refined bound of $\text{PoA} \leq 5 + 2\rho(G[E_c])$ for clustering games with equal-split distribution rule which reveals that the maximum

---

[2] The game is called a *coordination game* if all edges are coordination edges and an *anti-coordination game* (or *cut game*) if all edges are anti-coordination edges.

[3] In this paper, we use $[k]$ to denote the set $\{1, \ldots, k\}$ for a given integer $k \geq 1$.

Table 1. Overview of our topological Price of Anarchy bounds for symmetric and asymmetric clustering games. A "+" or "1" in the column "distr. α" indicates whether the distribution rule α is positive or equal-split, respectively. $\bar{\alpha}$ is the maximum disparity, and c is the number of colors. $\rho(G)$ and $\Delta(G)$ refer to the maximum subgraph density and the maximum degree of G, respectively. The stated bounds for random graphs hold with high probability.

Symmetric clustering games					
Graph topology	Coord. only	Indiv. pref.	Distr. α	Topological PoA (our bounds)	PoA (prev. work)
Arbitrary	✗	✓	+	$1 + (1+\bar{\alpha})\,\rho(G)$ (Theorem 1)	c [3,11]
Planar	✗	✓	+	$\leq 4 + 3\bar{\alpha}$ (Corollary 1)	
Arbitrary	✗	✓	1	$1 + 2\rho(G)$ (Corollary 2)	
Arbitrary	✗	✓	1	$\leq 5 + 2\rho(G_c)$ (Theorem 2)	
Sparse random	✓	✓	1	$\Theta(1)$ (Corollary 3)	
Dense random	✓	✗	1	$\Omega(c)$ (Theorem 3)	
Asymmetric clustering games					
Graph topology	Coord. only	Indiv. pref.	Distr. α	(ϵ, k)-topological PoA (our bounds)	(ϵ, k)-PoA (prev. work)
Arbitrary	✓	✗	1	$\leq 2\epsilon\Delta(G)$ (Theorem 5)	$\leq 2\epsilon\frac{n-1}{k-1}$
Arbitrary	✓	✗	1	$\geq \epsilon(\frac{\Delta(G)}{k-1}-1)$ (Theorem 5)	$\geq 2\epsilon\frac{n-k}{k-1}+1$
Dense random	✓	✗	1	$\Omega(\epsilon n)$	[21]
Sparse random	✓	✗	1	$\Theta(\frac{\epsilon \ln(n)}{\ln\ln(n)})$ (Theorem 6)	
+ common color	✓	✗	1	$O(1)$ (Theorem 7)	

subgraph density with respect to the graph $G[E_c]$ (or simply G_c) induced by the *coordination edges* E_c *only* is the crucial topological parameter determining the Price of Anarchy.

These bounds provide more refined insights than the known (tight) bound of PoA $\leq c$ (number of colors) on the Price of Anarchy for (i) symmetric coordination games with individual preferences and arbitrary distribution rule [3], and (ii) clustering games without individual preferences and equal-split distribution rule [11] (both being special cases of our model). An important point to notice here is that this bound indicates that the Price of Anarchy is unbounded if the number of colors $c = c(n)$ grows as a function of n. In contrast, our topological bounds are independent of c and are thus particularly useful when this number is large (while the maximum subgraph density is small). Moreover, our refined bound of $5 + 2\rho(G[E_c])$ mentioned above provides a nice bridge between the facts that for max-cut (or anti-coordination) games the price of anarchy is known to be constant, whereas for coordination games the price of anarchy might grow large.

2. Price of Anarchy for Random Coordination games. We derive the first price of anarchy bounds for coordination games on random graphs. We focus on the *Erdős-Rényi random graph model* [13] (also known as $G(n,p)$), where each graph consists of n nodes and every edge is present (independently) with probability $p \in [0,1]$. More specifically, we show that the Price of Anarchy is constant (with high probability) for coordination games on sparse random graphs (i.e., $p = d/n$ for some constant $d > 0$) with equal-split distribution rule. In contrast, we show that the Price of Anarchy remains $\Omega(c)$ (with high probability) for dense random graphs (i.e., $p = d$ for some constant $0 < d \leq 1$).

Note that our constant bound on the Price of Anarchy for sparse random graphs stands in stark contrast to the deterministic bound of PoA $= c$ [3,11] (which could increase with the size of the network). On the other hand, our bound for dense random graphs reveals that we cannot significantly improve upon this bound through randomization of the graph topology.

It is worth mentioning that all our results for random graphs hold against an *adaptive adversary* who can fix the input of the clustering game *knowing* the realization of the random graph. To obtain these results, we need to exploit some deep probabilistic results on the maximum subgraph density and the existence of perfect matchings in random graphs.

3. Convergence of Best-Response Dynamics. In general, pure Nash equilibria are not guaranteed to exist for clustering games with *arbitrary* distribution rules α, even if the game is symmetric (see, e.g., [3]). While some sufficient conditions for the existence of pure Nash equilibria, or, the convergence of best-response dynamics (see also [3]) are known, a complete characterization is elusive so far.

In this work, we obtain a complete characterization of the class of distribution rules which guarantee the convergence of best-response dynamics in clustering games on a fixed network topology. Basically, we prove that best-response dynamics converge if and only if α is a *generalized weighted Shapley distribution rule* (Theorem 4). Our proof relies on the fact that there needs to be some form of *cyclic consistency* similar to the one used in [14].

Prior to our work, the existence of pure Nash equilibria was known for certain special cases of coordination games only, namely for symmetric coordination games with individual preferences and $c = 2$ [3], and for symmetric coordination games without individual preferences [11]. To the best of our knowledge, this is the first characterization of distribution rules in terms of best-response dynamics (which, in particular, applies to the settings in which pure Nash equilibria are guaranteed to exist for every distribution rule [3,11]).[4]

Related Work. The literature on clustering and coordination games is vast; we only include references relevant to our model here. The proposed model above is a mixture of (special cases of) existing models in [3,4,11,21].

Anshelevich and Sekar [3] consider symmetric coordination games with individual preferences and (general) distribution rules. They show existence of ϵ-*approximate k-strong equilibria*, (ϵ, k)-equilibria for short, for various combinations; in particular, $(2, k)$-equilibria always exist for any k. Moreover, they show that the number of colors c is an upper bound on the PoA. Apt et al. [4] study asymmetric coordination games with unit weights, zero individual preferences, and equal-split distribution rules. They derive an almost complete picture of the

---

[4] In the full version, we extend our ideas and provide a characterization of the existence of pure Nash equilibria in symmetric coordination games, complementing a result by Anshelevich and Sekar [3].

existence of $(1, k)$-equilibria for different values of c. Feldman and Friedler [11] introduce a unified framework (as introduced above) for studying the (strong) Price of Anarchy in clustering games with individual preferences set to zero and equal-split distribution rules. In particular, they show that the number of colors is an upper bound on the PoA and that $2(n-1)/(k-1)$ is an upper bound on the $(1, k)$-PoA. Rahn and Schäfer [21] consider the more general setting of polymatrix coordination games with equal-split distribution rule, of which our asymmetric coordination games with individual preferences are a special case. They show a bound of $2\epsilon(n-1)/(k-1)$ on the (ϵ, k)-PoA and that an (ϵ, k)-equilibrium is guaranteed to exist for any $\epsilon \geq 2$ and any k.

There is also a vast literature on different variants of anti-coordination (or cut) games, see, e.g., [16,18] and the references therein, which are also captured by our clustering games. In a recent paper, Carosi and Gianpiero [8] consider so-called k-coloring games. Moreover, clustering and coordination games were also studied on directed graphs [4,7]. Finally, certain coordination and clustering games can be seen as special cases of hedonic games [10]; we refer the reader to [6] for, in particular, a survey of recent literature on (fractional) hedonic games. Identifying topological inefficiency bounds for these type of games, as well as for clustering games on directed graphs, could be an interesting direction for future work.[5]

Regarding the study of the inefficiency of equilibria on random graphs, closest to our work seems to be the work by [23]. They study the Braess paradox on large Erdős-Rényi random graphs and show that for certain settings the Braess paradox occurs with high probability as the size of the network grows large. The study of randomness in games has also received some attention in other setting, see, e.g., [1,5]. These are mostly settings with small strategy sets and random utility functions, and are not comparable with ours.

Finally, our characterization results regarding the existence of pure Nash equilibria and convergence of best-response dynamics are conceptually similar to the work of Chen et al. [9] and Gopalakrishnan et al. [14].

2   Preliminaries

Clustering Games. As introduced above, an instance of a *clustering game* $\Gamma = (G, c, (S_i), (\alpha_{ij}), w, q)$ is given by:

- an undirected graph $G = (V, E)$, where the set of edges $E = E_c \cup E_a$ is partitioned into coordination edges E_c and anti-coordination edges E_a;
- a subset $S_i \subseteq [c]$ of colors available to player $i \in V$;
- a split parameter $\alpha_{ij} \geq 0$ for every player $i \in V$ and incident edge $\{i, j\} \in E$;
- a weight function $w : E \to \mathbb{R}_{\geq 0}$ on the edges;
- a vector $q = (q_i)_{i \in V}$ of individual preference functions $q_i : S_i \to \mathbb{R}_{\geq 0}$.

---

[5] Our results do not seem to extend to clustering games on directed graphs. One could model a directed edge $e = (i, j)$ by setting $\alpha_{ij} = 0$ and $\alpha_{ji} > 0$. E.g., Theorem 1 does not apply then as $\bar{\alpha} = \infty$ in this case.

Whenever we refer to a *clustering game* below, we assume that all of the above input parameters are non-trivial; we specify the respective restrictions otherwise.

Each node $i \in V$ corresponds to a player whose goal is to choose a color $s_i \in S_i$ from the set of colors available to her to maximize her utility

$$u_i(s) = q_i(s_i) + \sum_{\{i,j\} \in E_c : s_i = s_j} \frac{\alpha_{ij}}{\alpha_{ij} + \alpha_{ji}} w_{ij} + \sum_{\{i,j\} \in E_a : s_i \neq s_j} \frac{\alpha_{ij}}{\alpha_{ij} + \alpha_{ji}} w_{ij}.$$

We call $\alpha = (\alpha_{ij}) \geq 0$ a *distribution rule*. We assume that α satisfies $\alpha_{ij} + \alpha_{ji} > 0$ for every edge $e = \{i,j\} \in E$; in particular, not both i and j have a zero split for edge e. We say that α is *positive* if $\alpha_{ij} > 0$ and $\alpha_{ji} > 0$ for all $e = \{i,j\} \in E$; we also write $\alpha > \mathbf{0}$. Further, α is called the *equal-split* distribution rule if $\alpha_{ij} = \alpha_{ji}$ for all $e = \{i,j\} \in E$; we also indicate this by $\alpha = \mathbf{1}$. The *disparity* of an edge $e = \{i,j\}$ is defined as $\bar{\alpha}_e = \max\{\alpha_{ij}/\alpha_{ji}, \alpha_{ji}/\alpha_{ij}\}$ and we use $\bar{\alpha} = \max_{e \in E} \bar{\alpha}_e$ to denote the maximum disparity.

We say that the clustering game is *symmetric* if $S_i = \{1, \ldots, c\}$ for every player $i \in V$ and *asymmetric* otherwise. If we focus on symmetric clustering games, we omit the explicit reference of the strategy sets (S_i) with $S_i = [c]$. A clustering game is called a *coordination game* if $E_a = \emptyset$ and an *anti-coordination game* (or *cut game*) if $E_c = \emptyset$. We use $n = |V|$ to refer to the number of players.

We consider the utilitarian *social welfare* objective $u(s) = \sum_{i \in V} u_i(s)$. The *Price of Anarchy* of an instance Γ is defined as $\mathrm{PoA}(\Gamma) = \max_{s \in \mathrm{NE}(\Gamma)} u(s^*)/u(s)$, where $\mathrm{NE}(\Gamma)$ is the set of all pure Nash equilibria of Γ and s^* is a socially optimal strategy profile. Given a class of clustering games $\mathcal{G}$, the Price of Anarchy is defined as $\mathrm{PoA}(\mathcal{G}) = \sup_{\Gamma \in \mathcal{G}} \mathrm{PoA}(\Gamma)$.

Random Clustering Games. In our probabilistic framework to study the Price of Anarchy of random clustering games, we use the well-known *Erdős-Rényi random graph model* [13], denoted by $G(n, p)$:[6] There are n nodes and every (undirected) edge is present (independently) with probability $p = p(n) \in [0, 1]$. We say that a random graph is *sparse* if $p = d/n$ for some constant $d > 0$, and it is *dense* if $p = d$ for some constant $0 < d < 1$. In this paper, we focus on random graph instances with equal-split distributions rules.[7]

Fix some probability $p = p(n) \in [0, 1]$ and let $\beta = \beta(n, c(n))$ be a given function. Define $\mathcal{G}_{G_n}$ as the set of all clustering games on random graph $G_n \sim G(n, p)$. We say that the *Price of Anarchy for random clustering games is at most* β *with high probability* $(\mathrm{PoA}(\mathcal{G}_{G_n}) \leq \beta, \text{for short})$ if $\mathbb{P}_{G_n \sim G(n,p)}\{\mathrm{PoA}(\mathcal{G}_{G_n}) \leq \beta\} \geq 1 - o(1)$. We use a similar definition if we want to lower bound the Price of Anarchy. Finally, for a constant β (independent of n and c) we say that the *Price of Anarchy for random clustering games is* β *with high probability* $(\mathrm{PoA}(\mathcal{G}_{G_n}) \to \beta$, *for short*) if for all $\varepsilon > 0$ $\mathbb{P}_{G_n \sim G(n,p)} \{|\mathrm{PoA}(\mathcal{G}_{G_n}) - \beta| \leq \varepsilon\} \geq 1 - o(1)$. All our results for clustering games on random graphs hold with high probability.

---

[6] Although this model was first introduced by Gilbert, it is often referred to as the *Erdős-Rényi random graph model.*

[7] Some of our results naturally extend to more general distribution rules, but we omit the (technical) details here because they do not provide additional insights.

Shapley Distribution Rules. We adapt the definition of Shapley distribution rules for resource allocation games [14] to our setting.

A distribution rule α corresponds to a *generalized weighted Shapley distribution rule* if and only if there exists a permutation σ of the players in V and weight vector $\gamma \in \mathbb{R}^V_{\geq 0}$ such that the following two conditions are satisfied for every edge $e = \{i,j\}$: (i) If $\alpha_{ij} = 0$, then $\sigma(i) < \sigma(j)$. (ii) If $\alpha_{ij} > 0$, then $\frac{\alpha_{ij}}{\alpha_{ij}+\alpha_{ji}} = \frac{\gamma_i}{\gamma_i+\gamma_j}$. If all weights are strictly positive, then the resulting distribution rule is a *weighted Shapley distribution rule*. If $\gamma_i = \gamma_j$ for all $i,j \in V$ the resulting distribution rule is an *unweighted Shapley distribution rule*. Note that this case corresponds to an equal-split distribution rule.

Due to space restrictions, some proofs below are omitted and will be given in the full version of the paper.

3 Refined Bounds on the Price of Anarchy

In this section, we first establish our topological bound on the Price of Anarchy for symmetric clustering games and then use it to derive new bounds for some special cases as well as random clustering games.

3.1 Topological Price of Anarchy Bound

Our topological bound depends on the *maximum subgraph density* of G which is defined as $\rho(G) = \max_{S \subseteq V}\{|E[S]|/|S|\}$, where $|E[S]|$ is the number of edges in the subgraph induced by S. Recall that $\bar{\alpha}$ refers to the maximum disparity.

Theorem 1 (Density bound). *Let $\Gamma = (G, c, \alpha, w, q)$ be a symmetric clustering game with $\alpha > 0$. Then $PoA(\Gamma) \leq 1 + (1 + \bar{\alpha})\rho(G)$ and this is tight.*

Proof (upper bound). Let s and s^* be a Nash equilibrium and a social optimum, respectively. Consider an edge $\{i,j\} \in E$ and assume without loss of generality that $u_i(s) \leq u_j(s)$. If $\{i,j\}$ is a coordination edge, then $u_i(s) \geq u_i(s_{-i}, s_j) \geq \alpha_{ij}/(\alpha_{ij}+\alpha_{ji})w_{ij}$, where (s_{-i}, s_j) is the strategy profile in which player i deviates to the color of player j and all other players play according to s. Suppose $\{i,j\}$ is an anti-coordination edge. If $s_i \neq s_j$, then we trivially have $u_i(s) \geq \alpha_{ij}/(\alpha_{ij}+\alpha_{ji})w_{ij}$ by non-negativity of the weights and individual preferences. If $s_i = s_j$, then the same inequality holds by using the Nash condition for some arbitrary color which is not s_j. (We may assume that every player has at least two colors in her strategy set.) In either case, we conclude that

$$w_{ij} \leq \left(1 + \frac{\alpha_{ji}}{\alpha_{ij}}\right)u_i(s) \leq \left(1 + \max_{e \in E}\bar{\alpha}_e\right)u_i(s) = (1+\bar{\alpha})\,u_i(s). \quad (1)$$

Moreover, by exploiting that s is a Nash equilibrium and the non-negativity of the edge weights, we obtain for every $i \in V$, $u_i(s) \geq u_i(s_{-i}, s_i^*) \geq q_i(s_i^*)$.

Using that the sum of the weights of all satisfied edges in s^* is at most the sum of all edge weights, we obtain

$$u(s^*) \le \sum_{i \in V} q_i(s_i^*) + \sum_{e=\{i,j\} \in E} w_{ij} \le \sum_{i \in V} u_i(s) + (1 + \bar{\alpha}) \sum_{\{i,j\} \in E} \min\{u_i(s), u_j(s)\}.$$

If we can find a value M such that

$$\sum_{\{i,j\} \in E} \min\{u_i(s), u_j(s)\} \le M \cdot \sum_{i \in V} u_i(s) \qquad (2)$$

then it follows that $u(s^*) \le (1 + (1 + \bar{\alpha}) \cdot M) u(s)$. We show that $M = \max_{S \subseteq V}\{|E[S]|/|S|\}$ satisfies (2).

Let $N(i) = \{j \in V : \{i,j\} \in E\}$ be the set of neighbors of i. Define $m_i = |\{j \in N(i) : u_i(s) < u_j(s) \text{ or } (u_i(s) = u_j(s) \text{ and } i < j)\}|$ and note that $\sum_{i \in V} m_i = |E|$. We can assume without loss of generality that $\sum_{i \in V} u_i(s) = 1$, since the expression in (2) is invariant under multiplication with a constant positive scalar. Moreover, the players may be renamed such that $u_1(s) \le u_2(s) \le \cdots \le u_n(s)$.

We continue by showing that M is an upper bound for the linear program below (in which $u_i = u_i(s)$ and the m_i are considered constants).

$$\max \sum_{i \in V} u_i m_i \quad \text{s.t.} \quad u_1 + u_2 + \cdots + u_n = 1$$
$$0 \le u_1 \le u_2 \le \cdots \le u_n$$

The dual of this program is given by

$$\min z \quad \text{s.t.} \quad -\pi_i + \pi_{i+1} + z = m_i, \quad i = 1, \ldots, n-1$$
$$-\pi_n + z = m_n$$
$$\pi_i \ge 0, \quad i = 1, \ldots, n$$
$$z \in \mathbb{R}$$

We now construct a feasible dual solution. Set $z^* = \max_{l \in V}\{\sum_{i=l}^{n-1} m_i/(n-l)\}$. We will often use that $(n-l)z^* \ge \sum_{i=l}^{n-1} m_i$ for any fixed l. In particular, with $l = n-1$, we find $z^* \ge m_n$, so that $\pi_n^* := z^* - m_n \ge 0$. Then we define $\pi_{n-1}^* := \pi_n^* + z^* - m_{n-1} = 2z^* - (m_{n-1} + m_n) \ge 0$. Using induction it then easily follows that $\pi_i^* := \pi_{i+1}^* + z^* - m_i \ge 0$ for all $i = 1, \ldots, n-2$ as well. We have constructed a feasible dual solution with objective function value z^*. Using weak duality it follows that for any feasible primal solution $u = (u_1, \ldots, u_n)$, we have

$$\sum_{\{i,j\} \in E} u_i m_i \le \max_{l \in V}\left\{\frac{\sum_{i=l}^{n-1} m_i}{n-l}\right\} \le \max_{S \subseteq V}\left\{\frac{|E[S]|}{|S|}\right\},$$

since the term in middle is precisely the density of the induced subgraph on the nodes $l, \ldots, n$. This completes the upper bound proof. $\qquad\square$

We use our topological bound to derive deterministic bounds on the Price of Anarchy for two special cases of clustering games. Note that these bounds cannot be deduced from [3,11].

Corollary 1 (Planar clustering games). *Let $\Gamma = (G, c, \alpha, w, q)$ be a symmetric clustering game on a planar graph G with $\alpha > 0$. Then $PoA(\Gamma) \leq 4 + 3\bar{\alpha}$.*

Proof. By Euler's formula, $|E(H)|/|V(H)| \leq 3$ for any planar graph H. Further, any induced subgraph H of a planar graph G is again planar. Using this in Theorem 1 proves the claim. □

Corollary 2 (Equal-split coordination games). *Let G be a given undirected graph, and let $\mathcal{G}_G$ be the set of all symmetric coordination games $\Gamma = (G, c, 1, w, q)$ with equal-split distribution rule on G. Then $PoA(\mathcal{G}_G) = 1 + 2\rho(G)$.*

We emphasize that the bound in Corollary 2 is tight on *every* fixed graph topology G, rather than only in the *value* of $\rho(G)$.

It is known that the Price of Anarchy of anti-coordination games is 2 (see, e.g., [18]), which is not reflected by our bound in Theorem 1. Intuitively, this suggests that a large Price of Anarchy is caused by the coordination edges of the graph. Theorem 2 reveals that this intuition is correct: it shows that the maximum subgraph density with respect to the *coordination edges only* is the determining topological parameter.

Theorem 2 (Refined density bound). *Let $\Gamma = (G, c, 1, w, q)$ be a symmetric clustering game with equal-split distribution rule. Then $PoA(\Gamma) \leq 5 + 2\rho(G[E_c])$, where $G[E_c]$ is the subgraph induced by the coordination edges E_c.*

Using a similar construction as in the proof of Corollary 2 we can also establish a lower bound of $1 + 2\max_{S \subseteq V} \{|E_c[S]|/|S|\}$.

Note that for anti-coordination games we obtain an upper bound of 5 which is inferior to the known (tight) bound of 2. It would be interesting to see whether our topological bound in Theorem 2 can be improved to match this bound.

3.2   Price of Anarchy for Random Coordination Games

We now turn to our bounds for random coordination games. Recall that for random graphs we consider equal-split distribution rules only. We first show that for sparse random graphs the Price of Anarchy is constant with high probability.

Corollary 3 (Sparse random coordination games). *Let $d > 0$ be a constant. Let $\mathcal{G}_{G_n}$ be the set of all symmetric coordination games $\Gamma = (G_n, c, 1, w, q)$ on graph $G_n \sim G(n, d/n)$ with equal-split distribution rule. Then there is a constant $\beta = \beta(d)$ such that $PoA(\mathcal{G}_{G_n}) \to \beta$.*

Proof. The maximum subgraph density of a random graph G_n approaches a constant $\beta = \beta(d)$ with high probability [2] (see [17] for approximations of this constant). Combining this with the bound in Corollary 2 proves the claim. □

As we show in Theorem 3, the result of Corollary 3 does not hold for sufficiently dense random graphs if the number of available colors grows large.

Theorem 3 (Dense random coordination games). *Let $0 < d \leq 1$ be a constant and let $(c_n)_{n \in \mathbb{N}} \to \infty$ be a sequence of available colors. Let $\mathcal{G}_{G_n}(c_n)$ be the set of all symmetric coordination games $\Gamma = (G_n, c_n, 1, w, 0)$ on graph $G_n \sim G(n, d)$ with c_n colors, equal-split distribution rule and no individual preferences. Then there is a constant $\beta = \beta(d)$ such that $PoA(\mathcal{G}_{G_n}(c_n)) \geq \beta c_n$.*

We note that this lower bound holds even for coordination games without individual preferences (as studied in [11]). Basically, this bound implies that for dense graph topologies we cannot significantly improve upon the Price of Anarchy bound of c by [3,11], even if we randomize the graph topology.

Proof (Theorem 3). We first construct a deterministic instance Γ with Price of Anarchy $\Omega(c_n)$ and then show that we can embed this construction into a random graph with high probability.

Consider a graph $G = (V, E)$ and let c be the number of available colors. Let $M = \{e_1, \ldots, e_q\} \subseteq E$ be a matching of size at most c. Let V_M be the set of nodes which are matched in M. Define the weight of an edge $e \in E$ as $w(e) = 2$ if $e \in M$, $w(e) = 1$ if precisely one of e's endpoints is matched in M, and $w(e) = 0$ otherwise.

Consider the strategy profile s in which the nodes adjacent to e_i play color i, for $i = 1, \ldots, q$. Note that this is possible because $q \leq c$ by assumption. All other nodes play an arbitrary color; these nodes are irrelevant as all the edges that they are adjacent to have weight zero. In a social optimum s^* all players choose a common color. It follows that $PoA(\Gamma) \geq |E[V_M]|/(2q)$, where $|E[V_M]|$ is the number of edges in the induced subgraph of V_M. Note that all these edges have weight at least one.

Now, let $G_n = (V_n, E_n) \sim G(n, d)$ and assume without loss of generality that $V_n = \{1, \ldots, n\}$. We claim that with high probability the induced subgraph on nodes $W_n = \{1, \ldots, \lceil c_n/4 \rceil\}$ contains both $\Omega(c_n^2)$ edges and a perfect matching (if $\lceil c_n/4 \rceil$ is odd, we consider the first $\lceil c_n/4 \rceil + 1$ nodes).[8]

The first claim follows from standard arguments. Note that $\mu = \mathbb{E}\{E_n[W_n]\} = d\binom{\lceil c_n/4 \rceil}{2} = \Omega(c_n^2)$. Using Chernoff's bound, it follows that $\mathbb{P}\{E_n[W_n] < \mu/2\} \leq \exp(-\mu/8) = \exp(-\Omega(c_n^2)/8) \to 0$ as $n \to \infty$ as $(c_n) \to \infty$. The second claim relies on the following result (see, e.g., [12]): For every fixed $0 < d \leq 1$ it holds that $\lim_{n \to \infty} \mathbb{P}_{G_n \sim G(n,d)}\{G_n \text{ contains a perfect matching}\} = 1$. By applying this result to the induced subgraph on W_n and using that c_n approaches infinity as $n \to \infty$, the claim follows.[9]

---

[8] One may focus on any set of $\lceil c_n/4 \rceil$ nodes. The important thing to note is that we need a set of nodes with many edges on its induced subgraph *and* a perfect matching (it is not sufficient to find two different sets each satisfying one of these properties). Moreover, if $c_n \geq 4n$, we consider $W_n = \{1, \ldots, n\}$ and then the same argument works.

[9] Note that here we implicitly use that the intersection of two probabilistic events which occur with high probability also occurs with high probability.

Combining this with the deterministic bound on the Price of Anarchy derived above concludes the proof.   □

4 Convergence of Best-Response Dynamics

We provide a characterization of distribution rules that guarantee the convergence of best-response dynamics in symmetric clustering games.

Theorem 4 (Best-response convergence). *Let $\mathcal{G}_{G,c,\alpha}$ be the set of all symmetric clustering games $\Gamma = (G, c, \alpha, w, q)$ on a fixed graph G with c common colors and distribution rule α. Then best-response dynamics are guaranteed to converge to a pure Nash equilibrium for every clustering game in $\mathcal{G}_{G,c,\alpha}$ if and only if α corresponds to a generalized weighted Shapley distribution rule.*

Remark 1. Theorem 4 remains valid also for various settings without individual preferences. For example, this holds for coordination games (corresponding to certain models in [3,11]) and for general clustering games with $c = 2$.[10]

For symmetric coordination games with $c \geq 3$ colors, we can strengthen the condition in Theorem 4 to "guaranteed existence of a pure Nash equilibrium", which complements the result in [3] (details will be given in the full version).

5 Results for Asymmetric Clustering Games

We give an overview of our results for asymmetric clustering games. We focus on coordination games with equal-split distribution rule and no individual preferences.

Apt et al. [4] show that the Price of Anarchy of coordination games is unbounded if $c \geq n + 1$; notably, this holds for arbitrary graph topologies. We slightly generalize this observation by showing that the Price of Anarchy is unbounded if and only if $c \geq \chi(G) + 1$, where $\chi(G)$ is the chromatic number of G. We exploit this insight to prove that if the number of colors c is a constant then the Price of Anarchy is unbounded for sparse random graphs, while it is bounded by some constant for dense random graphs (details will be given in the full version).

Subsequently, we focus on the Price of Anarchy of ϵ-*approximate k-strong equilibria*, called (ϵ, k)-*equilibria* for short.[11] The Price of Anarchy naturally

---

[10] In general, this is not true if $c \geq 3$. For example, consider a cycle of length three with only anti-coordination edges.

[11] A strategy profile s is an (ϵ, k)-*equilibrium* with $\epsilon \geq 1$ and $k \in [n]$ if for every set of players $K \subseteq V$ with $|K| \leq k$ and every deviation $s'_K = (s'_i)_{i \in K}$, there is at least one player $j \in K$ such that $\epsilon \cdot u_j(s) \geq u_j(s_{-K}, s'_K)$. We turn to (ϵ, k)-equilibria because pure Nash equilibria are not guaranteed to exist in asymmetric coordination games (see, e.g., [4]).

extends to the set of (ϵ, k)-equilibria. It is known that the (ϵ, k)-PoA of coordination games is between $2\epsilon(n-1)/(k-1) + 1 - 2\epsilon$ and $2\epsilon(n-1)/(k-1)$ for $k \geq 2$ [21]. In particular, the Price of Anarchy grows like $\Theta(\epsilon n)$ if k is a constant.

We derive a topological bound on the (ϵ, k)-Price of Anarchy which depends on the maximum degree $\Delta(G)$ of the graph G.

Theorem 5 (Degree bound). *Let* $\epsilon \geq 1$, $k \geq 2$, $c \geq 3$, *and let* G *be an arbitrary graph. Let* $\mathcal{G}_G(c)$ *be the set of all coordination games* $\Gamma = (G, c, (S_i), \mathbf{1}, w, \mathbf{0})$ *on graph* G *with* c *colors, equal-split distribution rule and no individual preferences. Then* $\epsilon \cdot \max\{1, \Delta(G)/(k-1) - 1\} \leq (\epsilon, k)\text{-}PoA(\mathcal{G}_G(c)) \leq 2\epsilon \cdot \Delta(G)$.

We use this result to bound the (ϵ, k)-Price of Anarchy for random graphs. It is known that the maximum degree of a dense random graph is $\Theta(n)$ (see, e.g., [12]). So for these graphs the (ϵ, k)-Price of Anarchy still grows like $\Omega(\epsilon n)$ (as in the worst case). In contrast, we obtain an improved bound for sparse random graphs.

Theorem 6. *Let* $\epsilon \geq 1$, $k \geq 2$ *and* $d > 0$ *be constants. Let* $(c_n)_{n \in \mathbb{N}}$ *be a sequence of integers with* $c_n \geq 3$ *for all* n. *Let* $\mathcal{G}_{G_n}(c_n)$ *be the set of all coordination games* $\Gamma = (G_n, c_n, (S_i), \mathbf{1}, w, \mathbf{0})$ *on graph* $G_n \sim G(n, d/n)$ *with* c_n *colors, equalsplit distribution rule and no individual preferences. Then* $(\epsilon, k)\text{-}PoA(\mathcal{G}_{G_n}(c_n)) = \Theta(\epsilon \ln(n)/\ln \ln(n))$.

If, in addition, the strategy sets are drawn according to a sequence of distributions that satisfy the so-called *common color property*, and all weights are equal to one (corresponding to the games studied in [4]), then we can even prove that the (ϵ, k)-Price of Anarchy is bounded by a constant. Intuitively, the common color property requires that with positive probability any two players have a color in common in their strategy sets.[12] In particular, this condition is satisfied if we draw the strategy sets uniformly at random from $2^{[c]} \setminus \emptyset$.

Theorem 7. *Let* $\epsilon \geq 1$, $k \geq 2$ *and* $d > 0$ *be constants. Let* $(c_n)_{n \in \mathbb{N}}$ *be a sequence of integers with* $c_n \geq 3$ *for all* n *and let* $(\mathcal{F}_n)_{n \in \mathbb{N}}$ *be a sequence of strategy set distributions satisfying the common color property. Let* $\mathcal{G}_{G_n, (S_i)}(c_n)$ *be the set of all coordination games* $\Gamma = (G_n, c_n, (S_i), \mathbf{1}, \mathbf{1}, \mathbf{0})$ *on graph* $G_n \sim G(n, d/n)$ *with* c_n *colors, strategy set* $S_i \sim \mathcal{F}_n$ *for every* i, *equal-split distribution rule, unit weights and no individual preferences. Then there exists a constant* $\beta = \beta(d, \epsilon)$ *such that* $(\epsilon, k)\text{-}PoA(\mathcal{G}_{G_n, (S_i)}(c_n)) \leq \beta$.

Theorem 7 does not hold for $k = 1$. To see this, consider the uniform distribution over strategy sets $\{s_0, s_1\}, \ldots, \{s_0, s_n\}$. In the strategy profile where every player picks her color different from s_0, at most a constant number of edges will be satisfied with high probability. Thus, $(\epsilon, 1)$-PoA $\geq \beta n$ for some β with high probability.

Acknowledgements. The first author thanks Remco van der Hofstad for a helpful discussion on random graph theory and, in particular, the results in [2].

---

[12] Note that in the deterministic setting the Price of Anarchy does not improve if all players have a color in common (see [21]).

References

1. Amiet, B., Collevecchio, A., Scarsini, M.: Pure nash equilibria and best-response dynamics in random games. CoRR abs/1905.10758 (2019)
2. Anantharam, V., Salez, J.: The densest subgraph problem in sparse random graphs. Ann. Appl. Probab. **26**(1), 305–327 (2016)
3. Anshelevich, E., Sekar, S.: Approximate equilibrium and incentivizing social coordination. In: Proceedings of the 28th AAAI Conference on Artificial Intelligence, pp. 508–514 (2014)
4. Apt, K.R., de Keijzer, B., Rahn, M., Schäfer, G., Simon, S.: Coordination games on graphs. Int. J. Game Theory **46**(3), 851–877 (2017)
5. Bárány, I., Vempala, S., Vetta, A.: Nash equilibria in random games. Random Struct. Algor. **31**(4), 391–405 (2007)
6. Bilò, V., Fanelli, A., Flammini, M., Monaco, G., Moscardelli, L.: Nash stable outcomes in fractional hedonic games: existence, efficiency and computation. J. Artif. Intell. Res. **62**, 315–371 (2018)
7. Carosi, R., Flammini, M., Monaco, G.: Computing approximate pure nash equilibria in digraph k-coloring games. In: Proceedings of the 16th Conference on Autonomous Agents and Multi Agent Systems, pp. 911–919 (2017)
8. Carosi, R., Monaco, G.: Generalized graph k-coloring games. In: Wang, L., Zhu, D. (eds.) COCOON 2018. LNCS, vol. 10976, pp. 268–279. Springer, Cham (2018). https://doi.org/10.1007/978-3-319-94776-1_23
9. Chen, H.L., Roughgarden, T., Valiant, G.: Designing network protocols for good equilibria. SIAM J. Comput. **39**(5), 1799–1832 (2010)
10. Drèze, J.H., Greenberg, J.: Hedonic coalitions: optimality and stability. Econometrica **48**(4), 987–1003 (1980)
11. Feldman, M., Friedler, O.: A unified framework for strong price of anarchy in clustering games. In: Halldórsson, M.M., Iwama, K., Kobayashi, N., Speckmann, B. (eds.) ICALP 2015. LNCS, vol. 9135, pp. 601–613. Springer, Heidelberg (2015). https://doi.org/10.1007/978-3-662-47666-6_48
12. Frieze, A., Karoński, M.: Introduction to Random Graphs. Cambridge University Press, Cambridge (2015)
13. Gilbert, E.N.: Random graphs. Ann. Math. Stat. **30**(4), 1141–1144 (1959)
14. Gopalakrishnan, R., Marden, J.R., Wierman, A.: Potential games are necessary to ensure pure nash equilibria in cost sharing games. Math. Oper. Res. **39**(4), 1252–1296 (2014)
15. Gourvès, L., Monnot, J.: On strong equilibria in the max cut game. In: Leonardi, S. (ed.) WINE 2009. LNCS, vol. 5929, pp. 608–615. Springer, Heidelberg (2009). https://doi.org/10.1007/978-3-642-10841-9_62
16. Gourvès, L., Monnot, J.: The max k-cut game and its strong equilibria. In: Kratochvíl, J., Li, A., Fiala, J., Kolman, P. (eds.) TAMC 2010. LNCS, vol. 6108, pp. 234–246. Springer, Heidelberg (2010). https://doi.org/10.1007/978-3-642-13562-0_22
17. Hajek, B.E.: Performance of global load balancing of local adjustment. IEEE Trans. Inf. Theory **36**(6), 1398–1414 (1990)
18. Hoefer, M.: Cost sharing and clustering under distributed competition. Ph.D. thesis (2007)
19. Koutsoupias, E., Papadimitriou, C.: Worst-case equilibria. In: Meinel, C., Tison, S. (eds.) STACS 1999. LNCS, vol. 1563, pp. 404–413. Springer, Heidelberg (1999). https://doi.org/10.1007/3-540-49116-3_38

20. Kun, J., Powers, B., Reyzin, L.: Anti-coordination games and stable graph colorings. In: Vöcking, B. (ed.) SAGT 2013. LNCS, vol. 8146, pp. 122–133. Springer, Heidelberg (2013). https://doi.org/10.1007/978-3-642-41392-6_11

21. Rahn, M., Schäfer, G.: Efficient equilibria in polymatrix coordination games. In: Italiano, G.F., Pighizzini, G., Sannella, D.T. (eds.) MFCS 2015. LNCS, vol. 9235, pp. 529–541. Springer, Heidelberg (2015). https://doi.org/10.1007/978-3-662-48054-0_44

22. Roughgarden, T., Tardos, E.: How bad is selfish routing? J. ACM **49**(2), 236–259 (2002)

23. Valiant, G., Roughgarden, T.: Braess's paradox in large random graphs. Random Struct. Algor. **37**(4), 495–515 (2010)

Outsourcing Computation: The Minimal Refereed Mechanism

Yuqing Kong[1] , Chris Peikert[2] , Grant Schoenebeck[2] ,
and Biaoshuai Tao[2(✉)]

[1] Peking University, 5 Yiheyuan Rd, Haidian 100871, China
yuqing.kong@pku.edu.cn
[2] University of Michigan, 500 S State St, Ann Arbor, MI 48109, USA
{cpeikert,schoeneb,bstao}@umich.edu

Abstract. We consider a setting where a verifier with limited computation power delegates a resource intensive computation task—which requires a $T \times S$ computation tableau—to two provers where the provers are rational in that each prover maximizes their own payoff—taking into account losses incurred by the cost of computation. We design a mechanism called the Minimal Refereed Mechanism (MRM) such that if the verifier has $O(\log S + \log T)$ time and $O(\log S + \log T)$ space computation power, then both provers will provide a honest result without the verifier putting any effort to verify the results. The amount of computation required for the provers (and thus the cost) is a multiplicative log S-factor more than the computation itself, making this schema efficient especially for low-space computations.

Keywords: Outsourcing · Minimal refereed mechanism · Merkle hash tree · Prisoner's dilemma

1 Introduction

The growing number of computationally intensive tasks has led to the delegation of computation to "computing as a service" platforms such as Amazon's EC2, Microsoft's Azure, etc. This enables users with widely varying loads to only pay for the computation they need. This mirrors a larger trend to out-source: Uber (car as a service), Amazon Turk (computer plugged in worker), etc. When outsourcing tasks, some labors may perform the task honestly due to their intrinsic preference for honesty; however, often labors need incentives which encourage them to dutifully perform the task. If the requester has ability to (cheaply) verify the completion of tasks, the incentive problem can be solved naturally by only providing payment for satisfactory results. However, in the case of outsourcing

The first and third authors gratefully acknowledge the support of the National Science Foundation under CCF #1618187. The last two authors gratefully acknowledge the support of NSF under Career Award #1452915.

© Springer Nature Switzerland AG 2019
I. Caragiannis et al. (Eds.): WINE 2019, LNCS 11920, pp. 256–270, 2019.
https://doi.org/10.1007/978-3-030-35389-6_19

computation, the verifier cannot necessarily verify the task's completion. What should an incentive system look like for outsourcing computation?

Motivated by the need for verifiable computations, recent results have drawn on the work of interactive proof systems (IP)—where a resource-limited verifier can verify an extremely complicated proof provided by a untrusted prover—as main ingredients. However, the classical IP work diverges from the outsourced computation application in two ways: (1) in the crowdsourcing setting, the cost an honest prover incurs in performing the proof must be taken into consideration, while in the classical IP, the honest prover may suffer a heavy (and uncompensated) burden in proving her result; (2) in the crowd-sourcing setting provers can be assumed rational rather than merely untrusted, while the classical IP setting work does not assume or make use of the rationality of the prover.

Several works (e.g. [1,9,25]) either take point (1) or (2) into consideration. But few works consider the both divergences. In this paper, we consider the relation between the related IP work and outsourced computation applications. We take the effort of the provers into consideration, and provide a mechanism—that we call the Minimal Refereed Mechanism—which harnesses the rationality of provers in that it is individual rational, and has the truthful computation as the only equilibrium. In particular, this means that our protocol is robust against agents communicating, as long as they cannot make binding commitments to one another (for example, to redistributing the payoffs in the future). Moreover, an honest prover always obtains a positive utility even if her opposite is irrational. While our mechanism requires that the verifier *can* perform a computation requiring $O(\log S + \log T)$ time and space, in equilibrium the verifier need only check the equality of answers.

Each prover that faithfully follows our mechanism must spend a factor of $\log(S)$ more computational effort than is required to simply run the computation. This, of course, must be compensated by the verifier. However, in the case where the verifier has many different processes to run, we can reduce this overhead by a factor of nearly two. Instead of having two provers run every program, the vast majority will only be run by one prover.

A key ingredient in the construction of the minimal refereed mechanism is from the "prisoner dilemma". When provers are paid based on whether they have the same output, they may collude to obtain agreement without exerting any effort. To solve the "collusion" problem, our minimal refereed mechanism pays an agent who betrays the collusion and *tells the truth* a large reward. We also draw on techniques form IP so that the verification is possible with dramatically fewer resources than the computation itself requires.

1.1 Related Work

Outsourced Computation Literature. The most closely related works in this area to the current paper are Belenkiy et al. [5], Dong et al. [11]. We all implement the idea of the "prisoner dilemma" in outsourced computation. Dong et al. [11] also employ smart contract to implement the "prisoner dilemma" based outsourced computation. However, Belenkiy et al. [5], Dong et al. [11] require that the verifier has the ability to run the program by himself and infrequently performs the whole computation to verify the correctness of the prover's output. Our work only requires that the verifier has the ability to perform a simple $O(\log T + \log S)$ time arbitration process when the provers disagree where the computation size is $T \times S$.

Canetti et al. [9] also designs a $O(\log T + \log S)$ time process where a verifier can determine which prover is honest with the help of Merkle hash tree. However, they do not make use of the rationality of the provers but instead assume one of the provers must be honest.

Conceptually, our paper combines the results of the two aforementioned works. However, naively combining them does not work. Game theory and computation are notoriously tricky to combine [20,21]. For example, our results do not yield a dominant strategy equilibrium as those of Belenkiy et al. [5], and using a collision resistant hash function as in Canetti et al. [9] seems not to be enough for our setting. We carefully integrate the two ideas, and, moreover, provide a delicate game theoretical analysis to show that rational provers must be honest even if the arbitration process gives an arbitrary answer when both of them are dishonest.

Interactive Proof (IP) Literature. Since the seminal work of Goldwasser et al. [17] and Babai and Moran [3] introducing interactive proofs (IP), a host of results in closely related models have followed (see, e.g., [4,7,15,16]). In the classical model (e.g., Lund et al. [24], Shamir [26]), a verifier with limited computation power has the ability to verify statements provided by a untrustworthy prover with unlimited computation power. This desirable property makes IP work an important ingredient in many outsourced computation applications. However, in the classical IP work, the verifier usually employs an arithmetization method that imposes a heavy computational burden on the prover even when the prover is honest. Moreover, the classical IP work always consider the worst case—the prover is an adversary.

Azar and Micali [1] assume that the prover is rational. With this assumption, Azar and Micali [1] show that the verifier can easily incentivize a rational prover to provide the answer of $\sharp SAT$ in the following manner: the verifier asks the prover to report $\frac{\sharp SAT}{2^n}$ which can be seen as the prover's prediction for the event that a randomly chosen assignment is satisfied. The verifier uses a tool called proper scoring rules [8,14] to measure the accuracy of the prover's prediction via only one sample and pays the prover the score of the accuracy. For a SAT instance with n variables, uniformly randomly picking an assignment, the assignment is satisfied with probability $\frac{\sharp SAT}{2^n}$, and so a property of proper scoring rule implies that the prover should provide the exact value of $\frac{\sharp SAT}{2^n}$ to maximize her expected payment. This clever design works with the assumption that the prover can obtain the exact answer without any effort. However, in real life applications, the exponential precision required in some of the reports is very costly to provide. This influential work has been extended to work for different complexity classes, to improve the efficiency of the verifier, and to improve the efficiency of the prover [2,18,19]. However, while this line of work does explicitly have incentives, the costs of computation are ignored while computing these incentives.

Several works successfully design an interactive proof system where the computational resources of both the verifier and honest prover run are limited, but they do not take the rationality of the prover into consideration. The most closely related work in this area to the current paper are refereed games [12] and doubly efficient IP [25]. The arbitration process in the current paper is designed based on the idea of the refereed game in Feige and Kilian [12]. However, [12] do not make use of the rationality of provers and still put a heavy burden on the honest prover. Reingold et al. [25] designs a doubly efficient and constant-round interactive proofs for languages that have a unique witness—if $x \in L$ there exists a unique witness y, of polynomial size, that attests to this. In their proof system the verifier runs in linear time with respect to $|y|$, and the honest provers run in polynomial time with respect to $|y|$. However, if we do not have better than polynomial bound of $|y|$ in terms of $|x|$ this tells us little about the required run time of verifier. Note that the prover's polynomial time bound does not account for the time it takes the prover to find $|y|$, which could be super-polynomial, if L is a hard language (e.g. $L \notin P$). Reingold et al. [25] do not explicitly take the rationality into consideration. Moreover, even if we use the prisoner dilemma technique to modify Reingold et al. [25] to a mechanism where the verifier does not need to spend effort when the provers are rational, that modified mechanism still requires the verifier has the ability to run a linear time verification (in the size of $|y|$), while our mechanism only requires a sublinear time verification in $|x|$ (as long as the computation itself is computable in subexponential time).

Kalai and Yang [22] update this work to include various additional settings such as making the computation publicly verifiable (while keeping the result private), non-interactive, and employing standard cryptographic assumptions. Moreover, their work applies to polynomial computation rather than NP computations. The running time required by the verifier is still polynomially related (T^ϵ) to the actual running time of the delegated computation T, and the verifier incurs an additional polynomial overhead.

The aforementioned Canetti et al. [9] uses interactive proofs with multiple provers to design schemes with increased efficiency. aforementioned Canetti et al. [10] extends this line of results to be more efficient and apply to more realistic architectures (instead of Turing Machines), but both assume one honest prover.

Gennaro et al. [13] gives a construction that allows the outsourcing of a single function for multiple inputs, a different setting that considered here. The verifier's need for computational power scales linearly with the output size of the computation by cleaverly employing techniques from Yao's garbled circuit and fully-homomorphic encryption.

Teutsch and Reitwießner [27] produce a white paper for TrueBit, a system which allows out-sourced computation via smart contracts for the digital currency Ethereum. The system allows users to post computations with a reward for the answer. A user proposing to have solved the computation must also post a bounty. The proposed answer then can be challenged by any user. A challenge results in an arbitration process where the solver must prove the validity of her solution. If she fails, she loses her bounty. If no successful challenge occurs before a deadline, the solver collects the original reward and reclaims her bounty. Unfortunately, in the equilibrium, agents should shirk the task and report randomly with a small probability.

2   Preliminaries

Consider the scenario where a verifier wants to solve a question q and has program $\mathcal{M}$ that can solve the question. The verifier, however, only has *limited computational power* and cannot run the code by himself. Therefore, the verifier gives the program to two agents: Alice and Bob. In this paper, we design a mechanism for the verifier which collects reports from Alice and Bob, and rewards them based on their reports in a way that incentivizes both agents to faithfully execute the program. In this section, we first review cryptographical hash functions and the Merkle hash tree which are used by our mechanism, and then discuss the mechanism design goals.

2.1   Merkle Hash Tree $H(\mathcal{T})$ of Computation Table $\mathcal{T}$

In our setting, Alice and Bob use the same code $\mathcal{M}$ to solve q if both of them are honest. We assume the program $\mathcal{M}$ requires at most time T and space S.

Definition 1 (computation table). *The computation table $\mathcal{T}$ of a Turing machine $\mathcal{M}$ that calculates question q is a $T \times S$ matrix. The first row encodes the input and initial configuration of $\mathcal{M}$. Each row has an active region around where the read/write head of $\mathcal{M}$ is located. The last non-blank row has only one non-blank entry—the answer of question q.*

Definition 2 (hash function [23]). *A hash function (with output length ℓ) is a pair of probabilistic polynomial-time algorithms (Gen, H) satisfying the following:*

- *Gen is a probabilistic algorithm which takes as input a security parameter 1^n and outputs a key k. We assume that 1^n is implicit in k.*
- *H takes as input a key k and a string $x \in \{0,1\}^*$ and outputs a string $H^k(x) \in \{0,1\}^{\ell(n)}$ (where n is the value of the security parameter implicit in s).*

We call $H^k(x)$ the hash value of x.

A standard property that a hash function (Gen, H) has is the *collision-resistance*, meaning that it is computationally infeasible to find a collision—$x, x' \in \{0,1\}^*$ such that $H^k(x) = H^k(x')$, even if the algorithm knows the key k.

Definition 3 (collision-resistance). *Given a hash function* (Gen, H), *an adversary* $\mathcal{A}$ *is a probabilistic algorithm which takes as inputs the security parameter* n *and a key* k *generated by* $\mathsf{Gen}(1^n)$, *and outputs* $x, x' \in \{0,1\}^*$. *The hash function is* collision-resistant *if* $\Pr(H^k(x) = H^k(x')) \leq \frac{t^2}{2^n}$ *for all probabilistic adversaries* $\mathcal{A}$ *that run in time at most* t *(where the randomness in this probability comes from* $\mathcal{A}$, *not the key generation* $k \sim \mathsf{Gen}(1^n)$*).*

For simplicity, we refer to H or H^k instead of (Gen, H) as a hash function, and all the hash functions in this paper satisfy collision-resistance. Throughout the paper, we make a standard assumption that the hash function (Gen, H) can only be accessed as a *random oracle* [6]. As a result, for a fixed message x, we assume that the time required to compute the hash value depends only on n. Moreover, it is infeasible to obtain the value $H^k(x)$ without knowing x.

Definition 4 (Merkle (hash) tree). *A Merkle tree is a binary tree in which every internal node stores the hash value of the concatenation (denoted by symbol* $\|$*) of its two children and the leaves are the hash values of different data blocks.*

We are interested in constructing a Merkle tree $\mathcal{MT}_H(\mathcal{T})$ for a computation table $\mathcal{T}$. Definition 5 illustrates the construction.

Definition 5 (Merkle tree for a computation table). *Given a computation table* $\mathcal{T}$ *of a Turing machine* $\mathcal{M}$ *and a Hash function* H, *the Merkle tree for* $\mathcal{T}$, *denoted by* $\mathcal{MT}_H(\mathcal{T})$, *is constructed as follows.*

1. *The Lower Part of* $\mathcal{MT}_H(\mathcal{T})$*: For each row* $\mathcal{T}_i$ *of* $\mathcal{T}$, *we split it into several data blocks of size* λ, *and construct a Merkle tree* $\mathcal{MT}_H(\mathcal{T}_i)$ *where each leaf is the hash value of a data block.*
2. *The Upper Part of* $\mathcal{MT}_H(\mathcal{T})$*: The upper part of* $\mathcal{MT}_H(\mathcal{T})$ *is a binary tree with* T *leaves such that the* i-th *leaf is the root of* $\mathcal{MT}_H(\mathcal{T}_i)$. *Each internal node has value which is the hash value of the concatenation of its two children as it is in a Merkle tree.*

Throughout the paper, we use r to denote the value of the root node of $\mathcal{MT}_H(\mathcal{T})$, r_i to denote the value of the root of the subtree $\mathcal{MT}_H(\mathcal{T}_i)$ which corresponding to the i-th row of $\mathcal{T}$, and r_{ij} to denote the value of the leaf corresponding to the j-th block of the i-row. Denote the j-th block of the i-row of $\mathcal{T}$ by b_{ij}, and then r_{ij} is the hash value of b_{ij}. We use $r^A, r_i^A, r_{ij}^A, b_{ij}^A$ to refer to the corresponding values that Alice provides (which may be subjected to Alice's strategical manipulation), and let $r^B, r_i^B, r_{ij}^B, b_{ij}^B$ have similar meanings. We sometimes abuse the notations a little bit and use r, r_i, r_{ij} to refer to the nodes themselves instead of the values stored in these nodes.

An advantage of the Merkle tree is that we can verify the consistency between a single data block b_{ij}^A (or b_{ij}^B) and the value r^A (or r^B) with time complexity only $O(\log T + \log S)$, as we will see soon.

Definition 6 (consistent path). *Given* $\mathcal{MT}_H(\mathcal{T})$ *for a computation table* $\mathcal{T}$ *and two nodes* u, v *of* $\mathcal{MT}_H(\mathcal{T})$ *such that* u *is an ancestor of* v, *we say the path* from u to v is consistent *if for each node w on the (shortest) u-v path the value of w is the hash value of the concatenation of the values stored in w's children. In particular, for $w = v$ being a leaf, the value must be the hash value of the corresponding data block.*

From the definition above, to check the consistency of a path from u to v, we need the values of all the nodes on the path and all their children. For example, to check the consistency between b_{ij}^A and r^A, we need to check if the path from the root to the leaf corresponding to this data block is consistent. Since this path has length $O(\log(ST)) = O(\log S + \log T)$ and each node on the path has at most two children, this consistency can be checked in time $O(\log S + \log T)$.

2.2   An Informal Description of Mechanism Design Goals

In this section, we describe our mechanism design goals in an informal way. Formal descriptions are deferred to Sect. 4.

We say a mechanism is *truthful* if the strategy profile where each of the agents plays a truthful strategy that always submits the correct report to the verifier is a Nash equilibrium. We have two goals for our mechanism design. Other than the truthfulness, our second goal is that, through an iterative query process, the mechanism must be able to verify the correctness of the answer that Alice and Bob provide in logarithmic time: $O(\log S + \log T)$. As we will see later, our mechanism satisfies a stronger notion of truthfulness, for which we name *strong truthfulness*.

3   Minimal Refereed Mechanism

Remember that the high level idea is from *the prisoner's dilemma*. When Alice and Bob are paid based on whether they have the same output, they may collude to obtain agreement without exerting any effort. To solve this "collusion" problem, our *minimal refereed mechanism* pays an agent who betrays the collusion and *tells the truth* a large reward. We also draw on techniques from IP so that the verification is possible with dramatically fewer resources than the computation itself requires.

Minimal Refereed Mechanism ($\mathcal{M}$, $f_H(\cdot)$, $\mathcal{AP}$, d_1, d_2):

Step 1 The verifier samples a hash key $k \sim \text{Gen}(1^n)$ and assigns a program $\mathcal{M}$ to both Alice and Bob and asks them to commit to $\mathbf{r} = f_H(\mathcal{M})$. We call $f_H(\cdot)$ the *commitment function*, which is a mapping from a program $\mathcal{M}$ to a report profile (a, t, r), where a is the output of $\mathcal{M}$, t is the time spent in computing $\mathcal{M}$ (i.e., the number of non-blank rows in $\mathcal{T}$), and r is the value of the root of the Merkle hash tree $\mathcal{MT}_H(\mathcal{T})$, for $\mathcal{T}$ being the computation table of $\mathcal{M}$.

Step 2 (Computation Stage) Alice and Bob do the computation separately and commit $\mathbf{r}^A$ and $\mathbf{r}^B$ to the verifier privately.

Step 3 (Arbitration Stage) If $r^A = r^B$, the verifier pays both Alice and Bob the amount $d_1(t)$ that depends on and is monotone in t, the time spent as reported by both agents. Otherwise, the verifier runs an *arbitration process* in which the verifier asks both agents several questions and finally announces for each of Alice and Bob if she(he) is a *winner*. The verifier pays each winner $d_2 \gg d_1(T)$ and each loser 0 (recall that T is the number of rows in $\mathcal{T}$ including blank rows, which is an upper bound on t).

MRM: Arbitration Process $\mathcal{AP}$. The arbitration process takes in the two commitments r^A, r^B that are different, and outputs either "winner" or "loser" for each of Alice and Bob. Below we give a verbal summary of the arbitration process, while the precise description of the process is available in the full version of this paper.

When Alice and Bob agree with the value of the root of $\mathcal{MT}_H(\mathcal{T})$, then they must disagree on either a or t. The verifier first checks, in the case $t^A \neq t^B$, if the last rows from both agents contains the halting state, and if the agent reporting the larger running time has a halting state in the middle row $\min\{t^A, t^B\}$. Notice that in a correct execution of $\mathcal{M}$, the halting state should appear and only appear in the last non-blank row. The arbitration process terminates immediately if an agent is caught for violating this, and moves on otherwise.

The verifier then asks their values for the root of the subtree corresponding to the $\min\{t^A, t^B\}$-th row:

- If they agree with each other, the verifier checks the path from the root of this subtree to the first block of the $\min\{t^A, t^B\}$-th row, and announces the winner or the loser based on if the agent can provide a consistent path.
- If they disagree, then the verifier checks the consistency of the path from the root of this subtree to the root of the entire tree $\mathcal{MT}_H(\mathcal{T})$, and announces the winner or the loser based on the consistency.

When Alice and Bob disagree on the value of the root of $\mathcal{MT}_H(\mathcal{T})$, the verifier runs a subroutine $\texttt{FirstDivergence}(r^A, r^B, r)$ (with the precise definition in the full version of this paper) to figure out *the first place on which Alice disagrees with Bob in $\mathcal{T}$*. The subroutine $\texttt{FirstDivergence}$ takes in three inputs: a hash value v^A, a hash value v^B, and a node v in the Merkle tree, where v^A and v^B are the values Alice and Bob provide (respectively) for the node v, and $v^A \neq v^B$. It outputs either the identity of the agents (either one or two) which are identified as "liars", or a block b_{ij} in $\mathcal{T}$. As a brief description, $\texttt{FirstDivergence}$ travels from the node v to a leaf based on the following rules: at a node u with children u_1, u_2 during the traversal, $\texttt{FirstDivergence}$ checks if the hash is consistent, i.e., if $H(u_1^A \| u_2^A) = u^A$ and $H(u_1^B \| u_2^B) = u^B$, and moves on to the left-most child u_i with $u_i^A \neq u_i^B$. If an inconsistency in the hash computation is found during the traversal, $\texttt{FirstDivergence}$ terminates and outputs the identity of the agent(s) with the inconsistent computation as the liar(s). Otherwise, the traversal process will not end until a leaf is reached. This is because we start at v on whose value Alice and Bob disagree, and Alice and Bob must disagree on at least one of the children u_1, u_2 if they disagree on the parent u. When the traversal ends at a leaf r_{ij}, assuming both agents have not broken the hash function, we know that b_{ij} is the first block where Alice and Bob disagree. Intuitively, FirstDivergence performs a binary search, viewing the Merkle tree as the binary search tree, and checks the consistency of hashing during the search.

If FirstDivergence(r^A, r^B, r) outputs the identity of the liar(s), the algorithm terminates by announcing the liar(s) being the loser(s). If the output is a block b_{ij}, then we consider two cases: $i = 1$ and $i > 1$.

- If $i = 1$, i.e., the block is in the first row, since the first row of $\mathcal{T}$ encodes the input of $\mathcal{M}$, it is easy for the verifier to check the correctness of b_{ij}^A and b_{ij}^B by herself.
- If $i > 1$, i.e., the block is in a middle row, the verifier asks Alice and Bob the value of the corresponding block $b_{(i-1)j}$ in the previous row which contains the active region. If Alice and Bob agree on $b_{(i-1)j}$, the verifier calculates b_{ij} by himself and spot the liar(s) who has a different value than the verifier. If Alice and Bob disagree on $b_{(i-1)j}$, the verifier checks the consistency of the path from the leaf $r_{(i-1)j}$ all the way to the root r of the Merkle tree.

Complexity Analysis of f_H and $\mathcal{AP}$: The time complexity of computing f_H is $O(S+T\log S+T)$ since for every i-th, $(i+1)$-th row, given the hash tree of the i-th row, we only need to modify the path from the active region to the root $(O(\log S))$ to obtain the hash tree of $(i+1)$-th row. The time complexity of $\mathcal{AP}$ is $O(\log S + \log T)$. The main computations are the computation of FirstDivergece and the consistency check of paths. Both of them require $\log S + \log T$ time. The verifier needs $O(\log S + \log T)$ space to record the position of the leaf (which represents the path from the root to that leaf). Thus, a verifier, who has the ability to run a computation that needs $O(\log S + \log T)$ time and $O(\log S + \log T)$ space, can run an MRM with $\mathcal{AP}$ as the arbitration process. This shows the achievement of the second goal mentioned in the last section.

4   Mechanism Design Goals Revisited

We define *strategy* and *effort* in a natural way, and each agent's *utility* is quasi-linear. Once we have defined strategies and utilities, the definition of Nash equilibrium becomes standard. The precise definitions of these terms are omitted due to the space limit, and they are available in the full version of this paper.

We say a strategy is *truthful* if it specifies the correct report in the computation stage, and let **T** be the set of all truthful strategies. We call the strategy that correctly reports **r** in the computation stage and truthfully responds to the verifier in the arbitration stage *absolutely truthful*, and we denote it as τ. The precise definitions for the truthfulness and the absolute truthfulness of a strategy, which depend on the precise definition of strategy, are available in the full version of this paper. We say the mechanism MRM is *truthful* if (τ, τ) is a Nash equilibrium, and is *strongly truthful* if, in addition, (s^A, s^B) being a Nash equilibrium implies $s^A, s^B \in \mathbf{T}$.

Throughout the paper, we use $M(i)$ to denote the (minimum) amount of effort required to compute the first i rows of T and the Merkle tree $\mathcal{MT}_H(T)$, $M_c := M(T)$ to denote the maximum effort a truthful agent can spend in the computation stage, and M_{ap} to denote the maximum possible effort a truthful agent can spend in the arbitration stage. In particular, for the absolutely truthful strategy $\tau = (\tau_c, \tau_{ap})$, the effort of computing $\tau_c(\mathcal{M}, H) = (a, t, h)$ is $M(t)$, and we use M_c^τ to denote this. From our discussion earlier, we have $M_c = O(S + T \log S + T)$ and $M_{ap} = O(\log S + \log T)$.

5 Strong Truthfulness of MRM

In this section, we prove that the mechanism MRM is strongly truthful with appropriate choices of parameters.

Theorem 1. *For any program $\mathcal{M}$, if we choose large enough security parameter n such that $n > 2\log(M_c + M_{ap}) + C$ for some constant C, there exists b such that MRM ($\mathcal{M}$, f_H, $\mathcal{AP}$, d_1, d_2) with $d_2 = 2(M_c + M_{ap}) + 2b$ and $d_1(t) = M(t) + b$ is strongly truthful, where t is the time spent in computing $\mathcal{M}$ as reported by both agents (their reports are the same if payment $d_1(\cdot)$ is considered).*

This main theorem is straightforwardly implied by the following four lemmas. The proofs of Lemmas 1, 2 and 3 are available in the full version of this paper.

Lemma 1. *Given a program $\mathcal{M}$, a hash function $(\textbf{Gen}, H)$ and a pure strategy $s = (s_c, s_{ap}) \notin \mathbf{T}$ such that the total effort of computing $s_c(\mathcal{M}, H^k)$ is strictly less than M_c^τ, there exists $\epsilon < 1$ such that $\Pr_{k \sim \textbf{Gen}(1^n)} \left(s_c(\mathcal{M}, H^k) = f_{H^k}(\mathcal{M}) \right) < \epsilon$.*

Lemma 2. *An agent playing the absolutely truthful strategy τ always wins in the arbitration process $\mathcal{AP}$, regardless of the strategy the other agent plays. Moreover, when the security parameter n is large enough with $n > 2\log(M_c + M_{ap}) + 15$, if there exists a dishonest agent that plays a pure strategy $s \notin \mathbf{T}$ and all dishonest agents spend effort at most $\zeta := 2^{(n-15)/2}$, the probability that $\mathcal{AP}$ announces two winners is smaller than $\delta := 2^{-10}$.*

Note that Lemma 2 does not say anything about the situation where both two agents are dishonest and only one of them wins $\mathcal{AP}$.

Lemma 3. *MRM($\mathcal{M}$, f_H, $\mathcal{AP}$, d_1, d_2) is truthful if $d_1(t) = M(t) + b$, $b > \delta d_2 + \frac{\epsilon M_c}{1-\epsilon}$ and $\zeta > d_2$.*

Lemma 4. *MRM($\mathcal{M}$, f_H, $\mathcal{AP}$, d_1, d_2) is strongly truthful if $d_1(t) = M(t) + b$, $d_2 = 2(M_c + M_{ap}) + 2b$ for $\frac{\zeta - 2(M_c + M_{ap})}{2} > b > \frac{2\delta(M_c + M_{ap}) + \frac{\epsilon M_c}{1-\epsilon}}{1-2\delta} > 0$.*

Proof. It is easy to see $\zeta > d_2$. By some calculations, we also have $b > \delta d_2 + \frac{\epsilon M_c}{1-\epsilon}$. Thus, we know MRM is truthful by Lemma 3.

To show MRM is strongly truthful, we consider any (pure or mixed) strategy Nash equilibrium (s^A, s^B). We will show that (s^A, s^B) is a Nash equilibrium if and only if both agents tell the truth in the computation stage: $s^A, s^B \in \mathbf{T}$.

We classify the possible outcomes of (s^A, s^B) into the below disjoint cases:

O Alice and Bob agree with each other and both of them tell the truth.

A Alice and Bob agree with each other on correct commitment but at least one of them is dishonest.

A_1 Alice is truthful but Bob spends effort less than the effort of $\tau_c(\mathcal{M}, H)$.

A_2 Bob is truthful but Alice spends effort less than the effort of $\tau_c(\mathcal{M}, H)$.

A_3 Both Alice and Bob spend effort less than the effort of $\tau_c(\mathcal{M}, H)$.

B Alice and Bob agree with each other on a wrong commitment.

C Alice wins in $\mathcal{AP}$ via a non-truthful strategy. Bob loses.

D Alice wins in $\mathcal{AP}$ via a truth-telling strategy. Bob loses.

E Bob wins in $\mathcal{AP}$ via a non-truthful strategy. Alice loses.

F Bob wins in $\mathcal{AP}$ via a truth-telling strategy. Alice loses.

G Both lose in $\mathcal{AP}$.

H Both win in $\mathcal{AP}$.

H_1 Alice is honest in the computation stage. Bob is dishonest.

H_2 Bob is honest in the computation stage. Alice is dishonest.

H_3 Both of them are dishonest in the computation stage.

In the remaining part of this proof, when we mentioned probability of certain event, the randomness is from both the hash key generation $k \sim \texttt{Gen}(1^n)$ and the mixed strategy. We will show that (s^A, s^B) *is a Nash equilibrium if and only if the probability that outcome O happens is 1.* The same arguments in the proof of Lemma 3 show the if direction, so we focus on the only-if direction.

Let $M^* = M + M_{ap}$ be the maximum effort the truth-telling strategy can cost in the whole MRM game. For convenience, we write $\Pr(A, B)$ as the probability event A or event B happens. Since the cases we consider are disjoint, we can see $\Pr(A, B) = \Pr(A) + \Pr(B)$.

First of all, any pure strategies that spend effort at least ζ is strictly dominated, since the maximum possible payment d_2 is less than ζ. Therefore, in the remaining part of this proof, we assume with probability 0 that one of Alice and Bob will spend effort at least ζ.

We compare Alice's expected utility when Alice plays τ and Bob plays s_B with the expected utility of (s^A, s^B). Notice that a truthful agent always has utility $M(t) + b - M(t) = b$ if $\mathcal{AP}$ is not launched, and has utility at least $d_2 - M^*$ if $\mathcal{AP}$ is launched.

$$\mu^A(s^A, s^B) - \mu^A(\tau, s^B) \leq \Pr(A_2, A_3) \cdot (M_c + b - b) + \Pr(B) \cdot (M_c + b - (d_2 - M^*)) + \Pr(C) \cdot (d_2 - (d_2 - M^*)) + \Pr(E) \cdot (0 - (d_2 - M^*)) + \Pr(F) \cdot (0 - b) + \Pr(G) \cdot (0 - (d_2 - M^*)) + \Pr(H_2) \cdot (d_2 - b) + \Pr(H_3) \cdot (d_2 - (\epsilon b + (1 - \epsilon)(d_2 - M^*)))$$

Since (s^A, s^B) is a Nash equilibrium, $\mu^A(s^A, s^B) - \mu^A(\tau, s^B) \geq 0$. By simplification, rearranging terms and substituting $d_2 - (\epsilon b + (1 - \epsilon)(d_2 - M^*)) < d_2 - b$ (which is straightforward to show) for the coefficient of $\Pr(H_3)$, we have

$$\Pr(A_2, A_3) \cdot M_c + \Pr(C) \cdot M^* + \Pr(H_2, H_3) \cdot (d_2 - b)$$
$$\geq \Pr(B) \cdot (d_2 - M_c - b - M^*) + \Pr(E, G) \cdot (d_2 - M^*) + \Pr(F) \cdot b. \quad (1)$$

Moreover, let Σ be the event that Alice spends effort less than the effort of $\tau_c(\mathcal{M}, H)$, we know $\Pr(A_2, A_3) = \Pr((A_2, A_3) \wedge \Sigma) = \Pr(\Sigma) \Pr(A_2, A_3 \mid \Sigma) \leq$

$\epsilon \Pr(\Sigma)$ by Lemma 1, which implies $\Pr(B, C, E, F, G, H_2, H_3) \geq (1 - \epsilon) \Pr(\Sigma)$, and which further implies

$$\Pr(A_2, A_3) \leq \frac{\epsilon}{1 - \epsilon} \Pr(B, C, E, F, G, H_2, H_3)$$
$$= \frac{\epsilon}{1 - \epsilon} \left(\Pr(B, C, E, F, G) + \Pr(H_2, H_3) \right). \qquad (2)$$

Let Π be the event that Alice is dishonest in the computation stage and $\mathcal{AP}$ is implemented. We know $\Pr(H_2, H_3) = \Pr((H_2, H_3) \wedge \Pi) = \Pr(\Pi) \Pr(H_2, H_3 \mid \Pi) \leq \delta \Pr(\Pi)$ by Lemma 2 (as mentioned earlier, we can assume no one spends at least ζ effort), which implies $\Pr(C, E, F, G) \geq (1 - \delta) \Pr(\Pi)$, and which further implies

$$\Pr(H_2, H_3) \leq \frac{\delta}{1 - \delta} \Pr(C, E, F, G). \qquad (3)$$

After replacements according to (2) and (3), we can rewrite (1) as

$$\Pr(C) \left(M^* + \frac{\epsilon \cdot M_c}{1 - \epsilon} + \frac{\delta \cdot (d_2 - b + \frac{\epsilon \cdot M_c}{1 - \epsilon})}{1 - \delta} \right)$$
$$\geq \Pr(B) \left((d_2 - M_c - b - M^*) - \frac{\epsilon \cdot M_c}{1 - \epsilon} \right) + \Pr(E, G) \left(d_2 - M^* - \frac{\epsilon \cdot M_c}{1 - \epsilon} \right.$$
$$\left. - \frac{\delta \cdot (d_2 - b + \frac{\epsilon \cdot M_c}{1 - \epsilon})}{1 - \delta} \right) + \Pr(F) \left(b - \frac{\epsilon \cdot M_c}{1 - \epsilon} - \frac{\delta \cdot (d_2 - b + \frac{\epsilon \cdot M_c}{1 - \epsilon})}{1 - \delta} \right). \quad (4)$$

Since $b > \delta d_2 + \frac{\epsilon M_c}{1 - \epsilon}$, we have the coefficient of $\Pr(F)$ in (4) satisfies $b - \frac{\epsilon \cdot M_c}{1 - \epsilon} - \frac{\delta \cdot (d_2 - b + \frac{\epsilon \cdot M_c}{1 - \epsilon})}{1 - \delta} = \frac{1}{1 - \delta} \left(b - \delta d_2 - \frac{\epsilon \cdot M_c}{1 - \epsilon} \right) > 0$. This further implies

$$d_2 = 2M^* + 2b > 2M^* + 2 \frac{\epsilon \cdot M_c}{1 - \epsilon} + 2 \frac{\delta \cdot (d_2 - b + \frac{\epsilon \cdot M_c}{1 - \epsilon})}{1 - \delta}, \qquad (5)$$

so the coefficients of $\Pr(G)$ in (4) is positive. By $b > \delta d_2 + \frac{\epsilon M_c}{1 - \epsilon}$ again and $d_2 = 2M^* + 2b$, $(d_2 - M_c - b - M^*) - \frac{\epsilon \cdot M_c}{1 - \epsilon} = b + M^* - M_c - \frac{\epsilon \cdot M_c}{1 - \epsilon} > \delta d_2 + M^* - M_c = \delta d_2 + M_{ap} > 0$, so the coefficients of $\Pr(B)$ in (4) is also positive. Therefore, we have

$$\Pr(C) \left(M^* + \frac{\epsilon M_c}{1 - \epsilon} + \frac{\delta (d_2 - b + \frac{\epsilon \cdot M_c}{1 - \epsilon})}{1 - \delta} \right)$$
$$\geq \Pr(E) \cdot \left(d_2 - M^* - \frac{\epsilon M_c}{1 - \epsilon} - \frac{\delta (d_2 - b + \frac{\epsilon \cdot M_c}{1 - \epsilon})}{1 - \delta} \right). \qquad (6)$$

Symmetrically, by analyzing Bob, we have

$$
\Pr(E) \left(M^* + \frac{\epsilon M_c}{1 - \epsilon} + \frac{\delta(d_2 - b + \frac{\epsilon \cdot M_c}{1 - \epsilon})}{1 - \delta} \right)
$$

$$
\geq \Pr(C) \cdot \left(d_2 - M^* - \frac{\epsilon M_c}{1 - \epsilon} - \frac{\delta(d_2 - b + \frac{\epsilon \cdot M_c}{1 - \epsilon})}{1 - \delta} \right). \tag{7}
$$

Equation (5) implies the coefficient of $\Pr(E)$ is strictly greater (less) than the coefficient of $\Pr(C)$ in (6) (in (7)), then $\Pr(C) = \Pr(E) = 0$ for otherwise (6) and (7) cannot be valid at the same time. When $\Pr(C) = \Pr(E) = 0$, (4) implies that $\Pr(B) = \Pr(F) = \Pr(G) = 0$, which, by (2) and (3), further implies that $\Pr(A_2, A_3) = 0$ and $\Pr(H_2, H_3) = 0$. Combining with a similar analysis for Bob, we will have $\Pr(O) = 1$ in every pure or mixed equilibrium.

6   On Other Notions of Truthfulness

The mechanism MRM is *not dominant-strategy truthful* (meaning τ or any $s \in \mathbf{T}$ is a dominant strategy), unlike the prisoner's dilemma game. If fixing Bob's strategy such that Bob only computes $\mathcal{M}$ up to the i-th row and reports it as a, then τ (or any other truthful strategies) is not a best respond to Alice, as Alice only needs to compute $\mathcal{M}$ up to the $(i + 1)$-th row (maybe also manually inserts a halting state in the $(i + 2)$-th row) and wins in $\mathcal{AP}$.

Notice also that (τ, τ) is not a *subgame perfect Nash equilibrium* (SPNE). For our problem, SPNE is difficult to achieve, but it is also unnecessary and unnatural in some sense. We further remark on this in the full version of this paper. Our notion of strong truthfulness ensures that the mechanism MRM will obtain the correct output of $\mathcal{M}$ if the two agents are rational (by playing any equilibrium strategy).

References

1. Azar, P.D., Micali, S.: Rational proofs. In: Proceedings of the Forty-Fourth Annual ACM Symposium on Theory of Computing, pp. 1017–1028. ACM (2012)
2. Azar, P.D., Micali, S.: Super-efficient rational proofs. In: Proceedings of the Fourteenth ACM Conference on Electronic Commerce, pp. 29–30. ACM (2013)
3. Babai, L., Moran, S.: Arthur-Merlin games: a randomized proof system, and a hierarchy of complexity classes. J. Comput. Syst. Sci. **36**(2), 254–276 (1988)
4. Badrinarayanan, S., Kalai, Y.T., Khurana, D., Sahai, A., Wichs, D.: Succinct delegation for low-space non-deterministic computation. In: Proceedings of the 50th Annual ACM SIGACT Symposium on Theory of Computing, STOC 2018, pp. 709–721. ACM, New York (2018). https://doi.org/10.1145/3188745.3188924
5. Belenkiy, M., Chase, M., Erway, C.C., Jannotti, J., Küpçü, A., Lysyanskaya, A.: Incentivizing outsourced computation. In: Proceedings of the 3rd International Workshop on Economics of Networked Systems, pp. 85–90. ACM (2008)

6. Bellare, M., Rogaway, P.: Random oracles are practical: a paradigm for designing efficient protocols. In: Proceedings of the 1st ACM Conference on Computer and Communications Security, pp. 62–73. ACM (1993)
7. Bitansky, N., Canetti, R., Chiesa, A., Tromer, E.: From extractable collision resistance to succinct non-interactive arguments of knowledge, and back again. In: Proceedings of the 3rd Innovations in Theoretical Computer Science Conference, pp. 326–349. ACM (2012)
8. Brier, G.W.: Verification of forecasts expressed in terms of probability. Mon. Weather Rev. **78**(1), 1–3 (1950)
9. Canetti, R., Riva, B., Rothblum, G.N.: Practical delegation of computation using multiple servers. In: Proceedings of the 18th ACM Conference on Computer and Communications Security, pp. 445–454. ACM (2011)
10. Canetti, R., Riva, B., Rothblum, G.N.: Refereed delegation of computation. Inf. Comput. **226**, 16–36 (2013)
11. Dong, C., Wang, Y., Aldweesh, A., McCorry, P., van Moorsel, A.: Betrayal, distrust, and rationality: smart counter-collusion contracts for verifiable cloud computing. In: Proceedings of the 2017 ACM SIGSAC Conference on Computer and Communications Security, pp. 211–227. ACM (2017)
12. Feige, U., Kilian, J.: Making games short. In: Proceedings of the Twenty-Ninth Annual ACM Symposium on Theory of Computing, pp. 506–516. ACM (1997)
13. Gennaro, R., Gentry, C., Parno, B.: Non-interactive verifiable computing: outsourcing computation to untrusted workers. In: Rabin, T. (ed.) CRYPTO 2010. LNCS, vol. 6223, pp. 465–482. Springer, Heidelberg (2010). https://doi.org/10.1007/978-3-642-14623-7_25
14. Gneiting, T., Raftery, A.E.: Strictly proper scoring rules, prediction, and estimation. J. Am. Stat. Assoc. **102**(477), 359–378 (2007)
15. Goldwasser, S., Kalai, Y.T., Rothblum, G.N.: Delegating computation: interactive proofs for muggles. In: Proceedings of the Fortieth Annual ACM Symposium on Theory of Computing, pp. 113–122. ACM (2008)
16. Goldwasser, S., Kalai, Y.T., Rothblum, G.N.: Delegating computation: interactive proofs for muggles. J. ACM **62**(4), 27 (2015)
17. Goldwasser, S., Micali, S., Rackoff, C.: The knowledge complexity of interactive proof systems. SIAM J. Comput. **18**(1), 186–208 (1989)
18. Guo, S., Hubáček, P., Rosen, A., Vald, M.: Rational arguments: single round delegation with sublinear verification. In: Proceedings of the 5th Conference on Innovations in Theoretical Computer Science, pp. 523–540. ACM (2014)
19. Guo, S., Hubáček, P., Rosen, A., Vald, M.: Rational sumchecks. In: Kushilevitz, E., Malkin, T. (eds.) TCC 2016. LNCS, vol. 9563, pp. 319–351. Springer, Heidelberg (2016). https://doi.org/10.1007/978-3-662-49099-0_12
20. Halpern, J.Y., Pass, R.: Algorithmic rationality: game theory with costly computation. J. Econ. Theor. **156**, 246–268 (2015)
21. Halpern, J.Y., Pass, R., Seeman, L.: Computational extensive-form games. In: Proceedings of the 2016 ACM Conference on Economics and Computation, pp. 681–698. ACM (2016)
22. Kalai, Y.T., P.O., Yang, L.: How to delegate computations publicly. In: STOC 2019: Proceedings of the 51th Annual ACM SIGACT Symposium on Theory of Computing. ACM (2019)
23. Lindell, Y., Katz, J.: Introduction to Modern Cryptography. Chapman and Hall/CRC, Boca Raton (2014)
24. Lund, C., Fortnow, L., Karloff, H., Nisan, N.: Algebraic methods for interactive proof systems. J. ACM (JACM) **39**(4), 859–868 (1992)

25. Reingold, O., Rothblum, G.N., Rothblum, R.D.: Constant-round interactive proofs for delegating computation. In: Proceedings of the 48th Annual ACM SIGACT Symposium on Theory of Computing, pp. 49–62. ACM (2016)
26. Shamir, A.: IP = PSPACE. J. ACM (JACM) **39**(4), 869–877 (1992)
27. Teutsch, J., Reitwießner, C.: A scalable verification solution for blockchains. https://people.cs.uchicago.edu/teutsch/papers/truebitpdf (2017)

On Core-Selecting and Core-Competitive Mechanisms for Binary Single-Parameter Auctions

Evangelos Markakis and Artem Tsikiridis$^{(\boxtimes)}$

Department of Informatics, Athens University of Economics and Business,
Athens, Greece
{markakis,artem}@aueb.gr

Abstract. Our work concerns the class of core-selecting mechanisms, as introduced by Ausubel and Milgrom [3]. Such mechanisms have been known to possess good revenue guarantees and some of their variants have been used in practice especially for spectrum and other public sector auctions. Despite their popularity, it has also been demonstrated that these auctions are generally non-truthful. As a result, current research has focused either on identifying core-selecting mechanisms with minimal incentives to deviate from truth-telling, such as the family of Minimum-Revenue Core-Selecting (MRCS) rules, or on proposing truthful mechanisms whose revenue is competitive against core outcomes. Our results contribute to both of these directions. We start with studying the core polytope in more depth and provide new properties and insights, related to the effects of unilateral deviations from a given profile. We then utilize these properties in two ways. First, we propose a truthful mechanism that is $O(\log n)$-competitive against the MRCS benchmark. Our result is the first deterministic core-competitive mechanism for binary single-parameter domains. Second, we study the existence of *non-decreasing* payment rules, meaning that the payment of each bidder is a non-decreasing function of her bid. This property has been advocated by the core-related literature but it has remained an open question if there exist MRCS non-decreasing mechanisms. We answer the question in the affirmative, by describing a subclass of rules with this property.

1 Introduction

The VCG mechanism has been undoubtedly one of the early landmarks within the field of mechanism design. At the same time however, VCG is rarely preferred in more complex real-life auction scenarios, such as allocation of spectrum or other governmental licences. The shortcomings that have led to this situation have been well summarized by [4], and one of the most prominent drawbacks is the unacceptably low revenue that VCG generates on instances that do not lack

A. Tsikiridis—Research was supported by the Hellenic Foundation for Research and Innovation (HFRI) under the HFRI PhD Fellowship grant (Fellowship Number: 289).

© Springer Nature Switzerland AG 2019
I. Caragiannis et al. (Eds.): WINE 2019, LNCS 11920, pp. 271–285, 2019.
https://doi.org/10.1007/978-3-030-35389-6_20

competition. In worst case, one can have even zero payments for the winners, giving rise to *free-riders* [2].

To counterbalance this issue, Ausubel and Milgrom [3,4] adapted the notion of the *core* from the theory of cooperative games and introduced the class of *core-selecting* mechanisms. These mechanisms first select an optimal (welfare-maximizing) allocation as in VCG, but then the payments are set in a way that no coalition of bidders together with the auctioneer can switch to a better outcome, of higher revenue for the auctioneer. It was argued in [4] that a mechanism is of suboptimal performance in terms of revenue precisely when the payments it assigns may *not* be in the core, which is quite common for VCG when the goods exhibit complementarities. Over the last years, core-selecting mechanisms gained even higher support especially among practitioners, due to the fact that they have been successfully implemented for a number of high-profile public sector auctions in several countries [8].

Interestingly, for complement-free settings, the VCG payments can lie in the core. When there are complementarities however, core payments do not generally yield truthful mechanisms [13]. With this negative aspect in mind, research on this topic has focused mainly on two directions. The first one concerns a game-theoretic analysis of core-selecting mechanisms so as to identify which payments from the core polytope have better incentive properties. As an example, it has been shown in [10] that selecting a minimum revenue core outcome also minimizes in a certain sense, the total gain from unilateral deviations. When the minimum revenue does not prescribe a unique outcome, a further refinement needs to take place, guided again by incentives. This has led to the family of quadratic payment rules (see Sect. 5). In parallel to this, another way to evaluate such mechanisms is by analyzing the performance of their Bayes Nash equilibria, e.g., [2]. At the moment, these works have not yet led to definite conclusions and there is still a lively debate on what are the best core-selecting mechanisms, given also the recent experimental evaluation of [7].

The second direction was initiated by [12] and concerns the design of truthful (hence, not core-selecting) mechanisms whose revenue is competitive against a core outcome. The core benchmark was naturally taken to be the minimum revenue core outcome, given the properties highlighted in the previous paragraph. Hence, a mechanism is then called α-*core-competitive* when it achieves a $1/\alpha$ fraction of the minimum revenue core outcome, for $\alpha \geq 1$. The main results of [12] involved the design of core-competitive mechanisms for a particular single-parameter domain motivated by online ad auctions. For more general combinatorial auctions, one can also obtain core-competitive mechanisms using the results of [17], where a stronger benchmark has been considered. This approach is still worth further investigation, as finding the best ratio against the core benchmark has remained open for various domains of interest.

Our Contribution. We focus on binary single-parameter domains where each bidder is either accepted or rejected in every outcome. We start in Sect. 3, with providing new insights and properties on the geometry of the core polytope. Our aim is to understand how the polytope is affected by a unilateral deviation of a bidder from a given profile. To do this, we perform a kind of sensitivity analysis for the core constraints. In the remaining of the paper, we make use of the results of Sect. 3 in two ways. First, in Sect. 4, we derive a deterministic $O(\log n)$-core-competitive strategyproof mechanism, where n is the number of bidders. So far, only a randomized mechanism with the same ratio was known, implied by [17]. Our result is the first deterministic core-competitive mechanism for arbitrary single-parameter domains. It also provides a separation between core-competitiveness, and the stronger benchmark of [17], for which an impossibility result of $\Omega(n)$ for deterministic mechanisms has been known even for single-parameter environments. Second, in Sect. 5, we focus on the class of minimum revenue core-selecting (MRCS) payment rules, and study the existence of *non-decreasing* payment rules, where the payment of each bidder is a non-decreasing function of her bid [6,11]. This property has been advocated, among others, for minimizing the marginal incentive to deviate, but it has remained an open question if there exist MRCS rules satisfying it. We provide a positive answer by describing a subclass of rules possessing the property, which can be seen as a further refinement towards selecting MRCS mechanisms with the most desirable attributes. Overall, our results shed more light on understanding core-selecting and core-competitive mechanisms, and expect that the properties established here can have even broader appeal and applicability.

1.1   Related Work

The core in the context of auctions was introduced in [3,4], as a suitable formalism to understand settings where the VCG mechanism underperforms in terms of revenue. In [3], Ausubel and Milgrom also proposed core-selection as a standalone auction design goal by introducing an ascending auction format called the ascending-proxy auction, whose equilibrium outcomes are in the core. The topic gained popularity both in theory and in practice, and several follow up works emerged on exploring different core-selecting Pareto-efficient rules with minimal incentives to deviate or mechanisms that are core-selecting at equilibrium, see e.g., [2,8–11,19]. The incentives to deviate from truth-telling have been quantified under different metrics and, to our understanding, no consensus on the most acceptable metric has been reached. Recently, an experimental comparison was also conducted by [7] in an attempt to offer more insights on that front.

Regarding truthfulness and core-selection, the work of [13] showed that when VCG payments lie in the core, then this is the only truthful mechanism in the core, whereas when VCG is not in the core, there exists no other truthful core-selecting mechanism. This reveals a severe incompatibility between truth-telling and core-selection, especially for auction domains that exhibit complementarities. Such domains can arise naturally in spectrum auctions or in auctions related to online advertising. Motivated by these considerations, Goel et al. suggested in [12] the use of the minimum revenue core-selecting (MRCS) outcome, as a competitive benchmark for truthful mechanisms. In their work, they focus on the so called *Text and Image Ad-Auctions*, a special case of knapsack auctions, where k ad slots are being auctioned and each bidder is known to require 1 or k ad slots. They proposed a truthful deterministic mechanism that is $O(\sqrt{\log k})$-core-competitive and a randomized one which is $O(\log \log k)$-core-competitive. To our knowledge, this is the only work where a core benchmark has been explicitly used for truthful revenue maximization.

Clearly, the problem of designing mechanisms with revenue guarantees is a fundamental question that has attracted considerable attention. For example, the notion of envy-free pricing [14] gave rise to various revenue benchmarks, with several follow up papers. These lines of inquiry mostly focused on environments where goods are substitutes (for which VCG payments are in the core), whereas the core-benchmark is meaningful for environments with complementarities. For such environments, two notable benchmarks have been proposed in [1] for knapsack auctions and in [17] for general combinatorial auctions. We refer the reader to [12] for a detailed comparison of all these benchmarks with the MRCS benchmark. The two main takeaways are that, the mechanism of [1] performs arbitrarily bad against the MRCS benchmark, whereas the benchmark of [17] is stronger than MRCS. The results of [17] imply a truthful randomized mechanism for general combinatorial auctions that is $O(\log n)$-core-competitive.

2   Definitions and Preliminaries

2.1   Single-Parameter Domains and Mechanisms

Our work focuses on mechanisms for *binary, single-parameter* domains. We consider a set of bidders $N = \{1, 2, \ldots, n\}$, who can express a request for some type of service (e.g., for obtaining a set of goods, or access to a facility). Each bidder $i \in N$ has a single private parameter v_i, which denotes the value derived by bidder i if she is granted the service. The environment is binary and every bidder will be either accepted or rejected. For every $S \subseteq N$, we let $\mathcal{F}(S) \subseteq 2^S$ be the set of feasible allocations for the bidders of S. Unless otherwise stated, we assume that $\mathcal{F}(N)$ is *downward-closed*, i.e., for every $X \in \mathcal{F}(N)$ and every $Y \subseteq X$ it holds that $Y \in \mathcal{F}(N)$. We also assume that for every $S \subseteq T$, $\mathcal{F}(S) \subseteq \mathcal{F}(T)$.

An auction mechanism $\mathcal{M} = (X, \mathbf{p})$, in this setting, when run on the set N of agents, consists of an *allocation algorithm* $X : \mathbb{R}_+^n \mapsto 2^N$ and a *payment rule* $\mathbf{p} : \mathbb{R}_+^n \mapsto \mathbb{R}^n$. Initially, the auctioneer collects the vector of bids $\mathbf{b} = (b_i)_{i \in N}$, where $b_i \in [0, \infty)$ denotes the bid declared by bidder $i \in N$. Then, given a bidding profile $\mathbf{b}$, the auctioneer runs the allocation algorithm to determine a feasible allocation $X(\mathbf{b}) \in \mathcal{F}(N)$, and the payment rule to determine the payment vector $\mathbf{p}(\mathbf{b}) = (p_1(\mathbf{b}), \ldots, p_n(\mathbf{b}))$, where $p_i(\mathbf{b})$ is the payment requested by bidder i.

We will often need to refer to sub-instances defined by a coalition of bidders. Given a bidding vector $\mathbf{b}$, and a subset of bidders $S \subseteq N$, we denote by $\mathbf{b}_S$ the projection of $\mathbf{b}$ on S. We also denote by $\mathbf{b}_{-i}$ the vector of all bids except for some bidder i. Given a profile $\mathbf{b}$, if we run a mechanism $\mathcal{M} = (X, \mathbf{p})$ on a sub-instance defined by $S \subseteq N$, then $X(\mathbf{b}_S) \in \mathcal{F}(S)$ will be the resulting allocation and $\mathbf{p}(\mathbf{b}_S)$ will be the corresponding payment vector for the members of S.

We assume that bidders have quasi-linear utilities and hence, given a mechanism $\mathcal{M} = (X, \mathbf{p})$, the final utility of bidder $i \in N$ for a profile $\mathbf{b}$ is

$u_i^{\mathcal{M}}(\mathbf{b}) = v_i - p_i(\mathbf{b})$, when $i \in X(\mathbf{b})$, and 0 otherwise. We say that $\mathcal{M}$ satisfies individual rationality if for every profile $\mathbf{b}$ and for every bidder $i \in N$ it holds that $u_i^{\mathcal{M}}(\mathbf{b}) \geq 0$. Additionally, a mechanism is truthful, or strategyproof, if for every bidder $i \in N$, every $b_i \geq 0$ and every profile $\mathbf{b}_{-i}$ it holds that $u_i^{\mathcal{M}}(v_i, \mathbf{b}_{-i}) \geq u_i^{\mathcal{M}}(b_i, \mathbf{b}_{-i})$.

Since we are in a single-parameter environment, in order to design truthful mechanisms, we use the characterization of Myerson [18]. In particular, we say that an allocation algorithm X is *monotone* if for every agent $i \in N$ and every profile $\mathbf{b}$, if $i \in X(\mathbf{b})$, then $i \in X(b_i', \mathbf{b}_{-i})$ for $b_i' \geq b_i$. Thus, if a bidder is selected by declaring a bid b_i, then she should also be selected when declaring a higher bid. Any monotone algorithm can be turned to a truthful mechanism by using the so called *threshold payments* described in [18].

2.2 Welfare Maximization and VCG Payments

For a mechanism $M = (X, \mathbf{p})$, the social welfare produced when run on a profile $\mathbf{b}$ (from the viewpoint of the mechanism since each b_i may differ from v_i) is equal to $\sum_{i \in X(\mathbf{b})} b_i$. Furthermore, for any coalition $S \subseteq N$, the *optimal* allocation with respect to $\mathbf{b}_S$ is the one achieving maximum welfare, defined as

$$X^*(\mathbf{b}_S) := \arg\max_{T \in \mathcal{F}(S)} \sum_{i \in T} b_i$$

We will denote by $W(\mathbf{b}_S)$ the social welfare achieved by an optimal allocation. This is also referred to as the *coalitional value* of S: $W(\mathbf{b}_S) := \max_{T \in \mathcal{F}(S)} \sum_{i \in T} b_i = \sum_{i \in X^*(\mathbf{b}_S)} b_i$. When $S = N$, we refer to an optimal allocation by $X^*(\mathbf{b})$ instead of $X^*(\mathbf{b}_N)$, and to the optimal welfare by $W(\mathbf{b})$.

Regarding tie-breaking issues, throughout this work, we assume that a consistent (deterministic) tie-breaking rule is used to select an allocation, whenever there are multiple optimal allocations at a given profile. For example a fixed ordering on subsets of bidders would suffice to resolve ties.

A mechanism is called efficient or welfare-maximizing if for every input profile, it outputs an optimal allocation. The VCG mechanism is the most popular example of an efficient and strategyproof mechanism, where for a bidding profile $\mathbf{b}$, the payment of bidder $i \in X^*(\mathbf{b})$ is the externality she imposes to the other bidders (i.e., the loss to their welfare), defined as

$$p_i^{VCG}(\mathbf{b}) = W(\mathbf{b}_{-i}) - \sum_{j \in X^*(\mathbf{b}) \setminus \{i\}} b_j \tag{1}$$

2.3 Core-Selecting and Core-Competitive Payment Rules

The notion of the core as a solution concept originates from cooperative game theory where it captures the fact that coalitions of agents do not have incentives to appeal to a payoff division. To adjust these ideas to the auctions context, we first define the following quantity, for every $S \subseteq N$ and bidding profile $\mathbf{b}$.

$$\beta(S, \mathbf{b}) := W(\mathbf{b}_S) - \sum_{j \in X^*(\mathbf{b}) \cap S} b_j.$$

This quantity is a generalization of the VCG payment formula, and can be interpreted as the *collective externality* that bidders in $N \setminus S$ impose to the bidders in S. Indeed, with this notation we can restate VCG payments in Eq. (1) as $p_i^{VCG}(\mathbf{b}) = \beta(N \setminus \{i\}, \mathbf{b})$, for every bidder $i \in X^*(\mathbf{b})$.

Core-selecting payment rules were initially defined in the space of utility vectors by [3]. In our work we follow the equivalent formulation of [8] that recasts them to the space of payment vectors. For a profile $\mathbf{b}$, the core polyhedron is defined w.r.t. an optimal allocation $X^*(\mathbf{b})$ as follows

$$CORE(\mathbf{b}) = \{\mathbf{p} \in \mathbb{R}^n : \sum_{j \in X^*(\mathbf{b}) \setminus S} p_j \geq \beta(S, \mathbf{b}) \ \forall S \subseteq N, \ p_j = 0 \ \forall j \notin X^*(\mathbf{b})\}. \quad (2)$$

Definition 1. *A payment rule is called core-selecting, if it is individually rational w.r.t. the reported bids, and* $\mathbf{p}(\mathbf{b}) \in CORE(\mathbf{b})$ *for every profile* $\mathbf{b}$*. Furthermore, a mechanism* $\mathcal{M} = (X, \mathbf{p})$ *is core-selecting if (i)* $X(\mathbf{b})$ *is a welfare-maximizing allocation for every profile* $\mathbf{b}$*, and (ii)* $\mathbf{p}$ *is a core-selecting payment rule.*

The constraints of the core polytope in (2) require that every coalition of bidders pays at least their collective externality, i.e., the damage their presence inflicts on the remaining bidders. An equivalent way to view this is that under a core payment vector, every coalition S, together with the auctioneer creates a collective utility at least as high as $W(\mathbf{b}_S)$, which is the best they could achieve if they ran an auction among themselves. Using this interpretation, if a payment vector is not in the core, this implies that there was a coalition that could offer the auctioneer a higher revenue and yet this did not happen. For further intuition on the core polytope, we refer the reader to [4].

As an example, it is easily verifiable that the pay-your-bid mechanism, coupled with the optimal allocation, is a core-selecting mechanism (referred to also as the *seller-optimal* payment rule). Given that core-selecting mechanisms are not truthful in general, see also [13], a natural quest has been to identify payments in the core where the incentives to misreport are minimized. Formalizing this idea, Day and Milgrom [9] proposed the use of *Pareto-efficient* core payments, which, in the core-literature are also referred to as *bidder-optimal* payment rules. We say that a payment vector $\mathbf{p}$ is a Pareto-efficient core payment if for every other payment $\mathbf{p}'$ such that $p_i' \leq p_i$ for every bidder $i \in X^*(\mathbf{b})$, with strict inequality for at least one bidder, we have that $\mathbf{p}' \notin CORE(\mathbf{b})$.

A prominent class of Pareto-efficient payment rules in the literature are the Minimum Revenue Core-Selecting (MRCS) rules, i.e., the minimum revenue points in the core, first introduced in [10]. An MRCS rule assigns payments given a profile **b**, that are optimal solutions of the linear program:

$$\min_{\mathbf{p} \in \mathbb{R}^n} \left\{ \sum_{j \in N} p_j : \quad \mathbf{p} \in CORE(\mathbf{b}), \quad \mathbf{p} \le \mathbf{b} \right\}. \tag{3}$$

It is straightforward to see that this is indeed a Pareto-efficient core payment rule. We denote by $\mathsf{MREV}(\mathbf{b})$ the optimal value of the objective function in (3). As shown in [9], the minimum core revenue still gives a better revenue guarantee than VCG, i.e., for a profile **b**, $\mathsf{MREV}(\mathbf{b}) \ge \sum_{i \in N} p_i^{VCG}(\mathbf{b})$. A further advantage of MRCS rules, established in [10], is that they minimize the *total gains from unilateral deviations*. Finally, it is also interesting to note that whenever the VCG payment belongs to the core, it is the unique MRCS rule, because it is the unique Pareto-efficient point [9]. Otherwise, the linear program in (3) has a continuum of solutions and a secondary refinement is required in practice to select a particular MRCS payment rule in a disciplined way. We continue this discussion in Sect. 5, by studying Quadratic Payment Rules.

Core-Competitive Mechanisms. A different approach has been initiated in [12] concerning revenue guarantees in relation to the core outcomes. Since core-selecting mechanisms are not always truthful, [12] proposed the design of truthful mechanisms whose revenue is competitive against a core outcome. Given the discussion in Sect. 2.3, it is quite natural to use as a core benchmark the revenue attained by the MRCS rules. One can evaluate then truthful mechanisms as follows:

Definition 2 ([12]). *Let* $\mathcal{M} = (X, \mathbf{p})$ *be a truthful mechanism. We say that* M *is* α-core-competitive, *with* $\alpha \ge 1$, *if for any bidding profile* **b** *it assigns a payment vector* $\mathbf{p}(\mathbf{b})$ *such that* $\sum_{i=1}^n p_i(\mathbf{b}) \ge \frac{1}{\alpha} \mathsf{MREV}(\mathbf{b})$.

3   Insights on the Geometry of the Core

We focus first on some properties of the core polytope with regard to how the polytope changes when a single bidder declares a higher bid, i.e., we study the relation between $CORE(\mathbf{b})$ and $CORE(b_i', \mathbf{b}_{-i})$, with $b_i' > b_i$ for some $i \in X^*(\mathbf{b})$. Throughout this section, we assume that for all payment vectors that we consider, we have set $p_j = 0$ for every $j \notin X^*(\mathbf{b})$, and a profile **b**. Finally, we defer all missing proofs in the remainder of this paper to the full version of our work.

3.1   Pareto-Efficiency and Individual Rationality Within the Core

According to Definition 1, a core-selecting mechanism must be individually rational with respect to the reported bids. We show that for Pareto-efficient core-selecting payment rules, we have individual rationality for free, and there is, in fact, no need for the auctioneer to explicitly enforce the IR constraints.

Lemma 1. *A payment rule that for a profile* **b** *prescribes a Pareto-efficient vector of payments* $\mathbf{p} \in CORE(\mathbf{b})$, *satisfies* $p_i \leq b_i$ *for every bidder* $i \in X^*(\mathbf{b})$.

Lemma 1 allows us to focus only on the core constraints, when reasoning about Pareto-efficient payment rules. Moreover, using the fact that MRCS payments are Pareto-efficient, we can now simplify the linear program of Eq. (3).

Corollary 1. *A payment rule is* MRCS *if, given a profile* **b**, *it assigns payments that are optimal solutions of the linear program*

$$\min_{\mathbf{p}\in\mathbb{R}^n} \left\{ \sum_{j\in N} p_j : \quad \mathbf{p} \in CORE(\mathbf{b}) \right\}. \tag{4}$$

3.2   The Effects of Unilateral Deviations on the Core

We now aim to understand how the core polytope that forms after a unilateral deviation of a winning bidder is related to the initial core polytope. Initially, we focus on how each of the constraints in the polytope is modified and perform a sensitivity analysis for the term $\beta(S, \mathbf{b})$, the collective externality in the core constraints in (2), for every $S \subseteq N$.

To proceed, our analysis will be dependent on the following quantity, defined for an input profile **b**, a bidder $i \in X^*(\mathbf{b})$, and a coalition $S \subseteq N$ with $i \in S$.

$$t_i(\mathbf{b}_{S\setminus\{i\}}) = \min\{z : \exists T \subseteq S, s.t.\ i \in T \text{ and } \sum_{j\in T\setminus\{i\}} b_j + z = W(z, \mathbf{b}_{S\setminus\{i\}})\}$$

The term $t_i(\mathbf{b}_{S\setminus\{i\}})$ is the minimum bid i should declare to be included in some optimal allocation in an auction where only the bidders from S are present. The following key lemma encapsulates the effects on the collective externality of S by a unilateral deviation of a bidder $i \in S$.

Lemma 2 (Sensitivity analysis for $\beta(S, \mathbf{b})$). *Let* **b** *be a bidding profile. Fix a bidder* $i \in X^*(\mathbf{b})$, *and a coalition* $S \subseteq N$. *Suppose that bidder* i *unilaterally deviates to* $b_i' > b_i$. *Then:*

1. *If* $i \notin S$ *or if* $i \in S$ *and* $b_i \geq t_i(\mathbf{b}_{S\setminus\{i\}})$ *then* $\beta(S, (b_i', \mathbf{b}_{-i})) = \beta(S, \mathbf{b})$.
2. *Otherwise, it holds that* $\beta(S, (b_i', \mathbf{b}_{-i})) = \beta(S, \mathbf{b}) - (\min\{b_i', t_i(\mathbf{b}_{S\setminus\{i\}})\} - b_i)$.

Lemma 2 enables us to prove the two theorems that follow.

Theorem 1. *Let* **b** *be a bidding profile and* $i \in X^*(\mathbf{b})$. *Then, for every* $b_i' > b_i$, $CORE(\mathbf{b}) \subseteq CORE(b_i', \mathbf{b}_{-i})$.

Proof. Note first that for $b_i' > b_i$, since the optimal allocation algorithm is monotone and $i \in X^*(\mathbf{b})$, it holds that $X^*(b_i', \mathbf{b}_{-i}) = X^*(\mathbf{b})$. Consider now a vector **p** in $CORE(\mathbf{b})$. We will show that **p** is also a member of $CORE(b_i', \mathbf{b}_{-i})$. This is equivalent to showing that for every $S \subseteq N$, $\mathbf{p}$ satisfies $\sum_{j \in X^*(\mathbf{b}) \backslash S} p_j \geq \beta(S, (b'_i, \mathbf{b}_{-i}))$.

When $S \subseteq N$ is a coalition such that either $i \notin S$ or $i \in S$ and $b_i \geq t_i(\mathbf{b}_{S \backslash \{i\}})$, then by Lemma 2 (Condition 1), we immediately have

$$\sum_{j \in X^*(\mathbf{b}) \backslash S} p_j \geq \beta(S, \mathbf{b}) = \beta(S, (b'_i, \mathbf{b}_{-i})).$$

On the other hand, when $i \in S$ and $b_i < t_i(\mathbf{b}_{S \backslash \{i\}})$, then again by Lemma 2 (Condition 2), and since $\mathbf{p} \in CORE(\mathbf{b})$, we obtain

$$\sum_{j \in X^*(\mathbf{b}) \backslash S} p_j \geq \beta(S, \mathbf{b}) = \beta(S, (b'_i, \mathbf{b}_{-i})) + \min\{b'_i, t_i(\mathbf{b}_{S \backslash \{i\}})\} - b_i > \beta(S, (b'_i, \mathbf{b}_{-i})),$$

where the last inequality follows from the facts that $b'_i > b_i$ and $t_i(\mathbf{b}_{S \backslash \{i\}}) > b_i$. $\quad\square$

We note that the set inclusion claimed in Theorem 1 can be strict. Theorem 1 also has the following corollary for MRCS core payments, defined in (4).

Corollary 2. *Let* $\mathbf{b}$ *be a bidding profile, and* $i \in X^*(\mathbf{b})$. *For* $b'_i > b_i$, *we have* $\mathsf{MREV}(b'_i, \mathbf{b}_{-i}) \leq \mathsf{MREV}(\mathbf{b})$.

Corollary 2 states that a higher willingness to pay will never lead to an increase of the auctioneer's revenue under MRCS. This may look counter-intuitive on a first reading, and is commonly mentioned as a violation of *revenue monotonicity*[1]. Pareto-efficient core payments have been known to be susceptible to violating this property. Namely, it has been shown by [5,16] that in a multi-parameter domain with at least three items, revenue-monotonicity is violated. In fact we can strengthen these results to single-parameter auctions by exhibiting instances where we can have strict inequality in the statement of Corollary 2. We defer a further analysis of these issues to our full version.

Aside from this discussion, and quite surprisingly, Corollary 2 also plays a crucial role in the analysis of the mechanism we present in Sect. 4.

The next theorem says that in order to obtain a payment that is in the enlarged polyhedron after a bidder's deviation, the deviating bidder should be charged a payment that exceeds her previous bid. This will be particularly useful in Sect. 5.

Theorem 2. *Let* $\mathbf{b}$ *be a bidding profile and fix a bidder* $i \in X^*(\mathbf{b})$. *For* $b'_i > b_i$, *let* $\mathbf{p} \in CORE(b'_i, \mathbf{b}_{-i})$ *be a payment vector with* $p_i \leq b_i$. *Then,* $\mathbf{p} \in CORE(\mathbf{b})$.

4   An $O(\log n)$-core-competitive Mechanism

In this section, we present a first application of the properties derived in Sect. 3. We move away from core-selecting mechanisms and our main result is a deterministic, truthful mechanism that is also $O(logn)$-core-competitive with respect

---

[1] There are several facets in studying revenue monotonicity, as it concerns the effects on revenue when adding new bidders, or increasing the offers of the current bidders.

to the MRCS benchmark. Although we are not analyzing core-selecting mechanisms in this section, the properties of the core, (namely Corollary 2 of Theorem
1), will still come in handy for the analysis of our mechanism.

Mechanism $\hat{\mathcal{M}} = (\hat{X}, \hat{p})$.

Input: A value profile $v \in \mathbb{R}^n_+$.
Output: An allocation $\hat{X}(v) \in \mathcal{F}(N)$ and a vector of payments $\hat{p}(v)$.

1. Find an optimal allocation $X^*(v)$. Let $m = |X^*(v)|$.
2. Let $s_1, \dots, s_m$ be an ordering of the bidders in $X^*(v)$ such that $v_{s_1} \geq \cdots \geq v_{s_m}$. Let $k \leq m$ be the largest index such that

$$k \cdot v_{s_k} \geq \frac{\mathsf{MREV}(v)}{H_n}. \tag{5}$$

3. Set $\hat{X}(v) = \{s_1, \dots, s_k\}$ and $\hat{p}(v)$ according to Myerson's Lemma.

Fig. 1. An $O(\log n)$-core-competitive and strategyproof mechanism.

The mechanism is described in Fig. 1, where we have used the real valuation
profile for the bidders ($b = v$). We also denote the n-th harmonic number
by $H_n = \sum_{i=1}^n 1/i$. In the first step, we find a welfare-maximizing allocation.
However, instead of accepting all bidders in the optimal solution, the second step
disqualifies some bidders with values that do not meet a certain cutoff. In case
of ties in step 2, it suffices to have a consistent deterministic tie-breaking rule,
e.g., given by an ordering on the set of bidders. The mechanism tries, in some
sense, to be as inclusive as possible, as long as the value of the last member of
$\hat{X}(v)$ is not too small for the coalition to collectively miss the cutoff.

Theorem 3. *The mechanism $\hat{\mathcal{M}}$ is individually rational, truthful, and $O(\log n)$-core-competitive.*

Section 4.2 is devoted to the proof of Theorem 3. Before this, we discuss first
some aspects of the mechanism, and comparisons with other results.

4.1 Remarks on Tightness, Complexity and Other Implications

Prior to our work, a randomized, exponential, strategyproof mechanism was
known that is also $O(\log n)$-core-competitive [17]. This result is based on establishing competitiveness against a stronger benchmark, which is the maximum
welfare when the highest bidder is ignored. What we find most valuable in our
deterministic matching upper bound is that it yielded a better understanding
of the core polytope, through the properties of Sect. 3. On the other hand, the
mechanism of [17] does not reveal any properties for the core, since it is centered
around a different benchmark. Moreover, our result provides a strict separation

on the performance of the two benchmarks, since [17] shows that deterministic mechanisms cannot perform better than $\Omega(n)$ for their benchmark. Hence, our mechanism illustrates that the benchmark of [17] is much more stringent.

Regarding complexity, our mechanism clearly has a worst-case exponential running time, because it requires the computation of an optimal allocation and of MREV(**b**). This bottleneck is not uncommon in the core auction literature, and it is often assumed that the mechanism has oracle access to a welfare maximization algorithm. Given the results in [10] for computing MREV(**b**), we can conclude that our mechanism can be implemented with a polynomial number of oracle calls to welfare maximization. Faster algorithms have also been proposed for MREV(**b**), e.g., [15], but these compute ϵ-bidder-optimal core points and are not suitable for our mechanism. Finally, for settings where there exist efficient algorithms for welfare optimization, our mechanism is also implementable in polynomial time.

As for tightness, recall that the mechanism selects a subset of the optimal allocation $X^*(\mathbf{v})$ as the set of winning bidders. For the special case studied in [12], it is shown that mechanisms whose allocation is a subset of an optimal allocation, cannot perform better than $O(\log n)$. This directly implies that our result is tight, and among such mechanisms, it achieves the best possible core-competitiveness.

4.2   Feasibility, Monotonicity and Competitiveness of $\hat{X}$

To show that the mechanism always outputs a feasible allocation, we use the fact that for a given $\mathbf{v}$, $\hat{X}(\mathbf{v}) \subseteq X^*(\mathbf{v})$. Since the optimal allocation $X^*(\mathbf{v}) \in \mathcal{F}(N)$ and since we have assumed that $\mathcal{F}(N)$ is downward-closed, then $\hat{X}(\mathbf{v})$ is feasible.

Moreover, we claim that the allocation algorithm $\hat{X}$ always outputs a non-empty allocation, i.e., the cutoff set in (5) is always achievable by at least one index $k \in \{1, \ldots, |X^*(\mathbf{v})|\}$. This is precisely what the next lemma establishes.

Lemma 3. *Let* $\mathbf{v}$ *be a value profile, and* $m = |X^*(\mathbf{v})|$. *Let* $s_1, s_2, \ldots s_m$ *be an ordering of the bidders in* $X^*(\mathbf{v})$ *by their value in a non-increasing order. Then*
$$\max_{j \in \{1, \ldots, m\}} j \cdot v_{s_j} \geq \frac{\mathsf{MREV}(\mathbf{v})}{H_n}.$$

Next, we show that the allocation algorithm $\hat{X}$ is monotone. Lemma 4 will be the key to establish this argument, which is in turn based on Corollary 2 from Sect. 3. Lemma 4 states that when a winning bidder increases her bid, the allocation algorithm $\hat{X}$ may only increase the number of bidders it serves.

Lemma 4. *For every value profile* $\mathbf{v}$, *bidder* $i \in \hat{X}(\mathbf{v})$ *and every* $v_i' > v_i$ *it holds that* $|\hat{X}(\mathbf{v})| \leq |\hat{X}(v_i', \mathbf{v}_{-i})|$.

Proof. Suppose for contradiction that there exists a profile $\mathbf{v}$ with a bidder $i \in \hat{X}(\mathbf{v})$ and a bid $v_i' > v_i$ for which $|\hat{X}(\mathbf{v})| > |\hat{X}(v_i', \mathbf{v}_{-i})|$. Since $i \in X^*(\mathbf{v})$ and due to the fact that the welfare-maximizing algorithm is monotone, it holds that $i \in X^*(v_i', \mathbf{v}_{-i})$ as well. Let $\mathbf{s}$ be the ordering of the players in $X^*(\mathbf{v})$, produced by the mechanism at step 2, on input $\mathbf{v}$, and let $\mathbf{s}'$ be the corresponding ordering of bidders in $X^*(v_i', \mathbf{v}_{-i})$. Let $k = |\hat{X}(\mathbf{v})|$ and $k' = |\hat{X}(v_i', \mathbf{v}_{-i})|$. By our assumption, $k' < k$. Bidder i can only be at a lower index in the ranking $\mathbf{s}'$ compared to her position at $\mathbf{s}$, since she has deviated to $v_i' > v_i$. This implies that $v_{s_k'} \geq v_{s_k}$. To verify this, either the bidder at position k in $\mathbf{s}'$ has remained the same but with equal or higher value (in case bidder i is at position k) or bidder i has moved up in the ranking and it has displaced some bidder with a higher value to position k. However, this yields

$$k \cdot v_{s_k'} \geq k \cdot v_{s_k} \geq \frac{\mathrm{MREV}(\mathbf{v})}{H_n} \geq \frac{\mathrm{MREV}(v_i', \mathbf{v}_{-i})}{H_n}.$$

The second inequality follows from what we assumed for the execution of the mechanism on $\mathbf{v}$, whereas the third inequality follows from Corollary 2. Thus, k bidders can still be served on input $(v_i', \mathbf{v}_{-i})$, and k' is not the largest index of bidders who can meet the cutoff of (5) under $(v_i', \mathbf{v}_{-i})$, which is a contradiction.   □

By using Lemma 4, we can prove the monotonicity of the allocation algorithm.

Lemma 5. *The allocation algorithm $\hat{X}$ is monotone.*

Hence, the mechanism is truthful, and all that is left to prove is that $\hat{M}$ is $O(\log n)$-core-competitive. The following lemma provides a relationship for the threshold payment of each bidder and is crucial to obtain our revenue guarantee.

Lemma 6. *Given a value profile $\mathbf{v}$, the threshold payment $\hat{p}_i(\mathbf{v})$ of every bidder $i \in \hat{X}(\mathbf{v})$ for the mechanism $\hat{M}$ satisfies $\hat{p}_i(\mathbf{v}) \geq p_i^{VCG}(\mathbf{v})$ and, additionally,*

$$\hat{p}_i(\mathbf{v}) \geq \frac{\mathrm{MREV}(\hat{p}_i(\mathbf{v}), \mathbf{v}_{-i})}{|\hat{X}(\hat{p}_i(\mathbf{v}), \mathbf{v}_{-i})| \cdot H_n}.$$

The proof of Theorem 3 is completed by exploiting Lemma 6 and establishing the following lemma.

Lemma 7. *The mechanism is $O(logn)$-core-competitive.*

5   A Class of Non-decreasing Quadratic Payment Rules

In this section, we illustrate a second application of our results from Sect. 3.

5.1   Quadratic Payment Rules

As mentioned in Sect. 2, when VCG is not in the core, the linear program of Eq. (3) that determines the MRCS payments has a continuum of solutions. Even though all these solutions have been shown in [10] to minimize the gain of deviating, the question remained whether one of these points should be more preferred over others. This motivated [8,11] to propose a class of core-selecting mechanisms, based on the idea of picking the point on the minimum revenue face of the core that is the closest in Euclidean distance to a given reference point in the vector space. This payment rule can be expressed using the quadratic program defined below, and are called quadratic rules.

Definition 3. *Let* $\mathbf{r} \in \mathbb{R}_+^n$. *We call a payment rule* $\mathbf{r}$-*nearest when, for every vector* $\mathbf{b}$, *it assigns the payment*

$$\mathbf{p}^{\mathbf{r}}(\mathbf{b}) = \arg\min_{\mathbf{p} \in \mathbb{R}^n} \left\{ \sum_{j \in X^*(\mathbf{b})} (p_j - r_j)^2 : \ \mathbf{p} \in CORE(\mathbf{b}), \ \sum_{j \in X^*(\mathbf{b})} p_j = \mathsf{MREV}(\mathbf{b}) \right\}.$$

The vector $\mathbf{r}$ is referred to as the reference point of the rule. Note that, since this quadratic program expresses a minimization of Euclidean distance from a convex set to a fixed point, the payment vector $\mathbf{p}^{\mathbf{r}}(\mathbf{b})$ is *unique*.

A number of vectors have been proposed as potential reference points for this class of payments. Initially, in [8] Day and Cramton used the VCG payments for a reference point, $\mathbf{r} = \mathbf{p}^{VCG}(\mathbf{b})$. The motivation came from the findings of [20] who observed that the quantity $p_i - p_i^{VCG}(\mathbf{b})$ represents the bidder's "residual incentive to misreport". Hence, minimizing this quantity seemed a reasonable choice with good incentive properties. In parallel to this, Erdil and Klemperer [11] leaned more towards constant payment rules with reference points that do not depend on the bidding profile, motivated by minimizing *marginal* incentives to deviate. One well-studied and intuitive example is the **0**-nearest mechanism: pick the point in MRCS that is closest to **0**. Yet another perspective was given in [2] who proposed the **b**-nearest rule, i.e., the MRCS payments closest to the actual bids. Overall, such quadratic rules have formed the basis for many deployments in practice in several countries, especially for public sector auctions [8].

5.2   Non-decreasing Payment Rules

We now consider the following desirable property for payment rules.

Definition 4. *A payment rule is called non-decreasing, if for every profile* $\mathbf{b}$, *every bidder* $i \in N$ *and every* $b_i' > b_i$ *it holds that* $p_i(b_i', \mathbf{b}_{-i}) \geq p_i(\mathbf{b})$.

This notion has been defined independently in [11] and [6], with a different motivation in mind. In [11], it is argued that payment rules satisfying this property weakly dominate all other rules in terms of the so called *marginal incentive to deviate*. Hence, even though such mechanisms may not be truthful, they possess very desirable incentive guarantees. In [6], another advantage is highlighted, of computational nature: limiting our attention to non-decreasing rules makes the daunting task of computing Bayes Nash equilibria much simpler.

Hence, it becomes important to understand which mechanisms satisfy this property. It can be seen that the VCG mechanism and the pay-your-bid auction do satisfy Definition 4. In the context of MRCS rules, it is shown in [6], that $\mathbf{p}^{VCG}$-nearest is *not* non-decreasing. To our knowledge, it has remained an open question whether there exist MRCS rules that satisfy Definition 4.

We answer this question in the affirmative for single parameter domains, by providing a class of quadratic rules that are non-decreasing. To proceed, given a vector $\mathbf{b}$, for all $i \in N$, define $f_i(b_i)$ to be any non-decreasing function of b_i. Let $\mathbf{f}(\mathbf{b}) = (f_1(b_1), \ldots, f_n(b_n))$. The following is the main result of this section, and we also note that it does not require the assumption that $\mathcal{F}(N)$ is downward-closed.

Theorem 4. *For all* $\mathbf{f} = (f_1(\cdot), \ldots, f_n(\cdot))$, *where each* $f_i(\cdot)$ *is a non-decreasing function of* b_i, *the* $\mathbf{f}(\mathbf{b})$-*nearest payment rule is non-decreasing.*

Notice that as a corollary, we have that the well known **0**-nearest and **b**-nearest mechanisms that were advocated by [11] and [2] respectively, are non-decreasing. The proof of Theorem 4, is based on Theorems 1 and 2 from Sect. 3.

References

1. Aggarwal, G., Hartline, J.: Knapsack auctions. In: Proceedings of the 17th Annual ACM-SIAM Symposium on Discrete Algorithms, pp. 1083–1092 (2006)
2. Ausubel, L., Baranov, O.: Core-selecting auctions with incomplete information. Int. J. Game Theor. **36**(3–4), 393–407 (2019)
3. Ausubel, L., Milgrom, P.: Ascending auctions with package bidding. Adv. Theor. Econ. **1**(1), 1–42 (2002). https://doi.org/10.2202/1534-5963.1019
4. Ausubel, L., Milgrom, P.: The lovely but lonely vickrey auction. In: Cramton, P., Shoham, Y., Steinberg, R. (eds.) Combinatorial Auctions (2006)
5. Beck, M., Ott, M.: Revenue monotonicity in core-selecting auctions. Technical Report Stanford University (2010)
6. Bosshard, V., Wang, Y., Seuken, S.: Non-decreasing payment rules for combinatorial auctions. In: Proceedings of the 27th International Joint Conference on Artificial Intelligence, pp. 105–113 (2018)
7. Bünz, B., Lubin, B., Seuken,S.: Designing core-selecting payment rules: a computational search approach. In: Proceedings of the 19th ACM Conference on Economics and Computation, p. 109 (2018)
8. Day, R., Cramton, P.: Quadratic core-selecting payment rules for combinatorial auctions. Oper. Res. **60**(3), 588–603 (2012)
9. Day, R., Milgrom, P.: Core-selecting package auctions. Int. J. Game Theor. **36**(3–4), 393–407 (2008)
10. Day, R., Raghavan, S.: Fair payments for efficient allocations in public sector combinatorial auctions. Manage. Sci. **53**(9), 1389–1406 (2007)
11. Erdil, A., Klemperer, P.: A new payment rule for core-selecting package auctions. J. Eur. Econ. Assoc. **8**(2–3), 537–547 (2010)
12. Goel, G., Khani, M.R., Leme, R.P.: Core-competitive auctions. In: Proceedings of the 16th ACM Conference on Economics and Computation, pp. 149–166 (2015)
13. Goeree, J., Lien, Y.: On the impossibility of core-selecting auctions. Theor. Econ. **11**(1), 41–52 (2016)
14. Guruswami, V., Hartline, J., Karlin, A., Kempe, D., Kenyon, C., McSherry, F.: On profit-maximizing envy-free pricing. In: Proceedings of the 16th Annual ACM-SIAM Symposium on Discrete Algorithms, pp. 1164–1173 (2005)
15. Hartline, J., Immorlica, N., Khani, M.R., Lucier, B., Niazadeh, R.: Fast core pricing for rich advertising auctions. In Proceedings of the 19th ACM Conference on Economics and Computation, pp. 111–112 (2018)
16. Lamy, L.: Core-selecting package auctions: a comment on revenue-monotonicity. Int. J. Game Theor. **39**(3), 503–510 (2010)

17. Micali, S., Valiant, P.: Collusion-resilient revenue in combinatorial auctions. Technical Report MIT-CSAIL-TR-2007-052, MIT-CSAIL (2007)
18. Myerson, R.: Optimal auction design. Math. Oper. Res. **6**(1), 58–73 (1981)
19. Ott, M., Beck, M.: Incentives for overbidding in minimum-revenue core-selecting auctions. Tech. rep. Working paper, Stanford University (2013)
20. Parkes, D., Kalagnanam, J., Eso, M.: Achieving budget-balance with Vickrey-based payment schemes in exchanges. In: Proceedings of the 17th International Joint Conference on Artificial Intelligence, pp. 1161–1168 (2001)

Scheduling Games
with Machine-Dependent Priority Lists

Marc Schröder[1]([✉]), Tami Tamir[2], and Vipin Ravindran Vijayalakshmi[1]

[1] Chair of Management Science, RWTH Aachen, Aachen, Germany
{marc.schroeder,vipin.rv}@oms.rwth-aachen.de
[2] School of Computer Science, The Interdisciplinary Center, Herzliya, Israel
tami@idc.ac.il

Abstract. We consider a scheduling game in which jobs try to minimize their completion time by choosing a machine to be processed on. Each machine uses an individual priority list to decide on the order according to which the jobs on the machine are processed. We characterize four classes of instances in which a pure Nash equilibrium (NE) is guaranteed to exist, and show by means of an example, that none of these characterizations can be relaxed. We then bound the performance of Nash equilibria for each of these classes with respect to the makespan of the schedule and the sum of completion times. We also analyze the computational complexity of several problems arising in this model. For instance, we prove that it is NP-hard to decide whether a NE exists, and that even for instances with identical machines, for which a NE is guaranteed to exist, it is NP-hard to approximate the best NE within a factor of $2 - \frac{1}{m} - \epsilon$ for every $\epsilon > 0$.

In addition, we study a generalized model in which players' strategies are subsets of resources, where each resource has its own priority list over the players. We show that in this general model, even unweighted symmetric games may not have a pure NE, and we bound the price of anarchy with respect to the total players' costs.

Keywords: Scheduling games · Priority lists · Price of anarchy

1   Introduction

Scheduling problems have traditionally been studied from a centralized point of view in which the goal is to find an assignment of jobs to machines so as to minimize some global objective function. Two of the classical results are that Smith's rule, i.e., schedule jobs in decreasing order according to their ratio of weight over processing time, is optimal for single machine scheduling with

T. Tamir—This research is supported by The Israel Science Foundation (ISF). Grant No. 1036/17.

V. R. Vijayalakshmi—This work is supported by the German research council (DFG) Research Training Group 2236 UnRAVeL.

© Springer Nature Switzerland AG 2019
I. Caragiannis et al. (Eds.): WINE 2019, LNCS 11920, pp. 286–300, 2019.
https://doi.org/10.1007/978-3-030-35389-6_21

the sum of weighted completion times as the objective [23], and list scheduling, i.e., greedily assign the job with the highest priority to a free machine, yields a 2-approximation for identical machines with the minimum makespan objective [14]. Many modern systems provide service to multiple strategic users, whose individual payoff is affected by the decisions made by others. As a result, non-cooperative game theory has become an essential tool in the analysis of job-scheduling applications. The jobs are controlled by selfish users who independently choose which resources to use. Job-scheduling games have by now been widely studied and many results regarding the inefficiency of equilibria in different settings are known.

A particular focus has been placed on finding coordination mechanisms [6], i.e., local scheduling policies, that induce a good system performance. In fact, recently Caragiannis et al. [4] proposed a framework that uses such policies to come up with combinatorial approximation algorithms for the underlying optimization problem. It is common to assume that ties are broken in a consistent manner (see, e.g., Immorlica et al. [17]), or that there are no ties at all (see, e.g., Cole et al. [7]). In practice, there is no real justification for this assumption, except that it avoids subtle difficulties in the analysis. In this paper we relax this restrictive assumption and consider the more general setting in which machines have arbitrary individual priority lists. That is, each machine schedules those jobs that have chosen it according to its priority list. The priority lists are publicly known to the jobs.

In this paper we analyze the effect of having machine-dependent priority lists on the corresponding job-scheduling game. We study the existence of Nash equilibrium, the complexity of identifying whether a NE profile exists, the complexity of calculating a NE, in particular a good one, and the equilibrium inefficiency.

1.1 The Model

An instance of a *scheduling game with machine-dependent priority lists* is given by a tuple $G = \langle N, M, (w_i)_{i \in N}, (c_j)_{j \in M}, (\pi_j)_{j \in M} \rangle$, where N is a finite set of $n \geq 1$ jobs, M is a finite set of $m \geq 1$ machines, $w_i \in \mathbb{R}_+$ is the weight of job $i \in N$, $c_j \in \mathbb{R}_+$ is the processing delay of machine $j \in M$, and $\pi_j : N \to \{1, \ldots, n\}$ is the priority list of machine $j \in M$. In the literature, it is common to characterize the jobs by their *processing time* and the machines by their *speed*. We prefer to refer to weight instead of to processing time, and to delay, which is the inverse of speed, in order to be consistent with the general definition of congestion games.

A strategy profile $s = (s_i)_{i \in N}$ assigns a machine $s_i \in M$ to every job $i \in N$. Given a strategy profile s, the jobs are processed according to their order in the machines' priority lists. The set of jobs that delay job i in s is $B_i(s) = \{i' \in N | s_{i'} = s_i \wedge \pi_{s_i}(i') \leq \pi_{s_i}(i)\}$. Note that job i itself also belongs to $B_i(s)$. Let $w^i(s) = \sum_{i' \in B_i(s)} w_{i'}$. The cost of job $i \in N$ is equal to its completion time in s, given by $cost_i(s) = c_j \cdot w^i(s)$.

A more general model is that of a *congestion game with resource-dependent priority lists*, in which the strategy space of a player consists of *subsets of resources.* Formally, an instance of the general game is given by a tuple $G = \langle N, E, (\Sigma_i)_{i \in N}, (w_i)_{i \in N}, (c_e)_{e \in E}, (\pi_e)_{e \in E} \rangle$, where N is a finite set players, E is a finite set of resources, $\Sigma_i \subseteq 2^E$ is the set of feasible strategies for player $i \in N$, $w_i \in \mathbb{R}_+$ is the weight of player $i \in N$, $c_e \in \mathbb{R}_+$ is the cost coefficient of resource $e \in E$, and $\pi_e : N \to \{1, \dots, n\}$ is the priority list of resource E that defines its preference over the players using it.

Scheduling games are symmetric singleton congestion games in which the strategy space of each job is the set of all machines. For the general setting, the players' costs are defined as follows. Given a strategy profile $s = (s_i)_{i \in N} \in \times_{i \in N} \Sigma_i$, for every player $i \in N$, and resource $e \in s_i$, let $B_{ie}(s) = \{i' \in N \mid e \in s_{i'} \wedge \pi_e(i') \leq \pi_e(i)\}$, and define $w_e^i(s) = \sum_{i' \in B_{ie}(s)} w_{i'}$. The cost of a player $i \in N$ is given by, $cost_i(s) = w_i \cdot \sum_{e \in s_i} c_e \cdot w_e^i(s)$.

Notice that for general congestion games, we assume that players' costs are multiplied by their weight, whereas we do not make that assumption for scheduling games. This has no implications for the existence of Nash equilibria, but only affects the efficiency result.

Each job chooses a strategy so as to minimize its cost. A strategy profile s is a *pure Nash equilibrium (NE)* if for all $i \in N$ and all $s_i' \in \Sigma_i$, we have $cost_i(s) \leq cost_i(s_i', s_{-i})$. Let $\mathcal{E}(G)$ denote the set of Nash equilibria for a given instance G. Notice that $\mathcal{E}(G)$ may be empty.

For a profile s, let $cost(s)$ denote the cost of s. The cost is defined with respect to some objective. For example, the total players' cost or the maximum cost of a player. It is well known that decentralized decision-making may lead to sub-optimal solutions from the point of view of the society as a whole. For a game G, let $P(G)$ be the set of feasible profiles of G. We denote by $OPT(G)$ the cost of a social optimal (SO) solution; i.e., $OPT(G) = \min_{s \in P(G)} cost(s)$. We quantify the inefficiency incurred due to self-interested behavior according to the *price of anarchy* (PoA) [19] and *price of stability* (PoS) [2] measures. The PoA is the worst-case inefficiency of a pure Nash equilibrium, while the PoS measures the best-case inefficiency of a pure Nash equilibrium.

Definition 1. *Let $\mathcal{G}$ be a family of games, and let G be a game in $\mathcal{G}$. Let $\mathcal{E}(G)$ be the set of pure Nash equilibria of the game G. Assume that $\mathcal{E}(G) \neq \emptyset$.*

- *The price of anarchy of G is the ratio between the maximal cost of a NE and the social optimum of G. That is, $PoA(G) = \max_{s \in \mathcal{E}(G)} cost(s)/OPT(G)$. The price of anarchy of the family of games $\mathcal{G}$ is $PoA(\mathcal{G}) = sup_{G \in \mathcal{G}} PoA(G)$.*
- *The price of stability of G is the ratio between the minimal cost of a NE and the social optimum of G. That is, $PoS(G) = \min_{s \in \mathcal{E}(G)} cost(s)/OPT(G)$. The price of stability of the family of games $\mathcal{G}$ is $PoS(\mathcal{G}) = sup_{G \in \mathcal{G}} PoS(G)$.*

1.2   Our Contribution

We start by studying scheduling games, i.e., each job has to choose one machine to be processed on, and then based on the choices of the jobs, each machine schedules the jobs according to its individual priority list. We first show that a

Nash equilibrium in general need not exist, and use this example to show that it is NP-complete to decide whether a particular game has a Nash equilibrium. We then extend known results in order to provide a characterization of instances in which a pure Nash equilibrium is guaranteed to exist. Specifically, existence is guaranteed if the game belongs to at least one of the following four classes: $\mathcal{G}_1$: all jobs have the same weight, $\mathcal{G}_2$: there are two machines, $\mathcal{G}_3$: all machines have the same processing delay (shown in [9]), and $\mathcal{G}_4$: all machines have the same priority list (shown in [11]). For all four of these classes, there is a polynomial time algorithm that computes a Nash equilibrium. In fact, if jobs are unweighted, better-response dynamics converge to a Nash equilibrium in polynomial time. This characterization is tight in a sense that our inexistence example disobeys it in a minimal way: it describes a game on three machines, two of them having the same processing delay and the same priority list.

We analyze the inefficiency of Nash equilibria by means of two different measures of efficiency: the makespan, i.e., the maximum completion time of a job, and the sum of completion times. For all four classes of games with a guaranteed Nash equilibrium we provide tight bounds for the price of anarchy and the price of stability with respect to both measures. Our results are summarized in Table 1. For two machines with processing delays $c_1 = 1$ and $c_2 = c \geq 1$, we prove that the PoA and the PoS are at most $1 + \frac{c}{c+1}$ if $c \leq \frac{\sqrt{5}+1}{2}$, and $1 + \frac{1}{c}$ if $c \geq \frac{\sqrt{5}+1}{2}$. Our analysis is tight for all $c \geq 1$. The maximal inefficiency, listed in Table 1, is achieved with $c = \frac{\sqrt{5}+1}{2}$.

Table 1. Our results for the equilibrium inefficiency.

Instance class\objective	Makespan		Sum of completion times	
	PoA	PoS	PoA	PoS
$\mathcal{G}_1$: Unweighted jobs	1	1	1	1
$\mathcal{G}_2$: Two machines	$(\sqrt{5}+1)/2$	$(\sqrt{5}+1)/2$	$\Theta(n)$	$\Theta(n)$
$\mathcal{G}_3$: Identical machines	$2-1/m$	$2-1/m$	$\Theta(n/m)$	$\Theta(n/m)$
$\mathcal{G}_4$: Global priority list	$\Theta(m)$	$\Theta(m)$	$\Theta(n)$	$\Theta(n)$

In terms of computational complexity, we prove that it is NP-hard to approximate the best NE within a factor of $2 - \frac{1}{m} - \epsilon$ for all $\epsilon > 0$, if machines have identical processing delays and the minimum makespan objective is considered. Recall that $2 - \frac{1}{m}$ is the price of anarchy for these instances. In particular, this implies that the simple greedy algorithm that computes a Nash equilibrium by letting each machine with the current least load get the most preferred unassigned job, is the best one can hope for.

We finally generalize the model to allow for arbitrary strategy sets. We show that in general, even with unweighted jobs, a Nash equilibrium need not exist by making use of the famous Condorcet paradox [8]. We then use this example to prove that the question whether a Nash equilibrium exists is NP-hard, even with unweighted jobs. We lastly study the price of anarchy with respect to the sum of weighted costs and show that the upper bound of 4 proven by Cole et al. [7] for unrelated machine scheduling with Smith's rule also extends to congestion games with resource-dependent priority lists. This ratio is smaller than the price of anarchy of the atomic game with priorities defined by Farzad et al. [11].

Due to space constraints, some of the proofs are omitted. A full version of this paper with all the proofs can be found at https://arxiv.org/abs/1909.10199.

1.3   Related Work

Scheduling Games. The existence and inefficiency of Nash equilibria in scheduling games gained lots of attention over the recent years. We refer to Vöcking [24] for a recent overview. For existence, Immorlica et al. [17] proved that for unrelated machines, i.e., different machines can have different processing times for jobs, and priority lists based on shortest processing time first with consistent tie-breaking, the set of Nash equilibria is always non-empty and corresponds to the set of solutions of the Ibarra-Kim algorithm [16].

The standard measure for the inefficiency of Nash equilibria is the price of anarchy [19]. This measure has been widely studied for different measures of efficiency. Most attention has been addressed on minimizing the makespan. Czumaj and Vöcking [10] gave tight bounds for related machines that grow as the number of machines grows, whereas Awerbuch et al. [3] and Gairing et al. [12] provided tight bounds for restricted machine settings. An alternative measure of efficiency is utilitarian social welfare, that is, the sum of weighted completion times. Correa and Queyranne [9] proved a tight upper bound of 4 for restricted related machines with priority lists derived from Smith's rule. Cole et al. [7] generalized the bound of 4 to unrelated machines with Smith's rule. Hoeksma and Uetz [15] gave a tighter bound for the more restricted setting in which jobs have unit weights and machines are related.

Congestion Games with Priorities. Rosenthal [21] proved that congestion games are potential games and thus have a pure Nash equilibrium. Ackermann et al. [1] were the first to study a congestion game with priorities. They proposed a model in which users with higher priority on a resource displace users with lower priority. Similar to our model, Farzad et al. [11] studied priority based selfish routing for non-atomic and atomic users. Gourvès et al. [13] studied capacitated congestion games to characterize the existence of pure Nash equilibria and computation of an equilibrium when they exist. Piliouras et al. [20] assumed that the priority lists are unknown to the players a priori and consider different risk attitudes towards having a uniform at random ordering.

2   Equilibrium Existence and Computation

In this section we give a precise characterization of instances that are guaranteed to have a NE. The conditions that we provide are sufficient but not necessary. A natural question is to decide whether a given game instance that does not fulfill any of the conditions has a NE. We show that answering this question is a NP-complete problem.

We first show that a NE may not exist, even with only three machines, two of which have the same delay and the same priority list.

Example 1. Consider the game G^* with 5 jobs, $N = \{a, b, c, d, e\}$, and three machines, $M = \{M_1, M_2, M_3\}$, with $\pi_1 = (a, b, c, d, e)$, and $\pi_2 = \pi_3 = (e, d, b, c, a)$. The first machine has delay $c_1 = 1$ while the two other machines have delay $c_2 = c_3 = 2$. The job weights are $w_a = 5, w_b = 4, w_c = 4 + 2\epsilon, w_d = 9 + \epsilon$, and $w_e = 2$, where $\epsilon > 0$ but small.

Job a is clearly on M_1 in every NE. It is easy to see that in every NE at least one of b, c and d is on M_1. Therefore, job e is first on M_2 or M_3. Since these two machines have the same priority list and the same delay function, we can assume w.l.o.g., that if a NE exists, then there exists a NE in which job e is on M_3. We show that no NE exists by considering the three possible strategies of job b.

1. b is on M_1: If d is not on M_2 or M_3, then b prefers M_2 to M_1. If d is on M_2, then c is on M_3 (since $12 + 4\epsilon < 13 + 2\epsilon$). As a result, d prefers M_1 (since $18 + \epsilon < 18 + 2\epsilon$), so b prefers M_2. Finally, given that e is on M_3, d is not on M_3.
2. b is on M_2: job c prefers M_1, where it completes at time $9 + 2\epsilon$, while after e on M_3 it completes at time $12 + 4\epsilon$. Now d prefers M_2, (since $18 + 2\epsilon < 18 + 3\epsilon$). So b prefers M_1.
3. b is on M_3: Being after e, job b prefers M_1.

Thus, the game G^* has no pure Nash equilibrium.

We can use the above example to show that deciding whether a game instance has a NE is NP-complete by using a reduction from 3-bounded 3-dimensional matching. The proof is omitted. A more involved hardness proof that uses a similar technique is given in the proof of Theorem 12.

Theorem 1. *Given an instance of a scheduling game, it is NP-complete to decide whether the game has a NE.*

Our next results are positive. When combined with known results regarding equilibrium existence, and our example above, we get a tight characterization of classes of instances with a guaranteed Nash equilibrium.

The following algorithm is intended for instances in the class $\mathcal{G}_1$, that is, for all $i \in N$, $w_i = 1$. It assigns the jobs greedily, where in each step, a job is added on a machine on which the cost of the next job is minimal.

Algorithm 1. Calculating a NE of unit-weight jobs on related machines

1: Let ℓ_j denote the number of jobs assigned on machine j. Initially, $\ell_j = 0$ for all $1 \leq j \leq m$.
2: **repeat**
3:    Let $j^* = \arg\min_j \ c_j \cdot (\ell_j + 1)$.
4:    Assign on machine j^* the first unassigned job on its priority list.
5:    $\ell_{j^*} = \ell_{j^*} + 1$.
6: **until** all jobs are scheduled

Theorem 2. *If $w_i = 1$ for all jobs $i \in N$, then Algorithm 1 calculates a NE.*

In fact, for the unweighted case, every sequence of better responses converges in polynomial time. Given a strategy profile s, a strategy s_i' for job $i \in N$ is a better response if $cost_i(s_i', s_{-i}) < cost_i(s)$. The proof of the following theorem is omitted, but analyzes a potential function that is introduced by Gourvès et al. [13].

Theorem 3. *If $w_i = 1$ for all jobs $i \in N$, then jobs reach an equilibrium after polynomially many better response moves.*

Our next result considers the number of machines and completes the picture. Since our inexistence example uses three machines, out of which two are identical (in both delay and priority list), we cannot hope for a wider positive result.

Theorem 4. *If $m \leq 2$, then a NE exists and can be calculated efficiently.*

Proof. For a single machine, the priority list defines the only feasible schedule, which is clearly a NE. For $m = 2$, assume w.l.o.g., that $c_1 = 1$ and $c_2 = c \geq 1$. Consider the following algorithm, which initially assigns all the jobs on the fast machine. Then, the jobs are considered according to their order in π_2, and every job gets an opportunity to migrate to M_2.

Algorithm 2. Calculating a NE schedule on two related machines

1: Assign all the jobs on M_1 (the fast machine) according to their order in π_1.
2: For $1 \leq k \leq n$, let the job i for which $\pi_2(i) = k$ perform a best-response move (migrate to M_2 if this reduces its completion time).

Denote by s^1 the schedule after the first step of the algorithm (where all the jobs are on M_1), and let s denote the schedule after the algorithm terminates. We show that s is a NE.

Claim. No job for which $s_i = 1$ has a beneficial migration.

Proof. Assume by contradiction that job i is assigned on M_1 and has a beneficial migration. Assume that $\pi_2(i) = k$. Job i was offered to perform a migration in the k-th iteration of step 2 of the algorithm, but chose to remain on M_1. The only migrations that took place after the k-th iteration are from M_1 to M_2. Thus, if migrating is beneficial for i after the algorithm completes, it should have been beneficial also during the algorithm, contradicting its choice to remain on M_1.

Claim. No job for which $s_i = 2$ has a beneficial migration.

Proof. Assume by contradiction that the claim is false and let i be the first job on M_2 (first with respect to π_2) that may benefit from returning to M_1. Let s^1 denote the schedule before job i migrates to M_2 - during the second step of the algorithm. Recall that $cost_i(s)$ is the completion time of job i on M_2, and $cost_i(s^1)$ is its completion time on M_1 before its migration.

Since the jobs are activated according to π_2 in the 2-nd step of the algorithm, no jobs are added before job i on M_2. Job i may be interested in returning to M_1 only if some jobs that were processed before it on M_1, move to M_2 after its migration. Denote by Δ the set of these jobs, and let δ be their total weight. Let i' be the last job from Δ to complete its processing in s. Since job i' performs its migration out of M_1 after job i, and jobs do not join M_1 during step 2 of the algorithm, the completion time of i' when it performs the migration is at most $cost_{i'}(s^1)$. The migration from M_1 to M_2 is beneficial for i', thus, $cost_{i'}(s) < cost_{i'}(s^1)$.

The jobs in Δ are all before job i in π_1 and after job i in π_2. Therefore, $cost_{i'}(s^1) < cost_i(s^1)$, and $cost_{i'}(s) \geq cost_i(s) + c\delta$. Finally, we assume that s is not stable and i would like to return to M_1. By returning, its completion time would be $cost_i(s^1) - \delta$. Given that the migration is beneficial for i, and that i is the first job who likes to return to M_2, we have that $cost_i(s^1) - \delta < cost_i(s)$.

Combining the above inequalities, we get

$$cost_i(s^1) < cost_i(s) + \delta \leq cost_{i'}(s) - (c-1)\delta < cost_{i'}(s^1) - (c-1)\delta < cost_i(s^1) - (c-1)\delta.$$

This contradicts the fact that $c \geq 1$ and $\delta \geq 0$.

By combining the two claims, we conclude that s is a NE.   □

3   Equilibrium Inefficiency

Two common measures for evaluating the quality of a schedule are the makespan, given by $C_{max}(s) = \max_{i \in N} cost_i(s)$, and the sum of completion times, given by $\sum_{i \in N} cost_i(s)$. In this section we analyze the equilibrium inefficiency with respect to each of the two objectives, for each of the four classes for which a NE is guaranteed to exist.

We begin with $\mathcal{G}_1$, the class of instances with unweighted jobs. For this class we show that allowing arbitrary priority lists does not hurt the social cost, even on machines with different speeds.

Theorem 5. $PoA(\mathcal{G}_1) = PoS(\mathcal{G}_1) = 1$ *for both the min-makespan and the sum of completion times objective.*

In Theorem 4 it is shown that a NE exists for any instance on two related machines. We now analyze the equilibrium inefficiency of this class. Let $\mathcal{G}_2^c$ denote the class of games played on two machines with delays $c_1 = 1$ and $c_2 = c \geq 1$.

Theorem 6. *For the min-makespan objective, $PoA(\mathcal{G}_2^c) = PoS(\mathcal{G}_2^c) = 1 + \frac{1}{c}$ if $c \geq \frac{\sqrt{5}+1}{2}$, and $PoA(\mathcal{G}_2^c) = PoS(\mathcal{G}_2^c) = 1 + \frac{c}{c+1}$ if $c \leq \frac{\sqrt{5}+1}{2}$.*

Proof. Let $G \in \mathcal{G}_2^c$. Let $W = \sum_i w_i$ be the total weight of all jobs. Assume first that $c \geq \frac{\sqrt{5}+1}{2}$. For the minimum makespan objective, $OPT(G) \geq W/(1+1/c)$. Also, for any NE s, we have that $C_{max}(s) \leq W$, since every job can migrate to be last on the fast machine and have completion time at most W. Thus, PoA $\leq 1 + 1/c$.

Assume next that $c < \frac{\sqrt{5}+1}{2}$. Let job a be the last job to complete in a worst Nash equilibrium s, w_1 be the total weight of all jobs different from a on machine 1, and w_2 be the total weight of all jobs different from a on machine 2 in s. Then since s is a Nash equilibrium, $C_{max}(s) \leq w_1 + w_a$ and $C_{max}(s) \leq c \cdot (w_2 + w_a)$. Combining these two inequalities yields

$$C_{max}(s) \leq \frac{W + w_a}{1 + \frac{1}{c}} \leq (1 + c/(c+1)) \cdot OPT(G),$$

where for the inequality we use that $OPT(G) \geq W/(1+1/c)$ and $OPT(G) \geq w_a$, and thus PoA$\leq 1 + c/(c+1)$.

For the PoS lower bound, assume first that $c > \frac{\sqrt{5}+1}{2}$. Consider an instance consisting of two jobs, a and b, where $w_a = 1$ and $w_b = c$. The priority lists are $\pi_1 = \pi_2 = (a, b)$. The unique NE is that both jobs are on the fast machine. $cost_a(s) = 1, cost_b(s) = c + 1$. For every $c > \frac{\sqrt{5}+1}{2}$, it holds that $c + 1 < c^2$, therefore, job b does not have a beneficial migration. An optimal schedule assigns job a on the slow machine, and both jobs complete at time c. The corresponding PoS is $\frac{c+1}{c} = 1 + \frac{1}{c}$.[1]

Assume now that $c < \frac{\sqrt{5}+1}{2}$. Consider an instance consisting of three jobs, x, y and z, where $w_x = 1, w_y = \frac{1+c-c^2}{c^2}$, and $w_z = \frac{1+c}{c}$. The priority lists are $\pi_1 = \pi_2 = (x, y, z)$. Note that $w_y \geq 0$ for every $c \leq \frac{\sqrt{5}+1}{2}$. The unique NE is when jobs x and z are on the fast machine, and job y on the slow machine. Indeed, job y prefers being alone on the slow machine since $\frac{1+c}{c^2} > \frac{1+c-c^2}{c}$. Job z prefers joining x on the fast machine since $1 + w_z < c(w_y + w_z)$. The makespan is $1 + w_z = \frac{1+2c}{c}$. In an optimal schedule, job z is alone on the fast machine, and jobs x and y are on the slow machine. Both machines have the same completion time $\frac{1+c}{c}$. The PoS is $\frac{1+2c}{1+c} = 1 + \frac{c}{c+1}$. $\square$

Theorem 7. *For the sum of completion times objective, $PoA(\mathcal{G}_2^c) = \Theta(n)$ and $PoS(\mathcal{G}_2^c) = \Theta(n)$ for all $c \geq 1$.*

---

[1] For $c = \frac{\sqrt{5}+1}{2}$, by taking $w_b = c + \epsilon$, the PoS approaches $1 + c/(c+1)$ as $\epsilon \to 0$.

We turn to analyze the equilibrium inefficiency of the class $\mathcal{G}_3$, consisting of games played on identical-speed machines, having machine-based priority lists. The proof of the following theorem is based on the observation that every NE schedule is a possible outcome of Graham's *List-scheduling* (LS) algorithm [14].

Theorem 8. *For the min-makespan objective, $PoA(\mathcal{G}_3) = PoS(\mathcal{G}_3) = 2 - \frac{1}{m}$.*

Theorem 9. *For the sum of completion times objective, $PoA(\mathcal{G}_3) \leq \frac{n-1}{m} + 1$, and for every $\epsilon > 0$, $PoS(\mathcal{G}_3) \geq \frac{n}{m} - \epsilon$.*

The last class of instances for which a NE is guaranteed to exist includes games with a global priority list, and is denoted by $\mathcal{G}_4$. It is easy to verify that for this class, the only NE profiles are those produced by List-Scheduling algorithm, where the jobs are considered according to their order in the priority list. Different NE may be produced by different tie-breaking rules. Thus, the equilibrium inefficiency is identical to the approximation ratio of LS [5]. Since the analysis of LS is tight, this is also the PoS.

Theorem 10. *For the min-makespan objective, $PoS(\mathcal{G}_4) = PoA(\mathcal{G}_4) = \Theta(m)$.*

For the sum of completion times objective, we note that the proof of Theorem 7 for two related machines uses a global priority list. The analysis of the PoA is independent of the number and delays of machines.

Theorem 11. *For the sum of completion times objective, $PoA(\mathcal{G}_4) = \Theta(n)$ and $PoS(\mathcal{G}_4) = \Theta(n)$.*

3.1   Hardness of Approximating the Minimum Makespan NE

Correa and Queyranne [9] showed that if all the machines have the same speeds, but arbitrary priority lists, then a NE is guaranteed to exist, and can be calculated by a simple greedy algorithm. In Theorem 8, we have shown that the PoA is at most $2 - \frac{1}{m}$. In this subsection, we show that we cannot hope for a better algorithm than the simple greedy algorithm. More formally, we prove that it is NP-hard to approximate the best NE within a factor of $2 - \frac{1}{m} - \epsilon$ for all $\epsilon > 0$.

Theorem 12. *If for all machines $c_j = 1$, then it is NP-hard to approximate the best NE w.r.t. the makespan objective within a factor of $2 - \frac{1}{m} - \epsilon$ for all $\epsilon > 0$.*

Proof. We show that for every $\epsilon > 0$, there is an instance on m identical machines for which it is NP-hard to distinguish whether the game has a NE profile with makespan at most $m + 2\epsilon$ or at least $2m - 1$.

The hardness proof is by a reduction from 3-bounded 3-dimensional matching (3DM-3). The input to the 3DM-3 problem is a set of triplets $T \subseteq X \times Y \times Z$, where $|X| = |Y| = |Z| = n$. The number of occurrences of every element of $X \cup Y \cup Z$ in T is at most 3. The number of triplets is $|T| \geq n$. The goal is to decide whether T has a 3D-matching of size n, i.e., there exists a subset $T' \subseteq T$, such that $|T'| = n$, and every element in $X \cup Y \cup Z$ appears exactly once in T'. 3DM-3 is known to be NP-hard [18].

Given an instance of 3DM-3 and $\epsilon > 0$, consider the following game on $m = |T| + 2$ machines, $M_1, M_2, \ldots, M_{|T|+2}$. The set of jobs includes job a of weight m, job b of weight $m - 1$, a set D of $|T| - n$ dummy jobs of weight 3ϵ, two dummy jobs d_1, d_2 of weight 2ϵ, a set U of $(m - 1)^2$ unit-weight jobs, and $3n$ jobs of weight ϵ - one for each element in $X \cup Y \cup Z$.

We turn to describe the priority lists. When the list includes a set, it means that the elements can appear in an arbitrary order. For the first machine, $\pi_1 = (d_1, b, a, U, X, Y, Z, D, d_2)$. For the second machine, $\pi_2 = (d_2, X, Y, Z, b, U, a, d_1)$. The $m - 2$ right machines are *triplet-machines*. For every $t = (x_i, y_j, z_k) \in T$, the priority list of the triplet-machine corresponding to t is $(D, x_i, y_j, z_k, U, X \setminus \{x_j\}, Y \setminus \{y_j\}, Z \setminus \{z_j\}, d_1, d_2, a, b)$.

The heart of the reduction lies in determining the priority lists. The idea is that if a 3D-matching exists, then job b would prefer M_2 and let job a be assigned early on M_1. However, if there is no 3D-matching, then some job originated from the elements in $X \cup Y \cup Z$ will precede job b on M_2, and b's best-response would be on M_1. The jobs in U have higher priority than job a on all the machines except for M_1, thus, unless job a is on M_1, it is assigned after $|U|/(m - 1)$ unit-jobs from U, inducing a schedule with high makespan.

Observe that in any NE, the two dummy jobs of weight 2ϵ are assigned as the first jobs on M_1 and M_2. Also, the dummy jobs in D have the highest priority on the triplet-machines, thus, in every NE, there are $|D| = |T| - n$ triplet-machines on which the first job is from D.

The following two claims complete the proof. Figure 1 provides an example for $m = 5$.

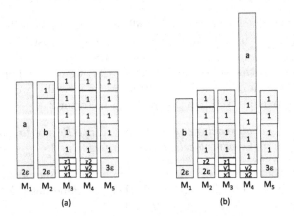

Fig. 1. (a) A NE schedule for $n = 2$ and $T = \{(x_1, y_1, z_1), (x_2, y_2, z_2), (x_1, y_2, z_2)\}$. A matching of size 2 exists. The makespan is $5 + 3\epsilon$. (b) A NE schedule for $T = \{(x_1, y_1, z_1), (x_2, y_2, z_1), (x_1, y_2, z_2)\}$. A matching of size 2 does not exist. The makespan is $9 + 2\epsilon$.

Claim. If a 3D-matching of size n exists, then the game has a NE schedule whose makespan is $m + 2\epsilon$.

Proof. Let T' be a matching of size n. Assign the jobs of $X \cup Y \cup Z$ on the triplet-machines corresponding to T' and the jobs of D on the remaining triplet-machines. Also, assign d_1 and d_2 on M_1 and M_2 respectively. M_1 and M_2 now have load 2ϵ while the triplet machines have load 3ϵ. Next, assign job a on M_1 and job b on M_2. Finally, add the unit-jobs as balanced as possible: m jobs on each triplet-machine and a single job after job b on M_2. It is easy to verify that the resulting assignment is a NE. Its makespan is $m + 3\epsilon$.

Claim. If a 3D-matching of size n does not exist then every NE schedule has makespan at least $2m - 1$.

Proof. Let s be a NE profile of an instance for which a matching does not exist. From the above observations, there are exactly n triplet-machines on which the first element is not from D. Since a matching does not exist, for at least one such machine, there are at most two jobs from $X \cup Y \cup Z$ whose priority is higher than the priority of the unit jobs. Thus, at least one job from $X \cup Y \cup Z$ prefers M_2, and is assigned after d_2. As a result, job b prefers M_1, where it can start being processed at time 2ϵ. Given that job b is on M_1, and that there are at least $m - 1$ unit jobs on each machine, job a cannot start its processing earlier than $m - 1$, implying that its completion time is at least $2m - 1$. □

4 General Congestion Games with Priority Lists

In this last section we consider a generalization of the model that allows for arbitrary strategy sets. First, we show that a Nash equilibrium need not exist and in fact, the question whether a Nash equilibrium exists is NP-complete, even for unweighted players. Recall that in our unweighted singleton game a NE is guaranteed to exist. Second, we show a tight upper bound on the price of anarchy for the sum of weighted costs.

4.1 Unweighted Games

In this subsection, we restrict ourselves to unweighted congestion games with priority lists, i.e., $w_i = 1$ for all $i \in N$. We first provide an example that shows that a Nash equilibrium need not exist. Farzad et al. [11] give a different example with two players for which a NE need not exist. Our example describes a symmetric game.

Example 2. The game, G^* contains 3 unweighted players, $w_i = 1$ for all $i \in N$, and 6 resources. Each players $i \in N$ has two pure strategies: $\{e_1, e_2, e_3\}$ and $\{e_4, e_5, e_6\}$. The delays are equal to 1 for all resources, and the priority lists are $\pi_j(i) = i + j - 1$ (modulo 3) for all $j \in E$ and $i \in N$. Observe that there is no Nash equilibrium if all three players choose the same three resources. Also, due to the Condorcet paradox [8], there is no Nash equilibrium in which two players choose one subset of resources and the other player chooses the other. Specifically, one of these two players has cost 5 and the other has cost 4. By deviating to the other triplet of resources, the player whose cost is 5 can reduce its cost to 4.

A natural question is to decide whether a game instance with unweighted players have a NE profile. Our next result shows that this is NP-complete. The hardness proof is different from the one in Theorem 1, since this proof considers unweighted players and multiple-resources strategies, while that proof is for weighted players and singleton strategies.

Theorem 13. *Given an instance of a congestion game with priority lists, it is NP-complete to decide whether the game has a NE profile. This is valid also for unweighted players.*

4.2   Equilibrium Inefficiency

We consider the sum of weighted players' costs as a measure of the quality of a strategy profile. Our analysis below is for linear cost functions, and is trivially extended to affine cost functions. A game G is said to be (λ, μ)-*smooth* if for all strategy profiles s, s' we have

$$\sum_{i \in N} cost_i(s'_i, s_{-i}) \leq \lambda \cdot cost(s') + \mu \cdot cost(s).$$

Roughgarden [22] showed that if a game G is (λ, μ)-smooth with $\lambda > 0$ and $\mu < 1$, then PoA(G)$\leq \frac{\lambda}{1-\mu}$.

Theorem 14. *Every congestion game with resource-specific priority lists is* $\left(2, \frac{1}{2}\right)$-*smooth. Hence* $PoA(\mathcal{G}) \leq 4$.

Proof. Given a strategy profile s, define $w_e(s) = \sum_{i' \in N: e \in s_{i'}} w_{i'}$. For all s, s',

$$\sum_{i \in N} cost_i(s'_i, s_{-i})$$

$$\leq \sum_{i \in N} \sum_{e \in s'_i} w_i \cdot c_e \cdot (w_e(s) + w_i) = \sum_{e \in E} c_e \cdot \left(w_e(s') \cdot w_e(s) + \sum_{i \in N: e \in s'_i} w_i^2 \right)$$

$$\leq \sum_{e \in E} c_e \cdot \left(w_e(s')^2 + \frac{1}{4} \cdot w_e(s)^2 + \sum_{i \in N: e \in s'_i} w_i^2 \right) \leq 2 \cdot cost(s') + \frac{1}{2} \cdot cost(s),$$

where the second inequality follows from $\left(w_e(s') - \frac{1}{2} \cdot w_e(s) \right)^2 \geq 0$ and the third inequality from $cost(s) = \sum_{e \in E} \frac{1}{2} \cdot c_e \cdot \left(w_e(s)^2 + \sum_{i \in N: e \in s_i} w_i^2 \right)$ for all s.   □

Correa and Queyranne [9] give an example that shows that the bound of 4 is tight for restricted singleton congestion games with priority lists derived from Smith's rule.

References

1. Ackermann, H., Goldberg, P., Mirrokni, V.S., Röglin, H., Vöcking, B.: A unified approach to congestion games and two-sided markets. Internet Math. **5**(4), 439–457 (2008)
2. Anshelevich, E., Dasgupta, A., Kleinberg, J., Tardos, E., Wexler, T., Roughgarden, T.: The price of stability for network design with fair cost allocation. SIAM J. Comput. **38**(4), 1602–1623 (2008)
3. Awerbuch, B., Azar, Y., Richter, Y., Tsur, D.: Tradeoffs in worst-case equilibria. Theor. Comput. Sci. **361**(2–3), 200–209 (2006)
4. Caragiannis, I., Gkatzelis, V., Vinci, C.: Coordination mechanisms, cost-sharing, and approximation algorithms for scheduling. In: Devanur, N.R., Lu, P. (eds.) WINE 2017. LNCS, vol. 10660, pp. 74–87. Springer, Cham (2017). https://doi.org/10.1007/978-3-319-71924-5_6
5. Cho, Y., Sahni, S.: Bounds for list schedules on uniform processors. SIAM J. Comput. **9**(1), 91–103 (1980). https://doi.org/10.1137/0209007
6. Christodoulou, G., Koutsoupias, E., Nanavati, A.: Coordination mechanisms. In: Díaz, J., Karhumäki, J., Lepistö, A., Sannella, D. (eds.) ICALP 2004. LNCS, vol. 3142, pp. 345–357. Springer, Heidelberg (2004). https://doi.org/10.1007/978-3-540-27836-8_31
7. Cole, R., Correa, J., Gkatzelis, V., Mirrokni, V., Olver, N.: Decentralized utilitarian mechanisms for scheduling games. Games Econ. Behav. **92**, 306–326 (2015)
8. Marquis de Condorcet, M.J.A.: Essai sur l'application de l'analyse a la probabilite des decisions: rendues a la pluralite de voix. De l'Imprimerie royale (1785)
9. Correa, J., Queyranne, M.: Efficiency of equilibria in restricted uniform machine scheduling with total weighted completion time as social cost. Naval Res. Logistics **59**(5), 384–395 (2012)
10. Czumaj, A., Vöcking, B.: Tight bounds for worst-case equilibria. ACM Trans. Algorithms **3**(1), 4 (2007)
11. Farzad, B., Olver, N., Vetta, A.: A priority-based model of routing. Chicago J. Theor. Comput. Sci. **1** (2008)
12. Gairing, M., Lücking, T., Mavronicolas, M., Monien, B.: Computing nash equilibria for scheduling on restricted parallel links. Theory Comput. Syst. **47**(2), 405–432 (2010)
13. Gourvès, L., Monnot, J., Moretti, S., Thang, N.K.: Congestion games with capacitated resources. Theory Comput. Syst. **57**(3), 598–616 (2015)
14. Graham, R.: Bounds for certain multiprocessing anomalies. Bell Syst. Tech. J. **45**(9), 1563–1581 (1966)
15. Hoeksma, R., Uetz, M.: The price of anarchy for utilitarian scheduling games on related machines. Discrete Optim. **31**, 29–39 (2019)
16. Ibarra, O.H., Kim, C.E.: Heuristic algorithms for scheduling independent tasks on nonidentical processors. J. ACM (JACM) **24**(2), 280–289 (1977)
17. Immorlica, N., Li, L.E., Mirrokni, V., Schulz, A.: Coordination mechanisms for selfish scheduling. Theor. Comput. Sci. **410**(17), 1589–1598 (2009)
18. Kann, V.: Maximum bounded 3-dimensional matching is MAX SNP-complete. Inf. Process. Lett. **37**(1), 27–35 (1991)
19. Koutsoupias, E., Papadimitriou, C.: Worst-case equilibria. In: Meinel, C., Tison, S. (eds.) STACS 1999. LNCS, vol. 1563, pp. 404–413. Springer, Heidelberg (1999). https://doi.org/10.1007/3-540-49116-3_38

20. Piliouras, G., Nikolova, E., Shamma, J.S.: Risk sensitivity of price of anarchy under uncertainty. ACM Trans. Econo. Comput. **5**, 5–27 (2016)
21. Rosenthal, R.: A class of games possessing pure-strategy nash equilibria. Int. J. Game Theory **2**(1), 65–67 (1973)
22. Roughgarden, T.: Intrinsic robustness of the price of anarchy. J. ACM **62**(5), 32 (2015)
23. Smith, W.E.: Various optimizers for single-stage production. Naval Res. Logistics Q. **3**(1–2), 59–66 (1956)
24. Vöcking, B.: Algorithmic Game Theory, Chap. 20: Selfish Load Balancing. Cambridge University Press (2007)

Optimal Search Segmentation Mechanisms for Online Platform Markets

Zhenzhe Zheng[1]($\boxtimes$) and R. Srikant[2]

[1] Coordinated Science Lab, University of Illinois at Urbana-Champaign,
Champaign, USA
zhenzhe@illinois.edu
[2] Coordinated Science Lab, Department of Electrical and Computer Engineering,
University of Illinois at Urbana-Champaign, Champaign, USA
rsrikant@illinois.edu

Abstract. Online platforms, such as Airbnb, hotels.com, Amazon, Uber and Lyft, can control and optimize many aspects of product search to improve the efficiency of marketplaces. Here we focus on a common model, called the discriminatory control model, where the platform chooses to display a subset of sellers who sell products at prices determined by the market and a buyer is interested in buying a single product from one of the sellers. Under the commonly-used model for single product selection by a buyer, called the multinomial logit model, and the Bertrand game model for competition among sellers, we show the following result: to maximize social welfare, the optimal strategy for the platform is to display all products; however, to maximize revenue, the optimal strategy is to only display a subset of the products whose qualities are above a certain threshold. This threshold depends on the quality of all products, and can be computed in linear time in the number of products.

Keywords: Online platform markets · Bertrand competition game · Search segmentation

1 Introduction

In recent years, we have witnessed the rise of many successful online platform markets, which have reshaped the economic landscape of modern world. The online platforms facilitate the exchange of goods and services between buyers and sellers. For example, buyers can purchase goods from sellers on Amazon, eBay and Etsy, arrange accommodation from hosts on Airbnb and Expedia, order transportation services from drivers on Uber and Lyft, and find qualified workers on online labor markets, such as Upwork and Taskrabbit. The total

Research supported by NSF grants NeTS 1718203, CPS ECCS 1739189, CMMI 1562276, ECCS 16-09370, China Postdoctoral Science Foundation NO. 2018M642018.

I. Caragiannis et al. (Eds.): WINE 2019, LNCS 11920, pp. 301–315, 2019.
https://doi.org/10.1007/978-3-030-35389-6_22

market value of online platforms has exceeded 4.3 trillion dollars worldwide, and is growing quickly [10].

Compared with traditional markets, the modern online marketplaces have greater controls over price determination, search and discovery, information revelation, recommendation, etc. For example, Uber and Lyft adopt the *full control model*, in which the ride-sharing platforms use online matching algorithms to determine matches between drivers and riders as well as the fee for the route. Amazon and Airbnb use the *discriminatory control model*, where the platforms only control the list of products to display for each buyer's search, and the potential matches and transaction prices are determined by the preference of buyers and the competition among sellers. The platform can also use other types of control, such as commissions/subscriptions fees [7], to influence the outcomes of markets. The rich control options for online platforms have led to an increasing discussion about the design of online marketplaces with different optimization objectives [4,5,14].

In this paper, we investigate social welfare and revenue optimization under the discriminatory control model for online marketplaces. In the discriminatory control model, the platform has only control over *search segmentation mechanisms - which products to display for each buyer's search*, and the transaction prices are endogenously determined by the competition among sellers. Unlike traditional firms, most online platforms do not manufacture goods or provide services, and thus they also do not dictate the specific transaction prices. Instead, buyers and sellers jointly determine the prices at which the goods or services will be traded. For example, sellers set prices for their goods on Amazon, hosts decide on the price for their properties on Airbnb, and freelancers negotiate employers with hourly fee on Upwork. These prices depend on the demand and supply for comparable goods and services in the market, and choosing different products to display for buyers impacts the transaction prices and then the social welfare and revenue. Motivated by this, we study the role of search segmentation mechanisms in social welfare and revenue optimization in the discriminatory control model with endogenous prices.

To calculate the social welfare and revenue, we first need to specify demand and supply in online marketplaces. Much of prior work simply represent the demand/supply curves with non-increasing/non-decreasing distributions [5,7]. Instead, we consider a demand and supply function derived from a basic market setting in which each seller has one unit of product to offer, and each buyer demands at most one unit of product chosen from the products displayed to her[1]. Given the quality and prices of products, the demand for each product is equivalent to the proportion of potential buyers that purchase such a product. Thus, the demand function is closely related to the purchase behaviors of buyers who face multiple substitutable products. We adopt the standard multinomial logit (MNL) model [16] to describe buyers' choice behaviors, and then derive the demand as a softmax function. With such a specific demand function,

---

[1] Throughout the article, we use product to refer good/service, and use the terms of product and seller interchangeably.

we can model the competition among sellers via a Bertrand price competition game, which is a useful model for investigating oligopolistic competition in real markets [23]. For instance, the Bertrand game can model the situation where the hosts on Airbnb compete for potential guests by setting prices for their properties. The basic questions for the Bertrand competition game are existence, uniqueness, closed-form expression and learning algorithm of the equilibrium. The results in [2,11] have shown that there exists a unique (pure) Nash equilibrium in the Bertrand game with a MNL model. Furthermore, the Nash equilibrium coincides with the solution of a system of first-order-condition equations. We can then characterize the Nash equilibrium in a "closed" form, and express the equilibrium social welfare/revenue by employing a variant of Lambert W function [8]. We also derive myopic learning strategies, *i.e.*, best response dynamics, for sellers to reach the Nash equilibrium in practice.

The online platform can further optimize the equilibrium social welfare/revenue by employing search segmentation mechanisms. Different sets of sellers involved in the Bertrand competition game lead to different equilibrium solutions. The goal of the search segmentation mechanisms is to efficiently choose a set of products to display for buyers (or in other words, choose a set of sellers to compete in the Bertrand game) that maximizes the equilibrium social welfare or revenue. This display control optimization problem is combinatorial in nature and the number of possible product sets can be very large, particularly when there are many potential products to offer. One of our main contributions is to identify the efficient and optimal search segmentation mechanism, which turns out to have a simple structure. We show that the online platform *will display all products to maximize equilibrium social welfare, but just display the top k^* highest quality products to maximize equilibrium revenue*. We also refer the optimal mechanism for revenue maximization as *quality-order mechanism*. The optimal threshold k^* depends on the quality of all products, and can be calculated in linear time in terms of the number of products. The optimality of such simple search segmentation mechanisms has crucial theoretical and practical implications. On the theoretical side, this result allows the platform to find the optimal set of displayed products in linear time, significantly reducing the computational complexity. On the practical side, optimality of quality-order mechanism is quite appealing as it guarantees that a lower quality product will not be chosen for display over a higher quality product. Moreover, in order to increase the opportunity of being selected, sellers would improve the quality of their products as product quality is the selection criteria of the optimal mechanism, which will benefit all the market participants in the long term.

The optimality of the quality-order mechanism for revenue maximization is established by making a novel connection between the quasi-convexity of equilibrium revenue function and the optimal control decision on selecting displayed products. We show that in the Bertrand game with a given subset of sellers, the equilibrium revenue can be expressed as a quasi-convex function with respective to an independent variable, which is a one-to-one transformation of the quality of a candidate product. The property of quasi-convexity guarantees that the maximum revenue can be obtained at one of the two endpoints, which corresponds to the options of displaying the current set of products or involving a new product with the highest quality among the remaining products. With this critical observation, if the platform decides to add a new product, it will always select the available product with the highest quality. Thus, we can efficiently construct the optimal set of displayed products from any product set. Specifically, if the current product set does not contain all the top k^* products, we can further improve the equilibrium revenue by repeatedly replacing one currently selected product with an unselected product with a higher quality.

Our work in this paper is related to work on the design of markets for networked platforms [1,5,6,15,19]. We present a detailed discussion of related work towards the end of the paper. Here, we briefly discuss the similarities and differences between our work and prior work on networked market platforms. In networked markets, there are buyers and sellers connected by a bipartite graph, where each link indicates that a specific buyer is allowed to buy from a specific seller. The goal is to remove links from the complete bipartite graph to maximize either social welfare or revenue. However, much of the prior work focuses on a linear price-demand curve which does not explicitly model situations where each buyer is interested in buying only one product (such as one copy of a book) and each buyer takes into account the quality of each product (available typically in the form of reviews) while making a buying decision. For such situations, economists use the MNL model, which we have adopted in this paper. On the other hand, compared to prior work on networked markets, we only consider a much simpler bipartite graph where there is only one representative buyer. Such a model is appropriate when there are no capacity constraints for products at a seller, for example, each seller may have many copies of a book and there is no danger of immediately selling out a particular book title. The model is also appropriate for hotels.com-type settings in situations when most hotels have multiple available rooms. In situations where multiple buyers are performing searches simultaneously and hotels are about to sell out of rooms, capacity constraints do matter. Such capacity-constrained situations have not been studied either in this paper or in prior work, and is a topic for future research.

We now summarize the main contributions of this paper.

- We introduce a stylized model to capture the main features of online platform markets. We explicitly model the market, where each buyer is interested in purchasing one product, and takes into account the quality of products when making choice. Specifically, the demand function for products is derived from the multinomial logit (MNL) choice model, and the supply response of sellers is described by the outcome of Bertrand competition game. We show that the Bertrand game exists a unique (pure) Nash equilibrium, and the best response dynamics converge to the equilibrium. We also explicitly express the social welfare and revenue under the equilibrium.

- We design efficient search segmentation mechanisms to optimize equilibrium social welfare and revenue under the Bertrand model of competition. We first prove that it is optimal to display all products to maximize social welfare. For revenue maximization, we then show that the optimal mechanism, referred to as quality-order mechanism, only needs to display the top k^* highest quality products, where the optimal number of products k^* can be found in linear time.

- We prove the result for social welfare maximization by showing the equilibrium social welfare function is decreasing with respective to an independent variable, which also decreases for involving a new product. We establish the optimality of the quality-order mechanism for revenue maximization by making a novel connection between the quasi-convexity of equilibrium revenue function and the optimal decision on selecting displayed products.

2   Preliminaries

We consider a two-sided market with n sellers $\mathbb{S} = \{1, 2, \cdots, n\}$ and one *representative* buyer, representing a set of homogeneous buyers. Each seller $i \in \mathbb{S}$ offers a product with quality θ_i and price p_i. We denote the quality and price vectors by $\boldsymbol{\theta} = (\theta_1, \theta_2, \cdots, \theta_n)$ and $\boldsymbol{p} = (p_1, p_2, \cdots, p_n)$, respectively. The quality vector $\boldsymbol{\theta}$ is fixed, while the price vector $\boldsymbol{p}$ is determined by the competition among sellers. Without loss of generality, we assume the products' quality and prices are non-negative, *i.e.*, $\theta_i \geq 0$ and $p_i \geq 0$, and the sellers are sorted according to the product quality in a non-decreasing order, *i.e.*, $\theta_1 \geq \theta_2 \geq \cdots \geq \theta_n$. Given the quality $\boldsymbol{\theta}$ and prices $\boldsymbol{p}$ of all products, the buyer purchases one of the n products, or adopts an outside option, *i.e.*, buys nothing from this market. We normalize the problem parameters so that outside option's quality θ_0 and price p_0 are zero, *i.e.*, $\theta_0 = p_0 = 0$.

In the random utility model [17], the buyer derives utility u_i from purchasing the product $i \in \mathbb{S}$ or selecting the outside option $i = 0$ as follows

$$u_i \triangleq \theta_i + \xi_i - p_i,$$

where ξ_i is a random variable representing buyer's (private) preference about the ith alternative. Given the $n+1$ choices (n products and the outside option), the buyer selects the alternative with the maximum utility. Under the standard assumption that the random variables $\{\xi_i\}$ are independent and identically distributed (i.i.d.) with Gumbel distribution [3,12], it can be shown [3,16] that the buyer selects the alternative $i \in \{0\} \cup \mathbb{S}$ with probability

$$q_i(\boldsymbol{p}) \triangleq Pr(u_i = \max_{j \in \{0\} \cup \mathbb{S}} u_j) = \frac{a_i}{1 + \sum_{j \in \mathbb{S}} a_j}, \tag{1}$$

where $a_i = \exp(\theta_i - p_i)$ for all $i \in \mathbb{S}$. We refer to q_i as *demand* or *market share* of the alternative $i \in \{0\} \cup \mathbb{S}$. We can also interpret q_i as the expected sales of quantity of product i normalized by the total number of potential buyers. This choice model is known as multinomial logit (MNL) model in economic literature [3,12,16]. We use $\boldsymbol{q} = (q_0, q_1, \cdots, q_n)$ to denote the demands of products.

Under the above model, we can also obtain an explicit form for the utility $\bar{u}$ of the representative buyer

$$\bar{u} \triangleq \mathbb{E}[\max_{i \in \{0\} \cup \mathbb{S}} u_i] = \log(1 + \sum_{i \in \mathbb{S}} a_i).$$

From the demand $q_i(\boldsymbol{p})$ in (1), we can express seller i's expected revenue $r_i(\boldsymbol{p})$ in terms of prices

$$r_i(\boldsymbol{p}) \triangleq p_i \times q_i(\boldsymbol{p}) = p_i \times \frac{a_i}{1 + \sum_{j \in \mathbb{S}} a_j}. \tag{2}$$

The social welfare of the two-sided market is measured by the sum of buyer's utility and the total revenue of sellers, $i.e.,$

$$sw(\boldsymbol{p}) \triangleq \bar{u} + \sum_{i \in \mathbb{S}} r_i(\boldsymbol{p}) = \log(1 + \sum_{j \in \mathbb{S}} a_j) + \sum_{i \in \mathbb{S}} p_i \times \frac{a_i}{1 + \sum_{j \in \mathbb{S}} a_j}. \tag{3}$$

The revenue of the market is the total revenue of all sellers, $i.e.,$

$$re(\boldsymbol{p}) \triangleq \sum_{i \in \mathbb{S}} r_i(\boldsymbol{p}) = \sum_{i \in \mathbb{S}} p_i \times \frac{a_i}{1 + \sum_{j \in \mathbb{S}} a_j}. \tag{4}$$

We now note the relation between price and demand in the MNL model, which would be quite useful for optimization and analysis later. Using the price-demand model in (1), we can express the price p_i in terms of demands $\boldsymbol{q}$:

$$p_i(\boldsymbol{q}) = \theta_i + \log(1 - \sum_{j \in S} q_j) - \log(q_i). \tag{5}$$

The social welfare and revenue optimization would become convenient if we work with the demands **q** rather than the prices **p**. For example, the social welfare and revenue functions are not concave in **p**, but become jointly concave if we express the functions in terms of **q** [9,13,21]. We can leverage this property to derive the optimal prices for social welfare and revenue maximization in the full control model, where the platform can control both price and displayed products. We leave the detailed discussion in Appendix A of technical report [24].

3   Bertrand Competition Game

In discriminatory control model, the online platform can only control the list of products to display for buyers, and the transaction prices are endogenously determined by the oligopolistic competition among sellers. In a Bertrand competition game, the seller of each product sets a price. Based on the prices of the products and the set of available products, the market produces a certain demand for each product. In our MNL model, the demand is simply the probability with which a product will be purchased by the buyer. This is the typical situation in a Airbnb-like model, where the owner of each rental unit sets a price, the platform controls the manner in which the rental units are displayed, and the renter selects a unit to rent.

In this section, we investigate the existence and uniqueness of equilibrium in the Bertrand competition game, explicitly express the equilibrium social welfare/revenue, and derive the best response dynamics to reach the Nash equilibrium. We assume that only a subset $S \subseteq \mathbb{S}$ of sellers are involved in the game. In other words, we assume that the platform has chosen to display the products of a subset S of the sellers. In the next section, we will show how the choice of S can be optimized by the platform to maximize either social welfare or revenue.

In the Bertrand competition game, seller $i \in S$ selects price p_i to maximize her revenue $r_i(\boldsymbol{p}) = p_i \times q_i(\boldsymbol{p})$, where the demand $q_i(\boldsymbol{p})$ is determined by the prices $\boldsymbol{p}$ of all products in (1). We can formally represent the Bertrand game as a triplet $G^b = (S, (\mathcal{P}_i)_{i \in S}, (r_i)_{i \in S})$, where S is a set of players, $\mathcal{P}_i$ is the strategy space of player $i \in S$ (i.e., $\mathcal{P}_i \triangleq \{p_i | p_i \geq 0\}$), and $r_i(\boldsymbol{p})$ is the payoff of player $i \in S$. We represent the set of strategy profiles by $\mathcal{P} = \mathcal{P}_1 \times \mathcal{P}_2 \times \cdots \times \mathcal{P}_n$. We also denote the strategy profile $\boldsymbol{p} \in \mathcal{P}$ as $\boldsymbol{p} = (p_i, \boldsymbol{p}_{-i})$, where $\boldsymbol{p}_{-i}$ is the strategies (or prices) of all the players except i. For such Bertrand game, we have the following result from [11].

Theorem 1. *There exists a unique (pure) Nash equilibrium in the Bertrand game $G^b = (S, (\mathcal{P}_i)_{i \in S}, (r_i)_{i \in S})$. A vector of prices $\bar{\boldsymbol{p}} = (\bar{p}_1, \bar{p}_2, \cdots, \bar{p}_n) \in \mathcal{P}$ satisfies $\partial r_i(\bar{\boldsymbol{p}})/\partial p_i = 0$ for all $i \in S$ if and only if $\bar{\boldsymbol{p}}$ is a Nash equilibrium in $\mathcal{P}$.*

We next calculate a closed-form expression for the Nash equilibrium prices $\bar{\boldsymbol{p}}$. For each seller $i \in S$, by the first-order condition $\partial r_i(\bar{\boldsymbol{p}})/\partial p_i = 0$, we have the following relation for $\bar{p}_i$:

$$\bar{p}_i = \frac{1 + \sum_{j \in S} \bar{a}_j}{1 + \sum_{j \in S} \bar{a}_j - \bar{a}_i} = \frac{1}{1 - \bar{q}_i}, \tag{6}$$

where $\bar{a}_i \triangleq \exp(\theta_i - \bar{p}_i)$ and $\bar{q}_i$ is the demand of product i at the equilibrium, i.e., $\bar{q}_i \triangleq \bar{a}_i/(1 + \sum_{j \in S} \bar{a}_j)$. From the price function in (5) and with some calculations applied to (6), we have the following equations

$$\bar{q}_0 \times \exp(\theta_i - 1) = \bar{q}_i \times \exp(\frac{\bar{q}_i}{1 - \bar{q}_i}), \quad \forall i \in S, \tag{7}$$

where $\bar{q}_0 \triangleq 1 - \sum_{j \in S} \bar{q}_j$ is the probability of the buyer that purchases nothing. We introduce a function $V(x) : (0, +\infty) \to (0, 1)$, such that for any $x \in (0, \infty)$, $V(x)$ is the solution $v \in (0, 1)$ satisfying

$$v \times \exp(\frac{v}{1 - v}) = x. \tag{8}$$

We can verify that $V(x)$ is a strictly increasing and concave function over $[0, +\infty)$. This function is similar to the Lambert function $W(x)$ [8], which is the solution w satisfying $w \times exp(w) = x$. With the function $V(x)$ and (7), we can obtain a closed-form expression for the demand $\bar{q}_i = V(\bar{q}_0 \times \exp(\theta_i - 1))$.

Combing with the definition of $\bar{q}_0$, we can determine $\bar{q}_0$ by solving the following single-variable equation

$$\sum_{i\in S} V(\bar{q}_0 \times \exp(\theta_i - 1)) = 1 - \bar{q}_0. \tag{9}$$

This equation has a unique solution because $V(x)$ is a strictly increasing function. We also refer this equation as the equilibrium constraint. The next theorem presents a closed-form expression for the Nash equilibrium solution in the Bertrand competition game.

Theorem 2. *In the Bertrand game $G^b = (S, (\mathcal{P}_i)_{i\in S}, (r_i)_{i\in S})$, the Nash equilibrium price $\bar{p}_i$ and the demand $\bar{q}_i$ for each product $i \in S$ are given by*

$$\bar{p}_i = \frac{1}{1 - V(\bar{q}_0 \times \exp(\theta_i - 1))} \quad and \quad \bar{q}_i = V(\bar{q}_0 \times \exp(\theta_i - 1)),$$

where $\bar{q}_0$ is the unique solution to (9).

Substituting the equilibrium solutions into (3), we obtain the equilibrium social welfare in the Bertrand game with the sellers $S \subseteq \mathbb{S}$

$$\overline{sw}(S) = -\log(\bar{q}_0) + \sum_{i\in S} \frac{\bar{q}_i}{1 - \bar{q}_i}. \tag{10}$$

By (4), we can similarly get the equilibrium revenue in the Bertrand game with the set of sellers $S \subseteq \mathbb{S}$

$$\overline{re}(S) = \sum_{i\in S} \frac{\bar{q}_i}{1 - \bar{q}_i}. \tag{11}$$

Instead of directly deriving the equilibrium strategies in one single step, in practice, the sellers may employ some simple, natural and myopic learning algorithms, such as best response, fictitious play or no-regret learning algorithm, to interact with each other and eventually reach the equilibrium. One straightforward procedure for sellers in online platform markets to reach the Nash equilibrium is best response dynamics. Specifically, suppose that the current vector of price $\mathbf{p}$ is not a Nash equilibrium, and a seller $i \in S$ deviates by setting a new p_i^*, which is the optimal price with respective to the other prices $\mathbf{p}_{-i}$, *i.e.*,

$$p_i^* = B(\mathbf{p}_{-i}) \triangleq \arg\max_{p\in[0,+\infty)} r_i(p, \mathbf{p}_{-i}).$$

We can verify that the revenue function $r_i(p, \mathbf{p}_{-i})$ is strictly quasi-concave in p, and thus it is not easy to explicitly solve the above optimization problem. One key observation is that the revenue function is strictly concave in the domain of the demand, which enables us to obtain closed-form expressions for the best response strategies, as shown in the following lemma.

Lemma 1. *The best response price p_i^* with respective to a fixed price vector $\boldsymbol{p}_{-i}$ can be calculated as*

$$p_i^* = \theta_i - log((1 + \sum_{j \in S \setminus \{i\}} a_j) \times W(\frac{exp(\theta_i - 1)}{1 + \sum_{j \in S \setminus \{i\}} a_j})),$$

where $W(x)$ is the Lambert function and $a_j = exp(\theta_j - p_j)$ for all $j \in S$.

The proof of Lemma 1 is in Appendix B of technical report [24]. We further have the following result for such best response dynamics in the Bertrand game.

Lemma 2. *From an arbitrary price vector $\boldsymbol{p}$, the best response dynamics converge to the Nash equilibrium of the Bertrand game in a finite number of steps.*

The basic idea to derive this result is to show the Bertrand game is an ordinal potential game [18] with a finite value; the detailed proof of Lemma 2 is in Appendix C of technical report [24].

4 Optimal Segmenting Mechanisms

In online marketplaces, the platform has control over search segmentation mechanisms - which set of products to display for a buyer. The platform can display any set of products, and the competition among selected sellers then takes place endogenously through the Bertrand game in Sect. 3. The goal of the platform is to decide the optimal products $S^* \subseteq \mathbb{S}$ to display, in order to maximize the equilibrium social welfare/revenue. For n potential products in the market, there are $2^n - 1$ possible sets of products, thus an exhaustive search to determine the optimal set of displayed products is infeasible. We also note that the equilibrium constraint (9) imposed by the Bertrand competition game is highly nonlinear, which presents another challenge in deriving the optimal search segmentation mechanisms. In this section, we exploit the structure of social welfare/revenue functions to efficiently design the optimal search segmentation mechanisms.

4.1 Social Welfare Maximization

In the following theorem, we show the online platform would display all products to maximize social welfare.

Theorem 3. *For social welfare maximization, the optimal search segmentation mechanism is to display all products $\mathbb{S}$ in the platform.*

Proof. We prove this theorem by showing that adding a new product will always improve the equilibrium social welfare. Suppose the platform has already selected sellers $S \subset \mathbb{S}$, and consider introducing a new product $j \in \mathbb{S} \setminus S$. According to (10), we can express the equilibrium social welfare $\overline{sw}$ as

$$\overline{sw} = -\log \bar{q}_0 + \sum_{i \in S} \frac{\bar{q}_i}{1 - \bar{q}_i} + \frac{x_j \times \bar{q}_j}{1 - x_j \times \bar{q}_j}. \tag{12}$$

Here, $\bar{q}_i$ is a function of q_0, *i.e.*, $\bar{q}_i = V(\bar{q}_0 \times \exp(\theta_i - 1))$ and x_j is an indicator for product $j \in \mathbb{S}\backslash S$, where $x_j = 1$ denotes product j is selected for display; otherwise $x_j = 0$. It is difficult to directly compare $\overline{sw}$ with $x_j = 1$ and the one with $x_j = 0$. From (9), the demands $\boldsymbol{q}$ satisfy the equilibrium constraint:

$$1 - \bar{q}_0 = \sum_{i \in S} \bar{q}_i + x_j \times \bar{q}_j = \sum_{i \in S} V(\bar{q}_0 \exp(\theta_i - 1)) + x_j \times V(\bar{q}_0 \exp(\theta_j - 1)). \quad (13)$$

Since $V(x)$ is an increasing function, we can observe from the above equation that $\bar{q}_0$ decreases when x_j changes from 0 to 1. Furthermore, with (12) and (13), we can express the equilibrium social welfare as a function of $\bar{q}_0$:

$$\overline{sw}(\bar{q}_0) = -\log \bar{q}_0 + \sum_{i \in S} \frac{\bar{q}_i}{1 - \bar{q}_i} + \frac{1 - \bar{q}_0 - \sum_{i \in S} \bar{q}_i}{\bar{q}_0 + \sum_{i \in S} \bar{q}_i}. \quad (14)$$

Thus, we only need to prove $\overline{sw}(\bar{q}_0)$ is a decreasing function. The basic idea is to explicitly calculate the first derivative of $\overline{sw}(\bar{q}_0)$, and show $\overline{sw}'(\bar{q}_0) < 0$. We put the detailed proof of the following lemma in Appendix D of technical report [24].

Lemma 3. *The social welfare $\overline{sw}(\bar{q}_0)$ is a decreasing function.*

From this lemma and the above discussion, we can always improve the equilibrium social welfare by adding a new product, which completes the proof. □

4.2 Revenue Maximization

The optimal search segmentation mechanism with the objective of revenue maximization is different from the optimal mechanism when the platform attempts to maximize social welfare. To illustrate this difference, we consider two cases: a low quality case, *e.g.*, $\theta_1 = \theta_2 = \cdots = \theta_n = 0.5$, and a high quality case, *e.g.*, $\theta_1 = \theta_2 = \cdots = \theta_n = 10$. From the result in Theorem 3, the optimal mechanisms for social welfare maximization in these two cases are to display all products. However, for revenue maximization, it can be verified that the platform still displays all products in the low quality case, but only selects the first product in the high quality case. The intuition behind this difference is that in some scenarios, the platform can further improve price and then revenue by reducing the competition among sellers. We next show the design rationale for the optimal search segmentation mechanisms for the revenue maximization.

One critical decision the platform has to make is the following: given a set of products $S \subset \mathbb{S}$, whether to just display the currently selected product set S, or add a new product j from $\mathbb{S}\backslash S$. We refer to such a decision problem as the "incremental" problem. Similar to the discussion on social welfare maximization, given a set of selected products $S \subset \mathbb{S}$, we can represent the equilibrium revenue under these two decision options with the following function:

$$\overline{re} = \sum_{i \in S} \frac{\bar{q}_i}{1 - \bar{q}_i} + \frac{x_j \times \bar{q}_j}{1 - x_j \times \bar{q}_j}. \quad (15)$$

We recall that x_j is an indicator for product $j \in \mathbb{S} \backslash S$, where $x_j = 1$ indicates that product j is selected for display; otherwise $x_j = 0$. The demands $\bar{q}_i$'s need to satisfy the following equilibrium constraint:

$$1 - \bar{q}_0 = \sum_{i \in S} \bar{q}_i + x_j \times \bar{q}_j = \sum_{i \in S} \bar{q}_i + x_j \times V(\bar{q}_0 \times \exp(\theta_j - 1)). \qquad (16)$$

Since $V(x)$ is an increasing function, we have a critical observation from (16): given a selected product set S, *the quality θ_j of the potential product $j \in \mathbb{S} \backslash S$ has a one-to-one and inverse relation with the demand $\bar{q}_0$*, i.e., when $x_j = 1$, involving the product with a higher quality θ_j leads to the lower value of q_0. With this observation, we can derive the feasible range of the independent value $\bar{q}_0$. On the one hand, when the platform selects the available product with the highest quality, i.e., the product $j \in \mathbb{S} \backslash S$ with $\theta_j \geq \theta_{j'}$ for all $j' \in \mathbb{S} \backslash S$, the demand $\bar{q}_0$ achieves its lower bound at $\bar{q}_0^{min}$. On the other hand, setting x_j to 0 represent the case that the platform does not select any new product, and the corresponding demand $\bar{q}_0^{max}$ in this case is the upper bound of $\bar{q}_0$. Thus, we have $\bar{q}_0 \in [\bar{q}_0^{min}, \bar{q}_0^{max}]$ for the decision on selecting different product $j \in \mathbb{S} \backslash S$.

Using Eq. (16), we can replace $x_j \times \bar{q}_j$ with $1 - \bar{q}_0 - \sum_{i \in S} \bar{q}_i$ in (15) to express the equilibrium revenue as a function of $\bar{q}_0$:

$$\overline{re}(\bar{q}_0) = \sum_{i \in S} \frac{\bar{q}_i}{1 - \bar{q}_i} + \frac{1}{\bar{q}_0 + \sum_{i \in S} \bar{q}_i} - 1. \qquad (17)$$

Such revenue function indeed captures the equilibrium revenue of making different decisions in the "incremental problem". Specifically, adding a new product $j \in \mathbb{S} \backslash S$ (i.e., $x_j = 1$) or do not add anything (i.e., $x_j = 0$ for all $j \in \mathbb{S} \backslash S$) can obtain different values $\bar{q}_0$ calculated by (16), and then $\overline{re}(\bar{q}_0)$ from (17) is the corresponding equilibrium revenue. The property of the revenue function in (17), especially the quasi-convexity, is a key step to derive the optimal search segmentation mechanisms for revenue maximization.

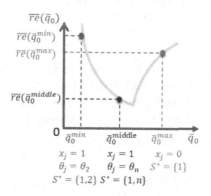

Fig. 1. $\overline{re}(\bar{q}_0)$ is a quasi-convex revenue function for the possible product set to display when the product 1 has been selected. $\overline{re}(\bar{q}_0^{min})$ is the revenue obtained by displaying $S^* = \{1, 2\}$, $\overline{re}(\bar{q}_0^{middle})$ is the revenue from showing $S^* = \{1, n\}$, and $\overline{re}(\bar{q}_0^{max})$ is the revenue of displaying $S^* = \{1\}$.

Based on the above discussion, we show that the optimal search segmentation mechanism is to choose the k^* products with the best quality, for an appropriate value of k^*, using the following steps:

- First, we show that one should always display the product with the best quality to maximize revenue (Lemma 4).
- Then, we consider the decision of adding one product to display. As discussed previously, we show that $re(q_0)$ is quasi-concave in q_0 which implies that the optimal decision is to add the next highest quality product or to not add a product at all, as illustrated in Fig. 1. The quasi-convexity of $re(q_0)$ is shown in Lemma 5 under a certain condition. Using the quasi-convexity of $re(q_0)$, in Lemma 6, we prove that if the optimal display set consists of k^* products, then one should select the top k^* products in terms of quality.
- The final step is to find the optimal k^*. This can be done by the following calculation. For each possible value of $k^* \in \{2, \cdots, n\}$, we select the top k^* products and calculate the revenue. We choose k^* to maximize this revenue. This is clearly a linear-time algorithm in n, since one has to add one term to the expression for the revenue when we increase k^* by one. This result is summarized in Theorem 4.

We first show that revenue maximization implies that the highest quality product is always selected for display.

Lemma 4. *For revenue maximization, it is optimal to always display the product with the highest quality.*

The intuition behind the proof is to show that for any displayed product set, the revenue function in (17) increases with the quality of the product with the highest quality in this set. The proof is in Appendix E of technical report [24].

Lemma 4 implies that when the optimal search segmentation mechanism is to display one product, *i.e.*, $k^* = 1$, the platform will choose the first product. To obtain the result for the general case with $k^* \geq 2$, we need to establish the quasi-convexity of the revenue function in (17). It is non-trivial to directly verify this property because the first term in the revenue function, *i.e.*, $\sum_{i \in S} \frac{\bar{q}_i}{1 - \bar{q}_i}$, is increasing and concave with respective to q_0, while the remaining term $\frac{1}{\bar{q}_0 + \sum_{i \in S} \bar{q}_i} - 1$ is decreasing and convex. We first prove the desired quasi-convexity by assuming all demands $\bar{q}_i$'s are less than 0.5, *i.e.*, $q_1 < 0.5$, due to $q_i \leq q_1$ for $i \in S$, meaning that no seller dominates the market. This assumption simplifies the analysis, but still preserves the major intuition. Our results also hold without this assumption, as shown in Appendix H of technical report [24].

Lemma 5. *For any selected product set S, the revenue function $\overline{re}(\bar{q}_0)$ in (17) is quasi-convex in the range $\left[\bar{q}_0^{min}, \bar{q}_0^{max}\right]$, under the assumption of $q_1 < 0.5$.*

The basic idea to prove this result is to check the second-order conditions of a quasi-convex function, *i.e.*, at any point with zero slope, the second derivative is non-negative, *i.e.*, $\overline{re}'(\bar{q}_0) = 0 \Rightarrow \overline{re}''(\bar{q}_0) > 0$. The details are in Appendix F of technical report [24]. Equipped with Lemma 5, we can derive the optimal search mechanism for the case with $k^* \geq 2$.

Lemma 6. *For revenue maximization, the optimal search segmentation mechanism is to display the top k^* products if the cardinality of the optimal product set is $k^* \geq 2$, under the assumption of $q_1 < 0.5$.*

The optimality of the top k^* mechanism in this lemma can be established by showing that replacing any product with a product of higher quality will increase the revenue (see Appendix G in technical report [24] for the proof).

While the specific value of k^* depends on the quality of all products θ, The platform can find the optimal k^* in linear time by computing the revenue of each set with the top $k \in [1, n]$ products, and selecting the one with the maximum revenue. Thus, from Lemmas 4 and 6, we obtain the main result for the case of revenue maximization.

Theorem 4. *For revenue maximization, the optimal search segmentation mechanism is to display the top k^* products, where k^* is determined by the quality of all products θ, and can be calculated in linear time.*

5 Related Work

Our work is related to the burgeoning literature that studies online platform marketplaces of using control levels other than pricing to influence the market outcomes [4,5,7,14]. Kanoria and Saban designed a framework to facilitate the search for buyers and sellers on matching platforms, and found that simple restrictions on what buyers/sellers can access would boost social welfare [14]. Arnosti et al. investigated the welfare loss due to the uncertainty about seller availability in asynchronous dynamic matching markets, and also found that limiting the visibility of sellers can improve social welfare [4]. Our result, displaying only a subset of products to buyers can increase the equilibrium revenue, extends the findings in these two pieces of work to the context of revenue optimization. Banerjee et al. studied how the platform should control which sellers and buyers are visible to each other, and provided polynomial-time approximation algorithms to optimize social welfare and throughput [5]. In their model, supply and demand are associated with public distributions. By contrast, we adopt the MNL model to derive a specific demand system, and use the Bertrand game to capture supply response to this demand system, doing so leads to very different optimization problems.

Revenue management under general demand model has been extensively studied in economics, marketing and operation management [9,20–22]. The model considered in this paper is closely related to that in assortment optimization, which is an active area in revenue management research. For assortment optimization, the demand of products are governed by the variants of attraction-based choice models [3], e.g., MNL model, mixed nested logit model and nested logit model, and each product is associated with a fixed price. The objective is to find a set of products, or an assortment to offer that maximizes the expected revenue. In [22], Talluri and van Ryzin studied the assortment optimization problem under the MNL model, and showed that the optimal assortment includes a certain number of products with the highest prices. We also derive a similar result, but use the criteria of quality rather than price to rank the potential products. In our setting a key difference from this line of work is that the product prices are determined endogenously by the outcome of oligopolistic competition games instead of being given beforehand. Pricing multiple differentiated products in the context of the MNL model is another fairly active direction [9,13,21]. In this setting, all products are displayed, and the objective is to choose pries of products to maximize revenue. In contrast, we focus on search segmentation mechanisms with endogenous prices, where the platform only controls the set of displayed products, to optimize the equilibrium social welfare/revenue.

6   Conclusion

In this paper, we have studied the problems of social welfare maximization and revenue maximization in designing search space for online platform markets. In the discriminatory control model, the platform can only control the search segmentation mechanisms, i.e., determine the list of products to display for buyers, and the products' prices are determined endogenously by the competition among sellers. Under the standard buyer choice model, namely the multinomial logit mode, we have developed efficient and optimal search segmentation mechanisms to maximize the equilibrium social welfare and revenue under Bertrand competition game. For social welfare maximization, it is optimal to display all the products. For revenue maximization, the optimal search mechanism, referred as quality-order mechanism, is to display the top k^* highest quality products, where k^* can be computed in at most linear time in the number of products.

References

1. Abolhassani, M., Bateni, M.H., Hajiaghayi, M.T., Mahini, H., Sawant, A.: Network cournot competition. In: Liu, T.-Y., Qi, Q., Ye, Y. (eds.) WINE 2014. LNCS, vol. 8877, pp. 15–29. Springer, Cham (2014). https://doi.org/10.1007/978-3-319-13129-0_2
2. Aksoy-Pierson, M., Allon, G., Federgruen, A.: Price competition under mixed multinomial logit demand functions. Manage. Sci. 59(8), 1817–1835 (2013)
3. Anderson, S.P., De Palma, A., Thisse, J.-F.: Discrete Choice Theory of Product Differentiation. MIT Press, Cambridge (1992)
4. Arnosti, N., Johari, R., Kanoria, Y.: Managing congestion in decentralized matching markets. In: EC, p. 451 (2014)
5. Banerjee, S., Gollapudi, S., Kollias, K., Munagala, K.: Segmenting two-sided markets. In: WWW, pp. 63–72 (2017)
6. Bimpikis, K., Ehsani, S., Ilkiliç, R.: Cournot competition in networked markets. Manage. Sci. 65(6), 2467–2481 (2019)
7. Birge, J., Candogan, O., Chen, H., Saban, D.: Optimal commissions and subscriptions in networked markets. In: EC, pp. 613–614 (2018)
8. Corless, R.M., Gonnet, G.H., Hare, D.E.G., Jeffrey, D.J., Knuth, D.E.: On the lambertw function. Adv. Comput. Math. 5(1), 329–359 (1996)
9. Dong, L., Kouvelis, P., Tian, Z.: Dynamic pricing and inventory control of substitute products. Manufact. Serv. Oper. Manag. 11(2), 317–339 (2009)

10. Evans, P.C., Gawer, A.: The rise of the platform enterprise: a global survey (2016)
11. Gallego, G., Huh, W.T., Kang, W., Phillips, R.: Price competition with the attraction demand model: existence of unique equilibrium and its stability. Manufact. Serv. Oper. Manag. **8**(4), 359–375 (2006)
12. Guadagni, P.M., Little, J.D.C.: A logit model of brand choice calibrated on scanner data. Mark. Sci. **2**(3), 203–238 (1983)
13. Hanson, W., Martin, K.: Optimizing multinomial logit profit functions. Manage. Sci. **42**(7), 992–1003 (1996)
14. Kanoria, Y., Saban, D.: Facilitating the search for partners on matching platforms: restricting agent actions. In: EC, p. 117 (2017)
15. Lin, W., Pang, J.Z.F., Bitar, E., Wierman, A.: Networked cournot competition in platform markets: access control and efficiency loss. In: CDC, pp. 4606–4611 (2017)
16. McFadden, D.: Conditional logit analysis of qualitative choice behaviour. In: Zarembka, P. (ed.) Frontiers in Econometrics, pp. 105–142. Academic Press, New York (1974)
17. McFadden, D.: The choice theory approach to market research. Mark. Sci. **5**(4), 275–297 (1986)
18. Monderer, D., Shapley, L.S.: Potential games. Games Econ. Behav. **14**(1), 124–143 (1996)
19. Pang, J.Z.F., Fu, H., Lee, W.I., Wierman, A.: The efficiency of open access in platforms for networked cournot markets. In: INFOCOM, pp. 1–9 (2017)
20. Rusmevichientong, P., Shmoys, D., Tong, C., Topaloglu, H.: Assortment optimization under the multinomial logit model with random choice parameters. Prod. Oper. Manag. **23**(11), 2023–2039 (2014)
21. Song, J.-S., Xue, Z.: Demand management and inventory control for substitutable products. Working paper (2007)
22. Talluri, K., van Ryzin, G.: Revenue management under a general discrete choice model of consumer behavior. Manage. Sci. **50**(1), 15–33 (2004)
23. Vives, X.: Oligopoly Pricing: Old Ideas and New Tools. MIT Press, Cambridge (2001)
24. Zheng, Z., Srikant, R.: Optimal search segmentation mechanisms for online platform markets. Technical report (2019). https://drive.google.com/file/d/18esA_BjxMvJbEkIvbdBruU1Ji5Am0KxJ/view

On the Price of Anarchy for High-Price Links

Carme Àlvarez and Arnau Messegué[(⊠)]

ALBCOM Research Group, Computer Science Department, UPC, Barcelona, Spain
{alvarez,amessegue}@cs.upc.edu

Abstract. We study Nash equilibria and the price of anarchy in the classic model of Network Creation Games introduced by Fabrikant, Luthra, Maneva, Papadimitriou and Shenker in 2003. This is a selfish network creation model where players correspond to nodes in a network and each of them can create links to the other $n-1$ players at a prefixed price $\alpha > 0$. The player's goal is to minimise the sum of her cost buying edges and her cost for using the resulting network. One of the main conjectures for this model states that the price of anarchy, i.e. the relative cost of the lack of coordination, is constant for all α. This conjecture has been confirmed for $\alpha = O(n^{1-\delta})$ with $\delta \geq 1/\log n$ and for $\alpha > 4n - 13$. The best known upper bound on the price of anarchy for the remaining range is $2^{O(\sqrt{\log n})}$.

We give new insights into the structure of the Nash equilibria for $\alpha > n$ and we enlarge the range of the parameter α for which the price of anarchy is constant. Specifically, we prove that for any small $\epsilon > 0$, the price of anarchy is constant for $\alpha > n(1 + \epsilon)$ by showing that any biconnected component of any non-trivial Nash equilibrium, if it exists, has at most a constant number of nodes.

1 Introduction

Many distinct network creation models trying to capture properties of Internet-like networks or social networks have been extensively studied in Computer Science, Economics, and Social Sciences. In these models, the players (also called nodes or agents) buy some links to other players creating in this way a network formed by their choices. Each player has a cost function that captures the need of buying few links and, at the same time, being well-connected to all the remaining nodes of the resulting network. The aim of each player is to minimise her cost following her selfish interests. A stable configuration in which every player or agent has no incentive in deviating unilaterally from her current strategy is

We thank D. Bilò, P. Lenzner and our anonymous reviewers for their helpful comments. This work has been partially supported by funds from the Spanish Ministry for Economy and Competitiveness (MINECO) and the European Union (FEDER funds) under grant GRAMM (TIN2017-86727-C2-1-R) and from the Catalan Agency for Management of University and Research Grants (AGAUR, Generalitat de Catalunya) under project ALBCOM 2017-SGR-786.

© Springer Nature Switzerland AG 2019
I. Caragiannis et al. (Eds.): WINE 2019, LNCS 11920, pp. 316–329, 2019.
https://doi.org/10.1007/978-3-030-35389-6_23

called a *Nash equilibrium* (NE). In order to evaluate the social impact of the resulting network, the *social cost* is introduced. In this setting the social cost is defined as the sum of the individual costs of all the players. Since there is no coordination among the different players, one can expect that stable networks do not minimise the social cost. The *price of anarchy* (PoA) is a measure that quantifies how far is the worst NE (in the sense of social cost) with respect to any optimal configuration that minimises the social cost. Specifically, the PoA is defined as the ratio between the maximum social cost of NE and the social cost of the optimal configuration. If we were able to prove formally that the PoA is constant, then we could conclude that the equilibrium configurations in the selfish network·creation games are so good in terms of social cost.

Since the introduction of the classical network creation game by Fabrikant et al. in [8], many efforts have been done in order to analyse the quality of the resulting equilibrium networks. The *constant PoA conjecture* is a well-known conjecture that states that the PoA is constant independently of the price of the links. In this work we provide a new understanding of the structure of the equilibrium networks for the classical network creation game [8]. We focus on the equilibria for high-price links and show that in the case that an equilibrium is not a tree, then the size of any of its biconnected components is upper bounded by a constant. This is the key ingredient to prove later that, for any small $\epsilon > 0$, the PoA is constant for $\alpha > n(1 + \epsilon)$ where α is the price per link and n is the number of nodes.

Let us first define formally the model and related concepts.

1.1 Model and Definitions

The *sum classic network creation game* Γ is defined by a pair $\Gamma = (V, \alpha)$ where $V = \{1, 2, ..., n\}$ denotes the set of players and $\alpha > 0$ a positive parameter. Each player $u \in V$ represents a node of an undirected graph and α represents the cost of establishing a link.

A *strategy* of a player u of Γ is a subset $s_u \subseteq V \setminus \{u\}$, the set of nodes for which player u pays for establishing a link. A strategy profile for Γ is a tuple $s = (s_1, \ldots, s_n)$ where s_u is the strategy of player u, for each player $u \in V$. Let $\mathcal{S}$ be the set of all strategy profiles of Γ. Every strategy profile s has associated a *communication network* that is defined as the undirected graph $G[s] = (V, \{uv \mid v \in s_u \vee u \in s_v\})$. Notice that uv denotes the undirected edge between u and v.

Let $d_G(u, v)$ be the distance in G between u and v. The cost associated to a player $u \in V$ in a strategy profile s is defined by $c_u(s) = \alpha|s_u| + D_{G[s]}(u)$ where $D_G(u) = \sum_{v \in V, v \neq u} d_G(u, v)$ is the sum of the distances from the player u to all the other players in G. As usual, the social cost of a strategy profile s is defined by $C(s) = \sum_{u \in V} c_u(s)$.

A Nash Equilibrium (NE) is a strategy vector s such that for every player u and every strategy vector s' differing from s in only the u component, $s_u \neq s'_u$, satisfies $c_u(s) \leq c_u(s')$. In a NE s no player has incentive to deviate individually her strategy since the cost difference $c_u(s') - c_u(s) \geq 0$. Finally, let us denote by

$\mathcal{E}$ the set of all NE strategy profiles. The price of anarchy (PoA) of Γ is defined as $PoA = \max_{s \in \mathcal{E}} C(s) / \min_{s \in \mathcal{S}} C(s)$.

It is worth observing that in a NE $s = (s_1, ..., s_n)$ it never happens that $u \in s_v$ and $v \in s_u$, for any $u, v \in V$. Thus, if s is a NE, s can be seen as an orientation of the edges of $G[s]$ where an arc from u to v is placed whenever $v \in s_u$. It is clear that a NE s induces a graph $G[s]$ that we call *NE graph* and we mostly omit the reference to such strategy profile s when it is clear from context. However, notice that a graph G can have different orientations. Hence, when we say that G is a NE graph we mean that G is the outcome of a NE strategy profile s, that is, $G = G[s]$.

Given a graph G we denote by $X \subseteq G$ the subgraph of G induced by $V(X)$. In this way, given a graph $G = G[s] = (V, E)$, a node $v \in V$, and $X \subseteq G$, the *outdegree of* v in X is defined as $deg_X^+(v) = |\{u \in V(X) \mid u \in s_v\}|$, the *indegree of* v in X as $deg_X^-(v) = |\{u \in V(X) \mid v \in s_u\}|$, and, finally, the *degree of* v in X as $deg_X(v) = deg_X^+(v) + deg_X^-(v)$. Notice that $deg_X(v) = |\{u \in V(X) \mid uv \in E\}|$. Furthermore, the average degree of X is defined as $deg(X) = \sum_{v \in V(X)} deg_X(v)/|V(X)|$.

Furthermore, remind that in a connected graph $G = (V, E)$ a vertex is a *cut vertex* if its removal increases the number of connected components of G. A graph is biconnected if it has no cut vertices. We say that $H \subseteq G$ is a *biconnected component* of G if H is a maximal biconnected subgraph of G. More specifically, H is such that there is no other distinct biconnected subgraph of G containing H as a subgraph. Given a biconnected component H of G and a node $u \in V(H)$, we define $S(u)$ as the connected component containing u in the subgraph induced by the vertices $(V(G) \setminus V(H)) \cup \{u\}$. The *weight* of a node $u \in V(H)$, denoted by $|S(u)|$ is then defined as the number of nodes of $S(u)$. Notice that $S(u)$ denotes the set of all nodes v in the connected component containing u induced by $(V(G) \setminus V(H)) \cup \{u\}$ and then, every shortest path in G from v to any node $w \in V(H)$ goes through u.

In the following sections we consider G to be a NE for $\alpha > n$ and $H \subseteq G$, if it exists, a non-trivial biconnected component of G, that is, a biconnected component of G of at least three distinct nodes. Then we use the abbreviations d_G, d_H to refer to the diameter of G and the diameter of H, respectively, (although $d_G(u, v)$ denotes the distance between u, v in G), and n_H the size of H.

1.2   Historical Overview

We now describe the progress around the central question of giving improved upper bounds on the PoA of the network creation games introduced by Fabrikant et al. in [8].

First of all, let us explain briefly two key results that are used to obtain better upper bounds on the PoA. The first is that the PoA for trees is at most 5 [8]. The second one is that the PoA of any NE graph is upper bounded by its diameter plus one unit [6,7]. Using these two results it can be shown that the PoA is constant for almost all values of the parameter α. Demaine et al. in [6,7] showed constant PoA for $\alpha = O(n^{1-\delta})$ with $\delta \geq \frac{1}{\log n}$ by proving that the diameter of equilibria is constant for the same range of α. In the view that the PoA is constant for a such a wide range of values of α, Demaine et al. in [6,7] conjectured that the PoA is constant for any α. This is what we call the *constant PoA conjecture*. More recently, Bilò and Lenzner in [5] demonstrated constant PoA for $\alpha > 4n - 13$ by showing that every NE is a tree for the same range of α. For the remaining range Demaine et al. in [6,7] determined that the PoA is upper bounded by $2^{O(\sqrt{\log n})}$.

The other important conjecture, the *tree conjecture*, stated by Fabrikant et al. in [8], still remains to be solved. The first version of the tree conjecture said that there exists a positive constant A such that every NE is a tree for $\alpha > A$. This was later refuted by Albers et al. in [4]. The reformulated tree conjecture that is believed to be true is for the range $\alpha > n$. In [11] the authors show an example of a non-tree NE for the range $\alpha = n-3$ and then, we can deduce that the generalisation of the tree conjecture for $\alpha > n$ cannot be extended to the range $\alpha > n(1-\delta)$ with $\delta > 0$ any small enough positive constant. Notice that the constant PoA conjecture and the tree conjecture are related in the sense that if the tree conjecture was true, then we would obtain that the PoA is constant for the range $\alpha > n$ as well.

Let us describe the progress around these two big conjectures considering first the case of large values of α and after the case of small values of α.

For *large values* of α it has been shown constant PoA for the intervals $\alpha > n^{3/2}$ [9], $\alpha > 12n \log n$ [4], $\alpha > 273n$ [10], $\alpha > 65n$ [11], $\alpha > 17n$ [1] and $\alpha > 4n - 13$ [5], by proving that every NE for each of these ranges is a tree, that is, proving that the tree conjecture holds for the corresponding range of α.

The main approach to prove the result in [1,10,11] is to consider a biconnected (or 2-edge-connected in [1]) component H from the NE network, and then to establish non-trivial upper and lower bounds for the average degree of H, noted as $deg(H)$. More specifically, it is shown that $deg(H) \leq f_1(n, \alpha)$ for every $\alpha \geq c_1 n$ and $deg(H) \geq f_2(n, \alpha)$ for every $\alpha \geq c_2 n$, with c_1, c_2 constants and $f_1(n, \alpha), f_2(n, \alpha)$ functions of n, α. From this it can be concluded that there cannot exist any biconnected component H for any α in the set $\{\alpha \mid f_1(n, \alpha) < f_2(n, \alpha) \wedge \alpha \geq \max(c_1, c_2)n\}$, and thus every NE is a tree for this range of α.

In [10,11], to prove the upper bound on the term $deg(H)$ the authors basically consider a BFS tree T rooted at a node u minimising the sum of distances in H and define a *shopping vertex* as a vertex from H that has bought at least one edge of H but not of T. The authors show that every shopping vertex has bought at most one extra edge and that the distance between two distinct shopping vertices is lower bounded by a non-trivial quantity that depends on α and n. By combining these two properties the authors can give an improved upper bound on $deg(H)$ which is close to 2 from above when α is large enough in comparison to n. On the other hand, to prove a lower bound on $deg(H)$ the authors show that in H there cannot exist too many nodes of degree 2 close together.

In [1], the authors use the same upper bound as the one in [11] for the term $deg(H)$ but give an improved lower bound better than the one from [11]. To show this lower bound they introduce the concept of *coordinates* and *2-paths*. For $\alpha > 4n$, the authors prove that every minimal cycle is directed and then use this result to show that there cannot exist long 2−paths.

In contrast, Bilò and Lenzner in [5] consider a different approach. Instead of using the technique of bounding the average degree, they introduce, for any non-trivial biconnected component H of a graph G, the concepts of *critical pair*, *strong critical pair*, and then, show that every minimal cycle for the corresponding range of α is directed. The authors play with these concepts in a clever way in order to reach the conclusion.

In a very preliminary draft [2], we take another perspective and conclude that given $\epsilon > 0$ any positive constant, the PoA is constant for $\alpha > n(1 + \epsilon)$. Specifically, in [2], we prove that if the diameter of a NE graph is larger than a given positive constant, then the graph must be a tree. Such proposal represents an interesting approach to the same problem but the calculations and the proofs are very involved and hard to follow. In this work we present in a clear and elegant way the stronger result that, for the same range of α, the size of any biconnected component of any non-tree NE is upper bounded by a constant.

For *small values* of α, among the most relevant results, it has been proven that the PoA is constant for the intervals $\alpha = O(1)$ [8], $\alpha = O(\sqrt{n})$ [4,9] and $\alpha = O(n^{1-\delta})$ with $\delta \geq 1/\log n$ [6,7].

The most powerful technique used in these papers is the one from Demaine et al. in [6,7]. They show that the PoA is constant for $\alpha = O(n^{1-\delta})$ with $\delta > 1/\log n$, by studying a specific setting where some disjoint balls of fixed radius are included inside a ball of bigger radius. Considering the deviation that consists in buying the links to the centers of the smaller balls, the player performing such deviation gets closer to a majority of the nodes by using these extra bought edges (if these balls are chosen adequately). With this approach it can be shown that the size of the balls grows in a very specific way, from which then it can be derived the upper bounds for the diameter of equilibria and thus for the PoA.

1.3   Our Contribution

Let us consider a weaker version of the tree conjecture that considers the existence of biconnected components in a NE having some specific properties regarding their size.

Conjecture 1 (The biconnected component conjecture). For $\alpha > n$, any biconnected component of a non-tree NE graph has size at most a prefixed constant.

Let $\epsilon > 0$ be any positive constant. We show that the restricted version of this conjecture where $\alpha > n(1 + \epsilon)$ is true (Sect. 5, Theorem 3). This result jointly with $d_G \leq d_H + 250$ (Theorem 1, Sect. 4) for $\alpha > n$, whenever H exists, imply that d_G is upper bounded by a prefixed constant, too. Recall that, the diameter of any graph plus one unit is an upper bound on the PoA and the price of anarchy for trees is constant. Hence, we can conclude that the PoA is constant for $\alpha > n(1 + \epsilon)$.

In order to show these results, we introduce a new kind of sets, the A sets, satisfying some interesting properties and we adapt some well-known techniques and then, combine them together in a very original way. Let us describe the main ideas of our approach:

- Inspired by the technique considered in [6,7] which is used to relate the diameter of G with the size of G, we obtain an analogous relation between the diameter of H and the size of H (Sect. 3, Proposition 4), that can be expressed as $d_H = 2^{O(\sqrt{\log n_H})}$.
- We improve the best upper bound known on $deg(H)$ (Sect. 5, Theorem 2). We show this crucial result by using a different approach than the one used in the literature. We consider a node $u \in V(H)$ minimising the sum of distances and, instead of lower bounding the distance between two shopping vertices, we introduce and study a natural kind of subsets, the A sets (Sect. 2). Each A set corresponds to a node $v \in V(H)$ and a pair of edges e_1, e_2 where $v \in V(H)$ and $e_1, e_2 \in E(H)$ are two links bought by v. The A sets play an important role when upper bounding the cost difference of player v associated to the deviation of the same player that consists in selling e_1, e_2 and buying a link to u (Sect. 2, Proposition 1 and Proposition 2). By counting the cardinality of these A sets we show that the term $deg(H)$ can be upper bounded by an expression in which the terms n, α, n_H, and d_H appear (Sect. 2, Proposition 3). By using the relation $d_H = 2^{O(\sqrt{\log n_H})}$ we can refine the upper bound for the $deg(H)$ even more. Subsequently, we consider the technique used in [1,10,11], in which lower and upper bounds on the average degree of H are combined to reach a contradiction whenever H exists, i.e. whenever G is a non-tree NE graph.

Due to space constraints we refer to [3] for all omitted details.

2   An Upper Bound for $deg(H)$ in Terms of the Size and the Diameter of H

Remind that in all the sections we consider that G is a NE of a network creation game $\Gamma = (V, \alpha)$ where $\alpha > n$. If G is not a tree then we denote by H a maximal biconnected component of G.

In this section we give an intermediate upper bound for the term $deg(H)$ that will be useful later to derive the main conclusion of this paper.

Let $u \in V(H)$ be a prefixed node and suppose that we are given $v \in V(H)$ and $e_1 = (v, v_1), e_2 = (v, v_2)$ two links bought by v. The A set of $v, e_1 = (v, v_1), e_2 = (v, v_2)$, noted as $A_{e_1, e_2}(v)$, is the subset of nodes $z \in V(G)$ such that every shortest path (in G) starting from z and reaching u goes through v and the predecessor of v in any such path is either v_1 or v_2.

Therefore, notice that $v \notin A_{e_1, e_2}(v)$ and the following remark always holds:

Remark 1. Let e_1, e_2, e_1', e_2' be four distinct edges such that e_1, e_2 are bought by v and e_1', e_2' are bought by v'. If $d_G(u, v) = d_G(u, v')$ then the A set of v, e_1, e_2 and the A set of v', e_1', e_2' are disjoint even if $v = v'$.

Notice that the definition of the A sets depends on $u \in V(H)$, a prefixed node. For the sake of simplicity we do not include u in the notation of the A sets. Propositions 1 and 2 are stated for any general $u \in V(H)$ but in Corollary 1 we impose that u minimises the function $D_G(\cdot)$ in H.

For any $i = 1, 2$, we define the A^i set of $v, e_1 = (v, v_1), e_2 = (v, v_2)$, noted as $A^i_{e_1,e_2}(v)$, the subset of nodes z from $A_{e_1,e_2}(v)$ for which there exists a shortest path (in G) starting from z and reaching u such that goes through v and the predecessor of v in such path is v_i.

With these definitions, $A_{e_1,e_2}(v) = A^1_{e_1,e_2}(v) \cup A^2_{e_1,e_2}(v)$ and $A^i_{e_1,e_2}(v) = \emptyset$ iff $d_G(u, v_i) = d_G(u, v) - 1$ or $d_G(u, v_i) = d_G(u, v)$. Furthermore, the subgraph induced by $A^i_{e_1,e_2}(v)$ is connected whenever $A^i_{e_1,e_2}(v) \neq \emptyset$.

Now, suppose that $e_1, e_2 \in E(H)$ and think about the deviation of v that consists in deleting e_i for $i = 1, 2$ and buying a link to u. Let ΔC be the corresponding cost difference and define $crossings(X, Y)$ for subsets of nodes $X, Y \subseteq V(G)$ to be the set of edges xy with $x \in X$, $y \in Y$. Then we derive formulae to upper bound ΔC in the two only possible complementary cases: (i) $crossings(A^1_{e_1,e_2}(v), A^2_{e_1,e_2}(v)) \neq \emptyset$ and (ii) $crossings(A^1_{e_1,e_2}(v), A^2_{e_1,e_2}(v)) = \emptyset$.

In case (i), $A^1_{e_1,e_2}(v), A^2_{e_1,e_2}(v) \neq \emptyset$ so that the subgraphs induced by $A^1_{e_1,e_2}(v)$, $A^2_{e_1,e_2}(v)$ are both connected. This trivially implies that the graph induced by $A_{e_1,e_2}(v) = A^1_{e_1,e_2}(v) \cup A^2_{e_1,e_2}(v)$ is connected as well. Therefore, since H is biconnected and $e_1, e_2 \in E(H)$ by hypothesis, there must exist at least one connection distinct from e_1, e_2 joining $A_{e_1,e_2}(v)$ with its complement. Taking this fact into the account we obtain the following result:

Proposition 1. *Let us assume that* $crossings(A^1_{e_1,e_2}(v), A^2_{e_1,e_2}(v)) \neq \emptyset$ *and* xy *is any connection distinct from* e_1, e_2 *between* $A_{e_1,e_2}(v)$ *and its complement, with* $x \in A_{e_1,e_2}(v)$. *Furthermore, let* l *be the distance between* v_1, v_2 *in the subgraph induced by* $A_{e_1,e_2}(v)$. *Then* ΔC, *the cost difference for player* v *associated to the deviation that consists in deleting* e_1, e_2 *and buying a link to* u, *satisfies the following inequality:*

$$\Delta C \leq -\alpha + n + D_G(u) - D_G(v) + (2d_G(v, x) + l)|A_{e_1,e_2}(v)|$$

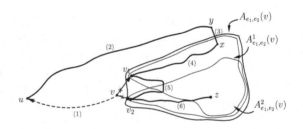

Fig. 1. The new path from z to v in the deviated graph G'

Proof. The term $-\alpha$ is clear because we are deleting the two edges e_1, e_2 and buying a link to u. Now let us analyse the difference of the sum of distances in the deviated graph G' vs the original graph. For this purpose, suppose wlog that $x \in A^1_{e_1,e_2}(v)$ and let z be any node from G. We distinguish two cases:

(A) If $z \notin A_{e_1,e_2}(v)$ then:
(1) Starting at v, follow the connection vu.
(2) Follow a shortest path from u to z in the original graph.

In this case we have that $d_{G'}(v, z) \leq 1 + d_G(u, z)$.

(B) If $z \in A_{e_1,e_2}(v)$ then there exists some i such that $z \in A^i_{e_1,e_2}(v)$. Consider the following path (see the Fig. 1 above for clarifications):
(1) Starting at v, follow the connection vu, which corresponds to one unit distance.
(2) Follow a path from u to y contained in the complementary of $A_{e_1,e_2}(v)$. Since $y \notin A_{e_1,e_2}(v)$ we have that $d_G(u, y) \leq d_G(u, v) + d_G(v, x) + 1$. Therefore, in this case we count at most $d_G(u, v) + d_G(v, x) + 1$ unit distances.
(3) Cross the connection yx, which corresponds to one unit distance.
(4) Go from x to v_1 inside $A_{e_1,e_2}(v)$ giving exactly $d_G(x, v) - 1$ unit distances.
(5) Go from v_1 to v_i inside $A_{e_1,e_2}(v)$ giving at most l unit distances.
(6) Go from v_i to z inside $A_{e_1,e_2}(v)$ giving exactly $d_G(v, z) - 1$ unit distances.

In this case we have that:

$$d_{G'}(v,z) \leq \overbrace{1}^{(1)} + \overbrace{d_G(u,v) + d_G(v,x) + 1}^{(2)} + \overbrace{1}^{(3)} + \overbrace{d_G(x,v) - 1}^{(4)} + \overbrace{l}^{(5)} + \overbrace{d_G(v,z) - 1}^{(6)}$$
$$= 1 + d_G(u,z) + (2d_G(v,x) + l)$$

Combining the two inequalities we reach the conclusion:

$$\Delta C \leq -\alpha + n + D_G(u) - D_G(v) + (2d_G(v,x) + l)|A_{e_1,e_2}(v)|$$

In case (ii), we assume that $crossings(A^1_{e_1,e_2}(v), A^2_{e_1,e_2}(v)) = \emptyset$. Since H is biconnected and $e_1, e_2 \in E(H)$ by hypothesis, for each i such that $A^i_{e_1,e_2}(v) \neq \emptyset$ there must exist at least one connection distinct from e_i joining $A^i_{e_1,e_2}(v)$ with its complement. Taking this fact into the account we obtain the following result:

Proposition 2. *Let us assume that* $crossings(A^1_{e_1,e_2}(v), A^2_{e_1,e_2}(v)) = \emptyset$ *and let* $I \subseteq \{1, 2\}$ *be the subset of indices* i *for which* $A^i_{e_1,e_2}(v) \neq \emptyset$. *Furthermore, suppose that for each* $i \in I$, $x_i y_i$ *is any connection distinct from* e_i *between* $A^i_{e_1,e_2}(v)$ *and its complement, with* $x_i \in A^i_{e_1,e_2}(v)$. *Then* ΔC, *the cost difference of player* v *associated to the deviation that consists in deleting* e_1, e_2 *and buying a link to* u, *satisfies the following inequality:*

$$\Delta C \leq -\alpha + n + D_G(u) - D_G(v) + \max(0, 2 \max_{i \in I} d_G(v, x_i))|A_{e_1,e_2}(v)|$$

Now, notice the following simple fact:

Remark 2. If $z_1, z_2 \in V(H)$ then any shortest path from z_1 to z_2 is contained in H. This is because otherwise, using the definition of cut vertex, any such path would visit two times the same cut vertex thus contradicting the definition of shortest path. Therefore, if $z_1, z_2 \in V(H)$ then $d_G(z_1, z_2) = d_H(z_1, z_2) \leq d_H$.

Combining the formulae from Proposition 1 and Proposition 2 together with this last remark, we can obtain a lower bound for the cardinality of any A set of v, e_1, e_2 when u satisfies a very specific constraint:

Corollary 1. *If $u \in V(H)$ is such that $D_G(u) = \min_{z \in V(H)} \{D_G(z)\}$, then* $|A_{e_1,e_2}(v)| \geq \frac{\alpha - n}{4d_H}$.

Now we use this last formula to give an upper bound for the average degree of H. Recall that we are working in the range $\alpha > n$:

Proposition 3.

$$deg(H) \leq 2 + \frac{16d_H(d_H + 1)n}{n_H(\alpha - n)}$$

Proof. For any node $v \in V(H)$ let $Z(v)$ be any maximal set of distinct and mutually disjoint pairs of edges from H bought by v. Let X be defined as the set of tuples $(\{e_1, e_2\}, v)$ with $v \in V(H)$ and $\{e_1, e_2\}$ a pair of edges from $Z(v)$. Now define $S = \sum_{(\{e_1,e_2\},v) \in X} |A_{e_1,e_2}(v)|$. On the one hand, using Corollary 1 we deduce that $S \geq \frac{\alpha - n}{4d_H}|X|$.

On the other hand, for each distance index i, let S_i be the sum of the cardinalities of the A sets for all the tuples $(\{e_1, e_2\}, v) \in X$ with $d_G(u, v) = i$. By Remark 1, $S_i \leq n$. Therefore:

$$|X|\frac{\alpha - n}{4d_H} \leq S = S_0 + ... + S_{d_H} \leq n(d_H + 1)$$

Next, notice that there are exactly $\lfloor \frac{deg_H^+(v)}{2} \rfloor$ pairs in $Z(v)$ for each v considered. Furthermore, $\lfloor \frac{deg_H^+(v)}{2} \rfloor = deg_H^+(v)/2$ if $deg_H^+(v)$ is even and $\lfloor \frac{deg_H^+(v)}{2} \rfloor = (deg_H^+(v) - 1)/2$ otherwise. Hence:

$$|X| \geq \sum_{v \in V(H)} \frac{deg_H^+(v) - 1}{2} = \frac{|E(H)| - |V(H)|}{2}$$

Finally:

$$deg(H) = \frac{2|E(H)|}{|V(H)|} \leq 2 + \frac{4|X|}{|V(H)|} \leq 2 + \frac{16(d_H + 1)nd_H}{n_H(\alpha - n)}$$

3   The Diameter of H vs the Number of Nodes of H

In this section we establish a relationship between the diameter and the number of the vertices of H which allows us to refine the upper bound for the term $deg(H)$ using the main result of the previous subsection.

We start extending the technique introduced by Demaine et al. in [6,7]. Instead of reasoning in a general G, we focus our attention to the nodes from H reaching an analogous result. Since for $\alpha > 4n - 13$ every NE is a tree it is enough if we study the case $\alpha < 4n$.

For any integer k and $u \in V(H)$, let $N_{k,H}(u) = \{v \in V(H) \mid d_G(u,v) \le k\}$ be the set of nodes from $V(H)$ at distance at most k from u. With this definition in mind then $S_k(u) = \cup_{v \in N_{k,H}(u)} S(v)$ is the set of all nodes inside $S(v)$ for all $v \in V(H)$ at distance at most k from u. In other words, $S_k(u)$ is the set of all nodes z such that the first cut vertex that one finds when following any shortest path from z to u is at distance at most k from u.

Furthermore, for any integer k we define $m_k = \min_{u \in V(H)} |N_{k,H}(u)|$. That is, m_k is the minimum cardinality that any k-neighbourhood in H can have.

Lemma 1. *For any integer $k \ge 0$, either there exists a node $u \in V(H)$ such that $|S_{4k+1}(u)| > n/2$ or, otherwise, $m_{5k+1} \ge m_k k/4$.*

Proof. If there is a vertex $u \in V(H)$ with $|S_{4k+1}(u)| > n/2$, then the claim is obvious. Otherwise, for every vertex $u \in V(H)$, $|S_{4k+1}(u)| \le n/2$. Let u be any node from $V(H)$ minimising the cardinality of the balls of radius $5k + 1$ intersected with $V(H)$. That is, u is any node from $V(H)$ with $|N_{5k+1,H}(u)| = m_{5k+1}$. Let $Z = \{v_1, ..., v_l\}$ be any maximal set of nodes from $V(H)$ at distance $4k + 1$ from u (in H) with the property that every two distinct nodes $v_i, v_j \in Z$, we have that $d_G(v_i, v_j) \ge 2k + 1$.

Now, consider the deviation of u that consists in buying the links to every node from Z and let G' be the new graph resulting from such deviation. Let $z \in S(w)$ with $w \in V(H)$ and $d_G(w,u) \ge 4k + 1$ and consider any shortest path (in H) from w to u. Let w_π be the node from any such shortest path at distance $4k + 1$ from u. By the maximality of Z there exists at least one node $v_w \in Z$ for which $d_G(v_w, w_\pi) \le 2k$. The original distance between z and u is $d_G(z,u) = d_G(z,w) + d_G(w,u)$. In contrast, the distance between z and u in G' satisfies the following inequality:

$$d_{G'}(z,u) \le 1 + d_G(v_w, w_\pi) + d_G(w_\pi, w) + d_G(w,z)$$

$$\le 1 + 2k + (d_G(u,w) - (4k + 1)) + d_G(w,z) = -2k + d_G(u,w) + d_G(w,z)$$

Therefore, $d_G(z,u) - d_{G'}(z,u) \ge 2k$. Since we are assuming that $|S_{4k+1}(u)| \le n/2$ then this means that $\sum_{\{v \in V(H) \mid d_G(v,u) > 4k+1\}} |S(v)| \ge n/2$, that is, the sum of the weights of the nodes from H at distance strictly greater than $4k + 1$ from u is greater than or equal $n/2$. Then ΔC, the cost difference for u associated to such deviation, satisfies:

$$\Delta C \le l\alpha - 2k \left(\frac{n}{2}\right) \le 4nl - kn$$

Since G is a NE then from this we conclude that $l \geq k/4$.

Finally, notice that the distance between two nodes in Z is at least $2k + 1$ implying that the set of all the balls of radius k with centers at the nodes from Z are mutually disjoint. Therefore, $m_{5k+1} = |N_{5k+1,H}(u)| \geq lm_k \geq m_k k/4$.

Lemma 2. *If $r < d_H/4 - 4$ then $|S_r(u)| \leq n/2$ for every node $u \in V(H)$.*

Combining these results we are able to give an extension of the result from Demaine et al. in [6,7]:

Proposition 4. $d_H < 5^{\sqrt{2\log_5 n_H}+5}$.

4   The Diameter of G vs the Diameter of H

In this section we establish a relationship between the diameter of G and the diameter of H when $\alpha > n$. Since for $\alpha > 4n - 13$ every NE is a tree it is enough if we study the case $n < \alpha < 4n$.

We show that in this case, the distance between any pair $w, z \in V(G)$ where $z \in S(w)$, is upper bounded by 125 from where we can conclude that $d_G < d_H + 250$. To obtain these results we basically exploit the fact that G is a NE graph together with key topological properties of biconnected components:

Proposition 5. *Let $w \in V(H)$ and $z \in S(w)$ maximising the distance to w. Then $d_G(z, w) < 125$.*

Proof. Let Z be the subgraph of G induced by $S(w)$ and W the subgraph of G induced by w together with the set of nodes $V(G) \setminus S(w)$. Then, define $r = d_G(z, w) = \max_{t \in V(Z)} d_G(w, t), s = \max_{t \in V(W)} d_G(w, t)$. With these definitions it is enough to show that $r < 125$. Notice that, for instance, if $S(w) = \{w\}$ then the result trivially holds.

First, let us see that $\min(r, s) \leq 8$.

Let v any node maximising the distance to w in W and ΔC_1 and ΔC_2 the corresponding cost differences of players z and v, respectively, associated to the deviations of the same players that consist in buying a link to w. Then $\Delta C_1 \leq \alpha - |V(W)|(r - 1)$ and $\Delta C_2 \leq \alpha - |V(Z)|(s - 1)$. Adding up the two inequalities and using that $\alpha < 4n$:

$$\Delta C_1 + \Delta C_2 \leq 2\alpha - (\min(r, s) - 1)(|V(Z)| + |V(W)|) < 8n - (\min(r, s) - 1)n$$

Since G is a NE graph then $\Delta C_1 + \Delta C_2 \geq 0$ and from here we deduce that $\min(r, s) \leq 8$, as we wanted to see.

If $r \leq 8$ then we are done. Therefore we must address the case $s \leq 8$.

Next, since H is a non-trivial biconnected component, there exist nodes $t, t' \in V(H)$ such that they are adjacent in H, t has bought the link $e = (t, t')$ and one of the two following cases happen: either (i) t is at distance 1 from w, t' is at distance 1 or 2 from w or (ii) t' is at distance 1 from w and t at distance 2 from w.

In case (i) we deduce that $|S(w)| = |V(Z)| \leq n\frac{4s-2}{4s-1} \leq n\frac{30}{31}$. This is because of the following reasoning. Let ΔC_{delete} be the corresponding cost difference of player t associated to the deviation of the same player that consists in deleting the edge e. Since H is biconnected then there exists a loop going through e and contained in H of length at most $4s + 1$. Notice that when deleting e, t only increases the distances maybe to the nodes from $V(W) \setminus \{w\}$ but not to the nodes from $V(Z)$ by at most $4s - 1$ distance units. Therefore:

$$\Delta C_{delete} \leq -\alpha + (4s - 1)(n - |V(Z)|) < -n + (4s - 1)(n - |V(Z)|)$$

Since G is a NE graph then $\Delta C_{delete} \geq 0$ and from here, using the hypothesis $s \leq 8$, we deduce the conclusion:

$$|V(Z)| < \frac{-n + n(4s - 1)}{4s - 1} = n\frac{4s - 2}{4s - 1} \leq \frac{30}{31}n$$

In case (ii) we deduce that $|S(w)| = |V(Z)| \leq n/2$. This is because of the following reasoning. Let ΔC_{swap} be the corresponding cost difference of player t associated to the deviation of the same player that consists in swapping the edge e for the link (t, w). Notice that when performing such swap, t only increases the distances maybe to the nodes from $V(W) \setminus \{w\}$ but strictly decreases for sure, one unit distance to all the nodes from $V(Z)$. Therefore:

$$\Delta C_{swap} \leq -|V(Z)| + (n - |V(Z)|) \leq n - 2|V(Z)|$$

Since G is a NE graph then $\Delta C_{swap} \geq 0$ and from here we deduce the conclusion $|V(Z)| \leq n/2$.

Hence, we have obtained that either $|S(w)| \leq \frac{30}{31}n$, in case (i), or $|S(w)| \leq \frac{n}{2}$, in case (ii).

Finally, consider the deviation of z that consists in buying the link to w. Then the corresponding cost difference ΔC_{buy} satisfies the following inequality:

$$\Delta C_{buy} \leq \alpha - (r - 1)(n - |S(w)|) < 4n - (r - 1)(n - |S(w)|)$$

Since G is a NE graph, then $\Delta C_{buy} \geq 0$ so that we conclude that $r < \frac{4n}{n - |S(w)|} + 1$. Using this property we conclude that $r < 125$ in case (i) and $r \leq 8$ in case (ii), so we are done.

As a consequence:

Theorem 1. $d_G < d_H + 250$.

5 Combining the Results

Finally, in this section we combine the distinct results obtained so far to prove the main conclusion.

On the one hand, combining Proposition 3 with Proposition 4 we reach the following result for the average degree of H:

Theorem 2.

$$deg(H) < 2 + \frac{16n}{\alpha - n} \frac{5^{2\sqrt{2\log_5 n_H}+10}}{n_H}$$

On the other hand, recall that from Lemma 4 and Lemma 2 from [10] and [11], respectively, the general lower bound $deg(H) \geq 2 + \frac{1}{16}$ that works for any α can be obtained.

With these results in mind we are now ready to prove the following strong result:

Theorem 3. *Let $\epsilon > 0$ be any positive constant and $\alpha > n(1 + \epsilon)$. There exists a constant K_ϵ such that every biconnected component H from any non-tree Nash equilibrium G has size at most K_ϵ.*

Proof. Let G be any non-tree NE graph. Then there exists at least one biconnected component H. By Theorem 2 when $\alpha > n(1 + \epsilon)$ we have that $deg(H) < 2 + \frac{16}{\epsilon} \frac{5^{2\sqrt{2\log_5 n_H}+10}}{n_H}$. On the other hand, we know that for any α, $deg(H) \geq 2 + \frac{1}{16}$. Then this implies that there exists a constant K_ϵ upper bounding the size of H, otherwise we would obtain a contradiction comparing the asymptotic behaviour of the upper and lower bounds obtained for $deg(H)$ in terms of n_H.

In other words, the restricted version of the biconnected component conjecture where $\alpha > n(1 + \epsilon)$ holds.

Furthermore, recall that it is well-known that the diameter of any graph plus one unit is an upper bound for the PoA and the PoA for trees is constant. Therefore, we conclude that:

Theorem 4. *Let $\epsilon > 0$ be any positive constant. The price of anarchy is constant for $\alpha > n(1 + \epsilon)$.*

Proof. Let G be a NE. If G is a tree we are done, because the PoA for trees is at most 5. Therefore to prove the result consider that G is a non-tree configuration. Then, G has at least one non-trivial biconnected component H. On the one hand, by Theorem 3, there exists a constant K_ϵ that upper bounds the size of H. This implies that $d_H \leq n_H \leq K_\epsilon$. On the other hand, by Theorem 1, $d_G \leq d_H + 250$. In this way, $d_G \leq K_\epsilon + 250$ and since $K_\epsilon + 250$ is a constant, then the conclusion follows because the PoA is upper bounded by the diameter plus one unit.

6   The Conclusions

The most relevant contribution we have made in this article is to show that the price of anarchy is constant for $\alpha > n(1 + \epsilon)$. The technique we have used relies mostly on the improved upper bound on the term $deg(H)$ for $\alpha > n$. However, as in [10,11], our refined upper bound still depends on the term $n/(\alpha - n)$, that tends to infinity when α approaches n from above. This makes us think that either our technique can be improved even more to obtain the conclusion that the tree conjecture claims or it might be that there exist some non-tree equilibria when α approaches n from above.

References

1. Àlvarez, C., Messegué, A.: Network creation games: structure vs anarchy. CoRR, abs/1706.09132. http://arxiv.org/abs/1706.09132 (2017)
2. Àlvarez, C., Messegué, A.: On the constant price of anarchy conjecture. CoRR, abs/1809.08027. http://arxiv.org/abs/1809.08027 (2018)
3. Àlvarez, C., Messegué, A.: On the price of anarchy for high-price links. CoRR, abs/1909.09799. http://arxiv.org/abs/1909.09799 (2019)
4. Albers, S., Eilts, S., Even-Dar, E., Mansour, Y., Roditty, L.: On Nash equilibria for a network creation game. ACM Trans. Econ. Comput. 2(1), 2 (2014)
5. Bilò, D., Lenzner, P.: On the tree conjecture for the network creation game. STACS 2018, 14:1–14:15 (2018)
6. Demaine, E.D., Hajiaghayi, M.T., Mahini, H., Zadimoghaddam, M.: The price of anarchy in network creation games. In: PODC 2007, pp. 292–298 (2007)
7. Demaine, E.D., Hajiaghayi, M.T., Mahini, H., Zadimoghaddam, M.: The price of anarchy in network creation games. ACM Trans. Algorithms 8(2), 13 (2012)
8. Fabrikant, A., Luthra, A., Maneva, E.N., Papadimitriou, C.H., Shenker, S.: On a network creation game. In: PODC 2003, pp. 347–351 (2003)
9. Lin, H.: On the price of anarchy of a network creation game. Class final project (2003)
10. Mihalák, M., Schlegel, J.C.: The price of anarchy in network creation games is (Mostly) constant. Theor. Comput. Syst. 53(1), 53–72 (2013)
11. Mamageishvili, A., Mihalák, M., Müller, D.: Tree Nash Equilibria in the network creation game. Internet Mathe. 11(4–5), 472–486 (2015)

Abstracts

Competition in Ride-Hailing Markets

AmirMahdi Ahmadinejad[1], Hamid Nazerzadeh[2,4], Amin Saberi[1],
Nolan Skochdopole[3(✉)], and Kane Sweeney[4]

[1] Department of Management Science and Engineering, Stanford University,
Stanford, USA
{ahmadi, saberi}@stanford.edu
[2] Marshall School of Business, University of Southern Califorina, Los Angeles, USA
hamidnz@uber.com
[3] Institute for Computational and Mathematical Engineering, Stanford University,
Stanford, USA
naskoch@stanford.edu
[4] Uber Technologies Inc., San Francisco, USA
kane@uber.com

One of the salient and understudied features of ride-hailing markets is that riders and drivers can move between platforms with relatively low friction or have a presence on several applications at the same time. This feature of the market has created an intense competition among platforms. The goal of this paper is to understand the dynamics and outcome of this competition. We aim to answer the following questions: What is the impact of platform competition on prices as well as the overall throughput of the market? Could competition lead to a "tragedy of the commons" and market failure as the platforms compete over the shared resource of open cars?

To address these questions, building on the market dynamics framework developed in [1] for a single platform, we propose and study a game-theoretic model in which two ride-hailing platforms compete for market share via pricing. Riders and drivers seek to maximize their own utilities and can choose to be present on only a single platform or participate in both platforms simultaneously. We see that at any equilibrium, all users will patronize both platforms which must offer equal prices; an equilibrium that results in a potential market failure always exists, but we show surprisingly that under many realistic settings, other more promising equilibria also exist.

This result is additionally supported by numerical analysis, using parameters estimated from Uber data to define the demand model, and simulations. We observe that if riders are not very sensitive to waiting times, the loss of efficiency due to competition could be small, corresponding to the second equilibrium outcome of the above theorem.

Reference

1. Castillo, J.C., Knoepfle, D., Weyl, G.: Surge pricing solves the wild goose chase. In: Proceedings of the 2017 ACM Conference on Economics and Computation, pp. 241–242. ACM (2017)

The full paper can be found here: http://ssrn.com/abstract=3461119.

© Springer Nature Switzerland AG 2019
I. Caragiannis et al. (Eds.): WINE 2019, LNCS 11920, p. 333, 2019.
https://doi.org/10.1007/978-3-030-35389-6

Persuading Risk-Conscious Agents:
A Geometric Approach

Jerry Anunrojwong[1,2]([✉]), Krishnamurthy Iyer[3][iD], and David Lingenbrink[4][iD]

[1] Massachusetts Institute of Technology, Cambridge, USA
[2] Chulalongkorn University, Bangkok, Thailand
jerryanunroj@gmail.com
[3] University of Minnesota, Minneapolis, MN 55455, USA
kriyer@umn.edu
[4] Cornell University, Ithaca, NY 14853, USA
dal299@cornell.edu

Abstract. Motivated by practical concerns in applying information design to markets and service systems, we consider a persuasion problem between a sender and a receiver where the receiver may not be an expected utility maximizer. In particular, the receiver's utility may be non-linear in her belief; we deem such receivers as *risk-conscious*. Such utility models arise, for example, when the receiver exhibits sensitivity to the variability and the risk in the payoff on choosing an action (e.g., waiting time for a service). In the presence of such non-linearity, the standard approach of using revelation-principle style arguments fails to characterize the set of signals needed in the optimal signaling scheme. Our main contribution is to provide a theoretical framework, using results from convex analysis, to overcome this technical challenge. In particular, in general persuasion settings with risk-conscious agents, we prove that the sender's problem can be reduced to a convex optimization program. Furthermore, using this characterization, we obtain a bound on the number of signals needed in the optimal signaling scheme.

We apply our methods to study a specific setting, namely *binary persuasion*, where the receiver has two possible actions (0 and 1), and the sender always prefers the receiver taking action 1. Under a mild convexity assumption on the receiver's utility and using a geometric approach, we show that the convex program can be further reduced to a linear program. Furthermore, this linear program yields a canonical construction of the set of signals needed in an optimal signaling mechanism. In particular, this canonical set of signals only involves signals that fully reveal the state and signals that induce uncertainty between two states. We illustrate our results in the setting of signaling wait time information in an unobservable queue with customers whose utilities depend on the variance of their waiting times.

Keywords: Bayesian persuasion · Non-expected-utility-maximizers · Revelation principle

The full paper is available at https://ssrn.com/abstract=3386273. K. Iyer gratefull acknowledges support from the NSF under grant CMMI-1633920.

© Springer Nature Switzerland AG 2019
I. Caragiannis et al. (Eds.): WINE 2019, LNCS 11920, p. 334, 2019.
https://doi.org/10.1007/978-3-030-35389-6

Scrip Systems with Minimal Availability

Itai Ashlagi and Süleyman Kerimov$^{(\boxtimes)}$

Department of Management Science and Engineering, Stanford University,
Stanford, CA 94305, USA
{iashlagi, kerimov}@stanford.edu

Abstract. In economies without monetary transfers, scrip systems serve
an alternative to sustain cooperation, improve efficiency and mitigate free
riding. This paper considers a marketplace, in which at each time period,
one agent requests a service, one agent provides the service, and a unit
of artificial currency is used to pay for service provision. We ask whether
agents can sustain cooperation when the market is thin, in the sense that
only few agents are available to provide the requested service. To study
this problem, we analyze the stability of the scrip distribution assuming that among the available agents, the one with the minimum amount
of scrips is selected to provide service. When exactly one random agent
is available to provide service, the scrip distribution is unstable, since
the number of scrips each agent has behaves like a simple random walk
in one dimension. However, already when just two random agents are
available to provide service, the scrip distribution is stable, in the sense
that agents do not deviate much from their initial endowment, with high
probability. This suggests that even with minimal liquidity in the market, cooperation can be sustained by balancing service provisions among
agents. We further explore cases, in which agents request and become
available to provide service at different rates, and generalize our positive
results to the case, in which the request and availability rates of each
agent are equal. Our theory builds on the literature on the power of two
choices paradigm and load balancing problems. Finally, our results suggest that scrip systems can lead to efficient outcomes in kidney exchange
platforms by sustaining cooperation between hospitals.

Keywords: Scrip systems · The power of two choices ·
Kidney exchange

A full draft of the paper is available at https://web.stanford.edu/iashlagi/papers/
scrips.pdf
S. Kerimov—Supported by the Stanford Management Science & Engineering Graduate
Fellowship, the Nakagawa Special Steel-Mitani Fellowship, and the Jerome Kaseberg
Doolan Fellowship.

© Springer Nature Switzerland AG 2019
I. Caragiannis et al. (Eds.): WINE 2019, LNCS 11920, p. 335, 2019.
https://doi.org/10.1007/978-3-030-35389-6

The Capacity Constrained Facility Location Problem

Haris Aziz[1], Hau Chan[2]([✉]), Barton E. Lee[1], and David C. Parkes[3]

[1] UNSW Sydney and Data61 CSIRO, Sydney, NSW 2052, Australia
[2] University of Nebraska-Lincoln, Lincoln, NE 68588, USA
hchan3@unl.edu
[3] Harvard University, Cambridge, MA 02138, USA

Abstract. We initiate the study of the capacity constrained facility location problem from a mechanism design perspective. In the capacity constrained setting, the facility can serve only a subset of the population, assumed to be the k-closest with respect to agents' true locations (this can be justified as the essentially unique equilibrium outcome of a first-come-first-serve game induced by the facility location). The main result is a complete characterization of dominant-strategy incentive compatible (DIC) mechanisms via the family of generalized median mechanisms (GMMs). Thus, the framework we introduce surprisingly provides a new characterization of GMMs, and is responsive to gaps in the current social choice literature highlighted by Border and Jordan [1983] and Barberà, Massó and Serizawa [1998]. We also provide algorithmic results and study the performance of DIC mechanisms in optimizing welfare. Adopting a worst-case approximation measure, we attain tight lower bounds on the approximation ratio of any DIC mechanism. Interestingly, the standard median mechanism achieves the optimal approximation ratio for smaller capacity settings.

ArXiv link: https://arxiv.org/abs/1806.00960.

Keywords: Facility location · Mechanism design without money · Capacity · Approximation

© Springer Nature Switzerland AG 2019
I. Caragiannis et al. (Eds.): WINE 2019, LNCS 11920, p. 336, 2019.
https://doi.org/10.1007/978-3-030-35389-6

The Price of Anarchy in Routing Games as a Function of the Demand

Roberto Cominetti[1], Valerio Dose[2], and Marco Scarsini[2(✉)]

[1] Facultad de Ingeniería y Ciencias, Universidad Adolfo Ibáñez, Santiago, Chile
roberto.cominetti@uai.cl
[2] Dipartimento di Economia e Finanza, LUISS, Viale Romania 32, 00197 Rome, Italy
{vdose, marco.scarsini}@luiss.it

Most of the literature concerning the price of anarchy (PoA) has focused on the search of tight worst case bounds for specific classes of games, such as congestion games and, in particular, routing games. Some papers have studied the PoA as a function of some parameter of the model, such as the traffic demand in routing games, and have provided asymptotic results in light or heavy traffic. Other studies have empirically shown that in real networks, for intermediate levels of traffic the PoA oscillates and exhibits some kinks at specific values of the demand, often without reaching the worst case bounds.

The shape and number of these oscillations is the object of this paper, where we provide theoretical results for the behavior of the PoA. We first present some results for general nonlinear costs, and then we focus on affine cost functions. We establish some smoothness properties of Wardrop equilibria and social optima. Under mild assumptions, we show that the price of anarchy is a smooth function of the traffic inflow, except at values of the demand where the set of paths used in equilibrium changes. We call these values *break points*. We then turn our attention to a class of cost functions that are heavily used in applications, namely, the ones proposed by the Bureau of Public Roads, and we show that for these costs we have a scaling law between the equilibrium and optimum flows which induces a similar scaling for the break points. Moreover, for affine cost functions we show that the number of break points is finite for any given network, and we present an example showing that this number can be exponential in the number of paths.

The relevance of break points is due to the fact that between break points the PoA is either monotone or it has a unique minimum, therefore, the PoA can have a local maximum only at a break point. The main fact that supports these results is that, with affine costs, if an equilibrium uses a certain set of paths at two different demand levels, then it uses the same set of paths at all intermediate demands. Finally, we show that this does not hold for less regular cost functions.

The details of the proofs and the relevant references can be found in [1].

Reference

1. Cominetti, R., Dose, V., Scarsini, M.: The Price of Anarchy in Routing Games as a Function of the Demand (2019). https://arxiv.org/abs/1907.10101

© Springer Nature Switzerland AG 2019
I. Caragiannis et al. (Eds.): WINE 2019, LNCS 11920, p. 337, 2019.
https://doi.org/10.1007/978-3-030-35389-6

The Value of Personalized Pricing

Adam N. Elmachtoub[1] (ID), Vishal Gupta[2] (ID), and Michael L. Hamilton[3](✉) (ID)

[1] Department of Industrial Engineering and Operations Research,
Columbia University, New York, NY 10027, USA
adam@ieor.columbia.edu
[2] Marshal School of Business, University of Southern California,
Los Angeles, CA 90007, USA
guptavis@usc.edu
[3] Katz Graduate School of Business, University of Pittsburgh,
Pittsburgh, PA 15260, USA
mhamilton@katz.pitt.edu

Abstract. Increased availability of high-quality customer information has fueled interest in personalized pricing strategies, i.e., strategies that predict an individual customer's valuation for a product and then offer a customized price tailored to that customer. While the appeal of personalized pricing is clear, it may also incur large costs in the form of market research, investment in information technology and analytics expertise, and branding risks. In light of these trade-offs, our work studies the value of personalized pricing strategies over a simple single price strategies.

We first provide tight, closed-form upper and lower bounds on the ratio between the profits of an idealized personalized pricing strategy and a single price strategy. Our upper bounds depend on simple statistics of the valuation distribution and shed light on the types of markets for which personalized pricing has the most potential. Our lower bounds depend on simple statistics as well as a unimodal assumption and shed light on which markets are ill served by a fixed price. Second, we demonstrate how to obtain bounds that depend on arbitrary moments of the valuation distribution via infinite dimensional linear programming duality. Finally, we show how to transform our upper and lower bounds on idealized personalized pricing strategies to stronger bounds on feature based personalized pricing strategies that better model current industry practices.

Keywords: Price discrimination · Personalization · Market segmentation

A full version is available at: https://papers.ssrn.com/sol3/papers.cfm?abstract_id=3127719.

© Springer Nature Switzerland AG 2019
I. Caragiannis et al. (Eds.): WINE 2019, LNCS 11920, p. 338, 2019.
https://doi.org/10.1007/978-3-030-35389-6

Sophisticated Attacks on Decoy Ballots: A Devil's Menu

Hans Gersbach, Akaki Mamageishvili$^{(\boxtimes)}$, and Oriol Tejada

CER-ETH – Center of Economic, Research at ETH Zurich, Zürichbergstrasse 18, 8092, Zurich, Switzerland
amamageishvili@ethz.ch

Abstract. Voting systems based on decoy ballots aim at preventing real ballots from being bought. Decoy ballots do not count in election outcomes, but are indistinguishable from real ballots. We introduce a "Devil's Menu" consisting of several price offers and allocation rules, which can be used by a malevolent third party—called the adversary—to curb the protection offered by decoy ballots. In equilibrium, the adversary can buy the real ballots of any strict subset of voting districts at a price corresponding to the willingness to sell them. By contrast, the voters holding decoy ballots are trapped into selling them at a low or negligible price. Decoy ballots may thus be ineffective against vote-buying even if the adversary's budget is limited.

Keywords: Voting · Decoy ballots · Adversary · Mechanism design · Attacks · Adverse selection

JEL Classifications: C72 · D4 · D82 · D86

We would like to thank David Basin, Afsoon Ebrahimi, Georgy Egorov, Lara Schmid, Larry Samuelson, Salvador Barberà and seminar participants at ETH Zurich for valuable comments. All errors are ours. The authors declare that they have no relevant or material financial interests that relate to the research described in this paper.
A full draft of the paper is available at https://papers.ssrn.com/sol3/papers.cfm?abstract_id=3088508.

I. Caragiannis et al. (Eds.): WINE 2019, LNCS 11920, p. 339, 2019.
https://doi.org/10.1007/978-3-030-35389-6

Markets Beyond Nash Welfare
for Leontief Utilities

Ashish Goel, Reyna Hulett, and Benjamin Plaut[(✉)]

Stanford University, Stanford, USA
{ashishg, rmhulett, bplaut}@stanford.edu

Abstract. We study the allocation of divisible goods to competing agents via a market mechanism, focusing on agents with Leontief utilities. The majority of the economics and mechanism design literature has focused on *linear* prices, meaning that the cost of a good is proportional to the quantity purchased. Equilibria for linear prices are known to be exactly the maximum Nash welfare allocations.

Price curves allow the cost of a good to be any (increasing) function of the quantity purchased. We show that price curve equilibria are not limited to maximum Nash welfare allocations with two main results. First, we show that an allocation can be supported by strictly increasing price curves if and only if it is *group-domination-free*. A similar characterization holds for weakly increasing price curves. We use this to show that given any allocation, we can compute strictly (or weakly) increasing price curves that support it (or show that none exist) in polynomial time. These results involve a connection to the *agent-order matrix* of an allocation, which may have other applications. Second, we use duality to show that in the bandwidth allocation setting, any allocation maximizing a CES welfare function can be supported by price curves.

The full version of the paper can be found at https://arxiv.org/pdf/1807.05293.pdf.

Acknowledgements. This research was supported in part by NSF grant CCF-1637418, ONR grant N00014-15-1-2786, and the NSF Graduate Research Fellowship under grant DGE-1656518.

© Springer Nature Switzerland AG 2019
I. Caragiannis et al. (Eds.): WINE 2019, LNCS 11920, p. 340, 2019.
https://doi.org/10.1007/978-3-030-35389-6

Capacity and Price Competition in Markets with Congestion Effects

Tobias Harks and Anja Schedel[(✉)]

Institute of Mathematics, University of Augsburg, 86159 Augsburg, Germany
{tobias.harks, anja.schedel}@math.uni-augsburg.de

We study oligopolistic competition in service markets where firms offer a service to customers. The service quality of a firm – from the perspective of a customer – depends on the level of congestion and the charged price. A firm can set a price for the service offered and additionally decides on the service capacity in order to mitigate congestion. The total profit of a firm is derived from the gained revenue minus the capacity investment cost. Firms *simultaneously* set capacities and prices in order to maximize their profit and customers *subsequently* choose the services with lowest combined cost (congestion and price). For this basic model, Johari, Weintraub and Van Roy [1] derived the first existence and uniqueness results of pure Nash equilibria (PNE) assuming mild conditions on congestion functions. Their existence proof relies on Kakutani's fixed-point theorem and a key assumption for the theorem to work is that demand for service is *elastic*, that is, there is a smooth inverse demand function determining the volume of customers given the effective customers' costs.

In this paper, we consider the case of *perfectly inelastic demand*. This scenario applies to realistic cases where customers are not willing to drop out of the market, e.g., if prices are regulated by reasonable price caps. We investigate existence, uniqueness and quality of PNE for models with inelastic demand and price caps. We show that for linear congestion cost functions, there exists a PNE. This result requires a completely new proof approach compared to previous approaches, since the best response correspondences of firms may be empty, thus standard fixed-point arguments are not directly applicable. We show that the game is *C*-secure (see Reny [3], and McLennan, Monteiro and Tourky [2]), which leads to the existence of PNE. We furthermore show that the PNE is unique, and that the efficiency compared to a social optimum is unbounded in general.

A full version of this paper is available at https://arxiv.org/abs/1905.05683.

References

1. Johari, R., Weintraub, G.Y., Van Roy, B.: Investment and market structure in industries with congestion. Oper. Res. **58**(5), 1303–1317 (2010)
2. McLennan, A., Monteiro, P.K., Tourky, R.: Games with discontinuous payoffs: a strengthening of Reny's existence theorem. Econometrica **79**(5), 1643–1664 (2011)
3. Reny, P.J.: On the existence of pure and mixed strategy Nash equilibria in discontinuous games. Econometrica **67**(5), 1029–1056 (1999)

Funded by the Deutsche Forschungsgemeinschaft (DFG, German Research Foundation) - HA 8041/1-1.

© Springer Nature Switzerland AG 2019
I. Caragiannis et al. (Eds.): WINE 2019, LNCS 11920, p. 341, 2019.
https://doi.org/10.1007/978-3-030-35389-6

Equality of Power and Fair Public Decision-Making

Nicole Immorlica[1], Benjamin Plaut[2(✉)], and E. Glen Weyl[1]

[1] Microsoft Research, Redmond, USA
{nicimm, glenweyl}@microsoft.com
[2] Stanford University, Stanford, USA
bplaut@cs.stanford.edu

Abstract. Ronald Dworkin's *equality of resources* and the closely related concept of envy-freeness, are two of the fundamental ideas behind fair allocation of private goods. The appropriate analog to these concepts in a public decision-making environment is unclear, since all agents consume the same "bundle" of resources (though they may have different utilities for this bundle). Drawing inspiration from equality of resources and the Dworkin quote below, we propose that equality in public decision-making should allow each agent to cause equal cost to the rest of society, which we model as equal externality. We term this *equality of power*. The first challenge here is that the cost to the rest of society must be measured somehow, and it is generally impossible to elicit the scale of individual utilities (in the absence of monetary payments). Again drawing inspiration from foundational literature for private goods economies, we normalize each agent's utility so that every agent's marginal utility for additional power is the same. We show that for quadratic utilities, in the large market limit, there always exists an outcome that simultaneously satisfies equal power, equal marginal utility for additional power, and social welfare maximization with respect to the normalized utilities.

The full version of the paper can be found at: https://papers.ssrn.com/sol3/papers.cfm?abstract_id=3420450.

"Equality of resources supposes that the resources devoted to each person's life should be equal. That goal needs a metric. The auction proposes what the envy test in fact assumes, that the true measure of the social resources devoted to the life of one person is fixed by asking how important, in fact, that resource is for others. It insists that the cost, measured in that way, figure in each person's sense of what is rightly his and in each person's judgment of what life he should lead, given that command of justice."

Ronald Dworkin, *What is Equality? Part II: Equality of Resources*, 1981

This research was supported in part by the NSF Graduate Research Fellowship under grant DGE-1656518.

I. Caragiannis et al. (Eds.): WINE 2019, LNCS 11920, p. 342, 2019.
https://doi.org/10.1007/978-3-030-35389-6

How to Hire Secretaries with Stochastic Departures

Thomas Kesselheim[1], Alexandros Psomas[2], and Shai Vardi[3(✉)]

[1] Institute of Computer Science, University of Bonn, 53115 Bonn, Germany
thomas.kesselheim@uni-bonn.de
[2] Simons Institute for the Theory of Computing, Berkeley, CA, USA
alexpsomi@cs.berkeley.edu
[3] Krannert School of Management, Purdue University, West Lafayette, IN, USA
svardi@purdue.edu

Abstract. We study a generalization of the secretary problem, where decisions do not have to be made immediately upon candidates' arrivals. After arriving, each candidate stays in the system for some (random) amount of time and then leaves, whereupon the algorithm has to decide irrevocably whether to select this candidate or not. The goal is to maximize the probability of selecting the best candidate overall. We assume that the arrival and waiting times are drawn from known distributions.

Our first main result is a characterization of the optimal policy for this setting. We show that when deciding whether to select a candidate it suffices to know only the time and the number of candidates that have arrived so far. Furthermore, the policy is monotone non-decreasing in the number of candidates seen so far, and, under certain natural conditions, monotone non-increasing in the time. Our second main result is proving that when the number of candidates is large, a single threshold policy is almost optimal.

Keywords: Secretary problem · Online algorithms · Threshold policy

The full paper can be found at http://arxiv.org/abs/1909.08660.

Part of this work was done while the authors were visiting the Simons Institute for the Theory of Computing.

Almost Quasi-linear Utilities in Disguise: Positive-Representation an Extension of Roberts' Theorem

Ilan Nehama$^{(\boxtimes)}$ (iD)

Bar-Ilan University, Ramat Gan, Israel
ilan.nehama@mail.huji.ac.il

Abstract. This work deals with implementation of social choice rules using dominant strategies for unrestricted preferences. When monetary transfers are allowed and quasi-linear utilities w.r.t. money is assumed, Vickrey-Clarke-Groves (VCG) mechanisms were shown to implement any affine-maximizer, and by the work of Roberts only affine-maximizers can be implemented whenever the type sets of the agents are rich enough.

In this work, we generalize these results and define a new class of preferences: Preferences which are *positive-represented by a quasi-linear utility*. That is, preferences which can be modeled using quasi-linear utilities on a subspace of the outcomes: outcomes with non-negative utility. We show that the characterization of VCG mechanisms as the incentive-compatible mechanisms extends naturally to this domain. We show that the original characterization of VCG mechanism is an immediate corollary of our generalized characterization. Our result follows from a simple reduction to the characterization of VCG mechanisms. Hence, we see our result more as a fuller more correct version of the VCG characterization than a new non quasi-linear domain extension.

This work also highlights a common misconception in the community attributing the VCG result to the usage of transferable utility. Our result shows that these results extend naturally to the non-transferable utility domain. That is, that the incentive-compatibility of the VCG mechanisms does not rely on money being a common denominator, but rather on the ability of the designer to fine the agents on a continuous (maybe agent-specific) scale.

We would like to thank Reshef Meir and Hongyao Ma for stimulating early discussions on the topic. We also would like to thank the anonymous reviewers for their detailed reviews, which helped us to improve the presentation of this work.

This work was supported in part by Israel Science Foundation (ISF) Grant 1626/18.

A full version of this paper is available at https://arxiv.org/abs/1805.05094v2.

© Springer Nature Switzerland AG 2019
I. Caragiannis et al. (Eds.): WINE 2019, LNCS 11920, pp. 344–345, 2019.
https://doi.org/10.1007/978-3-030-35389-6

We think these two insights, considering the utility as a representation and not as the preference itself (which is common in the economic community) and considering utilities which represent the preference only for the relevant domain, would turn out to fruitful in other domains as well.

Keywords: Mechanism design · Strategy-proofness · Dominant strategy incentive compatibility · Non Quasi-linear Utilities · Positive-representation · Roberts' Theorem

Information Design in Spatial Resource Competition

Pu Yang[1]([✉])[iD], Krishnamurthy Iyer[2][iD], and Peter I. Frazier[1][iD]

[1] Cornell University, Ithaca, NY 14853, USA
{py75, pf98}@cornell.edu
[2] University of Minnesota, Minneapolis, MN 55455, USA
kriyer@umn.edu

Abstract. We consider information design in spatial resource competition, motivated by ridesharing platforms sharing information with drivers about rider demand. Each of N co-located agents (drivers) decides whether to move to another location with an uncertain and possibly higher resource level (rider demand), where the utility for moving increases in the resource level and decreases in the number of other agents that move. A principal who can observe the resource level wishes to share this information in a way that ensures a welfare-maximizing number of agents move. Analyzing the principal's information design problem using the Bayesian persuasion framework, we study both private signaling mechanisms, where the principal sends personalized signals to each agent, and public signaling mechanisms, where the principal sends the same information to all agents. We show:

(1) For private signaling, computing the optimal mechanism using the standard approach leads to a linear program with 2^N variables, rendering the computation challenging. We instead describe a computationally efficient two-step approach to finding the optimal private signaling mechanism. First, we perform a change of variables to solve a linear program with $O(N^2)$ variables that provides the marginal probabilities of recommending each agent move. Second, we describe an efficient sampling procedure over sets of agents consistent with these optimal marginal probabilities; the optimal private mechanism then asks the sampled set of agents to move and the rest to stay.

(2) For public signaling, we first show the welfare-maximizing equilibrium given any common belief has a threshold structure. Using this, we show that the optimal public mechanism with respect to the sender-preferred equilibrium can be computed in polynomial time.

(3) We support our analytical results with numerical computations that show the optimal private and public signaling mechanisms achieve substantially higher social welfare when compared with no-information and full-information benchmarks.

Keywords: Bayesian persuasion · Spatial resource competition

The full paper is available at http://arxiv.org/abs/1909.12723. K. Iyer gratefully acknowledges support from the NSF under grants CMMI-1462592 and CMMI-1633920. P. Frazier gratefully acknowledges support from NSF and AFOSR.

I. Caragiannis et al. (Eds.): WINE 2019, LNCS 11920, p. 346, 2019.
https://doi.org/10.1007/978-3-030-35389-6

Author Index

Abramowitz, Ben 3
Aggarwal, Gagan 17
Ahmadinejad, AmirMahdi 333
Alaei, Saeed 31
Àlvarez, Carme 316
Anshelevich, Elliot 3
Anunrojwong, Jerry 45, 334
Arunachaleswaran, Eshwar Ram 57
Ashlagi, Itai 335
Aziz, Haris 336

Babaioff, Moshe 71
Badanidiyuru, Ashwinkumar 17, 31
Barman, Siddharth 57
Boone, Victor 85
Brandt, Felix 100

Chan, Hau 336
Chen, Yiling 45
Cohen, Avi 114
Cominetti, Roberto 337
Curry, Michael 129

Dickerson, John P. 129
Dose, Valerio 337
Dughmi, Shaddin 142

Echzell, Hagen 156
Elmachtoub, Adam N. 338

Feige, Uriel 71
Ferraioli, Diodato 171
Filos-Ratsikas, Aris 186
Frazier, Peter I. 346
Friedrich, Tobias 156

Georgoulaki, Eirini 200
Gersbach, Hans 339
Giannakopoulos, Yiannis 186
Goel, Ashish 340
Gupta, Vishal 338

Hamilton, Michael L. 338
Harks, Tobias 341
Hollender, Alexandros 214
Hulett, Reyna 340

Immorlica, Nicole 342
Iyer, Krishnamurthy 334, 336

Jin, Yaonan 228

Kerimov, Süleyman 335
Kesselheim, Thomas 343
Kleer, Pieter 241
Kollias, Kostas 200
Kong, Yuqing 256
Kumar, Rachitesh 57

Lazos, Philip 186
Lee, Barton E. 336
Lenzner, Pascal 156
Li, Weian 228
Lingenbrink, David 334

Mahdian, Mohammad 31
Mamageishvili, Akaki 339
Markakis, Evangelos 271
Mehta, Aranyak 17
Meier, Adrian 171
Messegué, Arnau 316
Molitor, Louise 156

Nazerzadeh, Hamid 333
Nehama, Ilan 344
Niazadeh, Rad 142

Pappik, Marcus 156
Parkes, David C. 336
Peikert, Chris 256
Peleg, David 114
Penna, Paolo 171
Piliouras, Georgios 85

Plaut, Benjamin   340, 342
Psomas, Alexandros   142, 343

Qi, Qi   228

Rathi, Nidhi   57
Ravindran Vijayalakshmi, Vipin   286

Saberi, Amin   333
Sankararaman, Karthik Abinav   129
Scarsini, Marco   337
Schäfer, Guido   241
Schedel, Anja   341
Schoenebeck, Grant   256
Schöne, Friedrich   156
Schröder, Marc   286
Skochdopole, Nolan   333
Sommer, Fabian   156
Srikant, R.   301
Srinivasan, Aravind   129
Stangl, David   156
Sweeney, Kane   333

Tamir, Tami   286
Tao, Biaoshuai   256
Tejada, Oriol   339
Tsikiridis, Artem   271

Vardi, Shai   343
Ventre, Carmine   171

Waggoner, Bo   45
Wan, Yuhao   129
Weinberg, S. Matthew   142
Weyl, E. Glen   342
Wilczynski, Anaëlle   100

Xu, Haifeng   45
Xu, Pan   129

Yang, Pu   346
Yazdanbod, Sadra   31

Zheng, Zhenzhe   301
Zhu, Wennan   3

Printed in the United States
By Bookmasters